# Max Weber
## *Modernisation as Passive Revolution*

# Historical Materialism Book Series

The Historical Materialism Book Series is a major publishing initiative of the radical left. The capitalist crisis of the twenty-first century has been met by a resurgence of interest in critical Marxist theory. At the same time, the publishing institutions committed to Marxism have contracted markedly since the high point of the 1970s. The Historical Materialism Book Series is dedicated to addressing this situation by making available important works of Marxist theory. The aim of the series is to publish important theoretical contributions as the basis for vigorous intellectual debate and exchange on the left.

The peer-reviewed series publishes original monographs, translated texts, and reprints of classics across the bounds of academic disciplinary agendas and across the divisions of the left. The series is particularly concerned to encourage the internationalization of Marxist debate and aims to translate significant studies from beyond the English-speaking world.

*For a full list of titles in the Historical Materialism Book Series*
*available in paperback from Haymarket Books, visit:*
www.haymarketbooks.org/category/hm-series

# Max Weber

## Modernisation as Passive Revolution

*A Gramscian Analysis*

By
Jan Rehmann

Translated by
Max Henninger

Haymarket Books
Chicago, IL

First published in 2015 by Brill Academic Publishers, The Netherlands
© 2015 Koninklijke Brill NV, Leiden, The Netherlands

Published in paperback in 2015 by
Haymarket Books
P.O. Box 180165
Chicago, IL 60618
773-583-7884
www.haymarketbooks.org

ISBN: 978-1-60846-551-4

Trade distribution:
In the US, Consortium Book Sales, www.cbsd.com
In Canada, Publishers Group Canada, www.pgcbooks.ca
In the UK, Turnaround Publisher Services, www.turnaround-uk.com
In all other countries, Publishers Group Worldwide, www.pgw.com

Cover design by Ragina Johnson.

This book was published with the generous support of
Lannan Foundation and the Wallace Global Fund.

Printed in Canada by union labor.

10 9 8 7 6 5 4 3 2 1

Library of Congress Cataloging-in-Publication data is available.

# Contents

PART 4

# The Ideal-Typical Construction of an Originary Protestant-Capitalist Spirit

# Preface to the English Edition

It is one of the basic insights of critical theories of ideology and discourse that every society must, in order to reproduce itself, bring forth appropriate subjects and subjectivities. They must 'function' within that society or rather make it possible, time and again, for the society to function. Althusser accounted for this in terms of ideological state apparatuses, by virtue of which individuals recognise themselves and submit to the given order as 'subjects' (in the twofold sense of 'free' agents and subordinates). Judith Butler has attempted to demonstrate how closely the processes of ideological subjection and subjectivation interlink. On Pierre Bourdieu's view, social 'fields' are what leads to the unconscious introjection of a bodily-engrained 'habitus'. If Weber is generally not discussed in relation to such approaches, this is mainly due to the fact that he, in spite of being a contemporary of Freud and familiar with some of his works,[1] essentially wrote *before* the psychoanalytic paradigm shift without which the 'ideology-theoretical turn' of the 1970s and 80s would not have been possible. Notwithstanding this historical distance, his relevance to the investigation of ideology is obvious. The way he defines the interaction of economic and ethico-religious motivational forces within the overall complex of social action and subjective experience remains relevant both to the theory of ideology and to psychoanalysis. A key reason for Weber's ongoing relevance lies in the theme of *subject constitution*, which runs through his writings on politics and the sociology of religion, even if it is never referred to under that name.

• • •

The theme of subject constitution '*avant la lettre*' manifested itself in a twofold way. On the one hand, the *Protestant Ethic* laid a claim to explain the emergence of an early bourgeois 'type of *human being* [*Menschentum*] that was created out of the confluence of the religious and economic components'.[2] On this account, religious subordination to the Calvinist doctrine of predestination's absolutist and inscrutable God engendered an individual solitude hitherto unknown; the fears triggered by this solitude were then compensated for by 'restless activity' and a consistently implemented rationalisation of life

---

1  Due to his concept of a value-related 'personality', Weber did not know what to make of Freudian psychoanalysis (see Marianne Weber 1975, pp. 38off).

2  Weber 2001, p. 1010, in Chalcraft and Harrington (eds) 2001, p. 106.

praxis.[3] Practising active self-control and the control of one's affects led to the emergence of a bourgeois 'personality' in the 'formal psychological sense of the term'.[4] What was now bred, in lieu of Luther's 'humble sinners', were 'those self-confident saints whom we can rediscover in the hard Puritan merchants of the heroic age of capitalism'.[5] The clear separation from 'depraved humanity', particularly that of society's lower strata, procured businessmen and entrepreneurs an 'amazingly good, we may even say a pharisaically good, conscience in the acquisition of money' and the 'comforting assurance that the unequal distribution of the goods of this world was a special dispensation of Divine Providence'.[6]

That Weber described this early modern subject constitution in a onesided way and by means of the inadequate method of a 'spirit'-focused and confessionalist reductionism is something I have attempted to demonstrate by reference to numerous examples in this book. These examples include: Weber's isolation of the 'mental and spiritual particularities' from the social conditions within which the various confessions operated (see below, Chapter 24); his adoption of the stereotypes associated with German 'cultural Protestantism' as understood by Ritschl (although Weber did give these stereotypes a specific Anglo-American twist) (chapters 25.4 and 25.5); a onesided choice of material, limited almost entirely to the post-revolutionary and depoliticised Puritanism of the late seventeenth century, which was already in the process of entering into an organic relationship with capitalism (chapters 26 and 28); his severance of the 'spirit of capitalism' from actually-existing capitalism and its economic forms (Chapter 28.4); the narrowing down of sociology of religion to a bourgeois 'occidental-protestant' teleology that views the non-European religions through an 'orientalist' lens (Chapter 30),[7] and so on. But even if one reaches the conclusion that Weber's was an ideologically overdetermined search for an originary 'spirit' of capitalism that can be neither verified nor falsified empirically (chapters 29.2 and 29.3), Weber's work does have the merit of raising an issue relevant to the theory of hegemony: unlike Sombart, Weber has a sharp intuitive grasp of the key difference between a private bourgeois entrepreneurial spirit and an expansive bourgeois ideology that aims to reshape life practices

---

3   Weber 1950, pp. 70–1, 107–8.
4   Weber 1950, p. 119.
5   Weber 1950, p. 112.
6   Weber 1950, pp. 176–7.
7   Sara Farris has analysed an 'orientalist' framework in Weber's comparative study of world religions that operates with the dichotomy between an occidental-protestant 'personality' and an Asiatic 'non-personality' (Farris 2013).

and subjectivities in their entirety (chapter 29.3). According to Kathi Weeks, Weber offers an archaeology of capitalist development that is complementary to the one Marx proposed in *Capital*'s chapter on the 'So-Called Primitive Accumulation': both offer an account of how the two main classes came into being, but whereas Marx focuses on their relations to the means of production as propertied owners and propertyless workers, Weber 'concentrates on the development of their consciousnesses as employers and employees'.[8] 'Thus to Marx's account of the primitive accumulation of private property, Weber adds a story about the primitive construction of capitalist subjectivities'.[9]

What is however often overlooked in the secondary literature is the fact that, superimposed upon Weber's historical theme, one finds the contemporary theme of a second *subject constitution*, this one taking the form of a future-oriented project of political education. It has almost become a commonplace of Weber scholarship that the *Protestant Ethic* should not be read, first and foremost, as a historical inquiry into the early modern period, but rather as 'an implicitly political text from cover to cover',[10] or as 'an allegory about Weber's Germany and its alternative possible futures, based on different projects of political education'.[11] It is a key hypothesis of this book that Weber presents himself, by virtue of his conception of history, as an 'ethico-political reformer' (Chapter 29.3) who wished to modernise German capitalism according to a Puritan-Americanist blueprint. He was concerned with morally reforming Germany's upper strata and enabling those strata to hegemonically integrate skilled labour. At heart, this modernisation project was about preparing a new stage of capitalist development, one that would later—and following Gramsci—be termed Fordism. As early as his 1904 journey to America, Weber was fascinated by early American Fordism, which he studied, for example, in the Taylorist organisation of Chicago's stockyards.[12] In the *Protestant Ethic*, the ethical resources of 'ascetic Protestantism' (essentially Calvinism and the Baptist sects) are arranged in such a way as to procure the anticipated Fordist bloc—the industrial bourgeoisie and the 'labour aristocracy'—with an underlying 'mythistory'.

---

8    Weeks 2011, p. 39.
9    Weeks 2011, p. 40.
10   Gosh 2008, p. 14.
11   Barbalet 2008, p. 9.
12   'Assembly-line mechanization was already well advanced in the packing plants...The plants served as a perfect illustration of Fordism in practice well before Henry Ford's first automotive assembly line in 1913, though one should note that the change at Ford was accompanied by an extraordinary increase in wages to $5,00 a day' (Scaff 2011, p. 45).

Thus Weber becomes relevant to a critical theory of ideology by virtue of the twofold character of his approach: he is both the perceptive observer of a historically constituted bourgeois subjectivity and the ideological designer of another bourgeois subjectivity that still needs to be constituted. The challenge lies in the fact that these two aspects of Weber interpenetrate constantly. We need nevertheless to distinguish between them analytically; this will make it possible for us to learn from Weber's approach while critically decoding its ideological import. In this context, it is relevant that, in his 1895 Freiburg inaugural address, Weber already thought of himself as the organic intellectual of a bourgeoisie that had yet to come into its own, in his view, and which he consequently attempted to prepare for the period of Fordism. Herbert Marcuse expressed the scholarly cost of this ideological commitment particularly succinctly when he remarked that Weber's analysis 'took into its "pure" definitions of formal rationality valuations peculiar to capitalism'.[13] Thus Weber's endorsement of capitalist modernisation continues to exert its effect within the formation of scientific concepts: Weber's ' "reason" remains *bourgeois* reason, and, indeed, only one part of the latter, viz. capitalist technical reason'.[14] At the same time, the force of his historico-sociological analysis consists in the fact that it takes account of the relative autonomy of the ideological, whereas economistic variants of Marxism often treated the ideological as a mere expression of class interests. Quoting Marx's appraisal of idealism in the first thesis on Feuerbach, one might say that, differently from mechanical materialism, Weber's *Protestant Ethic* developed the '*active* side', albeit 'only abstractly', since it remained ignorant of 'real, sensuous activity as such'.[15]

• • •

With regard to Marxism, there is a hidden and even uncanny dialectic of contradiction. It is already evident in the fact that Weber, who set out to overcome Marx's historical materialism, nevertheless absorbed so much of it that his conservative opponents accused him of thinking in terms of class struggle like a Marxist. The same Weber who had only vitriolic expressions of contempt for the revolutionaries of 1918/19, and who called for Karl Liebknecht and Rosa Luxemburg to be sent to the 'madhouse' or the 'zoological garden' shortly before they were murdered, admitted left-wing intellectuals such as Ernst Bloch and György Lukács to his Heidelberg circle of discussion. He met the sociologist

---

13      Marcuse 1969, p. 223.
14      Marcuse 1969, p. 208.
15      Marx and Engels 1975–2005, vol. 5, p. 6.

and future leading intellectual of the civil rights movement W.E.B. Du Bois in the 1890s, when Du Bois was in Germany as an exchange student, remained in contact with him and convinced him to write an article on the 'Negro Question' for the journal *Archiv für Sozialwissenschaft und Sozialpolitik* (1906). With a nod to Bloch's dictum that the best thing about religion is its creation of heretics, one might say that Weber's most valuable pedagogical achievement consisted in his contribution to the training of critical and extraordinarily productive left-wing intellectuals. Michael Löwy speaks of a 'Weberian Marxism' that picks up some of Weber's core arguments and brushes them against the grain to formulate a critique of the 'capitalist religion'.[16]

As is well known, highly diverse currents, including conservative and fascist ones, have laid claim to Weber's approach. It can nevertheless be said that it found a particularly fertile ground in critical theories that strove to liberate themselves from economistic reductionisms. When in 1923 György Lukács sought to account for socialist revolution's failure to materialise in Western Europe by invoking the 'ideological phenomenon of reification', he made recourse, on the one hand, to Marx's analysis of commodity fetishism, and on the other, to Weber's 'formal rationalisation', in which capitalist economy, state and civil society fuse to produce an 'iron cage' of bondage. This metaphor resurfaced, in an updated form, in Horkheimer's and Adorno's *Dialectic of Enlightenment*, where aesthetically homogenised mass culture is described as a 'completely closed existence' [*lückenlos geschlossenes Dasein*], in which even political antagonists 'are one in their enthusiastic obedience to the rhythm of the iron system'.[17] While Weber lived on in this tradition, as it were, in an apocalyptic diagnosis, one can observe, on the opposite pole of critical theory, how Ernst Bloch's understanding of the utopian potentials of Judaeo-Christian religion allowed itself to be inspired by the sociology of religion developed by Ernst Troeltsch and Weber; as far as Weber is concerned, Bloch was especially influenced by his study *Ancient Judaism*. To be sure, Bloch replaced Weber's bourgeois tailoring of religious sociology to a Western capitalist ideal type of rationality with the wholly different principle of reason associated with a

---

16    The term 'marxisme wébérien' was coined by Merleau-Ponty in *Les Aventures de la dialectique* to characterise Lukács in particular (Merleau-Ponty 1955, pp. 42ff). Löwy uses the concept in a wider sense to describe a heterogeneous field methodologically inspired by both Marx and Weber (notwithstanding their opposite political perspectives), which includes among others the Frankfurt School, Gramsci, Mariátegui (via Ramiro de Maeztu), Merleau-Ponty, Jean-Marie Vincent and Catherine Colliot-Thélène (see Löwy 2013, part III).

17    Adorno and Horkheimer 1997, p. 120.

society that is classless and free of domination. Left-wing historians and social scientists ranging from Henry Tawney, Christopher Hill and Franz Borkenau to Leo Kofler, Wolfgang Lefèvre and E.P. Thompson strove to combine historical materialist and Weberian methods; in doing so, they needed of course to free the latter from the reductionism of an 'isolating causal' deduction (Borkenau). They searched for the dialectical interaction of economic and ideological components, and in the course of this search, it emerged that the bourgeois dominance of Protestantism developed only gradually and in the course of the bourgeoisie's overall attainment of hegemony.[18] In developing his concept of the 'religious field', Pierre Bourdieu started from his lectures on Weber's religio-sociological definition of the relationship between priests, prophets, magicians and laymen in ancient Israel. In the process, he realised that the mutual relations of religious specialists and their relations to laymen can no longer be conceptualised in terms of 'interaction', as in Weber, but need rather to be thought of as 'objective relations' related to the social division of manual and intellectual labour as analysed by Marx and Engels in *The German Ideology*.[19] As the German editors of Bourdieu's book on the 'religious field' note, Bourdieu initially made use of Weber's sociology of religion in order to conceptualise, against economistic reductionism, the autonomy of the religious; subsequently, he used the concept of the field to try to 'overhaul Weber by means of Marx' and pose the Weberian question 'in Marxian terms'.[20]

Gramsci, in turn, put Weber's critique of Bismarck's 'Caesarism' to use in his own critique of the 'passive revolution' that developed in Italy and throughout Europe as a 'reaction' to and 'transcendence' of [*reazione-superamento*] the French Revolution. One has the impression of reading a modified extension of Weber's *Protestant Ethic* when Gramsci analyses the function of Puritanism within the framework of US Fordism as a component of a new type of hegemony, in which 'the "structure" dominates the superstructure more directly', and in which hegemony is 'born in the factory and does not need so many political and ideological intermediaries'.[21] In this context, there develop massive entrepreneurial and state campaigns against the sexual promiscuity and licentious drinking habits of the working class. 'The new industrialism requires monogamy; it does not want the workingman to squander his nervous energies in the anxious and unruly search for sexual gratification'.[22] According

---

18    See Rehmann 2008, pp. 40ff.
19    Bourdieu 2000, pp. 16, 50–1, 56–7, 118; see Marx and Engels 1845, p. 45.
20    Bourdieu 2000, p. 156.
21    Gramsci 1992, p. 169.
22    Gramsci 1996, p. 217.

to Gramsci, this is in fact 'the biggest collective effort [ever made] to create, with unprecedented speed and a consciousness of purpose unique in history, a new type of worker and of man'.[23] While in Weber the 'spirit' of capitalism anticipates the emergence of the capitalist order, Gramsci observes the 'forced development of a new human type', which takes the form of a 'psycho-physical adaptation to the new industrial structure'.[24] In contrast with Weber's project of bourgeois self-moralisation, the link between ideological subjection and structural violence emerges clearly: what is at stake is a process in which 'one class [imposes itself] over another', and by which the weak and recalcitrant are '[hurled] into the hell of the underclasses'.[25] In this context, Puritan ideology brings about adjustment to the new forms of work by giving 'to the intrinsic brutal coercion the external form of persuasion and consent'.[26]

Plainly, the ideological shaping of subjects evident after the crisis of Fordism and the transition to a transnational high-tech capitalism since the 1970s could no longer be analysed according to the paradigm of a 'disciplinary society' (Foucault); it called, rather, for new instruments of analysis. Various approaches ranging from Foucault-inspired 'governmentality studies' and Boltanski/Chiapello's inquiries into the 'new spirit of capitalism' to Frigga Haug's critical discourse analysis of Peter Hartz's programmatic book on the 'job revolution' have used the example of neoliberal management literature to investigate the development of new leadership techniques, by which persons can be mobilised for heteronomous goals in the name of personal responsibility and self-activity.[27] The question concerning the constitution of a new 'type of *human being*' [*Menschentum*], raised by Weber, poses itself differently again in a period when the hegemony of neoliberalism—its ability to activate subjects in terms of both a political and an economic ethics—has 'exhausted' itself in the face of multiple crises superimposed one upon the other, such that repressive and disciplinary aspects move to the fore.

•••

---

23    Gramsci 1996, p. 215.

24    Gramsci 1992, p. 169.

25    Gramsci 1992, p. 235.

26    Ibid.

27    See, among others, Bröckling, Krassmann and Lemke 2000; Boltanski and Chiapello 2005; F. Haug 2003. See also the evaluation in Rehmann 2013, pp. 296ff, as well as 301ff. With regard to the neo-Weberian approach of Boltanski and Chiapello, see Baratella and Rehmann 2005.

What is commonly published under the label of 'Weber scholarship' is a far cry from such productive extensions of Weberian queries and impulses. Instead, one finds, for the most part, a combination of ever more perfectly executed research into specific details of Weber's work with theoretical vacuity, periodically interspersed with 'divulgements' decked out as sensations. In what follows, and by way of ideal-typical simplification, I select from a broad range of recent publications one 'apologetic', one 'critical' and one 'divulging' example.

In 2001, Guenther Roth, whose earlier research I have profited from and some of which I have made use of in this book, published a detailed investigation of 'Max Weber's German-English Family History, 1800–1950'. One can confidently assume that the standards of archival diligence have therein been met, so that no relevant component of the genealogical table is missing. When, however, one looks for a theoretically grounded organising principle, one meets instead with a familiar ideological narrative: on the one hand, there prospered an open minded, multi-ethnic capitalism with its 'cosmopolitan bourgeoisie', while on the other, 'authoritarian and totalitarian powers' threatened to rise and replace the peaceful competitive order by an 'epoch of growing nation-state rivalries'.[28] Once the 'prosperous, intelligent and energetic individuals' of the mid-nineteenth century had built a cosmopolitan economic liberalism 'from below' (a feat achieved, however, 'under the protection of the British fleet'), the conservative turn associated with Bismarck and Disraeli brought the breakthrough of a nationalism that turned cosmopolitanism into a term of abuse.[29] Now, since Weber did not just descend, on his father's side, from Bielefeld's export-oriented textile patriciate, but was also, on his mother's side, the 'late descendant' of one of the wealthiest Anglo-German merchant families, he naturally belonged in the camp of the Anglophile cosmopolitan bourgeoisie, for which a world war was 'sheerly unimaginable'.[30]

Of course, Roth cannot avoid reporting that Weber vilified Polish immigrant workers as a bestial and barbaric cultural threat to 'Germanness', speaking out against 'sentimental cosmopolitanism'; that he was an enthusiastic supporter both of Germany's 1897 naval armament drive and of the country's 1914 entry into the war; or that even after the USA's entry into the war, he gasconaded about the global political tasks of a German 'master people'.[31] Roth believes he can get rid of Weber's cultural racism and imperialism by characterising him as a 'cosmopolitan nationalist', thereby setting him off from 'xenophobic

---

28    Roth 2001, p. 5.
29    Roth 2001, pp. 25–8.
30    Roth 2001, pp. 2–3, 29.
31    Roth 2001, pp. 30ff, 46ff.

nationalists', and by portraying him as someone who struggled time and again to heroically defend himself against the lures of chauvinism and nationalism.[32] After all, Weber allowed himself to get 'carried away' with enthusiasm for the war only 'initially', when he justified the war as a 'gamble', but then 'he wanted to see the war end soon, so that German capital would not be exhausted and Germany's position on the world market would not be undermined for a con- siderable time'—Roth praises this as an example of 'superior insight' into the domestic and foreign threats faced by Germany,[33] and he asserts that said insight set Weber off 'fundamentally' from social Darwinist nationalism and Prussian militarism.[34] Much as with Nietzsche's 'wicked' sister, the blame for a distorted reception is placed on a woman: the 'nationalist' Marianne Weber, who 'downplayed Weber's family relationship to England' in her biography of Weber, neglecting to 'start from the cosmopolitan and Anglophile great grand- father Carl Cornelius Souchey'.[35] By shedding light on the rarely mentioned 'cosmopolitan' branch of Weber's genealogy, Roth exonerates Weber from the fatal German 'Sonderweg' and 'rescues' him—as if that were still necessary— for a broad reception in 'Western' dominated transnational capitalism. In his ideologically overzealous effort to neatly distinguish between the good and the bad aspects of imperialism, it never even occurs to Roth that for signifi- cant parts of the German bourgeoisie of the period, the 'cosmopolitan' and the 'nationalist-chauvinistic' orientation did not necessarily present themselves as mutually exclusive options: one was quite happy to opt for the variant of 'ultra-imperialism' (Kautsky) whenever one was united by a common anti- 'Southern' or anti-'Eastern' cause, as was the case, for example, in the colonial war to defeat the Chinese 'Boxer Rebellion' around 1900, but one readily advo- cated intra-imperialist war when one held that irreconcilable aspirations to world power rendered it 'inevitable'. Even in the view of the German bourgeoi- sie's 'liberal' intellectuals, it was genuinely in the latecomer nation's legitimate interest to prepare for war, since this would secure it adequate 'elbow room' on the cosmopolitan world market. To express indignation over certain national- ist 'delusions' and 'misjudgements' is diversionary and misleading. It amounts to distracting from the tasks of critical social analysis, for such analysis is faced

---

32    Roth 2001, p. 2; Andrew Zimmerman described Weber's position as 'neoracism', i.e. 'a rac-
      ism that denies the importance of biological race while working out a system of cultural
      differences that functions as effectively as race as a means of underwriting political and
      economic inequality' (2006, p. 53; see Zimmerman 2010, pp. 100ff, 205ff, 212ff).

33    Roth 2001, p. 35.

34    Roth 2001, p. 37.

35    Roth 2001, p. 40.

with a bourgeois imperial configuration of interests that was oriented towards colonialist exploitation and imperial domination of the world market and made millions of persons pay with death and immiseration.

Compared to Roth's apologetic genealogical research, Jack Barbalet's *Weber, Passions and Profits* is situated on the opposite front, that of a critique of Weber. Barbalet recognises clearly that Weber presented himself, in his Freiburg inaugural address, as a class conscious defender of the German national interest, calling for a political education in preparation for the role of leader. Barbalet posits a continuity between this address and the *Protestant Ethic*, which transposed the educational mandate to a different 'key', namely that of religious 'vocation'.[36] What links the two, according to Barbalet, is Weber's recurrent interest in national politics, his 'nationalist enthusiasm'.[37] As a programme of political education, the *Protestant Ethic* is 'a rallying cry to wake and encourage the proto-political class of the then backward German people to stand up' and 'strive for self-assertive and self-directed commitment to nation-state building and political leadership'.[38]

But what direction was the German nation to follow, once it had 'awoken', 'stood up' and 'asserted itself'? Barbalet addresses the link between Weber's project of modernisation and its primary national addressees, but he is not interested in the strategic coordinates of the project itself. He even overlooks that in the Freiburg inaugural address, in the midst of an unrelenting national chauvinist discourse, Weber formulates a political class analysis that amounts to a rescission of the Junker-bourgeois class compromise and aims at the possibility of coupling the bourgeoisie with the 'highest strata' of the working class. Barbalet then quotes extensively from the opening passage of the *Protestant Ethic*, where Weber emphasises the predominantly Protestant character of capital ownership and entrepreneurism on the one hand, and of the higher, skilled strata of the working class and the elevated technical personnel of the modern firm on the other.[39] But in his discussion of the quotation, Barbalet focuses exclusively on an incidental remark by Weber on the relationship between Germans and Poles in East Germany, interpreting this remark as evidence that the passage is continuous with the nationalism of Weber's early studies on agrarian life. In making this point, he misses what is essential, namely that Weber has already in his first sentence decided upon the strategic arrangement of the entire study: his reference to modern entrepreneurs, the 'labour

---

36    Barbalet 2008, pp. 8–9, 17.

37    Barbalet 2008, pp. 34ff, 41.

38    Barbalet 2008, pp. 216, 224.

39    Barbalet 2008, pp. 23–4; compare Weber 1950, pp. 35–6.

aristocracy' and the scientific technical intelligentsia denominates the key components of the anticipated Americanist-Fordist bloc. If the *Protestant Ethic* were no more than a politico-pedagogical pamphlet of German nationalism, it would not have met with as broad a reception following the German Reich's defeat in the First World War. By focusing onesidedly on German nationalism, Barbalet prevents himself from explaining why the ascetic virtues outlined in the *Protestant Ethic* were able to merge so seamlessly with America's self-perception.[40] Yet this becomes immediately comprehensible as soon as one takes into account Weber's ethico-political anticipation of US Fordism.

German newspapers ranging from the conservative *Frankfurter Allgemeine Zeitung* and *Die Welt* to the liberal *Frankfurter Rundschau* celebrated Joachim Radkau's biography *Max Weber: A Biography* (2011; German edition 2005). It was praised as a 'riveting life-story', a 'fascinating biography', and so on. The book's sensational character was mainly due to its attempt to understand Weber's life and work primarily in terms of his nervous disease, with its associated sexual misery (avolition, impotence, nocturnal emissions, dreams of torture, etc.) The drama is presented in three acts, all of which revolve around 'nature as the generator of dramatic tension':[41] Part One, 'The Violation of Nature', by which Weber's physical and mental health is lastingly damaged—with his mother and wife as the main culprits (with regard to the latter, Radkau allows himself to speculate on a 'suspicion that suggests itself', namely that she was the 'main cause' of Weber's sexual troubles);[42] Part Two, 'Nature's Revenge', which manifests itself in the onset of 'sexual neurasthenia', in seven years of ill health and in vain attempts both to cure the disease and to overcome it by way of compensatory behaviour; Part Three, 'Salvation and Illumination', also effected by means of two women, namely by Weber's love for Mina Tobler and Else Jaffé-Richthofen.

It cannot be a question here of entering into a general discussion of psychoanalytically-oriented historiography and its methodological fruitfulness or lack thereof. In principle, Dirk Käsler's criterion seems plausible, namely that revelations about a person's private and intimate life are significant when they are indispensable for reconstructing the relationship between life and work, and when they 'shed light on the work under examination'.[43] This is precisely what is doubtful in Radkau's case. In fact, Radkau is struck with blindness whenever the coordinates of Weber's political, religio-sociological and

---

40    Barbalet 2008, pp. 2–3.
41    Radkau 2011, p. 2.
42    Radkau 2011, p. 19.
43    Käsler 2006.

epistemological interventions are at issue. For example, in discussing Weber's 1895 inaugural address, he does not even notice that Weber presents himself there as a class conscious 'member of the bourgeois classes', one that is, however, obliged to tell his 'own class' what it does not want to hear. Weber criticises the power political 'immaturity' of this economically dominant class and argues that said immaturity needs to be overcome, as quickly as possible, by means of 'political educative work', but all Radkau notices is that the expression 'mature' derives from an 'organological vocabulary', thereby indicating an underlying naturalism and social Darwinism.[44] Weber's imperialist call for an aggressive German imperialist politics is interpreted by Radkau as one of the spontaneous 'outbursts' by which Weber allegedly vented his deep seated inner turmoil.[45] During his visit to the USA Weber is fascinated by the 'strongholds of capital' in Manhattan, by the Taylorist work organisation of Chicago's stockyard and by the brutal militancy of the class struggles, but Radkau perceives only 'vitalist enthusiasm', an obsession with 'vital wildness' and a society in its 'raw state'.[46] If Weber refuses an invitation to the White House and chooses to visit Oklahoma instead, then this is because he seeks 'immediate contact with the wilderness', according to Radkau, but when he enjoys the turbulent noise of a petroleum-producing town, he is again fascinated by 'wildness',[47] so that in the end, even the spoils system serves as an example of the 'wildness of American politics'.[48] And so it comes as no surprise that Weber's subsequent investigations of the Russian Revolution, taken up in 1905, are accounted for in terms of a 'fascination for the wildness of nature in man'.[49]

These and other platitudes confirm Käsler's verdict: Radkau engages in an 'exhibitionist historiography', and the 'indiscrete brightness' of its exposures 'obfuscates' Weber's work.[50] Barbara Hahn sees a 'normalising discourse' at work in Radkau's focus on intimate matters, a discourse that 'threatens to neutralise the intellectual and political brisance of Weber's writings'.[51] To refer to Weber's political interventions only so as to illustrate his personal struggle with his inner demons is, as Peter Thomas has politely noted, not a particularly

---

44   Radkau 2011, pp. 126ff, 131–2.
45   Radkau 2011, p. 130.
46   Radkau 2011, pp. 224–5.
47   Radkau 2011, p. 230.
48   Radkau 2011, p. 231.
49   Radkau 2011, p. 239.
50   Käsler 2006.
51   Hahn 2006.

fruitful approach.[52] According to Sara Farris, Radkau engages in a 'lewd' reading of Weber that 'naturalises' his intellectual life and fails to do justice to his 'political drives'.[53]

By no means does it necessarily follow from such criticisms that a psycho-analytic approach to Max Weber is principally inappropriate. There can be of course no question of defending the imaginary unity of a 'great' personality against demonstrations of that personality's contradictory and fractured nature. One also needs to distinguish between the contribution Radkau's approach makes to our understanding of 'neurasthenia' as a disease of civilisation typical, in Weber's time, of society's upper echelons,[54] and the contribution it makes to our understanding of Weber's scholarly work. As far as the latter is concerned, it holds true that even if one follows Freud in understanding an intellectual's thought and research as the sublimation of unconscious and sometimes agonising drive destinies, one nevertheless needs to take that thought and that research seriously as instances of a *successful* sublimation (at whatever cost), and hence as intellectual interventions into the historical conjuncture. To refer to an intellectual's work only sporadically and so as to illustrate a putatively fundamental struggle with 'nature' leads, despite the interesting observations it may occasionally yield, to a reductionist and banalising *rendezvous manqué*.

•••

The present book has largely been ignored by mainstream Weber scholarship, as is hardly surprising given the way the latter has shut itself off from the traditions of critical theory. The book was however received with much interest and positively reviewed where there is openness for the formulation and development of critical theory. Writing in *Z. Zeitschrift für Marxistische Erneuerung*, Sebastian Herkommer has emphasised that the book's approach to Weber's work follows the method by which Gramsci engaged with Croce. It is guided, according to Herkommer, by a technique of decipherment indebted to the theory of hegemony, one that asks 'to what extent Weber needs to be understood as an "organic intellectual" of the bourgeois class, as the committed advocate and trailblazer of a historical bloc consisting of the modern bourgeoisie and the so-called labour aristocracy'. Herkommer's review arrives at the conclusion that the *Protestant Ethic* can no longer be read, after this study, 'without

---

52    Thomas 2006, pp. 150, 156.
53    Farris 2010a, p. 339.
54    Radkau has published a separate study on this subject (Radkau 1998).

bearing in mind its "hidden telos", that of combining a "neutral", "purely historical account" with a specific form of partisanship for bourgeois supremacy'.[55]
Writing in *Süddeutsche Zeitung*, Claudius Rosenthal confirmed that the book
has shown how Weber's political commitment can indeed be 'conceptualised,
explained and understood in a Gramscian manner': 'By means of the hunch-
backed Italian, Marx catches up with the great national economist and sociologist, whom we think of mostly as the bourgeois response to Marx'.[56]

W.F. Haug's book review for the journal *Sozialismus* was titled *'Eine neue
Entschlüsselung Max Webers'* ['A New Decipherment of Max Weber']; it concluded that this multi-layered contextual study is something more than simply
one more 'refutation' of Weber. It is, according to Haug, 'critique in the serious
sense of the word: a reconstruction, in terms of social analysis and the theory
of hegemony, of the political and scholarly posing of the problem, one that
exposes the ideological arrangement of theoretical concepts and is thereby
able to integrate and inherit Weber's achievements'.[57] Writing for German
weekly *Freitag*, Willi Brüggen attested to the book's achievement of 'combining the numerous explicit and implicit strands of the debate conducted at the
beginning of this century to produce a clear, detailed and informed account'.
In particular, the book has successfully demonstrated, according to Brüggen,
that the 'politically fatal equation of rationality with conformity is the product of an ideologically motivated conceptualisation that starts, *inter alia*, with
Max Weber'.[58] In his review for the Swiss journal *Widerspruch*, Ruedi Graf
stressed that the importance of the study lies mainly in its crafting of a set
of methodological instruments that moves beyond the 'objectivism' often
encountered within Marxism while sidestepping the poststructuralist pitfall of
'isolating forms of thought from their social background'. The book's approach
has made it possible, on Graf's view, to interpret Weber's work in terms of his
own political project, and to read it against the grain from the perspective of a
Marxian project of liberation.[59] In the journal *Das Argument*, Wolfgang Küttler
concludes that the study makes use of extensive materials and provides not
just many stimulating impulses but also much matter for further thought and
research. Its original approach, he writes, proves itself to be 'extraordinarily
fruitful, particularly with regard to the issues that remain inconclusive or

---

55    Herkommer 1998.
56    Rosenthal 1999.
57    Haug 1999, p. 56.
58    Brüggen 1999.
59    Graf 2001, p. 198.

prompt critical inquiry'.[60] In an omnibus review for the *International Review of Social History* (*IRSH*), Sara Farris has pointed out that the book's key finding, namely that Weber's *Protestant Ethic* essentially constitutes the ethico-political project of an early Fordist self-moralisation of the bourgeoisie, has yet to be picked up on in recent Anglo-American Weber scholarship.[61]

•••

Apart from some amendments, this English edition is basically a translation of the second German edition, published by Argument-Verlag in 2013.[62] It was supported, on the international level, by expert assessments penned, among others, by Fredric Jameson, Richard D. Wolff, Bob Jessop, Josef Buttigieg, Domenico Losurdo and W.F. Haug. Their contribution was essential to the book receiving funding, in April 2012, from the German Publishers and Booksellers Association [*Börsenverein des deutschen Buchhandels e.V.*]. In the context of its translation programme ['*Geisteswissenschaften International— Preis zur Förderung der Übersetzung geisteswissenschaftlicher Literatur*'], the Association declared the book an 'excellent publication' that merits translation. This has made it possible to prepare an English edition. My heartfelt thanks to everyone.

> *Jan Rehmann*
> New York, December 2013

---

60    Küttler 1999, p. 121.
61    Farris 2010a, p. 340.
62    With regard to the amendments, I would like to thank Wulf D. Hund for his advice to connect my analysis of the social components in Weber's sociology of religion more clearly with his cultural racism.

# Introduction to the First Edition (1998)

1

Paying tribute to Weber as an outstanding pioneer and theorist of 'modernity' has become a commonplace in the scholarly literature, one that unites the most disparate Weber interpretations. Conversely, whoever articulates himself from within the paradigm of a modernisation approach needs to refer to Weber. Reference to him is often not so much a matter of scholarly analysis as it is an ideological ritual: to bow briefly before Weber's path-breaking contribution to 'modernity' has become a shibboleth by which intellectuals in the humanities and social sciences can let it be understood that they belong to the discursive world of a 'Western' scientific community.

The present work attempts to identify the concrete significance of the modernisation pursued by Weber within the political, philosophical and religious contexts of Wilhelmine society. The underlying methodological choice—that of deducing Weber's approach not primarily from the historical objects of his analyses, but mainly from the ideological relations of his time—is not new. As demonstrated by the anthologies edited by Mommsen and Schwentker (1988) and Lehmann and Roth (1993), much of Weber scholarship has proceeded to attempt 'to newly situate Max Weber within the intellectual and political constellation at the transition from the 19th to the 20th century'.[1] Of course, this poses the problem that, absent a precisely formulated question, such attempts can quickly lead to a boundless and arbitrary stringing together of intellectual analogies.

The present contextual studies rely on an approach drawn from the theory of ideology that has been influenced mainly by Gramsci, Althusser and the work of the German research group *Projekt Ideologietheorie*. The point is not to comprehensively reconstruct Weber's intellectual influences as such, but rather to understand his contradictory relationship to the influential ideological formations of Germany's ruling bourgeois-Junker power bloc. On the one hand, Weber inserts himself within these formations; on the other, he transforms them with an eye to capitalist modernisation. His political interventions span the arc from the Prussian-German statism of the 'Katheder-socialists' to the development of a flexible model of conflict designed to lastingly integrate the labour movement in bourgeois society. In his writings on the theory of science, Weber initially adopts the key categories of southwest German

---

1  Mommsen 1988a, p. 19.

neo-Kantianism (Windelband, Rickert), but then replaces its model of an ahistorical 'system of values' with the concept of a 'clash of values' by which he renders the theory of science sensitive to social antagonisms. With his hypothesis of a specific Protestant-capitalist business ethic, he latches onto the widespread self-conception of a German-Lutheran 'cultural Protestantism'. But a comparison of Weber with the leading cultural Protestant theologian Albrecht Ritschl reveals that Weber's distinctiveness lies in the Anglo-American twist he gives his religio-historical material.

## 2

Marxism constitutes a special sort of context. It represents a counter-discourse that persistently accompanies and significantly shapes Weber's engagement with economic, socio-political, neo-Kantian and cultural Protestant ideologies. Weber's manifest critique is directed primarily against an economistic and determinist Marxism of the Kautskyian variety, and his followers found a similarly rewarding opponent in the official 'Marxism-Leninism' of the Third International. The sterile confrontation predetermined by this constellation has for a long time shaped discussion of the relationship between Marx and Weber. For example, Johannes Weiß claims to present an overview of Weber's 'Marxist' reception and critique, but refers almost exclusively to the Marxist-Leninist reception.[2] By contrast, I am interested mainly in confronting Weber the 'overcomer' of Marx with the renewed approaches of a critical (and self-critical) Marxist thought. In this endeavour, I have found valuable resources in the *Dictionnaire critique du marxisme*, and, even more so, in the hitherto published volumes of the German 'Historical-Critical Dictionary of Marxism' [*Historisch-Kritisches Wörterbuch des Marxismus*, HKWM], both of which allow the reader to distinguish historico-critically between the multiple and sometimes contrary uses to which certain concepts have been put within the traditions of Marxist thought.

In this attempt at a dialogue, I focus mainly on two core themes: on the one hand, I wish to demonstrate that Weber's writings on politics, philosophy and religion react to Marx at decisive moments, albeit to a Marx perceived through the lens of the Second International's 'orthodox Marxism'. Rosa Luxemburg described the 'younger historical school', to which Weber and Sombart belong,

---

2  Weiß 1981; see also Böckler and Weiß 1987 and Weiß in Gneuss and Kocka 1988, pp. 126ff. A positive counter-example of a rigorous comparison between Marx and Weber can be found in the introduction to social theory edited by Bader, Berger, Ganßmann and Knesebeck 1987.

as 'digestive science', and she identified Marx as its secret cause.[3] But at times it seems as if a giant snake had swallowed an elephant, whose contours can still be clearly recognised. A scholarly literature on Weber that feels it needs to defuse the original challenge posed by Marx ends up defusing Weber himself more than anything else; this is because Weber owes a significant part of his analytic wealth to his having wrestled with the Marxian analysis of society.

On the other hand, I confront Weber's 'overcoming' of Marx with Gramsci, who picked up on and pondered many Weberian proposals in his *Prison Notebooks*. Both Weber and Gramsci speak out against the notion of an 'objective reality' that exists independently of subjects and needs only to be 'represented' within consciousness. They both oppose economism and determinism, which had largely imposed themselves within the official Marxism of the Second and Third Internationals. But while the Weber of the *Protestant Ethic* opposes to the vulgar materialist theory of reflection a mirror-inverted ethico-religious deduction of the spirit of capitalism, Gramsci attempts, in his engagement with Croce, to re-integrate 'ethico-political history' in a 'theory of superstructures'.

To the extent that a comparison between Weber and Gramsci is attempted in the scholarly literature published to date, this is done primarily with an eye to answering the question of how strongly Gramsci was influenced by Weber.[4] It appears to me to be more fruitful to pursue the opposite path, taking Gramsci's theory of hegemony as the starting point for an interrogation of Weber's approach to modernisation: how does Weber define his relationship to 'his' class, the modern bourgeoisie? What social constellations does he situate this class in with regard to the agrarian class on the one hand and the industrial proletariat on the other? In what direction does he wish to transform relations of hegemony? What type of intellectual does he oppose, and what type does he himself represent?

3

That Weber's political interventions are highly important for understanding his approach to modernisation has been undeniable at least since the second edition of Mommsen's great study *Max Weber and German Politics, 1890–1920* (1984 [1974]). But the explanatory value of this connection depends on how, and from what viewpoint, Weber's politics are interpreted. Here too, the scholarly

---

3  Luxemburg 1970–5a, p. 491.
4  See Paggi 1970, pp. 377–8; Mangoni 1977, p. 409; Levy 1988, pp. 534ff.

literature on Weber is concerned primarily with intellectual labels; they range from German 'nationalism' and 'Machiavellianism' to 'liberalism', 'pluralism of values' and 'democracy'. The US reception of Weber was long dominated by a harmonising interpretation that was developed first by Parsons and then by Bendix: one wanted to see Weber as laying the intellectual groundwork for a free and liberal society. In Germany, it is mainly Schluchter who propounded this sort of interpretation by relegating the German-nationalist 'undertones' of an early Weber and presenting the mature Weber as the exponent of a liberal pluralist and specifically 'occidental' modernity.[5] The new bourgeois class constellation Weber strove for, without reference to which such a label remains meaningless, is not analysed. This is related to the fact that Schluchter's 'modernity' boils down to a bourgeois class project of its own, a neoliberal one. Thus, in his more recent apology for the dismantling of the German Democratic Republic, he sees East Germany's modernisation gap as consisting in the fact that its citizens have yet to sufficiently interiorise the 'distinction between economic liberty and social security'.[6]

As far as the Weber reception in post-1945 US sociology is concerned, portraying Weber as a 'good', viz. 'liberal' German amounted to a precondition for 'importing' him, as Hennis has remarked.[7] To be sure, Hennis himself has no more to offer than another intellectual contextualisation of Weber, this time one that situates Weber within the 'specific history of "German spirit"', and more specifically within the tradition of a Nietzschean 'voluntarism' that has thoroughly dismantled the illusions of a 'liberal-optimistic thought'.[8] Hennis, whom the German conservative daily *Frankfurter Allgemeine Zeitung* celebrates as an unconventional outsider distinct from the 'sociologically inflected interpretation of Weber',[9] has provided the keywords for a Nietzschean faction of scholars that discovers in Weber a heroic, *fin-du-siècle* pessimism. This interpretation is no less apologetic than that of the scholarly mainstream, for Hennis strives, out of a nonsensical opposition to sociology as such, to thoroughly suppress the social components of Weberian 'spirit'. After promising to

---

5  See Schluchter 1991, pp. 177–8, note 18, and pp. 306, 328 and 333.
6  Schluchter 1996, p. 23. While the institutions have been successfully 'Westernised', 'in the hearts and minds of many East German citizens, questions of economic efficiency, social security and political legitimacy remain amalgamated...Their dissociation proceeds only slowly' (Schluchter 1996, pp. 22–3). This 'dissociation' is a neoliberal ideal that it has never been possible to impose fully in the 'West' either, especially not in the corporatist Federal Republic.
7  Hennis 1987, p. 203.
8  Hennis 1987, pp. 42, 219, 222, 233.
9  Käsler 1996.

examine Weber's practico-political and value-free scholarly positions with an eye to their 'internal relation', the only answer he provides is the lofty phrase that the 'development of humanity' is to be seen as the key category of Weber's inquiry, one by which he putatively continues Nietzsche's basic endeavour.[10]

Hennis and Schluchter may serve as examples of a German debate on Weber that has largely suppressed the challenge of a Marxist critique—a suppression from which the theoretical standard of the debate has not benefited. The extent of what has been lost becomes clear when one compares *Critical Theory's* analyses of Weber, formulated, during the 1960s and 70s, mainly by Marcuse and Lefèvre. At the 1964 Heidelberg Sociological Conference, Marcuse propounded that Weber's theory 'took into its "pure" definitions of formal rationality valuations peculiar to capitalism'.[11] The strength of this critique consisted precisely in the fact that, unlike the critique of Weber formulated by 'Marxism-Leninism', it did not lay claim to a 'materialist' (i.e. economic) refutation, but focused rather on the internal relationship between 'theoretical form' and the underlying social formation.[12] The present work attempts to latch on to this ideology-critical reading of Weber in order to continue it in various ways, sometimes extending and sometimes correcting it. In the main, what I adopt is the basic objective of exposing the theory's ideological configuration. I lay no claim to oppose to Weber's analyses an alternative account of 'reality'; rather, I wish to identify the rules of composition by which he construes his ideal-typical concepts. The strategic orientations and blind spots of his scholarship are most evident in what he chooses to emphasise and what he chooses to suppress. In order to understand Weber as a scholar, one needs to observe how he organises his ideological concatenations.

This, however, is an endeavour that goes beyond the critique of ideology formulated by Critical Theory. In its framework, 'ideology' referred primarily to a consciousness that is necessarily 'false', one that reflects the reifications of the bourgeois exchange of commodities. This suggests a methodological reductionism that traces bourgeois ideology—exposed as 'topsy-turvy'—directly back to an economic inversion, thereby failing to take account of the proper materiality and relative autonomy of ideological powers, practices and

---

10    Hennis 1987, pp. 22, 32–3, 46, 192. In continuation of this approach, Hennis proposes replacing the 'sociological' reading of Weber with an 'anthropological' one; he also proposes replacing Weber's concept of the 'science of reality' [*Wirklichkeitswissenschaft*] with that of a 'science of essentiality' [*Wesentlichkeitswissenschaft*]. Hennis 1996, pp. 15, 19.

11    Marcuse 1969, p. 223.

12    Compare Lefèvre 1971, pp. 10, 44.

discourses.[13] A critique of ideology that limits itself to demonstrating that Weber's 'value-free' social science in fact only reproduces the capitalist logic of valorisation misses what is specifically 'modern' about his approach: both the analytic acuity of his critique of Germany's bourgeois-feudal compromises and his early orientation toward the model of 'Americanism'. A study of ideology that accounts for the fascination exerted by these interventions (thereby demystifying them) needs to consider more closely the ideological formations of the turn of the century, within which Weber operates; it needs to identify the traditions that he picks up on, as well as the elements he adopts and the strategies he employs in order to integrate those elements into a new arrangement.

The specificity of Weber's approach to modernisation consists not in its capitalist orientation as such, but in its anticipation of the rising new formation of Fordism.

## 4

As Domenico Losurdo rightly observes, Weber was one of the first to recognise the emergence of the 'American era'.[14] The present work begins with Weber's 1904 visit to America and his articles on the Protestant sects, a direct result of his journey. What fascinates Weber about America is not simply the diligence of the Americans or the restlessness that characterises their life, as the literature on Weber reports; rather, he is fascinated by the first elements of a new formation of capitalism, one that will later be referred to as 'Fordism'. In the Chicago stockyards he takes a guided tour of, he admires the 'utterly amazing work performance' of a Taylorist production that already disposed of automatic conveyor belts before Henry Ford had the assembly line moved from the ceiling to the floor in his automobile factory. In parallel with this, Weber's first articles on the Protestant sects aim at revealing to the German readers of *Frankfurter Zeitung* and *Christliche Welt* the link between the religiosity of 'Americanism' and its 'superiority in the struggle for existence'. Weber's hypothesis on the sects is itself a contribution to the constitution of a modern capitalist hegemony; a hegemony intended to achieve, by the 'cool dispassion

---

13  The late Engels coined the concept of 'ideological powers' (Marx and Engels 1975–2005, vol. 26, pp. 392–3). On the concept of the ideological as a 'functional complex of ideal societalisation-from-above', see Rehmann 2013, pp. 241ff; on the Lukács paradigm and Critical Theory, see Rehmann 2013, pp. 77ff.

14  '*Weber è tra i primi a segnalare l'avvento di quello che due decenni più tardi verrà chiamato il "secolo Americano"*' (Losurdo 1996, p. 145).

of societalisation', an ideal selection of bourgeois economic subjects while simultaneously integrating the workers in a lasting way. In the *Grundrisse*, Marx spoke of the capitalist relations of production as a 'foreshadowing of the future' of new relations;[15] in Weber's approach to modernisation, one discerns a first 'foreshadowing' of Fordism.

Thus what is 'modern' in Weber resides mainly in his project of a new bourgeois hegemony in the transition to Fordism. In Gramsci, 'hegemony' refers in particular to the consensual, intellectual and moral 'leadership' [*direzione*] of a class, as opposed to its 'domination' [*dominio*].[16] The backdrop to this distinction is the experience that the Western European attempts at socialist revolution have been foiled not just by military relations of force, but also by bourgeois society's internal stability. If the centre of state power could be successfully conquered in Russia in 1917, this was because there, the state was 'everything', whereas civil society was only 'gelatinous'; in the most developed capitalist countries, by contrast, the state was merely a 'forward trench', behind which lay the resilient structure of civil society.[17] Within the elaborate system of trenches made up of civil society's apparatuses and associations, the ruling class successfully 'obtained the active consensus of the governed'.[18] It is here, Gramsci concludes, that the socialist labour movement must 'take positions' as well, working its way from an 'economic-corporative' stage of development to an 'ethico-political' one that will allow it to constitute, along with allied classes, a 'historical bloc' with majority appeal.[19]

Weber made a conceptual contribution to the differentiation of modern civil society. He presents himself as the general 'organic' intellectual of a bourgeois class that has yet to find itself, and that can only develop the capacity to lead by means of 'political education'.[20] As early as his 1895 Freiburg inaugural address, considered the most important document of Weber's political stance prior to the First World War, one discerns a project of attaining hegemony that consists of two interrelated components: that of separating the bourgeoisie from its Caesaristically mediated alliance with the agrarian class and that of

---

15　Marx 1973, p. 461.

16　Gramsci 1992, pp. 136–7.

17　Gramsci 2007, pp. 162, 169.

18　Gramsci 1975c, pp. 1765–6.

19　See Gramsci 1975b, pp. 1053–4, 1244–5, 1291–1301, 1315–17, 1318–23, 1505–6. On the concepts of 'hegemony', 'civil society', the 'historical bloc', 'war of manoeuvre' and 'war of position', see for example Buci-Glucksmann 1975; Anderson 1979; Projekt Ideologietheorie 1982, pp. 61ff; Schreiber 1984.

20　On Gramsci's distinction between 'organic' and 'traditional' intellectuals, see Gramsci 1975c, pp. 1513–40.

integrating the upper strata of the working class into a modernised, 'rational'
capitalism. The more clearly the defeat of the ruling power bloc announced
itself during the First World War, the more clearly the contours of a new class
alliance emerged in Weber's analyses: an alliance between capitalists and
the labour aristocracy, whose common interest, according to Weber, is that
of the 'greatest possible rationalisation of economic labour'. This 'industrial-
productive bloc', as Gramsci will go on to call it in his analyses of Fordism,
is not just meant to replace the Junker-bourgeois class compromise of the
Wilhelmine period, but also to pre-empt the danger of the formation of a socialist bloc of workers, peasants and soldiers. The same Weber who denounces the
subordination of the bourgeoisie to the aristocracy propagates the subordination of the labour movement to the class interests of the bourgeoisie.

5

In order to understand this two-front struggle, I refer to Gramsci's considerations on 'passive revolution'. The concept refers initially to those countries
'that modernize the state through a series of reforms or national wars without undergoing a political revolution of a radical-Jacobin type'.[21] Gramsci has
in mind those European states that constituted themselves after 1815, both in
'reaction' to the French revolution and as its 'national overcoming' ['"*reazione-
superamento nazionale" della Rivoluzione francese*'].[22] These states developed
'flexible frameworks' for a bourgeois seizure of power without spectacular ruptures; instead of eliminating the feudal classes, they downgraded them to mere
'governing' castes devoid of any economic function.[23] In analysing this type of
'passive revolution', Gramsci can draw directly on Weber's critique of German
'Caesarism'.[24]

In a wider sense, the concept refers to a social modernisation that occurs in
the 'absence of popular initiative'. It occurs under the direction of the ruling
power bloc, which adopts some of the demands formulated from below.[25] This
amounts to the description of a constellation of forces within which attain-

---

21    Gramsci 1996, p. 232.
22    Gramsci 1992, pp. 229–30; Gramsci 1975b, p. 1361.
23    Gramsci 1975b, p. 1358.
24    See Gramsci 1996, pp. 105–6; Gramsci 1975c, pp. 1527, 1809.
25    Gramsci 1975b, pp. 1324–7.

ment of hegemony is rendered impossible for the subalterns.[26] Rather than referring to 'backward' variants of development, Gramsci's concept of 'passive revolution' described processes that were endogenous to developed capitalism and showed its malleability in times of crisis. Gramsci 'in no way underestimated the ability of capitalism to "restructure" itself'.[27] What now emerges is a modern variant of passive revolution: a 'Caesarism without a Caesar' that reproduces itself by means of an entire system of parliamentarism, industrial organisation, liberalism, trade-union and party organisations.[28] According to Gramsci, what such a 'syndicalist phenomenon' achieves is, first and foremost, a new kind of 'transformism', within which it is no longer merely individuals from the opposition that are integrated into the camp of the 'moderates', but the opposing class's representation of interests as a whole.[29] 'The dialectical process of historical change is blocked by the ability of the capitalist order to absorb even the so-called representatives of its antithesis'.[30]

Weber is the critic of a German passive revolution that maintains the bourgeoisie in a state of political and cultural subalternity vis-à-vis the agrarian class; at the same time, he represents what was in his day the most modern variant of a passive revolution against the socialist labour movement. He looked to the well-paid 'Yankee worker', who had adopted the forms of bourgeois society in full. The bourgeois-proletarian industrial bloc Weber propagated would then go on to constitute the hegemonic core structure of mature Fordism, up until the latter's crisis in the 1970s.[31] In the interest of such a bloc, Weber calls on the bourgeoisie to recognise the reality of 'class struggle' and recast it as an 'orderly', purely economic struggle. His model of integration by means of a circumscribed conflictuality correlates with what political theory describes as the transition from 'state corporatism' to a 'societal corporatism'

---

26    In this sense, Schreiber defines passive revolution as the 'forcing back of a class that is "working its way up" from the "ethico-political" phase to the "economic-corporative" one' (Schreiber 1984, p. 105).

27    Buci-Glucksmann 1980, p. xi; see 1977, p. 15.

28    Gramsci 1975c, pp. 1619–22, 1822–4.

29    Gramsci 2007, pp. 257–8. The concept of 'transformism' [*trasformismo*], already employed by Gramsci in the first prison notebook (Gramsci 1992, p. 137), was initially coined by him when discussing Lamarck's theory of evolution; after 1882, Gramsci transposed it to politics, in order to refer to the elimination of clear dividing lines between political parties. See Migliorini 1983, pp. 711–12.

30    Sen 1989, p. 204.

31    In part, his influence continues to be felt in the social democratic and 'Kalmarist' variants of 'post-Fordism'. On Swedish 'Kalmarism' (Volvo) and the ideal type of 'negotiated involvement' it represents, see Leborgne and Lipietz 1996, pp. 697ff.

that transfers the regulation of social antagonisms from the state to the representatives of the economic classes.[32]

What can be analysed, with reference to Weber's political interventions, as a
passive revolution against the dangers of a socialist revolution, also reproduces
itself, in different variants, within Weber's social theory. The transformation of
acquisition from a means to an end in itself, by which Weber characterises the
'spirit of capitalism', is already discussed in Marx's *Capital*. But Weber takes
the idea from Simmel's *Philosophy of Money*, which wants to 'deepen' Marxism
by adding an underlying psychologico-metaphysical storey and transforms
Marxian value-form analysis back into an anthropological contemplation of
essences. Thus Weber already draws upon an 'overcoming' of Marx that has
adopted certain components of the Marxian analysis in a mitigated form.
Accordingly, one finds in his usage of the capitalist spirit a peculiar shift of
meaning, from an ethically charged capitalist interest in valorisation to the
ethos of an 'acquisition' become autonomous and general, and from there to
the work ethic. Since no distinction is made between the standpoint of use
value and the capitalist standpoint of valorisation, the concept oscillates
across a broad spectrum of meanings.

Weber's relationship to the young Sombart, who first developed the concept of the 'capitalist spirit', allows one to observe how different strategies
of passive revolution compete with one another within the field of theories
on the genesis of capitalism. In his history of capitalism's emergence (1902),
Sombart wishes to oppose a 'historical psychology' to the 'economic' approach
of Marxism. But his refutation of Marxism is still too busy wrestling with the
Marxian original for it to win recognition as a sustainable overcoming of Marx.
Sombart wishes to reject Marx's claim that capital comes into the world 'dripping from head to foot ... with blood and dirt',[33] but his capitalist spirit is still
imbued with too much ruthlessness, state despotism and genocide. Weber will
purge his ideal type of these brutal realities of domination by consistently situating spirit where the power centres of commercial capitalism are *not* located.

6

As soon as one conceptualises Weber's politics not in the narrow sense of the
history of political ideas, but strategically, as a project of bourgeois hegemony,
the internal links to the theoretical concept of a science that is both 'commit-

---

32    Schmitter 1979, pp. 20ff.
33    Marx and Engels 1975–2005, vol. 35, p. 748.

ted to values' [*wertgebunden*] and 'value-free' [*wertfrei*] become apparent. This leads us to the controversial issue of Weber's relationship to the 'southwest German neo-Kantianism' of Windelband and Rickert, which was an ultimately counter-Enlightenment philosophy of values that pandered to the ruling power bloc's need for values and had more in common with the metaphysics of Lotze than with the Kantian Enlightenment. Weber adopts its central concepts while simultaneously making them amenable to contrary value choices. If his project of modernisation is concerned with a social integration that operates by means of a system of circumscribed corporatist conflicts, Weber now delineates a system of contrary and incompatible 'value spheres' that are neatly set off one from the other. The concept of value spheres is the theoretical formula for the corporatist 'compartmentalisation' by which the antagonisms of class society are to be regulated. Weber first develops the concept of a 'polytheism of values' in 1916, with an eye to shielding German war policy from Christian pacifist interventions of whatever sort. Opposing the 'ethics of conviction' to the 'ethics of responsibility' fulfils a similar function of securing distinctions; the opposition delegitimises every fundamental critique of given relations as a form of otherworldly irresponsibility.

The *Protestant Ethic*, which Weber calls a 'purely historical account', is also calibrated, from the outset, to the modernisation aimed at by German capitalism. Its significance consists in the 'ethical' mobilisation of economic subjects in the transition to Fordism. The book's first sentence emphasises the 'predominantly *Protestant* character' of capitalists on the one hand and of the upper, skilled strata of the workforce on the other; the social subjects addressed are precisely those whose alliance Weber's political analyses look to. 'Ascetic Protestantism' consists primarily of two components, Calvinism and Baptism, which represent, in the cultural Protestant semantics of Ritschl, the liberal (Anglo-American) bourgeoisie on the one hand and Social Democracy on the other. The *Protestant Ethic*'s hidden *telos* is the historical bloc of Fordism.

In Weber, the capitalist spirit has the hue of the Reformation, and in Sombart, that of the Renaissance. It can be demonstrated by reference to their controversy over Leon Battista Alberti (1404–72) that specifications within the history of thought remain speculative to the extent that they abstract from the forms of social praxis and from given relations of hegemony. It is more fruitful to re-interpret the very search for capitalism's originary spirit in terms of the theory of hegemony. According to Gramsci, Alberti represents the apolitical Renaissance man, the private *borghese*, who subordinates himself to the old ideological powers, whereas the Reformation constitutes a 'popular-national bloc' that lastingly transforms society's superstructures. Unlike Sombart, Weber has an acute intuitive sense of the difference between a private bourgeois entrepreneurial spirit and the revolutionary ideology of a popular-bourgeois mass movement: he presents himself as an ethico-political reformer, one who hopes to modernise German capitalism with the aid of such a mass mobilisation and in accordance with a Puritan-American blueprint.

### 7

In a concluding chapter (see below, 30), I develop the hypothesis that the Fordist perspective also determined the arrangement of Weber's material on the history of religion in his comparative *Economic Ethics of the World Religions*. Weber sets off his ideal type of Western rationalisation both against what is situated 'above' and against what is situated 'below' it: against lofty ideologies of a 'Renaissance' that generate too little popular cohesion, and against chiliastic movements that seek to bring heaven down to earth. In his history of religion, as elsewhere, he applies the method of retaining only the 'passive' aspect of a revolution and eliding the struggle by which a new ethico-political system develops.[34] The fundamental difference between Weber's sociology of religion and Marxist-inspired or liberation-theological approaches is to be sought in this cropping of the subject matter; it consists in a perspective of inquiry that eliminates from the subject matter's definition the 'sigh of the oppressed creature' and '*protest* against real suffering'.[35]

### 8

Before the presentation can begin, Marx comments in his 1873 afterword to *Capital*, inquiry has to appropriate the material in detail and trace out the 'inner connection' of its forms of development.[36] The present study has also involved learning the difference between presentation and inquiry. What was difficult was not so much the writing process itself, but rather the identification of a subject matter that is both central and amenable to being circumscribed and engaged with. In search of Weber's theory of religion, I began with *Ancient Judaism*, worked my way through to the *Protestant Ethic* and then proceeded

---

34  Gramsci criticised such a 'passive revolution' within historiography by reference to Croce, who began his history of Europe not with the French Revolution, but with the Restoration, i.e. in 1815 (Gramsci 1975b, p. 1227).

35  Marx and Engels 1975–2005, vol. 3, p. 175.

36  Marx and Engels 1975–2005, vol. 35, p. 19.

from there to his study of *Confucianism and Taoism*. It took considerable time for me to realise that I could not hope to decipher the peculiarity of Weber's theoretical setup by starting from one of his various religio-historical subject matters; I needed to proceed, instead, from the discursive formations of the early twentieth century. In engaging with Weber's ideological contexts, I gradually began to understand that the key to understanding his intellectual mode of production lay in the ethico-political project of a modern bourgeois hegemony. It was only from this vantage point that the extensive material could be newly and differently ordered.

I wish to thank Brigitte Kahl for putting up with this writing process for so long. Her liberation-theological perspicacity saved me from succumbing to the lure of Weber's cultural Protestantism. My teacher and dissertation supervisor W.F. Haug sharpened my sense of the struggles and compromise-formations that characterise the ideological during our multi-year collaboration within the *Projekt Ideologietheorie*. In so far as he has passed on to me his enthusiasm for Gramsci, he is co-responsible for the present work's specific hegemony-theoretical approach. I also thank him for the stamina with which he pushed me to complete a project whose sprawl had at times assumed a forbidding quality.

The doctoral colloquium at the Philosophical Institute of the Free University of Berlin was a great aid to me. The discussions there forced me to socialise my own work, and thus, to some extent, to step outside my framework of thought. In particular, I thank Peter Jehle, Thomas Laugstien and Susanne Lettow for thorough criticism and valuable suggestions. A final word of thanks goes out to Mrs. Dr. Hanke, who granted me valuable access to the Max Weber Archive in Munich.

# PART 1

## *The Model of Americanism*

∴

# CHAPTER 1

# Weber's 1904 Journey to America

In the summer of 1904, Max Weber travelled to America for several months, accompanied by his wife, as well as by Ernst Troeltsch and other Heidelberg professors. The occasion was provided by an invitation to an international scholarly congress in St. Louis, the Congress of Arts and Science, organised in conjunction with the St. Louis world exhibition by the industrial psychologist and founder of 'psycho-technics' Hugo Münsterberg, who had moved from Freiburg to Harvard, and who invited German scholars from every faculty to hold lectures—'for a substantial honorarium', as Marianne Weber notes in her biography of Weber.[1] There were thirty-two German participants, among them Adolf Harnack, Karl Lambrecht, Ferdinand Tönnies and Werner Sombart, so that in his concluding report, Münsterberg was able to inform the German Reich commissioner that the number of Germans 'was greater than that of any other country' and that 'German scholarship and German erudition represented the most distinguished contribution to the intellectual work of the congress'.[2] While Troeltsch lectured on 'Psychology and Epistemology in the Study of Religion',[3] Weber spoke about 'German Agrarian Relations Past and Present', which allowed him, among others, to compare the German-Polish race relations in Eastern Germany and the race relations between white landowners and black sharecroppers in the American South. What connected the two experiences was for Weber the problem of how to control formally 'free' agricultural labour (after the abolition of serfdom in Eastern Germany and of slavery in the US). This commonality and the interconnection of race and class were the major motives prompting Weber to reach out to W.E.B. DuBois (whom he also met in St. Louis) and convince him to write an article on the 'Negro Question' for the *Archiv für Sozialwissenschaft und Sozialpolitik*.[4] 'You can imagine how I felt when I saw him standing before an attentively listening

---

1  Marianne Weber 1975, p. 279.

2  Quoted in Roth 1987, p. 182. 'In hindsight, the world exhibitions themselves appear as manifestations of nationalism, imperialism and racism', writes Roth (1987, p. 187). In this context, Roth also discusses Münsterberg's work as the 'cultural ambassador' of a 'Wilhelmine scholarly nationalism' in the USA, as well as Münsterberg's failure to realise his vision of an alliance between the 'three teutonic master nations' (pp. 175–7, 180, 193).

3  Troeltsch 1905.

4  Du Bois 1906. See Zimmerman 2010, pp. 207ff.

audience again for the first time in six and a half years!', writes Marianne Weber: 'It was to be hoped that Weber's breaking of the spell of silence would have an important effect on his recovery'.[5]

The visit to America, which included stops in New York, Chicago, Oklahoma, New Orleans, Tuskegee, Philadelphia and Boston, among other places, is of crucial importance to Weber in several respects. Biographically, it represented a turning point in his gradual recovery, persistently threatened by relapses, from the nervous disease whose onset, around 1897 or 1898, had been preceded by Weber's dispute with his father and the latter's death. Weber's disease had rendered all teaching and research impossible. Socio-politically, Weber's visit to America provided him with the vivid experience of a 'modern' capitalism that he contrasted, as a model to be replicated, with Germany's backward condition. Finally, in terms of the sociology of religion, the visit provided Weber with new inspiration for his work on the *Protestant Ethic*, which was itself both the starting point and the teleological endpoint of the later *Economic Ethics of the World Religions*. Weber completed the first of the *Protestant Ethic*'s two parts, on which he had probably begun working during the second half of 1903, just prior to his departure for America; the second part, which he penned during the three months following his return to Germany (January to March 1905), 'reveals the influence of his recent experiences'.[6]

Rarely has the internal link between the spheres of life and work, and more specifically between Weber's life and his political and religio-sociological reflections, been as evident as here. The greatest insights are still to be gained from the impressions Marianne Weber recorded in her biography, partly on the basis of the letters by Weber available to her, and partly on that of her own recollections.[7]

---

5   Marianne Weber 1975, pp. 290–1.

6   Marianne Weber 1975, p. 326; compare Lehmann 1988, p. 538.

7   Rainer Lepsius, the editor of Weber's correspondence (Weber 1984–2009, vol. 11/4) assures me that Marianne Weber has published Weber's surviving letters from America 'almost in full' (letter dated 3 July 1996). In order to distinguish between the various types of text, I use 'Marianne Weber 1975' to refer to passages written by Marianne Weber herself, and 'quoted in Marianne Weber 1975' to refer to letters by Max Weber that she cites.

# CHAPTER 2

# The Ambivalent Fascination of Capitalism

The new is joyously anticipated even before there is anything to see: the very preparations for the journey 'acted as a tonic', and during the boat trip, Weber 'cheerfully eats his way through the whole menu every day', to the point that Marianne Weber expresses 'concern about the increase in his bulk'.[1] He can hardly await the procedure of coming ashore and passing through customs: 'When they went ashore he darted ahead with long, elastic strides, leaving his companions behind'.[2] While some of his colleagues develop nervous disorders due to their sense of being lost in Manhattan, Weber 'has never been better since his illness'; 'he at first finds everything beautiful and better than in our country on principle'.[3] The prohibition on alcohol notwithstanding, he claims not to have been 'so merry as I have been here with these people, who are as naïve as children and yet handle any situation'.[4] On the journey back, Marianne Weber feels she is bringing a 'convalescent' home with her, 'a man who had again become conscious of the reserves of energy that had slowly accumulated'.[5] Weber's renewed brio continues to unfold its effects following the return journey. At an 'American evening' organised by Heidelberg's 'National Social Association' on 20 January 1905, during which Marianne Weber speaks about the condition of women in America, '[h]is impromptu remarks in the discussion were longer than those of the two main speakers put together; all the impressions he had stored up poured out irresistibly'.[6]

In general, there is much talk, in the scholarly literature, of Weber's enthusiasm for the hectic activity and zealous lifestyle of the Americans, but little of the social context within which he observed these phenomena.[7]

---

1  Marianne Weber 1975, p. 280.
2  Marianne Weber 1975, p. 281.
3  Marianne Weber 1975, pp. 281–2.
4  Quoted in Marianne Weber 1975, p. 293.
5  Marianne Weber 1975, p. 304.
6  Marianne Weber 1975, p. 355.
7  'With congenial, massive sensuous pleasure, he abandoned himself to the wildness of activity that presented itself to him there', writes Baumgarten, for example (1964, p. 450). Rollmann, analysing the letters Troeltsch wrote to his wife from America, mainly emphasises Weber's admiration for American diligence: 'American life rejuvenated him, and he threw himself into its stream with abandon, almost intoxicated by the dynamic of American work and industry' (1993, p. 373). According to Scaff, the Webers 'marveled at the extreme

The images garnered in America are, first and foremost, attempts to perceive an 'Americanist' formation of capitalism that seems to Weber to be superior to the German condition. The contrast between a dynamically advancing development in America and a stalled, retarded development in Europe is not new; it is typical of the German bourgeois perception of America, particularly in the first half of the nineteenth century.[8] Writing for the *Neue Rheinische Zeitung* in 1850, Marx and Engels interpreted the discovery of gold mines in California as heralding a shift of the world economy's barycentre to America and argued that this shift was capable of prompting a decline of old Europe comparable to the one suffered by northern Italy from the sixteenth century onward.[9] Europe's only chance, they wrote, consisted in 'a different distribution of property—indeed the total abolition of private property'.[10]

At the beginning of the twentieth century, there emerged in America the first elements of a formation that would later, following Gramsci, be called 'Fordism'. In 1903, one year before Weber's visit to America, Henry Ford set up his company in Detroit, employing eight persons; by 1926, he was director of a corporation that boasted 88 factories, 600,000 employees and an output of two million automobiles a year, securing it a roughly 50 percent share of the US auto market.[11] What Weber perceived in the new capitalism was first and foremost its developmental dynamic: 'With almost lightning speed everything that stands in the way of capitalistic culture will be crushed'.[12] Standing on New York's Brooklyn Bridge, he is impressed by the pulsating traffic and the trams crowded with passengers, but especially by the 'magnificent view of the fortresses of capital'.[13] The aesthetics of the new capitalism becomes tangible in the skyscrapers: 'The resulting picture is that of a streaked rock with a den of thieves on top. This is certainly not "beautiful", but neither is it the opposite; rather, it is beyond both, and . . . it is the most appropriate symbol that I can imagine of what goes on here'.[14] The 'monstrous' city of Chicago,

---

contrasts: wealth and comfort alongside poverty and squalor, civility together with criminality, decency with vice' (2011, p. 42).

8     On the various phases the German perception of America passed through, compare for example Fraenkel 1959, pp. 11–48, Mommsen 1971, pp. 358–9, and Roth 1987, pp. 170ff.

9     Marx and Engels 1975–2005, vol. 10, pp. 265–6.

10    Marx and Engels 1975–2005, vol. 10, p. 266.

11    See Hirsch and Roth 1986, p. 45.

12    Quoted in Marianne Weber 1975, p. 293.

13    Quoted in Marianne Weber 1975, p. 282.

14    Ibid. On the capitalist symbolism of skyscrapers, compare the sociological study of D'Eramo 2002, pp. 53–8: built by and for the large corporations, they reproduced 'the vertical organization of a huge company, as huge as the building itself. The height of the

with its blatant contrast between wealth and 'unkempt poverty', appears to the Webers as the point where the 'American spirit' consolidates; the city is driven by the 'breathless pursuit of loot' and shrouded in a dense fog, 'which placed a black veil over every stone and every blade of grass'.[15] What would today be considered a vision of ecological disaster presents itself here as the fascination of industrialism: to Max Weber, when the wind is blowing from a certain direction and the sun is setting, the coal fog that prevents one from seeing more than three blocks in the daytime makes the city look 'fantastic'.[16]

Weber attentively notes the modes in which class antagonism plays out, modes reminiscent of civil war. He perceives class struggle in violent street crime and in a 'pell-mell of nationalities' that produces a 'strange flowering of culture': 'All hell had broken loose in the "stockyards": an unsuccessful strike, masses of Italians and Negroes as strikebreakers; daily shootings with dozens of dead on both sides; a streetcar was overturned and a dozen women were squashed because a "non-union man" had sat on it'.[17] This description refers to the major strike Chicago's meatpackers organised against the beef cartel in 1904—one of the bloodiest labour struggles of the period.[18] What fascinates Weber about American capitalism is not just the level of technological development and the intensity of work, but also the brutal visibility of class struggles. Marx and Engels claimed in 1847/48, in the *Manifesto of the Communist Party*, that the bourgeoisie has stripped every occupation of its halo, made all that is solid melt into air and left no other nexus between man and man than 'naked self-interest';[19] the process seems to repeat itself before Weber's eyes half a century later, in the transition from Heidelberg to Chicago: '[T]he whole tremendous city ... is like a man whose skin has been peeled off and whose intestines are seen at work. For one can see everything—in the evening, for example, on a side street in the "city" the prostitutes are placed in a show window with electric light and the prices displayed'.[20] Skinned people and intestines—these are the metaphors by which Weber describes the 'nakedness' of a society that had remained unknown to him in turn-of-the-century Germany.

---

building is a concrete metaphor of the company turnover, with the leadership occupying its uppermost reaches' (p. 53).

15   Marianne Weber 1975, p. 285.

16   Quoted in Marianne Weber 1975, p. 286.

17   Ibid.

18   See Rifkin 1992, pp. 119–20; Scaff 2011, 40.

19   Marx and Engels 1975–2005, vol. 6, p. 487. The hypothesis is disputable, as it overlooks the significance and functional necessity of the ideological under capitalism, its specific 'halo' and compensating function.

20   Quoted in Marianne Weber 1975, p. 286.

In a contribution to 'transcultural psychiatry', Erich Wulff has shown what an important role the protected inner space that is bounded by skin, the demarcation line between the inner and the outer world, plays in the emergence of European and North American self-consciousness; Wulff points out how sensitively the bourgeois private individual responds to any injury done to this partition, as when the individual is faced with the sight of raw, skinned innards.[21] Similar 'socially specific idiosyncrasies' may result whenever the ideological estates of a class society, which are concerned primarily with the autonomous motion of 'spirit', are confronted with the 'innards' of the capitalist mode of production. The 'nervous disturbances of all kinds' that Marianne Weber notes in some of the German professors who participated in the journey might be seen as an example.[22] In Weber's case, this sort of idiosyncrasy seems however to assume something lewdly attractive, in part because of its association with prostitution: contemplating the idiosyncrasy becomes a taboo violation to be savoured with relish. The sensuousness of the new capitalism appears as something forbidden that comprises both maximum performance and destruction. It seems to him that one cannot be had without the other, and so the productive is simultaneously feared, and the destructive desired.

One discerns here, as in a magnifying glass, an ambivalence that runs through both Weber's political statements and the conceptual arrangement of his sociologies of domination and religion: his political struggle in Germany is directed against all those who attempt to resist capitalist 'modernity' (be they agrarian and conservative or revolutionary and socialist; see below, chapters 12 and 13), and at the same time, modern capitalism is the tacit ideal to which his concept of 'occidental rationality' is oriented. His ' "reason" remains *bourgeois* reason, and, indeed, only one part of the latter, viz. capitalist technical reason', Marcuse remarks.[23] But as soon as this same capitalism emancipates itself from its religious buttresses, Weber diagnoses that it rigidifies into an 'iron cage', in which material assets act upon men with 'irresistible force', 'until the last ton of fossilized coal is burnt'.[24] To the extent that the motif of

---

21    Wulff 1969, pp. 245–6. Wulff's analysis is based on a comparison of the European and North American social type with Vietnamese culture; according to Wulff, Vietnamese culture produces not an individual ego but the psychic structures of a 'group ego' (Wulff 1969, pp. 234ff).

22    Marianne Weber 1975, p. 281.

23    Marcuse 1969, p. 208.

24    Weber 1950, p. 181.

the 'iron cage' refers to the capitalist economy,[25] it expresses a reified form of domination that Marx analysed as the 'dull compulsion of economic relations' under capitalism.[26] But what is criticised by Marx, from the standpoint of a self-determined 'association of free men',[27] presents itself as an ineluctable fate in Weber.

It is one of the aporias of Weber's approach that an 'understanding' sociology, which repudiates Marxist analysis of the 'system' in order to emphasise 'social' action and its 'subjectively intended' meaning,[28] ends up establishing a fateful development of society and thus the utter disempowerment of subjective sense.[29] The apology for capitalist rationality switches abruptly into an apocalyptic account that no longer allows for any rational way out, but knows only 'pathos-laden images of the decline of one's own civilisation',[30] much like Nietzsche's cultural criticism. Weber's oscillation between the apologetic and the apocalyptic, which the most diverse interpretations have been able to latch on to, from Carl Schmitt and Parsons to the Frankfurt School, is itself the parable of a limited bourgeois conception of rationality: it expresses a rationality that veers into destruction at the very moment when it unfolds.

---

25    See for example Weber 1984–2009, vol. I/15, pp. 356, 464; Weber 1988a, pp. 331–2, 354. A different usage refers to the state bureaucracy (see 12.2), but in Weber's interpretation of modern capitalism, both usages are linked.

26    Marx and Engels 1975–2005, vol. 35, p. 726.

27    Marx 1976, p. 171; see Marx and Engels 1975–2005, vol. 35, p. 89.

28    Weber 1978, p. 3.

29    On Weber's approach to the theory of action and its critique, see Bader 1987, pp. 66ff, 99ff, 108ff, 492–3.

30    Peukert 1989, p. 27.

# CHAPTER 3

# Taylorism and Fordism in the Stockyards

Skinned persons and innards—what has just been used as a metaphor to describe a 'naked' capitalism seems to stem directly from Weber's visit to the Chicago stockyard. For when Weber attempts to describe the development of the forces of production and the intensity of work, he does so by reference to 'the "stockyards" with their "ocean of blood" ', which he was guided through by a boy: 'From the moment when the unsuspecting bovine enters the slaughtering area, is hit by a hammer and collapses, whereupon it is immediately gripped by an iron clamp, is hoisted up, and starts on its journey, it is in constant motion—past ever-new workers who eviscerate and skin it, etc., but are always (in the rhythm of work) tied to the machine that pulls the animal past them. One sees an absolutely incredible output in this atmosphere of steam, blood, and hides in which I teetered about together with a "boy" who was giving me a guided tour for fifty cents, trying to keep me from being buried in the filth. There one can follow a pig from the sty to the sausage and the can'.[1]

Weber's visit to the stockyard allows us to identify more precisely the elements of a new capitalist formation. The observed linking of the workpace to the machine presupposes, first and foremost, a Taylorist division of the work process into elementary and repetitive motions: in order to break workers' resistance to increases in work intensity, the ex-foreman and ergonomist Frederic W. Taylor (1856–1915) developed a 'scientific management' that deprived productive workers of their traditional work skills and transferred them to an office of engineers working for the company management. There, those skills were classified and reduced to rules in such a way that daily class struggle over norms of production could be replaced by a scientifically determined 'fair wage'. The classic example is the rationalisation of pig iron conveyance that Taylor imposed at the Bethlehem Steel Company from 1899 onward. In 1903, Taylor published the results in a report, *Shop Management*. The same year, the 'Taylor system' began to be presented and discussed in the periodicals of Germany's engineering associations.[2] What proved essential to a broader German reception was however Taylor's main work, *The Principles of Scientific*

---

1  Quoted in Marianne Weber 1975, p. 286.
2  Ebbinghaus 1984, p. 188.

*Management*, which was translated into German in 1913 as *Die Grundsätze wissenschaftlicher Betriebsführung*.[3]

A number of affinities with Taylorism can be discerned in Weber's writings. Weber already uses the term 'Americanism' prior to his visit to America, in the first part of the *Protestant Ethic*, although the term does not there refer to a new mode of production.[4] After his return from America, he speaks of a 'powerful tendency toward uniformity of life, which to-day so immensely aids the capitalistic interest in the standardization of production'.[5] However, and in accordance with his hypothesis on Protestantism, he does not elaborate on the connection with Taylorism, since he wishes to trace the uniformisation of lifestyles back to an 'ideal foundation', the Puritan rejection of 'idolatry of the flesh'.[6] Then again, it is no coincidence that the German Association for Social Policy's 1908 inquiry into the 'selection and adaptation' of workers in large industry, which Weber played an important role in organising, is often discussed, in industrial sociology, as a study that parallels Taylor's research.[7] In his 1908/09 study '*Zur Psychophysik der industriellen Arbeit*' ['On the Psychophysics of Industrial Labour'] Weber investigates (without reference to Taylor) how the ' "dissection of work tasks" within large firms' affects workers' 'psychophysical apparatus'.[8] But he leaves open the question concerning the 'labour-economic expediency of the dissection of work tasks', since he concludes that in spite of the advantages accruing from the 'mechanisation' of work and from rendering it 'rhythmical', combining individual tasks into a simultaneously performed overall activity may, under certain circumstances, be more effective.[9]

---

3    With regard to the expropriation of skills organised by Taylor, compare his motif of the 'intelligent gorilla' (Taylor 1911, p. 40). For an overview, see, *inter alia*, André Philip (1926, pp. 42ff), whose sociological study informed Gramsci's reflections on Fordism, and Angelika Ebbinghaus (1984, pp. 48–68).

4    Weber 1950, p. 62.

5    Weber 1905, p. 96; Weber 1950, p. 169.

6    Ibid.

7    On the relationship between Taylorism and the German approaches known as 'psychophysics' and 'psycho-technics', whose exponents range from Kraepelin to Weber and Münsterberg, see for example Eliasberg 1966, pp. 46–7, Fürstenberg 1966, p. 36, Hinrichs 1981, pp. 92ff, 102ff, and Ebbinghaus 1984, pp. 183ff, 218–19.

8    Weber 1984–2009, vol. I/11, p. 163; Weber 1988b, pp. 61–2.

9    Weber 1984–2009, vol. I/11, pp. 178, 208–9; Weber 1988b, pp. 73–4, 100–1. While rendering work 'rhythmical', for example, may have the advantage of producing typical reactions 'without an articulated impulse from worker's will', whether or not this benefit will accrue depends to a considerable extent 'on whether the rhythm that is imposed upon the worker from outside is characterised by a pace adequate to him' (Weber 1984–2009, vol. I/11, p. 178; Weber 1988b,

Weber returns to these issues of optimal adaptation and work performance in *Economy and Society*, where he explicitly relates them to their 'rational' implementation within the 'Taylor system'.[10] Finally, in *Politics as a Vocation* (1919), Weber observes that 'the soviets are keeping, or rather, reintroducing, high pay for the factory owners, piece work, the Taylor system, military and factory discipline'.[11]

The combination of the Taylorisation of work with mechanised mass production that Weber observed in the stockyards is, in turn, fundamental to the mode of production that is *Fordism*: 'The workpiece wandered through the various workstations, where there now remained only work operations that had been reduced and simplified as far as possible. The collective worker was thereby segmented in a way that made him virtually intangible'.[12] Braverman has illustrated how this segmentation of the work process was developed, in microscopic detail, in the meatpacking industry.[13] As shown, among others, by Rifkin,[14] the automatic conveyor belt was originally introduced not in the steel industry but in the stockyards, so that even Henry Ford, who presents himself as the inventor of the assembly line in his autobiography, had to admit that the assembly line as employed in the automobile industry was inspired by the overhead trolley in Chicago's meat factories.[15] D'Eramo situates the origin of the Fordian assembly line even further in the past, drawing attention to the 'disassembly line' invented, for the purpose of butchering pigs, in Cincinnati in 1830.[16] Chicago's stockyard was famous, until its closure in 1970, for its degree of mass production and its high technological standards. Bertolt Brecht was

---

p. 73). Moreover, combined activities are superior to segmented ones to the extent that a coherent whole is more easily comprehended than meaningless single motions (Weber 1984–2009, vol. I/11, pp. 208–9; Weber 1988b, pp. 100–1).

10      Weber 1978, p. 150.

11      Weber 2008, p. 177. One year earlier, Lenin wrote in 'The Immediate Tasks of the Soviet Government' that Taylorism combines 'the refined brutality of bourgeois exploitation and a number of the greatest scientific achievements in the field of analysing mechanical motions during work, the elimination of superfluous and awkward motions, the elaboration of correct methods of work, the introduction of the best system of accounting and control' (Lenin 1960–78a, vol. 27, p. 259).

12      Haug 1987, p. 672.

13      Braverman 1974, pp. 79ff.

14      Rifkin 1994, pp. 82–3.

15      Ford 1922, p. 81. After claiming his assembly line, first tested in 1913/1914, was 'the first moving line ever installed', he adds: 'The idea came in a general way from the overhead trolley that the Chicago packers use in dressing beef' (ibid).

16      D'Eramo 2002, pp. 29–30.

inspired by them to write his play *Saint Joan of the Stockyards* in 1929/30.[17] The stockyard *Armour & Company*, which Weber took a tour of,[18] belonged to one of the five major producers of the 'beef cartel', who had imposed themselves on the market between 1869 and 1890.[19] Much as cattle transportation acted as an economic motive for the construction of transcontinental railway lines in the 1870s and 1880s, thereby driving the colonisation of the West, meat-processing corporations dictated the country's capitalist development at the beginning of the twentieth century. The fact that economic theorists have looked mainly to the steel and automobile industries when discussing American industrialisation is explained by Rifkin in terms of the numbing smell of death, the inhuman objectification of killing and the catastrophic work conditions in the meatpacking industry, which would have dampened the enthusiasm of even the most convinced advocate of the new concepts of production.[20] If it is true that under Fordism, hegemony is 'born in the factory', as diagnosed by Gramsci,[21] then this requires a sunny side, that of a model that is presentable.[22]

By admiring the 'absolutely incredible output' of the stockyard in an atmosphere of smoke, excrement, blood and hide, Weber has one foot in the new capitalist era, so to speak, the era that will put its mark on the world economy until the crisis of the 1970s. It is still too early, in 1904, for the development of a theoretical concept of Fordism. When Gramsci, writing 25 years later, included Fordism in the list of 'main themes' discussed in his *Prison Notebooks*,[23] the underlying insight was that capitalism had not just achieved a state of relative

---

17     See for example the passage on the 'cunning' technology of self-slaughter: 'On a belt of plaited wire, the hog ascends / To the top floor; that's where the slaughtering starts. / Almost unaided, the hog goes plunging down / From the heights onto the knives. You see? The hog / Slaughters itself. And turns itself into a sausage. / For now, falling from floor to floor, deserted / By its skin, which is transformed to leather / Then parting from its bristles, which become / Brushes, at last flinging aside its bones—/ Flour comes from them—its own weight forces it / All the way down into the can. You see?' (Brecht 1976, p. 16).

18     See Marianne Weber 1975, p. 286.

19     Rifkin 1994, p. 80; compare D'Eramo 2002, pp. 37–9.

20     Rifkin 1994, pp. 82 and 84.

21     Gramsci 1992, p. 169; Gramsci 1975c, p. 2146.

22     For contrast, compare Upton Sinclair's novel *The Jungle*, on conditions in the meatpacking industry, with those passages in Ford's autobiography in which Ford describes his clean, well-lit factory buildings, linking cleanliness to morality: 'The dark corners which invite expectoration are painted white. One cannot have morale without cleanliness' (1922, p. 114).

23     Gramsci 1992, p. 174.

stability, as assumed by Bukharin, but that it was experiencing a new heyday thanks to 'Americanism' and 'Fordism'.[24] In Gramsci, the concept is intended mainly to describe a radical transformation of Europe's society, economy and civilisation that occurred under the pressures of the USA's economic predominance,[25] a transformation achieved, in part, in the fascist forms of a Fordism bent on violent catch-up development.

In the literature produced by the regulation school, Fordism's expansion, as a 'regime of accumulation', is usually dated to the 1920s, whereas its imposition across society, as a 'mode of regulation', tends to be situated in the period between the 1930s and the 1950s: the rift between the strategy of accumulation and the structure of politico-ideological hegemony culminates in a comprehensive crisis of regulation during the late 1920s; both the American 'New Deal' and the economic policy of German fascism can be seen as strategies to impose 'a structure of hegemony that corresponds to the changed conditions of accumulation'.[26] Aside from its combination of Taylorism and the assembly line, the new formation is characterised mainly by a combination of higher wages with affordable mass produced goods; this combination is considered the paradigm of a new model of consumption, based on cars and electrical appliances. Its corollary is the emergence of a new model of integration, by which working conditions and wages are negotiated in regulated, circumscribed conflicts between entrepreneurial associations and trade unions, assuring the ' "passive incorporation" of the working class into the state'.[27]

To what extent Weber's political and theoretical project of modernisation is bound up with the emergence of Fordism and anticipates the latter's imposition will emerge in the course of this study. This is also true with regard to the *Protestant Ethic*'s putatively 'purely historical discussion',[28] which correlates conspicuously with the ideological need for a Fordist regulation of lifestyles. A characteristic feature of American Fordism consists in company

---

24      Baratta 1990, p. 158.

25      According to Gramsci, the question is not whether there exists in America a new civilisation or culture; rather, '[t]he problem is this: whether America, with the implacable preponderance of its economic production, will force or is already forcing Europe to undergo an upheaval of its socioeconomic alignment ... [which] will bring about the overthrow of existing civilization itself and the birth of a new one' (Gramsci 1996, p. 17; Gramsci 1975c, p. 2178).

26      Hirsch and Roth 1986, pp. 49–50; compare pp. 46ff. See also Hirsch 1985, p. 325; Häusler and Hirsch 1987, p. 659; Haug 1987, p. 672; Peukert 1989, pp. 70–91; Haug 1996a, p. 190. On some difficulties of definition and periodisation, see Jessop 1988, pp. 385–6.

27      Hirsch 1990, p. 102.

28      Weber 1950, p. 182.

managers' forced recourse to the traditional ideologies of Puritanism, with the aid of which they hope to adjust the life habits of their workers to the exigencies of Taylorist production. Gramsci warns against interpreting this engagement with workers' morality as being no more than a hypocritical form of 'Puritanism', arguing that by adopting such an interpretation, one forfeits every chance of understanding 'the *objective import* of the American phenomenon, which is *also* the biggest collective effort [ever made] to create, with unprecedented speed and a consciousness of purpose unique in history, a new type of worker and of man'.[29] The creation of such a new type of individual is analysed by him as a violent psychophysical process of subordination and adjustment by which to bring about 'the imposition of one class over another' while 'hurling the weak and the unruly into the hell of the underclasses'. In this context, Puritan ideology has the function of exerting pressure on the social field and giving 'to the intrinsic brutal coercion the external form of persuasion and consent'.[30]

Considered against this backdrop, Weber's *Protestant Ethic* reveals itself as making a relevant contribution to the 'consensual' buttressing of Fordist socialisation. One of the ways in which it does so, and not the least important, is by underpinning Fordist systemic functioning with a complementary counter image. By deducing the 'capitalist spirit' from the ethos of Puritan Calvinism and the Baptist sects, the *Protestant Ethic* articulates a narrative on the spiritual 'origins' of capitalism that is a mirror inverted version of the relationship between consensus and structural coercion, moving from 'spirit' to 'system' and from the capitalist economic ethic to the 'iron cage'.[31]

---

29    Gramsci 1996, p. 215; compare Gramsci 1975c, p. 2165.

30    Gramsci 1992, p. 235; Gramsci 1975c, p. 2163.

31    'In Baxter's view the care for external goods should only lie on the shoulders of the "saint like a light cloak, which can be thrown aside at any moment". But fate decreed that the cloak should become an iron cage' (Weber 1950, p. 181).

# CHAPTER 4

# The Alliance of Religion and Business

In a brief note, Marianne Weber refers to the founder of the *Women's International League for Peace and Freedom*, Jane Addams: the 'angel of Chicago' who 'provided the proletarians who were thrown together from all over the world with all the things that they could not provide for themselves'.[1] When Brecht demonstrates, in *Saint Joan of the Stockyards*, the contradictory ways in which Christian religion functions within Chicago's class struggles and the manner in which it ultimately fails, he is thinking of this sort of 'worker priestess'. But in Weber's perception of 'Americanist' religion, it is neither the working environment and lifeworld of the Chicago stockyard nor large capital's 'fortresses', with their Puritan methods of socialisation, that serve as the starting point.[2] As the visit to America proceeds, there occurs a peculiar shift, whereby the social poles of capitalist socialisation, around which religious articulations group themselves and between which they seek to mediate, are elided within Weber's reflections on the relationship between religion and the 'capitalist spirit'.

For these reflections are preceded, in the journey, by a change of scene, from the world of capitalist production to Chicago's colleges, 'far outside the metropolis set among carefully tended green lawns and in the shade of old trees'.[3] Weber believes he can recognise that what students learn there is 'habituation to work', 'far more...than there is among our students', and this appears to him to result from the fact that the colleges were founded by Puritan sects. To be sure, the 'religious spirit' has already 'mixed with uncongenial components', the sectarian organisations have been transformed into sports clubs—'Their "cricket team" is regarded as the best in the country'—, and asceticism has become prosperity: 'the young rascals are rolling in money'. But when attending the Quaker service, he still encounters a certain 'special' silence: in the wholly undecorated, altarless room, there is nothing to be heard except 'the crackling of the fireplace and muffled coughing', until, in an odd combination

---

1  Marianne Weber 1975, p. 288.

2  On the uses to which Puritanism is put within corporate ideological strategies, see André Philip 1926, pp. 126–7, note 1.

3  Marianne Weber 1975, p. 288.

of spontaneity and planning, someone 'moved' by the spirit holds a 'carefully prepared' speech.[4]

Religious relations also appear to him as 'utter chaos'. He notes both the 'tremendous power' of the church congregations and the fact that they are exposed to a much stronger process of secularisation. Students are required to attend three-fifths of the religious services that are held on a daily basis. If they fail to do so, they are expelled after two years, but if their 'chapel record' is higher than required, their surplus attendance is added to their record the following year. Sometimes the service consists in a theological lecture on Harnack's history of dogma. 'At the conclusion the dates of the next "foot-ball," "cricket," etc. are announced, as the harvesting used to be announced in German villages'.[5]

Following his return to Germany, Weber uses the 'chapel record' as the opener of a two-part feature article on 'Churches and Sects' first published in the *Frankfurter Zeitung* on 13 and 15 April 1906 and then re-published, in a slightly expanded form, in *Christliche Welt* on 14 and 21 June 1906. These articles constitute the foundation for Weber's essay 'The Protestant Sects and the Spirit of Capitalism', which he completed shortly before his death in 1920 and appended to the essay on the 'Protestant Ethic' in the first volume of his *Collected Essays on the Sociology of Religion*.[6]

While he does not do so in the 1920 essay, the two 1906 versions see Weber employing the 'chapel record' as an example by which to illustrate to his German readers the relationship between the religiosity of 'Americanism' and its 'superiority in the struggle for existence'.[7] Weber argues that in spite of its rigid separation of church and state, America has developed a far more intense 'churchliness' than Germany.[8] He traces this phenomenon back mainly to the fact that the place of religious commitment to the state has been taken, in America, by a close alliance between religion and commerce. While the American authorities never display any interest in one's religious affiliation, the people one does business with ask about it almost every time. 'Why pay

---

4   Quoted in Marianne Weber 1975, pp. 288–9.

5   Quoted in Marianne Weber 1975, p. 289.

6   I will henceforth cite the expanded version from *Christliche Welt* as 'Weber 1906a' (Part I) and 'Weber 1906b' (Part II), whereas I will cite Gerth and Mill's translation of Weber's 1920 version as 'Weber 1946a'.

7   Weber 1906a, p. 559.

8   For example, the dues paid for church activities sometimes amounted to as much as eight percent of the average income: even a fraction of this financial imposition would have led to mass secession from the church in Germany (Weber 1946a, p. 302; compare Weber 1906a, p. 559).

me, if he doesn't believe in anything?', says one salesman quoted by Weber.[9] Without membership in a sect, one has no chance of a career in the world of medium-sized business. What matters is not what sect one belongs to, but that one has been admitted to it, after examination and trial, by means of 'ballotage', a secret vote involving the use of white (yea) and black (nay) tokens. Thus, for example, a banker in need of credit joins a Baptist congregation not so much for the sake of the congregation as for that of his non-Baptist customers; joining the congregation involves an examination of his moral and commercial conduct that is considered to be far and away the strictest and most reliable.[10] Pointing out one's membership in the congregation during a visit to the doctor amounts to offering a guarantee of one's payment morale.[11] Unlike the 'church', which one is born into, membership in a sect amounts to 'a certificate of moral qualification and especially of business morals for the individual'.[12]

In this way, the sect becomes the key to understanding American commercial life and its 'ethic'. As foreshadowed by the change of scene during his visit to America, Weber explicitly focuses his analysis on the upwardly mobile strata of the bourgeois middle class 'outside of the quite modern metropolitan areas and the immigration centers', as he holds that the ruling economic spirit originates within these strata, and not among the 'economic supermen' of large capital.[13] The fact that Weber regularly situates his concept of a 'capitalist spirit' in the places where capital's centres of power are *not* located results from a peculiar 'ideal-typical' method of concept formation that I will return to in greater detail below (see chapters 22 and 28). I am not concerned here with the questions of how and with what justification Weber deduces his 'capitalist spirit' from the Protestant ethic or the sects. I wish to inquire, rather, into his specific manner of posing the problem and his underlying epistemological interest.

---

9       Weber 1946a, p. 303.
10      Weber 1946a, p. 305.
11      Weber 1946a, p. 304.
12      Weber 1946a, p. 305.
13      Weber 1946a, pp. 307–8.

# CHAPTER 5

# The 'Displacement' of Religion from the State into Civil Society (Marx)

Noting the country's particularly intense bond between religion and bourgeois commercial life was already a commonplace of the literature on America before Weber. The best known example is Tocqueville's 1835/40 investigation *Democracy in America*, which Weber never mentions, in spite of the conspicuous parallels with his own claims. Visiting America in 1833, Tocqueville also encountered a peculiar contradiction between the outward powerlessness of a religion separated from the state and an inner power of religion that was simultaneously imbued with an enlightened 'doctrine of interest rightly understood'.[1] 'The Americans not only follow their religion from interest, but they often place in this world the interest which makes them follow it'.[2] American priests—including Catholic priests![3]—attentively observe the successes of acquisition and 'applaud its results'. Instead of opposing religion and prosperity to one another, 'they study rather to find out on what point they are most nearly and closely connected'.[4] In 'On the Jewish Question', Marx refers, *inter alia*, to Tocqueville's book on America and to the report of Tocqueville's travelling companion Beaumont (*Marie ou l'esclavage aux Etats-Unis*, 1835). He also quotes an 1834 inquiry into Americans and their customs by Hamilton, according to which 'the devout...inhabitant of New England...adores [his idol Mammon] not only with his lips but with the whole force of his body and mind', even the preaching of the gospel having become an article of trade.[5]

While Marx's 1844 essay 'On the Jewish Question' was written in a completely different context—that of Marx's engagement with the critique of

---

1   Tocqueville 1904, p. 609.
2   Tocqueville 1904, p. 614.
3   The fact that Tocqueville considers Catholicism a part of America's democratic and republican religion jars with Weber's denominational approach and may explain why Weber never mentions Tocqueville: as French foreign minister (prior to the Bonapartist coup of 1851), and more importantly, as a decidedly Catholic politician and scholar, Tocqueville belongs to a national and confessional discursive world that Weber is not inclined to refer to or to cite.
4   Tocqueville 1904, p. 41.
5   Marx and Engels 1975–2005, vol. 3, p. 170.

religion formulated by the Young Hegelian Bruno Bauer—,[6] it could be fruit-
fully compared with Weber's account, in order to highlight both the limits and
the strengths of the way in which Weber poses the problem. Marx also considers North America 'pre-eminently the country of religiosity', American religion being characterised by 'a fresh and vigorous vitality'; religion's separation
from the state is described by Marx as a 'big step forward'.[7] According to Marx,
this step forward consists mainly in the state's *political* emancipation' from
religion, whereby the state no longer '[professes] any religion', like Germany's
'Christian state', but rather '[asserts] itself as a state'.[8] The phenomenon Weber
describes as a specific combination of religion and bourgeois commercial life
corresponds to what Marx conceptualises as the '*displacement* of the state from
religion into civil society'.[9] From the religious fragmentation in North America
he concludes that religion has become a 'purely individual affair'. 'Banished'
from the sphere of public law to that of private law, relegated to the elements
of bourgeois society, 'thrust' among the multitude of private interests, it has
gone from being the 'spirit of the state' to being the 'spirit of *civil society*'.[10] As
an integral component of the sphere of egoism and the *bellum omnia contra
omnes*, religion is 'no longer the essence of *community*, but the essence of *difference*' and has become 'the expression of man's *separation* from his *community*, from himself and from other men'.[11] By virtue of the 'most diverse world
outlooks' being 'grouped alongside one another in the form of Christianity',
Christianity finally attains 'the *practical* expression of its universal-religious
significance': 'The religious consciousness revels in the wealth of religious contradictions and religious diversity'.[12]

Weber, who considers the separation of religion and state policy indispensable, would surely have endorsed the way Marx contrasts the religious
situation in Germany (and Bauer's critique of religion, bound up with that

---

6    Marx's immediate point of criticism concerns Bauer's impertinently anti-Judaist position
     that Jews need to relinquish their religion, as well as religion in general, before human
     and civil rights can be bestowed upon them. Marx responds by arguing that political
     emancipation leads not to the abolition of religion, but rather to 'freedom of religion'—as
     in America. Marx then proceeds to transform Bauer's 'religious' argument into the ques-
     tion concerning the relationship between bourgeois-political and 'human' emancipation.
     For a theoretical appraisal of the essay, see Haug 1993, pp. 210–16.

7    Marx and Engels 1975–2005, vol. 3, pp. 151, 155.

8    Marx and Engels 1975–2005, vol. 3, p. 152.

9    Marx and Engels 1975–2005, vol. 3, p. 155.

10   Marx and Engels 1975–2005, vol. 3, p. 159.

11   Ibid.

12   Ibid.

situation) with America's separation of church and state, its 'displacement' of religion into civil society. But for Marx, this is only the starting point from which to transform the critique of religion, initially adopted from Feuerbach, into a critique of the capitalist economy and its 'emancipated' political state: what appears as a 'step forward' when comparing Germany with North America simultaneously reveals itself to be a new type of alienation. The bourgeois revolution withdraws the dispersed political competencies from society and pools them in an ideological instance of the political that administers the community's affairs separately from the real community, in an 'ideally independent' way.[13] Above the world of a materialist bourgeois life there arises the imaginary beyond of a state idealism, and this structure, which continues to be 'religious',[14] causes man to lead 'a twofold life, a heavenly and an earthly life': it splits him into the egotistic private individual of bourgeois society on the one hand and the moral person of the 'abstract' citizen on the other.[15]

These considerations on the cleavage within both bourgeois society and its subjects remain relevant to understanding alienated sociability as it presents itself within bourgeois society. The phenomenon Weber describes in terms of the alliance of religion and commerce has here been integrated in a comprehensive model of the compensation associated with ideological societalisation, a model within which state policy and apolitical private life, bourgeois materialism and state idealism, public morality and private egotism oppose, mutually implicate and stabilise one another. Weber observes religion's relocation from the state to bourgeois society without taking account of, for example, the religious form of the political public sphere, which it would later become common to describe, within the Anglo-American debate, by concepts such as 'civil religion' or 'civic religion'. The 'genius' of the American solution consists in the fact that the public *civil religion* and the private religions of the church congregations constitute a twofold religious superstructure, writes Bellah, for

---

13    Marx and Engels 1975–2005, vol. 3, p. 166: 'The political revolution ... set free the political spirit, which had been, as it were, split up, partitioned, and dispersed in the various blind alleys of feudal society. It gathered the dispersed parts of the political spirit ... and established it as the sphere of the community, the *general* concern of the nation, ideally independent of those *particular* elements of civil life'.

14    Man merely emancipates himself from religion in a manner that is itself 'religious', in 'a *roundabout way*', 'through the *medium of the state*', which becomes—like Christ—the mediator between man and his freedom (Marx and Engels 1975–2005, vol. 3, p. 152). One can see from this extension of the concept of religion how Marx leaves behind Feuerbach's critique of religion, which he had initially adopted, transposing its categories to the critique of the political state and of political economy (see Rehmann 2013, pp. 34–41).

15    Marx and Engels 1975–2005, vol. 3, pp. 153–4.

example.[16] In 1967, Bellah introduced Rousseau's concept of *religion civile* into the American debate, without however making reference to Marx's 'On the Jewish Question' or Gramsci's concept of *società civile*.[17] What interests Weber in the alliance of religion and bourgeois commerce is its superiority, in terms of 'economic ethics', vis-à-vis Germany's state church. Weber is not, however, interested in the question raised by Marx, namely how 'man's *separation* from his *community*' manifests itself within this alliance.[18] Bourgeois society's 'egotistic individual', which Marx presents to us as restricted, as a segregated 'monad', a degraded 'partial being', the 'passive result of the dissolved society',[19] is uncritically presupposed in Weber.

In this sense, Tocqueville, with his critique of the bourgeois private individual in America, is closer to Marx than to Weber:[20] in this country where the love of property is more 'restless and ardent' than elsewhere, one need not fear a revolution so much as a withdrawal of citizens into the 'narrow circle of domestic interests' that causes every innovation to be seen as an annoying disturbance, such that 'man will waste his strength in bootless and solitary trifling' and humanity, 'though in continual motion, will cease to advance'.[21] Above the isolated private individuals, there could arise a new despotism that succeeds in '[interfering] more habitually and decidedly within the circle of

---

16   Bellah 1978, p. 20.

17   In his theory of *religion civile*, Rousseau envisioned the state formulating a 'purely civic profession of faith' [*profession de foi purement civile*], so as to ensure that its citizens love their duties. This profession of faith was to include the basic sentiments of sociability [*sentiments de sociabilité*] as well as a number of general dogmas on divinity, the rewards and punishments of the hereafter and the sanctity both of the social contract and of law (Rousseau 1959, pp. 340–1). In Bellah, the concept of 'civil religion' refers to a firmly institutionalised religious aspect of American public life that involves ritualised invocations of the Almighty (in political speeches), a specific festival calendar (Thanksgiving, Memorial Day), a religiously idealised conception of history, and so on (Bellah 2002, pp. 513–14, 516). 'Though much is selectively derived from Christianity, this religion is clearly not itself Christianity' (Bellah 2002, p. 517). Bailey renders the concept more nuanced by using 'civic religion' to refer to its official aspect and 'civil religion' to refer to its popular, 'do-it-yourself' aspect (Bailey 1985). For a presentation and critique of the 'civil religion' approaches of Luhmann, Lübbe, Böckenförde, Spaemann and Koslowski, see Kleger and Müller 1986.

18   Marx and Engels 1975–2005, vol. 3, p. 155.

19   Marx and Engels 1975–2005, vol. 3, pp. 163, 164, 167.

20   It is no coincidence that Croce will claim, in his *History of Europe*, that Tocqueville's 'prejudices' derive from the doctrine of communism (Croce 1935, p. 140; compare p. 155).

21   Tocqueville 1904, pp. 754–5.

private interests' than ever before:[22] one that bends and leads the will instead of breaking it, thereby transforming the people into a 'flock of timid and industrious animals, of which the government is the shepherd'.[23]

Thus, amidst the points on which Marx and Weber agree, we also discern different perspectives. The fact that Weber perceives North America's religious life as an achievement for economic ethics, while Marx also perceives the alienated community, is accounted for by the different standpoints from which they conduct their inquiries. Considered from Marx's point of view, Weber resembles the 'old materialism' criticised in the 'Theses on Feuerbach' insofar as he assumes the 'standpoint of bourgeois society',[24] or, more precisely, the standpoint of a 'developed bourgeois society', devoid of feudal privileges,[25] contrasting it with the condition of Germany. To the extent that he formulates a critique of ideology in his political and sociological writings, this critique would be largely one of 'traditionalism', one that limits itself to those structures and attitudes that stand in the way of a 'developed bourgeois society'. By contrast, it is one of the strengths of Marx's critique of ideology that it begins with those manifestations of bourgeois society that are, relatively speaking, the most advanced, discussing bourgeois society's 'modern' structures of domination from the perspective of horizontal 'self-societalisation'.[26] Sixty years before Weber's visit to America, Marx opposes to the 'old' standpoint of bourgeois society his own 'new' standpoint, that of a 'human emancipation' or 'social humanity'.[27] What is fundamental is his anticipation of a 'human emancipation' in which the 'individual human being' no longer 'separates social power from himself in the shape of *political* power', but rather 're-absorbs in himself the abstract citizen'.[28]

And yet it is precisely in this strength of the Marxian critique that one finds, on the other hand, a weakness, one that was not overcome, within Marxism,

---

22  Tocqueville 1904, p. 808.

23  Tocqueville 1904, p. 811.

24  Marx and Engels 1975–2005, vol. 5, p. 5 (translation modified). In the *Marx Engels Collected Works*, Marx's notion of '*bürgerliche Gesellschaft*' (Marx and Engels 1975–2005, vol. 3, p. 7) is rendered as 'civil society' (Marx and Engels 1975–2005, vol. 5, p. 5), which demonstrates a fundamental ignorance of the ambiguity of the term '*bürgerlich*'. On the misleading and detrimental effect of such fallacious translations, see Rehmann (1999).

25  Marx and Engels 1975–2005, vol. 4, p. 116 (translation modified).

26  On the concept of 'self-societalisation' [*Selbstvergesellschaftung*], see Haug 1993, pp. 81–2, 154, 173 and Rehmann 2013, pp. 248–54.

27  Marx and Engels 1975–2005, vol. 5, p. 5.

28  Marx and Engels 1975–2005, vol. 3, p. 168. On the reciprocal relation between critique and anticipation within Marxism, see Rehmann 1994, pp. 364ff.

until Gramsci. By limiting himself to opposing the 'political state' and 'bourgeois society' to one another, Marx leaves no room for attention to the institutions of civil society, in which different social forces struggle for hegemony. This
is mainly because Marx progressively narrows the meaning of the polysemous
German expression 'bürgerliche Gesellschaft' ['bourgeois society' and/or 'civil
society']: Marx uses the expression to refer to bourgeois property relations,
but he fails to analytically distinguish between these relations and the idea of
the civic.[29] Thus Marx's reduction of bourgeois human rights to the illusory
freedom of the 'monad' forgets that individuals also engage in societalisation
outside of the state (in the narrow sense),[30] by entering into relationships of
cooperation, founding associations, and so on, and that human rights may perform a socially protective function in this context. Because Marx never develops a concept by which to describe the contested space of social institutions
and attitudes, he reduces the religion that has been 'displaced' from the state
to a mere expression of bourgeois private property, without displaying much
interest in the structure and workings of its 'apparatuses', organisations and
forms of socialisation. 'The religious appears to him as a sort of mirage appearing in the haze that . . . arises from capitalist practice'.[31] The point at which the
key lacuna of the Marxian critique of ideology and religion is located (a lacuna
that was to prove consequential in the history of Marxism) is the very point
at which the strengths of Weber's approach become apparent. What interests
Weber about North American religion is, first and foremost, the sect as a form
of societalisation [Vergesellschaftung], and its consequences for the 'selection'
of bourgeois economic subjects.

---

29    See for example the passages in which Marx stipulates that '[c]ivil society as such only
      develops with the bourgeoisie' (Marx and Engels 1975–2005, vol. 5, p. 189), civil society
      being characterised by the commodity form as the 'economic cell form' (Marx and Engels
      1975–2005, vol. 35, p. 8) and by capital as the 'all-dominating economic power' (Marx and
      Engels 1975–2005, vol. 28, p. 44), and so on. For an in-depth discussion, see Markner 1995,
      pp. 380–8, and Rehmann 1999.
30    See for example Marx and Engels 1975–2005, vol. 3, p. 162, and Marx and Engels 1975–2005,
      vol. 4, p. 116.
31    Haug 1993, p. 215.

# CHAPTER 6

# The Sect as Germ Cell of a Superior Model of Societalisation

By accounting for the transformation of religion into an 'economic ethic' in terms of the sect, Weber moves beyond his original hypothesis on Protestantism. The essay on the American sects (particularly the late, 1920 version) differs from the *Protestant Ethic* mainly insofar as it no longer explains the connection between Protestantism and the 'capitalist spirit' purely in terms of (Calvinist or Baptist) theology, but also provides an account of this connection on the 'structural-organisational' level.[1] The sociological distinction between the church as an 'institution' and the 'voluntarist' sect, commonly attributed to Ernst Troeltsch, can already be found in Weber's first, 1906 version of his essay on the American sects.[2] It is from there that Troeltsch adopted the concept of the sect for his 1912 work *The Social Teaching of the Christian Churches*, expanding it into a 'great sociological collective type of Christian thought' that stands opposed both to the 'ecclesiastical' and to the 'mystical' social type.[3] This typological distinction is, in turn, picked up on by Weber, who generalises it in two ways: first, he transposes it from the history of Christianity to the comparative religio-sociological study of the world religions; second, he reformulates it in terms of his sociology of domination, where it appears as the opposition between 'institution' and 'association'.[4]

---

1  Berger 1973, p. 251. Berger holds that the 'socio-structural' links between Protestantism and capitalism are stronger than the 'theologico-cultural' ones; referring mainly to the example of Talcott Parsons, he shows that a misguided focus on 'value systems' has led to Weber's key question, the question concerning the influence of churches and sects on everyday life, 'being lost out of sight almost entirely' (Berger 1973, pp. 247–8, 251, 254).

2  See Weber 1906b, pp. 577ff.

3  Troeltsch 1960, p. 689. Compare Troeltsch 1960, pp. 204–46, 328ff, 347–9, 379ff, 689ff, 700ff, 802ff, 817ff. That Troeltsch adopted the religio-sociological concept of the sect from Weber's 1906 article is confirmed both by Troeltsch himself (Troeltsch 1960, p. 433, note 164) and by Weber (Weber 1950, p. 255, note 173).

4  For examples of Weber's general religio-sociological usage of the term, see his studies of Confucianism and Taoism (Weber 1951, pp. 215ff, 218ff, 223ff; see Weber 1984–2009, vol. 1/19, pp. 433–4, 437ff, 446ff) and of Hinduism and Buddhism (Weber 1958, pp. 193–4, 293ff, 318ff; see Weber 1984–2009, vol. 1/20, pp. 307, 464ff, 509ff), the introduction to 'The Economic Ethics of the World Religions', translated as 'The Social Psychology of the World Religions'

Weber's deduction of the 'capitalist spirit' in America from the organisational structure of the Baptist sect is as controversial as his deduction of the 'capitalist spirit' from a specifically Protestant ethic. The criticisms levelled against him address different aspects of his explanatory model. Very roughly, one can distinguish three arguments: (1) Weber's focus on the American middle class ignores the fact that in New England, for example, 'possessive individualism' (Macpherson) imposed itself in parallel with the economic influence of the major export salesmen and against the resistance of the Puritan clergymen;[5] (2) both in the case of the Baptist and in that of the later Puritan sects, Weber systematically elides eschatology and its associated 'Ebionite' and anticapitalist dimensions;[6] (3) in analysing middle-class activism itself, Weber excludes other relevant factors from his explanatory model, such as the Protestants' social status as fugitive 'heretics' and 'strangers', emphasised by Sombart.[7]

The weaknesses indicated in these objections are overwhelmingly related to the ideal type of the 'capitalist spirit', whose underlying compositional principle will be analysed later (see below, chapters 28 and 29). This should be distinguished from the status of the Puritan sect within the ideological superstructure of American society, and in particular within its imaginary. One of the strengths of Weber's hypothesis on sects consists precisely in the fact that it engages with this imaginary—in part as its critical analysis, in part as an integral component of this imaginary, an instance of American 'mythistory'.[8] In what follows, I am not concerned with historically verifying or falsifying the essay on the sects within the framework of an 'American road' to capitalism; rather, I am concerned with the contemporary political stakes of its framing of the problem.

Formulated as it is (in the essay on the sects), namely in terms of the sociology of organisations, Weber's hypothesis on Protestantism is a hypoth-

---

(Weber 1946b, pp. 287ff; see Weber 1984–2009, vol. 1/19, pp. 111ff) and *Economy and Society* (Weber 1978, pp. 456–7, 479–80, 866–8, 1204–10). On the reformulation of the religiosociological opposition between 'church' and 'sect' into the sociology of domination's opposition between 'institution' and 'association', see Weber 1978, pp. 52–3, 55–6.

5  See for example Kilian 1979, pp. 35ff.

6  See for example Samuelsson 1961, pp. 27ff; Kofler 1966, pp. 240ff; Lehmann 1980, pp. 134ff; Lehmann 1988, pp. 540–1.

7  See Sombart 1916, pp. 878ff, 885ff; Sombart 1920, pp. 385, 392–3.

8  This is argued, for example, in Roth 1993a, pp. 3–4. Roth adopts the concept of 'mythistory' from McNeill, who uses it in an excessively general and therefore uncritical sense; in McNeill, the concept refers to any sort of search for historical truth: 'Myth lies at the basis of human society. That is because myths are general statements about the world and its parts ... that are believed to be true' (McNeill 1986, p. 23).

esis on the peculiarity and superiority of US civil society. The modern secular clubs that recruit their members by ballotage and accompany Weber's 'typical Yankee' from the cradle to the grave are products of a 'characteristic process of "secularization" '.[9] It is mainly to the sects that American democracy owes 'the elastic structure proper to it', and thus the strength of not constituting 'a formless sand heap of individuals, but rather a buzzing complex of strictly exclusive, yet voluntary associations'.[10] The German counterparts are the acquisition of 'titular nobility' through the purchase of a manor, 'which in turn facilitated reception of the grandchildren in aristocratic "society" ', and the major importance, within estates-based society, of 'qualifying to give satisfaction by duel'.[11] In the 1910 report on the Frankfurt Sociological Congress, Weber will use America, 'the land of associations *par excellence*', to illustrate the project of a 'sociology of associations' that examines the 'social' formations situated between the state and the family, 'from the bowling club to the political party and the religious, artistic or literary sect'.[12]

In the first (1906) version of the essay on the sects, it is more apparent than in the final (1920) version that Weber's line of argument is directed against a German conservatism that criticises democracy as 'atomisation': 'Those who think of "democracy" in the manner so dear to our romantics, which is to say as a mass of people ground into atoms, are thoroughly mistaken: it is not democracy but rather bureaucratic rationalism that tends to produce such "atomisation", which the popular imposition of "structures" from above then fails to eliminate'.[13] The first thing to be noted here is a new way of framing the problem: the conservatives traced atomisation, which Marx had traced back to commodity production, back to 'democracy'. Weber does not question this new framing of the problem in terms of a particular political form. Instead, he limits himself to shifting the blame to the bureaucracy. What both interpretations have in common is their elision of the capitalist economy's isolating effects.

Having returned the accusation of atomisation to the conservatives, Weber dispels their concern over the equalisation putatively associated with democracy: far from being a 'sand heap', American society was and continues to be 'shot through with "exclusivities" of all sorts', replacing an estates-based 'aristocracy of "rank" ' with an 'aristocracy of "quality" ' based on the individual's

---

9   Weber 1946a, pp. 309, 307; see Weber 2001, p. 77.

10  Weber 1906b, p. 580; Weber 1946a, p. 310.

11  Weber 1946a, pp. 310–11.

12  Weber 1988b, pp. 441–2.

13  Weber 1906b, p. 580.

personal achievements.[14] Weber's broadening of the concept of aristocracy, such that the term now refers to the 'social exclusiveness of a group of people' as such,[15] is part of a conceptual strategy suited for convincing at least part of the aristocracy of the benefits of a transition to democracy, while simultaneously providing non-aristocratic citizens with the self-confident conviction that they are the bearers of the genuine aristocratic values: the feared combination of democracy and social equality yields to a combination of democracy and 'aristocracy'.

At the heart of Weber's comparison of religions lies the diagnosis that in Germany, capitalist modernisation is being stalled by a statist and authoritarian form of religious life: it is 'our fate' that the German Reformation 'benefited not the practical vigour of individuals, but the mystique associated with an "office"'. That is why every effort at individual emancipation had to 'lead to hostility towards religious communities'.[16] This rift between religion and bourgeois private initiative seems to him to have been overcome in America's congregationalist system.[17] For it was in this system that individual autonomy obtained 'a foundation that rested not on indifferentism, but on religious positions': 'during the period of its heroic youth, individualism developed an eminently community-instituting power'.[18]

While the sects are still addressed, in this passage, as 'communities', this is corrected shortly thereafter: 'The "artefacts" are always, to use the terminology of Ferdinand Tönnies, "societies" and not "communities"'.[19] In his 1887 work *Community and Society*, Tönnies had defined the former as a 'living organism', whereas he described the latter as a 'mechanical aggregate and artefact' consisting of 'individuals living alongside but independently of one another'.[20] In essence, Tönnies is concerned with distinguishing, in an ideal-typical manner, a purely bourgeois-capitalist form of socialisation from pre-bourgeois forms of

---

14    Ibid.

15    Ibid.

16    Weber 1906b, p. 581.

17    Similarly, but from a Catholic standpoint, Tocqueville laments the difficult relationship between religion and 'freedom' in France: 'The religionists are the enemies of liberty, and the friends of liberty, and the friends of liberty attack religion; the high-minded and the noble advocate subjection, and the meanest and most servile minds preach independence; honest and enlightened citizens are opposed to all progress, whilst men without patriotism and without principles are the apostles of civilization and of intelligence' (1904, p. xli). Tocqueville also believes these difficulties have been overcome in America.

18    Weber 1906b, p. 579.

19    Weber 1906b, p. 581.

20    Tönnies 2001, p. 19.

socialisation, the latter being mystified as 'organic'. The community is rooted in the 'all-embracing character of the ... "vegetative" life that stems from birth'.[21] From the germ cell of the family, one line of continuity leads to relatives, neighbours, friends, common ownership of goods, and so on, while another leads, via patriarchy and gerontocracy, to princely rule.[22] Thus *community* encompasses the most contrary phenomena: pre-bourgeois authority *and* confraternity, the spirit of brotherhood *and* the presiding status of the father, the village community *and* the manor house.[23] By contrast, Tönnies's remarks on *society*, which follow, by and large, the structure of the first volume of Marx's *Capital*, focus on the exchange of commodities, exchange value, the generalised 'willingness to exchange', money and the capitalist production of surplus value.[24] To this Tönnies adds the associated contracts and the legal order that ensures they are respected, as well as an—at best—'*conventional sociability*' in which '[t]he primary rule is politeness'.[25] The nature of 'bourgeois society' or 'exchange society' is defined in terms of a 'situation in which, to use Adam Smith's expression, "everyone is a merchant" '.[26]

Tönnies's opposition between *community* and *society* is useful to Weber because it dissimulates the very social antagonisms of a given society which a Marxist critique of domination is mostly interested in. It focuses instead on the opposition between 'traditional' and 'rational' (or personified and reified) forms of domination, as well as between 'emotional' and 'impersonal' varieties of socialisation. Weber adopts this dualist construct in his sociology of domination, tacitly ignoring what stands in the way of such an adoption: for a start, Tönnies linked his concept of society to a specific tendency towards rationalisation that starts from the community and then develops, via individualism, into a 'state-based and international *socialism*'. This notion of socialism is 'already latent in the concept of *Gesellschaft* [society], although it begins only in the form of practical links between all the forces of capitalism and the state'.[27] Moreover, religion is treated as the form of volition proper to the community; its corollary in society is the form of volition known as 'public

---

21    Tönnies 2001, p. 22.

22    Tönnies 2001, pp. 25ff.

23    Tönnies 2001, pp. 41–2.

24    Tönnies 2001, pp. 52ff, 72–3.

25    Tönnies 2001, p. 65.

26    Tönnies 2001, p. 64.

27    Tönnies 2001, p. 260. To be sure, Tönnies's statist socialism transitions into state capitalism, as when, for example, he holds that it can be realised 'without needing to remove the fundamental division between the social classes': 'The state would become a coalition of capitalists that excluded all competition' (Tönnies 2001, p. 238). 'One can think of Tönnies

opinion'.[28] Thus religious societies exist only 'for some extraneous goal, such as serving the state or to promote some theory'.[29]

Without engaging with the basic conceptual setup, Weber reconfigures Tönnies's (state) socialist perspective as an 'Americanist' one,[30] transposing the opposition of community and society into the domain of religion itself. In *Economy and Society*, he refers to Tönnies's 'fine work' and characterises the sect as being, along with market exchange and purposive association, one of the 'purest' varieties of societalisation, 'insofar as it does not cultivate emotional and affective interests, but seeks only to serve a "cause"'.[31] The social community of the sect is not a collective being that hovers mystically above the individuals, Weber writes in the 1906 version of his essay on the sects; rather, it is consciously employed as a 'mechanism by which to achieve one's material or ideal aims'. Far from the 'undifferentiated, rustic-vegetative "cosiness" without which Germans believe no community can be cultivated', the sect is characterised by a ' "cool" objectivity of societalisation' [*kühle Sachlichkeit der Vergesellschaftung*] that rests on the 'accurate integration of the individual into the group's purposive action'.[32]

As if to confirm Marx's 'On the Jewish Question', religion is conceptualised as a purposive bourgeois undertaking, which is, however, accounted for not in terms of the workings of bourgeois society, but in terms of the voluntarist character of the 'believer's church'. The strength of Weber's approach is that one can now examine a mode of societalisation where Marx postulated only an asocial 'monad'. However, this possibility is compromised from the outset insofar as Weber insists the ideological societalisation of the sect is, by definition, of a purely 'objective' nature, and insofar as he elides, in an a priori manner, the sect's emotional and 'community'-constituting effects. In the 1920 version of his essay, Weber defines the type of societalisation proper to the sects firstly in terms of its bourgeois 'direction', the 'breeding of personal qualities suitable for *business*', and secondly in terms of the new 'means' by which the desired effects were produced: primarily, a continuous 'selection' differing

---

as the early exponent of a corporatism that oscillates between conservatism and socialism', writes Krüger (1988, p. 103).

28    Tönnies 2001, pp. 239–40.

29    Tönnies 2001, p. 18.

30    Kühne points out that Tönnies's ideal types are contrary to those of Weber: 'instead of providing an apology for the rationality of liberal capitalism, they are intended to demonstrate the ineluctability and necessity of a rational, "scientific socialism" ' (Kühne 1971, p. 222).

31    Weber 1978, p. 41.

32    Weber 1906b, p. 581.

from Catholic and Lutheran church discipline in that it does not occur in an
'authoritarian' manner, or via a spiritual office, but by virtue of the 'necessity of holding one's own in the circle of one's associates' ['*Notwendigkeit der
Selbstbehauptung im Kreise der Genossen*'].[33] What Weber contrasts with the
German condition is a mobilisation of subjects that promises freedom from
ideological subordination while simultaneously consolidating a new type of
ideological subordination. By speaking of *Genossen* [comrades, associates], he
adopts a horizontalist appellation from the socialist labour movement, and
he also adopts part of that movement's anti-ideological critique of traditional
hierarchies. But equality must not be understood as a horizontal relationship
of cooperation; instead, it is hybridised—by its association with 'self-assertion'
and 'selection'—with a social Darwinist discourse that transposes the bourgeois competition over achievement (a competition based on formal equality) to the internal structure of a religious association. In contrast with the
churchly institution of a grace that shines its light on the just and the unjust
alike, the sect qua association of 'persons with full religious qualification' is
nothing less than an 'aristocratic group'.[34] The elision of emotional and affective interests in favour of a 'cool objectivity of societalisation' delineates an
ideological subordination to alienated ends that is as closed to debate, in its
logic of 'practical constraints', as the ousted pre-bourgeois 'authorities'. This
correlates, on the level of the mode of production, with the process by which
the form of authority proper to the factory is transposed to the organisation
of the work process itself; Taylor's 1903 *Shop Management* summarises this
transposition by stating that the system of subordination yields to a 'system of
functions or activities'.[35] Much in the same vein, Henry Ford would later present himself, in his autobiography, as struggling against 'unjust' hierarchies and
honorary titles within the world of production, declaring the despotism of the
assembly line to be nothing but subordination to the work itself: 'The work and
the work alone controls us'.[36]

---

33    Weber 1946a, p. 320. Compare the identical formulation in the study on Confucianism
      (Weber 1951, p. 218; Weber 1984–2009, vol. I/19, p. 437) and the analogous formulation in
      Weber 1978, p. 1204.
34    Weber 1978, pp. 1204–5.
35    Quoted in Ebbinghaus 1984, p. 59.
36    Ford 1922, p. 93. Ford praises his new entrepreneurial principle of first stripping the single
      productive worker of as much knowledge and as many skills as possible and then pooling
      that knowledge and those skills in the bureau of engineers. He responds to the accusation
      of having undermined skilled productive work by claiming that he has, on the contrary,
      introduced a higher level of skill: 'We have not [taken skill out of work]. We have put in
      skill. We have put a higher skill into planning, management, and tool building, and the

What has changed is the mode in which the vertical dimensions are merged with the potentials of self-directed activity. The selective advantage consists precisely in the combination of a horizontal community, based on the 'spirit of early Christian brotherliness',[37] with an objectified process of elite formation, within which each member needs to constantly 'prove' himself: 'The continuous and unobtrusive ethical discipline of the sects was, therefore, related to authoritarian church discipline as rational breeding and selection are related to ordering and forbidding'.[38]

Thus, when Weber takes into account the institutional structure of American civil society (something Marx fails to do in 'On the Jewish Question'), he does so with an eye to its more efficient selection of bourgeois economic subjects. The sect is 'a selection apparatus for separating the qualified from the unqualified'.[39] It is around this selective function that a new kind of ideological 'mastic' will form, binding together bourgeois society's principal classes. For while the Protestant sect represents a 'particularist' formation, it also constitutes a vibrant, and not merely a traditional form of popular religiosity: 'The sects alone have been able to imbibe, on the basis of Protestant religiosity, broad masses of people and, more specifically, modern workers, with an intensity of clerical interest such as one will otherwise meet with only in the form of the bigoted fanaticism of retrograde peasants'.[40] The secularised result consists, according to Weber, in a specific adjustment to the habitus of the bourgeoisie: at the club, relations between the boss and his subordinate are characterised by the 'equality of gentlemen', and the wife of the American union man has fully adapted her dress and behaviour to that of the bourgeois lady; it is merely 'somewhat plainer and more awkward'.[41]

The genesis and the structure of the most modern form of bourgeois hegemony constitute the immediate political stakes both of the essay on the sects and of Weber's hypothesis on the link between ascetic Protestantism and the 'capitalist spirit' as such, and this hypothesis is, in turn, the starting point and the endpoint of his entire sociology of religion. Thus the astounding diffusion

---

results of that skill are enjoyed by the man who is not skilled' (Ford 1922, p. 78). Those performing their work need not know about the work of others: 'It is the business of those who plan the entire work to see that all of the departments are working properly toward the same end' (Ford 1922, p. 92).

37   Weber 1946a, p. 318.
38   Weber 1946a, p. 320.
39   Weber 1978, p. 1204.
40   Weber 1906b, p. 580.
41   Weber 1946a, pp. 310–11.

and lasting appeal of the *Protestant Ethic* is not due, primarily, to its scholarly soundness, which was questioned from the outset, and with good reason, but rather to the relevance, in terms of hegemonic strategy, of its framing of the problem.

Understanding what precisely this relevance consists in requires a change of scene, from America to Germany, as it is from within the German context that Weber looks to America.

# PART 2

*Outlines of a Fordist Project of Modernisation for Germany*

∵

# CHAPTER 7

# The Programme of the 1895 Freiburg Inaugural Address

Weber's May 1895 inaugural address, 'The Nation State and Economic Policy', is considered the most important document of his political stance prior to the First World War. Weber himself notes the lecture left his listeners appalled by the 'brutality' of his views.[1] He was thinking mainly of his argument that the national economy ought to be oriented to the 'economic and political power interests of our nation':[2] 'We do not have peace and human happiness to hand down to our descendants, but rather the eternal struggle to preserve and raise the quality of our national species ... Our successors will hold us answerable to history not primarily for the kind of economic organisation we hand down to them, but for the amount of elbow-room in the world which we conquer and bequeath to them'.[3]

'What use is the best social policy, when the Cossacks come?' Friedrich Naumann commented in an enthusiastic review. 'We need a socialism that is capable of governing. ... Such a socialism capable of governing must be nationalistic [*deutschnational*]'.[4] The impression left by Weber's lecture was not the least important factor contributing to the foundation, in 1896, of the 'National Social Association' [*National-Sozialer Verein*]. Weber and the younger members of the Christian Social Workers Party founded it with the aim of winning the workers who adhered to Social Democracy back to the cause of a 'national state' and 'a social empire'.[5] During this period—that is, between 1893 and 1899—Weber was also a member of the 'Pan-German Union' [*Alldeutscher Verband*] led by Alfred Hugenberg, Carl Peters and others; it called for a policy of expansion and Germanisation in Central and Southeastern

---

1 In a letter to his brother Alfred Weber dated 17 May 1895 (Weber 1984–2009, vol. I/4, p. 538 FN 12; compare Marianne Weber 1975, p. 216).

2 Weber 1994a, p. 17; see Weber 1984–2009, vol. I/4, p. 561.

3 Weber 1994a, 16; see Weber 1984–2009, vol. I/4, p. 560.

4 *Die Hilfe*, 14 July 1895, quoted in Marianne Weber 1975, p. 220; compare Mommsen 1974, pp. 74–5.

5 See Mommsen 1974, pp. 134–5; Theiner 1983, pp. 53ff.

Europe, prefiguring the key goals of German fascism within both domestic and foreign policy.[6]

Mommsen sees the inaugural address as having 'sparked the development of a liberal imperialism in Wilhelmine Germany';[7] Marcuse uses it to illustrate his critique of the concept of scientific neutrality, arguing that Weber 'with ruthless frankness subordinates value-free economics to the claims of national power politics'.[8] Nolte comments that the address 'far exceeds Treitschke in terms of its ruthlessness and exclusive orientation to national power'. He notes a 'striking resemblance' to certain passages of Hitler's *Mein Kampf*, but adds that the address is in some ways contrary to that work and represents a possible alternative solution.[9] Wehler describes it as documenting a 'goal-conscious imperialism' and calls it the 'fanfare flourish' of an industrial bourgeoisie representing 'the fundamental process that affected the overall development of society more powerfully than any other', a bourgeoisie pressing for a basic social decision in its favour.[10] By contrast, Hennis attempts to treat the Freiburg inaugural address as evidence supporting his hypothesis on the question that 'actually' interested Weber, that of the 'development of humanity'; in doing so, he is forced to elide the internal links between the address and the requirements of imperial power politics.[11] Schluchter believes he can counter such a 'peculiar rehabilitation' of the inaugural address by admitting that there are 'nationalist and Nietzschean undertones' in the early Weber but claiming that they have been overcome in Weber's later, scholarly and value-free work.[12]

---

6    See Wehler 1995, p. 1075.

7    Mommsen 1974, p. 76.

8    Marcuse 1969, p. 202.

9    Nolte 1963, pp. 2–3, 9, 12. According to Nolte, both the inaugural address and *Mein Kampf* begin from an 'imperialist nationalism that inclines toward raciology', a 'residual and extreme form of classic liberalism' that detaches the struggle of economic subjects from the notion of harmony and relates it to the 'cultivation of one's own nature' (Nolte 1963, p. 4). However, the contrariety of the two texts already emerges, according to Nolte, from their contrary definitions of the domestic foe: the labour movement and the Jews in Hitler, and the Prussian Junkers in Weber (ibid.).

10   Wehler 1995, pp. 620, 1140.

11   While Weber relates the value judgements of political economy to 'the particular strain of humankind [*Menschentum*] we find in our own nature', namely, and as emerges clearly from the context, the 'German state' (Weber 1994a, p. 15), Hennis perceives a first indication of the anthropological question concerning the 'development of humanity' as such (Hennis 1987, p. 46).

12   Schluchter 1991, pp. 177–8.

The significance of the Freiburg inaugural address is however not to be sought in particular 'undertones' but in the fact that it synoptically presents the strategic statement of the problem and the proposals that underpin Weber's political interventions. The general context is that of a critical sea change within Wilhelmine society. The extraordinarily rapid industrialisation process of 1873–95 followed Germany's relatively late industrial revolution. This process led to the expansion of major corporations, a predominance of financial capital and the increased significance of state intervention, thus transcending the framework of the 'private' and 'anarchic' capitalism analysed by Marx. Schumpeter speaks, in this context, of 'the watershed between two epochs in the social history of capitalism'.[13] The explanatory approaches developed within the social sciences largely fall into two groups: some adopted the concepts of 'state monopoly capitalism' or 'organised capitalism', inspired by Lenin and Hilferding; others, influenced by the Anglo-American debate, resorted to concepts such as 'corporation capitalism' or 'corporate capitalism'.[14] In contrast with a terminology that is often vague and unspecific, Gramsci's concept of Fordism has the advantage of conceptualising the transition from economic individualism to a 'planned economy' [*economia programmatica*] in terms of the specific requirements of a new mode of production.[15]

In Germany, the accelerated industrialisation process led to a crisis of modernisation and of hegemony. Weber held his Freiburg inaugural address in the final phase of an economic slump that lasted from 1890 until 1895 and was often perceived, by contemporaries and in the older economic literature, as part of a much longer, more than 22-year 'Great Depression' lasting from 1873 until 1895.[16]

---

13   Schumpeter 1934, p. 67.

14   Lenin, for example, speaks in 1917 of the transition from 'monopoly capitalism' to 'state-monopoly capitalism', and he sees the latter as 'the complete *material* preparation for socialism' (Lenin 1960–78b, vol. 25, pp. 360–1). The term 'organised capitalism' first appears in a 1915 essay by Hilferding, where it refers to the 'transformation of an anarchic capitalist into an organised capitalist economic order', achieved by the dominance of financial capital and monopolistic industry (Hilferding 1915, p. 322). On the rediscovery of the concept in the 1970s, see the essays by Kocka, Wehler, Feldmann, Puhle and Maier in Winkler 1974. Also note Wehler's later rejection of the concept and his replacement of it with the—overly general—concept of corporatism: Wehler 1995, pp. 663ff. References to 'corporation capitalism' or 'corporate capitalism' can be found, for example, in Maurice Dobb (Kocka 1974, p. 24).

15   Gramsci 1975c, p. 2139.

16   This interpretation, which Lenin's 1916 pamphlet on imperialism still appears to endorse (Lenin 1960–78c, vol. 22, p. 199), is rightly criticised for ignoring that the volume of productivity, commodity consumption and other significant indicators continued to

The fact that the boom of the *'Gründerjahre'* was followed, as early as 1873, by a severe downturn led many entrepreneurs, investors, politicians and journalists to develop an overwhelmingly pessimistic 'economic mentality inclined to constant lamentation'.[17] To this was added the traumatic experience of the rise of the Social Democrats, who emerged as the strongest party from the 1890 Reichstag elections, winning 19.7 percent of the vote and increasing their number of seats threefold in spite of the Anti-Socialist Laws. The non-continuation of the Anti-Socialist Laws, defeat in the *Kulturkampf* against Catholicism and Bismarck's 1890 dismissal marked a moment of painful defeat for the ruling power bloc. The subsequent attempts of the 'Caprivi era' (1890–4) to reconfigure the relations of power in favour of the bourgeoisie by adopting a pro-industry foreign trade policy were foiled by the resistance of major conservative landowners. It is within this context of economic and political crisis that Weber formulates his assessment that the foundation of the Reich has not been followed by the 'inner unification of the nation'.[18]

It is one of the distinctive features of Weber's analysis that he considers the deadlock of state politics in terms of the underlying class relations. In order to understand the significance of the Freiburg inaugural address to Weber's socio-political project, one needs therefore to consider, first and foremost, the way he assesses, from the perspective of the nation's 'elbow room', the 'political maturity' of the classes:

– The Junkers have done their meritorious work, but they now find themselves 'in the throes of an economic death-struggle'.[19] The retention of political power by an economically declining class is incompatible with the nation's interests. For it has always been the attainment of economic power 'which has led any given class to believe it *is a candidate for political leadership*'.[20]
– It is even more pernicious 'when classes which are moving *towards* economic power, and therefore expect to take over political rule, do not yet have the political maturity to assume the direction of the state'.[21] Weber

increase during the period. See, *inter alia*, Mottek 1974, pp. 175ff; Wehler 1995, pp. 552ff, 579ff.

17  Wehler 1995, pp. 578–9, 593–4.
18  Weber 1994a, p. 22. This formulation is obviously a variation on the widespread talk of the need for an 'inner founding of the Reich' by which to complete its 'outer' founding. See Sauer 1970, pp. 429, 548.
19  Weber 1994a, p. 22; Weber 1984–2009, vol. I/4, p. 567.
20  Weber 1994a, p. 21; Weber 1984–2009, vol. I/4, p. 566.
21  Ibid.

accounts for the bourgeoisie's political immaturity in terms of Bismarck's Caesarist founding of the Reich, Bismarck having been 'made of distinctly un-bourgeois stuff'.[22] A significant part of the upper bourgeoisie 'longs all too clearly for the coming of a new Caesar to protect it'; another part has sunk to the political Philistinism of the petty bourgeoisie.[23] What is lacking, first and foremost, is an adequate way of 'educating the people politically', something that cannot be substituted for by anything economic, and something that needs now to finally be tackled with the utmost urgency.[24]

– Weber deduces from the economic maturity of the working class, or at least of its 'highest strata', the right of the trade union 'to stand up for its interests in the shape of the openly organised economic struggle for power'.[25] He accounts for the political immaturity of the working class in terms of its leadership: a 'clique of journalists' that lacks both the 'Catilinarian energy to *act*' and the national fervour of the French Revolution. In other words, it lacks 'the great *power* instincts of a class with a vocation for political leadership'.[26]

In spite of a vague 1913 statement to the effect that he can 'no longer identify with the inaugural address on numerous important points',[27] the strategic axes of Weber's class analysis remain stable and structure not just his political interventions, but also, as will be shown in Parts Three and Four, the conceptual setup of his scholarly work. One feature of Weber by which he differs from most of the writers that invoke him, and not the least important, is that he lays bare the social standpoint from which he formulates his political interventions. He presents himself as a 'member of the bourgeois classes' who identifies with their views and ideals, adding however that his scholarly vocation makes it his duty 'to say things people do not like to hear—to those above us, to those below us, and also to our own class'.[28] Thus he speaks as the general intellectual of a bourgeoisie that has yet to find itself, in his view. He wishes to contribute to making the bourgeoisie capable of leadership, by means of 'political education'. In his first *Prison Notebook*, Gramsci argues that

22    Weber 1994a, p. 23; Weber 1984–2009, vol. I/4, p. 568.

23    Weber 1994a, p. 24; Weber 1984–2009, vol. I/4, pp. 569–70.

24    Weber 1994a, p. 25; Weber 1984–2009, vol. I/4, p. 570.

25    Ibid.

26    Weber 1994a, p. 26; Weber 1984–2009, vol. I/4, p. 571.

27    In the expert assessment on freedom from value judgements written for the committee of the Association for Social Policy in 1913 (quoted in Baumgarten 1964, p. 127).

28    Weber 1994a, p. 23; Weber 1984–2009, vol. I/4, p. 568. All that Hennis perceives in Weber's definition of his social position is a 'polemical concept by which to distance himself from flippant attitudes to the world' (Hennis 1987, p. 213).

before a class can seize power, it needs to assume a leading [*dirigente*] position; that is, it needs to attain 'political hegemony'.[29] As Gramsci looks to the hegemony of the proletariat, so Weber looks to that of the bourgeoisie. His claim to intellectual neutrality, which he will later elaborate theoretically in his statements on 'freedom from value judgements', does not stand opposed to this task; rather, it is what allows him to criticise and move beyond the 'average judgements' of his class.[30]

If the deciphering of Weber's social standpoint is removed, attempts to identify him politically with 'nationalism', 'liberalism' or 'modernity' remain superficial and incoherent. Wehler, for example, is led to the false conclusion that Weber was, much like Schmoller, and 'in spite of his differentiations and criticisms on points of detail', of the view that German monarchy and German 'spirit' were superior to the American hunt for filthy lucre.[31] The opposite is the case: Weber was always at pains to distance himself from such German chauvinism. His orientation of the national economy to the interests of German imperialism is not a claim about German superiority. For this reason, it is also misleading to contrast Weber's identification with 'German imperialist nationalism' with a later, 'modern' orientation to America.[32] For Weber does both things at the same time: he looks to America in order to strengthen the position of the German 'nation' within the imperialist power struggle.

What Schluchter describes as 'nationalist and Nietzschean undertones' and associates only with the early Weber may display the specifically 'German' features of a belated imperialism, but it is also part of the quite 'modern' discursive formation of an international 'social Darwinism' that accompanied

---

29    Gramsci 1992, p. 137. This is the first time Gramsci employs the term 'hegemony' as a synonym for the category of 'leadership' [*direzione*], which he distinguishes from the concept of 'domination' [*dominio*]. From this passage onward, the concept of hegemony serves to develop a '*differential analysis of the structures of bourgeois power in the West*' (Anderson 1976, p. 20). In the *Southern Question*, Gramsci uses the concept of proletarian 'leadership' with an eye to the formation of a common bloc uniting the northern labour movement and the peasants of southern Italy. The workers, Gramsci argues, need to overcome their prejudices vis-à-vis the peasants, thereby enabling themselves to win over the majority of workingmen and intellectuals by means of a new system of class alliances (Gramsci 1971, pp. 135, 145; compare Gramsci 1966, pp. 17ff).

30    See Weber 1988b, p. 419.

31    Wehler 1995, p. 463.

32    See for example Mommsen 1971, p. 359.

the emergence and breakthrough of Fordism.[33] The debates on Weber's 'liberalism' are largely dominated by ideological reception interests: while it was essential to American sociology's post-1945 reception of Weber that he be presented as a 'liberal' German, a different interpretation focuses on Weber as a 'German thinker' and sees him as continuous with a Nietzschean 'voluntarism' that has thoroughly done away with the illusions of 'liberal optimistic thought'.[34] Arguments can be found for each of these interpretations; what both have in common is their elision of the class constellation Weber had in mind; it is this class constellation that gives his 'liberal' or 'voluntarist' articulations their social significance.

Gramsci speaks of the emergence of a new, 'organic' type of intellectual in America. This intellectual is no longer the inorganic element of the 'corporatist' interests of his class; rather, he is capable of representing the 'self-critique' of that class, to detach himself from it in order to 'unite [himself] to it more closely', thus constituting its genuine 'superstructure'.[35] While this remark was made in a different context,[36] it nevertheless expresses the social significance of Weber's intervention. This is especially true of the two interrelated projects that recur in his political statements and analyses: on the one hand, he is concerned to free the bourgeoisie from its 'Caesaristically' mediated alliance with the agrarian class, providing it with a class self-consciousness of its own; on the other hand, he wants to attempt to win the 'higher strata' of the working class over to an alliance with the bourgeoisie. As will be seen in the following chapters, Weber is both a critic of Germany's 'passive revolution', which keeps the bourgeoisie in a politically and culturally subaltern position vis-à-vis the agrarian class, and the protagonist of a new constellation of 'passive revolution', one that aims at creating a Fordist bloc of modern entrepreneurs and workers.

---

33  On the association of 'scientific management' with social Darwinism in the USA, see for example Ebbinghaus 1984, pp. 25ff, 45ff, 220–1. Henry Ford also represents an anti-Semitic variant of social Darwinism; he devoted an entire book to the struggle against Jews (*The International Jew*). His puritan mobilisation is directed against the 'unpleasant orientalism' of the Jews, which he claims has 'insinuated itself' in all walks of life (Ford 1923, p. 293; compare Ford 1922, p. 251).

34  Hennis 1987, pp. 219, 222, 233.

35  Gramsci 1996, p. 355.

36  The example used by Gramsci is Sinclair Lewis's novel *Babbit*, whose critique of habits appears to Gramsci as the symptom of a new alliance between the ruling class and the intellectuals (Gramsci 1996, p. 355).

This strategic project is part of a more general paradigm shift within 'socio-political' engagement with the issue of class during the transition to the twentieth century: Weber does not develop his political positions on his own, but in relation to and by means of his engagement with the other 'social reformers' who organised themselves in the Association for Social Policy [*Verein für Sozialpolitik*] and the Evangelical Social Congress [*Evangelisch-sozialer Kongress*].

# The Katheder Socialist Milieu

Weber's transition from jurisprudence to political economy begins with an orientation towards 'Katheder Socialism' (or 'armchair Socialism'). Mommsen sees it as the 'turning point' of Weber's political biography, one by which Weber emancipated himself from the older liberalism.[1] From 1886 onward, Weber frequents a circle of young political economists and 'socio-politically interested civil servants of various kinds', whose key feature he describes in an 1888 letter to his uncle Hermann Baumgarten. There, Weber writes that what one banked upon now was 'state intervention in the so-called *social question*', so that the National Liberal era of the 1870s now appeared only as the 'transition to greater tasks for the state'.[2] While Weber concedes to the disillusioned liberal Baumgarten that he is not comfortable with the circle's 'strongly bureaucratic vein',[3] what strikes him as more important is the consideration that these elements are 'the only ones who perceive themselves clearly and proceed vigorously, which is why they will be the dominant ones in the future'.[4] Their view, he claims, 'will emerge as the dominant one, because it is the clearest'.[5]

Thus Weber's career as a political economist begins—after the successful defence, in 1889, of his legal dissertation on the history of the medieval trading companies—within the milieu of 'Katheder socialism'. Both of the two associations he joins around 1890, the Association for Social Policy [*Verein für Sozialpolitik*] and the Evangelical Social Congress [*Evangelisch-sozialer Kongress*] had been founded and influenced by leading 'Katheder socialists'. Both explicitly opposed the rise of Social Democracy and promised to avert the threat of revolution by integrating those worker demands they considered justified into a state social policy. The term 'Katheder Socialism' was first used by Oppenheim on 17 December 1871, in the right-wing newspaper *Nationalzeitung*, and Oppenheim intended it as a derisive moniker.[6] Those thus attacked were

---

1  Mommsen 1974, pp. 16–17.
2  Letter dated 30 April 1888, in Weber 1936, p. 299. Compare Marianne Weber 1975, pp. 124–5. See also Mommsen, who, however, wrongly states that the letter was written on 20 July 1888 (Mommsen 1974, pp. 16–17).
3  Ibid.
4  Weber 1936, p. 298.
5  Weber 1936, pp. 299–300.
6  Conrad 1906, p. 37.

indignant that they should be described as 'socialists',[7] but the name stuck. It was used to characterise an academic current that marks the transition of bourgeois economics from 'Manchesterism' to an ethically motivated and authoritarian-statist form of social reform.

Marx and Engels considered the ethicisation of political economy a symptom of its decline. In 1879/80, Marx uses the term 'Katheder socialist' to refer to Adolf Wagner's misinterpretation of his analysis of the value form: the analytic observation that, according to the law of value, surplus value belongs not to the worker but to the capitalist is turned by Wagner into the ethical judgement that net profits are not distributed 'properly', i.e. that they are distributed 'to the detriment of the workers'.[8] Also in 1879, Marx describes the Katheder socialists as 'poor *counter-revolutionary* windbags' [*Zungendrescher*] who wish to 'draw the teeth of socialism (which they have rehashed in accordance with academic formulae) and of the Social-Democratic *Party* in particular'.[9] In 1882, Engels includes the Katheder socialists with the mass of vulgar economists, 'who after all live solely off our leavings'.[10] But two years later, he is forced to take note that the transition to Katheder socialism has assumed the character of an international paradigm shift: in every industrialised country, the pressure exerted by the proletarian movement forced Manchesterism back and 'caused bourgeois economists, almost without exception, to acquire an armchair-socialist cum philanthropic complexion'.[11] Compared to classical economy, the new current strikes him as 'an uncritical, benevolent eclecticism ... a soft elastic, gelatinous substance that can be compressed into any desired shape and, for that very reason, exudes an excellent nutrient fluid for the culture of careerists just as does real gelatine for the culture of bacteria', and this 'even within the very confines of our party'.[12] In an 1886 letter to Bebel, Engels rates it 'an excellent sign' that the bourgeois are already constrained to 'sacrifice their pet classical economic theory' so soon: 'The real contradictions engendered by the mode of production have in fact become so glaring that no theory will now serve to conceal them save the hotch-potch of armchair socialism which, however, is not a theory but sheer drivel'.[13]

---

7       Brentano, for example, preferred the term 'realistic economists' (quoted in Conrad 1906, p. 39).

8       Marx and Engels 1975–2005, vol. 24, p. 558.

9       Marx and Engels 1975–2005, vol. 45, p. 413 (Marx to Sorge, 19 September 1879).

10      Marx and Engels 1975–2005, vol. 46, p. 416 (Engels to Bebel, 22 December 1882).

11      Marx and Engels 1975–2005, vol. 47, p. 184 (Engels to Vollmar, 13 August 1884).

12      Ibid.

13      Marx and Engels 1975–2005, vol. 47, p. 390 (Engels to Bebel, 20–23 January 1886).

Marx and Engels's critique focused on the question of theoretical consistency or inconsistency and was thus not interested in the ideological significance 'ethical' political economy had to a statist social policy conceived of as a 'Bonapartist method of stabilisation'.[14] According to Lindenlaub, who has reconstructed the debates held within the Association for Social Policy on the basis of a broad range of materials, 'the constitution of "ethical political economy" was what, methodologically, rendered social policy possible in the first place'.[15] The step from the lectern to effective political lobbying was taken in 1872/73, when Schmoller, Brentano, Wagner and other leading Katheder socialists founded the Association. Memories of the Paris Commune were still fresh. Germany's focus shifts from the founding of the Reich to the project of 'national and social unification', and in parallel with this, 'the political economists assume, within the German professoriate, the leading role hitherto held by historians'.[16] Schmoller's inaugural address at the 1872 Eisenach congress justifies the founding of the Association by reference to the 'deep division' between the property owning and the propertyless class, arguing that this division bears within it the threat of social revolution.[17] In the double struggle against the 'one-sided class standpoints' of Social Democracy and Manchesterism, the Katheder socialists place their trust in the state, which they feel has become sufficiently strong, since the founding of the Reich, to intervene in economic relations. Schmoller notes there is a consensus that the state can be seen as the 'greatest ethical institution for the education of human kind'. He strives for a strong state power that stands above the various interest groups, 'whose just hand protects the weak and elevates the lower classes'.[18]

The Association supports the Bismarck regime as embodying such a state power. In 1898, Schmoller says of this regime that it has understood what the great task of the day consists in: 'the state and the monarchy need to extend a helping hand to the labouring classes; they need to lighten their burden and reconcile them'.[19] Naturally, such acts of 'extending a helping hand' and 'reconciliation' require a framework of state violence: the social reformers—from Schmoller to Naumann—are united on a cross-party basis and in agreement with the policy of the conservative-liberal Reichstag majority on the question

---

14   Wehler 1973, p. 136.

15   Lindenlaub 1967, p. 4.

16   Lindenlaub 1967, p. 15. 'After unification was achieved in 1871, political economists gradually replaced historians as the leading professorial publicists' (Barkin 1970, p. 10).

17   Quoted in Boese 1939, p. 8.

18   Quoted in Boese 1939, p. 8; see also Conrad 1906, pp. 59–60.

19   Quoted in Lindenlaub 1967, p. 144.

of the Anti-Socialist Laws,[20] which they view as a necessary safeguard of their attempts to aid the state in furthering the 'worker's moral and economic invigoration'.[21] Weber also felt, in 1884, that it was necessary to adopt coercive measures against the Social Democrats, since they were just about to subvert fundamental institutions of public life. However, he problematises the method used, that of passing a special law, and states his preference for a universal restriction of freedom of speech and assembly.[22] In public, the Association for Social Policy presents itself as an exponent of the Reich's economic and social policies at least since its 1879 endorsement of Bismarck's protectionism. Engels notes in 1885 that the philanthropists 'have sunk to the level of simple apologists of Bismarck's *Staats-Sozialismus*',[23] and in her May 1914 article '*Hammer und Amboß*' ['Hammer and Anvil'], Rosa Luxemburg characterises the Association's endorsement of the 1899/1900 naval law as the 'fateful hour' of bourgeois social reform, arguing that the latter has 'eviscerated' itself.[24]

Weber's 1888 judgement that the concepts of the Katheder socialists would become 'dominant' was not unfounded. As an influential brain trust promoting the social enlightenment and education of the bourgeoisie, and of the state's political class, the Association for Social Policy made a major contribution to the pre-emptive struggle against Social Democratic hegemony. In 1919, Herkner expressed the view that the inaugural address on the social

---

20    That both Schmoller and Naumann supported the Anti-Socialist Laws prior to their blatant failure can be demonstrated conclusively (see for example Lindenlaub 1967, pp. 144, 375). Wehler nevertheless attempts to create the impression (by an adroit selection of undated quotations) that the two were among the critics of the Anti-Socialist Laws (Wehler 1995, pp. 905, 907).

21    Quoted in Conrad 1906, p. 68.

22    'I sometimes have the impression', he writes to his uncle Hermann Baumgarten on 8 November 1884, 'that universal equal rights for everyone does take precedence over everything else, and that it would be better to muzzle everyone than to put some in irons' (Weber 1936, p. 143). Mommsen seeks all too uncritically to agree with Weber, seeing in the proposal of a general restriction of fundamental rights, which is hardly original, an 'astonishing independence of political judgement'; the power-political consideration by which Weber responds to the blatant ineffectiveness of the Anti-Socialist Laws is glorified as an expression of Weber's 'sense of justice' (Mommsen 1974, p. 13).

23    Marx and Engels 1975–2005, vol. 47, p. 348 (Engels to Danielson, 13 November 1885).

24    According to Rosa Luxemburg, the social reformers among Germany's professoriate have forfeited all respect and sympathy by supporting the imperial propaganda for a doubling of the country's battle fleet: 'The apostles of "social truce" exchanged the gentle palm frond of social reform for the unsheathed sword of militarism and voluntarily offered their services to the Moloch... that crushes all social reform under its iron heel' (Luxemburg 1970–5b, p. 448).

question held by Schmoller on the occasion of the founding of the Association in 1872 was as important for the dissemination of socio-political ideas within the bourgeoisie as the *Manifesto of the Communist Party* was to the socialism of the working class.[25] However, this assessment does not hold true for large industry, as the capital factions led by Baron von Stumm, the owner of an iron mill in the Saarland, began to distance themselves from the Association in the 1880s, criticising Katheder socialism as 'demagogic socialism'. The assessment is more accurate when applied to those parts of the educated middle class [*Bildungsbürgertum*] that had understood repressive measures were insufficient for containing the threat of revolution. The Association influenced Protestant circles via the Evangelical Social Congress, and it influenced the Catholic Centre Party and its intellectual milieu via the theologian and social scientist Franz Hitze. The government officials Miquel, Berlepsch, Rottenburg and Thiel put it in direct contact with Germany's governments, some of which would financially support the Association's surveys from 1890 onward. The relationship between the Reich chancellor and Prussian prime minister von Bülow and the Association's president Schmoller was especially close; Schmoller was himself a member of the state council and the Prussian upper house and participated in numerous administrative and legislative commissions.[26] The Association exercises 'intellectual control over those who govern. And that is what is essential', Schmoller writes to Brentano in 1912.[27]

In parallel with this, the Association, via its 'younger' members, among them Max and Alfred Weber, exerts an intellectual influence on the reformist wing of Social Democracy. These efforts find direct political expression in Naumann's decision to approach Bernstein's circle and propose (in 1909) the formation of a centre-left coalition 'from Bassermann to Bebel',[28] as well as in the recruitment of leading Social Democrats by Brentano's student Schulze-Gaevernitz immediately prior to the August 1914 vote on war credits.[29] However, the Association's ideological influence goes well beyond such direct establishing of contacts. If it was possible, in the context of the 'political truce' during the First World War, to integrate the Social Democratic Party as a system-stabilising force, and if the November Revolution ended, in 1918/19, in the corporatist

---

25    Lindenlaub 1967, p. 29.

26    For a general account of the Association for Social Policy's influence, see Lindenlaub 1967, pp. 29ff, 34ff; on the Association's contacts with entrepreneurs, see pp. 44–83; on Schmoller's influence in particular, see pp. 141–53.

27    Quoted in Lindenlaub 1967, p. 149.

28    See Theiner 1983, pp. 97–8, 194, 208ff.

29    See Krüger 1983, pp. 214ff.

'Central Consortium' [*Zentralarbeitsgemeinschaft*] of entrepreneurs and trade unions, then this was due in no small part to the conceptual preparatory work and intellectual nimbus of the 'modernisers' within the Association for Social Policy. The Association's key role in the socio-political orientation of the ruling bloc has as its corollary an internal balance of power marked by the predominance of state capitalist approaches. In his *Foundations of Political Economy*, the leading 'state socialist' Adolf Wagner posited growing state intervention as a 'law of development', whereby state services 'in the fields of culture and welfare expand continuously and grow richer and more varied in content'.[30] While Schmoller refuses to accept such a 'law', he deduces the state's social policy mission from his research into the history of the Prussian state, which was able, by virtue of its morally advanced civil service, to impose itself as a neutral entity, against the resistance of the feudal aristocracy.[31] During the Association's 1905 debate on cartels, Schmoller proposes extending state control by giving civil servants positions in joint-stock companies (one-fourth of the votes on the board of directors and one-fourth of directorial positions),[32] the idea being that this will help ensure 'educators' and 'persons with non-commercial interests, a statesman's eye and a superior intellectual point of view get to the top', rather than egotistic, moneyed and 'violent men', as in America.[33] 'Professor Schmoller's great works on the history of the Prussian civil service number among ... our scholarly classics', Weber responds during the same general assembly of the Association in Mannheim, in order then to continue: 'But Goethe's dictum holds true here as elsewhere: "We all live by the past and perish by it"'.[34] It is mainly against the Prussian-German continuity between the traditions of a pre-capitalist absolute state and a modern state capitalism whose acme will be the 'corporate capitalism' of the First World War, a continuity articulated by Schmoller, that Weber will formulate his critique of bureaucracy from 1905 onward.

This is the field within which Weber's political analyses and statements inscribe themselves, and which they seek at the same time to transform. Along with his brother Alfred Weber, Sombart, Naumann, Tönnies, Schulze-Gaevernitz and others, he becomes the spokesperson of the 'young' members,

30 Quoted in Lindenlaub 1967, p. 112.
31 See for example the essay on the Prussian electoral reform in Schmoller 1920, pp. 65ff; see also the accounts in Lindenlaub 1967, pp. 114ff, 240ff; Krüger 1983, pp. 78ff; Schön 1988, pp. 93–4.
32 Verein für Socialpolitik 1905, pp. 265, 271.
33 Verein für Socialpolitik 1905, pp. 267, 422.
34 Weber 1988b, p. 402.

whose critique will shape the Association's debates following the turn of the century. To represent this as a generational conflict is however to obscure that the socio-political disputes were already conducted, and along similar frontlines, within the Association's founding generation, particularly between Schmoller and Brentano. Brentano's work on the *Labour Guilds of the Present* (1871, 1872) constitutes, along with his student Schulze-Gaevernitz's work on the social question in England (1890) and on British imperialism (1906), the basis for the project of an integration of the working class on the British model, ideas Weber will tacitly draw on as well. Brentano and the 'young' are no longer concerned with the harmonisation of social antagonism by a state that stands 'above' such antagonism; rather, they wish to develop adequate forms in which social struggles can play out. A highly controversial issue debated in the general assemblies is that of workers' freedom of association; some reject it as a socialist threat, while others favour it because they consider it a device by which to overcome class struggle.[35] Within the Evangelical Social Congress, where the disputes are conducted along similar frontlines, Weber joins forces with Friedrich Naumann and Paul Göhre to develop a critique of East Elbia's large estates that causes major controversy within the Association and leads eventually, in 1895, to the break with one of its co-founders, the anti-Semite Adolf Stoecker.

What conceptual classification of the strategic controversies within the Association for Social Policy one opts for depends largely on one's standpoint and epistemological interest. A 'liberal' historiography that accounts for the 'aberrations of Germany's pre-1945 history' mainly by reference to the country's '*Sonderweg*'—'late' industrialisation, the roughly equal power of the Junkers and the bourgeoisie, the predominance of pre-capitalist powers and dispositions, and so on—will tend to read the differences within the ruling power bloc in terms of a struggle between 'modern' and 'traditional' tendencies.[36] The ideological benefit of such a method of classification consists mainly in exonerating the 'modern' factions of capital and the state from their contribution to fascism's ascent and seizure of power. When applied to the turn of

---

35  The basic pattern of the disputes emerges clearly from the Association for Social Policy's 1890 general assembly in Frankfurt. There, Brentano claims that the British trade unions have overcome the class struggle by means of cooperation, whereas the director of the Central Association of German Industrialists [*Centralverband deutscher Industrieller*], Bück, claims that in England, freedom of association has led to permanent class war. Schmoller attempts to mediate between the two contrary views (see Verein für Socialpolitik 1890, pp. 119ff, 133ff, 201ff).

36  Wehler 1995, p. 1295.

the century's socio-political controversies, dichotomies such as 'conservatives' versus 'social liberals' or 'left liberals' obscure the lines of continuity and fluent passages between the two sides.[37]

To present Weber as the 'modern' antipode of the conservative current associated with Schmoller is to fail to recognise that Schmoller's ideas about the extension of the interventionist state were also part of the socio-political 'modernisation' of the Wilhelmine class state. In Germany, the initial phase of Taylorisation occurred during the First World War and in a 'state capitalist' manner; Rathenau, a leading rationaliser of production, was at the same time a proponent of economic planning by the state and was considered a follower of Saint Simon.[38] Of course Weber and the 'young', in calling for a rationalised capitalism, also presupposed a strong imperialist state, albeit one whose object of intervention and mode of integration they wished to revise. As Andreas Anter has shown, in Weber, 'two traditions of state theory converge: a statist tradition that is interested in the functionality and efficiency of the state, and an anti-statist tradition'.[39]

In a letter to Hermann Baumgarten (3 January 1891), Weber placed his hopes in a division between the interests of large landowners and a 'bureaucratically enlightened conservatism that is open to rational arguments'.[40] That he does not simply fit into the rubric of 'left liberalism' can already be seen from his six-year membership in the 'Pan-German Union' [Alldeutscher Verband], the 'spearhead of the new right-wing opposition' that substantially shaped, by its anti-Semitic agitation, the ideology of early fascism.[41] In an 1893 letter to Althoff, Schmoller praises Weber for combining excellent knowledge with the 'moderate' standpoint of a Prussian patriotism that is free both of the 'Anglomania' of Brentano and his followers and of any socialist

---

37    Krüger employed, *inter alia*, the distinction between 'conservatives' and 'social liberals' (1983, pp. 16ff). Barkin considers Schmoller a 'mild-mannered conservative' (1970, p. 93). Wehler believes that Naumann, for example, can be described as a 'left liberal' (1995, p. 1003).

38    See Schulin 1988, pp. 442ff. Wehler is aware of this too. He points out that state interventionism was far from being 'a foreign element grafted onto the system', as the neoliberals of the 1950s still claimed; state interventionism was 'immanent to the system' (Wehler 1974, p. 49). The liberal critique misconstrued those elements of Wilhelmine corporatism that were 'modern' and 'fit for the future'; it was Wilhelmine corporatism that laid the foundations for the 'new real type of state interventionist and regulated productive capitalism' (Wehler 1995, pp. 675, 1266).

39    Anter 1995, p. 129; see also pp. 160ff, 178–9.

40    Weber 1936, pp. 328–9.

41    See Bracher 1978, p. 100; Wehler 1995, pp. 1074–5.

tendency. Weber returns the compliment in a letter addressed to Schmoller on the occasion of the latter's seventieth birthday (in 1908, i.e. after the intense controversy of 1905 and shortly before the renewed controversy of 1909); there, Weber credits Schmoller's 'prudence and moderation' with imposing the socio-political idealism of the academically educated 'not just within public opinion, but also among those who *held power*'.[42] Even during the most trying periods of the Association's history, Weber is at pains to avoid a division that might make it more difficult for him to access the ruling power bloc. If the 'left' social reformers' 1912 plans for a special rally came to naught, this was mainly because Weber, concerned to maintain the Association's unity, rejected Brentano's proposal of inviting representatives of Social Democracy and the trade unions.[43] Thus when push came to shove, solidarity with the Association's 'right-wing' members took priority over efforts to link up with the reformist wing of the Social Democracy.

The heterogeneity of the 'young' makes it difficult to clearly define the frontlines of the debate. Politically, the group is divided into a number of factions, including for example a vaguely 'socialist' current associated with the early Sombart, Tönnies, Wilbrandt and Goldscheid, and a much more recognisable and assertive capitalist current associated with Max Weber, Schulze-Gaevernitz and Naumann. Seen from the perspective of this second, dominant current, the 'generational conflict' presents itself as a strategic dispute over the question of whether to strive for a 'Prussian' or an 'American' type of capitalism. The former represents a model of development in which the feudal-absolutist state apparatuses impose the capitalist mode of production 'from above' and by extra-economic means, while in the latter, capitalism develops 'from below' and on its own basis.[44] In the field of social policy, which is where Brentano and the 'young' develop most of their concepts, the dispute concerns the model of integration associated with 'corporatist pluralism',[45] whereby

---

42  Quoted in Schön 1988, pp. 90, 84.

43  See, *inter alia*, Schäfers 1967, pp. 263–4; Lindenlaub 1967, pp. 412–13, 419, 423–4; Mommsen 1974, pp. 128ff; Krüger 1983; pp. 109ff; Theiner 1983, pp. 205–6.

44  See Pêcheux 1983, pp. 379, 381–2. The distinction between a 'Prussian' and an 'American' road to capitalism is already drawn in Lenin. In 1907/08, Lenin looked to the American model of development in his outline of an agrarian programme of the Russian Social Democrats (Lenin 1960–78d, vol. 13, pp. 241, 254ff, 331ff). Pêcheux attributes different ideological mechanisms to the two models: the 'peripheral' Prussian model is associated with the ideological 'fortress' and authoritarian hierarchies, whereas the American model is associated with a 'paradoxical space' that lacks stable objects with clearly defined contours (Pêcheux 1983, pp. 379, 381–2).

45  Maier 1974, p. 202.

regulation of the market and of social antagonism is transferred from the state to the representatives of the economic classes themselves (see below, 13.5). Their political differences notwithstanding, the 'young' are also united by a context of discussion that coheres thematically by virtue of their common task, that of 'adequately interpreting the present as a "capitalist" era'.[46] In his 1904 editorial for the *Archiv für Sozialwissenschaft und Sozialpolitik*, Weber confronts the newly acquired journal with the task of identifying, historically and theoretically, *'the general cultural significance of the capitalistic development'.*[47]

This is indicative of a fundamental commonality: what most distinguishes the 'young' from the Association's founding generation is a reception of Marxism that does not begin, within German political economy, until 1894, the year the third volume of *Capital* is published, and which takes shape from 1896 onward, with the publication of Bernstein's writings. Instead of focusing on Lassalle and Rodbertus, the 'young' have 'trained themselves by engaging with Marx'.[48] They thereby become part of the diverse efforts to 'overcome' Marxism intellectually. These efforts occur almost simultaneously in a number of European countries: in Prague, there is Masaryk, who coins the expression 'crisis of Marxism' in 1898; in France, there are Sorel and Durkheim; in Italy, there is, first and foremost, Croce, whose essays influenced Bernstein, among others.[49] Looking back in 1955, Alfred Weber remarked that the Association's older members were not prepared to 'digest Marxism intellectually, as they considered it taboo'.[50] In speaking of intellectual 'digestion', Alfred Weber refers to a neutralising process of appropriation and revision that one might describe, following Gramsci, as a 'passive revolution' within social theory.

What needs now to be investigated is how Weber puts to use, in his analysis of East Elbian agrarian relations, the analytic tools he has largely borrowed from Marx.

---

46    Lindenlaub 1967, p. 289.

47    Quoted in Marianne Weber 1975, p. 278.

48    Lindenlaub 1967, p. 279.

49    Gramsci reports that Sorel wrote the following to Croce on 9 September 1899: 'Bernstein has just written to me that he has remarked in issue 46 of *Die Neue Zeit* that he has to a certain extent allowed himself to be inspired by your work' (Gramsci 1975b, p. 1213). For an account of the turn of the century's international debate on the 'crisis of Marxism', see Bensussan 1986, pp. 719ff.

50    A. Weber 1955, p. 163.

# CHAPTER 9

# The Imperialist Critique of the Agrarian Class

Weber's hostility towards the Junker landowners can be traced back to his first major sociological analysis of contemporary issues, written in 1892 and at the request of the Association for Social Policy: *The Condition of Farm Labour in Eastern Germany* (MWG I/3). The most important component of the Association's inquiry into farm labour, Weber's almost 900-page study was written in a mere six months.[1] It was followed by several evaluative contributions; of these, I will refer mainly to 'The Rural Labour Constitution', a lecture held by Weber at the Association's 1893 conference,[2] and the 1894 essay 'Developmental Tendencies of East Elbian Farm Labour'.[3]

'Weber's evaluation of the inquiry established his reputation as a political economist at a stroke', writes Mommsen.[4] It was not a foregone conclusion that Weber should be asked to write the strategically crucial and politically charged part of the inquiry; the agrarian question had already been the Association's core theme in the 1880s, so that there was no lack of experts.[5] What made the 27-year-old Weber appear qualified was the fact that his habilitation thesis on *Roman Agrarian History and its Significance for Public and Private Law* (MWG I/2), completed a short while earlier and published in October of 1891, won him the reputation of being an expert on agrarian issues. What was probably decisive was the recommendation of Weber's professor and habilitation supervisor

---

1   According to Riesebrodt's editorial report in Weber's *Collected Works*, organisational preparation of the inquiry, which was headed by H. Thiel, began in July of 1891. The 'special' questionnaires were distributed to 3,180 'rural employers' in December of the same year; another 562 'general' questionnaires were distributed in February of 1892. This means that Weber cannot have begun evaluating the results before February of 1892; by early September, his report had already been typeset (see Weber 1984–2009, vol. I/3, pp. 22ff).

2   Weber 1984–2009, vol. I/4, pp. 165–98; Weber 1988c, pp. 444–69.

3   Weber 1984–2009, vol. I/4, pp. 425–62; Weber 1988c, pp. 470–507. I cite from the second, abridged version of the essay published in the *Preußische Jahrbücher*, as it was intended for a broader public and therefore argues in layman's terms and in a more 'political' manner than the original version published in the *Archiv für soziale Gesetzgebung und Statistik* (see the editorial report in Weber 1984–2009, vol. I/4, pp. 365–6).

4   Mommsen 1974, p. 23.

5   According to Irmela Gorges's overview of the Association's activities, eight of the 22 volumes published during the 1880s were devoted to the agrarian question (Gorges 1980, pp. 158ff).

August Meitzen, a member of the Prussian bureau of statistics and author of the statistical standard work on Prussian agrarian relations.[6]

To say that Weber was hostile to the East Elbian landowners may appear paradoxical at first: from the outset, the inquiry is criticised for attempting to obtain its data on the condition of farm labour on the basis of question-naires sent exclusively to rural employers. In order to make the landowners willing to participate, the sociologists appeal to their fear of Social Democracy, which had begun, in 1890, to focus its agitative efforts on 'conquering the countryside'.[7] How pronounced this fear was can be deduced by implica-tion if one considers the hopes expressed by Engels in April of 1890. Engels believed Social Democracy was capable of conquering the rural proletariat of the Eastern provinces, and with it the soldiers of Prussia's core military regi-ments: 'That will bring down the old order with a vengeance, and we shall govern'.[8] Ultimately, Engels's expectation of collapse would not be confirmed. In fact Social Democracy proved unable to take root in the countryside.[9] But in 1891, shortly after the repeal of the Anti-Socialist Laws and given the Social Democrat Party's consistent electoral successes, these expectations and fears appeared so realistic that the anti-socialist cover letters mailed with the Association's questionnaires fell on fertile ground. That the inquiry was not 'free of value judgements' also emerges from the conclusion of Weber's study, where he indulges in ostentatious praise of the 'master estate' [*Herrenschicht*] of the Junkers,[10] praise that the rural conservative newspaper *Kreuz-Zeitung*

---

6    See Tribe 1983, pp. 195–6. See also, *inter alia*, Riesebrodt's editorial report on the inquiry
      (Weber 1984–2009, vol. 1/3, pp. 18ff, 22ff) and Deininger's introduction to Weber's *Roman
      Agrarian History* (Weber 1984–2009, vol. 1/2, p. 50). In 1886, when writing 'On the History
      of the Prussian Peasants' (Marx and Engels 1975–2005, vol. 26, pp. 341ff), Engels also drew
      on Meitzen's four volume statistical study of Prussia (*The Soil and the Agrarian Condition
      of the Prussian State*, 1868/71).

7    For example, Thiel's July 1891 circular letter points out that it is in the farmers' own best
      interest not to leave materials on rural labour relations to malicious people but rather to
      place them 'in the most competent hands' (Weber 1984–2009, vol. 1/3, p. 34). The letter
      accompanying the special questionnaire assures its readers the study may prove useful in
      confronting 'unjustified demands' (Weber 1984–2009, vol. 1/3, p. 36).

8    Marx and Engels 1975–2005, vol. 48, p. 474 (Engels to Sorge, 12 April 1890).

9    Expectation of the imminent 'conquest' of farm labour is a leitmotif in the political analy-
      ses of agrarian life penned by Engels (see for example Marx and Engels 1975–2005, vol. 4,
      p. 545; vol. 21, p. 100; vol. 27, p. 591; vol. 50, p. 170). What is most problematic about this
      expectation is the elision of small and medium-sized farmers it involves.

10   For example, Weber writes that the sons of the Junkers have led the nation to 'unprec-
      edented military success' and associated its name with memories 'that will always stir our
      blood' (Weber 1984–2009, vol. 1/3, p. 922).

was able, on 2 February 1893, to cite as proof of the historical achievements of the East Elbian landowners.

Yet such statements tell us more about the ideological power relations within which the inquiry inscribes itself than about the actual research strategy pursued by Weber within this predetermined framework. As Riesebrodt argues convincingly, Weber probably had no part in formulating the questionnaires,[11] and he distanced himself from the one-sided choice of addressees by pointing out, in his preface, that the data obtained do not provide a reliable account of farm workers' economic circumstances, but rather 'a fairly clear impression of the attitudes the employers have developed with regard to the interests of the two sides and the expediency of the various forms the labour relation might be given'.[12] Even Social Democratic scholars and journalists praised his skilful way of dealing with the inquiry's methodological deficits.[13] In a second inquiry into farm work, developed for the Evangelical Social Congress by Weber and Göhre in 1892/93, the questionnaires were mailed to all Protestant priests in Germany. And Weber's praise for the Junkers, which refers to what they have achieved for the nation historically, contrasts with the demonstration that they have assumed an anti-national character in the present: Weber's demonstrative curtsy occurs in his concluding appeal to the Prussian dynasty, whose hard real-political core consists in demonstrating the forlornness of the large East Elbian landowners, who can continue to exist only at the expense of the 'nation's vital interests'.[14]

The survey and its evaluation address the capitalist disintegration of the old patriarchal labour constitution by considering the social consequences of that disintegration: with the transformation of patriarchal lordship into a capital-intensive business, the former '*Instmann*' [farm worker], who laboured on the lordly estate with his family and a '*Scharworker*' [a co-worker remunerated by the *Instmann*], receiving a small plot of land on which to perform subsistence farming and other payment in kind (e.g. a share of threshed straw), increasingly becomes a 'free' day labourer working under precarious circumstances. In the east, the farm worker's social position has been forced down to the subsistence minimum, and 'there has emerged a potato-eating proletariat from a population whose diet once consisted of cereals and milk'.[15] Accompanying

---

11    See Weber 1984–2009, vol. I/3, pp. 18–19.

12    Weber 1984–2009, vol. I/3, p. 64; compare vol. I/4, p. 425; Weber 1988c, p. 470.

13    See Weber 1984–2009, vol. I/3, p. 15.

14    Weber 1984–2009, vol. I/3, p. 923.

15    Weber 1984–2009, vol. I/4, p. 174; Weber 1988c, p. 450. This, Weber argues, entails 'a threat to the rational alimentation of the people', for the shift to potatoes means 'that ...

immiseration is an exodus of the better-off German farm workers in particular; they are replaced by Polish immigrant labour [the so-called 'Sachsengänger'']. What makes this Polish labour so attractive to landowners, according to Weber, is not necessarily the lower wages, but rather the absence of poor relief payments ('once their labour power has been exploited, they are simply deported from the country'), as well as a docility that is created by the permanent threat of expulsion from Germany:[16] 'There are no limits to the landowners' ability to dispose over the Poles. At a wink, the neighbouring head official—who is also a landowner—will send the Pole back over the border'.[17]

Mommsen sees Weber's argument as 'clearly influenced by Marxist thought',[18] and Riesebrodt holds that Weber has adopted the 'hypothesis on class struggle' from the *Manifesto of the Communist Party*.[19] Weber's analysis of the social recomposition of farm labour as part of rural class struggle is indeed striking: given the fragmented nature of the rural workforce and its 'dispersal across the countryside', its inability to articulate common class interests and the absence of a 'labour aristocracy',[20] recruitment of Polish immigrant labour proves to be a 'weapon in the anticipated class struggle against the emergent self-consciousness of the workers'.[21]

To what extent Weber's class analysis and hypothesis on proletarianisation are 'directly' influenced by Marx, as Riesebrodt assumes,[22] and to what extent the parallels result from the 'object' itself (the capitalist developmental tendencies within agriculture) is a question that is difficult to decide, and it is only of secondary importance to evaluation of the farm labour inquiry. It is obvious that the majority of Weber's sociological observations can already be found in the political analyses of agrarian life penned by Marx and Engels, analyses that were available to Weber. For example, the observation that the dislocation of

---

hunger is satisfied, but muscular power is not reproduced, whereupon the attempt is made to compensate for this through the consumption of alcohol' (Weber 1984–2009, vol. I/3, p. 898).

16    Weber 1984–2009, vol. I/4, p. 176; Weber 1988c, p. 452.

17    Weber 1984–2009, vol. I/4, p. 457; Weber 1988c, p. 502.

18    Mommsen 1974, p. 27.

19    Riesebrodt 1985, p. 553.

20    Weber 1984–2009, vol. I/4, pp. 429, 443ff, 456; Weber 1988c, pp. 474, 488ff, 502.

21    Weber 1984–2009, vol. I/4, p. 457; Weber 1988c, p. 502. Emigration and immigration 'mutually reinforce one another, because they ... represent means of struggle employed in the latent conflict between property and labour. Emigration is a latent strike, and the recruitment of Poles is the corresponding weapon by which to combat it' (Weber 1984–2009, vol. I/4, p. 457; Weber 1988c, p. 503).

22    Riesebrodt 1985, p. 553.

farm labour prevents the development of a coherent class consciousness can already be found in the first volume of *Capital*, published in 1867.[23] There, Marx uses the 'classic example' of England to engage extensively with the relationship between agrarian capitalism's development of the forces of production and the 'laying [to] waste and consuming by disease [of] labour-power itself',[24] supporting his analysis with comprehensive sociological materials on population development, living conditions, nutrition, disease, crime, child labour (the 'gang system'), immigrant labour, and so on.[25] Nowhere, he argues, 'does the antagonistic character of capitalistic production and accumulation assert itself more brutally than in the progress of English agriculture...and the retrogression of the English agricultural labourer'.[26] Of course, Weber would have rejected such an explanatory approach, since he was working to distinguish the agrarian capitalism of the Junkers from a specifically bourgeois productive capitalism.

Another difference consists in the fact that Marx points out that it is not just labour power that is laid to waste, but also the aggregate 'metabolic interaction between man and the earth'.[27] In doing so, he addresses early on the tendency towards ecological devastation inherent in a mode of production that operates by 'sapping the original sources of all wealth—the soil and the labourer'.[28] Notwithstanding Marxism's longstanding negligence of both the ecological crisis and eco-socialist alternatives, Marx's metabolic analysis of industrialised

---

23    'The dispersion of the rural labourers over larger areas breaks their power of resistance while concentration increases that of the town operatives' (Marx and Engels 1975–2005, vol. 35, p. 507). In his 1865 pamphlet *The Prussian Military Question*, Engels writes: 'The agricultural proletariat is the section of the working class which has most difficulty in understanding its own interests and its own social situation and is the last to do so, in other words, it is the section which remains the longest as an unconscious tool in the hands of the privileged class which is exploiting it' (Marx and Engels 1975–2005, vol. 20, p. 25; compare vol. 21, p. 21).

24    Marx and Engels 1975–2005, vol. 35, p. 507.

25    See especially Section 10 of Chapter xv on 'Modern Industry and Agriculture' (Marx and Engels 1975–2005, vol. 35, pp. 505ff) and Section 5 of Chapter xxv, where Marx examines the effects of capital accumulation on the rural populations of England and Ireland (Marx and Engels 1975–2005, vol. 35, pp. 642ff).

26    Marx and Engels 1975–2005, vol. 35, p. 665.

27    Marx 1976, p. 637; see Marx and Engels 1975–2005, vol. 35, p. 505.

28    Marx 1976, p. 638; see Marx and Engels 1975–2005, vol. 35, p. 507. In the third volume of *Capital*, Marx criticises agrarian capitalism from the perspective of an agriculture that ministers to 'the entire range of permanent necessities of life required by the chain of successive generations' (Marx and Engels 1975–2005, vol. 37, p. 611, note 27; compare pp. 762–3, 798).

agriculture turned out to be a fruitful inspiration for a theoretical understanding of the 'metabolic rift' of the carbon cycle and global climate change.[29]

The specific development of agrarian capitalism in Prussia was mainly analysed by Engels, who was especially interested in the rise and socio-economic significance of the Junker potato spirit distillery.[30] Weber argues in 1894 that East Elbia's landed nobility is yielding to a 'class of agricultural entrepreneurs' whose 'social features are in principle not distinct from those of commercial entrepreneurs';[31] Engels already pointed out such a shift in 1847, when he wrote that, to the extent that the rural Junkers do not squander their wealth, they merge with the rising bourgeois estate owners to form a 'new class of *industrial landowners*', a 'section of the bourgeoisie which exploits agriculture'.[32] Even prior to the 1848 Revolution, part of the landed nobility 'so far changed into producers of mere marketable commodities, as to have the same interests and to make common cause with the middle class'.[33] 'The aristocracy itself was largely bourgeoisified', Marx and Engels wrote in the *Neue Rheinische Zeitung* in late 1848. 'Instead of dealing in loyalty, love and faith, it now dealt primarily in beetroot, liquor and wool. Its tournaments were held on the wool market'.[34] In 1870, Engels wrote: 'The rural nobility, who have been industrialists for a long time as manufacturers of beet sugar and distillers of brandy, have long left the old respectable days behind and their names now swell the lists of directors of all sorts of sound and unsound joint-stock companies'.[35]

In addition, there is another, rather problematic commonality between Weber, Marx and (especially) Engels: their rejection of small peasant holdings, which however is motivated in contrary ways. In Engels, the abandonment of small and medium-sized farmers is linked to expectations of the imminent proletarianisation and 'conquest' by the Social Democratic Party of East Elbian rural labour: while the French socialists wish to protect small farmers from

---

29    See Foster, Clark, York 2010, pp. 123ff.

30    See especially the article 'Prussian Schnapps in the German Reichstag', published in *Der Volksstaat* in 1876; there, Engels attempts to demonstrate that the agrarian capitalist production of spirits constitutes the 'real material basis of present-day Prussia' (Marx and Engels 1975–2005, vol. 24, p. 120). For later restatements of this argument, see for example Marx and Engels 1975–2005, vol. 26, p. 498 and Marx and Engels 1975–2005, vol. 27, pp. 500–2.

31    Weber 1984–2009, vol. I/4, p. 432; Weber 1988c, pp. 476ff.

32    Marx and Engels 1975–2005, vol. 6, p. 91.

33    Marx and Engels 1975–2005, vol. 11, p. 25.

34    Marx and Engels 1975–2005, vol. 8, p. 158.

35    Marx and Engels 1975–2005, vol. 23, p. 364.

capitalism, the Engels of 1894 considers the small farm to be 'irretrievably' lost and considers small farmers a transitional phenomenon leading from the traditional peasantry to the rural proletariat.[36] The *Manifesto of the Communist Party*, with its orientation towards a capitalist progress that liberates the populace from the 'idiocy of rural life',[37] has distracted from the fact that Marx later, particularly in his 1881 letter to Vera Zasulich, also developed a different line of thought, one that builds on the cooperative tradition of the Russian peasant commune.[38] Suppression of this line of thought has entailed disdain both for the archaic traditions of the village community and for small peasant forms of existence (some of which were still bound up with the village community), and this in turn has helped make it possible for an industrialism that is hostile to peasants and ecologically disastrous to assert itself, particularly within 'Marxism-Leninism'.[39]

The link between the original village commune and the relations of reciprocity within the small peasantry is precisely what Weber attacks during the Association for Social Policy's 1893 debate on agrarian life. The traditions of cooperation found in the agriculture of southern and western Germany appear to him as an 'inorganic' residue of the 'old organised commons of the village commune'.[40] The aftereffects of the village commune seem to him to consist mainly in the absence of a 'social partition' between the large farmer and the smallholder who works for him as a day labourer. Weber assumes that his readers endorse the economic argument according to which hereditary law is inefficient because it leads to the parcelling of landed property. He concentrates on a 'psychological aspect', namely that the land worker likes to consider his labour 'almost a form of neighbourly and friendly support', to be 'reciprocated in kind'; in other words, he asks to be treated 'as an equal party, stripping away

---

36    See Marx and Engels 1975–2005, vol. 27, pp. 484ff. If we succeed in sowing the seed of Social Democracy among the agricultural workers, the great reactionary power of Junkerdom 'will collapse like a pricked bubble' (Marx and Engels 1975–2005, vol. 27, p. 502).

37    Marx and Engels 1975–2005, vol. 6, p. 488.

38    Marx and Engels 1975–2005, vol. 46, p. 71.

39    Lenin failed to take note of Marx's reflections on the Russian village commune both in his 1899 work *The Development of Capitalism in Russia* (Lenin 1960–78e, vol. 3, pp. 21–608), and in his 1905/07 article on 'Social Democracy's Attitude Towards the Peasant Movement' (Lenin 1960–78f, vol. 9, pp. 280–239). On the status of the 'agrarian question' within Marxism, see Bergmann 1994, pp. 75ff. On the Marxist suppression and later rediscovery of the 'village commune', see Wielenga 1995, pp. 825ff. On the *Manifesto*'s 'undifferentiated discourse of modernisation', see Jacobs 1995, pp. 615–16.

40    Weber 1984–2009, vol. I/4, p. 168; Weber 1988c, p. 444.

all the trappings of a relationship of authority'.[41] This sort of labour constitution, which 'would be identical to the radical abolition of all large property', cannot be a desired goal, according to Weber, for the rural workers lack 'the characteristically Prussian notion of "darn duty and obligation"': 'They do not know the kind of work that we are familiar with in the East: the strict, dutiful and lifelong exercise of one's capacity for labour'.[42]

Riesebrodt holds that Weber's inquiry into rural labour is a 'theoretical synthesis', essentially of Rodbertus, Schmoller and Marx.[43] Riesebrodt's demonstration limits itself, for the most part, to listing various points of agreement (e.g. elements of Rodbertus's 'Oiken theory', of Gierke's concept of Germany's law of associations, of Marx's concept of class, of Schmoller's emphasis on psychological drives),[44] but none of them is examined in its argumentative context. The search for intellectual analogies misses the strategic stakes of Weber's studies of agrarian life, which are decisive to the specific manner in which he puts his sources to use. The search for intellectual traces that Riesenbrodt engages in fails to take into account, for example, that if Weber appropriates some categories of Marx's analysis of agrarian life, he does so only in order to integrate those categories into an agrarian political project that is contrary to Marx's.

Riesebrodt formulates a widespread commonplace of the literature on Weber when he defines the opposition between Marx and Weber by attributing to the former the standpoint of 'economic reductionism' and claiming that the latter understood that 'the "psyche" and the ethic of those participating in a process of transformation are also ... subject to structural change'.[45] This, of course, is precisely how the opposition is *not* to be defined, for Marx would by no means have disputed such psycho-ethical change, and the accusation of reductionism is formulated as if a critique and/or self-critique of economism had never been formulated by Marx, not to mention the late Engels.[46] Riesebrodt justifies his claim about the opposition between Marx and Weber by pointing out that Weber accounts for the exodus of rural workers to the city

---

41    Weber 1984–2009, vol. I/4, p. 168; Weber 1988c, p. 445.

42    Weber 1984–2009, vol. I/4, pp. 168–9; Weber 1988c, p. 445.

43    Riesebrodt 1985, p. 560.

44    Riesebrodt 1985, pp. 550ff.

45    Riesebrodt 1985, pp. 554, 560.

46    See for example Marx's critique of Mikhailkovsky's conversion of *Capital*'s 'historical sketch' of the emergence of Western European capitalism into the historico-philosophical theory of a universal and ineluctable development (Marx and Engels 1975–2005, vol. 24, pp. 196–201). For the self-critique of Engels, see for example Marx and Engels 1975–2005, vol. 49, pp. 33ff and Marx and Engels 1975–2005, vol. 50, pp. 163ff.

primarily in terms of the psychological allure of 'freedom' and considers the issue of 'bread and butter' secondary.[47] Weber explains the fact that it is mainly the better off who leave the countryside by arguing that they are emancipating themselves from patriarchal relations of servitude and seeking to break out of their 'dull resignation'.[48] 'In this inarticulate, half-conscious urge towards far-off places there is an element of primitive idealism', Weber sums up in his 1895 Freiburg inaugural address, adding that '[a]nyone who cannot decipher this does not know the magic of freedom'.[49] Weber also holds that the immigration of Polish workers is not to be explained primarily in terms of wage levels, but rather in terms of an 'unwillingness to commit to long-term work at home': 'The familiar work bell of the large landowner nextdoor has a particularly unpleasant ring to it'.[50] Much as in the *Protestant Ethic* (see below, Chapter 24.4), Weber discusses the socio-psychological element in an inconsistent manner: in some passages, he argues that people's behaviour is driven *not* by economic considerations, but by a 'mass-psychological mechanism'; in others, he speaks of a 'combination of economic and psychological aspects'.[51]

Here as elsewhere, Gramsci's observation that '[f]requently, people attack historical economism in the belief that they are attacking historical materialism' holds true.[52] While Weber refuses to reduce the complex reasons for migration to an issue of 'bread and butter', he by no means opposes a Marxist approach to the explanation of social action; what he opposes is a Chartist formula according to which what is needed is not just political democratisation as effected by electoral reform and the like, but also social improvements with regard to working hours, wages and housing conditions. This theme, coined by the Methodist minister J.R. Stephens at an 1838 rally, before an audience of 200,000, is taken up by Engels in his examination of *The Condition of the Working Class in England*; in doing so, Engels intends to illustrate Chartism's character as the first spontaneous proletarian mass movement.[53] At the same time, Engels notes that, as far as its theoretical development is concerned, Chartism lags far behind the intellectual socialists; generally speaking, he

47    Weber 1984–2009, vol. I/3, p. 920.

48    Weber 1984–2009, vol. I/4, pp. 174, 448; Weber 1988c, pp. 450–1, 493.

49    Weber 1994a, p. 8; Weber 1984–2009, vol. I/4, p. 552.

50    Weber 1984–2009, vol. I/4, p. 175; Weber 1988c, p. 451.

51    See for example Weber 1984–2009, vol. I/4, pp. 551–2; Weber 1988a, pp. 6–7; Weber 1984–2009, vol. I/4, p. 447; Weber 1988c, p. 493.

52    Gramsci 1996, p. 185.

53    Marx and Engels 1975–2005, vol. 4, pp. 518, 525. On Chartism's significance to Marx and Engels, see Kross 1995, pp. 465ff.

has the impression that for the British—and unlike the politicised French—'politics exist only as a matter of interest, solely in the interest of bourgeois society'.[54] Following Gramsci, we can say that issues of 'bread and butter' are to be interpreted as indicating the 'corporate phase' of a movement that has yet to work its way from society's 'base' to its ethico-political 'superstructure'.[55] In this sense, the 'economic reductionism' of which Riesebrodt speaks is characteristic of a form of protest that is still subaltern and not yet capable of hegemony, as it continues to operate upon the terrain of bourgeois society and according to the latter's rules.

Nevertheless, the contrast with Marx could not be more pronounced. It is not to be found in the weighing of 'economic' and 'psychological' causes, but rather in the place where any comparison that works only with the instruments of intellectual history has its blind spot: the social standpoint and the strategic arrangement resulting from it. Weber does not discuss the 'rural labour issue' as an 'issue of rural labourers', but purely 'from a reason-of-state perspective'.[56] It is from this perspective that he evaluates the rural-sociological findings and formulates his critique of large-scale landholding. While Weber's text praises the contributions made by the Junkers to the 'tight organisation of the state' and its military discipline,[57] his analysis amounts to the assessment that the Junkers are also responsible for the 'coercive force' of East Elbian economic relations, and thereby for the displacement of German farm labour.[58] East Elbia's manorial agriculture is no longer capable of binding the German farm worker to his home soil; it is promoting the 'Polonisation' of the German East. For this reason, the 'peaceful defence' of the eastern frontier needs to be undertaken against the interests of the large East Elbian landowner, who is the 'greatest Poloniser' and thereby the nation's most dangerous enemy.[59]

Moreover, in the case of Weber, to examine the Polish question from a 'reason-of-state' perspective is to articulate it in racist terms. He speaks of a 'Slavic deluge that would amount to being set back culturally by several generations',[60] of an 'ongoing incursion of swarms of Eastern nomads', who by their 'different physical constitutions', particularly their 'differently built

---

54      Marx and Engels 1975–2005, vol. 4, pp. 512, 525.

55      See Gramsci 1996, p. 179; Gramsci 1975b, pp. 1244–5.

56      Weber 1984–2009, vol. I/4, p. 180; Weber 1988c, p. 455.

57      See Weber 1984–2009, vol. I/3, p. 916.

58      See Weber 1984–2009, vol. I/3, pp. 915–16.

59      Weber 1984–2009, vol. I/4, p. 177; Weber 1988c, p. 453.

60      Weber 1984–2009, vol. I/4, p. 458; Weber 1988c, p. 504.

stomachs', would force Germany down to a 'lower, more Eastern cultural level'.[61] The Polish peasant 'gains more land because he is prepared even to eat grass, as it were', Weber remarks in his Freiburg inaugural address,[62] where the different 'level[s] of economic sophistication [*Kultur*]' are explained in terms of the 'psychological and physical racial characteristics' of Germans and Poles.[63]

At the 1896 founding meeting of Naumann's National Social Association, Weber rejects a criticism formulated by von Gerlach, namely that the Poles have been forced into the status of second-class citizens: 'The opposite is the case: we are the ones who have turned the Poles into human beings [in the first place]. It is also in your view of the "Polish question" that you display your usual apolitical trait of miserabilism'.[64] Gerlach replied, to considerable applause, that he would never subscribe to such a 'Nietzschean master morality' within politics.[65] At this point in time, there is no relevant difference between Weber and the 'Pan-Germans' to be discerned; one of the programmatic goals of the Pan-Germans is to 'cultivate awareness of the racial affiliation of all parts of the German people'.[66] Weber held several lectures on the 'Polish question' at the invitation of the Pan-German Union.[67] His 1899 break with the Pan-Germans was not due to a rejection of their racist imperialism; the reason Weber gave was that the Union had failed to promote the expulsion of Polish immigrants with sufficient vigour and displayed more consideration for the financial interests of agrarian capitalism than for what Weber considered 'a *vital question* for the Germans'.[68]

The impending 'Polonisation' of the East prompts Weber to speak of the necessity of a 'radical [state] intervention' into the distribution of land.[69] Sombart had already made a similar statement in his study on the Roman

---

61    Weber 1984–2009, vol. I/4, pp. 182, 176; Weber 1988c, pp. 452, 457.

62    Weber 1994a, p. 10.

63    See for example Weber 1994a, p. 5. For Weber's anti-Polish racism, see also Zimmerman 2006, pp. 57ff, 61ff.

64    Weber 1984–2009, vol. I/4, p. 622; Weber 1988c, p. 628.

65    Quoted in Mommsen 1974, p. 58.

66    Quoted in Wehler 1995, pp. 1073–4.

67    Marianne Weber 1975, p. 202.

68    Quoted in Marianne Weber 1975, p. 224. Of course, Weber's withdrawal from the Pan-German Union did not prevent him from continuing to be 'in sympathy with the Union's endeavors' (quoted in Marianne Weber 1975, p. 225). The reasons given by Weber for his withdrawal appear to be a pretence: in 1894, the Pan-German Union did in fact call for closure of the eastern frontier to Polish immigrant labour, placing the 'Polish question' at the centre of its agitational practice. See Mommsen 1974, pp. 58–9.

69    Weber 1984–2009, vol. I/4, p. 460; Weber 1988c, p. 505.

*campagna*;[70] in terms of its direction of inquiry and conclusions, the study displays the same general thrust as Weber's farm labour inquiry.[71] But the interventions proposed are as far a cry from the Jacobin smashing of large estates and redistribution of land to small peasants in 1793 as from the socialist call for setting up landworker cooperatives on confiscated land.[72] The first thing Weber calls for is closure of Germany's eastern frontier, something Bismarck had already decided in 1885, although the decision had been partly revoked, due to pressure from landowners, following Bismarck's resignation.[73] A second demand looked to the 'combination of small tenancy agreements with labour contracts', such that the tradition of *Instmann* labour might be preserved without the element of bondage associated with it.[74] Thirdly and finally, Weber calls for the purchase of land by the state. The state could then lease the land as part of a process of 'internal colonisation', but not to 'little pygmy peasants' who would only constitute a miserable 'landed proletariat'; instead, the land would go to 'well-funded estate tenants' who would, in addition, be supplied with melioration credits by the state.[75] In a contribution to a discussion held at the 1894 Evangelical Social Congress, Weber rejects the accusation that he is out to 'eradicate' the large estates. He proposes making the purchase of run-down estates a permanent budgetary item, thus increasing the state's estate holdings; he also proposes the planned parcelling of suitable estates. If this is 'expropriation', he argues, then so is the private slashing up of estates.[76] According to Tribe, the agrarian policy of the 1890s was the 'switchboard' by

70    Sombart 1888, pp. 161–2.

71    Those searching out connections within the history of ideas often overlook the rural-sociological parallel with Sombart. This is true both of the literature on the farm worker inquiry (see for example Schluchter 1980, pp. 134ff; Tribe 1983; Riesebrodt 1985) and of the literature on the relationship between Weber and Sombart (see for example Mitzman 1988, and Lehmann 1993). An allusion can be found in Hennis 1996, p. 200. Weber's habilitation thesis already makes reference to Sombart's study of the Roman *campagna* (see Weber 1984–2009, vol. I/2, pp. 299, 380), and Sombart extensively reviewed the thesis (Sombart 1893).

72    At the Basel Congress of the International Workingmens' Association (IWA), a resolution was passed (in September of 1869) that private property of land should be abolished and replaced by collective property. See Marx and Engels 1975–2005, vol. 21, p. 100, and vol. 27, p. 501.

73    Weber 1994a, p. 12.

74    Weber 1984–2009, vol. I/4, pp. 193–4, 460–1; Weber 1988c, pp. 466–7, 506.

75    Weber 1984–2009, vol. I/4, pp. 460ff; Weber 1988c, pp. 505ff.

76    Weber 1984–2009, vol. I/4, p. 344.

which a reconstitution of the entire political field was achieved.[77] For Weber too, engagement with agrarian relations in the East was the starting point for a comprehensive critique of Wilhemine society. His transition to the analysis of society as a whole occurred on two levels. On the one hand, East Elbian land-owners constituted a large part of the political class; on the other hand, they strongly influenced the lifestyle of their rivalling class, the bourgeoisie.

Before discussing Weber's critique of the bourgeois-feudal class compromise, I will outline his project of bourgeois class constitution by reference to the stock market.

---

77  'Engagement with the "agrarian problem"…during the 1890s brought with it automatically an engagement with the central field of German politics…Agrarian Germany became the switchboard through which a reconstitution of the political domain was effected' (Tribe 1983, p. 182).

# CHAPTER 10

# A Homogenous Stock Market Elite with a Coherent Concept of Honour

During the period 1894–6, Weber focuses his political interventions on the stock market reform planned by the Reichstag. Reich Chancellor Caprivi had set up a commission of inquiry in 1892; charged with examining the stock market, the commission suffered from a clash of interests between those members representing the banks and those representing landowners. The main controversy was over the restriction of futures trading, a measure demanded by landowners so as to shield grain prices from world-market pressures. In 1896, Weber was invited to participate in the commission's consultations; along with economist Wilhelm Lexis, he took on the task of reporting to Germany's federal assembly, the *Bundesrat*. During negotiations involving the representatives of large industry, the money market and large landowners, he incurs the hostility of the landowners and wins the sympathy of high finance.[1] Due to pressure exerted by the landowner representatives, he is not voted a member of the definite, 1897 stock market committee, thereby losing the ability to directly influence stock market legislation. The preponderance of the agrarians is evident in the 1896 stock market law, which restricts trade in grain futures at the Berlin commodity exchange until 1908.[2]

Weber's best-known statement on these issues is his article 'The Stock Market', published as part of Friedrich Naumann's Göttingen-based worker's library in 1894 and 1896, under the title of 'Stock Market and Bank Primer for Ten Pfennigs'.[3] I will also draw on Weber's 1894 essay 'The Results of the German Stock Market Inquiry', which develops the same line of thought with a slightly different emphasis. Weber rejects the notion that the stock market is a 'club of conspirators who engage in lies and deception at the expense of the

---

1   See the ironic comment in a letter dated 20 November 1896, where Weber writes to his wife that he appears to have 'met with the approval of the millionaires': '[A]t least Privy Councillor of Commerce x ... always squeezes my hand so vigorously that I am surprised at not finding a check for some 100,000 marks under my blotter' (quoted in Marianne Weber 1975, pp. 198–9).

2   See Bendix 1964, p. 18; Mommsen 1974, pp. 80–1, 143.

3   Weber 1988b, pp. 256–322.

righteously labouring people'.[4] In doing so, he is concerned, on the one hand, to demonstrate the stock market's economic necessity and usefulness, and on the other, to examine the legislative possibilities by which the state might curb speculative abuses. His argument is developed from the standpoint of a 'rational stock-market policy based on Germany's power interests'.[5] The essay ends with a polemic against the 'starry-eyed apostles of economic peace' who are out to disarm the nation, because they have confused the stock market with a 'club for "ethical culture"'. Against them, Weber insists 'there can no more be unilateral disarmament in the field of economics than elsewhere'.[6]

The backdrop to Weber's intervention is a shift in the stock market's significance, outlined by Engels the very same year (1894), in a postscript to the third volume of *Capital*. In the 1860s, Engels writes, the stock market was still a '*secondary* element in the capitalist system', whereas it now 'tends to concentrate all production, industrial as well as agricultural, and all commerce, the means of communication as well as the functions of exchange, in the hands of stock exchange operators', thereby becoming 'the most prominent representative of capitalist production itself'.[7] To be sure, production remains 'in the final analysis, the decisive factor', as Engels writes to Conrad Schmidt in 1890, but the more the money trade separates itself from and becomes independent of the commodity trade, the stronger and the more complex becomes its 'reaction' to production and the more it conquers for itself 'direct control of a section of production by which it is largely dominated'.[8]

In criticising the notion that a 'club of conspirators' is cheating the German people, Weber speaks out against a widespread critique of the stock market in which agrarian-conservative, petty bourgeois and popular socialist frontlines intersect. As someone who counts on accidents, natural disasters and crop failures to make him a profit, the speculator represents a personification that can easily become the focal point of a moral critique of capitalism. A criticism formulated from a capitalist perspective—partly by agrarians and partly by members of the bourgeoisie—, and one that extended far into the middle classes, was directed at the 'stock market Jews', who were held responsible for all destructive epiphenomena of capitalist development, from exploitation to economic crisis. Such 'outcry against the stock exchange' is 'petty-bourgeois', Engels writes to Bernstein in 1883, since it 'simply adjusts the *distribution* of

---

4   Weber 1988b, p. 256.

5   Weber 1988b, p. 320.

6   Weber 1988b, pp. 321–2.

7   Marx and Engels 1975–2005, vol. 37, p. 894; Marx 1981, p. 1045.

8   Marx and Engels 1975–2005, vol. 49, pp. 58–9.

the surplus value *already stolen* from the workers'.[9] As early as 1850, Marx and Engels already argued that insofar as the crisis first erupts in the field of speculation and affects production only subsequently, it appears to 'the superficial observer' that the cause of the crisis is not overproduction but 'excess speculation', although 'this is itself only a symptom of overproduction'.[10] In contrast with the harbingers of the later anti-Semitic dichotomy of 'money-grubbing' and 'productive' capital ['*raffendes*' versus '*schaffendes*' *Kapital*], Marx and Engels consider stock market speculation both a necessary systemic component of the capitalist mode of production and the most visible expression of its irrationality. Engels considers the stock markets 'temples of Mammon' and 'gambling houses', where capitalists who have in principle become superfluous rob each other of their capital.[11] They constitute the 'spearhead of capitalist gain where ownership becomes directly synonymous with theft',[12] a 'breeding ground of extreme corruption', where all 'obligatory moral concepts' of bourgeois society are turned upside down.[13] At the same time, Marx and Engels perceive in the autonomisation of financial capital an 'abolition of the capitalist mode of production within the capitalist mode of production itself', and thus a new form assumed by the contradiction between social and private wealth, one promoting the advent of socialism.[14] By providing, within the briefest of time spans, the capitals required by large industry, the stock market is 'as revolutionary as the steam engine'.[15]

In his popular discussion of the stock market, addressed 'first and foremost' to the 'labour movement',[16] Weber adopts the strategy of refuting unscientific prejudices about the stock market in order thereby also to render ineffective

---

9      Marx and Engels 1975–2005, vol. 46, p. 433; see vol. 50, p. 88.

10     Marx and Engels 1975–2005, vol. 10, p. 490.

11     See for example Marx and Engels 1975–2005, vol. 24, pp. 416–17; vol. 25, pp. 264–5.

12     Marx and Engels 1975–2005, vol. 46, p. 435.

13     Marx and Engels 1975–2005, vol. 50, p. 88.

14     Marx 1981, pp. 569ff; see Marx and Engels 1975–2005, vol. 37, pp. 434ff. 'What the speculating wholesale merchant risks is social property, not *his own*' (Marx and Engels 1975–2005, vol. 37, p. 437). Marx had originally planned to write a chapter on 'Capital as Money Market', but never did so. 'In the money market, capital is posited in its totality; there it *determines price, provides work, regulates production*, in a word, *source of production*' (Marx and Engels 1975–2005, vol. 28, p. 206). On later discussions of the stock market within Marxism, see Krätke 1995a, pp. 290ff.

15     Marx and Engels 1975–2005, vol. 46, p. 434. In a letter to Bernstein (24 January 1893), Engels praises the stock market as 'an incomparable element of destruction' and 'the most powerful accelerator of impending revolution' (Marx and Engels 1975–2005, vol. 50, p. 88).

16     Weber 1988b, p. 246.

all socialist critiques. At the heart of his argument lies the demonstration that one cannot deduce from the form of futures trading that it is characterised by 'unreality' or displays 'the character of a game'.[17] For example, a salesman who takes advantage of currency differentials, in order thereby to protect himself against the risk of price fluctuations, is pursuing a highly 'real' and 'sound' business goal, and to neglect this sort of insurance, which takes the form of futures trading, 'would be as unsound as to refrain from ensuring oneself against the risk of fire'.[18] 'Where the indispensable activity of brokers ends and straightforward speculation on price differentials begins, no one can say'.[19] This argument, directed against a critique of the stock market that invokes 'sound' revenue within agricultural and rural production, is one that Marx and Engels would have endorsed.

But Weber is not concerned with an analysis of the stock market's function within the reproduction of capital. What he actually wants to do is reintroduce the distinction between 'good' and 'bad' revenues, albeit in a way that differs from its usage by the stock market's conservative or populist critics. It is not the outward form of a business activity that determines its character, but rather 'the internal economic purpose, which one cannot recognise by considering only a specific business transaction', he concludes.[20] Weber uses the concept of the 'internal' purpose to displace the problem of speculation from the economic level, that of the capitalist realisation of profit, to the socio-psychological one of 'real' or 'unreal' businessmen: 'It is on the persons that everything ultimately depends'.[21]

In the scholarly literature on Weber, this displacement is generally considered evidence of the important role the subjective and the ideal play within his early economic works. Bendix believes he can show that, differently from Marxism, Weber emphasised the significance of ideas and of the individual.[22] This interpretation elides the argumentative strategy that gives Weber's emphasis on the 'ideal' its significance in the first place: in order to be able to plausibly demonstrate the economic usefulness of the stock market, Weber has to attempt to redirect the accusation of speculation, common in everyday thought, from the institution and the financial circles controlling it to small stock market speculators. While he declares large financial capitalists to be

---

17      Weber 1988b, p. 308.

18      Weber 1988b, p. 309.

19      Weber 1988b, p. 311.

20      Weber 1988b, p. 309.

21      Weber 1988b, p. 285.

22      Bendix 1960, pp. 66ff.

indispensable, because they prevent the nation from becoming dependent on foreign capital, he describes the small speculator as a 'parasite' who is superfluous from the point of view of political economy,[23] devoid of expertise and irresponsible with regard to profit and loss:[24] 'Almost everything one really can criticise futures trading for takes one back to the easy access enjoyed by speculators who lack sound judgement and significant assets'.[25] In doing so, he refers back to the concept of 'vocation' or 'calling', which will go on to play an important role in the *Protestant Ethic*, as well as in *Politics as Vocation* and *Science as Vocation*: what ought to be retained as a fundamental principle is that 'the one whose "calling" does not lie here—in the sense appropriate to this context—is primarily the small speculator with little capital'.[26]

Consequently, what appears to Weber to constitute a 'grave defect' is the fact that among the Prussian stock market operators, and differently from English stock market operators, there exist the starkest differences in wealth. Prussian stock market operators are an extremely 'mixed society', ranging from the representatives of major banks to the 'most pitiful little crook living hand to mouth off the minor price fluctuations he speculates on'.[27] Stock deals in particular display the tendency to 'attract elements of doubtful moral quality and equally doubtful solvency'.[28] That is why reform of the stock market must be concerned primarily with eliminating the participation of 'those "uncalled for" in the field of speculation' by making proof of substantial assets a condition of entry.[29]

Thus Weber's emphasis on the 'ideal' is both the premise and a mystification of the social distinction between the 'indispensable' large speculator and the 'harmful' small speculator. While the 'outcry' against the stock market that Engels criticised attributes all of capitalism's ills to 'stock market Jews', Weber simply passes the accusation on to the financially weakest faction of speculators. Economically, his justification is limited to the claim that as 'outsiders', small speculators lack the equity and expertise to 'even make and implement independent decisions', so that they tend to 'blindly follow a slogan issued "from above"', exaggerating the development of prices in the direction corresponding to the predominant trend'.[30] The argument is incoherent since it

---

23    Weber 1988b, p. 286.
24    Weber 1988b, p. 315.
25    Weber 1988b, p. 320.
26    Weber 1894, p. 127; compare p. 101.
27    Weber 1988b, pp. 283–4.
28    Weber 1894, p. 116.
29    Weber 1988b, pp. 316, 321.
30    Weber 1894, p. 130; compare Weber 1988b, p. 319.

entails that the putatively harmful activity is in no way distinct from that of the large banks, whom the small speculators merely follow as 'outsiders'. Even if their 'inner' economic purpose is morally questionable, as Weber insinuates, they are merely supporting the morally lofty purposes of large stock market operators. No evidence is provided for the claim that small-scale speculation is particularly 'harmful' economically.

The only level on which Weber's argument could be said to be coherent is that of an ideological class construction: the small speculator 'prevents the emergence of a class of traders that is *more homogeneous* in terms of its prior social qualification, upbringing and position', who develop a common 'concept of honour' and might be able to set up, on this basis, 'courts of honour' by which to curb abuses.[31] And vice versa: such a court of honour would presuppose 'that the quality of those subject to its jurisdiction is more or less the same in social terms and relatively high on average'; otherwise, one could not speak of the development of an 'authoritative concept of honour', according to Weber's paraphrase of the expert Eulenburg. Weber concludes: 'Once unsuited or "uncalled for" elements are permitted to participate in stock market activities, repressive measures are of no avail'.[32] Weber's ideal is the English and American stock market, openly organised as a 'monopoly of the rich', whose operators constitute a 'monetary aristocracy' of the stock market business.[33] Since large capital rules the stock market anyhow, it is only 'forthright' to 'leave the field to it formally as well'.[34]

In his considerations on how such a project might be implemented, Weber displays a vacillating stance towards state intervention. On the one hand, he endorses the state's right to supervise and intercede (much like Schmoller), speaking out in favour of, for example, the appointment of a state commissar within the bourgeois 'court of honour', similar to the state prosecutor.[35] On the other hand, he emphasises the limited nature of state supervision, arguing that the stock market is not a food market where the police can detect instances of fraud.[36] What thereby becomes decisive is the belated development of a specific business ethic: 'If one can *not* rely on the loftiest possible notion of social respectability asserting itself within the estate, the entire institution [the court of honour; J.R.] is a farce and it is better to avoid it altogether'.[37]

---

31    Weber 1988b, pp. 286–7.
32    Weber 1894, pp. 137–8.
33    Weber 1988b, pp. 279–80.
34    Weber 1988b, p. 287.
35    Weber 1988b, pp. 288, 321. For Schmoller's view, see the paraphrase in Weber 1894, p. 134.
36    Weber 1988b, p. 288.
37    Ibid.

What Weber articulates, in the terminology of an estates-based concept of honour, is the attempt to constitute a homogeneous stock market elite, thereby contributing to the ethical constitution of the bourgeoisie as an independent class. Weber's discussion of the stock market provides a first indication of the peculiarity of Weber's concept of ethics: the very Weber who condemns the 'ethicisation' of the stock market as an act of national self-disarmament ends up placing his hopes in an 'ethic' qua bourgeois business morality. What Weber rejects is an ideological subordination to universal moral norms, something he will later subsume under the rubric of the 'ethic of conviction' (see below, Chapter 21.3). What he strives for is the hegemonic quality of class-determined and class-constituting emotions and motivations. In this sense, 'ethics' will become part of his religious sociology also, determining concepts such as that of the 'Protestant ethic' and 'economic ethics'.

# CHAPTER 11

# The Critique of the 'Passive Revolution' in Germany

## 11.1    The 'Entailed Estate'

The transition from a critique of agricultural policy to a comprehensive critique of society is driven by the contradiction that in order to curb the power of large landowners, Weber must appeal to a state that is itself bound up with this class and shaped by it. The estates of the East are not just economic units; they are also 'local centres of political power'. As such, they entail the 'dislocation of a politically dominant class across the countryside'.[1] But while they once constituted the economic foundation of the state class, they are now no longer sufficient for financing the lifestyle dictated by the upper middle classes of the cities. The formerly 'economically "saturated" existences' yield to the phenomenon of the 'farmer in distress'. Political power lacks a secure 'material foundation' and needs now to 'be put in the service of economic interests'.[2]

This reversal of economy and politics had been described in similar terms, and not long before, by Engels, in *The Role of Force in History* (1887/88): 'The duty to live up to its [big landed property's; J.R.] status becomes more and more expensive every day . . . This artificially preserved class is doomed to extinction and no state assistance can keep it alive in the long run. But with it disappears also the old Prussian state'.[3] The disproportion between dwindling economic power and a power maintained by the state provides Weber with his key to the analysis of Wilhelmine society. He is especially interested in the institutional and ideological ways in which the state attempts to compensate for the decline of landed property by means of feudal-bourgeois compromises.

Weber formulates an exemplary critique of one such 'artificial' social-aristocratic institution in 'The Entailed Estate' [*Fideikommiss*].[4] The title refers to a legal institution whereby aristocratic landed estates were 'withdrawn from free commercial intercourse and the perpetuity of ownership by a given aristocratic family was ensured, along with forced heirship'.[5] The state's expansion of privileged entailed-estate ownership was a reaction to the rapidly rising debt

---

1    Weber 1984–2009, vol. I/4, p. 426; Weber 1988c, p. 471.

2    Weber 1984–2009, vol. I/4, p. 428; Weber 1988c, p. 473.

3    Marx and Engels 1975–2005, vol. 26, pp. 498–9.

4    Weber 1984–2009, vol. I/4, p. 794.

5    Wehler 1995, p. 814.

of the Junkers, as a result of which property fluctuations had become more marked in East Elbia than, for example, in the Rhineland or in Westphalia.[6] At the same time, the creation of the entailed estate allowed prosperous members of the bourgeoisie to purchase manors with royal approval, thereby joining the aristocracy, which then made it easier for family members to pursue a career in the civil service.

Weber's engagement with this phenomenon can be reconstructed almost continuously for the period from 1895 to 1920, but it peaked in 1904 and 1917. In 1904, a Prussian legal bill designed to facilitate the creation of entailed estates prompted Weber to pen—simultaneously with the first part of the *Protestant Ethic*—a systematic critique titled 'Considerations on the Question of Entailed Estates in Prussia from the Point of View of Agricultural Statistics and Social Policy'.[7] According to Marianne Weber, the subsequent withdrawal of the bill can be attributed to Weber's intervention.[8] In early 1917, the government yielded to conservative pressure and presented a new legal bill on the entailed estate, an act the bourgeois opposition denounced as a violation of the 'party truce' during the First World War. Weber's response, 'The Nobilitation of War Gains', was published in the *Frankfurter Zeitung* on 1 March 1917.[9] Criticism of the entailed estate was unable to prevent its expansion: in 1870, there were 700 entailed estates; by 1915, the number had tripled to 1,311, with entailed estates making up no less than 7.3 percent of state territory; during the war, the number continued to rise (to 1,369).[10]

Much as in his inquiry into farm labour, Weber's critique was initially (in the 1890s) formulated on the level of agricultural and demographic policy: the entailed estate promotes a 'feudal-aristocratic organisation of the countryside';[11] it displaces small peasant property by its orientation to maximum rent levels; and it leads to 'depopulation' and 'denationalisation'.[12] In the counties with the highest number of entailed estates, the rural population is 'almost like quicksand'.[13] The systematic critique formulated by Weber in 1904 provides ample statistical evidence for these tendencies. Because it is precisely the more

---

6    'In the case of two thirds of all major East Elbian farms, debt...exceeded half of total
     assets' (Wehler 1995, p. 815).
7    Weber 1988b, pp. 323–93.
8    Marianne Weber 1975, p. 327.
9    Weber 1984–2009, vol. I/15, pp. 206ff; Weber 1988a, pp. 183ff.
10   Wehler 1995, p. 814.
11   Weber 1984–2009, vol. I/4, p. 596.
12   Weber 1984–2009, vol. I/4, pp. 780, 782, 785.
13   Weber 1984–2009, vol. I/4, p. 832.

valuable land that is absorbed by capital and 'pegged down' in entailed estates, the creation of viable small and medium-sized farms is stalled.[14] Pressures to extend the volume of rent lead to the entailed estates becoming 'centres for the accumulation of land' that have to 'clear' small tenants on the purchased lands.[15] By facilitating the creation of entailed estates, the state sacrifices the best land to the 'contemptible pursuit of nobiliary particles'.[16] Weber calls for limiting the creation of entailed estates to large estates and woodlands, so as to redirect rent-seeking capital to the less valuable lands that are suitable for forestation.[17] Eventually, in the 1918/19 debates on a new German constitution, Weber calls for the complete abolition of the entailed estate.[18]

## 11.2    The 'Feudal Pretensions' of the German Bourgeoisie

But what is at issue is no longer merely a problem of agricultural policy. The critique's significance to the analysis of society derives from the fact that it decodes the legal institution of the entailed estate as a complex grouting of bourgeois and feudal interests that runs through the various functional levels of society, thereby shaping the social structure as a whole.

On the economic level, the entailed estate presents itself, first and foremost, as a 'modern capitalist form of rent formation' that serves both capital's interest in valorisation and the ruling strata's interest in a stable income appropriate to their social status.[19] Weber defines the entailed estate as the 'form in which "saturated" capitalist characters tend to steer their acquisitions from the stormy seas of economic struggle into the haven of the life led by rentiers ennobled by letters patent'.[20] Thus there emerges a compromise formation within which the capital function is subordinate to the interest of a particular social stratum, an interest pre-determined by feudalism. The search for a

---

14    Weber 1988b, pp. 332, 344.

15    Weber 1988b, pp. 371–2. It is precisely the owners of small entailed estates that 'must get all they can out of the land, the tenants and the workers in order to live in a manner "befitting their social status"', and they must use their revenue to purchase additional land: 'Because what he needs is rent and more rent: first to be ennobled, and then to become, in the course of generations, a baron, a count, and so on' (Weber 1984–2009, vol. I/15, p. 210; Weber 1988a, p. 187).

16    Weber 1988b, pp. 379, 393.

17    Weber 1988b, pp. 360–1, 378–9; compare Weber 1984–2009, vol. I/15, pp. 213–14.

18    Weber 1984–2009, vol. I/16, pp. 139, 212, 503.

19    Weber 1988b, p. 331.

20    Ibid.

'seigniorial' existence leads to the 'nobilitation' of capitals.[21] But while Weber's economic analysis positions itself critically vis-à-vis the transformation of capital into rent, it remains uncritical with regard to the underlying social relation, namely the capitalist appropriation of surplus value. The autonomisation of capital, interest and ground rent, analysed by Marx as a mystificatory 'religion of everyday life',[22] is presupposed by Weber and constitutes the basis for the distinction between 'good' and 'bad' revenue: during the war, Weber condemns the way the 'nobilitation of war profits' occurs behind the back of the fighting army and at the expense of the nation's vital interests, but at the same time, he exempts the economically 'useful' war profits of the Krupp corporation from all criticism.[23] What Weber criticises is that German capital has become distracted from its proper task, namely 'economic conquest in the wide world'.[24]

Instead of developing an ethic of its own, one compatible with the laws proper to the movement of capital, the bourgeoisie is 'taken with feudal pretensions'.[25] The legal construct of the entailed estate is nominally presided over by the king, who needs to personally approve the creation of each new entailed estate. Thus the transformation of capital into rent is gilded with the illusion, comforting to all monarchists, that the king himself has verified each family's 'worthiness'.[26] Underlying this is a political strategy of domination by which 'the bourgeois money-bag is reconciled to its minimal degree of political influence by granting it a sort of "second-rate right of presentation at court"' [Hoffähigkeit].[27] By allowing nobilitated family members to enter the civil service, the entailed estate guarantees that the civil service will be dominated by conservatives, something that no longer accords with capitalist relations of production: the civil service recruits persons 'who confront the broad strata of the modern middle and working classes without any knowledge or understanding, with nothing but a dull, semi-agrarian sense of antipathy'.[28] Weber

---

21    Weber 1988b, pp. 366, 379.

22    Marx and Engels 1975–2005, vol. 37, p. 817. According to this analysis, the economic 'trinity' capital/profit, land/rent and work/wages completes the reification of social relations: 'an enchanted, perverted, topsy-turvy world, in which Monsieur le Capital and Madame la Terre do their ghost-walking as social characters and at the same time directly as mere things' (ibid).

23    Weber 1984–2009, vol. I/15, pp. 206–7, 220, 349.

24    Weber 1988b, p. 391.

25    Ibid.

26    Weber 1988b, p. 380; compare Weber 1984–2009, vol. I/15, p. 211.

27    Weber 1988b, p. 379.

28    Weber 1988b, p. 389.

is concerned that the resulting state will be incapable both of promoting the interests of the bourgeoisie and of integrating those of the proletariat; it proves unsuited to the task of intervening in modern class relations in a regulatory manner. Behind this perceived asynchrony lies an image of social disintegration, a premonition of revolution.

The effects on political culture are devastating. Weber acutely observes that instead of a self-confident bourgeois culture, what is developing is a dangerous blend of subalternity and unchecked lordliness. What is being created is a set of state-sustaining forces without political competence, 'comfortable and sated upstarts (*parvenus*)... who feel the need to sun themselves in the graciousness of the court'.[29] A mentality widespread among civil servants combines 'privileged inactivity' with 'the arrogance of mandarins when it comes to professional communication with those lower in the hierarchy', and what results is an '"assessorialism" that behaves in an impertinent manner when dealing with those below it, and pliantly when dealing with those above it'.[30]

Weber places the blame for the emergence of such attitudes on two instances in particular: the body of *reserve officers*, within which professional officers decided on the co-optation of 'acceptable' members of the bourgeoisie after closely scrutinising the candidate's professional and family background, and the *student fraternities*, which place their members in coveted positions with the aid of influential 'old boys'. Weber criticises both institutions as surrogates by which the state attempts to compensate the reduced economic foundation of landed property by ideologically 'annexing' the 'governing classes' to the aristocracy.[31] Enlargement of the body of reserve officers constitutes an attempt to 'establish a relationship to the dynasty that is, as it were, that of vassals',[32] whereas the student fraternities function as 'institutions by which to secure one's advancement',[33] and as a typical social form of 'education' and 'selection' for the recruitment of young civil servants.[34]

In his critique of student fraternities, Weber can appeal to personal experience. As a student in Heidelberg, he joined the fraternity 'Alemannen'; during his third semester, he engaged in the usual student duels and received his stripes. As Marianne Weber reports, this education for manhood required that a young man be 'able to pour in the greatest amount of alcohol without losing

---

29    Weber 1988b, p. 393.

30    Weber 1988b, p. 390.

31    Weber 1984–2009, vol. I/3, p. 918.

32    Ibid.

33    Weber 1988b, p. 390, note 1.

34    Weber 1994b, pp. 115–16; Weber 1984–2009, vol. I/15, pp. 382–3.

his self-control'. She attributes to Weber an 'outstanding capacity for alcohol', one that led to the rather slender freshman becoming 'corpulent' for a brief period of time.[35] In retrospect, Weber would report on the difficulty of 'getting out of my system the gestures that are instinctively practiced at the university when one is immature'.[36]

The damage done is, if nothing else, economic. By spreading to technical and commercial colleges, the fraternities undermine the 'spirit of uncompromising bourgeois work' within this strategically important area, a spirit much needed in the competitive struggle with the 'major working nations of the world, especially the Americans'.[37] As we have seen (Chapter 6), the fraternity has its positive counterpart in the American associations as they have developed from the Puritan sects; Weber studied these associations at about the same time, during his visit to America. This contrast also structures Weber's later interventions. In presenting his project of a sociology of associations at the first Sociological Congress in Frankfurt in 1910, he contrasts the practically-oriented American association with the tranquillising effects of the German choral society, arguing that the latter habituates a person to 'let tremendous sentiments gush from his heart and through his larynx, free of any relationship whatsoever to his behaviour'.[38] When Weber reiterates his critique of commercial colleges at the Fourth German Professorial Congress in Dresden in 1911, he provokes a hostile press campaign that sees the directors of the commercial colleges of Cologne and Berlin backing the fraternities of their students. Weber responds by penning a special memorandum.[39] In his lecture 'Socialism', held before Austrian officers in Vienna in 1918, he formulates the criticism that, in Germany, attendance of commercial colleges, technical colleges and professional schools is associated with the wish 'to join a fraternity, get cuts on one's face, become capable of giving satisfaction in a duel and thus of becoming a reserve officer, in order to later, in the office, stand a better chance of being

---

35   'The increase in his physical girth was even more striking than the expansion of his intellect ... When his mother first saw him so changed, the vigorous woman could think of no other way to express her astonishment and fright than to give him a resounding slap in the face' (Marianne Weber 1975, p. 69).

36   Quoted in Marianne Weber 1975, p. 427.

37   Weber 1988b, p. 390, note 1.

38   Weber 1988b, p. 445. Whoever grows accustomed to this, Weber argues, very easily becomes a '"good citizen" ... in the passive sense of the word. It is no wonder that monarchs are so fond of this sort of thing. "Where people are singing, you can settle down and feel at ease"' (Weber 1988b, p. 445).

39   See Marianne Weber 1975, p. 428; Mommsen 1974, pp. 101–2.

allowed to marry the boss's daughter—in other words, to assimilate oneself to what is known as "society".[40]

Weber's critique assumes special significance in his series of articles 'Suffrage and Democracy in Germany', written in 1917, as Germany's defeat in the First World War gradually began to become apparent. In Weber's view, the German habitus is characterised by the fact that, within it, an outdated form of lordliness and Germany's status of international inferiority are bound up with and presuppose one another: on the one hand, what the fraternities produce, by their 'subaltern social forms', is the very opposite of a 'cosmopolitan education', namely 'upstart manners' [*Parvenümanieren*] that appear as an uncouth 'stroppiness' stemming from inner insecurity and awkwardness;[41] on the other hand, these conventions differ from those of the Romance and Anglo-Saxon countries insofar as they are not 'amenable to democratisation', meaning that they cannot serve as '*models* for the nation as a whole, right down to the lowest strata', thereby '*shaping* [the nation] into a "master people" [*Herrenvolk*] with a self-confident outward bearing' in a unified manner.[42] The imperialism articulating itself with the 'master people' is bound up, here, with 'democracy', which Weber judges to be superior in power-political terms (see below, Chapter 12.3). Of course, Weber's 'democratisation' is itself conceptualised from above and amounts to a cross-class generalisation of ideological societalisation that is designed to effectively 'shape' its subjects by means of the role models it presents. Weber's critique of ideology is formulated from the perspective of a more effective ideologisation. Seen from this perspective, the bureaucratically shaped conventions are *formally* 'conventions of caste' [*Kastenkonventionen*], because they cannot be democratised, but *in substance*, they are not of an aristocratic but of a 'plebeian' character: 'The Germans are a *plebeian people*—or, if people prefer the term, a bourgeois [*bürgerlich*] people, and this is the only basis on which a specifically "German form" could grow'.[43] This 'German form', whose rudiments in the Hanseatic towns have not been developed

---

40    Weber 1984–2009, vol. I/15, p. 623; Weber 1988b, p. 510.

41    Weber 1984–2009, vol. I/15, pp. 383ff; Weber 1994b, pp. 115ff.

42    Weber 1984–2009, vol. I/15, pp. 386–7; Weber 1994b, pp. 119–20. Of Romance conventions, Weber says they replicate the 'gesture of a cavalier' [*Kavaliersgeste*] as it has developed since the sixteenth century, and of Anglo-Saxon conventions that they stem from the social habits of the stratum of gentlemen, which he sees as having shaped English relations since the seventeenth century. 'The important thing was that in all these cases the decisive features of those conventions and gestures could be imitated readily by all, and were therefore capable of being *democratised* (Weber 1984–2009, vol. I/15, p. 387; Weber 1994b, p. 120).

43    Weber 1984–2009, vol. I/15, p. 388; Weber 1994b, p. 121.

further since 1870, ought now to found itself upon 'inner *distance* and *reserve* in a person's personal bearing', Weber argues.[44] It is not to be overlooked that this personality profile is modelled on the men of worldly asceticism portrayed in the *Protestant Ethic*, 'men who had grown up in the hard school of life … temperate and reliable … completely devoted to their business'.[45] By promoting his project of a 'German form' that is both distanced ('truly aristocratic') and amenable to democratisation, Weber opposes the given intellectual culture on two fronts: on the one hand, he turns against the 'ignoble' need of the 'newest literati' to obtrusively 'palaver' about their erotic or religious experiences (Weber is presumably thinking of the 'erotic movement' propagated, among others, by Otto Gross, a student of Freud; Max and Marianne Weber engaged intensely with this movement from 1905/06 onward);[46] on the other hand, he questions the 'misapprehension' of numerous 'prophets' who invoke Nietzsche and seek distance for the sake of setting themselves off, in a putatively aristocratic manner, from the 'all too many'.[47]

The significance of the entailed estate to Weber's critique of ideology also emerges from the fact that he transposes the concept from economic law to the sociology of religion, where he applies it—analogously to the governmental administration and awarding of manors—to the official church's administration and awarding of religious salvation: in contrast with the sect, a 'believer's church' based on self-responsibility, the official church functions as 'a sort of entailed-estate foundation for supernatural ends' ['*eine Art Fideikommissstiftung zu überirdischen Zwecken*'],[48] a 'grace corporation' [*Gnadenanstalt*] that encompasses the righteous and the unrighteous and which 'administers religious gifts of grace like an endowed foundation

---

44    Weber 1984–2009, vol. I/15, p. 389; Weber 1994b, p. 122.

45    Weber 1950, p. 69.

46    To Marianne Weber, 'socialistic theories of marriage, by Nietzsche, Ellen Key, the psychiatrist Sigmund Freud, and others' numbered among the intellectual originators of a 'force of dissolution', a current that criticises bourgeois sexual morality and seeks to liberate the 'life-enhancing value of eroticism' in a 'sexual communism' (Marianne Weber 1975, p. 374). In her 1907 book *Ehefrau und Mutter in der Rechtsentwicklung* ['Wife and Mother in the Development of Law'], she engages extensively with theories of matriarchy and with the erotically libertine lifestyle propagated by Gross (on her status within the bourgeois women's movement, see Roth 1989, pp. IX–LXXI). On Max Weber's critique of the 'new ethic', see his refusal, on 13 September 1907, to publish an essay by Gross in the *Archiv* (Baumgarten 1964, pp. 644ff). On Weber's critique of the 'eroticistic culture of sentiment', see Schwentker 1988, pp. 665ff.

47    Weber 1984–2009, vol. I/15, p. 389–90; Weber 1994b, p. 122.

48    Weber 1950, p. 154 (translation modified).

[*Fideikommissstiftung*].[49] Whether it presents itself in the form of a legal or in that of a religious institution, the entailed estate is perceived by Weber as an 'asset' that is received 'from above' (i.e. from the state or the official church), rather than being obtained through one's own efforts, and this, he argues, has a tranquillising effect on the bourgeois economic ethic. On the opposite pole of the conceptual arrangement is the combination of a 'free' capitalist (agricultural) market with the 'free' religiosity of the sects.

Weber's critique of society can largely be read as a specific contribution to the analysis of the ideological superstructures of a German 'Bonapartism'. Thus it seems appropriate to compare his critique of 'Caesarism' with the analyses of Bonapartism formulated by Marx and Engels, in order then to relate the latter to Gramsci's reflections on 'passive revolution'. Doing so will also involve verifying Marianne Weber's remark that Weber's rejection of state metaphysics accords with the Marxian 'conception of the state and its ideology'.[50]

## 11.3    Caesarism, Bonapartism and 'Passive Revolution'

The more severe the crisis, the more acute his insight into the fault lines of Germany's system of authority becomes: Weber systematises his critique during the critical year 1917, under the impression of the February Revolution in Russia, in the course of his engagement with Germany's strike movement and domestic political crisis and in expectation of the country's impending military defeat. Two of his more extensive texts from the period have become best known: his December 1917 essay on 'Suffrage and Democracy in Germany',[51] mentioned above, and a series of articles, published in the *Frankfurter Zeitung* between April and June of 1917, whose critique of the political system led to the newspaper being subjected to 'pre-emptive censorship'. Reworked as a pamphlet, the articles were published, in 1918, under the title 'Parliament and Government in Germany under a New Political Order'.[52]

---

49    Weber 1946a, pp. 305–6. According to Weber, one typical expression of the church's character as an institution is to be found in the view 'that it is not the holy writ which guarantees the truth of the tradition and of ecclesiastical doctrine but rather the holiness of the church and its tradition, to which God has given the truth in trust [*als Fideikommiss*] and which thus guarantees the genuineness of the holy writ' (Weber 1978, pp. 790–91; see Weber 1970, 460).

50    Marianne Weber 1975, p. 587.

51    Weber 1984–2009, vol. I/15, pp. 344ff; see Weber 1994b.

52    Weber 1984–2009, vol. I/15, pp. 421ff; see Weber 1994c.

Gramsci holds that in this pamphlet, Weber criticises, with reference to Wilhelmine Germany, a state of affairs similar to the one he himself has criticised with reference to the Italy shaped by the *Risorgimento*.[53] In a second remark, he specifies that the pamphlet held lessons on how the aristocracy's monopoly position within politics has prevented the emergence of a substantial body of experienced bourgeois politicians.[54] The state places itself above the political parties 'in order to disunite them, to separate them from the great masses, and to gain a "force of nonpartisans" who are attached to the government by paternalistic bonds of a Bonapartist-Caesarist type'.[55] The method employed to undermine political parties consists in 'absorbing their few indispensable intellectuals'.[56] The misery of parliamentary life corresponds to that of cultural life: 'sterile erudition in place of political history, superstition instead of religion'; personal faction building instead of serious politics; isolation of the universities from the 'living reality of national life'. The bureaucracy assumed the place of intellectual and political hierarchies, which thereby becomes a 'political', i.e. 'state-Bonapartist party' in its own right.[57]

Weber begins his series of articles for the *Frankfurter Zeitung* with remarks on the 'Legacy of Bismarck', summarising and systematising his earlier criticisms of the German statesman. The state's undermining of political parties and their separation from the masses, two phenomena by which Gramsci characterises the Caesarist-Bonapartist type of authority, is discussed with specific reference to the strategies Bismarck adopted against the pro-government National-Liberal Party: Bismarck used military bills and the special laws against the Social Democratic Party to manoeuvre the National-Liberal Party into intractable situations, veritable breaking tests.[58] Unable to tolerate any independent power beside him, Bismarck destroyed the political representative of the bourgeoisie. His legacy consisted in an impotent parliament with a 'seriously lowered level of intellectual ability' and a nation devoid both of a political education and of political will, one that had grown 'accustomed to assume that the great statesman at the head of the nation would take care of political matters for them'.[59]

---

53   Gramsci 1996, p. 106.
54   Gramsci 1975c, p. 1527.
55   Gramsci 1996, p. 106.
56   Ibid.
57   Ibid.
58   Weber 1984–2009, vol. I/15, pp. 441ff; see Weber 1994c, pp. 137ff.
59   Weber 1984–2009, vol. I/15, pp. 449–50; see Weber 1994c, pp. 144–5.

In terms of the theory of hegemony, Weber's critique of Bismarck's 'Caesarism' amounts to the accusation that Bismarck prevented the bourgeoisie from producing its own 'organic intellectuals', capable of adequately transposing the exigencies of the capitalist mode of production into the superstructure, civil society and the *'società politica'*.[60] Instead, Caesarism produces a type of intellectual that Weber describes and combats as 'literati'. Politically, the concept is as ambivalent as that of 'traditionalism', and Weber uses it to refer to various social forces ranging from the conservatives and the 'Pan-Germans' to the left socialists. What is common to these various referents, however, is that they do not accord with Weber's project of Fordist modernisation; specifically, they represent the inability to recognise and articulate the interests of capital's productive factions.

Weber perceives the 'political literati' as divided, since 1878, into two 'parts of unequal size'. The smaller of the two has responded to Bismarck's Caesarism with 'feeble resentment'—what Weber has in mind is left liberalism—, whereas the larger has merely glorified Bismarck's statesmanship for its 'element of violence and cunning ... the real or apparent brutality in his methods', crafting from this the historical legend of Germany's conservative politicians.[61] Weber speaks of a 'subaltern fashion among today's littérateurs' that seeks to deny that Germany's parliaments and political parties express the 'German spirit';[62] he chastises the 'bootlickers who follow whatever fashion happens to be considered "aristocratic"' and who are 'always there to applaud the given "developmental tendency"; behind them lies the anti-parliamentary resentment of the civil servants.[63] Accordingly, Weber uses the term 'literati' synonymously with 'ideologues'.[64]

---

60  Every social class 'organically' creates for itself 'one or more strata of intellectuals who provide it with homogeneity and a consciousness of its own function not only within the economic, but also within the social and the political sphere' (Gramsci 1975c, p. 1513). Textual version A had still limited this function to the 'economic sphere' (see Gramsci 1996, p. 199).

61  Weber 1984–2009, vol. I/15, p. 438; Weber 1994c, p. 135.

62  Weber 1984–2009, vol. I/15, p. 441; Weber 1994c, p. 138.

63  Weber 1984–2009, vol. I/15, p. 245; Weber 1988a, p. 203; Weber 1988d, p. 513. The original version of the text, published in the *Frankfurter Zeitung* on 27 May 1917, also contains gender-related invectives such as 'in a revoltingly feminine manner', 'hysterical' and 'eunuchism' (Weber 1984–2009, vol. I/15, p. 438).

64  Weber 1984–2009, vol. I/15, pp. 357, 505; Weber 1988a, pp. 254, 368. It was originally Napoleon I who introduced the pejorative term of 'ideologues' or *'idéologistes'* (see Rehmann 2013, pp. 18ff).

To the extent that Weber's critique of the literati is directed against this larger conservative 'half', it aims at a type of intellectual that one might follow Gramsci in describing as the 'traditional' or 'crystallised' intellectual of the ruling power bloc.[65] In Germany, 'the bourgeoisie gains industrial-economic control, but the old feudal classes remain as the governing stratum' and continue to enjoy 'wide caste privileges in the army, in state administration and on the land'. The literati performed the function of the bourgeoisie's 'traditional intellectuals', who joined forces with the petty bourgeoisie to maintain their intellectual and political leadership position.[66] In characterising the literati as representatives of a civil-service ideology, Weber attacks a specific alliance between intellectuals and the state bureaucracy, analysed by Gramsci as the distinctive feature of 'passive revolution': where 'passive revolution' developed as a 'reaction' and 'national overcoming' of the French Revolution, it was borne by intellectuals who were not associated with a strong bourgeois class, but rather understood the state as 'a thing in itself, as a rational absolute'.[67] Prussia is to German unification what the Piedmont is to the Italian *Risorgimento*.[68] The state assumes the position of local groups and exercises the function of authority, not that of leadership: a dictatorship without hegemony.[69]

Marianne Weber holds that Weber and Marx both reject the metaphysics of the state;[70] this is most true with regard to the analyses of Bonapartism formulated by Marx and Engels. These analyses refer not just to the regime of Napoleon III, but also to that of his 'imitator' Bismarck, who outgrew his teacher.[71] While Marx would have rejected the term 'Caesarism',[72] used by

---

65    Gramsci 1996, pp. 202–3; Gramsci 2007, pp. 332–3.

66    Gramsci 1992, pp. 150–1; Gramsci 2007, pp. 332–3; Gramsci 1975c, p. 1515.

67    Gramsci 1992, p. 229; compare Gramsci 1975b, p. 1362.

68    'Il ruolo del Piemonte nel Risorgimento italiano diviene cosí per Gramsci non dissimile da quello che Weber ha individuato per la Prussia' (Mangoni 1977, p. 409). In *The Role of Force in History*, Engels already speaks of 'Prussia's Piedmont mission in Germany' (Marx and Engels 1975–2005, vol. 26, p. 480).

69    Gramsci 1975c, pp. 1822–4; compare Gramsci 2007, p. 37.

70    Marianne Weber 1975, p. 587.

71    Marx and Engels 1975–2005, vol. 27, p. 513; vol. 42, pp. 292–3. 'Bismarck is Louis Napoleon translated from the adventurous French pretender to the throne into the Prussian backwoods Junker and member of the German students' association', writes Engels in 1887/88 (Marx and Engels 1975–2005, vol. 26, p. 475; compare vol. 22, pp. 5–6).

72    Talk of 'Caesarism' is described by Marx in the preface to the second, 1869 edition of *The Eighteenth Brumaire* as a 'superficial historical analogy', since in ancient Rome, class struggle only played out within a privileged minority, with the slaves merely forming the 'purely passive pedestal'. Given such differences in material conditions, the corresponding

Weber, it is striking to what extent the analytic interests and findings of the two coincide.

When Marx uses the case of France to analyse the political workings of Bonapartism,[73] his basic methodological operation consists in tracing what appears to be one-man rule back to its social conditions of existence. One of these conditions is the secular process of the state apparatus's growing autonomisation vis-à-vis society.[74] State power, 'divided and centralized as in a factory', begins to develop under absolute monarchy, which transforms feudal privileges into 'attributes of the state power' and feudal dignitaries into 'paid officials'; it then expands into a bureaucratic state machinery that parasitically 'enmeshes the body of French society and chokes all its pores'.[75] All revolutions 'perfected this machinery instead of breaking it'.[76]

Weber reiterates the observation: 'In France the Revolution and, more decisively, Bonapartism have made the bureaucracy all-powerful'.[77] The state-bureaucratic determinant of Bonapartism that Marx draws attention to recurs, in a similar form, in Weber's analyses of the emergence of the modern civil service.[78] And when, in his theory of bureaucracy, he makes the triumph of the bureaucratic life form end in an 'iron cage' or 'steel housing' [*stählernes Gehäuse*] of servitude,[79] this can be read as a continuation (and totalisation) of the explanatory model of Bonapartism—albeit one formulated from a perspective diametrically opposed to the Marxian critique of the state, a perspective that conceptualises bureaucratisation as an inevitable process and reduces

---

political phenomena cannot have more in common with one another 'than the Archbishop of Canterbury has with the High Priest Samuel' (Marx and Engels 1975–2005, vol. 21, pp. 57–8).

73  In particular, he does so in 1850 in *The Class Struggles in France* (Marx and Engels 1975–2005, vol. 10, pp. 45ff), in 1853 in *The Eighteenth Brumaire* (Marx and Engels 1975–2005, vol. 11, pp. 99ff) and in 1871 in *The Civil War in France* (Marx and Engels 1975–2005, vol. 21, pp. 307ff). On the various theories of Bonapartism within Marxism, see Mackenbach 1995, pp. 283ff.

74  Another condition cited by Marx, which I will not discuss here, is the isolation of small-holding peasants, which constrains the representation of class interests to assume the form of a relation of authority: 'Their representative must at the same time appear as their master, as an authority over them, an unlimited governmental power which protects them from the other classes' (Marx and Engels 1975–2005, vol. 11, p. 187).

75  Marx and Engels 1975–2005, vol. 11, p. 185.

76  Marx and Engels 1975–2005, vol. 11, p. 186.

77  Weber 1978, p. 985.

78  See for example Weber 1978, pp. 956ff.

79  Weber 1984–2009, vol. I/15, pp. 464–5, 593; see Weber 1994c, p. 157.

modern socialism to a necessary aggravation of bureaucratic authority from the outset (see below, Chapter 12.2).

What distinguishes the Bonapartist monarchy from absolute monarchy in Marx and Engels is the new class constellation engendered by the industrial revolution. The old monarchy's function was to establish an 'equilibrium' between the aristocracy and the bourgeoisie, but now all property-owning classes must be protected against the onslaught of the working class.[80] While the bourgeoisie has 'already lost' the faculty of ruling the nation, the working class has 'not yet acquired' it.[81] What proved decisive for the debates on Bonapartism within Marxism was Engels's formula of the '*balance of the contending classes of French society*'.[82] This formula, however, is all too easily understood as a general 'sociological model . . . of a mathematical type', as Gramsci has noted.[83] It has the disadvantage of focusing too strongly on a particular domestic constellation of forces and eliding Bonapartism's international determinants. These determinants are evident, for example, in the bourgeois-feudal power bloc's response to the upheavals of the French Revolution, a general European response that vacillated between repression and modernisation.[84] Yet even if the schematic notion of a domestic class 'equilibrium' leads astray, there is ample evidence for the relationship, analysed by Marx, between the need to

---

80    Marx and Engels 1957, vol. 7, p. 538; compare Marx and Engels 1975–2005, vol. 23, p. 626.

81    Marx and Engels 1975–2005, vol. 22, p. 330.

82    Marx and Engels 1975–2005, vol. 11, p. 215.

83    Gramsci 1975b, pp. 1197–8, 1194–5; Gramsci 1975c, pp. 1619–22.

84    Wehler mentions this formula in order to conclude that the concept of Bonapartism cannot be applied to Bismarck, although in 1973, he had himself invoked Marx to analyse Bismarck's rule as a 'Bonapartist' dictatorial regime (Wehler 1973, pp. 63ff). Wehler's main argument is that, unlike France, post-1849 Germany displayed no class equilibrium; the traditional elites with their army and civil service apparatus were clearly predominant (Wehler 1995, pp. 366–7). What Wehler overlooks is the fact that German Bonapartism was substantially determined by the European dynamic of 'passive revolution', which was anti-French (consider for example the fear of a spread of the Paris Commune). Moreover, when dealing with the period of rapid industrialisation and of the rise of the Social Democratic Party (the 1870s and 1880s), the question concerning relative class equilibrium needs to be posed in different terms than when dealing with the years after 1849. The Weberian concept of 'charismatic rule' that Wehler proposes (Wehler 1995, pp. 369ff) fails to resolve the issue, because it referred originally to a precarious and temporary type of authority *devoid of* traditional elites, a well-established administrative staff and so on (see for example Weber 1978, p. 244). Under close scrutiny, all that remains of the concept's putatively 'superior explanatory power' is the 'characteristic aura of the charismatic leader' (Wehler 1995, p. 373)—whose workings are, however, in need of socio-theoretical explanation (see below, Chapter 14.1).

fight back the revolution and the bourgeoisie's willingness to compromise with the Junkers: because of its fear of the proletariat, the bourgeoisie concludes a 'tacit agreement' with the government and obtains its gradual social emancipation in return for relinquishing political power in the present.[85]

The bourgeoisie's renunciation of hegemony is criticised by both Marx and Weber, albeit from divergent standpoints. Marx contends that when it comes under pressure from the proletariat, the bourgeoisie suddenly perceives its own democracy as a precursor of socialism: 'The parliamentary regime lives by discussion, how shall it forbid discussion? ... The parliamentary regime leaves everything to the decision of majorities; how shall the great majorities outside parliament not want to decide? When you play the fiddle at the top of the state, what else is to be expected but that those down below dance?'[86] In order to prevent the proclaimed political and legal equality from being extended to all of society, the bourgeoisie sacrifices 'its general class interests, that is, its political interests, to the narrowest and most sordid private interests'.[87] By virtue of this sacrifice, it admits 'that in order to save its purse it must forfeit the crown, and the sword that is to safeguard it must at the same time be hung over its own head as a sword of Damocles'.[88]

Weber observes the same development, but from the opposite perspective: what makes it so difficult for bourgeois reformers to endorse equal suffrage 'with unqualified inner forthrightness' is 'the effect of capitalism with its power to form classes', he writes in 1906, with reference to the bourgeois revolution in Russia. Weber puts himself in the position of the bourgeois who is threatened by the proletariat: 'The economic conflict of interest and the class character of the proletariat stabs specifically bourgeois reformers in the back: this is the fate of their work, here and everywhere else'.[89] What 'stabs' the bourgeoisie 'in the back' in Weber is the same class dynamic that drives it to discredit its own models of democracy as 'socialist' in Marx and Engels. What we are dealing with is a structural fear that, just like all ideologies formulated as expressions of the general interest, the general right to vote and parliamentarism could be employed for non-bourgeois purposes. Weber criticises 'Caesarism' for exploiting this class-determined ambivalence: in order to aggravate the bourgeoisie's nervelessness vis-à-vis democracy, Caesarism makes use of modern society's

---

85    Marx and Engels 1975–2005, vol. 23, p. 628.

86    Marx and Engels 1975–2005, vol. 11, p. 142.

87    Marx and Engels 1975–2005, vol. 11, p. 173.

88    Marx and Engels 1975–2005, vol. 11, p. 143.

89    Weber 1984–2009, vol. I/10, p. 117, Weber 1988a, p. 36.

division 'into two classes that are both intimately connected and, for this very reason, hostile to one another: the bourgeoisie and the proletariat'.[90]

The critiques are as similar as the perspectives from which they are formulated differ: while Marx and Engels seek to demonstrate that, given its class position, the bourgeoisie cannot but fall back behind its democratic ideologies,[91] Weber wants to help the bourgeoisie promote its ethico-political interest against Bonapartist temptations. In a letter to Marx dated 13 April 1866, Engels characterised Bonapartism as the 'true religion of the modern bourgeoisie' and the Bonapartist semi-dictatorship as its 'normal form' of rule;[92] Weber would have objected to this both politically and in terms of the sociology of religion: the *Protestant Ethic* can be read as an ambitious attempt to prove the opposite, namely that the bourgeoisie's 'true religion', its ideal-typical 'spirit of capitalism', is to be sought not in Caesarism but in ascetic Protestantism.

In an outline of the concluding section of *The Role of Force in History*, a text found in Engels's literary estate, Engels suggests that instead of the Bismarckian strategy of a 'strengthening of state power', the propertied classes would have been better advised to manoeuvre back and forth between the bourgeoisie and the proletariat.[93] This is Weber's assessment as well. Weber perceives the bourgeois-feudal compromise of interests that Caesarism secured as an existential threat: a 'passive revolution' that keeps the bourgeoisie in a politically and culturally subaltern position also renders the ruling power bloc incapable of action when faced with a socialist revolution.

The remedies developed and proposed by Weber towards the end of the First World War reveal another contrast between him and Marx: in criticising Bismarck's 'Caesarism', Weber merely seeks to impose more flexible forms of Caesarist rule.

---

90    Weber 1984–2009, vol. I/15, p. 347; Weber 1994b, p. 80.

91    The European bourgeoisie recognised in Louis Napoleon 'the first "great statesman", who was flesh of their flesh, and bone of their bone' (Engels, *The Role of Force in History*, Marx and Engels 1975–2005, vol. 26, p. 461). Once Bismarck had implemented the bourgeois project of national unity by 'Bonapartist means' in 1870/71, '[a]ll European philistines admired [him] as they had admired Louis Napoleon, Bismarck's model, in the fifties' (Marx and Engels 1975–2005, vol. 26, p. 497; compare p. 476).

92    Marx and Engels 1975–2005, vol. 42, p. 266.

93    Marx and Engels 1975–2005, vol. 26, p. 579.

# CHAPTER 12

# Proposals for the Development of a 'Caesarism without a Caesar'

## 12.1 The Shortcomings of a 'Value-Rational' Critique of Weber

In two texts written during the First World War, 'Suffrage and Democracy in Germany' and 'Parliament and Government in Germany under a new Political Order', Weber seeks to demonstrate that, contrary to what the 'political literati' claim, the foreign-policy and domestic crisis of 1917 should be attributed not to parliamentarism and the political parties, but to the powerlessness caused by Bismarckian Caesarism. This led to the 'Pan-Germans' accusing him of being a foreign agent.[1] From the 1920s onward, Weber's students begin disseminating and citing the same texts to show that he is a brilliant ethico-political leader who has simply never been given a chance to prove his mettle. For example, Jaspers claimed in his speech at the 1920 memorial funeral service in Heidelberg that what distinguished Weber from a politician was his unwillingness to seize power: Weber was able to live without power, 'like the Platonic philosopher who is only ready to govern the state out of duty'.[2] Weber's calls for parliamentarisation and democratisation tempted 1950s West German commentators to celebrate him as a kind of founding father of German democracy. This image of Weber has justifiably been criticised as a myth: according to György Lukács, Weber 'regarded democracy as the form most suited to the expansion of a better functioning imperialism',[3] and Mayer considers it a subordinate element within the 'Machiavellianism of the steel age' he sees Weber as having

---

1 Weber 1994c, p. 131; see Weber 1984–2009, vol. I/15, p. 433. On 22 December 1917, the *Alldeutsche Blätter* accused the *Frankfurter Zeitung* of being the organ of 'universal Jewry' and British high finance; on 20 December 1917, the *Göttinger Tageblatt* claimed Weber had founded an anti-Pan-German student committee, possibly with funding from the British government (see Weber 1984–2009, vol. I/15, p. 532, notes 6 and 7).

2 Jaspers 1989a, p. 18. Jaspers makes a similar claim in his 1932 publication 'Max Weber: Politician, Scientist, Philosopher', re-published under a new title (but without changes to the text) in 1946 (Jaspers 1989b): 'The time cried out for a strong personality, and was not able to use the greatest that it had. The consistency with which it eliminated Max Weber reveals something no longer shocking about the time itself' (Jaspers 1989b, p. 112).

3 Lukács 1980, p. 609 (translation modified).

bestowed upon the German nation.[4] Mommsen, who considers the accusations of Machiavellianism levelled against Weber to be 'quite sweeping',[5] nevertheless concludes that Weber treated the equal franchise and parliamentarism
purely as requirements of the international and domestic power struggle,
'implementing with utmost rigour the model of a top-down political decision-
making process':[6] 'democracy' does not refer to the self-determination of the
people, but to a 'functionalist system' whose selection process privileges political leaders instead of the conservative character type of the civil servant.[7]

In fact, what is absent in Weber's 1917 and 1918 interventions is nothing less
than the core of traditional liberal concepts of parliamentarisation, namely
the demand, realised in the November Revolution, to explicitly make the
power of the Reich chancellor conditional on the confidence of the Reichstag.
As far as this issue is concerned, Weber is far from being a theoretical pioneer
of the transition to democracy; in fact, he falls back behind the decisions taken
by the constitutional committee of the Reichstag, which had already decided
the introduction of a corresponding constitutional clause as early as May 1917.[8]
According to Hans Maier, one can see from this 'that as soon as democracy
draws closer, as soon as the nation state assumes republican forms, Weber
begins to hesitate and look about for balancing forces'.[9] The standpoint from
which Weber discusses democratisation corresponds to that of his Freiburg
inaugural address, the farm work inquiry and his articles on the stock market:
it is the standpoint of the nation's 'vital interests', which are principally situated
above 'all questions of its state form' and therefore 'obviously take precedence
over democracy and parliamentarism'.[10] Even when he calls for the equal franchise, Weber does not think of himself as addressing a matter of principle or
promoting a 'doctrinary "orthodoxy of suffrage"', as he says; rather, his considerations are guided by 'state-politically decisive' criteria. Thus he argues, for
example, that it would perhaps have been more advantageous, during the first
decades following German unification, to introduce an electoral law that privileges the 'economically and socially prominent strata'.[11]

4    Mayer 1956, p. 109; compare pp. 20–1, 117–18.
5    Mommsen 1974, p. 444; compare pp. 44–5, 48.
6    Mommsen 1974, p. 198.
7    Mommsen 1974, pp. 421, 447.
8    See Mommsen 1974, p. 196.
9    Maier in Gneuss and Kocka 1988, p. 35.
10   Weber 1984–2009, vol. I/15, pp. 432, 435; Weber 1994c, pp. 130, 133.
11   Weber 1984–2009, vol. I/15, pp. 348–9; Weber 1994b, p. 82.

To the extent that Weber's understanding of democracy is questioned, this usually occurs in accordance with a paradigm of normative critique whose arguments are formulated (in Weber's terminology) from the standpoint of a 'value-rational organisation of political communal life' and locate the decisive weak point in the 'purposive-rational' curtailment of political ethics.[12] Offe speaks of a 'state-technical' concept of institutions that endorses democratic institutions not because of their 'intrinsic ethical value', but because of their 'steering function with regard to the selection of elites'.[13] Habermas's critique of Weber's concept of rationality also boils down to the claim that in his understanding of rationality, Weber theoretically neglects 'value rationality', as opposed to 'purposive rationality'.[14]

Yet to the extent that the literature on Weber limits itself to criticising an insufficient engagement with 'values', it risks constantly being outrun by the realism of Weber's political analyses. Let us take as an example the fact that Weber refuses to invoke norms or natural law in order to equip positive law with a 'supernatural' dignity, choosing rather to think of it as the product and instrument of a 'pacified contest' and as a 'rational technical apparatus, which is continually transformable in the light of expediential considerations and devoid of all sacredness of content'.[15] This cannot be cited as proof of his 'purposive-rational' reductionism; rather, it constitutes one of the strengths of his sociology of law, one he owes, at least in part, to the critiques of legal ideology formulated by Marx and Engels.[16] If nothing else, renunciation of a normative account of democratic decision-making *also* implies the insight, proper to the critique of ideology, 'that given existing relations, counterfactual democratic ideals ... can easily lapse into ideology'.[17] Thus the normative critique of Weber's 'purposive rationality' not only misses the mark; in many ways, it also remains oddly uncritical. This is true, first, with regard to the systemic

---

12      Mommsen 1974, p. 441; compare pp. 430, 436.

13      Offe in Gneuss and Kocka 1988, p. 174.

14      Habermas 1984, pp. 281ff, 284–5.

15      Weber 1978, pp. 1053, 811, 895.

16      In a well-known formulation from the *Preface* to *A Contribution to the Critique of Political Economy* (1859), Marx considers law one of the 'ideological forms' in which men 'become conscious' of the conflict between the forces of production and the relations of production, and one of the forms in which they 'fight it out' (Marx and Engels 1975–2005, vol. 29, p. 263). Compare Weber's remarks on how the development of formal law is 'almost always' related to the growing importance of commodity exchange and its associated legal stakeholders, legal 'form' serving precisely to legalise the 'unequal distribution of economic power' (Weber 1978, pp. 755, 812; compare pp. 729–30, 979).

17      Bader, Berger, Ganßman and Knesebeck 1987, p. 466.

functionality of Weber's political analyses: by situating the problem on the level of a general engagement with values, the critique elides the link between Weber's 'purposive-rational' understanding of democracy and capitalism's political conditions of reproduction, with their inherent need for 'Caesarism'. Second, it is also true with regard to the theoretical implications of Weber's sociology of domination: Weber's 'purposive-rational' discussion of democracy has a reference point in his theory of bureaucratic rule, which constitutes, in turn, the centrepiece of his sociology of domination.

In the following sections, I will develop an interpretation that is based on the theory of hegemony and analyses Weber's political interventions during the First World War as proposals for the renewal of Germany's ruling power bloc, taking into account the links between their political *modus operandi* and their theoretical organisation of concepts. I will limit myself to discussing Weber's calls for parliamentarisation and democratisation, which amount to a 'Caesarism without Caesar'. For the time being, I will bracket the controversial question concerning the extent to which Weber revokes this new model of an integration of class struggle when he formulates his concept of charismatic-plebiscitary leadership; I will return to this question in a later section (see below, Chapter 14).

### 12.2    'Universal Bureaucratisation' as an Ineluctable Fate

Weber's calls for parliamentarisation have as their starting point an element of the sociology of domination, namely the theory of progressive bureaucratisation. Notwithstanding his critique of sociological and especially Marxist 'law-based thinking', Weber conceives of this bureaucratisation in terms of an iron law of development: firstly, it is 'completely homogeneous in its basic essence', imposing itself within the economy as much as within the military, the communal administration, the church and the political parties;[18] secondly, its character has been, since the First World War at the latest, that of a 'universal bureaucratisation' that proceeds triumphantly 'across the world';[19] thirdly, it is 'inexorable', 'inescapable', and like the factory, it leaves its mark on the present and the future age—'the future belongs to it', and the future is transformed by it into that 'cage of subservience' which people will be powerless to resist, like the fellahs in the ancient Egyptian state.[20]

---

18    Weber 1984–2009, vol. I/15, p. 452; Weber 1994c, pp. 146–7.

19    Weber 1984–2009, vol. I/15, pp. 461–62; Weber 1994c, pp. 155–6.

20    Weber 1984–2009, vol. I/15, pp. 462ff; Weber 1994c, pp. 156ff.

In Weber's typology of the forms of domination, the bureaucratic administrative staff belongs to the type of 'rational' domination whose legitimacy rests
on a 'belief in the legality of enacted rules and the right of those elevated to
authority under such rules to issue commands'.[21] In contrast with both 'charismatic' and 'traditional' rule, the administration of an office is governed by
'rules or norms', fixed in writing and structured in accordance with set, hierarchically organised responsibilities.[22] The main historical models of bureau-
cratism identified by Weber are Egypt, the Roman patriciate and China,[23] yet
he treats modern bureaucracy, on which the ideal type of legal authority is
modelled,[24] as a historical creation of capitalism: it is capitalism, first and foremost, that has produced the 'need for stable, strict, intensive, and calculable
administration'.[25] True, capitalism is capable of co-existing with the 'wide lati-
tude' of a 'ruler's unrestricted discretion', but pre-bourgeois forms of authority lack the 'political and procedural *predictability*, indispensable for capitalist
development, which is provided by the rational rules of modern bureaucratic
administration'.[26] Since the modern capitalist firm rests mainly on the possibility of calculation, it requires a judiciary and an administration that 'function
in a *rationally calculable* manner according to stable, general norms, just as
one calculates the predictable performance of a *machine*'.[27]

Thus, and contrary to what one might expect, Weber does not present us
with a 'liberal' critique of bureaucracy, but rather with the demonstration that
there is an internal link between bureaucracy and capitalism—not the pre-
bourgeois 'political' capitalism but the modern 'entrepreneurial' capitalism:
as the money and capital calculus embodies 'maximum formal rationality'
within the domain of economic activity,[28] so the bureaucratic administration
represents, within the comparative sociology of authority, the 'most rational
form' of authority.[29] What is formally rational in both domains is, for example,
the impersonal 'objectivity' with which authority is exercised: Marx characterised the form of domination proper to capitalism as the 'dull compulsion

---

21    Weber 1978, p. 215.
22    Weber 1978, p. 217–19.
23    Weber 1978, pp. 259–60.
24    Weber 1978, p. 215.
25    Weber 1978, p. 224.
26    Weber 1978, pp. 1094–5.
27    Weber 1984–2009, vol. I/15, p. 453; Weber 1994c, pp. 147–8.
28    Weber 1978, p. 161; compare pp. 93–94, 107–9.
29    Weber 1978, p. 224.

of economic relations';[30] Weber characterises bureaucracy as 'dominance of a spirit of formalistic impersonality'.[31]

One aspect of this formal rationality, evident on both functional levels, is the expropriation of the original proprietors: Marx analyses the so-called primitive accumulation of capital as the separation of the small peasant from all property of the means by which to realise his labour, the 'process of divorcing the producer from the means of production';[32] Weber conceptualises the emergence of the civil service in terms of the separation 'of the administrative staff... from ownership of the means of production or administration', by virtue of which the civil servant, differently from the purchaser of an official position or liege man, is no longer able to own his position and use it as a sinecure, but is obliged to account for his use of the means left at his disposal.[33] Marx assumed that a growing number of means of production would be concentrated in the hands of fewer and fewer capitalists;[34] to Weber, the advance of bureaucracy is associated with a simultaneous 'concentration of the material means of management in the hands of the master'.[35] Within both the political and the religious superstructure, he observes the progressive separation of the workers from their means of labour being 'implemented in exactly the same way' as in the capitalist economy: 'It runs fully parallel'.[36]

Krätke holds that in formulating this analysis, Weber was the first to 'succinctly describe, in historical-materialist terms,' the emergence of the modern civil servant, a judgement rendered all the more weighty by the assertion that 'there exists no Marxist theory of bureaucracy comparable even to Max Weber's basic concepts'.[37] This is however an unsustainable exaggeration. Weber's 'historical materialism' consists primarily in his taking concepts developed by Marx to describe the emergence of capitalist relations of production and *transposing* them to the emergence of the absolute state. On the abstract conceptual level of formal analogies, such a method of transposition can be heuristically fruitful, as long as it does not ignore the differences and autonomies of society's functional levels, in the manner of a mechanical theory of reflection that Weber rightly criticises. And yet Weber *does* ignore these

---

30    Marx and Engels 1975–2005, vol. 35, p. 726.

31    Weber 1978, p. 225.

32    Marx and Engels 1975–2005, vol. 35, p. 705.

33    Weber 1978, pp. 218–19; compare pp. 980–1.

34    See for example Marx and Engels 1975–2005, vol. 35, pp. 748ff.

35    Weber 1978, p. 980.

36    Weber 1946b, p. 295; Weber 1984–2009, vol. I/19, p. 120.

37    Krätke 1995b, p. 85; Krätke 1995c, pp. 406, 427.

differences and autonomies, because he is interested in describing the central-isation of power within production and politics as a 'homogeneous', 'univer-sal' and 'ineluctable' process of social 'rationalisation'. One might ask critically whether the 'separation from the means of administration' suffered by the pur-chasers of official positions in the course of their transformation into civil ser-vants does not constitute a quite different social process than the separation from the means of production evident, for example, in the expropriation and pauperisation of the rural population. The emergence of the industrial prole-tariat constitutes a fundamental process within capitalist relations of produc-tion, but the officials who putatively suffer 'the same' expropriation continue to be, as Engels says, organs of society standing '*above* society', bearers of a 'power that is becoming alien to society', who are no more satisfied by the 'free, voluntary respect that was accorded to organs of the gentile constitution': 'respect for them must be enforced by means of exceptional laws by virtue of which they enjoy special sanctity and inviolability'.[38] After all, the decisive import of Weber's critique is that Prussian Germany's disproportionately large bureaucracy is not an expression of capitalist progress, but an impediment to such progress.[39] Yet by confounding, within his theory of bureaucracy, the eco-nomic base with the state superstructure, Weber makes the differences within the social process of production (compare Adam Smith's distinction between 'productive' and 'unproductive' labour), within the division of manual and intellectual labour and within the ideological reproduction of class society disappear. When Weber returns to the issue in 1918, in his lecture 'Socialism', held before Austrian military officers, the exonerating function of the equation is more than evident: with regard to non-ownership of the means of labour, professors and officers are 'in exactly the same position as any worker', thus Weber's message, and this is due to the 'nature of technology today'.[40]

Here as elsewhere, comparisons between Weber and Marx must not stop at the identification of particular analogies. For Weber's adoption of Marxist terminology is part of a conceptual strategy for 'overcoming' Marxism.

---

38   Marx and Engels 1975–2005, vol. 26, p. 270.

39   'The bureaucratic order put an end not just to every political initiative on the part of its subordinates, but also to all economic initiative', Weber writes in 1909, with reference to rural relations in the late Roman Empire. He then generalises: '*Every bureaucracy tends to produce the same effect by virtue of its expansion, including our own*' (Weber 1988c, p. 277). Engels formulated a similar assessment in 1847: 'But the bureaucracy, which is a necessity for the petty bourgeoisie, very soon becomes an unbearable fetter for the bour-geoisie' (Marx and Engels 1975–2005, vol. 6, p. 88).

40   Weber 1984–2009, vol. I/15, pp. 607, 609; Weber 1988b, pp. 498–9.

The determinist evolutionary thought of the Second International (Bernstein's evolutionism included) is transposed to the level of political rule, where a similarly determinist evolutionary thought is set against it, one whose endpoint is not socialist society but progressive bureaucratisation. Robert Michels has encapsulated this second type of evolutionary thought in the formula 'iron law of oligarchy'.[41] If this approach were valid, a socialist and radically democratic politics would be discredited from the outset. In fact, Weber is primarily concerned with demonstrating that 'any rational type of socialism' will have to adopt and develop this bureaucracy.[42] By no means does the elimination of private capitalism lead to a 'crumbling of the iron cage of modern commercial labour'; rather, it gives rise to an amalgamation of private and public bureaucracy, by virtue of which the future definitively assumes the form of a 'cage' of officially managed 'subservience'.[43] The assumption of such a fateful bureaucratisation rests, first, on Weber's inability to conceptualise a 'rational' socialist society otherwise than as a bureaucratic state socialism—it is no coincidence that he refutes the critics of capitalism by pointing out the similarly alienated forms of life proper to Prussia's state-owned mining and railway administration—,[44] and second, on his refusal to distinguish analytically between the technical requirements of a professional administration and the social form of bureaucratic administration, such that bureaucratisation appears to result from the greater complexity of modern mass societies as such.[45]

By adopting this conceptual strategy, Weber has effectively enclosed his theory of bureaucracy in a cage of its own, and this makes it exceedingly difficult for him to formulate a rational critique of bureaucracy. Since the bureaucratic administration represents, by definition, a maximum of 'formal rationality', and since an alternative 'material' rationality plays no role within Weber's analysis of bureaucracy, '[t]he choice is only that between bureaucracy and dilettantism in the field of administration'.[46] Analytically, this excludes the possibility of identifying specific instances of irrationality within the bureaucracy, such as the discrepancy between expertise and rank or the inverted

41      Michels 1916, pp. 393–409. On the phraseology of certainty articulated in the word 'iron',
        and on its role within the labour movement and Marxism, see Haug 1997.

42      Weber 1978, p. 225.

43      Weber 1984–2009, vol. I/15, p. 464; see Weber 1994c, p. 157.

44      Weber 1984–2009, vol. I/15, p. 464; see Weber 1994c, p. 157.

45      See Bader, Berger, Ganßman and Knesebeck 1987, pp. 478, 488.

46      Weber 1978, p. 223.

relationship of means to ends that was already criticised by the young Marx.[47] Politically, the prospect of efficient control from below is eliminated, a prospect Marx and Engels sought to make a reality, as when they proposed, in their discussion of the Paris Commune, the implementation of the general right to the election and recall of administrative employees by the communes.[48] Much like that of capitalist rationalisation, the concept of bureaucratic rationalisation consists of an apologetic element, into which Weber is even able to effortlessly integrate Schmoller's ethical glorification of the Prussian-German civil service,[49] and an apocalyptic element, which sees Weber pathetically opposing the single individual, its freedom of movement and its 'charisma', to the supremacy of the bureaucracy, so as to 'salvage a vestige of humanity' from the bureaucratic dissection of the soul.[50]

Of course, when he speaks of 'individuals', Weber does not have in mind society's ordinary individuals: since controlling the bureaucracy from below is out of the question for Weber, all his proposals for curbing it are associated with the question of how one can create within society a 'leading spirit': first among entrepreneurs and then among politicians.[51] He considers the 'capitalist entrepreneur' the 'only type who has been able to maintain at least relative immunity from subjection to the control of rational bureaucratic knowledge';[52] he is in any case capable of 'keeping at bay' the state's public bureaucracy by means of his own, private bureaucracy.[53] Weber appeals to the 'leading politician' because this politician represents the non-bureaucratic apex of bureaucracy

---

47    On the critique formulated by organisational sociologists such as Merton, Litwak, Crozier and Offe, see the overview in Bader, Berger, Ganßman and Knesebeck 1987, pp. 454ff. Some of the objections were already developed by Marx in his 1843 *Critique of Hegel's Philosophy of Right*: 'Because the bureaucracy makes its formal aims its content, it comes into conflict everywhere with the real aims. Hence it is obliged to present what is formal for the content and the content for what is formal. The aims of the state are transformed into aims of bureaus, or the aims of bureaus into the aims of the state. The bureaucracy is a circle from which no one can escape' (Marx and Engels 1975–2005, vol. 3, p. 46).

48    Marx and Engels 1975–2005, vol. 22, pp. 331, 473, 490.

49    No one questions the 'high *moral* standards of our civil servants in particular', Weber claims in 1909, for example, during a debate within the Association for Social Policy. He adds that, from a pragmatic perspective, the democratic countries with their sometimes corrupt civil servants have nevertheless achieved more than our 'highly moral bureaucracy' (Weber 1988b, pp. 415–16). Compare the young Marx's critique of Hegel's moral glorification of the civil servant (Marx and Engels 1975–2005, vol. 3, pp. 49ff).

50    Weber 1988b, p. 414; compare Weber 1984–2009, vol. I/15, pp. 465–6; Weber 1994c, p. 159.

51    Weber 1984–2009, vol. I/15, p. 466; Weber 1994c, p. 159.

52    Weber 1978, p. 225.

53    Weber 1984–2009, vol. I/15, p. 464; Weber 1988a, p. 332; Weber 1994c, pp. 157–8.

and differs from the civil servant primarily 'in terms of the type of responsibility held': the civil servant is subject to official duty, and his 'honour' consists in implementing even those instructions that contradict his personal convictions 'as if they corresponded to his inmost beliefs'; by contrast, the political leader struggles passionately for power and bears 'exclusive personal responsibility' for what he does.[54] If Weber wishes to salvage a 'vestige of humanity' from progressive bureaucratisation, what he has in mind concretely is the personal 'freedom' both of the entrepreneur and of the politician to exercise his decision-making power on his own authority.

Here as elsewhere, it is worth distinguishing between the descriptive realism of Weber's analyses of bureaucracy and the way he theorises them. As Beetham observes,[55] Weber transposed the old liberal concept of individualism 'to the peak positions of the bureaucratic structures, where it was recognisable in the personality of the industrial or party leader'. This, however, renders the theoretical arrangement circular. For paradoxically, the instances Weber appeals to when it is a matter of curbing bureaucracy are the very ones that he has identified as being responsible for the rise of bureaucracy, instances that depend on the 'precision instrument' of a strong bureaucracy when exercising their authority.[56] Marx summarises the Hegelian glorification of the moral fibre of the civil servants in the formula that '[t]he man within the civil servant is supposed to secure the civil servant against himself';[57] something similar can be said about Weber's invocation of the leadership personality proper to entrepreneurs and politicians, a personality that is supposed to curb the very bureaucracy the entrepreneur and the politician require. That such a strategy entails dangerous implications emerges especially clearly from the concept of the 'plebiscitary leader', by means of which Weber seeks to contain the bureaucracy's supremacy during the constitutional debates of 1918/19 (see below, Chapter 14.3).

The theoretical 'cage' into which Weber has enclosed his analysis of bureaucracy lends a special character to all his proposals for countering the rise of bureaucratisation. This is also true of the proposals on the parliamentarisation of Germany that Weber develops in various political pieces penned during the First World War.

---

54    Weber 1984–2009, vol. I/15, pp. 467–8, Weber 1988a, pp. 334–5; vol. I/17, pp. 189–90, Weber 1988a, pp. 524–5.

55    Beetham 1988, pp. 237–8.

56    Weber 1978, p. 990.

57    Marx and Engels 1975–2005, vol. 3, p. 58.

## 12.3 Parliamentarism as a Superior Mechanism for the Selection of Leaders

Weber's 'state-political' derivation of the parliamentarisation of Germany is based on an ideal-typical opposition of 'civil servants' and 'political leaders'. Since Bismarck had eliminated all his potential political rivals, his resignation led to Germany being governed by '"officials" (in mentality)'.[58] The monarchy is unable to generate the battle-tried political leaders who would be capable of exercising effective control over the bureaucracy; it lacks the requisite expertise and is itself dependent on civil servants.[59] However, parliament is in a position to accomplish this task; its function is that of representing those ruled by the bureaucracy and manifesting their 'inner assent'.[60] Thus its significance results from the fact that it assumes a central position within the political reproduction of class society, being situated at the interface of domination and the dominated.

What Weber criticises in the 'authoritarian state' is not the rule of the few over the many, but a structural feature that leads to the people being subordinated not to genuine political leaders but to 'officials'.[61] The critique is formulated from the standpoint of a superior *mechanism for the selection of leaders*: 'The political aim of parliamentarisation is, after all, to turn parliament into a place where *leaders* are selected [*Auslesestätte für Führer*]'.[62] While the conditions for a successful career within a bureaucratic organisation are such as to promote, first and foremost, 'a person's compliance in relation to the apparatus', the only people suited to political leadership are those who have been 'selected in political *struggle*'.[63] Within a powerful working parliament, egotistic power interests can be organised in such a way as to ensure 'selection of the men endowed with leadership qualities', whereas in the authoritarian state, which lacks a strong parliament, the struggle for power proceeds 'in subaltern forms and directions', with the hunt for positions and patronage playing out behind the scenes, in a disingenuously covert form.[64] This characterisation can also be found in Gramsci's reflections on 'black parliamentarianism', within which the bureaucracy conceals the worst type of party rule: the political parties operate

---

58  Weber 1994c, p. 161; Weber 1984–2009, vol. I/15, p. 468.
59  Weber 1994c, pp. 162ff; Weber 1984–2009, vol. I/15, pp. 470–1.
60  Weber 1994c, p. 165; Weber 1984–2009, vol. I/15, pp. 472–3.
61  Weber 1994c, p. 175; Weber 1984–2009, vol. I/15, p. 484.
62  Weber 1994c, p. 251; Weber 1984–2009, vol. I/15, p. 574.
63  Weber 1994c, pp. 218–19; Weber 1984–2009, vol. I/15, pp. 536–7.
64  Weber 1994c, pp. 167–8, 176–7; Weber 1984–2009, vol. I/15, pp. 475, 485.

in a hidden and unchecked manner; they are replaced by the camarilla and by personal cliques that cannot be held accountable politically.[65]

That parliamentary delegates function as a mere 'entourage' of their party leaders for as long as the latter are successful, 'ought to be so', according to Weber, for: 'Political action is always governed by the "principle of small numbers", i.e. by the superior political agility of small groups that exercise leadership. In mass states, this "Caesaristic" streak will never be done away with'.[66]

As far as this 'principle of small numbers' is concerned, Weber is in agreement with the prevailing theories of the elite formulated in the sociology of his day, theories that set out to refute the socialist 'illusion' of a classless society free of domination. According to Beetham, Weber was concerned, just like Mosca and Pareto, to 'elaborate a new formulation of liberalism, couched in the concepts of the theory of elites, but it was only *his* new formulation that was immediately compatible with the formal requirements of parliamentary democracy'.[67] Parliament is precisely what renders possible the Caesarist rule of a minority endowed with leadership skills. '"Caesarist solutions" can also be obtained without a Caesar, without a great, "heroic" and representative personality', Gramsci remarks: 'The parliamentary system has provided the mechanism for such compromises'.[68] In Weber, the model of such a Caesarism without a Caesar is provided by the British parliament, which was capable of 'bringing a fourth of mankind under the rule of a tiny but state-politically sagacious minority. And the most important thing is that to a degree that is not negligible, subordination occurred voluntarily'.[69] Here, there is no need to dwell on the fact that Weber's image of a 'voluntary subordination' to the British colonial empire downplays the violent military and economic destruction involved. What is more important, in the present context, is that the formula 'voluntary subordination' addresses the core issue of any ideological societalisation from above.[70] The superiority of democracy, which Weber describes in terms of the ability to subordinate other nations, is also evident

65    Gramsci 1975c, pp. 1742–4, 1808–9.
66    Weber 1984–2009, vol. I/15, p. 483; see Weber 1994c, p. 174. The quotation is part of a larger passage that Weber inserted during his final revision of 'Parliament and Government' (see Weber 1984–2009, vol. I/15, pp. 483–5).
67    Beetham 1988, p. 240.
68    Gramsci 1975b, pp. 1194–5; Gramsci 1975c, pp. 1619–22.
69    Weber 1984–2009, vol. I/15, p. 491; see Weber 1994c, p. 181.
70    See Althusser 1971, pp. 182ff; Projekt Ideologietheorie 1982, pp. 109ff, 192; Rehmann 2013, pp. 248ff.

domestically, in the form of democracy's more developed cohesive force: a bureaucratic 'authoritarian state', which 'administers' its citizens like a herd of cattle, leads to the masses directing all of their forces '*against* a state . . . in which they are mere objects and in which they have no share'. By contrast, a 'master people' [*Herrenvolk*] must integrate the majority of citizens 'into the state as *co-rulers*' [*Mitherren*].[71] '*Only master peoples have the vocation of grabbing the spokes of the world's development*', and a nation that 'tolerates the unchecked authority of civil servants, decked out with pseudo-monarchist phrases . . . would be *no master people*'.[72] Instead of a 'dictatorship without hegemony',[73] which would entail defeat abroad and downfall or revolution domestically, Weber outlines a political system that is capable of hegemony, combining the domestic 'co-regency' of relevant segments of the population with the ability to exercise imperialist rule.

## 12.4    The Construction of an Industrial Bloc of Capitalists and Workers

Weber predicts that the post-war economic situation will be dramatic, regardless of the war's outcome: merely ensuring that the masses have enough to eat will require 'a tremendous intensification and rationalisation of economic work'.[74] The problem is aggravated by the fact that 'competition with the great working peoples of the world' is impeded by the existence of a broad stratum of persons who live off ground rent and subsidies of all varieties. The required modernisation process is faced with a 'stifling rent burden'.[75] Whoever chooses, in this situation, to criticise the German 'work spirit' from the standpoint of a more 'easygoing' existence, represents the 'parasitic ideals of a stratum of prebends and rentiers that have the audacity to compare their intellectually and physically labouring co-citizens to their own inkwell existence'.[76] Whoever persists in devising 'state socialist' or 'small business' experiments that involve state subsidies for the lifestyles of petty capitalists is promoting Germany's paralysis by means of its 'Austrification' [Verösterreicherung].[77]

---

71    Weber 1984–2009, vol. I/15, p. 396; Weber 1994b, p. 129.

72    Weber 1994c, p. 269

73    Gramsci 1975c, pp. 1822–4.

74    Weber 1984–2009, vol. I/15, p. 351; Weber 1994b, p. 84.

75    Weber 1984–2009, vol. I/15, pp. 351ff; Weber 1994b, pp. 84ff.

76    Weber 1984–2009, vol. I/15, p. 351; Weber 1994b, pp. 84–5.

77    Weber 1984–2009, vol. I/15, p. 354; Weber 1994b, p. 88.

The burden represented by the strata of pensioners and prebends, a burden Weber illustrates by reference to the German example, will be analysed by Gramsci in the late 1920s, within the context of his discussion of the contradiction between the European 'tradition' and the 'rationalization of the population' demanded by Fordism:[78] Americanism demands, as its precondition, '"the rationalization of the population"; that is, that there do not exist numerous classes without a function in the world of production', but the European 'tradition' is characterised by a number of 'sedimentations of lazy people': state employees, intellectuals, the clergy, landowners, predatory salesmen, the military. The rentification of the bourgeoisie diagnosed in Weber's critique of the entailed estate has its corollary in Gramsci's so-called 'producer of savings' [*produttore di risparmio*], a 'passive' stratum of profiteers which 'not only extracts its own sustenance from the primitive labor of a specific number of peasants, but also manages to save'. The anachronistic demographic composition is evident in the large number of urban agglomerations without industry. The unproductive bustle of Naples, determined by the city's landowning rentiers, presents itself as the paradigm of a parasitic economic structure that is also prevalent in the smaller cities of central and northern Italy.[79] 'Tradition' means, among other things, 'the passive residue of all the social forms that have faded away in history', Gramsci writes in another passage.[80] Where this leaden weight is absent, as in America, an enormous accumulation of capital can be achieved in spite of high wages, and the entire country can be founded on industry: 'Hegemony is born in the factory and does not need so many political and ideological intermediaries'.[81] It is against this background that Gramsci analyses Italian fascism as an inconsistent, statist and despotic form of catch-up Fordism: under pressure from America, the 'plutocratic stratum' itself attempts to impose some aspects of Fordism in a particularly brutal form, and to combine them with the parasitic social structure.[82]

Seen from this angle, Weber reveals himself to be an early exponent of Fordist 'population rationalisation'. His way of posing the problem splits society into two opposed socio-economic blocs. What is decisive is not the opposition, analysed by Marx, between societal labour and its capitalist form, but the one between industrial modernisation and 'traditionalist' counterforces:

---

78   Gramsci 1992, p. 167; Gramsci 1975c, pp. 2140ff.

79   Gramsci 1992, pp. 167–8; Gramsci 1975c, p. 2141.

80   Gramsci 1996, p. 218.

81   Gramsci 1992, p. 169; compare 1975c, p. 2145.

82   Gramsci 1975c, p. 2147. Europe would like 'the barrel full and the wife drunk'—'*la botte piena e la moglie ubriaca*' (Gramsci 1975c, p. 2141).

on one side stand the 'prebendary strata' and all their congenial parties with a stake in 'economic stagnation'; on the other side stands the alliance between 'organisationally high-ranking entrepreneurs' and the working class, both of whom have an interest in the 'maximum rationalisation of economic work', an interest that coincides, 'principally', with the 'political interest in preserving the nation's international standing'.[83] Thus the former Junker-bourgeois class compromise is to yield to an alliance of interests comprising the representatives of entrepreneurs and those of the workforce. In and of itself, the idea is not new; it can already be found, for example, in Saint-Simon, whose *Catéchisme politique des industriels* (1823/24) subsumes both workers and industrial capitalists under the concept of 'industrialists'.[84]

According to Gramsci, there are numerous points of contact between Saint-Simonism and the doctrines of Americanism,[85] and the crafting of such an alliance for productivity is one of the most important. Under the conditions proper to the emergent Fordist mode of production, it is given a new and realistic foundation. During the First World War, there develops, within the war-economic apparatuses, an intense cooperation between trade-union leaders and the exponents of 'scientific management', a development that leads, in Germany, to the foundation of the 'Central Work Group' [*Zentralarbeitsgemeinschaft*] in 1918, an organisation that united the trade unions and large capital. 'Due to the First World War, the conditions for the productivity-oriented integration of workers into mechanised mass production were in place'.[86] In *The Southern Question*, Gramsci coined the term 'industrial bloc' [*blocco industriale*

83    Weber 1984–2009, vol. I/15, p. 354; Weber 1994b, p. 87; Weber 1988a, p. 251.

84    To Saint-Simon, the 'idlers' were not just the privileged, but also all those who 'lived on their incomes', without contributing to production and distribution, as Engels summarises: 'And the workers were not only the wage-workers, but also the manufacturers, the merchants, the bankers' (Marx and Engels 1975–2005, vol. 24, pp. 290–1; see also vol. 5, pp. 500ff).

85    Gramsci 1996, p. 273.

86    Ebbinghaus 1984, p. 197. According to Ebbinghaus, in America, there emerged, within the framework of the war economy, an identity of interests between the 'industrial democracy' of the American Federation of Labor (AFL) and the 'industrial autocracy' of the Taylorist planners. By 1919, exponents of 'scientific management' had succeeded in 'conceptually integrating the organised labour movement into the interrelationship between "collective bargaining" and the high-wage policy, thereby Taylorising them from the inside out' (Ebbinghaus 1984, pp. 154, 168). In Germany, 'there are no differences to be discerned between the positions expressed in the publications of the later Social Democratic economic politician Wissell and the head of AEG, Rathenau—neither before nor after 1918' (Ebbinghaus 1984, p. 197).

*capitalistico-operaio*] to describe such a constellation of capitalists and workers; he was referring to the class constellation in northern Italy as opposed to the southern Italian 'agrarian bloc'.[87] In the first *Prison Notebook*, Gramsci speaks of an '"urban" (capitalists-workers) bloc', for which the *mezzogiorno* serves as a semi-colonial sales market.[88] The immediate context consisted of the temporarily liberal and pro-industrial policies of Prime Minister Giolitti, which yielded, however, to a bloc of northern Italian industrialists and southern Italian agrarians in 1910. If the coherence of the agrarian bloc is mainly ensured by a middle-class, state-bureaucratic type of intellectual who links the peasant masses to the state administration, the industrial bloc coheres by virtue of the 'technician' who implements the production plan developed by industry's general staff.[89]

Within this constellation, Gramsci sketches the contours of a socialist intellectual policy; it aims to bring about an 'organic rupture' within the majority of intellectuals associated with both blocs, thereby giving rise to a left tendency in the modern sense of a mass formation.[90] It is mainly the intellectual bloc ensuring the coherence of the agrarian classes that needs to be 'disunited',[91] thus rendering possible a common bloc of workers and peasants. This presupposes, first, overcoming, within the ideology of northern Italian workers, their racialised contempt for the south, and second, organising the poor peasants in 'autonomous and independent organisations'.[92]

Gramsci returns to the concept of the 'industrial bloc' in his discussion of N. Massimo Fovel's theory of corporatism. Fovel, a colourful figure who frequented both Turin's industrialists and its socialists, developed, in the late 1920s and on the basis of fascist corporatism, a concept of Fordist rationalisation directed against the 'producers of savings'. According to Gramsci, what is interesting about Fovel is his project of an 'autonomous industrial-productive bloc destined to resolve in a modern way the problem of the economic apparatus in an emphatically capitalistic manner'.[93] Of course, what Fovel fails to

---

87    Gramsci 1971, p. 146; Gramsci 1966, p. 18.

88    Gramsci 1992, p. 131.

89    See Gramsci 1961, p. 151; Gramsci 1992, p. 131. This distinction between the intellectuals associated with the northern Italian 'industrial bloc' and the southern Italian 'agrarian bloc' is the concrete starting point from which Gramsci develops his concepts of the 'organic' and the 'traditional' intellectual (see Gramsci 1996, pp. 201–2; Gramsci 1975c, pp. 1513ff).

90    Gramsci 1971, p. 158; Gramsci 1966, p. 35.

91    Ibid.

92    Gramsci 1971, pp. 140, 158; Gramsci 1966, pp. 12, 35.

93    Gramsci 1992, p. 221.

take into consideration is the fact that Italian corporatism originates in the 'policing' and not in the 'revolutionising' of the economy: Americanism requires a liberal state based on free initiative and economic individualism, one that has arrived at the regime of the monopolies 'by spontaneous means, by virtue of the historical development itself', i.e. by virtue of 'civil society', as Gramsci adds in version C of his text.[94] As we have seen, such a development of capitalism as 'civil society' constituted the strategic stakes of Weber's analysis of the American sects, which gave rise to a model of bourgeois hegemony superior to the German condition (see above, Chapter 6).

These considerations on Italy's agrarian and industrial blocs constitute the historical material from which Gramsci then developed, following Sorel, the theoretical concept of the 'historic bloc'. Aside from its inter-class composition, the historic bloc displays another feature that makes it significant to any analysis of Weber based on the theory of hegemony. The historic bloc is supposed to express the 'unity' of the economic base and the superstructures, the internal connection and interrelationship between them, their 'necessary and vital nexus'.[95] Weber was also concerned with such a coherent link between the economic base and the superstructures: not only in his political interventions, but also, and as will be shown later (see below, Part Four), in his sociology of religion.

Thus, for example, he accounts for the introduction of the equal franchise in terms of the 'imperative' necessity of granting the bearers of 'rational labour' a corresponding degree of political influence.[96] The distinctive feature of the 'political literati' is that they combat parliamentarism as a non-German 'import' and seek to stall the impending introduction of the equal franchise by means of variously graduated 'organic' models of representation based on the old model of the estates.[97] What Weber criticises these models for is their 'lack of adjustment to the modern economic structure, which is constantly undergoing transformation'.[98] For they do not do justice to the truly significant forces of the economic world, namely the associations of employers

94    Ibid. Gramsci 1975c, p. 2157.
95    See Gramsci 2007, pp. 271–2; Gramsci 1975b, pp. 1214–15, 1291–1301, 1315–23, 1505–6. Presumably, this necessary unity also constitutes the basis for the indirect adoption of the concept from Sorel, who explains, in the 'Introduction' to *On Violence*, that one cannot dissect the mythic 'warlike images' of social movements into distinct elements; one needs rather to grasp them 'as a whole' (*en bloc*), as an indivisible ensemble of historical forces (on this, see Gramsci 1996, pp. 156–8).
96    Weber 1984–2009, vol. I/15, p. 354; Weber 1994b, p. 87.
97    Weber 1984–2009, vol. I/15, pp. 358–9; Weber 1994b, 91–3.
98    Weber 1984–2009, vol. I/15, p. 360; Weber 1994b, p. 93.

and workers, who operate on the basis of 'legally free recruitment of members', which makes them 'organisations suited to *struggle* and *compromise*'.[99] In defining their specificity vis-à-vis state associations, Weber uses the same concept by which he distinguished the Protestant sects from the church: 'voluntary' membership.[100] From here, he contests the use his opponents make of the concept of the 'organic': it is precisely the '"*voluntarist*" basis of the organisation that is decisive, it being the organisation's only appropriate, and therefore its "organic" basis'.[101]

One argument used by Nolte to oppose Weber to fascism is that Weber criticised 'the social concept dearest to all fascists, that of parliamentarism yielding to a system of professional representative bodies and a "corporate" state structure'.[102] Yet this difference with regard to the model of political representation refers us to a different social composition of the projected 'historic bloc': the difference consists, firstly, in opposition to the landed property of the Junkers, and secondly, in the fact that Weber wishes to integrate the workforce into the productivist alliance by means of its 'voluntarist' organisations, as long as they are not revolutionary, whereas German and Italian fascism set out to smash the labour movement altogether.

## 12.5    A New Model for the 'Assimilation' of Hostile Groups into the State

Of course, what Weber and the emerging fascist movement do have in common is their hostility to the November Revolution. It will lead to a situation in which 'German workers will have to work for American entrepreneurs, who won't tolerate any drollery', Weber claims in a January 1919 campaign speech for the German Democratic Party.[103] That imperialist Germany's developmental lag vis-à-vis the USA results from the revolution is hardly a sustainable argument. But the revolution provides a projection surface and reflects catch-up Fordism's fear of being relegated to a peripheral position by the hegemonic power, America.

Weber's projected 'industrial bloc' is to replace the Junker-bourgeois power bloc of Wilhemine Germany while simultaneously pre-empting the possible formation of a bloc of workers, peasants and soldiers: if Prussia's three-class

99     Weber 1984–2009, vol. I/15, p. 364; Weber 1994b, p. 98.
100    Ibid.
101    Weber 1984–2009, vol. I/15, p. 365; Weber 1994b, p. 99.
102    Nolte 1963, p. 8.
103    Weber 1984–2009, vol. I/16, p. 441.

franchise is not reformed in time, before the end of the war, the returning soldiers will end up in the lowest class, devoid of influence, whereas those who stayed home and grew wealthy during the war will find themselves in the privileged classes. Thus the very people who risked their lives for the German nation would be excluded from its reorganisation. Such an injustice would violate the 'minimum', required even in politics, 'of shame and decency',[104] and it would ruin the nation's cohesiveness: '*Never* again would the nation stand united as it did in August 1914'.[105] The problem strikes Weber as being so urgent that he proposes, in the *Frankfurter Zeitung* on 28 March 1917, an 'emergency electoral law': if introducing an equal franchise should prove impossible in the short term, the soldiers should at least be placed in the most influential class of voters.[106] Weber's moral indignation is based primarily on his insight that an alliance of striking workers and soldiers could pose a threat to the ruling power bloc's military apparatus, which is what in fact occurred in Russia's October Revolution and Germany's November Revolution. Weber is at pains to prevent such a development by means of the enforced integration of the soldiers: the soldiers, he argues, are 'as little interested in insurrectionary as they are in pacifist utopias' and equipped with a 'sense of reality'.[107] In parallel with this argument, Weber seeks to demonstrate, in his essay 'Russia's Transition to Mock Democracy' (April 1917), that an alliance between the peasants and Marxist Social Democrats such as Plekhanov is impossible, due to contrasting economic interests, and that the socialists therefore remain dependent on the 'fraternal association of the only bourgeois strata that are *worthy of credit*'.[108] It is in keeping with the projected industrial bloc that Weber emphasises not the bourgeois integration of the peasants, but that of the workers. Half a year later, Lenin will oppose his party's central committee by summarising the needs of the workers, peasants and soldiers in the threefold call for an immediate end to the war, the distribution of land to the peasants and 'all power to the soviets'.[109]

As the November Revolution draws closer, Weber's critique of the feudal-bourgeois 'passive revolution' increasingly becomes the model of a new 'passive revolution' designed to contain and overcome the socialist labour movement. In his post-war scenario, there develops a 'syndicalism of immaturity': the 'Liebknecht group' grows larger while those with a stake in the old

104   Weber 1984–2009, vol. I/15, p. 349; Weber 1994b, pp. 82–3.
105   Weber 1984–2009, vol. I/15, p. 552; Weber 1994c, p. 233.
106   Weber 1984–2009, vol. I/15, pp. 217–18.
107   Weber 1984–2009, vol. I/15, p. 220.
108   Weber 1984–2009, vol. I/15, pp. 252–3; Weber 1988a, pp. 209–10.
109   See Lenin 1960–78g [1917], vol. 26, pp. 59ff.

order use left radicalism as an excuse to speculate on the cowardice of the bourgeoisie and the weak nerves of the philistines, preparing to establish a reign of violence. But the real problem is 'whether the masses will *stop* at the sterile negation of the state that is to be expected'.[110] To ward off Russian conditions, the government needs to forcefully put down every violent revolution, but it also needs to then reinstitute the guarantees of the liberal order, resolving the tensions that underlay the revolution in an 'objective' manner.[111]

Universal suffrage and a systematic process of parliamentarisation reveal themselves to be the only viable strategy against the 'rule of the street'. The only remedy against the unorganised masses, which Weber considers to be 'completely irrational in state-political terms', is the activity of the political parties, organised on the basis of 'rigidly organised political interest groups', and in particular the 'orderly' organisations of the industrial proletariat.[112] This assessment is based, in part, on Robert Michels's 1911 study *Political Parties*, which seeks to demonstrate the 'iron law of oligarchy' by reference to the bureaucratisation of Germany's Social Democratic Party.[113] The bureaucracy, whose overbearing power Weber otherwise laments, becomes a stronghold of 'rationality' when it is a matter of opposing the revolution. In 'state-political' terms, he argues, everything depends on increasing the power of the 'rationally thinking' labour leaders, and particularly the trade-union leaders, over and above their 'momentary instincts':[114] 'In our country ... organisations such as the trade unions, but also the Social Democratic Party, are a very important counterbalance to the current irrational rule of the street, which is typical of purely plebiscitary peoples'.[115] Weber is referring to the 'coffee house culture' of the Romance countries: in Paris and Rome, Weber claims, street politics was not determined by 'workers bound to their workplaces', but by 'dawdlers and coffee house intellectuals'.[116]

Similarly, with regard to the relationship between the government and parliament, Weber's proposals for reform aim not at a democratisation of political rule, but at the restoration of a homogeneous political leadership. Seen from this perspective, the main problem appears to him to consist in the fact that a parliament without the right to effectively monitor the government,

---

110   Weber 1984–2009, vol. I/15, p. 551; Weber 1994c, p. 231.

111   Weber 1984–2009, vol. I/15, p. 551; Weber 1994c, p. 232.

112   Weber 1984–2009, vol. I/15, pp. 49–50; Weber 1994c, p. 231.

113   Michels 1916, pp. 393–409.

114   Weber 1984–2009, vol. I/15, p. 392; Weber 1994b, p. 125.

115   Weber 1984–2009, vol. I/15, p. 550; Weber 1994c, p. 231.

116   Weber 1984–2009, vol. I/15, p. 392; Weber 1994b, p. 125.

a parliament that has no more than the right to refuse a budget, can engage only in a 'negative politics'.[117] This means that parliamentary leaders fall short of being 'positive co-bearers of state power'.[118] Using the example of the July crisis prompted by Erzberger,[119] Weber illustrates the problem that the government and parliament opposed one another 'as two distinct entities'; state leaders and party leaders did not communicate continuously with one another and were therefore unable to discuss possible solutions to the conflict in advance. When the parliamentary majority opposed the government, the 'perplexed government representatives' were forced to 'slacken the reins, because they had no foot in the party organisations'.[120] Weber criticises an organisation of political bodies that leads, in times of crisis, to a split within the ruling power bloc, threatening the development of a unified bourgeois hegemony from the top. His proposals aim at overcoming this split in the interest of governability.

As a precondition for any political reform, Weber calls for the abolition of article 9 of the 1871 constitution, which prohibits leading statesmen from holding seats in parliament. For this decreed incompatibility entails that every party leader who wishes to become a member of the government must abdicate his position within the party, thereby 'politically uprooting' himself: 'Thus, by proceeding in this manner, one "decapitates" the political parties but obtains only professional civil servants for the government, instead of usable politicians ... civil servants who lack the influence exercised by members of parliament'.[121] Gramsci also speaks of 'decapitation'; he uses the term to describe a key process of 'passive revolution', namely absorption of the active elements of both allied and hostile classes.[122] What Gramsci discusses with reference to the social structure of society as a whole is limited, in Weber, to relations within the political leadership. Weber's critique amounts to the claim that this sort of 'passive revolution' within the relationship between government and parliament has the effect of polarising the pro-state forces, such that they form two opposed camps. This blockade must yield to the integrating mode of a reciprocal interlocking of political bodies, one that allows the

117 Weber 1984–2009, vol. I/15, p. 497; Weber 1994c, pp. 186–7.

118 Weber 1984–2009, vol. I/15, p. 473; Weber 1994c, p. 166.

119 In July 1917, Erzberger, a member of the Centre Party, challenged the government to negotiate a peace treaty. The controversies this caused led to the fall of Reich Chancellor Bethmann-Hollweg.

120 Weber 1984–2009, vol. I/15, pp. 497–8; Weber 1994c, p. 186.

121 Weber 1984–2009, vol. I/5, p. 477; Weber 1994c, p. 169; compare Weber 1984–2009, vol. I/15, p. 499; Weber 1994c, pp. 188–9.

122 Gramsci 1992, p. 137.

political parties to influence the government while simultaneously ensuring a 'legitimate influence on the parliament':[123] when party leaders assume the responsibility of setting the political course, they also 'burden' their party with that responsibility.[124]

Of course, this is a 'passive revolution' as well, but it differs from the one Weber criticises insofar as it no longer involves individual party leaders being 'absorbed' into the government; instead, entire parties and their areas of influence are 'absorbed' into government policy. In his discussion of the Italian case, Gramsci distinguished between two periods of political 'absorption' into the ruling political class: '"molecular" transformism' integrates single members of the opposition into the 'moderate camp', but after 1900, it becomes possible to motivate 'whole groups of extremists' to change sides and join the pro-state, 'moderate' forces.[125] It is this modern variant of transformism that Weber propagates. His political model does not involve the parliament effectively 'checking and balancing' the government. This concept of a new transformism, one that aims at the absorption of entire groups into the state, will now be examined by reference to the class whose integration it was primarily designed to bring about.

---

123    Weber 1984–2009, vol. I/15, p. 574; Weber 1994c, p. 251.
124    Weber 1984–2009, vol. I/15, p. 571; Weber 1994c, p. 248.
125    Gramsci 2007, p. 257.

# CHAPTER 13

# The Integration of the Modern Industrial Proletariat into Bourgeois Society

## 13.1    Paul Göhre's Study on the Heterogeneity of Social Democratic Common Sense

The intellectual 'digestion' of Marxism Alfred Weber attributed to the 'younger' generation of social politicians (see above, Chapter 8) shapes a new type of social policy that is clearly distinct from the social-conservative opposition to socialism. I wish to demonstrate this, initially, by reference to Max Weber's interventions into the debates of the Evangelical Social Congress, which had been founded in the spring of 1890, mainly on the initiative of the former court chaplain and anti-Semitic politician Adolf Stoecker. The foundation of the Evangelical Social Congress was rendered possible by a declaration issued by the Kaiser in February, in which he announced an intensification of national industrial safety programmes and an international conference on industrial safety.[1] Subsequently to this, the Protestant High Consistory, a body directly subordinate to the head of state, issued a decree calling upon the clergy to continue combating Social Democracy while recognising the justified social needs of the workforce. 'Repression of the Social Democratic movement was now to yield to stronger socio-political efforts to solve social problems, especially those of the industrial workforce'.[2] But since the announced era of socio-political reform was not immediately successful in curbing Social Democracy's influence on the workforce, it was abandoned, both by the government and by the leadership of the Protestant church, in 1894/95.[3]

---

1   It 'reassured the rightists that in participating in the Congress they were not on the wrong track' (Marianne Weber 1975, p. 132). On the founding of the Evangelical Social Congress, see for example Göhre 1896, pp. 136ff; Apel 1939, pp. 30–1; Schick 1970, pp. 76–90, and Kouri, who emphasises the large number of government officials among its members (1984, pp. 99ff, 117ff, 120).

2   Aldenhoff 1988, p. 286.

3   Minister of Trade Berlepsch, who passed a law banning the employment of children younger than 13, was sidelined from 1894 onward, at the instigation of Saarland industrialist von Stumm, and resigned in 1896 (Wehler 1995, p. 1088). A decree issued by Prussia's Protestant High Consistory on 16 December 1895 banned pastors from participating in any kind of 'socio-political agitation' and threatened them with disciplinary measures if they failed to

The Evangelical Social Congress suffers from internal tensions similar to those within the Association for Social Policy. Weber, who attends the annual assemblies regularly until 1897, numbers among the 'younger' members, along with Naumann and Göhre; the 'young' opposed to the initially dominant 'state socialist' positions of Stoecker and Wagner an 'English conception of social policy'.[4] The Protestant controversies about the 'labour issue' are sparked by the general secretary of the Evangelical Social Congress, Paul Göhre; in 1891, Göhre published a study on the industrial workforce, written after he had spent three months working incognito at Chemnitz's engineering works (in what follows, I quote from the 1913 'popular edition', which is identical to the original edition).

What was offensive in Göhre's book was his demonstration that any strategy aiming to separate the workers from Social Democracy is doomed to fail: the entire workforce of Chemnitz and its environs is tied up with the Social Democratic Party and 'lives and breathes its ideas'.[5] The workforce is 'held together by the glue of Social Democratic agitation', and Social Democracy will continue to be its expression and representation within the foreseeable future; 'in fact today, Social Democracy is this movement itself'.[6] To eliminate Social Democracy would be neither sensible nor possible, 'but what is possible, desirable and necessary is that Social Democracy be educated, ennobled and sanctified'.[7] This presents engagement with Social Democracy with new challenges: on the one hand, one needs to 'break and remove the materialist backbone' of the Social Democratic worldview;[8] on the other hand, one must not overlook that the moral sensibility of the workers influenced by Social Democracy continues to be shaped by Christianity, and that Social Democratic agitation continues to arouse a number of 'ideal forces'.[9] It needs to be recognised 'that a Social Democrat can also be a Christian, and that a Christian can

---

comply; this led to numerous clergymen withdrawing from the Evangelical Social Congress (see Göhre 1896, pp. 172–3).

4   Apel 1939, p. 85. Apel's 1939 dissertation attempts to portray the Evangelical Social Congress as a precursor of the National Socialist 'new era' (Apel 1939, p. 122); accordingly, Apel sympathises with the 'state socialist' position, without however rejecting the 'English' position of the 'young' out of hand.

5   Göhre 1913, p. 108.

6   Göhre 1913, pp. 142, 214.

7   Göhre 1913, p. 215.

8   Göhre 1913, p. 216.

9   Göhre 1913, pp. 191, 194.

also be a Social Democrat'.[10] 'Let us join the professional associations of the workers, their electoral associations ... Let us offer them our services'.[11]

These are the two poles of an 'interruptive' discourse that inserts itself into the contradictions inherent in the enemy's formation. This discourse is intended to replace previous efforts to combat the Social Democrat Party by means of a frontal assault; that these previous efforts have failed is shown by the example of the Anti-Socialist Laws.[12] Göhre's *Drei Monate Fabrikarbeiter* ['Three Months as a Factory-Worker'] is not just one of the first well-founded studies on industrial workers' way of life; it is also, as Gramsci would have said, a study on the contradictory and 'bizarre' composition of Social Democratic 'common sense' [*senso comune*]: when a worldview is not critical and coherent, it contains 'elements of the caveman and principles proper to the most modern and advanced science, prejudices from every past ... historical phase and intuitions of a future philosophy that will belong to a humanity unified the world over'.[13] It is from here, and not from the philosophies of intellectuals, that Gramsci sets out in his attempt to develop a *philosophy of praxis* qua 'critique of "common sense"', a philosophy that simultaneously grounds itself in the spirit of experimentation and sense of reality inherent in '*buon senso*' in order to 'renew and render "critical" an activity already underway there'.[14]

In contrast with Gramsci's political perspective, Göhre searches for faultlines in order to mobilise the common sense of the workers against the Marxist hegemony within the workers' party. He observes that most 'average Social Democrats' do not think very highly of the official democratic republicanism or of economic communism; they are more interested in questions relating to their own employer, the modalities of payment, just wages and so on.[15] Including these workers in the activities of the professional and craft associations, of the health and accident insurance funds and so on would allow for the creation of an 'effective counterweight against dreams and utopian pursuits'.[16] Göhre notes a 'surprisingly sympathetic attitude' to the German fatherland, the Kaiser and the military (this being especially true of those workers who

---

10    Göhre 1913, p. 216.

11    Göhre 1913, p. 217.

12    On the concept of 'interruptive discourse', coined by Ernesto Laclau, see Projekt Ideologietheorie 1980, pp. 36–7.

13    Gramsci 1975b, p. 1376.

14    See Gramsci 1975b, pp. 1334–8, 1376, 1382, 1386, 1483. On the concepts of *senso comune* and *buon senso* in Gramsci, see Jehle 1994, pp. 162ff, and Rehmann 2013, pp. 126ff.

15    Göhre 1913, pp. 113, 115.

16    Göhre 1913, p. 131.

participated in the military campaign against France), an attitude that differs markedly from the republican, cosmopolitan and Marxist worldview of the 'elite Social Democrats' and conflicts with the 'nationless sentiment enforced by the party'.[17] The official 'phrase about the confraternisation of all nations' is confronted with the Social Democratic workers' aversion to the Czechs ['*Seffs*'] who have immigrated across the Bohemian and Saxon borders.[18]

Göhre's alliance with the 'average Social Democrats', against the Marxist 'elite Social Democrats', resembles the strategy of the Catholic Church as criticised by Gramsci, a strategy of 'leaving "simple minds" to their primitive philosophy of common sense' instead of 'constructing a new moral and intellectual bloc'.[19] Given the massive pressure of conservative criticism, which identified the Evangelical Social Congress with Social Democracy, the dividing line would be drawn more clearly again. In 1896, the year that he and Naumann founded the National Social Association, Göhre emphasised that the Evangelical Social Congress and Social Democracy had nothing in common: 'It [Social Democracy; J.R.] is democratic and republican, whereas the Evangelical Social Congress is monarchist and loyal to the Kaiser; Social Democracy is international, whereas the Evangelical Social Congress is national; Social Democracy strives for social revolution, whereas the Evangelical Social Congress strives for social reform; Social Democracy is materialist and atheist, whereas the Evangelical Social Congress is Christian. How could there be any more pronounced oppositions than these?'[20] At the same time, he hopes (and says so in an August 1895 letter to Naumann) to 'join forces with the reasonable majority of Social Democrats' and considers the foundation of the National Social Association a preparatory step by which to 'gain time until Vollmar, Schönlank, etc., bring about the split on the other side, so that we can join them, our people, all reasonable Social Democrats, the better Hirsch-Duncker people, in creating a truly radical German labour party, one that is national, not pledged to Marx, not anti-Christian, and one that obtains leadership of the Reich'.[21] This project is however not yet realistic, so that Göhre is compelled to change course. In April of 1899, he would leave the National Social Association, of which he was the vice chairman, and join the Social Democratic Party; later still, he would abandon his position as a clergyman and leave the Church.[22]

---

17    Göhre 1913, pp. 117, 121, 123, 142.
18    Göhre 1913, p. 129.
19    Gramsci 1975b, pp. 1384–5.
20    Göhre 1896, p. 171.
21    Quoted in Theiner 1983, p. 54.
22    See Aldenhoff 1988, p. 293.

## 13.2    'Class Struggle' as a Mode of Integration into Bourgeois Society

Göhre is Weber's main confidant within the Evangelical Social Congress, one who also shares his interest in sociological research.[23] Weber and Göhre elaborated the questionnaire for the farm worker inquiry, which differed from the questionnaires prepared by the Association for Social Policy insofar as it was no longer sent to landowners but to clergymen.[24] If the Weber obituary by Troeltsch (in the *Frankfurter Zeitung* of 20 June 1920) is to be believed, Weber was linked to Göhre by a strong, emotional friendship.[25]

When Göhre was sharply attacked for his study on factory workers by the orthodox consistorial councillor Cremer, Weber came to his aid in the newspaper *Christliche Welt* in 1892. He concentrates on formulating a critique of the patriarchal pastoral stance that treats workers with kind-hearted 'forbearance': 'With regard to his economic distress, the worker does not ask for alms, not for remedies that take the form of charity; he claims a *right* to a larger share of the world's goods'.[26] Weber posits a parallel between this consciousness of a social right and a new attitude towards the ideological powers: what the worker demands from the 'custodians of the moral powers in the life of the people' is positive recognition of his intellectual independence and respect for his own 'moral powers'. He needs to be addressed 'in his own language'.[27] However, such 'respectful' treatment is a far cry from the comprehensive emancipation of labour, understood as producer democracy and self-management: the 'interpellation' that Althusser discusses as a fundamental mechanism of ideological subjection is to be organised in such a way as to ensure that the interpellated workers 'recognise themselves' in it, thereby becoming capable of submitting to it 'voluntarily'. What Weber is looking for is a new ideological relationship of representation, one in which the workers no longer feature only as objects, but also as ideological subjects who subordinate themselves in the mode of 'autonomy' and 'free choice'.[28]

---

23    See Aldenhoff 1988, pp. 292–3.

24    Documented in Baumgarten 1964, pp. 376–86. According to Göhre, this new inquiry differed from that of the Association for Social Policy, which yielded 'purely economic results', insofar as it was especially concerned with the 'interaction between the economic situation and the whole mental, ethical and religious situation of the various strata of landworkers' (Göhre 1896, p. 150).

25    See Graf 1988, p. 321.

26    Weber 1984–2009, vol. I/4, p. 114.

27    Ibid.

28    In keeping with the French meaning of the word, Althusser uses the *concept of the subject* in a twofold sense: '(1) a free subjectivity, a centre of initiatives, author of and responsible

At the Frankfurt meeting of the Evangelical Social Congress in 1894, Weber confronts his listeners with the claim that if they wish to make any headway on the terrain of the 'worker question', they need to accept not only the reality of class struggle but also that of the 'objective hatred' between one class and the other:[29] 'Those who would rather not see the psychologically inevitable necessity of this phenomenon will have to blindfold themselves'.[30] Partisanship for the workers needs also to be tolerated. Weber states that personally, he would not be able to cast stones at a clergyman 'who is convinced that the emancipatory struggle of a rising class is a good struggle and one willed by God'.[31]

At first blush, it might seem as if what is being articulated here resembles the liberation-theological approach of a socialist worker-priest. But Weber is concerned with the development of an 'Evangelical-social labour movement' that can prevent the advance of Social Democracy, especially in rural areas. He is particularly concerned with not allowing the Social Democrats to take advantage of the farm workers' hunger for intellectual culture, a task to be coordinated (at least provisionally) by the rural clergy.[32] It is only if class relations are recognised as real that the emergence of class consciousness among the farm workers can occur under the leadership of Protestant worker associations.[33] Recognition of worker struggle intersects with the urgent requirement of modernising a church that has fallen back considerably with regard to the 'social question,' due to the authoritarian state-fixation it has developed by way of setting itself off from its Catholic rival.[34]

I have deliberately passed over the way in which Weber defines the class struggle he is asking the Protestants to recognise: 'Class struggle exists and is an

---

for its actions; (2) a subjected being, who submits to a higher authority' and freely recognises its subordination (Althusser 1971, p. 182). The *effet de reconnaissance*, which plays a central role in the constitution of individuals as subjects, is also ambiguous and refers to recognition in both senses of the word. By recognising itself in the Subject, the subject recognises the Subject as a higher instance and thereby makes itself a subordinated subject (pp. 177ff). For a discussion and critique, see Projekt Ideologietheorie 1982, pp. 116–25 and Rehmann 2013, pp. 155ff.

29    Weber 1984–2009, vol. I/4, pp. 327–8.
30    Weber 1984–2009, vol. I/4, p. 328.
31    Weber 1984–2009, vol. I/4, p. 330.
32    Weber 1984–2009, vol. I/4, pp. 332–3.
33    Weber 1984–2009, vol. I/4, p. 345.
34    Since the genesis of the organised labour movement, there has existed a Catholic current within it. As early as 1846, Kolping founded the first Catholic apprentice associations, and from the 1860s onward, Mainz's 'worker bishop' von Ketteler organised Catholic worker associations and trade unions. See Rehmann 1986, pp. 18–19.

*integrating* element of today's social order'.[35] Mommsen quotes this passage and concludes that Weber is following 'in the footsteps of Marxist thought'.[36] This remark is, at the least, imprecise. It takes note of Weber's adoption of one of the socialist labour movement's key concepts, but it overlooks the change of standpoint, from 'active' to 'passive revolution'. As is well known, integration into bourgeois society is not what Marx expected from proletarian class struggles; he looked to overcoming bourgeois society and to the prospect of a self-governing 'association' of free individuals.[37]

Weber's re-fashioning of the concept operates via the ideology of nationalism. Psychologically and ethically, class struggle within the nation is to him 'analogous to the struggles between nations',[38] just as 'class hatred' is comparable, in his view, to the 'national hatred of hostile nations', for which it 'often enough serves as a psychological replacement'.[39] The autonomous 'struggle' of the workers that Weber evokes with such pathos is conceived of according to the model of imperialist world power rivalry. Accordingly, the Protestant worker associations are charged with the educational task of taking burgeoning class consciousness beyond the 'philistine' orientation towards material goals and guiding it into the channels of an expansion of national power: 'No one has a greater interest in the power of the national state than the proletariat when it thinks more than one day ahead'.[40] Weber's modern variant of transformism looks to the workforce's active integration into a national bloc. Class struggle becomes a mode of integration into bourgeois society when the proletarian interest can be linked to the nation's imperialist power position.

This link occupies the very key position that Gramsci describes as *catharsis* when he conceives of the achievement of hegemony as a process: the transition from a merely economic aspect to an 'ethico-political moment'.[41] While what would be decisive for the rising class is the development of its own 'ethic', by which to transform the 'base' from an external, tranquillising force that oppresses people into a means of freedom,[42] Weber organises the subordination of the worker standpoint to imperialist nationalism. The ideological hub of 'worker honour' provides the medium of this foreign occupation.

---

35  Weber 1984–2009, vol. I/4, p. 329 (emphasis added).

36  Mommsen 1974, p. 109.

37  Marx and Engels 1975–2005, vol. 6, p. 505.

38  Weber 1984–2009, vol. I/4, p. 330.

39  Weber 1984–2009, vol. I/4, p. 328.

40  Weber 1984–2009, vol. I/4, p. 341.

41  Gramsci 1975b, pp. 1244–5.

42  Ibid.

## 13.3    Linking 'Worker Honour' to the Force Field of Nationalism

Both within the Evangelical Social Congress and within the Association for Social Policy, Weber's model of integration is understood as a risky case of playing with fire. The subverted appropriation of Marx sounds as if Marx were speaking through it. The German industrialists, whose interests Weber claims to understand well and to represent, almost universally endorse a 'patriarchalism' that combats even formal equality of rights for workers as tantamount to socialist revolution. Led by the owner of a Saarland iron mill, von Stumm, they raise the question, in the Prussian Upper House, of whether the Association for Social Policy is not itself guilty of socialism, as soon as it goes beyond the state's measures for worker protection and calls for worker rights of co-determination.[43] The trap threatens to spring shut, unless the representatives of the state can be convinced that the social reforms called for would in fact allow a more effective curtailment of the impending revolution.

The same discursive coercion reproduces itself in the controversies fought out within the Association. There, Brentano already took the view, as early as 1890, that the introduction of freedom of association in England had replaced struggle with negotiation, so that 'what was once unilaterally imposed and reluctantly suffered is now implemented and observed with the support of the workers'.[44] According to Brentano, the English example demonstrates 'how revolutionary convictions can become quite conservative if one allows their bearers to participate practically in the concrete tasks of the day', this being why Marx and his comrades so despised the old trade-union leaders.[45] In the view of the Association's leadership, recognition of an independent representation of worker interests would amount to overstepping the line that separates the Association from Social Democracy. For example, Schmoller considers it the greatest misfortune that the idea introduced into class relations by Marx is gaining ground throughout society, namely that 'all social relations . . . can be

---

43    In a speech held before the Upper House on 28 May 1897, Baron von Stumm claims that
      Katheder socialism has transformed from a royalist social policy into a 'demagogic social-
      ism' that proclaims the class struggle and has initiated 'rabble-rousing against capital and
      property' (quoted in Lindenlaub 1967, p. 66).

44    Verein für Socialpolitik 1890, p. 125.

45    Verein für Socialpolitik 1890, p. 128. Such arguments can already be found in Brentano's
      book on the 'Worker Gilds of the Present' (Brentano 1871b, pp. 331–2). There, Brentano
      traces the English trade unions back to the medieval gilds, who were initially prohibited,
      then tolerated and eventually recognised and integrated into the state body (Brentano
      1871a, pp. 9ff, 66ff, 89ff). On Brentano's conception of trade unions, see also Müssiggang
      1968, pp. 161ff, and Plessen 1975, pp. 20, 32–3, 98ff.

improved ... only through struggle ... The state order and the social order are seen not as orders of peace, but as a battleground'.[46]

The discursive arrangement has its own logic. The 'ethical' condemnation of class struggle leads, in the opposite camp, to an 'ethical' countermovement and idealisation. As entrepreneurs and conservatives warn against constantly referring workers to 'struggle' and handing them a weapon that they wield to the 'detriment of economic life in its entirety', the social-reformist counterfaction invokes the workers' 'sense of honour' and the 'decent' character of their struggle.[47] Now, by virtue of being articulated as a struggle for 'honour,' the workers' own organised representation of interests becomes the point from which to initiate a new type of ethicisation. An 'ethicisation [*Versittlichung*] of class struggle' replaces the strategy of ethical condemnation.[48]

Weber intervenes in this constellation in order to link the workers' standpoint to the force field of nationalism. Let us begin by observing how he intervenes in the controversies surrounding the right of association for workers. The context is that the strategy for containing the labour movement shifted, following the failure of the Anti-Socialist Laws, from penal measures to measures putatively intended to 'protect' the individual worker from the ostensibly coercive measures of the trade unions. The conflict within the Association for Social Policy turned mainly on paragraph 153 of the Reich's trade regulation act, which threatened striking workers and their trade unions with up to three months in prison if they should attempt to pressure colleagues 'willing to work' while simultaneously allowing entrepreneurs to threaten striking workers with dismissal with impunity. 'Today, if a striking worker were to say to one who is willing to work: "My Augusta isn't dancing with you unless you join the strike", he would render himself liable to prosecution', Weber scoffs during the Association for Social Policy's 1905 meeting in Mannheim.[49] What Weber criticises in the legislation is, first, the law's 'strident one-sidedness' and second, the fact that it promotes precisely those character traits that are least valuable, namely 'cowardice', the 'absence of convictions' and a 'lack of comradely honour': it is the 'so-called worker willing to work' who is legally protected, someone 'who enjoys all the advantages of the strike, but is not willing to pay for them; instead he means to stab those who struggle in the

---

46     Schmoller in the Prussian Upper House on 13 May 1904, quoted in Lindenlaub 1967, p. 217.

47     Quoted in Conrad 1906, pp. 139–40.

48     This is the title of an article by the liberal minister Ernst Lehmann, published in the *Süddeutsche Blätter* in 1911. In his call for the recognition of class struggle, Lehmann explicitly invokes the authority of Weber. See Hübinger 1994, pp. 104–5.

49     Weber 1988b, p. 397.

back'.[50] Those who are addressed, within the social-conservative discourse, as 'decent'—unorganised individual workers—are here exposed as spineless parasites. Thus the moral subject of Bonapartist social policy is annihilated, and annihilated *morally*. The view of the 'young' can be expressed formulaically as follows: a social policy capable of bringing about integration needs to ally itself not with the weak, but with the strongest characters within the class to be integrated.[51] In a 1912 circular letter on social policy, Weber portrays 'comradeliness' and 'class sentiment' developing within the 'orderly struggle' of the workers as a 'cultural asset in and of themselves'.[52] The unarticulated old moral subject yields to a new one, that of the union man who 'bravely stands up for his convictions', who fights for his 'honour' and who—according to 'unbiased' entrepreneurs—also ranks among the most productive of workers.[53]

This worker 'honour' has rich potential for being linked to various other ideological formations. That it is a *male* honour goes without saying. This association is an unquestioned commonplace within the worker movement itself, so that even Rosa Luxemburg feels she needs to praise the virtues of revolutionary persistence as 'manful'.[54] In Weber, it is of course unionism that contrasts, as a stronghold of 'idealist convictions', with Social Democratic 'party philistinism', thereby becoming the warrant of 'masculine, free independence'.[55] Another widespread tendency is that of combining, within worker honour, elements of an assertive defence of one's interests with social Darwinist

50  Ibid.

51  At the same meeting, Brentano describes those 'willing to work' as that 'peculiar sort of worker who allegedly wishes to work under worse conditions than those demanded by organised workers'. He says of them that they are either workers dragged along from abroad or workers permanently bound to a certain firm by certain welfare arrangements such as the provision of housing or credit (Verein für Socialpolitik 1905, pp. 139–40, 148). In 1906, Naumann states that the worker who is 'willing to work' is either an 'outdated trapping from the dawn of liberalism', a weak worker who 'seizes upon the opportunity to settle into the warm nest of his struggling colleagues out of fear, destitution, lassitude' or a 'straightforward overachiever who does not want to expose himself to the strains of the class movement' (Naumann 1911, pp. 282–3).

52  Quoted in Schäfers 1967, p. 266.

53  Weber 1984–2009, vol. I/11, p. 278; Weber 1988b, p. 160.

54  Thus she says, in 'The Crisis of Social Democracy', that the future of humanity depends on whether or not the proletariat 'resolves manfully to throw its revolutionary broadsword into the scales' (Luxemburg 1970–5c, p. 62). On Luxemburg's relevance to women's politics, see Frigga Haug (F. Haug 1988, and 2007, pp. 27ff).

55  Weber 1988b, p. 406; compare pp. 398–9.

notions.[56] Weber does this in his 1917 critique of Bismarck's social policies, which involved the elderly, the infirm and the disabled being provided with 'pensions' but failed to provide any guarantees 'for the possibility of an objective and self-confident *representation of the interests of the healthy and strong*'.[57]

Finally, the soldierly semantic core of the concept of honour makes it possible to tie the working class to militarism. When Bismarck smashed the trade unions, he not only eliminated 'the only possible candidate for an objective representation of the workforce's interests'; he also overlooked 'that a state wishing to base the spirit of its mass army on honour and comradeliness must not forget that in everyday life as well, in the economic struggles of the workforce, it is the sense of honour and comradeliness that engenders the only moral powers that are decisive for the education of the masses, and that one must therefore give them free rein'.[58] Thus, the economic class struggle is presented as a medium by which the military concepts of honour and camaraderie in 'everyday life' are to be anchored. While in fact striking workers exposed themselves (both before and after 1918/19) to the threat of being 'struck down' by soldiers, Weber wants to view both sides of the barricade as bound together by one and the same moral virtue. He returns to the idea in his 1918 lecture 'Socialism', held before Austrian military officers, where he celebrates Germany's legalisation of independent trade unions as an example of military prudence. After all, he argues, the trade unions are not just fighting for wages, but also for things of an ideal nature, namely 'for honour as the workers understand it': 'The sense of honour, of the companionship between the workers in a factory or in the same branch of industry, makes them stand together, and that feeling is, after all, one that the unity of military bodies also rests upon, even if it is there developed in a contrary direction'.[59]

The parallelisation of proletarian class consciousness and the 'unity of military bodies' shows that Weber's mobilisation of subjects maintains said subjects within a strictly heteronomous and alienated form of societalisation. In contrast with the traditional 'transformism' of social-conservative social policy, the collective representation of interests has now been integrated, on a corporatist economic level, into ideological subordination. This, however, requires keeping worker struggle all the more remote from the Marxian

---

56    W.F. Haug has used the examples of Otto Bauer and Karl Korsch to demonstrate how the left was informed, prior to the First World War, by a current of social Darwinism (Haug 1986, pp. 66ff).

57    Weber 1984–2009, vol. I/15, p. 448; Weber 1994c, p. 143; Weber 1988a, p. 318.

58    Ibid.

59    Weber 1984–2009, vol. I/15, p. 602; Weber 1988b, p. 494.

perspective of a self-governing association of producers.[60] This also explains why, in formulating his countermodel to patriarchal social policy, Weber does not look to Marx, but rather to social Darwinism: outward circumstances are explicitly not to be organised in such a way 'that people feel at ease', he lectures his audience, members of the Evangelical Social Congress, in 1894, but rather in such a way 'that, given the pressures of the inevitable struggle for existence, their best traits, the ones we want to preserve for the nation, are maintained'.[61] The 'we' Weber invokes speaks from above, from the imaginary observatory of the bourgeois intellectual who is an ally of the modern imperialist state. What needs to be promoted is 'what appears to us to be valuable in man: self-responsibility, the deep compulsion to rise up towards humanity's intellectual and moral assets'.[62]

The 'self-responsibility' conceded to the workers is determined by the will to social advancement. The social subject proper to this nexus is the 'labour aristocracy'.

### 13.4      The Absorption of the Labour Aristocracy into the Bourgeoisie

'We are still a long way from the day when we will be able to hand the responsibility of solving social problems to the urban proletariat. I hope that day will come', Weber says in his 1893 lecture on the 'rural labour constitution', held before the Association for Social Policy.[63] What is here still implied, in a general form, as a wish and with sceptical overtones, will be rendered more to-the-point in the 1895 Freiburg inaugural address, where Weber identifies the emergence of an 'aristocracy of labour' qua 'bearer of the political sense of purpose (*Sinn*)' as the core issue of the projected '*social unification* of the nation'. If this is achieved, he calls out pathetically, the 'spear of leadership' the arm

---

60    That Weber is familiar with the significance of this perspective in Marx can be seen, for example, from his lecture 'Socialism': the hope of fully overcoming the domination of man over man by creating an 'association of individuals' is 'the actual prophecy, the key sentence' of the *Manifesto of the Communist Party*, Weber writes, 'without which it would never have been written' (Weber 1984–2009, vol. I/15, pp. 616–17; Weber 1988b, p. 505).

61    Weber 1984–2009, vol. I/4, p. 340. In his rejection of a social policy motivated by social sentiment, Weber was 'remarkably close to the thought of Nietzsche, with its radical devaluation of "compassion"', Mommsen remarks (1974, p. 107; compare p. 136).

62    Ibid.

63    Weber 1984–2009, vol. I/4, p. 196; Weber 1988c, p. 468.

of the bourgeoisie is still too weak to hold could be 'transferred to the broader shoulders of the workers'.[64]

In this passage, Weber places the concept of the labour aristocracy in quotation marks. It remains unclear from whom he adopts it. Lenin's use of the term, intended to explain the interrelationship between 'imperialism' and the labour movement's political 'opportunism', only develops after the 1914 approval of the war by the Social Democratic parties, so that Weber cannot have been familiar with it in 1894.[65] The fact that the term is used, without quotation marks, in, for example, Schulze-Gaevernitz's study of British imperialism,[66] suggests it was already current in the social sciences before then. Marx used the term 'aristocracy,' in a rather *en passant* manner, to refer to the 'best-paid part of the working class' in England.[67] In 1895, Engels speaks of the 'aristocracy among the working class', which has forcefully secured for itself a relatively comfortable condition by means of strong trade unions, and which considers this condition 'final'.[68] He observes that the economic sectors concerned are those in which the workers are overwhelmingly adult men exposed neither to the competition of women's and children's work nor to that of machines (as is the case, for example, with engine fitters, construction workers and carpenters).[69] Engels related the economic possibility for such a privileged position to Great Britain's status as a world power.[70] Britain's loss of its industrial monopoly leads to the English working class losing its privileged status, and this is the reason, according to Engels, 'why there will be socialism again in England'.[71] The interrelationship between the worker aristocracy and the status of an imperial world power that Engels identifies can also be found in Weber, albeit under altogether different auspices. What was formulated as a critique in Engels now becomes the economic justification for a 'proletarian' imperialism: 'Regardless of their unions, the most high-standing worker groups in England

---

64    Weber 1994a, p. 27.

65    Lenin systematises the concept in his 1917 work *Imperialism, the Highest Stage of Capitalism* (Lenin 1960–78c [1916], vol. 22, pp. 276ff). On the concept's relevance and the problems associated with it, see Caire 1983 and Weinzen 1994.

66    Schulze-Gaevernitz 1906, p. 366.

67    Marx and Engels 1975–2005, vol. 35, p. 660.

68    Marx and Engels 1975–2005, vol. 26, p. 299; compare vol. 27, p. 265.

69    Ibid.

70    In an 1858 letter to Marx, Engels speaks of the English proletariat 'becoming more and more bourgeois'. The most bourgeois of all nations, which exploits the entire world, ultimately strives to 'possess *alongside* the bourgeoisie ... a bourgeois aristocracy and a bourgeois proletariat' (Marx and Engels 1975–2005, vol. 40, p. 344).

71    Marx and Engels 1975–2005, vol. 26, p. 300; compare vol. 27, p. 268.

would be unable to preserve their standard of life for a single day if the international political status of their empire were to decline. Our German proletariat should take note of this too'.[72] Thus Weber's 'ethical' association of class struggle with the national power interest is not at all devoid of a socio-economic foundation. Weber assumes a developmental tendency that is exactly contrary to the socialist prediction formulated by Engels. Engels views the British worker aristocracy as a kind of transitional stage on the road to unqualified proletarianisation, whereas in Weber, 'full proletarianisation constitutes the point of transition following which the highest strata of the workforce begin an upward movement'.[73] To the theory of immiseration that remained virtually unquestioned, within Social Democratic Marxism, until the 'revisionist' forays undertaken (from 1896/97 onward) by Bernstein,[74] Weber opposes the concept of an internal division within the proletariat.

That this division could not develop, in Germany, as a 'lasting phenomenon' is described by Weber, in 1895, as a 'disagreeable fact' and traced back to social backwardness: 'During times of crisis, this aristocracy falls back to the level of unskilled workers'.[75] By contrast, in the Anglo-Saxon countries, 'there is often not the least bit of social interaction between skilled unionists and the lower strata of the workforce; one knows that sometimes, they find it difficult to sit down at the same table'.[76]

In the methodological introduction to the Association for Social Policy's inquiry into 'Selection and Adaptation (Choice of Profession and Professional Destiny) Within the Workforce of Large Industry' (1908/09), where Weber formulates this observation, the problem of a new worker aristocracy poses itself as the scholarly question of how the development of the forces of production in large industry affects the 'selection' of highly paid and qualified workers. The aim is to investigate 'what type of worker is being eliminated, what type of worker is being fostered, what types of qualities these workers display and what sorts of technological changes are employed in the process'; Weber is

---

72    Weber 1984–2009, vol. I/4, p. 341.

73    Weber 1984–2009, vol. I/4, p. 444; Weber 1988c, p. 490.

74    It was, however, none other than Engels who criticised, in 1891, the hypothesis on progressive proletarianisation and immiseration formulated in the Social Democratic Party's Erfurt Programme: 'This is incorrect when put in such a categorical way. The organisation of the workers and their constantly growing resistance will possibly check the *increase of misery* to a certain extent. However, what certainly does increase is the *insecurity of existence*' (Marx and Engels 1975–2005, vol. 27, p. 223).

75    Weber 1984–2009, vol. I/4, p. 740.

76    Weber 1984–2009, vol. I/11, p. 145; Weber 1988b, p. 56.

also interested in the circumstances under which skilled workers 'are eliminated in favour of a narrower stratum of workers, perhaps with an even higher degree of qualification, or in favour of less skilled workers who can be easily replaced at any time'.[77] The summary of the seven-volume inquiry prepared by Weber's student Marie Bernays notes that the introduction of machines leads, among the majority of the workers, to 'a declining and an ascending process, an incredible . . . levelling of the worker masses which pushes the more intelligent common workers and women to the surface but in part also forces skilled workers to abandon their lofty position'.[78]

This finding points to two strategies of Taylorist-Fordist rationalisation that are both contradictory and complementary. On the one hand, Taylorism breaks the power of the highly qualified skilled workers who previously held a monopoly on producer's knowledge and controlled the recruitment of younger workers, i.e. it destroys the 'old' labour aristocracy that Engels had in mind, even if that labour aristocracy continued to dominate German mechanical engineering until 1914, due to the workshop principle in effect there.[79] Gramsci observes a 'forced selection' whereby 'a part of the old working class will be mercilessly eliminated from the world of production and from the world *tout court*'.[80] This tendency is also evident in the inquiry's studies on age selection, according to which mechanised large industry 'has used up its workers . . . at an age when the man employed in middle-class professions usually finds himself at the height of his powers'.[81] On the other hand, the Fordist industries can

---

77    Weber 1984–2009, vol. I/11, pp. 86–7; Weber 1988b, pp. 6–7. In order to be able to investigate this, the scholars involved in the inquiry should also be in the know about the '"organic" composition of the requisite capital' and its turnaround periods (Weber 1984–2009, vol. I/11, pp. 85–6; Weber 1988b, pp. 5–6).

78    Bernays 1912, p. 160.

79    Due to the predominance of skilled workers in mechanical engineering, the German scientific management movement lacked the 'unitary direction of US "scientific management"'. According to Ebbinghaus, Germany's scientific managers worked at the polytechnics, not in the machine-building industry (Ebbinghaus 1984, pp. 181–2, 187, 219). The Taylorisation of production occurred mainly under the exceptional circumstances of the First World War, when the metalworkers with their 'professional honour' were drafted into the military and replaced by unskilled women and adolescents (Ebbinghaus 1984, pp. 4, 6, 180–1, 194–5, 218).

80    Gramsci 1996, p. 215.

81    Quoted in Bernays 1912, p. 130. More than 90 percent of the workers in the large firms under study were younger than 40, and between 70 and 80 percent were younger than 40 (Bernays 1912, pp. 127–8). The selection of workers was less severe in smaller and less

use the introduction of machinery and cost-cutting measures to modify the tendential decline of the rate of profit, and they use their surplus profits to create a new labour aristocracy by means of high wages.[82] In order to impose psycho-physical adaptation to the new industrial structure, force (smashing the trade unions) is not sufficient; it needs rather to be combined with 'persuasion' in the 'forms proper to the society: money', Gramsci notes.[83] The ideal, usually unachieved paradigm of this strategy is provided by Ford, who more than doubled average wages in 1914, introducing a five-dollar minimum wage and coupling economic privilege with strict requirements on a clean, disciplined lifestyle and loyalty to the company.[84]

As can be seen in retrospect, Weber's expectation of a relatively stable worker aristocracy was more realistic than Engels's prediction of an unqualified proletarianisation leading to socialist revolution in capitalism's core country. In contrast with Kautskyan Marxism's theory of collapse, but also with Bernstein's delusional assumption of a gradual and peaceful transition to socialism, Weber noticed that capitalism's development contained within it enough capacity for transformation to allow for ongoing development on a capitalist basis.[85] In the *Grundrisse*, Marx had identified the 'foreshadowings of the future' with the overcoming of the 'present form of production relations'.[86] In the metropoles, it occurred not in the form of a socialist overcoming of capitalist relations of production, but as the transition to a Fordist regime of accumulation and the corresponding mode of regulation. Weber's strength consists in his registering and articulating the 'foreshadowing' of Fordism. Within

---

    mechanised firms (in this case, a leather workshop in Oldenburg) than in large firms involving the operation of machinery (Bernays 1912, pp. 155–6).

82    According to Gramsci, all industrial activity since Henry Ford constitutes 'an ongoing, interminable struggle to escape the law of the falling rate of profit and maintain a position of superiority vis-à-vis one's competitors' (Gramsci 1975b, pp. 1281–2; compare Gramsci 2007, p. 184; Gramsci 1975b, pp. 1312–13). On the modified operation of the tendential fall of the rate of profit under Fordism, see also Hirsch and Roth 1986, pp. 37ff.

83    Gramsci 1992, pp. 167–70; Gramsci 1996, pp. 215–20; Gramsci 1975c, pp. 2146, 2171–5.

84    See Ebbinghaus 1984, pp. 135ff. Henry Ford himself described this as the 'bonus-on-conduct-method' (Ford 1922, p. 130).

85    While he agreed with Bernstein in rejecting the theory of capitalism's breakdown, his lack of illusions with regard to class relations under capitalism meant that he was 'closer to Kautsky than to Bernstein', Breuilly observes (Breuilly 1988, p. 487). While Bernstein predicted the peaceful assertion of a capitalism with democratic and socialist values, Weber expected 'limited class conflict within the stable framework ... of the capitalist system', with the worker elites assuming a passive and subordinated stance (p. 482).

86    Marx 1973, p. 461.

Marxism, it was not until Gramsci that the success of the victorious formation was analysed from below, from the standpoint of the labour movement's efforts to develop 'an "Americanism" of its own', as represented by the current of Turin's *Ordine Nuovo*.[87] That Agnelli failed to 'absorb' this current within the complex of the FIAT Corporation, a failure repeatedly noted by Gramsci,[88] means that the 'industrial-productive bloc' aimed for by Weber encountered serious difficulties in Italy.

Of course, it is not primarily predictions on 'objective' developments that are at stake, but opposed political projects within the context of unequal power relations. As early as 1914, the European Social Democrats' approval of the war credits introduced by their governments showed that Weber's gamble on the internal division of the proletariat had paid off. As an organic intellectual of the bourgeoisie—and contrary to the neo-Kantian postulate of the separation of 'ought' and 'is' (see below, Chapter 17)—, he wants what he glimpses on the horizon to be implemented in the form of practical politics. What he looks to are the well-paid, 'real American Yankee workers', who have fully adopted the 'forms of bourgeois society': 'They appear in a tophat and in the company of their wife, who may be a little less smart and elegant than other ladies, but otherwise behaves just like them'.[89] As passionately as Weber combated the 'passive revolution' when it presented itself within the constellation between bourgeoisie and agrarian class, equally passionately does he propagate it as a strategy against the working class: integration by means of the absorption of its 'aristocracy' into the bourgeoisie.

## 13.5    A Graduated System of Corporatist Cooptation

Weber's proposals on the institutionalisation of a new mode of integration could also be read as a system of rules of 'controlled demarcation' between societal domains.[90] The dilettantism displayed by German foreign policy during the world war is traced back by him to a trespassing of the line of division between the military and the political. What had been disregarded was that 'the military commander wages war according to military criteria, whereas the

87    Gramsci 1992, pp. 169, 220–3; Gramsci 1975c, pp. 2147, 2156.

88    Ibid.

89    Weber 1984–2009, vol. I/15, p. 604; Weber 1988b, p. 496; compare Weber 1946a, p. 311.

90    On the significance of the 'function of controlled demarcation' to the ideological reproduction of relations of domination, see Nemitz 1979, pp. 67ff, and Projekt Ideologietheorie 1982, pp. 113–14, 199.

politician concludes peace according to political criteria'.[91] In order to keep the 'point of honour' remote from real politics, a line of division needs to be drawn between the leading politician and the monarch.[92] As we have seen, Weber derives his concept of parliamentarisation from a sharp division between the 'civil servant', who is obliged to be obedient, and the responsible leading politician. After 1918, this division will gradually yield to the dichotomy of the 'plebiscitary leader' and the parliamentary 'clique' (see below, Chapter 14.3). The state-held shares of cartels and joint-stock companies that present themselves as 'state socialism' in fact represent the domination of the state by industry, and so the state would be looked upon by the workers as a 'class state in the strictest sense of the word'.[93] Here, the destabilisation of the dominant order is caused only by the trespassing of a boundary that impairs the state's function as a socially transcendent ideological power: 'The state as such would only have to suffer the hostility of the workers, which is today directed at entrepreneurs'.[94]

If, as Friemert observes,[95] the Weimar Republic functioned according to the 'basic arrangement' of a consensus-building mechanism whose content was a legalised and strictly confined class struggle, then Weber was one of the main theoretical pioneers of this arrangement. Charles Maier has described this consensus-building mechanism as a 'corporatist pluralism' that transfers the regulation of the market and of social antagonism from the state to the representatives of the economic classes themselves.[96] In the terminology of Schmitter, who, differently from Maier, uses the terms 'corporatism' and 'pluralism' to denote two distinct modes of integration, one could describe this as the transition from a 'state corporatism' to a 'societal corporatism'.[97]

---

91      Weber 1984–2009, vol. I/15, p. 500; Weber 1994c, p. 189.

92      Weber 1984–2009, vol. I/15, p. 517; Weber 1994c, p. 203; compare Weber 1984–2009, vol. I/15, p. 511; Weber 1994c, p. 199.

93      Weber 1984–2009, vol. I/15, p. 614; Weber 1988b, p. 503. To Weber, the economy's potential for state-capitalist regulation is an illusion: 'Bankers and entrepreneurs would become the *unrestricted and unchecked* lords of the state! For who in the world is "the state", aside from this apparatus of large- and small-capitalist cartels of all kinds, within which the economy is "organised"'? (Weber 1984–2009, vol. I/15, p. 370; Weber 1994b, p. 104, Weber 1988a, p. 267).

94      Weber 1984–2009, vol. I/15, p. 615; Weber 1988b, p. 504.

95      Friemert 1980, p. 227.

96      Maier 1974, p. 202.

97      Schmitter uses the term 'corporatism' to refer, in a general way, to 'a system of interest and/or attitude representation, a particular ... institutional arrangement for linking the associationally organized interests of civil society with the decisional structures of the state' (Schmitter 1979, pp. 8–9). If 'state corporatism' refers to a model in which corporate

In Germany, the first model corresponds, for example, to the Supreme Army Command's policy of political truce, which made use of the trade unions to mobilise for the war economy (the Stinnes-Legien Agreement of 1917), whereas the second model takes shape in November 1918, with the foundation of the 'Central Work Group' [*Zentralarbeitsgemeinschaft*] that allied industrial associations with trade unions, and whose statutes first recognised the trade unions as 'chosen representatives of the workforce' with unqualified freedom of association.[98] To Weber, this agreement represents 'the only valuable socio-political achievement of the revolutionary period'.[99] Internationally, this variant of corporatism was mainly in effect during the period of stabilisation between 1924 and 1928, before imposing itself across Europe after 1948 (in a modified form characterised by the addition of Keynesian instruments of anti-cyclical economic policy). What is prefigured here is a politico-economic equilibrium 'that reserves central power either for conservatives willing to approve rising welfare spending or for Social Democrats willing to allow a reinforcement of capitalism'.[100] Buci-Glucksmann and Therborn speak of a 'corporatism-reformism' that relies on labour organisations (whereas fascism destroys them in order to install different, vertically structured organisations), and they follow Gramsci in analysing this 'corporatism/reformism' as a variant of 'passive revolution': the integrated working class 'remains corporatist and defends its ... interests within the given political framework, without transcending its own economic and class basis by means of a process of hegemonic unification of the various revolutionary subjects'.[101]

---

bodies are subordinated to the state and penetrated by them, then 'societal corporatism', by contrast, means that the legitimacy and the functioning of the state depend primarily on representative corporate bodies (Schmitter 1979, p. 20). 'Societal corporatism appears to be a typical, if not inevitable, component of the post-liberal, advanced capitalist, organized democratic welfare state; state corporatism seems to be a defining element, if not a structural necessity, of the anti-liberal, delayed capitalist, authoritarian, neo-mercantilist state' (Schmitter 1979, p. 22; see also Schmitter 1982, pp. 263–64, 266–67). In Wehler's view, the advantage of the term 'corporatism' lies at least partly in the fact that it focuses on the various forms of cooperation between firms, interest groups, trade unions and the state apparatus, referring to the balancing of interests within both 'authoritarian' and 'liberal democratic' states (Wehler 1995, pp. 664–5).

98    On this transition, see for example Feldmann 1974, pp. 158ff; see also Deppe, Fülberth and Harrer 1978, pp. 122ff, 149ff.

99    Weber 1984–2009, vol. I/16, p. 382; Weber 1988a, p. 486.

100   Maier 1974, p. 205.

101   Buci-Glucksmann and Therborn 1982, pp. 131, 135.

Weber's proposals for the institutionalisation of a new mode of integration can be used to show, in an exemplary fashion, that corporatism needs to be examined not only as an 'art of association', but also as a 'strategy of dissociation' and 'compartmentalisation'.[102] In any case, his strategy of a 'passive revolution' against the working class is also based on the drawing of a clear line of division, namely between economics and politics. We can see here a major difference between Weber and Brentano: Brentano had proposed a principle of organisation that encompassed all workers, the ones organised in trade unions as well as the unorganised ones, with the workers' elected representatives settling all disputes with the representatives of the employers under the chairmanship of a non-partisan third party.[103] Weber formulates the criticism that this 'compulsory organisation' cannot but involve the state in labour conflicts, leading to 'strike matters being informed by purely political criteria'.[104] The drawing of this line of division is, in turn, the reason why Weber needs to contrast the trade unions' representation of economic interests with 'party philistinism', glorifying the unions as a 'hub of idealist labour and ... convictions':[105] the idealisation of the trade unions is a compensation for their curtailed political competence. What strikes him as decisive is the prevention of any sort of political overdetermination of the trade unions' representation of interests. The question of whether to go on strike or not must not be decided according to party-political considerations; only economic considerations should play a role.[106]

This is why Weber also objects to the emergence of 'organic intellectuals' who 'transfer' the interests of the working class beyond the corporatist level and to the political levels of the superstructures. To the extent that they fail to subordinate themselves to the Fordist alliance for modernisation he calls for, he discredits them as 'literati'. While the term still referred, in 1917/18, to the conservative 'ideologues' of the ruling power bloc, the November Revolution causes the frontline to shift abruptly to the left. The 'literati government' of the Munich Council Republic under Kurt Eisner, within which writers and poets

---

102    Wassenberg 1982, pp. 86, 94–5. 'We can identify corporatism not just as an example of
        the "art of association", but as a strategy of dissociation as well' (Wassenberg 1982, p. 86).
        'The spectre of corporatism as a comprehensive, rational mode of governance fades away
        in the shadowy mists formed by the complex, compartmentalized structure of grouted
        public and private powers' (Wassenberg 1982, p. 95).
103    Verein für Socialpolitik 1905, p. 146.
104    Weber 1988b, pp. 397–8.
105    Weber 1988b, pp. 398–9.
106    Weber 1988b, p. 398.

(Toller, Mühsam, Landauer and others) played a key role, provided a direct target.[107] The testimony provided by Weber during Ernst Toller's trial on 16 July 1919 attributes to the man of letters, 'whom God, in his wrath, chose as a politician', an ethically sincere desire to do good, allied with unusual 'worldly innocence and ignorance of political and economic realities'.[108] As a rule, Weber accuses all those people of being 'literati' who attempt to advance democratisation beyond the point envisioned by him. In late 1918, he warns the 'economically progressive worker' that academic literati are attempting to undermine Germany's economic power by socialising heavy industry.[109] In polemicising against the 'utter inability of the radical literati to direct the economy', he attempts to demonstrate the necessity of a 'bourgeois-socialist administration convened on the basis of equal representation'.[110] Before 1918, he judged politicians primarily by reference to their willingness to engage in reform, but now the decisive criterion has become their willingness to recognise the indispensability and priority of the bourgeoisie.

Marcuse remarks that '[h]e raged against the intellectuals who had sacrificed their lives for the revolution'.[111] The radical left provokes scathing contempt from Weber. On 4 January 1919, he calls for Karl Liebknecht to be sent to a mental asylum, and for Rosa Luxemburg to be sent to Berlin's zoological gardens.[112] When he laments their murder (on 17 January 1919) in an article for *Der freie Volksstaat*, he misrepresents the contract killing as a reaction of 'the street' and ultimately lays the blame with Liebknecht and Luxemburg themselves: Liebknecht '*called for the struggle of the street. The street has struck him down*'.[113]

But a corporatist strategy of integration must be brought to bear on the political articulation of the labour movement as well. Weber recognised from the outset that Naumann's 1896 project of cutting the ground from under Social Democracy's feet by founding a Christian National Social Party would not be crowned with immediate success.[114] Göhre's *Three Months as a Factory Worker*

107  Weber 1984–2009, vol. I/16, p. 381; Weber 1988a, p. 485.
108  Weber 1984–2009, vol. I/16, pp. 489, 491. Weber believed that Toller benefited from his testimony, but Toller's defence lawyer Hugo Haase, the former representative of the USPD within the 'Council of People's Delegates', was less sure (see Weber 1984–2009, vol. I/16, p. 487).
109  Weber 1984–2009, vol. I/16, pp. 115–16; Weber 1988a, p. 460.
110  Weber 1984–2009, vol. I/15, p. 145; Weber 1988a, p. 482.
111  Marcuse 1969, p. 208.
112  Weber 1984–2009, vol. I/16, p. 441; compare pp. 443, 446.
113  Weber 1984–2009, vol. I/16, p. 461; compare pp. 468, 473.
114  Mommsen 1974, p. 135.

had already taught him that the spread of Social Democracy was not to be halted by Protestant worker associations, and that it was better to concentrate on 'refining' Social Democracy's own electoral base.[115] In 1906, Weber attends the Social Democratic Party's congress in Mannheim, and in 1907, he reports to the Association for Social Policy, speaking of a toothlessness that he seems at the same time to despise: his impression is that the Russian socialists that were invited to the congress ought to have thrown their hands up in horror at the sight of this party, 'in which the sedate publican's face and the physiognomy of the petty bourgeois emerged so dominantly ... lame rhetorical debates full of nagging and moaning' instead of the 'Catilinarian energy of faith they were used to from their assemblies'.[116] The description could just as well have been penned by Rosa Luxemburg, who attended the same congress and tried in vain to make her 'faint-hearted comrades' follow the example of the Russian Revolution and endorse her orientation towards the general strike.[117] When Robert Michels, who at the time was largely in agreement with Luxemburg on the question of the mass strike, protested against Weber's derogatory critique of Social Democracy, Weber replied to him, in a letter dated 6 November 1907, that he should simply consider 'his speech, which you find so puzzling, to be the speech of a *class-conscious bourgeois* addressing the *cowards* of *his own* class'.[118]

In fact, the main function of Weber's description is that of eliminating the bourgeoisie's fear of Social Democracy and helping it develop an interventionist strategy. To Weber, the starting point is to be found in a process of bureaucratisation that renders the contrast between revolutionary ideology and the material 'interest in advancement' more acute.[119] When ever more party members and officials are 'sustained at the manger of the commune', bourgeois society has less to fear than the Social Democrats: if one allowed them to join soldier associations and church administrations, instead of expelling them, it would transpire 'that instead of Social Democracy conquering the towns or the state, the opposite would occur: the state would conquer the party'.[120]

115   Göhre 1913, pp. 215, 222.
116   Weber 1988b, p. 410.
117   Luxemburg 1970–5d, pp. 171ff, 179.
118   Weber 1984–2009, vol. II/5, p. 423.
119   Weber 1988b, p. 408.
120   Weber 1988b, p. 409.

As with his anticipation of a Fordist reformation of capitalism, Weber's prognostic achievement is not to be denied. But what happens when the outlined parliamentarian or corporatist methods of absorbing hostile groups into the state do not suffice? The current of a modern 'Caesarism without a Caesar', which I have limited myself to discussing thus far, needs to be complemented by a personalist charismatic authority.

# CHAPTER 14

# The Return of the Charismatic 'Caesar' to Modern Politics

At the same time as Weber propagates, in 1917/18 and against the authority of the civil servants, a superior selection of leaders within and by means of parliament, he develops the parallel conception of an extra-parliamentary, charismatic-plebiscitary selection of leaders, expanding it 'in a clearly anti-parliamentary direction' during the November Revolution and the negotiations on the Weimar constitution.[1] In doing so, he articulates a position that has caused considerable difficulties for subsequent efforts to identify him with the liberal tradition and to set him off against fascism. In all honesty, writes Mommsen, following Nolte's lead, one ought to remark that the theory of charismatic authority contributed its share to 'making the German people inwardly willing to acclaim a leader [*Führer*], and thus to acclaim Adolf Hitler'.[2] In 1927, Robert Michels refers back to Weber's concept to justify his conversion from a left-wing syndicalist to a follower of Mussolini: there is no fundamental contradiction between popular sovereignty and dictatorship, because it is the people that gives itself 'absolute government by way of the plebiscite', and because Caesar presents himself as the 'incarnation of the popular will [*la volonté populaire faite homme*]'.[3] Carl Schmitt also invokes the concept of charismatic-plebiscitary authority, in order to replace the parliamentarian selection of leaders, still considered a counterbalance to plebiscitary authority by Weber,

---

1 Mommsen 1974, p. 199; see also pp. 448–9.

2 Mommsen 1974, p. 437; compare Nolte 1963, p. 11. Mommsen adopts a formulation proposed by Nolte, thereby qualifying his own, heavily criticised formulation from the first edition, according to which Weber's theory of charismatic leadership contributed to 'making the German people inwardly willing to acclaim Hitler's leadership position' (Mommsen 1959, p. 410).

3 Michels 1927, p. 293. 'In the case of charismatic leadership, the mass delegates its will to the leader almost in the manner of a natural, voluntary sacrifice, whereas in the case of democracy, the will is delegated in such a way as to preserve the *appearance* that it remains in the hands of the delegators' (Michels 1927, pp. 290–1; emphasis added). 'Today, aristocratic currents traverse the masses, and democratic tendencies lead to leadership' (Michels 1927, p. 294). On the indirect influence exerted on Michels by Weber during Michels's conversion to Italian fascism, see, *inter alia*, Röhrich 1972, pp. 143ff, and Mommsen 1988b, pp. 211ff.

with the 'forceful representation' of a political leadership and administration that is directly borne by the confidence of the masses.[4]

Here too, the problem cannot be discussed on the surface level of analogies and differences, as it touches on a more profound problem concerning the perspective and the arrangement of theoretical concepts. The figure of the charismatic-plebiscitary leader is a nodal point at which Weber's short-term political proposals intersect both with a basic concept from his sociology of domination and with a sociology of modern political parties. In order to render his analytic toolkit visible, I begin with the concept of charisma, which Weber subjects to a peculiarly narrow interpretation.

## 14.1  The Verticalist Narrowing of the Concept of Charisma

The term *charismata* is generally traced back to Saint Paul's first letter to the Corinthians and usually rendered as 'spiritual gifts' (e.g. 1 Corinthians 12,6). However, the etymology of the term leads us beyond its religious significance: the underlying Greek word *charis*, translated as 'grace' in English versions of the Bible, refers to 'everything that causes one joy',[5] the friendly powers or emissions of a living creature, the 'charm' of a beautiful person or the 'consciously enacted exchange of gifts and gifts in return'.[6] It is in this sense that Aristotle states, in the *Nicomachean Ethics*, that the *polis* coheres by virtue of 'proportionate reciprocity'.[7] 'And this is the moral of placing the Temple of the Graces [*charites*] in the public streets; to impress the notion that there may be requital, this being peculiar to *charis* because a man ought to requite with a good turn the man who has done him a favour'.[8] That the Graces are three in number is intended to express the fact that 'the *beneficium* goes from hand to hand, returning to the giver when it comes full circle'.[9]

Thus *charis* is originally associated with horizontal relations of reciprocity. Under the conditions associated with class societies constituted in the form of

---

4  Schmitt 2008, pp. 355–6. Schmitt held that Weber's ideal of a parliamentarian selection of leaders was, in 1917/18, 'the sole powerful idea system left for parliamentarianism', but given the divisions between Germany's political parties, 'this ideal... necessarily becomes problematical' (Schmitt 2008, pp. 362, 356).

5  Benseler 1990.

6  Dörrie 1981, p. 322.

7  Aristotle, *Nicomachean Ethics*, V8 1132 b34.

8  Aristotle, *Nicomachean Ethics*, 1133 a2.

9  Deichgräber 1971, p. 56.

the state, its significance verticalises itself and the term comes to refer to the 'grace' of the master as a response to the servant's services. This is the starting point for the religious semantic shift by which the term comes to refer to divine grace. It is against this background that Paul develops his concept of 'spiritual gifts' (*charismata*). In concrete terms, what is at issue is the problem of how to come to terms with men's 'different gifts' and 'ways of serving God', and with the 'different ways' in which God works through men (1 Corinthians 12,6), i.e. with the disputed matter of how to distribute tasks and competencies in the early communities of what will later be described as 'Christianity'. Within this context, 'divine gift' refers to the specific 'gift' that justifies one's claim to a leadership position. The criteria are as controversial and precarious as Paul's own position of authority. Institutionalised relations of ecclesiastic domination only imposed themselves after the turn of the century.[10]

Weber adopts the *concept of charisma* from the Protestant church historian Rudolf Sohm, who attempted to demonstrate, by reference to early Christian charisma, that every juridically organised church is 'Catholic' and in that sense 'un-Christian'—precisely because of its 'egalitarian' and 'democratic' character. Within this anti-democratic perspective, charisma is what licenses one to declare the word of God within the framework of 'divinely ordained relations of superiority and inferiority' and in an 'authoritarian' manner.[11] What is called for is obedience, but in the form of a voluntary recognition of charisma that can only be born from love.[12] By adopting this version of the concept, Weber surreptitiously introduces into sociology an element of Protestant theology. Within the concept of 'charismatic authority', the 'extraordinary' and hence provisional character of authority is linked, from the outset, to a personalised concept of the leader: charisma sets itself off from the regularity of 'traditional' and 'legal bureaucratic' authority insofar as it denotes 'a certain quality of an individual personality by virtue of which he is considered extraordinary and treated as endowed with supernatural, superhuman, or at least specifically exceptional powers or qualities . . . [O]n the basis of them the

---

10    See Meeks 1983, p. 135.

11    Sohm 1923, pp. 26–7, 29. At the same time, Sohm was a member of the 'right-wing' current within the National Social Association, and the antagonist of Paul Göhre, who was considered 'left wing'; see Themer 1983, pp. 8off. His conception of church law, which defined the genuine church as 'invisible' and abandoned the 'visible' church to the legal space organised by the state, served as a legitimation for clerical tendencies towards political conformity within the Nazi state and was only overcome within the fraternally organised Confessional Church. See Rehmann 1986, pp. 128ff.

12    Sohm 1923, p. 27.

individual concerned is treated as "leader".[13] Charismatic authority exists by virtue of 'affective devotion to the personality of the master and his gifts of grace ... Obedience is exclusively to the leader in a purely personal sense, and it is motivated in terms of his personal, extraordinary qualities, not in terms of his position or traditional authority'.[14] Thus the analysis is provided with an absolute verticalism as its underivable starting point.

The career of the concept of charisma is related to the variety of its colloquial, religious and sociological connotations, and it is partly accounted for by Marxism's denial of the problem of the personal capacity to lead.[15] On the other hand, the personal verticalism adopted from theology turned out to be the main obstacle to a sociological deciphering of charismatic phenomena. Gramsci is one of the few Marxists who partly adopted Weber's concept of charisma, having become aware of it via Robert Michels's sociology of political parties. Against Michels's personalist explanatory approach, Gramsci reinterprets the charismatic position in terms of the analyses of Bonapartism penned by Marx and Engels, i.e. as the phenomenon of a social balance of power.[16] Moreover, he associates the concept of charismatic leadership with a primitive stage in the development of political parties. As a more developed variety, he introduced the concept of 'organic' leadership, which elevates the competence of the masses and tends thereby to render itself superfluous.[17]

The main criticism directed at Weber's concept of charisma is that it does not lend itself to genealogical explanations and needs itself to be explained in terms of specific social relations. Many theories that look to Weber as a model have attempted to overcome his verticalist starting point by taking into account social conditions of development. The focus shifted from the person to the analysis of 'charismatic demand',[18] and of 'charismatic milieus',[19] 'movements',[20] 'interactions'.[21] Worsley emphasises the primacy of the 'message' and the mainly symbolic character of leadership as the nodal point of a system of relations. A leader only becomes charismatic by transforming 'latent solidarity' into ritual and political action.[22] Historical constellations are

---

13  Weber 1978, p. 241.
14  Weber 1988d, pp. 481–2; compare p. 485.
15  See Rehmann 1995, pp. 456ff.
16  See Gramsci 1992, p. 324.
17  See for example Gramsci 2007, pp. 83, 247; Gramsci 1975b, pp. 1428–31.
18  Wilson 1973, p. 499.
19  Mühlmann 1961, pp. 251ff.
20  Tucker 1968, pp. 738ff; Ebertz 1987, pp. 29ff.
21  Rustow 1970, p. 20; Goetze 1977, p. 14.
22  Worsley 1968, pp. 390ff.

considered charismatic when different forms of misery and desperation converge within them,[23] or when a society finds itself in a state of latent 'anomie'.[24]
In parallel with this, psychoanalytic approaches have referred back to Freud's
*Group Psychology and the Analysis of the Ego* (1921) in order to attempt to
account for the specificity of charisma in terms of the libidinous bond between
the leader and his followers.[25]

As soon as one returns from the theological and verticalist conception of
charisma to the actual meaning of the word, one is confronted with an aspect
that cannot be fully accounted for in terms of historical constellations. Weber
is also familiar with charisma as the 'spirit' or '*mana*' that provides living crea-
tures with their efficacy.[26] As such, it is akin to the heroic 'images of battle'
[*images de bataille*] that Sorel describes as 'myths': individuals who are participating in great social movements 'always picture their coming action as a battle
in which their cause is certain to triumph', examples being the glorious second
coming of Christ or the syndicalist general strike.[27] When an idea becomes a
'material force',[28] when it moves beyond intellectual circles and spreads among
the masses as a 'faith' and 'moral will',[29] then charismatic and energetic persons play a key role within popular movements, and the numinous quality of
these people can be accounted for in terms of certain leadership skills. Paul's
catalogue of charismatic qualities includes gifts of rhetoric and healing as
well as faith, which is able to move mountains, and the 'working of miracles'.
To this is added the 'ability to distinguish between spirits', which can be

---

23    Tucker 1968, pp. 742, 745.

24    Lipp 1985, p. 208. Lipp treats *charisma* as a liminal phenomenon and derives it from
      the opposite pole of *stigma*: under certain circumstances, stigmatised persons develop
      reactive powers that ultimately '"reverse" the stigma and convert it into positively
      valued, charismatic properties' (Lipp 1985, p. 76). The redefinition of stigma as charisma is
      brought about by an 'auto-stigmatisation' (exhibitionism, provocation, ascesis or ecstasy)
      that charges the field of action in such a way that deviant traits become the starting point
      for new solidarity (Lipp 1985, pp. 82, 204). By virtue of the process of 'charismatisation',
      marks of guilt become wondrous signs, and guilt becomes grace (Lipp 1985, pp. 204–5).
      The charismatic leader does not stand outside the new discursive formation, as a mere
      manipulator, he is rather co-produced by its effects of coherence and meaning: practi-
      cal anticipation of positive symbolic content retroactively affects and shapes the agents
      themselves (Lipp 1985, p. 266; see also Projekt Ideologietheorie 1980, pp. 66–7, 72).

25    See for example Reich 1971, pp. 71ff, 226–7; Downton 1973, pp. 222ff; Schiffer 1973, pp. 173ff.

26    Weber 1978, p. 401.

27    Sorel 1908, p. XXVI; Sorel 1916, p. 22.

28    Marx and Engels 1975–2005, vol. 3, p. 182.

29    Gramsci 1975b, pp. 1217–19, 1269ff.

interpreted, in terms of the theory of hegemony, as the ability to polarise and focus positions effectively.[30]

Machiavelli, who is aware of aspects of charisma insofar as they are part of techniques of domination, places the emphasis on the resolute will to create a *fait accompli*: nothing can ensure more lastingly that the prince will be revered than 'extraordinary undertakings'; in such undertakings, it is decisive that 'great deeds' succeed one another so rapidly that no one has time to develop a counterstrategy, such that there prevails a general sense of suspense and expectation of the outcome.[31] Machiavelli also considers the republic superior to autocracy, because the republic is better equipped to utilise people's different leadership qualities.[32] Lenin adopts Engels's view that insurrection is an 'art',[33] and shortly before the October Revolution, he renders this view more concrete by defining insurrection as the ability to make use of the 'turning point' during which both revolutionary fervour and the enemy's uncertainty reach their apex.[34] The ability to recognise the '*kairos*' of a crisis and translate it into effective action may be considered an element of 'charismatic leadership'.

In this broad sense, 'charisma' and 'charismatic leadership' can be analysed as aspects of hegemony. Considered against this background, Weber's concept of charisma reveals its one-sidedness. While the concept has inspired numerous fruitful investigations of 'charismatic' phenomena, it tends to elide the elements of a sociological or socio-psychological reconstruction. To the extent that 'charisma' informs Weber's analyses of contemporary politics, it refers less to the dynamics of non-institutionalised movements and communities than to a vertical relationship between leader and follower that cannot be rationally explained. Of course, such a relationship would require further theoretical mediation. For charismatic authority has been introduced as a typical, as yet unstable 'early phenomenon' of religious or political rule and refers to 'prerationalistic periods', in which virtually all models of action are associated either with tradition or charisma.[35] And yet it is precisely in the bureaucratic rationalisation of the Western world that charisma undergoes a process of 'becoming quotidian', such that it shifts from the concrete person to the institution and is objectified as 'charisma of office'.[36] This shift is, among other things,

---

30  1 Corinthians, 12–13.
31  Machiavelli 2005, pp. 76–9.
32  Machiavelli 1970, pp. 430–2.
33  Marx and Engels 1975–2005, vol. 11, p. 85.
34  Lenin 1960–78g, vol. 26, pp. 59ff.
35  Weber 1978, p. 245.
36  Weber 1978, p. 248.

the precondition for the church constituting itself as an 'institution', such that '[w]hoever works miracles on his own, without an office, is suspect as a heretic or magician'.[37] Thus, if one follows the line of development traced by Weber, that of Western rationalisation, there arises the problem of how charismatic leadership is to take shape in such a 'disenchanted world'.

## 14.2   Plebiscitary Charisma as Correlate of the Party Machine

In *Economy and Society*'s typology of domination, Weber defines 'plebiscitary rule' as the most important 'transitional type' between charismatic authority's authoritarian principle of legitimation and its redefinition in an 'anti-authoritarian' or 'democratic direction', according to which the community is the source of legitimacy.[38] It exists wherever 'the chief feels himself to be acting on behalf of the masses and is indeed recognized by them'.[39] Thus primary charisma, of which Weber has mainly retained its absolute, personalised verticalism, enters into a sort of compromise with the conditions of democratic legitimacy. Why and under what social conditions there persists a need for charismatic leadership is not a question that is discussed in this definition.

When, however, Weber sets out to formulate a party-sociological account of plebiscitary rule, a different picture emerges. In *Parliament and Government* and in *Politics as a Vocation*, he does not trace plebiscitary rule back to charismatic authority; on the contrary, he traces it back to a process of progressive bureaucratisation that is now—and this is due mainly to Weber's study of Ostrogorsky—shown to operate within the party system itself:[40] the old party of notables, which was led, on the local level, and on a voluntary basis, by the groups of intellectuals present in a given locality, while on the supralocal level, it cohered and was represented by its parliamentary faction, is overcome by means of a 'rationalisation of party activities'.[41] This rationalised party organisation consists first, in an extension of the party apparatus and its body of functionaries, and second, in the emergence of the 'professional politician', who obtains the trust of the masses 'by mass-demagogical means'.[42]

---

37   Weber 1978, p. 1165.
38   Weber 1978, pp. 266–7.
39   Weber 1978, p. 267.
40   Ostrogorsky 1903 a/b.
41   Weber 1984–2009, vol. I/15, p. 528; Weber 1994c, p. 211; Weber 1988a, p. 384.
42   Weber 1984–2009, vol. I/15, p. 539; Weber 1994c, p. 220.

Weber calls this a 'Caesarist turn within leader selection'.[43] Its hallmark is the plebiscite, meaning not a regular ballot or election but 'a profession of "faith" in the vocation as leader of the one who lays a claim to such acclamation',[44] or 'recognition of a pretender as a personally qualified, charismatic ruler'.[45] The plebiscitary charisma that presented itself, in the definition developed in the context of the sociology of domination, as an 'anti-authoritarian' redefinition of primary charisma, now turns out to be an element and a corollary of bureaucratic apparatuses of power.

The only thing this modern 'charisma' has in common with the original concept of a charismatic authority that functions without a constitution or rigid administrative apparatus is the word itself. Instead of operating at the opposite pole of traditional and bureaucratic authority, as a 'revolutionary' force for internal transformation,[46] it now correlates with the plebiscitary party 'machine' whose advance Weber notes in England and America, but also in Germany, where he agrees with Robert Michels in identifying it mainly with the Social Democratic Party.[47]

Where Weber attempts to describe the correlation between such plebiscitary 'charisma' and bureaucratisation, his account vacillates between two different explanatory approaches: on the one hand, the professional politician, and with him the plebiscitary leader, are inevitable products of the rationalisation of party work,[48] and the driving force behind this is the political 'corporation of interested parties [*Interessentenbetrieb*]',[49] particularly of the circles interested in local politics (the source of the greatest 'economic opportunities').[50] In England after about 1868, winning over the masses required one to create a large apparatus of apparently democratic associations while bureaucratising the party and concentrating power in the hand of a single leader:[51] 'The creation of such a party machine signifies ... the advent of plebiscitary democracy'.[52] It is also involved in the production of charisma itself. Not only does the American 'boss' of the party machine, whom Weber

---

43   Weber 1984–2009, vol. I/15, p. 539; Weber 1994c, pp. 220–1 (translation modified).
44   Weber 1984–2009, vol. I/15, p. 539; Weber 1994c, p. 221.
45   Weber 1978, p. 1126.
46   Weber 1978, p. 245.
47   According to Mommsen, Weber directed Michels's attention to James Bryce's and Maurice Ostrogorsky's studies of the American party system. See Mommsen 1988b, p. 202.
48   Weber 1984–2009, vol. I/15, p. 533; Weber 1994c, pp. 215–16.
49   Weber 1984–2009, vol. I/15, p. 547; Weber 1994c, p. 228 (translation modified).
50   Weber 2008a, p. 184.
51   Ibid.
52   Weber 2008a, p. 204.

describes as a 'capitalist entrepreneur of politics', devoid of basic political convictions, suggest to the party's electoral candidates 'what they would be well
advised to say'—'he himself remains silent'; he also organises, if necessary, the
candidacy of persons outside the party, and even of known critics of corruption, to the extent that he expects this to lead to electoral success.[53]

On the other hand, it is the plebiscitary leader who prompts or at least promotes the bureaucratisation of political parties. The fact that in America, the
party of notables transformed into a bureaucratic apparatus relatively early
(from about 1824 onward) is accounted for by Weber in terms of the strong
'president, elected by plebiscite', who was almost entirely independent of parliament, and because of whom all party activities were oriented to presidential elections. His position as boss of the party patronage leads to a situation
in which the competing parties are all devoid of convictions; they are simply
'parties for position hunters'.[54] In England, it was the firm faith of the masses
in the 'ethical character' of the politics and personality of the great dema-
gogue Gladstone that helped the party 'machine' triumph over the notables.[55]
What was decisive for the 'Caesarist, plebiscitary element', in this case, was the
'power of the demagogic speech'.[56]

What Weber is primarily interested in is how the plebiscitary leader, whom
he has hitherto described both as an effect of and as the driving force behind the
bureaucratisation of political parties, subordinates the party apparatus to himself. In Gladstone's case, the 'power of the demagogic speech' was so effective
that the party cliques (the caucus) oriented themselves 'completely ... toward
the charisma of the person' and submitted to their leader.[57] The parliamentarians function only as 'well-disciplined voting fodder', and above them arises
the 'de facto plebiscitary dictator, who gets the masses behind him by means
of the "machine"'.[58] Weber considers this development prototypical, and it is
on it that he bases his expectation that the bureaucratisation of political parties and electoral affairs could, thanks to the significance of emotional mass

---

53   Weber 2008a, p. 215ff. 'To be sure, the bosses will oppose an outsider who might pose a
     threat to their sources of money and power' (Weber 1984–2009, vol. I/17, p. 217; Weber
     1988a, p. 540). On the figure of the 'boss' as an 'incarnation of the machine', compare
     Ostrogorsky 1903b, pp. 375ff.

54   Weber 2008a, pp. 212–13.

55   Weber 2008a, p. 209.

56   Weber 2008a, p. 211.

57   Ibid.

58   Ibid.

impact, 'be forced into the service of charismatic hero worship' just when it reaches its apex.[59]

It is characteristic of the circular structure of Weber's sociology of domination that he can imagine an escape from the iron cage of bureaucracy only through the action of a plebiscitary leader who requires bureaucracy and perpetually creates it anew. For in essence, all that Weber has described by means of his explanatory approaches are the two poles of an ideological functional complex, poles that are linked to one another—in the normal case—by a dialectical interrelationship. The party apparatuses that woo the masses for support require not just a 'beyond' of universally acknowledged ideological values to which they demonstratively subordinate their policies; they also require suitable persons who embody those values in a credible and rousing manner. Considered in terms of the theory of ideology, charisma is not 'the value-instituting force as such', as Schluchter's interpretation of Weber would have it,[60] but the exemplary personification of ideological values. Following Freud, one can interpret the efficacy of charismatic leadership as a symptom that relevant ego ideals have been successfully addressed and focused on suitable persons.[61] The selection of the candidate by the 'boss' of the party apparatus that Weber refers to is only the comparatively harmless precursor of an increasingly industrialised production of charisma by employed psychologists and publicity experts.

On the other hand and in the long run, the charismatic bearers of values must be more than merely the puppets of party-political cliques; if they are to retain their credibility, they must make sure the party apparatus implements their decisions, rather than hiving itself off from them. This 'primacy' of politics vis-à-vis the apparatus must be aspired to by all political leadership, regardless of how democratically or undemocratically it came about. And like every ideological power, parties must seek to create at least a semblance of coherence between the interests of the apparatus and the values invoked. When they fail to do this and the contradictions become glaringly evident, hostile parties or popular charismatic movements may succeed in mobilising the values against the apparatus, thereby effectively undermining its hegemony.

---

59    Weber 1978, p. 1130.

60    Schluchter 1991, p. 143.

61    In such persons, 'the object serves as a substitute for some unattained ego ideal of our own. We love it on account of the perfections which we have striven to reach for our own ego, and which we should now like to procure in this roundabout way as a means of satisfying our narcissism', Freud writes in *Group Psychology and the Analysis of the Ego* (Freud 1949, p. 74).

To criticise Weber's concept of the plebiscitary leader for its 'personal-ist' thrust is nothing new; it is a commonplace of a sociology influenced by Parsons and Luhmann that has enacted the 'shift from the primacy of action theory to that of systems theory'.[62] The criticism is however frequently formu-lated in such a way as to render invisible the underlying verticalism of Weber's sociology of authority. By making the 'free' person the source of change and the decisive counterbalance of a bureaucratic system that became increasingly autonomous, Weber furthered 'a certain personalist and decisionist narrowing of the way political goals are defined', writes Schluchter, for example, invok-ing the critiques of Weber formulated by Luhmann and Ferber.[63] Following Habermas, one could trace this personalist reductionism back to the fact that Weber's model of action is still backed by an 'intentionalist', 'teleological' and 'monologically construed' theory of consciousness, one that does not recon-struct subjective meaning from linguistic interaction, in the manner of a the-ory of communication, but rather associates it with the 'beliefs and intentions of an acting subject, taken to begin with in isolation'.[64] While Marx attempted, in his writings on Bonapartism, to dissolve the 'charismatic' one-man rule of Napoleon III into its social conditions of existence, Weber reproduces the Bonapartist ideology that explains its 'charisma' by reference to the personal qualities of its leader. This is why Marcuse is able to consider the concept of charisma one of the most questionable of all of Weber's concepts; it 'gives every kind of successful, allegedly personal domination an almost religious consecration'.[65]

Weber's concept of 'plebiscitary rule' constitutes the opposite pole of Gramsci's concept of *political leadership*, notwithstanding the fact that Gramsci was able, in many of his analyses of 'passive revolution', to build upon Weber's critique of Bismarckian Caesarism. To begin with, Gramsci distinguishes political 'leadership' [*direzione*] from 'domination' [*dominazi-one*], linking it to the concept of 'hegemony' and relating it to the relation-ship between allied classes.[66] Furthermore, he discusses political leadership with an eye to its reabsorption into civil society and the achievement of hegemony by the subaltern. Like Weber, he does not invoke abstract postu-lates of equality, but takes differences in skill and actually-existing leadership

---

62    Habermas 1987a, p. 235.
63    Schluchter 1980, pp. 125, 130–1, note 233.
64    Habermas 1984, p. 279.
65    Marcuse 1969, p. 217.
66    Gramsci 1992, pp. 136–7.

functions into account.[67] What seems important to him, for example, is the formation, within the party, of an extensive 'middle stratum' between 'the leaders and the masses' that can 'prevent the leaders from deviating during periods of deep crisis'.[68] The most powerful counterforce against bureaucratisation is the party's 'organic' relationship to its followers. The philosophy of praxis is concerned with a 'moral and intellectual bloc that renders possible the intellectual progress of the masses'.[69] The formation of a 'historic bloc' requires, among other things, passion between intellectuals and the people; without such passion, the relationship between the two becomes bureaucratic.[70] A leader who accomplishes a 'constructive "constituent" task' attempts to 'foster potential "rivals" and peers, to elevate the capabilities of the masses, to produce individuals who can replace him as leader'.[71] By contrast, a charismatic leader 'posits himself as irreplaceable, he creates a desert around himself, he systematically crushes and eliminates potential rivals'.[72] His authority 'cannot be long lasting' and is 'not typical of the founding of new states or new national and social structures'.[73]

While Gramsci analyses charismatic leadership as an underdeveloped special case of political leadership, Weber proceeds in the opposite direction and works general issues of political leadership into the verticalist structure of his concept of charisma. 'It is not the politically passive "mass" that gives birth to the leader, but rather the political leader who recruits his entourage and wins the masses by means of "demagogy"'.[74] It is only the political leader's direct wooing of followers that renders 'the particular structure of responsibility associated with politics visible in an unadulterated form', preventing 'spontaneous, "idealist" politics from being reined in by the power of the politics of benefit', Schluchter summarises.[75] Here, everything that links the leadership to the followers 'organically' in Gramsci, from the critical labour of developing

---

67    On the one hand, the existence of leaders and followers, rulers and subjects remains a fact; on the other hand, it makes a decisive difference to the emergence of leaders whether one believes the division between rulers and subjects is eternal or whether one strives to create conditions 'under which this division ceases to be necessary' (Gramsci 1975c, p. 1752).

68    Gramsci 1992, p. 324.

69    Gramsci 1975b, pp. 1384–5.

70    Gramsci 1975b, pp. 1505–6.

71    Gramsci 2007, p. 83.

72    Ibid.

73    Gramsci 2007, p. 247.

74    Weber 1984–2009, vol. I/15, p. 547; Weber 1994c, p. 228; Weber 1988a, p. 401.

75    Schluchter 1980, p. 112.

a coherent everyday consciousness to 'co-sentiment',[76] becomes unthinkable. In part, 'political leadership' is reduced to mere manipulation—to the 'purely emotional' demagogic speech, whose content is secondary.[77] At the same time, political leadership is reabsorbed into the domain of domination, from which Gramsci sought to distinguish it. The production of political coherence within a political party is only conceivable in terms of the commands of the leader, which transform the party into an implementing 'machine', and the primacy of politics vis-à-vis the apparatus is conceivable only in terms of the 'blind obedience', 'soullessness' and 'intellectual proletarianisation' of the followers.[78] There is no possibility of reabsorbing hypostasised leadership competencies back into society, neither in the case of bureaucratisation, which is inevitable, nor in that of bureaucratisation being trumped by charisma.[79] The 'iron cage' that is so sombrely predicted is not to be dismantled at all; it merely needs to be crowned with a strong leader.

In conclusion, I want to consider the way the theoretical concepts of charisma and plebiscitary rule 'touch down' on the concrete level of political demands and programmes. What needs to be accounted for, among other things, is the shift from a parliamentarian to an extra-parliamentarian selection of leaders that Mommsen identifies with the period 'after 1918'.[80]

### 14.3 From the Parliamentary Selection of Leaders to 'Plebiscitary Leader Democracy'

During the November Revolution, Weber briefly has the opportunity to implement his political concepts for Germany's reorganisation in the form of provisions written into a new constitution. In November 1918, President Friedrich Ebert briefly considered making Weber, and not the professor of constitutional law Hugo Preuß, state secretary of the interior, a project he presumably dropped due to Weber's public polemics against the 'Council of People's Delegates' that

---

76  See Gramsci 1975b, pp. 1375ff, 1428–31.

77  Weber 1978, p. 1130.

78  Weber 1984–2009, vol. I/17, pp. 223–4; Weber 1988a, p. 544.

79  Merquior, among others, has noted that Weber's typology of legitimate authority is formulated 'entirely from the perspective of the rulers' (Merquior 1988, p. 251). According to Hennis, Weber's sociology 'is not a theory of society guided by the ideas of freedom and equality, but rather a theory of "complexes of domination" in the Nietzschean sense' (Hennis 1987, p. 218).

80  Mommsen 1974, p. 448.

emerged from the November Revolution and his uncompromising hostility to the representatives of the more left-wing Independent Social-Democratic Party of Germany [*Unabhängige Sozialdemokratische Partei Deutschlands*, USPD], which split from the SPD in 1917, but was now its coalition partner.[81] Preuß, who was subsequently charged with preparing a draft constitution, consulted Weber on the basic features of the Weimar constitution in December 1918. The debates on the draft constitution were concluded within three days (9–12 December). Weber had expected to be elected into parliament as a candidate of the German Democratic Party [*Deutsche Demokratische Partei*, DDP], where he would then have been able to participate in the further consultations on the constitution along with Preuß. But his candidacy turned out to be a failure, because he was unable to obtain a promising place on the DDP's list of candidates for Hesse-Nassau.[82] There is a consensus that Weber's concept of the plebiscitary leader influenced the constitution's provisions on the status of the Reich president. Max von Baden even attributes to Weber the 'great political achievement' of having ensured, against the admirers of the French political system, that the president of the Reich is elected not by the Reichstag, but by the people.[83] By contrast, Mommsen has indicated several currents within bourgeois constitutional theory that intersect with Weber's concept of the plebiscitary leader and amount to replacing constitutional monarchy with a sort of 'constitutional democracy'.[84] Moreover, Weber's demands regarding the status of the Reich president went far beyond the Weimar constitution. Weber called for the president to be equipped with his own set of officials, exempt from the powers of the chancellor; the president would then have been able to intervene in the Reich machine directly, by means of referendums, i.e. without the chancellor's signature.[85] On the other hand, Mommsen's suggestion that Weber failed because Preuß was more eager to compromise is rendered questionable by the fact that Weber explicitly welcomed Preuß's

---

81    See the minutes of the meeting of the Council of People's Delegates held on 15 November
        1918 (Mommsen 1974, p. 324). 'This government will never need me and I shall never serve
        it', Weber writes in a letter dated 29 November 1918. 'Herr Haase and company, in contrast
        to the trade unionists and Ebert, need only flatterers, flunkies, and people without char-
        acter, just as the princes do. The talkers and screamers are on top, and so is hate' (quoted
        in Marianne Weber 1975, p. 635).

82    See the editor's remarks in Weber 1984–2009, vol. I/16, pp. 152ff.

83    Von Baden 1927, p. 128.

84    Mommsen 1974, pp. 372ff, 377–8.

85    See Mommsen 1974, pp. 365, 392, 394, 404.

'smart' conduct of the negotiations and described the final constitutional draft as '*very* similar' to his own proposals.[86]

The contradiction between Weber's 'failure' and his 'success' could be resolved by assuming a division of labour that was at least implicit, and by which Weber, with his maximalist positions, allowed Preuß to make the representatives of the SPD agree to a 'compromise' that was a far cry from their own models. In fact, Weber consistently pursues a strategy of assuming the most extreme contrary position with regard to the standpoints of Social Democracy. While the SPD representatives Quarck and Herzfeld called for a 'unitary' constitution that placed all decisive competencies in the hands of the parliament, the Reichstag, with the federal representative of the states, the Reichsrat, being granted no more than an advisory function, Weber advocated a far-reaching federalism, pointing out that the 'old well-trained bureaucracies' were already functioning again in the single states.[87] When it is a question of defeating the revolution, the bureaucracy otherwise described in such apocalyptic terms becomes an indispensable buttress. The unitary counterbalance to the federalist representation of the states was to be provided not by the Reichstag or a Reich president dependent on the Reichstag, but by an independent leader who would be in a position, as head of the executive, to genuinely 'rule'.[88] The opposite position was that of the USPD representatives, who rejected the office of the Reich president altogether, whereas the SPD representatives were more inclined to replicate the Swiss model, by which the president would be elected by the Reichstag and the Reichsrat, 'so as not to create the possibility of a Bonapartist plebiscitary politics'.[89]

Given this constellation, Weber attempts to provide a 'socialist' justification of his concept of the plebiscitary leader. In order to win over the SPD, he argues that the socialisation it aims for can only be realised under a strong Reich president.[90] And yet he himself is opposed to socialisation on principle, for

---

86  Mommsen 1974, pp. 379, 391–2. Following the conclusion of the negotiations on the draft constitution, Weber wrote the following to Marianne Weber in a letter dated 13 December 1918: 'Preuss is doing his job very well; he is a very smart man ... [T]he Reich constitution is ready in principle, and it is *very* similar to my proposals' (quoted in Marianne Weber 1975, pp. 639–40).

87  While the Reich's authority was severely weakened, the authorities of the single states had already regained a firm footing and a 'firm grasp of the old, well-trained bureaucracies'—thus Mommsen's summary of the rationale offered by Weber (Mommsen 1974, p. 382).

88  Quoted in Marianne Weber 1975, p. 399.

89  Quoted in Marianne Weber 1975, p. 408.

90  See for example Weber 1984–2009, vol. I/16, pp. 128, 220; Weber 1988a, pp. 469, 498.

which reason he will leave the DDP in 1920, when it intended to make him a member of the commission on socialisation. As if to illustrate the charismatic 'power of demagogic speech', Weber's discursive strategy is characterised by a demagogic structure. The SPD, he says, ought to consider 'that the much discussed "dictatorship" of the masses calls for a "dictator", a self-elected ombudsman of the masses, to whom they subordinate themselves for as long as he enjoys their trust'.[91] While he appeals to a state-socialist Bonapartism when addressing the SPD, his constitutional proposals are supported, from the outset, not just by the DDP but also by the anti-parliamentarian right-wing parties who believe a plebiscitary president will protect them from the expected socialist majority in the Reichstag.[92] When parliament and 'party rule' turn out, during the late 1920s, to be bourgeois hegemony's weakest link, the parties of the right-wing 'Harzburg Front', i.e. the national-conservative German National People's Party [Deutschnationale Volkspartei, DNVP] and Hitler's NSDAP, will reactivate this animosity and mobilise it against the parliamentary institutions of the Weimar Republic.

We need now to consider how the relationship between parliament and plebiscite undergoes a shift within Weber's own thinking, so that his approach can then be used in such a reactionary and anti-parliamentarian way. We take as our starting point, for now, the fact that in 'Parliament and Government' in 1917 and 1918, Weber juxtaposed to the parliamentarian selection of leaders a 'plebiscitary' one, also associated, in his view, with democracy: since Pericles, democracy has 'always purchased its positive achievements through major concessions to the Caesarist principle of leader selection', and whenever a parliamentary democracy attempts to eliminate plebiscitary methods of leadership, it pays for this attempt 'with the kind of lack of authority of the highest powers that is typical of France and contrasts so characteristically with the powerful position of the American president'.[93] The negative example German parliamentarisation is set off against is that of the French republic, which had largely renounced plebiscitary elements, in part because of its negative experiences with Bonapartism.[94] What is decisive in Weber's comparison of the efficacy of the two models is that the 'highest powers' be considered 'authorities' by the masses. Even during the period when Weber seeks to strengthen parliament, because he conceives of it as the point where bureaucratic rule and its

---

91   Weber 1984–2009, vol. I/15, p. 221; Weber 1988a, p. 499.

92   See Mommsen 1974, pp. 372, 399, 401.

93   Weber 1984–2009, vol. I/15, pp. 539–40; Weber 1994c, p. 221.

94   'Weber rejects, not without a nationalistic bias, the system of the Third Republic', Mayer remarks (Mayer 1956, p. 100).

subjects meet, there is already a suggestion that it could one day lose its status as a decisive instance within ideological reproduction.

And so the opposition between the authority of civil servants and parliament's (still superior) selection of leaders is supplemented by a second opposition, between a 'plebiscitary leadership' that can rely on the 'devotion and trust which [the leader's; J.R.] political followers have in him personally' and a 'leaderless democracy' that is 'characterized by the attempt to minimize the domination of man over man' and can only operate in relatively small, poorly differentiated social bodies.[95] Prior to the outbreak of the November Revolution, the two oppositions still balance one another. For plebiscitary leadership democracy is 'democratic' insofar as it provides and underwrites bourgeois legal guarantees through its parliament while simultaneously ensuring that the 'Caesarist ombudsmen of the masses adhere to the fixed legal norms of the state and are not selected in a purely emotional manner'.[96] But to the extent that demands for parliamentarisation are implemented, the second opposition begins to prevail. In December of 1918, Weber states, in the prefatory remark to his article 'Germany's Future State Form', that his series of articles on 'Parliament and Government' is outdated, and cites as one reason that it 'could recognise our future condition only in parliamentarisation'.[97] Strictly speaking, the claim is false; it was precisely in 'Parliament and Government' that Weber developed the model of an equilibrium between the plebiscitary and the parliamentary principle. What was in fact 'outdated' was precisely this model of equilibrium from 1917/18. All that had remained from the envisioned permanent control of the Caesarist leader by parliament was the possibility for a qualified Reichstag majority to request a referendum on the president's dismissal.[98]

In *Politics as a Vocation*, Weber sees only 'the choice between leadership democracy with a "machine", or leaderless democracy. That means: rule by "professional politicians" with no vocation, without the inward, charismatic qualities that go to make the leader. And that in turn means having what the rebel faction within the party usually calls the rule of the "clique"'.[99] This dichotomy marks a clear shift in the coordinates of Weber's political analysis. The absence of charismatic qualities and the economy of the 'clique', associated, in the first dichotomy, with the authority of civil servants, against which Weber was

95    Weber 1978, pp. 268–9, 289–94, 979.
96    Weber 1984–2009, vol. I/15, pp. 540, 549; Weber 1994c, pp. 222, 229–30.
97    Weber 1984–2009, vol. I/16, p. 98; Weber 1988a, p. 448.
98    Weber 1984–2009, vol. I/15, p. 129; Weber 1988a, p. 470.
99    Weber 2008, p. 191.

able to present the selection of leaders in parliamentary 'struggle' as superior, now become traits of the parliamentarians themselves. The parliaments have also fallen into disrepute, Weber claims in late 1918, during the negotiations on the draft constitution.[100] In the authoritarian state, one needed to advocate an extension of the parliament's powers, but now, Weber claims in February of 1919, it is a matter of combating the 'blind charburner's faith' in the omnipotence and infallibility of the parliamentary majority.[101] The religious attributes—'faith' in 'omnipotence' and 'infallibility'—are demagogic articulations intended to discredit the constitutional demand for parliamentary control of the executive. Weber justifies this transition to an anti-parliamentary position by claiming that the 'professional associations' are taking the selection of party candidates into their own hands and transforming parliament into a body of 'philistines' to whom 'national politics is "Hecuba"', and who are instead acting in accordance with an '"imperative" mandate issued by economic stakeholders'.[102] In doing so, he has intensified his opposition between 'leaderless' and 'leader democracy' by supplementing it with an opposition between corporatist interests and a value-oriented 'national' politics. One could say that Weber confirms the claim, usually considered 'vulgar Marxist', that politics is determined by the economy, and that he reframes it in such a way as to ensure it is directed solely against parliament. To an extent, this prefigures his later hostility towards the 'failure' of parliament and party rule. The 'powerless abandonment to cliques' is now contrasted with 'real democracy', which Weber defines as 'subordination to self-elected leaders'.[103]

This is the definition by which he attempts, in May 1919, to win Ludendorff over to 'democracy'. During the talk, which lasted several hours,[104] Ludendorff accused Weber of being to blame for the new democracy, along with the *Frankfurter Zeitung*. 'Do you think I consider the mess we have now a *democracy?*', Weber replied—not, it should be noted, during the turmoil of the revolution, but after the election of the national assembly and the institution of the Reich government and the (provisional) Reich president, Ebert. Asked by

---

100   Quoted in Mommsen 1974, p. 391.

101   Weber 1984–2009, vol. I/16, p. 223; Weber 1988a, p. 500.

102   Weber 1984–2009, vol. I/16, p. 222; Weber 1988a, pp. 499–500.

103   Weber 1984–2009, vol. I/16, p. 224; Weber 1988a, p. 501.

104   The dialogue was reconstructed by 'friends', on the basis of Weber's anecdotes, according to Marianne Weber, who documents parts of the conversation (Marianne Weber 1975, p. 652). By his visit, Weber tried in vain to convince Ludendorff to hand himself over to the victorious powers—for the sake of the 'honor of the nation'. Ludendorff's reply was: 'The nation can go jump in the lake!' (ibid; see also Weber 1984–2009, vol. I/16, pp. 553, and the editor's remarks, pp. 545ff).

Ludendorff to explain his notion of democracy, Weber replied: 'In a democracy the people choose a leader whom they trust. Then the chosen man says, "Now shut your mouths and obey me". The people and the parties are no longer free to interfere in the leader's business'. Ludendorff replied: 'I could like such a "democracy"!' And Weber added: 'Later the people can sit in judgment. If the leader has made mistakes—to the gallows with him!'[105]

At the very least, the dialogue with Ludendorff marks a potential point of contact between Weber's 'plebiscitary leader democracy' and the anti-parliamentary articulations of a fascist movement that Ludendorff would adhere to early on.[106] Of course, one also needs to take into account Weber's 'demagogic' ability to speak in the language of the enemy.[107] Nor is it a matter of opposing to the common tendency to situate Weber within the democratic tradition an equally linear association of him with the ideology of fascism. For on the one hand, Weber's concept of 'plebiscitary leader democracy' is formulated in a deliberately polysemous way and can just as well be associated with the American or Gaullist presidential system, as is common in the literature on Weber, and on the other hand, Weber's social project of integrating the working class via its 'voluntarist' organisations remains something fundamentally different from the fascist destruction of the organised labour movement as a whole. And yet the oppositions are not fixed once and for all here either, for in the case of such an integration failing, as it seemed to have done to a large part of the bourgeoisie towards the end of the Weimar Republic, positions were likely to shift in favour of genuinely fascist solutions.

What is in question here is the explanatory value of associations and distinctions that are based on the history of ideas and abstract from underlying conceptions of the 'historic bloc'. Attempts to prove Weber's distance from fascism by reference to the counterbalance of a parliamentary principle of legitimation are not as perspicacious as is claimed. To Nolte, the 'European synthesis' represented by Weber ends, and 'pre-fascism' begins, only at the point 'where it is no longer the distribution of powers that is at issue, but where a principled turn against parliament is enacted'.[108] There remains the problem of what exactly constitutes such a 'principled turn'. After all, for

---

105   Quoted in Marianne Weber 1975, p. 653; Weber 1984–2009, vol. I/16, p. 553.

106   After 1918, he participated in the German *völkisch* movement; in 1923, he participated in Hitler's putsch; in 1925, he was the NSDAP's presidential candidate.

107   That Weber perceived Ludendorff as an enemy after this conversation, at the latest, emerges from his conclusion: 'If he should again meddle with politics, he must be fought remorselessly' (quoted in Marianne Weber 1975, p. 654).

108   Nolte 1963, p. 11.

Weber, parliament went, within a very brief time span,[109] from being the site of an effective selection of leaders to being the place where large-scale, 'national' politics is sacrificed to immediate corporatist interests. And at the same time, the position of power initially intended for parliament, one that would allow it to insert the president of the Reich in the 'fixed legal norms of the state', has underhandedly transformed into the subsequent function of 'overthrowing him as soon as his charisma fails'.[110] Thus the 'authoritarian reinterpretation' that Mommsen sees at work mainly in Carl Schmitt's adoption and development of Weber's 'leader democracy' is already evident, in a rudimentary form, in Weber's own work.[111]

Mommsen accounts for the return of Caesar in Weber's work by reference to the fact that the figure of Bismarck, criticised by Weber, still 'retained a secret power over his political thought': 'From 1917 onward, Weber propagated precisely what he had criticised Bismarck for'; Mommsen also speaks of Weber's adoption of an 'aristocratic individualism ... in which liberal notions blend with the Nietzschean idea of the value-instituting personality'.[112] But such explanations vacillate, in a speculative manner, between psychologisation and categorisation in terms of the history of ideas, unless they are combined with a socio-historical explanation of the structural need for a Caesar that Weber, the 'organic' collective intellectual of the modern bourgeoisie, was able to trace in a more empathetic and reflected manner than other ideologues of bourgeois authority. 'We have chosen the bourgeois Max Weber as a mirror of Germany's socio-economic and cultural developments ... not because he was a typical bourgeois, but because his analytic and reflective powers were such that in him one could focus the complicated and diversified threads which form the "German problem"', J.P. Mayer remarks.[113] It is as if Weber unwittingly confirmed Engels's claim that Bonapartism is the 'true religion of the modern bourgeoisie'.[114] As will be shown by reference to the example of Werner Sombart, one of Weber's most important political and socio-scientific companions, even the most 'modern' models of a negotiated integration of the working class were susceptible to conversion into the fascist project of the

---

109 Namely about one year, if one takes the final draft of the brochure on parliament (January 1918) as the starting point and the publication of the article 'The President of the Reich' (25 February 1919) as the endpoint.

110 Mommsen 1974, p. 369.

111 Mommsen 1974, pp. 436–7.

112 Mommsen 1974, pp. 202–3, 448, 451.

113 J.P. Mayer 1956, p. 119.

114 Marx and Engels 1975–2005, vol. 42, p. 266.

'people's community' [*Volksgemeinschaft*] as soon as the hegemonic relations changed (see below Chapter 27.5). What needs in any case to be grasped is the uncanny dialectic by which the very Weber who expressed, prior to 1918/19, the bourgeoisie's need for a parliamentary 'Caesarism without a Caesar', went on to articulate, during and after the November Revolution, the bourgeoisie's need for a 'Caesarism with a Caesar' and a 'machine' subordinated to that Caesar, a model that would go on to find a highly effective and terrifying 'German form' in the NSDAP. Weber's political analyses are themselves a symptom and the seismograph of catch-up Fordism's contradictory conditions of reproduction. Such Fordism vacillates between the flexible strategies of integration associated with modern transformism and the temptation to despotically 'resolve' class antagonism by annihilating the organisations of the labour movement.

# PART 3

# From the Neo-Kantian Philosophy of Values to the Weberian 'Theory of Science'

∵

# CHAPTER 15

# Formulating the Question in Terms of a Critical Theory of Ideology

## 15.1    A New Scientific Beginning on a Neo-Kantian Foundation

After years of being unable to work, Weber seems to fall back into step around 1903/04. It is as if he is now able to overcome the paralysis resulting from his depressive nervous disorder by writing in fits and starts and on the most varied subjects.[1] Having completed his work on Roscher and Knies, a methodological engagement with the 'older' historical school, in 1903,[2] he succeeds in writing, 'within a period of nine months in 1904 three major essays in completely different fields',[3] namely the epistemological essay on the 'Objectivity of Knowledge in Social Science and Social Welfare',[4] his engagement with the Prussian entailed estate and the first part of the *Protestant Ethic*, which will be published in 1904. 'Weber's regained productivity was constantly channelled into several streams that flowed along side by side', Marianne Weber reports.[5]

If one compares the works Weber wrote before and after his 1897/98 breakdown, one will not find any fundamental revisions on the level of political statements. To be sure, the political lines of division shift, as can be seen in the progressive redefinition of the main opponent not as right wing but as left wing and in the return of the charismatic leader. But this is primarily related to the changing constellations into which Weber intervenes; it does not modify his social project as such. What is astounding, rather, is the continuity with which he pursues and develops his critique of the bourgeois-feudal class compromise and his own modernisation project of a bloc comprising the bourgeoisie and the labour aristocracy. That Weber radicalises his critique of the state in

---

1 Marianne Weber reports the symptoms of the nervous disorder, which was kept a secret: 'These hours of sitting and *Stumpfen* [apathizing], as he calls it, just picking at his fingernails, always make me quite sad ... These men with a specialized education are completely at sea when their minds break down. If he could at least be sent to the kitchen!' (Marianne Weber 1975, p. 238).
2 Weber 1975; Weber 1988d, pp. 1–145.
3 Marianne Weber 1975, p. 279.
4 Weber 1988d, pp. 146ff.
5 Marianne Weber 1975, p. 326.

the course of his engagement with the 'Katheder socialist' milieu can already be gleaned from his 1893/94 essays on agricultural policy. By the same token, the nationalist 'brutalities' of his 1894 Freiburg inaugural address do not simply disappear after 1903; they recur whenever this seems opportune—witness his political statements on the First World War,[6] or the December 1918, 'post-revolutionary' appeal to his students to 'silently see to it that the first Polish official who dares to enter Danzig is hit by a bullet'.[7] The biographical rupture does not affect his political statements.[8]

What is new, however, is Weber's methodological distinction between socio-scientific work and 'ethical' or 'political' judgements. Following the dissolution of Naumann's National Social Party in the summer of 1903, Weber decides to turn his back on party politics and become, along with Edgar Jaffé and Werner Sombart, one of the editors of the journal *Archiv für Sozialwissenschaft und Sozialpolitik*. The 'essay on objectivity', which can be considered the journal's founding document, also constitutes the methodologically thought-out transition to a sociological 'science of reality' [*Wirklichkeitswissenschaft*] that conceives of itself as 'free of value judgements'.[9]

One important factor in this scholarly new beginning was the 1902 publication of the book *The Limits of Concept Formation in Natural Science* by Heinrich Rickert (1863–1936), the successor of Windelband and systematiser of the 'southwestern German school' of neo-Kantianism. Rickert's concept of a historical science that is at once 'value-oriented' and 'free of value judgements' helps Weber to frame his projected studies within a major philosophical

---

6  'For *regardless* of its outcome—this war is great and wonderful', he writes in a letter dated 28 August 1914 (quoted in Mommsen 1974, p. 206; compare Marianne Weber 1975, pp. 518–19). And in 1917/18, he argues, in his settling of accounts with Wilhelmine foreign policy, that instead of formulating annexation plans, one ought to have told soldiers the 'truth', namely 'that Germany continues to fight for its life against an army in which negroes, ghurkas and all sorts of other barbarians from every nook of the earth stand at the border, prepared to turn our country into a desert' (Weber 1984–2009, vol. I/15, p. 259; Weber 1994c, pp. 131–2; Weber 1988a, p. 307). Mommsen identifies a revision in the fact that Weber became, from 1905 onward, the 'advocate of a political settlement' of Prussia's Polish question and demanded extensive cultural autonomy for the Polish minority. To this was added, in 1916, the idea of annexing an internally autonomous Poland to the central powers (Mommsen 1974, pp. 61ff).

7  Quoted in Marianne Weber 1975, p. 631.

8  Mitzmann, who attempts to directly deduce Weber's political views from his Oedipal conflict with his father, limits himself to superficial analogies and therefore necessarily overlooks this discrepancy. See Mitzmann 1970, pp. 23ff; Mitzmann 1988, pp. 139ff. See also the apposite critique in Mommsen 1974, pp. 458ff.

9  Weber 1988d, p. 170.

current's epistemological theory while organising his copious material in a more manageable way. In his preface to the third and fourth editions, devoted to Weber, Rickert retrospectively emphasises the fact that after initial reservations with regard to Windelband and long-standing doubts about Rickert's book project, Weber allowed himself to be convinced 'that my concept of a theoretical value relation adequately characterises the conceptual procedure of scholarly historiography qua individualising human science'.[10] After receiving the last two book chapters from Rickert in the early summer of 1902, Weber himself wrote to his wife: 'I have finished Rickert. He is *very* good; in large part I find in him the thought that I have had myself, though not in logically finished form'.[11] In the course of his engagement with Roscher and Knies, he announces his endorsement of Rickert's 'main views',[12] and in the essay on objectivity, he also states his intention to follow in the footsteps of the work of the 'modern logicians', and in particular of Heinrich Rickert.[13]

The neo-Kantianism that Weber is here seeking to latch on to is the 'strongest force' in the German academic philosophy of the period from 1870 to 1920.[14] Köhnke's study on the *Development and Rise of Neo-Kantianism* [*Entstehung und Aufstieg des Neukantianismus*] distinguishes between an early phase, from the 1850s to the 1870s, during which neo-Kantianism was primarily a 'critical' and 'oppositional' current, and a later phase, during which it developed into a 'positive philosophy that once more boasted its own systems, claims to the absolute validity of its foundations, metaphysics, unassailable apriorism and doctrines of duty and value'.[15] What neo-Kantianism provides philosophy with is, first and foremost, a professional self-conception as the overriding 'instance of judgement and right' that shields the sciences from claims associated with particular worldviews and determines the limits of the sciences' competencies.[16] Bloch characterises neo-Kantianism as the 'altogether dominant current ... at all German universities', one that distorted Kant 'not in a pre-fascist, but in a national liberal manner, to the point that the Enlightenment philosopher ended up looking like a Bismarckian philistine

---

10    Rickert 1929, p. XXIV.

11    Quoted in Marianne Weber 1975, p. 260.

12    Weber 1975, p. 58, note 9. It is here in particular that one encounters Rickert at every turn. See for example Weber 1975, pp. 55, note 2; p. 63, note 22; p. 138, note 22; p. 131, note 25; p. 137, note 30; p. 145, note 39.

13    Weber 1988d, p. 146, note 1.

14    Lübbe 1960, p. 1421.

15    Köhnke 1986, p. 433; compare pp. 16–17.

16    Köhnke 1986, pp. 348–9.

with a parlour'.[17] This characterisation is certainly accurate with regard to a dominant formation within neo-Kantianism, one that includes Windelband and Rickert, but it cannot be extended to, for example, the equally 'neo-Kantian' efforts of F.A. Lange, Cohen, Staudinger and Vorländer to develop an 'ethical', 'idealist' or 'critical' socialism, efforts that influenced the Social Democratic labour movement via their association with Bernstein's 'revisionism'.[18] From the viewpoint of socialism's attainment of hegemony, Gramsci has characterised the relationship between the *philosophy of praxis* and Kantianism as a product and necessary counterbalance to vulgar Marxism, accounting for it in terms of the labour movement's ethico-political need to replace Kautskyan determinism with a socialism of ethical activation.[19]

Thus neo-Kantianism is not a homogeneous, unitary phenomenon but an ensemble of competing currents. While the 'Marburg School' of neo-Kantianism (Cohen, Natorp, Cassirer) makes use mainly of Kant's epistemological categories from the *Critique of Pure Reason*, the southwestern German or Heidelberg School around Windelband, Rickert and Rickert's student Emil Lask looks mainly to Kant's 'practical philosophy', starting from his 'fundamental ethical idea' in order to reintegrate criticism in a philosophy of values. The 'fluttering name of philosophy' can only gain a 'firm footing' if philosophy becomes the 'critical science of universally valid values', writes Windelband in his 1882 lecture 'What is Philosophy?' [*Was ist Philosophie?*].[20] Köhnke traces these value-philosophical aspirations back to an 'idealist turn' within philosophy, which he dates to 1878/79: two attempts on the life of the Kaiser (on 11 May and 2 June 1878) provoked such an anti-socialist 'fervour' within the bourgeoisie that it not only became possible to pass the anti-socialist laws a short time later (in September/October 1878), but, in addition to this, there occurred an

---

17    Bloch 1974, p. 350.

18    See Lübbe 1987; on Lange in particular, see also Köhnke 1986, pp. 233ff. Cohen was also 'one of the fathers of so-called revisionism's social reformist, socio-ethical programme' (Köhnke 1986, p. 300).

19    Gramsci 1975b, pp. 1507–9. To Gramsci, the relationship between the philosophy of praxis and Kantianism is part of the 'ensemble of all those tendencies which refuse to accept the so-called "orthodoxy" of German pedantry' (Gramsci 1975b, p. 1508). According to Gramsci, as soon as a subaltern group becomes autonomous and hegemonic, there arises the concrete exigency of 'constructing a new intellectual and moral order' and developing 'the most universal concepts' (Gramsci 1975b, p. 1509).

20    Windelband 1884, p. 28.

'epochal caesura within the development of philosophy', by virtue of which the reception interests of academic philosophers were abruptly altered.[21]

Volkelt, who describes the changes that occurred in 1882 in an essay on the rediscovery of Kant's ethics, writes that Kant was no longer praised 'one-sidedly' as the author of the *Critique of Pure Reason*; he was now also praised as the 'annunciator of the categorical imperative' and 'creator of an ethically grounded ideal world'. According to Volkelt, one could now no longer understand the 'return to Kant' as a recourse to the epistemological foundation of the system, 'which leads to modesty and scepticism', but rather as a renewed awareness of the lastingly true import of Kant's basic ethical ideas and their 'deployment...for the development of an ethics and metaphysics that of course go far beyond Kant'.[22] It was a matter of using a modified Kantianism to provide ideological socialisation's heightened need for values, expressed in the slogan 'inner founding of the Reich', with an epistemological foundation.[23]

## 15.2 Controversies Surrounding the Relationship between Weber and Rickert

This political need for a philosophically 'secure' foundation of ideological values provides the usually tacit context of the controversies, evident in the scholarly literature, over the extent to which Weber's theory of science should be considered an integral component of the neo-Kantian philosophy of values and the extent to which it has broken with that philosophical foundation. According to Schluchter, who attributes to Rickert an influence on Weber similar to that of Feuerbach on Marx, Rickert's concept of the cultural sciences needs to be seen as having provided the tentatively reconvalescent Weber with 'an intellectual confirmation, or even an intellectual liberation'.[24] The analogy between Feuerbach and Rickert was already drawn by Troeltsch in 1922: Troeltsch argued that while Marxian theory owed its 'grimacing severity' to Feuerbach's reversal of Hegel, Weber obtained his philosophical foundations mainly by latching on to Rickert's logic of history, 'thereby eliminating the

---

21  Köhnke 1986, pp. 410ff, 431. The '"social threat" that appeared to emerge in 1878 turned the "relativist" Windelband into a militant "value scholar" who assertively promoted the interests of the authoritarian Bismarckian state' (Köhnke 1986, p. 427).

22  Quoted in Köhnke 1986, p. 429.

23  See Sauer 1970, pp. 429, 548, note 58.

24  Schluchter 1991, pp. 44–5, 81.

Marxist onus of materialism'.[25] Oakes observes that the southwest German school provided Weber's theory of science not just with key concepts such as that of 'value-relatedness', that of the *'hiatus irrationalis'* between concept and reality or that of the 'historical individual', but also with central lines of argument.[26] According to Oakes, the more than 40 letters that Weber wrote to Rickert between June 1904 and April 1920 show that the two agreed not just on methodological issues, but also with regard to the theory of values: 'The letters make it implausible to suppose that Weber ever gave up his commitment to the neo-Kantian conceptual apparatus of Rickert's thought'.[27] According to Burger, Rickert's theory also provided Weber with the principle by which he selected theoretical elements from other authors.[28] Nusser holds that Weber's approach to the foundations of sociology has also been influenced by Weber's affinity for Rickert's philosophy;[29] Habermas, who speaks of 'Rickert's and Weber's theory of values',[30] takes the view that Weber's concept of Western rationalisation can only be understood within the context of the neo-Kantian philosophy of values.[31] Gerhard Wagner identifies a general consensus, within the literature on Weber, 'that Windelband's and Rickert's southwest German school of neo-Kantianism is to be seen as the source Weber drew on most strongly'.[32]

And yet it is equally undisputed that Weber rejected the neo-Kantian notion of a fixed and generally binding system of values more and more explicitly. After Weber's death, Rickert set about presenting his philosophy of values as concordant with Weber's scholarly approach, but even he had to admit, in the 1921 preface to the third and fourth editions of *The Limits of Concept Formation in Natural Science*, that Weber had always taken a sceptical view of Rickert's

---

25    Troeltsch 1922, pp. 565–6.

26    'Weber's critique of positivism, his method of demarcating the cultural sciences from the natural sciences, his distinction between value relevance and value judgements, and his conception of methodology as a theory of concept formation all appear to be based on arguments that are more fully developed in Rickert's work' (Oakes 1988a, p. 7; compare Oakes 1988b, p. 596).

27    Oakes 1988a, p. 166, note 38. For confirmation of this hypothesis, see Weber's letters to Rickert dated 9 May 1907 and 3 November 1907 (Weber 1984–2009, vol. II/5, pp. 297ff, pp. 414ff).

28    Burger 1976, p. XII; compare p. 8.

29    Nusser 1986, pp. 19–20, 61.

30    Habermas 1987a, p. 226.

31    Habermas 1984, p. 186.

32    Wagner 1987, p. 9.

projected 'doctrine of worldview based on a comprehensive system of values'.[33] Yet how one assesses this difference depends upon the status one attributes to the fixed system of values within the overall ideological configuration of neo-Kantianism's philosophy of values. The distance from Rickert emerges most clearly in the concept of an antagonistic 'clash of values'. This is one of the reference points of another current within the secondary literature, which calls for newly interpreting Weber's central query 'in the light of Nietzsche'.[34] According to this version, Weber only makes use of Rickert's conceptual apparatus in order to pursue an altogether different agenda. The specific question of Nietzsche's influence aside, the claim is supported by the consideration that Weber works not as a philosopher, but as a scholar in the social sciences, who also thinks of himself as a political strategist. Thus when Schluchter draws an analogy between Weber's relationship to Rickert and Marx's relationship to Feuerbach, one would need to inquire more specifically into whether the former involved a paradigm shift comparable to that associated with the latter.

Thus, while there is a general consensus within the literature that Weber relies primarily on Rickert, especially in his earlier methodological writings, it remains controversial what theoretical significance this has for the development of Weber's 'theory of science'. Henrich's view that Weber separated the theory of scientific methods completely from the philosophical context of neo-Kantianism contrasts with Burger's argument that Weber's modifications remain within Rickert's theoretical framework.[35] Most interpretations are situated somewhere between these two poles. For example, Kühne holds that the neo-Kantian system of values has been replaced by the 'analysis of specific meanings' and indicates that Weber determines the essence of value 'in the same way'.[36] Even if Weber should have made use of Rickert's terminology from a standpoint external to neo-Kantian philosophy, it is worth considering Oakes's objection that the neo-Kantian conceptual apparatus is not a cab one can stop at will.[37] Oakes identifies one similarity between Rickert

---

33    Rickert 1929, p. xxv. Jaspers reports that Rickert once elaborated on his 'areas of value' in Weber's presence, whereupon Weber exclaimed: 'Stop it with this summer house style, that's all nonsense!' (quoted in Hennis 1987, pp. 185–6, note 52).

34    Hennis 1987, p. 189.

35    Henrich 1952, pp. 5, 35. 'Weber enriched and elaborated on Rickert's account. These additions concern problems which Rickert either did not discuss at all or which he did not treat systematically and in detail. But they remain within Rickert's theoretical framework' (Burger 1976, p. 94).

36    Kühne 1971, pp. 307–8.

37    Oakes 1988a, p. 150. The argument alludes implicitly to Weber's formulation, in *Politics as a Vocation*, that the Sermon on the Mount is not 'like a cab to be entered at will' (Weber 2008, p. 203).

and Weber in their value-philosophical premise 'that values must be chosen rather than derived, and thus that our conception of the meaning of the world is not a product of research or analysis but rather an interpretation that we "create".[38] Others draw a line of demarcation between Weber's 'early writings', influenced by neo-Kantianism, and his subsequent emancipation from neo-Kantianism, which, it is claimed, finds its clearest expression in *Science as a Vocation* (1919/20). If Weber drew on Rickert's work initially, then he did so 'without knowing what he was getting into', says Wagner, who then goes on to credit Weber with having fully divested himself of the neo-Kantian philosophy of values in *Science as a Vocation*, under the influence of Nietzsche and in a manner that anticipates Horkheimer and Adorno.[39]

## 15.3    Paradigm Shift from the History of Ideas to a Critical Theory of Ideology

It cannot be a question, below, of simply extending the debates on continuity and change between Weber and Rickert. They can in any case not be resolved on the level of the history of ideas, which is where they are fought out. Most contributions are concerned with gauging intellectual influences, as if an intellectual's approach could be explained in terms of his intellect having developed organically from one or the other system of ideas. What underlies the development of ideas and concepts—the social and political frontlines, interests and discursive strategies—are hardly mentioned, and when they are, then only in a passing, almost inadvertent manner. While one learns which concepts and arguments Weber adopted from Rickert, one does not learn what ideological framework he positions himself within by virtue of these adoptions. Similarly, one learns that Weber historicises the neo-Kantian system of values and transforms it into a 'polytheism of values', but not to what extent this announces a new pattern, that of a more flexible integration of social contradictions.

The question to what degree there is continuity or discontinuity between Rickert and Weber can only be approached sensibly by enacting a paradigm shift, from a formulation of the problem in terms of the history of ideas to a formulation in terms of the theory of ideology. Thus, I shall not attempt the impossible, namely clearly staking out, within Weber's theory of science, the areas of influence proper to Rickert, Nietzsche, Marx and others. Instead, I will examine both the adoption of the neo-Kantian conceptual apparatus and its

---

38    Oakes 1988a, p. 146.
39    Wagner 1987, pp. 157ff.

modification with an eye to the underlying ideological workings. One expedient by which to uncover these workings is contrastive textual analysis. Since Weber employs and develops the theorems he adopts from neo-Kantianism against an objectivist and determinist Marxism, it seems appropriate to subject this widespread and influential refutation of Marx to a dialogue with Marx and Gramsci. By comparing the *southwest German school's* reception of Kant to the *Marburg School's* reception it can immediately be seen that the former is selective and one-sided almost to the point of distortion. Here, the comparison will be drawn by reference to the chapter on Kant in F.A. Lange's *History of Materialism*,[40] Gramsci having justly praised Lange as a scrupulous and astute historian of philosophy.[41] In order to be able to determine southwest German neo-Kantianism's conceptual strategy more accurately, I will also attempt to compare it to two other, rival currents claiming to have 'overcome' Marx: the hermeneutics developed by Dilthey and Croce's neo-Hegelian model of 'ethico-political history'. The main expedient by which I shall set about extrapolating the various neo-Kantian, neo-Hegelian and vitalist discourses is Troeltsch's broadly conceived 1922 attempt at a synthesis, *Der Historismus und seine Probleme* [*Historicism and its Problems*]. In order to evaluate the arguments of the 'Nietzsche faction', which are formulated in terms of the history of ideas, it will finally also be necessary to compare Weber's 'polytheistic' concept of spheres of values with Nietzsche's value antagonism between a 'master morality' and a 'moralism of resentment' associated with the inferior classes (see below, Chapter 20.3).

I will begin by focusing on the problem of what it means, theoretically and in terms of research strategy, that Weber attempts to engage Marxism on the basis of a neo-Kantian epistemology, adopted mainly from Rickert and Lask.

---

40    Lange 2000, vol. II, pp. 153ff.
41    Gramsci 1975b, pp. 1410–11.

# CHAPTER 16

# Theory of Reflection and Transcendental Idealism—An Epistemological *Rendezvous manqué*

## 16.1    The 'hiatus irrationalis' between Concept and Reality

In his essay on objectivity, Weber discusses the 'materialist conception of history' as part of the 'ancient scholastic theory of knowledge', according to which the purpose of concepts is to be 'representations, within the imagination, of "objective" reality'.[1] Against this position, he invokes the 'fundamental notion of modern epistemology as it has developed since Kant, namely that concepts are mental instruments employed for the purpose of mastering intellectually what is given empirically'.[2] This is to lay claim to an epistemology that Kant had described, in the *Critique of Pure Reason*, as 'formal' or 'transcendental idealism',[3] and which was considered 'modern' at the time when the essay on objectivity was written.

To what extent the 'modern epistemology' Weber lays claim to really 'goes back' to Kant is something that still needs to be verified. That Weber ever engaged thoroughly and firsthand with Kant's *Critique of Pure Reason* is not very likely. According to Marianne Weber, he read Kant the year before his school leaving examination (in the spring of 1882).[4] Weber himself reports, in a July 1887 letter to Emmy Baumgarten, that 'years ago', he 'righteously slogged away' at 'all the conceptual monstrosities', adding that this yields few results.[5] But the context indicates that Weber is not referring to Kant's epistemology, but rather to his moral philosophy, which is also what the 'southwest German school' was dealing with. The focus is on the demonstration that reason has 'no say' in moral judgements, i.e. with regard to the distinction between 'good' and 'evil', because the moral realm—just like that of 'taste'—is subject to 'laws of its own'.[6] Here, what interests Weber in Kant is his 'labour of dissociation', by

---

1    See Weber 1988d, pp. 166–7, 196, 204–5, 208.

2    Weber 1988d, p. 208.

3    Kant 1900, p. 879.

4    Marianne Weber 1975, p. 45.

5    Weber 1936, p. 262.

6    Weber 1936, pp. 260–1.

which he 'de-sensualises reason, de-rationalises the sensual and circumscribes a specific space for morality'.[7] It is here that Weber finds what he will later require for his 'compartmentalisation' of ideological socialisation by means of determinations of 'controlled demarcation' (see above, Chapter 13.5, and below, Chapter 21.2).

In the *Critique of Pure Reason*, Kant posed himself the question of how a finite intellect is able to perceive the infinite manifold of sense impressions as a coherent reality. The requisite connections are not to be found within objects, and so they cannot find their way into the intellect by means of perception; they are in fact 'determined ... purely and solely upon grounds determined by the understanding' itself, namely in the form of an a priori, 'originally synthetical unity of apperception' that is primordial with regard to all concrete cognition.[8] For example, in order to be able to relate impressions to something outside of me, I need to presuppose the concept of *space*, which thereby functions as an a priori, 'pure form of external intuition' and as a pre-condition of their contemplation.[9] Time is the 'form of the internal sense, that is, of the intuitions of self and of our internal state', whereby it directly conditions the inner phenomena of the soul, as well as (indirectly) those of the outside world.[10] On the other hand, external objects are only sense perceptions adapted to our mode of perception, and there can be no cognition of the corresponding 'things in themselves'.[11] All objects perceived within space and time are mere impressions, which, 'as presented to us ... have no self-subsistent existence apart from human thought'.[12] '[N]othing that can appertain to a thing in itself is to be found in them'.[13] Consciousness confronts 'things in themselves', which are devoid of time and space, 'and it has time and space

---

7    Haug 1993, p. 140.

8    Kant 1900, pp. 413, 130. 'Apperception' is perception that involves conceptual judgements, as distinct from 'perception', meaning sense impressions. Kant defines apperception as the subject having an 'internal intuition of itself' and a 'simple representation of the Ego' (Kant 1900, p. 86). By virtue of the synthetic unity that is primordial to concrete cognition, the cognitive subject is able to integrate the manifold of impressions within its self-consciousness, thereby making them its own impressions (Kant 1900, pp. 180–1). Thus the terms refer to a 'faculty that combines all my representations, considered as collectively belonging to me, in a self-consciousness' (Habermas 1987b, p. 37).

9    Kant 1900, p. 74.

10   Kant 1900, p. 73.

11   See Kant 1900, pp. 31, 70, 77, 248, 323.

12   Kant 1900, p. 879.

13   Kant 1900, p. 82.

beforehand present in it as the possibility of experience, just as in order to eat it has mouth and teeth', Hegel comments in his *Lectures on the History of Philosophy*: 'The things which are eaten have not the mouth and teeth, and as the eating is brought to bear on things, so space and time are also brought to bear on them; just as things are placed in the mouth and between the teeth, so it is with space and time'.[14]

In southwest German neo-Kantianism, Kant's 'thing in itself' was given a twist that would prove consequential for Weber's reception. Here, the existence of an 'insuperable opposition' between the concrete world and the human intellect was considered the 'core of transcendental-philosophical thought'.[15] 'Thought and being, form and content, the reality to be comprehended and the concept are starkly opposed to one another'.[16] Thus Rickert's student Emil Lask summarises Kant's epistemology by calling it the 'theory of empirical reality's irrationality'.[17] One cannot invoke Kant's *Critique of Pure Reason* in support of such a dichotomy, for in that work, the function of the 'thing in itself' is merely that of a liminal concept, and Kant displays no interest in its inner essence, as was already correctly noted by Lange.[18] 'The more the "thing in itself" dissolves into a mere notion, the more real the phenomenal world becomes'.[19] Unlike the 'innate ideas' of the old metaphysics, the a priori concepts of space and time only operate in connection with sense experience and mean nothing beyond it: they 'belong only to sense, and have no reality apart from it'.[20] Hegel, for example, considers this link between rational concepts and sense perception one of the 'most attractive sides of the Kantian philosophy', although he

---

14    Hegel 1896, p. 435. 'This would appear as though men could set forth upon the search for truth with spears and staves. And a further claim is made when it is said that we must know the faculty of knowledge before we can know. For to investigate the faculties of knowledge means to know them; but how we are to know without knowing, how we are to apprehend the truth before the truth, it is impossible to say. It is the old story of the man who would not go into the water till he could swim' (Hegel 1896, p. 428).

15    Wagner 1987, p. 113.

16    Wagner and Zipprian 1987, p. 192.

17    Lask 1902, p. 24.

18    Lange 2000, vol. II, pp. 216–18. When Kant points out that the thing in itself is not an object of cognition, he adds that in experience, 'no inquiry is ever made' with respect to it (Kant 1900, p. 71). 'What things may be in themselves, I know not, and need not know, because a thing is never presented to me otherwise than as a phenomenon' (Kant 1900, p. 282).

19    Lange 2000, vol. II, p. 217.

20    Kant 1900, p. 140.

goes on to criticise Kant for failing to genuinely link the two components, or for linking them in a purely formal manner, 'just as a piece of wood and a leg might be bound together by a cord'.[21]

Roscher's 'historical method', inspired by Hegel, is criticised by Weber for failing to recognise the '*hiatus irrationalis*' between concretely and individually given reality on the one hand and general concepts on the other; in other words, Roscher fails to recognise the 'irrationality of reality which resists subordination under "laws"'.[22] However, Weber adopts the expression '*hiatus irrationalis*' not from Kant but from Lask, and Lask did not adopt it from Kant either, but from Fichte, who used it to refer to the abrupt interruption of all speculation by the fact of 'brutal reality', by the elusiveness of knowledge and the dark centre between the projection and the projected.[23] Oakes mentions the two-stage adoption of this model (Weber-Lask-Fichte),[24] but he fails to notice that Lask invokes Fichte for the purpose of overcoming Kant's 'totality of reason', his 'ahistorical Enlightenment ideology', his 'atomistic individualism', 'formal rationalism' and 'abstract universalism of judgement'.[25] The shift of emphasis is not to be missed: critical examination of the faculty of cognition yields to an evocation of inscrutability and irrationality.

## 16.2   The Critique of the Subject/Object Dichotomy in the 'Theses on Feuerbach'

It is not just reality as a whole, but also each of its individual segments that presents itself as an infinite and vast manifold of individual manifestations and processes, such that there can be no cognition as 'reflection' [*Abbild*] of a given reality, Rickert and Weber agree.[26] Rather, all cognition is grounded in the cultural necessity of selecting a sensible segment from the 'meaninglessness of the endless flux of the infinite multiplicity of concrete reality'.[27]

---

21   Hegel 1896, p. 441.
22   Weber 1975, p. 85.
23   Lask 1902, p. 169; compare pp. 112–13.
24   Oakes 1988a, pp. 49ff; Oakes 1988b, p. 604.
25   See Lask 1902, pp. 5ff, 214ff, 245–46, 249, 259, 261. In Lask's construct, Fichte ultimately plays the role of 'Kant's genuine follower, the "greatest of all Kantians", who retains what is lastingly valuable in his master, and yet moves beyond him with creative energy' (Lask 1902, p. 270).
26   Rickert 1902, pp. 33–4; Weber 1975, p. 181.
27   Weber 1988d, 180.

That the way people select the objects of their perception and cognition depends on their standpoints and interests is not to be denied and is also accepted in epistemological theories that reject the dualist conception of thought and reality. At each moment, we have cognition of the history that is relevant to us, but we lack the 'means of knowing' the rest of history, writes Croce in his 1915 book *History, its Theory and Practice*, whereupon he deploys this argument against Kant: 'That "remaining" history is the eternal phantom of the "thing in itself," which is neither "thing" nor "in itself," but only the imaginative projection of the infinity of our action and our knowledge'.[28] If the 'philosophy of history' imagines itself to be faced only with 'brute facts', which are mute, and if it must not just relate them to one another but in fact provide them with meaning in the first place, then this appears, in Croce, as an effect of spirit itself, which only turns facts into brute facts by relating them to one another, by accepting them as such, 'because it is of use to it'.[29]

Whereas Croce formulates his critique starting from Hegel's concept of 'mind', Marx directs it against a conception of reality that ignores the way cognition is mediated by human practice. In Rickert, by contrast, a 'representation' is the 'complete' replica of 'perceptible physical reality . . . just as it is':[30] a figure of thought Marx already criticised, in the 'Theses on Feuerbach', by reference to the 'materialism . . . of contemplation', which does not grasp reality subjectively, as 'practice', but only 'in the form of the object, or of contemplation'.[31] Thus Rickert implies a mechanistic notion that is a far cry from the active and creative cognition process Marx described as the 'reproduction of the concrete by way of thought',[32] brought about by means of the synthesis of the concrete's analytically discovered determinations. When the human relationship to reality is conceived of not as a practical one, but as one of 'reflection' [*Abbild*], then rejection of such a mechanistic understanding entails the de-realisation

---

28    Croce 1921, p. 55. Troeltsch relates Croce's critique of the thing in itself to Croce's critique of religion, which borrows from Feuerbach: the thing in itself can only be meaningful to God (Troeltsch 1922, p. 629). Tugendhat holds that Kant's concept of synthetic a priori judgements is an 'unsuccessful attempt to secularise transcendence (in the religious sense of the word)', as it implies 'that we are not just beings in an earthly world, but also members of another, primordial, higher world' (Tugendhat 1984, p. 4).

29    Croce 1921, pp. 69, 73.

30    Rickert 1902, p. 33.

31    Marx and Engels 1975–2005, vol. 5, p. 3.

32    Marx and Engels 1975–2005, vol. 28, p. 37.

of reality itself: unable to become an object of cognition in and of itself, it becomes an 'irrational' variable.[33]

The fact that Weber conceptualises his opposition to Marxism in terms of an opposition between the theory of reflection and neo-Kantian transcendental philosophy is symptomatic of a *rendezvous manqué* between the two theoretical approaches. And yet the subsumption of the 'materialist conception of history' under the ancient and scholastic theory of 'reflection' is not unfounded, when one thinks of the Marxism of the Second and the Third International. As early as Engels's engagement with Dühring (1878), one notes a tendency to declare the idea a pale imitation of the world, and in Lenin's *Materialism and Empirio-criticism* (1909), the notion that in consciousness, 'objective reality' is 'copied, photographed, reflected' is pursued and developed.[34] Moreover, within the struggles between the various Marxist parties, the concept of 'reflection' functioned like a badge by which to identify the orthodox, and in 'Marxism-Leninism' it eventually became the power nexus of a philosophical and state function.[35] With regard to this 'Marxist' tradition, idealism certainly has the merit that Marx identified when distinguishing it from the 'materialism of contemplation', namely that of developing the 'active side', even if leaving real, sensuous activity aside and thus remaining 'abstract'.[36]

Weber fails to recognise that the 'thing in itself', which Kant considers to be principally unknowable, appertains to the same world of ideas as the 'objective reality' that 'Marxism-Leninism' posits as its philosophical starting point.[37] For what the contrary responses have in common is that they both respond to the same question, posed by a traditional philosophy of consciousness, in which a *subject*, detached from its respective societal relations and relations to nature, is opposed to the *object* that is its outer world. It is only in such a set-up that there arises the problem of how thought can access its object. To Sohn-Rethel, the 'great and fundamental question' concerning the relationship between thought and being, and by which 'being' is placed on one side and 'thought' on the other, is the 'centrepiece of the rigid, fetishistic oppositions' of philosophical thought.[38] Haug has shown, by reference to Descartes, that by

---

33    Rickert 1962, pp. 32–3; Rickert 1929, pp. 37, 78.

34    Lenin 1960–78h, vol. 14, p. 130.

35    See Haug 1994, pp. 13ff.

36    Marx and Engels 1975–2005, vol. 5, p. 3.

37    To Gramsci, for example, Kant's *thing in itself* is derived from the 'external objectivity of the real', and thus from Greco-Christian realism (Gramsci 1975b, p. 1333).

38    Sohn-Rethel 1971, p. 128.

being opposed to an 'outer world', the individual's inner world is systematically cleared, that is, severed from the mediations between the individual and social life practices, in order then to be inhabited by the 'ego', the 'subject', 'mind', 'consciousness' and the like.[39] The very opposition between transcendental reason and the 'thing in itself' is premised on the emergence of a stable division of manual and intellectual labour within society. It is only on the basis of its real and institutionally safeguarded autonomisation from the social life process that 'consciousness can really flatter itself that it is something other than consciousness of existing practice, that it really represents something without representing something real'.[40]

In the 'Theses on Feuerbach', Marx criticised the basic philosophical *dispositif* by which a cognitive subject is opposed to objects of cognition; in doing so, he moved beyond the responses both of the 'materialism of contemplation' and of idealism: what both have in common is that they do not grasp reality subjectively, as 'human sensuous activity, practice'.[41] Thus it is not a matter of opposing to ideas and concepts an 'objective reality' that exists independently of practice and which persons go on to 'represent'; on the contrary, even in our thinking about thought, we need to take as our starting point people's actual practices in production and reproduction.[42] In epistemological terms, the change of terrain consists in conceptualising the categories of cognition in terms of the contradictions of the social life process that necessitate their development.

## 16.3    The Sublation of the Kantian A Priori within the Concept of the 'Form of Thought'

Having shown, first, that Kant's transcendental idealism is not as far removed from its counterpart, the 'theory of reflection', as Weber assumes, and sec-

---

39    Haug 1984, p. 29. Haug identified the historical site of this clearing away as the absolutist state, in which the feudal state power reconstructs itself on the basis of an invigorated bourgeoisie. The new top-down administrative rationalism is supported, 'from below', i.e. mainly from within the bourgeoisie, by the emergence of a 'corresponding, accommodating reason' that conceptualises the totality anew and classifies it by means of concepts (Haug 1993, pp. 139–40).

40    Marx and Engels 1975–2005, vol. 5, p. 44.

41    Marx and Engels 1975–2005, vol. 5, p. 3.

42    Marx and Engels 1975–2005, vol. 5, pp. 35ff; 41ff; see Rehmann 2013, pp. 22ff.

ond, that Marx's standpoint is not that of the objectivism Weber would like to associate him with, I will now try to demonstrate that Weber overlooked that the 'new materialism' announced by Marx had incorporated relevant issues articulated by Kant's 'theory of cognition'. In the fragmentary 'Introduction' to the *Grundrisse* (1857), where the process of 'ascending' from a phenomenon's abstractly identified simple elements to the concrete totality is described by Marx as the 'scientifically correct method', an indirect indication of such a link between Marx and Kant can be found.[43] This ascending movement of categories, from the abstract to the concrete, now appears to philosophical consciousness as the 'real act of production', and this is correct insofar as the concrete, 'concrete in thought', is in fact a product of thought and cognition, albeit 'not in any way a product of the concept which thinks and generates itself outside or above observation and conception; a product, rather, of the working-up of observation and conception into concepts'.[44] Although it is addressed to Hegel, the passage could just as well be addressed to Kant. While Marx holds that deducing what is 'concrete in thought' from abstract categories is one-sided, because it is to fail to comprehend the process by which the concrete itself develops, he also sees such deduction as based on a real process proper to the intellectual appropriation of the world.

It is the critique of Kant formulated by Engels that has become well known: in the *Dialectic of Nature*, Engels describes the 'eternally unknowable thing-in-itself' as the element of Kantian philosophy that 'least merited preservation'.[45] In the 'Notes and Fragments' appended to the text, Engels points out the contradiction that the assumption of a principally unknowable 'thing in itself', which seems quite sensible when considered abstractly, is never actually applied, in scientific practice, by the scientists advocating it; it is only ever articulated 'in passing into philosophy'.[46] According to Engels, this shows 'how little seriously they take it and what little value it has itself'.[47] The most compelling refutation, according to Engels, is the artificial synthesis of chemical substances, by which the 'thing in itself' becomes a 'thing for us'.[48] Sometimes Engels's critique of Kant fails to resist the temptation Gramsci would later criticise Bukharin's *Historical Materialism* for yielding to, that of invoking

---

43    Marx and Engels 1975–2005, vol. 28, p. 37.
44    Marx and Engels 1975–2005, vol. 28, p. 38.
45    Marx and Engels 1975–2005, vol. 25, p. 340.
46    Marx and Engels 1975–2005, vol. 25, p. 520.
47    Ibid.
48    Marx and Engels 1975–2005, vol. 26, pp. 367–8; compare vol. 27, p. 287.

common sense to 'demolish the subjectivist view by rendering it "ridiculous"'.[49] But in the present context, what is more important than such 'refutations' is the transformation of the Kantian query that Engels follows Hegel in bringing about. 'Taken historically the thing would have a certain meaning: we can only know under the conditions of our epoch and *as far as these allow*'.[50] This historicisation corresponds to the proposal to investigate not the unanswerable philosophical question concerning the possibility of thought but the social 'forms of thought' and 'thought determinations'.[51]

As Haug shows, the concept of the 'form of thought' was itself used, in the early nineteenth-century debate on Kant's *Critique of Pure Reason*, to criticise the schematism of Kant's pure concepts of the understanding with its 'pure intuitions and a priori forms of thought'.[52] Hegel, whom Marx adopted the term from, prepares the ground for this historicisation, in his *Lectures on the Philosophy of History*, by associating the forms of thought proper to the sciences, which he defines as elements of 'forms of thought' common to the 'condition and culture of the time and of the people'.[53] What the concept adopts from Kant's apriorism is the aspect of not being a feature of individual consciousness, but of being primordial with regard to it—as, for example, in the case of language—and determining it like 'the net in which all concrete matter . . . is grasped',[54] such that consciousness knows within these forms of thought, 'but does not know them'.[55] In Marx too, the terms 'form of thought' and 'objective form of thought' indicate what remains unthought within thought and refer

---

49   Gramsci 1975b, p. 1412. As when he asks mockingly: 'What would one think of a zoologist who said: "A dog *seems* to have four legs, but we do not know whether in reality it has four million legs or none at all"? . . . But scientists take care not to apply the phrase about the thing-in-itself in natural science, they permit themselves this only in passing into philosophy' (Marx and Engels 1975–2005, vol. 25, p. 520).

50   Ibid.

51   Marx and Engels 1975–2005, vol. 25, p. 519. 'To know what can be discovered by our thinking, it is no use, a hundred years after Kant, to try and find out the range of thought from the critique of reason or the investigation of the instrument of knowing . . . On the other hand, the investigation of the *forms* of thought, the thought determinations, is very profitable and necessary' (Ibid).

52   Herder 1799, quoted in Haug 1995a, p. 590.

53   Hegel 1892, p. 57.

54   Ibid.

55   Ibid.

to the 'consciousness within the social form that has no consciousness of that form'.[56]

By conceptualising the 'objective forms of thought' not as mere illusions, but as real social forms with institutional stability, into which concrete modes of thinking and acting need to insert themselves, he treats them like an 'a priori' (in the literal sense of the term) that is primordial with regard to the individual, and which one might describe, following Max Adler and Otto Bauer, as a 'social a priori'.[57] The concepts of the understanding that Kant posits as a fixed and asocial point of departure have here been historicised and socialised, the forms of thought having been reconstructed, as structurally determined forms of practice, on the basis of the relations of production and domination proper to each social formation. In the 'Introduction' to the *Grundrisse*, Marx returns to the Kantian question of whether the abstract categories from which thought ascends to the composite categories that are 'concrete in thought' might not exist independently.[58] The careful answer he gives is: '*Ça dépend*', an answer whose implications he then examines by reference to the case of the category *labour*. On the one hand, this category appears as the abstract expression of the simplest and most ancient relationship between man and nature; on the other hand, '[i]ndifference towards any specific kind of labour presupposes a very developed totality of real kinds of labour', demonstrating in a striking fashion 'how even the most abstract categories, despite their validity—precisely because of their abstractness—for all epochs, are nevertheless, in the

---

56  Haug 1995a, p. 599. Thus the categories of bourgeois economy are based on the 'objective forms of thought [*objektive Gedankenformen*]' associated with private production of commodities based on the division of labour (Marx and Engels 1975–2005, vol. 35, p. 87; translation modified). The phenomenal forms known as the 'value and price of labour' and 'wages' reproduce themselves 'directly and spontaneously as current modes of thought [*gang und gäbe Denkformen*]', whereas the essential circumstances that bring these modes of thought about can only be discovered by science (Marx and Engels 1975–2005, vol. 35, p. 542; compare p. 540). Marx is able to say of the 'form of wages' that it 'forms the basis of all the juridical notions of both labourer and capitalist' (Marx and Engels 1975–2005, vol. 35, p. 540).

57  Bauer criticises Adler's 'social a priori' for referring, in an overly general manner, to the a priori preconditions of human experience as such. 'There exists not just a *social a priori* of human cognition in general; there are also, to use Kant's terminology, specific *social a prioris* associated with each historical epoch, each social order, each class' (Bauer 1980, p. 756).

58  Marx and Engels 1975–2005, vol. 28, p. 38.

specific character of this abstraction, themselves likewise a product of historic relations, and possess their full validity only for and within these relations'.[59]

Various epistemological approaches have been able to pick up on the Kantian problems preserved in Marx. Habermas develops the concept of a 'synthesis in the materialist sense', transferring Kant's concept from the sphere of transcendental consciousness to that of social labour. According to Habermas, the historical constitution of the human species as subject occurs not in the medium of thought, but in that of labour.[60] Of course this transposition of the concept entails that Marx's specific question concerning the *form* of thought and its historico-social structure is lost sight of. Moreover, Habermas uses his 'materialist concept of synthesis' to criticise Marx's putative reductionism, his focus on 'instrumental action'.[61] Sohn-Rethel relates the rift between thought and being, insuperable within philosophy, to the 'division between intellectual and manual labour' as it has emerged in commodity production.[62] Exploitation and class rule are characterised, among other things, by the fact that the 'synthesis' of societalisation rests on activities distinct from the work of production. But as a function of the work process, the synthesis is the basis for a communist society.[63] Sohn-Rethel's concept of the 'form of thought', with the aid of which he seeks to relate the process of cognition within natural science to the abstraction of exchange, is indebted not so much to Hegel's philosophy of identity as to Kant's concepts of the understanding, which are attributed with 'objective reality': 'While concepts belong "to us", because they are social products and not products of nature, they are nevertheless not made by us'.[64]

---

59    Marx and Engels 1975–2005, vol. 28, p. 39.

60    Habermas 1987b, pp. 25ff, 28, 31–2, 41–2.

61    Habermas 1987b, pp. 43ff. If for no other reason, the argument is flawed because Marx, as Habermas has to admit himself (Habermas 1987b, pp. 28–9), never attributed to labour such a general function of synthesis. For a critical overview of Habermas's dichotomies between labour and interaction, purpose-rational action and communicative action, system-world and life-world etc., see Rehmann 2013, pp. 99ff.

62    Sohn-Rethel 1970, p. 123.

63    Sohn-Rethel 1970, p. 140.

64    Sohn-Rethel 1971, p. 126; compare Sohn-Rethel 1970, pp. 20ff. Sohn-Rethel believes he has discovered 'that in the innermost core of the commodity structure there was to be found the "transcendental subject"' (Sohn-Rethel 1978, p. xiii). Against such a fixation on the reifying effects of the commodity fetish, a fixation influenced mainly by Lukács, Haug emphasises that what lies beyond the forms of thought is not just the abstraction of exchange, but a plurality of fields of action whose behavioural requirements and evidences do not need to harmonise with one another but can in fact be as starkly contradic-

A similar argument is presented by von Greiff: notwithstanding the fact that Kant was unable to genetically deduce the rational concepts of the understanding, his derivation of those concepts from 'transcendental consciousness'—an 'instance that is situated neither within the individual nor in nature'—comes close to an understanding of their societal conditions of emergence.[65] Within East German Marxism, Klaus, Kosing and Ruben were among those who attempted to articulate constructivist interpretative approaches that start from the activity of the cognitive subject, while of course remaining within the prescribed model of reflection, with its inner/outer world structure.[66] Holzkamp argues that when an individual consciousness 'reflects' something, then that something is not a reality independent from practice and untouched by thought, but rather something that has sedimented, by virtue of human practice, in 'cooperative and social forms of thought and speech'; moreover, such 'reflection' is to be understood as an active process of cognitive appropriation that also implies the possibility of change.[67] Lucien Sève has developed the concept of the 'form of individuality', by which he describes historical forms that impose certain social characters upon individuals by means of 'activity matrices'.[68]

## 16.4    Gramsci's Critique of Objectivism

Gramsci also refers back to Kant, being interested, among other things, in the subjective side of the cognitive process, by which the objects of cognition are constituted. The context is provided by the two-front struggle within the context of which he develops his philosophy of praxis:[69] on the one hand, he engages with an objectivism within Marxism, identifying Bukharin as one of its exponents, and on the other, he engages with the neo-Hegelianism of Croce, who attempts—similarly to Weber—to overcome Marxism by declaring it

---

tory as, for example, wage-oriented indifference and the pride of the professional worker when they co-exist in one and the same individual (Haug 1995a, p. 598).

65    Von Greiff 1976, p. 90.

66    See Haug 1994, pp. 15ff.

67    Holzkamp 1983, pp. 285–6; compare pp. 290, 317–18.

68    Sève 1972, pp. 101, 149, 152–3, 266–7.

69    Within Italian Marxism, Labriola coined the term 'philosophy of praxis'. Croce adopted the expression in his 1908 book *Philosophie der Praxis. Ökonomik und Ethik* ['Philosophy of Practice. Economics and Ethics'], integrating it into his neo-Hegelian philosophy of mind (see Gramsci 1995, p. 556, note 6a).

an economistic and mechanistic objectivism. Speaking at the International Congress of Philosophy in Oxford in 1930, Croce claims that Marxism splits the unitary process of reality into 'structure and superstructure, noumenon and phenomenon', instituting the economy as the hidden God 'that pulls all the threads and is the only reality within the phenomena of morality, religion, philosophy, art etc.'[70] Gramsci holds that Croce's accusation of metaphysics is justified insofar as it is directed at an 'inferior current within the philosophy of praxis', and he rejects the 'polemical trick' of presenting the critique of economism as a victory over Marxism, arguing that to do so is like presenting a critique of popular Catholic superstition as a critique of Catholic theology.[71]

Within this two-front struggle, the focus on practice within Marx's 'Theses on Feuerbach' becomes newly relevant: 'It is obviously neither idealistic nor materialistic "monism," neither "Matter" nor "Spirit," but rather "*historical materialism*," that is to say, concrete human activity (history): namely, activity concerning a certain organized "matter".'[72] This perspective leads him to formulate a call to study Kant and verify his concepts with precision.[73] Against the model of reflection presented in Bukharin's *Historical Materialism*, Gramsci proposes thinking of phenomena not as something 'objective' that exists 'in and of itself', but as 'qualities' that men have learned to distinguish between due to their practical and scientific interests. From the viewpoint of such interestedness, cognitions become our 'superstructures': what we encounter in things is nothing 'but ourselves, our needs and interests'.[74]

Implicit in this recourse to Kant are two lines of inquiry that Gramsci will pursue later, especially in Notebook 11: the disarticulation of the traditional concept of an 'objectively existing outside world' and the reinterpretation of the 'subjectivist' conception of reality within the framework of a Marxist 'theory of superstructures'. Belief in the objective existence of the outside world, in the sense of an 'objectivity that surpasses man ... and could also be intuited

70    See Gramsci 1975b, pp. 851–4.

71    On this, see for example Gramsci 2007, pp. 153, 271–2; Gramsci 1975b, pp. 1225–6, 1229–32, 1234–5, 1236, 1254, 1291–1301, 1318–23, 1418–20. Gramsci is able to speak of a 'polemical trick' because Croce had himself criticised such a vulgarisation of Marxism in the course of his earlier engagement with Marx in *Materialismo storico ed economia marxistica* (see for example Croce 1951, pp. 6–7, 11–12). In order to distinguish the new materialism from a metaphysical materialism, Croce defined it as a 'realistic conception of history' [*concezione realistica della storia*] (Croce 1951, p. 20).

72    Gramsci 1975b, pp. 1491–2; Gramsci 1996, pp. 176–7.

73    Gramsci 1975b, pp. 1290–1.

74    Gramsci 1975b, p. 1291.

beyond man', is religious by origin, according to Gramsci, and as a 'residuum
of the concept of God', it continues to operate within common sense thinking with iron persistence.[75] What Gramsci has in mind is a theology of creation according to which man finds the world, created by God prior to man's
own creation, 'ready-made', 'inventoried and defined once and for all'. Gramsci
holds that the 'materialist' ridicule of the subjectivist view invokes this
common-sense conception of reality, and he argues that such ridicule
is 'reactionary', because it makes use of the 'implicit return to religious
sentiment'.[76] Without human activity, objectivity would be chaos, nothing but
emptiness; in fact, not even this could be said of it, as language and thought are
not conceivable in the absence of man.[77] 'We are familiar with reality only in
its relation to man, and since man is a historical process, cognition and reality
are also processes, objectivity is a process etc.'[78] In Gramsci, the 'objective' is
not the conceptual counterpart of the 'subjective', but rather that of 'arbitrary',
'passing' or 'purely particular' processes. It refers to 'what exists necessarily in
our impressions', that which may become permanent and is common to everyone.[79] Against the particular standpoints of exploitation and domination, it
represents that which can be generalised, such that Gramsci is able to relate
the struggle for 'objectivity' to the abolition of class antagonism and the struggle for the 'cultural unification of the human race'.[80] Thus employed, the term
'objective' can only mean 'humanly objective', i.e. 'historically subjective' and
'universally subjective'.[81] This is similar to Kant's definition of objectivity; with
regard to 'accepting something as true' [*Fürwahrhalten*], Kant distinguishes
between 'objective' (intersubjective) *conviction* [*Überzeugung*] and purely
'subjective' *persuasion* [*Überredung*]: 'If a judgment is valid for every rational
being, then its ground is objectively sufficient, and it is termed a conviction. If,
on the other hand, it has its ground in the particular character of the subject,
it is termed a persuasion'.[82]

---

75    Gramsci 1975b, pp. 1411–16, 1455–7.
76    Gramsci 1975b, p. 1412.
77    Gramsci 1975b, p. 1457.
78    Gramsci 1975b, p. 1416.
79    Gramsci 1975b, p. 1456.
80    Gramsci 1975b, p. 1416.
81    Ibid.
82    Kant 1900, p. 692. Haug, who draws attention to this point of agreement between Gramsci
       and Kant, attributes to Kant a 'virtually socialised conception of objectivity' whose cat-
       egory of 'conviction' can moreover be conceptualised in terms of the theory of hegemony
       (Haug 1996b, p. 51).

Considered from the point of view of Gramsci's critique of objectivism, the commonly invoked opposition between 'conventional' and 'objective' concepts turns out to be merely apparent. Gramsci demonstrates this by reference to the concepts of 'east' and 'west': outside of real history, every point on earth would be east and west simultaneously, and so the concepts are historico-cultural 'constructs'. These constructs are not those of a hypothetical abstract man, but those of Europe's educated classes. Gramsci's argument can be seen as an insightful anticipation of Edward Said's critique of 'Orientalism': by their worldwide hegemony, these educated classes have imposed the concepts of 'east' and 'west' everywhere, and so these objects have come to be 'objectively real', i.e. standards of reference that correspond to real facts and orientations.[83] They owe their 'objectivity' to a hegemonic fact, such that Gramsci can say, in a different passage, that the *philosophy of praxis* conceives of the reality of human relations of cognition [*rapporti umani di conoscenza*] as an 'element of political "hegemony"'.[84]

Gramsci's response to Croce's critique of Marxism as metaphysical is a 'theory of superstructures', intended to translate what traditional philosophy expressed in a speculative form into a 'realist and historicist language'.[85] Instead of opposing to the 'subjectivist conception of reality' a metaphysical objectivism, Gramsci wishes to join forces with it, to 'absorb it' and 'translate' it into the terminology of a realist historicism.[86] It is only in such a 'translation' that it can achieve its 'vindication' [*inveramento*], whereas in its speculative form, it would remain a mere 'philosophical novel' [*romanzo filosofico*].[87] And vice versa: such a joining of forces would allow the *philosophy of praxis* to become the 'hegemonic exponent of the higher culture'.[88] 'What the idealists call "spirit" is not the starting point but the destination; it is the ensemble of superstructures as a process leading to concrete and objectively universal unification, and not a unitary premise, etc.'[89]

---

83    Gramsci 1975b, pp. 1419–20; see Said 2003.

84    Gramsci 1975b, p. 1245. Gramsci demonstrates that the practico-theoretical principle of hegemony also has 'epistemological implications' by reference to Lenin's political influence: by creating a 'new ideological terrain', the realisation of a hegemonic apparatus brought about a reform of the 'methods of cognition' and became a 'fact of cognition' in its own right (Gramsci 1975b, pp. 1249–50).

85    Gramsci 1975b, p. 1413.

86    Gramsci 1975b, p. 1244; compare p. 1292.

87    Gramsci 1975b, p. 1415.

88    Gramsci 1975b, p. 1413.

89    Gramsci 1975b, p. 1416.

## 16.5      F.A. Lange as Secret 'School Leader'?

The status of Marxist epistemology and the problems associated with it will not be discussed at greater length here.[90] Considered from the perspective of Marx and Gramsci, the commonalities with Weber's epistemological 'constructivism' appear more significant than the differences. At the same time, it ought to have become clear that the foundation upon which Weber engages with the 'objectivism' of the Marxism of his day was as outdated, when seen from the perspective of Marx's 'Theses on Feuerbach', as the theory of reflection that Weber rightly criticised.

Gramsci indicates a historico-cultural constellation that is highly significant to understanding the epistemological controversy: as a rule, Marxists began from the dogmatic premise 'that historical materialism is of course a slightly revised and corrected materialism ... We have studied Lange to learn what traditional materialism was, and its terms have been reintroduced as terms of historical materialism. Thus one can say that with regard to most of the conceptual items that present themselves under the rubric of historical materialism, Lange and no one else was the school leader and founder'.[91] And yet Lange had developed a 'limited' concept of materialism, namely a naturalist one. Feuerbach, for example, is excluded, because of the 'undue prominence given to man' in his work,[92] and Marx is never even mentioned.[93]

If Gramsci is right in calling Lange the secret 'school leader' of the historico-materialist conceptual apparatus, then the same is true, to a considerable extent, with regard to the instruments by which Marxism was 'triumphed over'. For example, in *Materialismo storico ed economia marxistica* ['Historical Materialism and Marxist Economics'], Croce still praised Lange's judiciousness in exempting historical materialism from his history of (metaphysical) materialism. However, Croce later went on to describe historical materialism in the terminology of a pre-Marxist vulgar Marxism, as a metaphysics whose hidden God is economics.[94] Weber read Lange's history of materialism as an

---

90    For such a discussion, see, *inter alia*, Laugstien 1997.

91    Gramsci 1975b, p. 1410; compare pp. 1064–5.

92    Lange 2000, vol. II, 248.

93    Except in the notes, although he is there paid homage to not as the founder of a 'new materialism' but as 'the most learned living historian of political economy' (Lange 2000, vol. I, p. 319, note 74; compare Lange 2000, vol. I, p. 295; see also Lange 2000, vol. II, p. 23).

94    Compare Gramsci 1975b, pp. 1318ff. Lange was of course familiar with Marxist socialism, Croce argues in *Materialismo storico*, but he was too judicious [*avveduto*] to confuse it

eighteen year old and found its sober account 'refreshing'.[95] Hennis holds that Lange conveyed to Weber, in a fashion more 'coherent' than Marx, the ethical problems associated with the modern economy, adding that the concept of the 'ideal type' also goes back to Lange, or at least its general import.[96] Presumably, Weber also took the association of materialism with naturalism not just from the Second International, but also from Lange.[97] However, he and the south-west German neo-Kantians differ from Lange in that they employ the concept of naturalism in such a way as to subsume under it every disclosure of social laws of tendency, including Marx's critique of political economy (see below, Chapter 17.2).

Both Marxists and their neo-Kantian and/or neo-Hegelian opponents failed to notice what Althusser called the 'epistemological break',[98] by which Marx opened up the 'continent of history' to scientific reconstruction and analysis. Given the positions taken, within the Second International, by the Marxism of the time, and given that Marx's original 1845 version of the 'Theses on Feuerbach' and the *German Ideology* had both still to be published,[99] Weber can perhaps be excused for this failure. But the same cannot be said for the mainstream current in the literature on Weber, which persists in suggesting, almost a century later, that Weber was combating, 'at Kant's side', the 'extreme objectivism' of Marx, the latter having been concerned only with a 'reconstruction in itself', whereas Weber was putatively concerned with a 'reconstruction for us', etc.[100] It is not in this outdated opposition that the stakes of a Marxist theory of cognition lie, but in the conception of the 'subjective' itself, or of the mediations between the subjective on the one hand and economic relations, social forms of practice (embedded in the 'metabolism' with nature) and hegemonic constellations on the other.

---

with metaphysical materialism, to which it has no internal relationship ['*che non ha con quello nessuna relazione intrinseca, ed è un semplice modo di dire*'] (Croce 1951, p. 6).

95   Weber 1936, p. 52.

96   Hennis 1996, pp. 196ff.

97   This is also suggested by Hennis, although Hennis fails to notice the problematic nature of this borrowing of ideas (Hennis 1996, p. 198).

98   Althusser 1974, p. 20.

99   Since 1888, the only version of the 'Theses on Feuerbach' to have been published was the one edited by Engels (see Marx and Engels 1975–2005, vol. 5, pp. 6–10); the *German Ideology* was not published until 1932.

100  See for example Schluchter 1991, pp. 71, 73, 76, 98–9.

CHAPTER 17

# The Dualism of Law-Determined 'Nature' and Value-Determined 'Culture'

Weber adopts from Rickert the opposition between 'scientific' and 'historical' thought, according to which empirical reality becomes *nature* when it is considered 'with regard to the general', whereas it becomes *history* when it is considered 'with regard to the particular'.[1] This distinction is new with regard to Kant, in whom 'the limits of the method of natural science coincide with those of the scientific method as such'.[2] Rickert adopted it from his teacher Windelband; in his 1894 rector's inaugural address, Windelband had defined the method of the natural sciences as 'nomothetic', i.e. as one that posits laws or seeks them, whereas he had defined the historical method as 'idiographic', i.e. as one that describes what is unique.[3] In Rickert, what Windelband states for 'history' is also applied to 'culture'. The opposition is intended as a methodological one, such that every fact can principally be dealt with by either method. Of course, the formulation of 'nomological' relations in the field of the cultural sciences would also have been justified, as Weber admits in his essay on objectivity,[4] but not as a goal, only as an expedient by which to achieve 'cognition of the socially real'. In any case, general 'laws' are inadequate to the comprehension of what is 'essential' in culture, e.g. the specific 'quality' of a socio-economic phenomenon, because they lead us away from the 'plenitude of reality'.[5] What is decisive is whether the cognitive interest aims 'merely' at

---

1  Rickert 1902, p. 255.
2  Schnädelbach 1974, p. 144.
3  Windelband 1915, pp. 145ff.
4  Weber 1988d, pp. 178ff.
5  Weber 1988d, pp. 161, 180. Wegener is wrong to believe he can play out Weber's acknowledgement that the nomothetic method can be applied, within historiography, against Rickert's and Windelband's dichotomy (Wegener 1962, p. 72), for similar arguments can be found in their work (see for example Rickert 1902, pp. 339–40; Windelband 1915, pp. 156–7). On the other hand, Schnädelbach is somewhat overhasty in using this as an opportunity to defend Rickert and Windelband against the criticism that they immunise the scientific disciplines in a sterile manner (Schnädelbach 1974, pp. 140ff, 145), for if what is 'essential' to history and culture can only be grasped idiographically, then 'immunisation' with regard to a 'science of laws' has been achieved as successfully as it would have been achieved by formal exclusion.

the detection of a law or at an 'active valuation of man' bound up with the 'singularity of the object'.[6]

Here, the general represents the 'law', such that it underhandedly becomes 'nature'; in the same way, 'value' represents what is 'particular' in history and culture. While Weber will give the concept of 'value' (and that of 'culture', defined by reference to 'value') a somewhat different twist than Windelband and Rickert (see below, Chapter 20), he does accept their fundamental opposition between law-governed 'nature' and value-determined 'culture'. What needs therefore to be investigated is what such a dualism entails for Weber's model of the historical and cultural sciences. Before I address the problems associated with the concept of 'value', I will focus on the philosophical hostility to 'naturalism', which extends far beyond southwest German neo-Kantianism.

### 17.1    The Common 'German-Italian' Front against 'Anglo-French' Naturalism

To Rickert, 'insight into the fundamental difference between historical thought and thought in the natural sciences' is the 'most important point' for comprehending both the activities of each individual science and most philosophical problems and questions of worldview. For it is here that 'logical theory is employed to oppose naturalism and also to ground a historically oriented philosophical idealism'.[7] Rickert legitimates his undertaking by describing the 'naturalist' foe as one who dominates not just the sciences but also philosophy.[8]

The categories 'naturalism' and 'scientific worldview' are open to the most diverse positions, from the 'metaphysics of materialism' as the most 'thoughtless form' via positivism to Dilthey's model of a human science based on psychology, although as I will go on to show (see below, Chapter 17.3), this last model also conceives of itself as a triumph over 'naturalism'.[9] Marxism, which the various combinations of 'history' and 'idealist philosophy' were mainly directed against during the early twentieth century, is not explicitly mentioned; it is combated, by way of displacement, in the figure of Comte. He is accused of having surrendered history to 'naturalism' by way of his 'law of the three stages' of intellectual development (from the theologico-fictional and the metaphysico-abstract phases to positive science, based on the cognition of

---

6   Windelband 1915, p. 155.

7   Rickert 1902, p. IV; Rickert 1986, p. 3.

8   Rickert 1902, pp. V, 1ff; Rickert 1986, pp. 4, 12ff.

9   Rickert 1902, pp. 3–4, 14–15, 27–8, 153–4.

laws).[10] If naturalism were right, Rickert argues, historical research would only be possible 'in the form of sociology', namely 'as a theory of the general natural laws that govern every process of historical reality in a uniform fashion'.[11] Here, 'sociology' is employed as a negative term, and this stance has surely contributed to the fact that Weber still hesitates, as late as 1913, to use the term to describe his own approach.[12]

Comte defined sociology, a term he had himself coined, as a 'social physics' [*physique sociale*] that supplements the natural sciences by examining the ensemble of basic laws governing social phenomena. His distinction between social stasis and social dynamics was conceived of as analogous to the distinction between anatomy and physiology within biology.[13] The critique of naturalism found an important point of attack in John Stuart Mill, who called for applying the inductive logic of the natural sciences to the 'moral sciences'. Herbert Spencer exerted a strong direct influence, of whom Troeltsch said he 'was the first to take the naturalisation of history to an extreme'.[14] Within German sociology, traces of Comte's approach are evident in the work of Paul Barth, Tönnies, Breysig, Müller-Lyer, Schäffle, Oppenheimer and—in the form of a 'psychogenetic' model of cultural development—Lamprecht.[15] Brentano also presents himself as a 'follower of Comte'; in particular, he invokes Comte's inductive method, which generalises from empirical data.[16]

Hostility towards 'naturalism' is not specific to southwest German neo-Kantianism, but rather common to various currents striving for a combination of history and idealist philosophy. Troeltsch discusses 'historicism' and 'naturalism' as the two 'great scientific creations of the modern world', tracing

---

10    Rickert 1902, pp. 18–19; Rickert 1986, pp. 24–7.

11    Rickert 1902, p. 19; Rickert 1986, p. 25.

12    Since Weber held that the 'sociological' approaches of Comte, Spencer and Tönnies were *natural-science* approaches and therefore fundamentally flawed, he 'remained distrustful of this term for a long time' (Schluchter 1991, p. 25). In spite of having co-founded the 'German Sociological Society' [*Deutsche Gesellschaft für Soziologie*] in 1909, he wrote to his publisher Siebeck, in November 1913, that his *Grundriss der Sozialökonomik* was becoming 'almost a "sociology" ... although I could never *call* it that' (quoted in Schluchter 1991, pp. 80–1, note 132). Accordingly, he points out, with reference to the basic *sociological* concepts of his 'theory of categories', that he is merely using the term in the sense of an 'understanding' sociology (Weber 1978, p. 3).

13    On organic metaphors in political philosophy, see Meyer 1969 (especially p. 134); a general overview of Comte's *Sociology* can be found, *inter alia*, in Massing 1976.

14    Troeltsch 1922, p. 420.

15    See Kühne 1971, pp. 72–3, 76ff, 90, 95ff, 233.

16    Brentano 1871, pp. 310–11, 312.

the former to the 'classical Romantic movement' in Germany and the latter to 'Anglo-French positivism and sociologism'.[17] One author the critics of naturalism invoke across Europe is Giambattista Vico (1668–1744), who opposed his 'New Science' to Cartesian 'naturalism' in 1725.[18]

Croce, for example, invokes Vico when setting his neo-Hegelian model of 'ethico-political history' off against both 'naturalism' and neo-Kantian dualism. In his *History of Europe in the 19th Century*, he speaks of the methods of the natural sciences conquering a field 'that only philosophico-historical thought has a claim to', thereby confusing people's minds 'by an Enlightenment abstractism'.[19] And like Rickert, Croce also describes sociology as the climax of a naturalist and positivist movement that has infused all of modern thought.[20] Dilthey also invokes Vico when he sets the historical world off from the natural, external world as one that has been constituted and shaped by the human intellect.[21] If naturalism is 'Anglo-French', as Troeltsch claims, then one could speak—in a similarly simplifying fashion—of a 'German-Italian' countermovement. Croce sees Dilthey and Troeltsch as exponents of a promising combination of philosophy and historiography and draws particular attention to Dilthey's studies of the Renaissance, praising them as exemplary intellectual histories of modern man.[22]

That the boundaries between southwest German neo-Kantianism and neo-Hegelianism are similarly unclear already emerges from the fact that in 1910, it is Windelband who delivers neo-Hegelianism's programmatic speech.[23]

---

17    Troeltsch 1922, pp. 104, 240.

18    See Vico 2001, pp. 13, 88–9.

19    Croce 1935, p. 245.

20    Croce 1930, pp. 246–7, 248. Croce, to whom the positivist or naturalist school is 'our present or recent adversary' (Croce 1921, p. 303), describes Vico's *New Science* as a 'very rich and organic anticipation of Romantic thought' (Croce 1921, p. 225). Whereas Croce praises Vico for his '*union of philosophy* with *philology*' (Croce 1921, p. 277), Gramsci criticises the philosophical construct of an 'eternal history' (Gramsci 1975b, p. 1372). Vico's genius consisted in his 'having grasped the wide world from a blind angle of "history", with the aid of Catholicism's unitary and cosmopolitan conception' (Gramsci 1975b, p. 1317). On Gramsci's view of Vico, see also Krebs 1990, pp. 535ff.

21    See for example Dilthey 2002, p. 334.

22    Croce 1930, pp. 278, 410. Croce invokes Dilthey's *Geschichte des modernen Geistes* in order to criticise Sombart's study on the intellectual history of the bourgeois (Sombart 1913a), which Croce sees as a failure: 'The emphasis ought always to have been sought in the intellectual and moral movement' (Croce 1930, p. 411).

23    'The direct renewal of Hegelianism was undertaken by neo-Kantians' (Schreiter 1988, p. 117).

It is to Windelband, 'one of the greatest masters in the modern history of philosophy', that Croce dedicates his 1911 book on Vico (*La filosofia di Giambattista
Vico*), and Troeltsch dedicates his book on historicism to both Dilthey and
Windelband. Such affinities are possible because, as Troeltsch recognises, 'all
of these teachers', whether it be Simmel or Windelband-Rickert, Husserl's phe-
nomenological school or the tradition that leads from Vico and Hegel to Croce,
agree in their acknowledgement of 'history's particular formative principles',
which are 'grouped around the concept of individuality'.[24]

The concept of individuality is, in turn, the starting point for efforts to posit
timeless values within history: 'All of us—Rickert, the phenomenologists, the
current that follows Dilthey—meet in our great struggle for what is *timeless
within the historical*, or above the historical, a struggle for the *realm of meaning* ... a *theory of values* that leads beyond what is merely subjective and to that
which is objective and valid', writes Dilthey's student Spranger.[25] The enumera-
tion is paradoxical, as the actual oppositions are diametrically opposed to the
labels attached to them: whereas *naturalism* stands for certain models of social
*development* and historical change, *historicism* stands for the search for *eternity*
within history.

The critique of 'naturalism' is politically overdetermined, as it believes it can
discern, behind the assumption of social laws of development, a democratic
or socialist tendency. Croce reports, in his *Cultura e vita morale*, how his horror of positivism became so overwhelming that for several years he stifled the
democratic leanings of his character.[26] Natural laws are always 'imbibed with
the ideals of the French Revolution, or the English gentleman, or American
democracy, or socialist brotherliness,' writes Troeltsch, going on to associate
the concepts of Saint-Simon, Comte, Mill and Spencer with the 'socialist philosophy of history developed by Fourier and Cabet, right up to Marx and the
syndicalists'.[27] In his posthumously published 'System of Ethics' [*System der
Ethik*], Dilthey also opposes the 'utilitarianism' of Comte, Hume and Bentham
by arguing that when it no longer stops at property and hereditary right, the
'principle of the greatest possible happiness' leads 'inevitably to the socialist
system, to social democracy'.[28] What is under attack here are the bourgeois-
liberal social strata, who promote socialism by their 'maladroit eudaimonism':

---

24    Troeltsch 1922, p. 30.
25    Spranger 1923, p. 193.
26    See Gramsci 1996, p. 196.
27    Troeltsch 1922, p. 143.
28    Dilthey 1958, p. 40.

the liberal bourgeoisie 'in its quasi-socialist exponents', as Kühne remarks.[29] The 'eudaimonism' attributed to Comtean positivism, i.e. the definition of general welfare as the greatest possible happiness of the greatest possible number, is also the opponent Weber sets out to combat in his socio-political interventions, as when he opposes to the 'soft eudaemonistic outlook' of 'amateur social politicians', who invoke peace and human happiness, the *eternal struggle* to preserve and raise the quality of our national species'.[30]

Within such political attributions, social distinctions, political hostilities and nationalist stereotypes blend to form an enemy stereotype that is difficult to unravel. Gramsci picks up on the combination of naturalism and democracy that Croce rejects and accounts for it by reference to the French materialism of the eighteenth century; in reducing man to a category of natural history, Gramsci argues, this materialism articulated a bourgeois call for equality that has gone on to become, within common sense, the popular postulate that 'we are all born naked'.[31] Thus the view that naturalism prepares the ground for socialism reflects the fear that the postulates of equality found within the bourgeois-popular bloc of the French Revolution, postulates based on 'natural law', might be dissociated from this context and used to socialism's advantage. As for the 'German-Italian' character of this perception, it is related to the fact that both nation states were constituted in the course of a 'passive revolution', by which they sought to resist the upheavals of the French Revolution.

In the course of this process of state formation, aristocratic and conservative resistance to revolution was reworked into a code of national distinction. To what extent nationalist stereotyping is capable, in the course of such a process, of losing touch with its social base can be seen, for example, in the fact that the fear of an egalitarian threat persists even when the characteristics of a hierarchical Catholicism have long since gained the upper hand—as in Comte's positivism—and 'positive' science operates in the service of the reaction.[32] Comte had already broken with his teacher Saint-Simon, whom Marx considered one of the 'patriarchs of socialism',[33] before he began elaborating his *philosophie positive*. The Paris workers knew him as 'the prophet in

---

29    Kühne 1971, pp. 122, 154–5.

30    Weber 1994a, pp. 16, 27.

31    Gramsci 1975b, pp. 1280–1. According to Gramsci, both conceptions of man as spirit and biological conceptions of human nature have been 'expressions of complex revolutionary movements' and need to be explained as scientific 'utopias' that have replaced the grandest utopia of all, that of a human 'nature' sought for within God (Gramsci 2007, p. 186).

32    See Gramsci 1975c, p. 1698.

33    Marx and Engels 1975–2005, vol. 23, p. 394.

politics of imperialism ... of capitalist rule in political economy, of hierarchy in all spheres of human action', Marx wrote in the first (1871) draft of *The Civil War in France*.[34] Comte's philosophy 'will have nothing to do with popular government, as we understand it', Marx stated in an interview, also from 1871; Comte merely sought to 'put a new hierarchy in place of the old one'.[35]

In 1895, Engels attributed to Comte a 'hierarchically organised religious constitution ... turned into something extremely sober, with a regular pope at the head, so that Huxley could say of Comtism that it was Catholicism without Christianity'.[36] What strikes Lange as Comte's 'most remarkable feature' is his 'decided predilection for a hierarchical guidance of the people': 'Here, then, is taken up a factor of the "outlived" Christian religion, which is unquestionably one of the most doubtful and dangerous of them all—Organised Priesthood and Official Authority'.[37] Gramsci, to whom Comte represents the alliance of Catholicism and positivism, pursues this tendency until he arrives at the 'naturalist positivism' of Maurras, who praises Catholicism as the Roman order's response to Jewish and early Christian anarchy.[38] Thus, while philosophies of history ranging from Rickert to Croce employ 'naturalism' as an enemy construct by which to combat 'Enlightenment abstractism', democracy and socialism, Lange, Marx and Gramsci discover an authoritarian naturalism that extends as far as the French forerunners of European fascism.

## 17.2   The Neo-Kantian Taboo on Social Laws

Our look at the political significance of Comteanism demonstrates, in an exemplary fashion, that the critique of naturalism can mean rather different things. In order to be able to confront the egalitarian articulations of naturalism, the historico-philosophical critique adopts an untenable counterposition that denies nature's basic significance to the human life process. It is as if human

---

34   Marx and Engels 1975–2005, vol. 22, p. 498.

35   Marx and Engels 1975–2005, vol. 22, pp. 605–6. The context of Marx's engagement with Comte was that the Paris-based, Comtean *Sociètè des prolètaires positivistes* wished to join the First International in 1870 but was rejected by the General Council, 'since the principles of Comtism directly contradict our Rules' (Marx to Engels, 19 March 1870, Marx and Engels 1975–2005, vol. 43, p. 460; compare vol. 23, p. 95).

36   Marx and Engels 1975–2005, vol. 50, p. 431.

37   Lange 2000, vol. III, p. 296.

38   Gramsci 1992, pp. 182, 194–5; Gramsci 1975c, pp. 1642ff.

history and culture were completely detached from nature and conceptualised as its beyond. Moreover, this critique's hostility to French 'intellectual life' causes it to succumb to the temptation of confusing the counterrevolutionary reaction to the French Revolution in France with the revolution itself. In the abstractness of intellectual history, the social and political context of the enemy formation is elided (as is one's own). The concept of 'naturalism' is dominated by a 'national' enemy stereotype that precludes the perception of congruence. It would, for example, be worth investigating to what extent the function the naturalist paradigm performed within the ideological reproduction of relations of domination in France was similar to the function performed by the philosophy of mind and value in Germany.

It is a different critique of naturalism one finds in Marx, who is subsumed under the rubric of 'naturalism' without further ado in the account provided by the philosophy of history, although he too invokes, in a footnote to *Capital*, Vico's view that 'human history differs from natural history in this, that we have made the former, but not the latter'.[39] But in contrast with later Marxist conceptions of nature, which are once more articulated in terms of the traditional subject/object dichotomy, Marx does not assume the imaginary standpoint, as if human animals were situated outside of nature; instead, he treats nature as the foundation both of the labour process and of the community.[40]

What Marx criticises Comte for is primarily the naturalisation by which the 'class form of property' appears as if it were property as such, and the apology

---

39    Marx and Engels 1975–2005, vol. 35, p. 375, note 2. In a letter to Lassalle dated 28 April 1862, Marx writes that Vico's *New Science* 'contains in embryo Wolf (Homer), Niebuhr (*Römische Königsgeschichte*), the fundamentals of comparative linguistics (even if in fanciful form) and a whole mass of really inspired stuff' (Marx and Engels 1975–2005, vol. 41, p. 353).

40    Thus, for example, in the *Critique of the Gotha Programme*, Marx insists on the fundamental significance of nature as 'the primary source of all instruments and subjects of labor' (Marx and Engels 1975–2005, vol. 24, p. 81). The critique is directed against the 'bourgeois phrase' that labour is the 'source of all wealth and all culture', which has found its way into the Social Democratic movement, a phrase by which a '*supernatural creative power*' is fictitiously attributed to labour (ibid). In *Capital*, the arms and legs, the head and the hand of man, employed in the appropriation of 'Nature's production', are also described as 'natural forces' (Marx and Engels 1975–2005, vol. 35, p. 187). Thus what is directed at the object of labour is itself an organised natural force. 'The earth is the great workshop, the arsenal which furnishes both means and material of labour, as well as the seat, the base of the community' (Marx and Engels 1975–2005, vol. 28, p. 400). On Marx's concept of nature, see Cachon 1986, pp. 922ff.

of the rule of capital as an eternal necessity.[41] But such a transformation of historical forms of society into immutable 'nature' is evident not just in 'Anglo-French' naturalism; it is equally evident in that naturalism's 'German-Italian' rejection in the name of spirit, soul or values. Engels pursued a similar conceptual strategy in his critique of the 'naturalistic conception of history'.[42] What he considers 'naturalistic' is the treatment of thought as 'something given, something opposed from the outset to being, to nature',[43] a description that applies precisely to the neo-Kantian opposition of culture and nature. What is addressed here is not just a certain intellectual current, but a dualistic framing of the problem: the natural sciences and philosophy 'know only nature on the one hand and thought on the other', and they neglect both human beings' modification of nature and the way their activities influence their thoughts.[44]

Within the 'historicist' philosophies of history, the concept of 'naturalism' is deployed in such a way as to allow for an indirect rebuttal of Marx. The critique has a rational kernel in so far as Marx was part of a tradition that transferred expressions from the natural sciences, and especially from micrological anatomy and the physiology of his day, to the theory of economy and society, as when society is described as a structured 'organic system', a formulation associated with metaphors of bourgeois society's 'anatomy' or 'internal physiology', complete with its own 'skeleton structure', 'cells', 'vascular system' and 'blood circulation'.[45] According to Gramsci, the social sciences of the period looked to the natural sciences as their 'model', so as to 'secure for themselves the same certainty and energy' in their quest for an objective and scientifically adequate foundation.[46] In the case of Marx, this invocation of the natural sciences, which Gramsci discusses mainly by reference to society's economic 'anatomy', is 'only a metaphor', albeit one that is easily re-materialised and mechanised when combined with common sense.[47] Such a re-substantiation of natural-

---

41   Marx and Engels 1975–2005, vol. 22, p. 504; compare vol. 35, p. 338, note 1.

42   Marx and Engels 1975–2005, vol. 25, p. 511.

43   Marx and Engels 1975–2005, vol. 25, p. 34.

44   Marx and Engels 1975–2005, vol. 25, p. 511.

45   See for example Marx and Engels 1975–2005, vol. 29, p. 262; Marx 1973, pp. 110, 278; Marx and Engels 1975–2005, vol. 35, pp. 7–8, 10–11, 189. On the concept of 'anatomy' in Marx, see T. Weber 1994, pp. 219ff. Breuer, who attempts to deploy Weber's conceptual apparatus in his study of Germany's 'conservative revolution', also lays a claim to having produced an 'anatomy' that has 'more in common with chemical analysis or anatomy than with moral or practico-political discourse' (Breuer 1993, p. 6).

46   Gramsci 1975b, pp. 1473–4.

47   Gramsci 1975b, p. 1091.

science metaphors has contributed its share to the assertion, within the Marxism of the Second International, of a determinism that argues in terms of natural laws. What was received as 'Marxism' within the labour movement was primarily a 'science of laws' and a 'theory of development'. In the course of this reception, it was possible to invoke not just the authority of Engels, who, in his funeral oration, juxtaposed Marx with Darwin,[48] but also Marx's own formulations, according to which, for example, the material transformation of the economic conditions of production could be 'determined with the precision of natural science';[49] in another passage, Marx wrote that capitalist production produces its own negation 'with the inexorability of a law of Nature'.[50]

However, as soon as one considers these quotes from the point of view of the 'Theses on Feuerbach', there arises the question of how the Marxian standpoint of 'praxis' is compatible with the assumption of such rigid determinations. Habermas has compiled a series of 'natural-science' formulations and concluded from them that Marx is dealing with the 'demand for a natural science of man, with its positivist overtones'.[51] But this interpretation, essentially nothing but an extension of the traditional historico-philosophical subsumption of Marxism under 'naturalism', not only overlooks the consistent critique of naturalism in Marx; it also ignores the difference between the linguistic material adopted and its operative use: the 'naturalist' terminology is to be accounted for in terms of the discursive scuffle with classical political economy, which articulated the relations proper to bourgeois production as eternal laws of nature that are immune to the influence of time, and against which Marx sought to demonstrate—in the currency of the natural sciences, so to speak—the exact opposite, namely the necessary development and demise of such 'eternal phenomena'.[52] Moreover, the parallelisation of social laws of tendency and natural laws has its rational kernel in the fact that both are deliberately reconstructed in the context of an experimental set-up that excludes counteracting

---

48    Marx and Engels 1975–2005, vol. 24, p. 467.

49    Marx and Engels 1975–2005, vol. 29, p. 263.

50    Marx and Engels 1975–2005, vol. 35, p. 751.

51    Habermas 1987b, p. 46.

52    Gramsci has traced Marx's concept of necessity to his engagement with Ricardo, upon whose 'abstract model of a certain economic society' was superimposed another abstraction, that of the 'ahistorical' human species: 'The "critique" of political economy starts from the concept of the historicity of the "particular market" and its "automatism", whereas the pure "economists" conceive of these elements as "eternal", "natural"' (Gramsci 1975b, p. 1478).

or modifying tendencies;[53] in other words, they are reconstructed according to a method that one might describe, following Weber, as 'ideal-typical' (see below, Chapter 22). This needs, in turn, to be distinguished from the instances in which Marx and especially Engels not only make use of linguistic material from the natural sciences, but also adopt the naturalist notions of authors such as Darwin and Morgan, as for example in their analyses of pre-state societies.[54] In any case, the generalised accusation of naturalism overlooks the fact that Marx does not reduce social phenomena to 'laws', but rather accounts for them by means of a historical-critical method of reconstruction.[55]

The neo-Kantian dichotomy of 'nomothetic' and 'idiographic' methods has not itself been developed from the innate logic of the objects of scientific inquiry; it rests, rather, on an extra-scientific and essentialist judgement that is valid neither for the natural nor for the social sciences: by binding the natural sciences to a nomothetic method, the dichotomy strips them of their descriptive and 'individualising' elements.[56] Moreover, it implicitly attributes to the natural sciences a monocausal concept of laws that has been obsolete since the development of quantum mechanics at the latest.[57] Most importantly, however, it declares the historical and cultural sciences unsuitable for examining the 'infinite manifold' of events with an eye to discovering structures of relative identity, functional modes and logics of development. 'Rickert also seems unable to confront the insight into capital's laws of motion in any other way than by attempting to demonstrate the limits of the cognitive aim of the

---

53    All laws of political economy are laws of tendency, according to Gramsci, because one 'obtains them by isolating a certain number of elements, that is, by eliding the counteracting forces' (Gramsci 1975b, p. 1279).

54    See the critique of Meillassoux 1994, pp. 311ff.

55    Marx did not conceptualise his project on the model of a 'deduction' of fundamental laws', but in terms of a 'development' that results from the contradictions of social life. According to Jäger, what separates Marx from Hegel is precisely the difference between 'developing' [Entwickeln] and 'deducing' [Ableiten] (Jäger 1994, p. 36). On Marxist 'determinism', see Laugstien 1995 and Giancotti 1995; on the concept of 'laws' in Marxism, see Assoun 1985.

56    According to Wegener, Rickert uncritically adopted the determinist concept of causality from Kant (Wegener 1962, pp. 70–1). The neo-Kantian conception of the natural sciences is also criticised by Schnädelbach 1974, pp. 164–5, and Habermas 1984, pp. 109–10.

57    Quantum mechanics's 'indeterminacy principle' rests on the insight that it is impossible to arrive at a precise definition of any one physical variable without simultaneously modifying another variable. Brecht integrated this indeterminacy principle into his conception of 'interventionist thought': 'The determining factors always include the behaviour of the one who defines' (Brecht 1968, p. 168). See also Haug 1996b, pp. 52–3.

science of laws as such', Wagner observes.[58] Because everything that can be generalised appears as a 'law', and because every 'law' is presented as a mono-causal 'law of nature', each and every exposure of social 'laws of tendency' is delegitimated. Within the imposed paradigm of individualisation, it becomes inconceivable that, in the context of social production, individuals might enter into definite 'relations ... independent of their will'[59]—relations that, in turn, shape the historical forms of individuality. A taboo is placed not just on eco-nomic laws, but also on the workings of ideological socialisation and the regu-larities evident within the construction of cultural hegemony.

The philosophical commonalities with regard to hostility towards Anglo-French 'naturalism' in general and Marxist 'naturalism' in particular do not preclude the various currents, which compete for the most effective remedy to 'naturalism', from associating one another with 'naturalism'. Croce, for example, considers naturalism and the neo-Kantian philosophy of history two pseudo-opposites, each of which engenders the other, and this allows him to treat Marxist 'determinism' as a transcendental dualism within which the eco-nomic base acts as a sort of hidden God.[60] By contrast, it is a distinctive feature of southwest German neo-Kantianism that it regards Hegelian 'emanationism' as an offshoot of naturalism and attacks Marxism on this basis. Thus the neo-Kantians find themselves opposed to the school of Dilthey, which dominates the historico-philosophical approaches within German historicism.

## 17.3    Competing with Dilthey

The hostility towards the assumption of social laws of tendency, which Weber shares,[61] is justified by Rickert in terms of the disintegrating effects of the very concept of development: this concept, he argues, has become a 'popular weapon of radicalism, which uses it to attempt to demonstrate the irrationality of all things historical'. Thus Hegel, for example, gave rise to the Hegelian left, 'which was great mainly when it came to destroying'. Even using the concept of

---

58    Wagner 1987, p. 111.

59    Marx and Engels 1975–2005, vol. 29, p. 263.

60    Croce argues that while the 'naturalism' of the determinist conception of history is immanent, its immanence is a 'false' one that perpetually transforms itself into transcen-dence, thereby bringing forth a dualist philosophy of history (Croce 1921, pp. 65, 67–8). 'Naturalism is always crowned with a philosophy of history, whatever its mode of formu-lation' (Croce 1921, pp. 67–8).

61    See for example Weber 1988d, pp. 22ff, 41, 203.

development in a non-revolutionary sense, to describe gradual change, is not sufficient, according to Rickert, 'to take the sting out of the notion that every-thing historical is relative and impermanent'.[62]

This hostility towards the Hegelian paradigm is related to the fact that Rickert also suspects Dilthey's distinction between the natural sciences and the humanities of being guilty of 'naturalism'. And yet Dilthey's is a rival proj-ect that is very much politically akin to Rickert's, one that aims to ward off 'naturalist' positions and has been characterised by Troeltsch as that of 'trans-forming the era of Goethe and Hegel into that of the Bismarckian German Reich, which looks to reality'.[63] Dilthey, who lays a claim, in his *Introduction to the Human Sciences*, to providing the historical school with a philosophical foundation,[64] is faced with the social upheaval since the French Revolution and seeks to establish a relationship between the human sciences, holding that cognition of the causes and forces at work within society is 'of vital concern to our civilisation'.[65] But differently from southwest German neo-Kantianism, he pursues the strategy of opposing to the naturalist concept of development a psychologico-hermeneutic deduction that traces historical development back to a structure of psychic life. His main aspiration is that of replacing the Kantian 'assumption of a rigid epistemological a priori' with a 'developmental his-tory' [*Entwicklungsgeschichte*] that starts from the 'totality of human nature'.[66] Considered from the standpoint of the unity of subject and object within expe-rience, nature and mind are products and subsequent interpretations of the dissociation of what was originally unified. Here too, natural science is defined in terms of the cognition of laws. In Dilthey, living emotion is relegated to an inferior position with regard to 'abstract comprehension', and man 'effaces him-self in order to construct—on the basis of his impressions—this great object, nature, as governed by laws'; but 'the same human being then turns back from it to life, to himself'.[67] This reflexive return of man to himself, which immerses itself in the character of experience, is what Dilthey calls *Verstehen*, in contrast with the mere cognition [*Erkennen*] of natural laws.[68] Dilthey makes the nexus

---

62     Rickert 1902, p. 741; Rickert 1929, p. 735.

63     Troeltsch 1922, p. 529. What is meant is a theory of society that 'blends the fortitude of the state order with the cultural content of education, thus corresponding roughly to national liberal policy at the time of the Reich's founding' (Troeltsch 1922, p. 528). See also Kühne 1971, pp. 120ff, 154–5.

64     Dilthey 1989, p. 49.

65     Dilthey 1989, p. 56.

66     Dilthey 1989, pp. 50–1.

67     Dilthey 2002. p. 104.

68     Dilthey 2002, pp. 104–5.

of 'life, expression and understanding' the foundation of the humanities, such that the cognition specific to the human sciences emerges 'insofar as human states are experienced, insofar as they come to expression in life-expression, and insofar as these expressions are understood'.[69] Their specificity consists in the fact that they 'translate objectified historical and social reality back into the intellectual vitality from which it emerged'.[70]

Gramsci says of Croce that one needs to acknowledge his efforts to reconnect idealistic philosophy to life [*per fare aderire alla vita la filosofia idealistica*], adding, however, that Croce did not pursue this aim consistently.[71] Much the same can be said of Dilthey. On the one hand, he wishes to overcome philosophical idealism by means of historical consciousness, but on the other hand, and in spite of all his historical rhetoric, history is rendered static insofar as it is reduced to a 'structure' of psychic life whose historical and social mediations are not reconstructed. In his correspondence with Count Yorck, he writes that he has found in psychologically discernible human nature a 'solid position' within the stream of evolution: 'something irreducible' within self-consciousness that cannot, he claims, be deduced from its elements or the relations between those elements.[72] In assuming such an indissoluble unity of the subject that manifests itself in every vital expression and can be comprehended starting from any of them, Dilthey shares the premises of an intentionalist psychology that was not overcome until Freud's distinction between antagonistic instances of the subject (id, ego, superego).[73] Starting from this imaginary unity of the subject, which appears to be unaffected by social contradictions and the contradictory demands on the individual that result from them, Dilthey reconstructs—primarily via the medium of biography and autobiography—the 'spirit' of generations, epochs and cultures. Thus the main

---

69    Dilthey 2002, pp. 108–9.
70    Dilthey 1924, p. 265.
71    Gramsci 1975b, pp. 1225–6.
72    Dilthey 1923, p. 90.
73    Compare the way Dilthey's *Ideen über eine beschreibende und zergliedernde Psychologie* ['Ideas on a Descriptive and Analytic Psychology'] divide the structure of the soul into the components will, drive, emotion and intelligence; Dilthey derives various character types from the 'proportions' of these components (Dilthey 1894, pp. 233ff). Habermas confronts Dilthey's hermeneutics, which goes back to the 'intentional structure of subjective consciousness as the ultimate experiential basis', with the 'depth hermeneutics' of the Freudian interpretation of dreams; the latter attempts to decipher the unconscious content of what is consciously intended by means of elisions and distortions (Habermas 1987b, pp. 214–78). The contrary concepts of the subject that underlie this opposition are not considered.

methodological problem emerging from his hermeneutics turns out to be that of how to elevate the sympathetic cognitions of singular states of mind to the status of 'objectivity' and 'universal validity'.[74]

That Dilthey never accomplished this transition from the biographical experience of the individual to 'historical' experience, in spite of his rapprochements with Husserl and Rickert, is a point that virtually all neo-Kantian and hermeneutic authors agree on. According to Gadamer, who holds that Dilthey's philosophical intention was not 'liberated' until Heidegger, Dilthey never produced more than preliminary sketches when it came to the transition from a psychological to a hermeneutical foundation.[75] Troeltsch, who speaks of an 'eventually very pronounced rapprochement with Rickert',[76] holds that in his last works, Dilthey attempted to reconfigure his entire approach, but lacked the strength to do so.[77] The critique of 'psychologism' and 'relativist scepticism' indicates that it was, in particular, Dilthey's claim to provide a philosophical foundation of 'objectively' valid ideological values that was seen as unreliable and problematic.[78] Within the reception of Dilthey, there is a continuous ambiguity between the temptation to receive an entirely 'unmetaphysical' deduction of the legitimacy of the dominant order of values from historical 'life' itself and the fear that the historicist paradigm might lead to a loss of validity for the ideological.

The attempt to trump Dilthey's approach ideologically results from this fear. What such an operation requires, as its first step, is an association of Dilthey with 'naturalism'. In order to reject a 'psycho-genetic' view, from which, according to Köhnke,[79] a 'German pragmatism' might have emerged, Rickert needs to demonstrate that the mental life by which Dilthey intends to parry 'naturalist' approaches is an unsuitable foundation for the science of history and culture, because its psychological investigation itself falls within the domain of the concept formation proper to the natural sciences.[80] In spite of his critique of southwest German neo-Kantianism, Gadamer adopts Rickert's interpretation, according to which Dilthey allowed himself to be

---

74    Dilthey 1900, p. 317.
75    Gadamer 2004, pp. 234–5, 249.
76    This accords, most importantly, with Rickert's own view; compare Rickert 1929, pp. XII, 183, 543.
77    Rickert 1929, pp. 519–20.
78    See for example Rickert 1929, pp. 529–30.
79    Köhnke 1986, p. 361.
80    Rickert 1929, pp. 126–7, 131, 154, 168, 181, 186.

'deeply' influenced by the model of the natural sciences,[81] and Gadamer's student Habermas also states that Dilthey transfers 'the natural sciences' ideal of objectivity' to the humanities.[82] Weber already picks up on Rickert's work in the first essay he writes after his illness ('Roscher and Knies'), engaging, without further reference to Dilthey himself,[83] with the approaches of 'psychologistic theorists of development' such as Wundt, Lamprecht, Simmel and Münsterberg,[84] whom he treats as examples of an abortive 'Hegelian form of emanatism'.[85]

Dilthey's humanities contain at least two elements that Rickert attributes to the natural sciences, namely a view of history as something 'objective' that arises from mental processes and the assumption of 'general' functional relations that need to be reconstructed in a gradually ascending manner, from private biographical experience to the systematic humanities, from language and forms of life to the institutions of the nation state.[86] Troeltsch, whose theory of religion frequently invokes southwest German neo-Kantianism, also criticises Dilthey's 'genetic psychologism' for placing too much emphasis on 'individual-intuitive interpretation', thus prompting a 'dissolution' of the comprehension of meaning into a 'causal genesis based on general laws'.[87] Thus, if neo-Kantianism extends its struggle against developmental conceptions of history to Dilthey's psychologico-hermeneutic approach, it is aiming not just at a Hegelian 'emanationism', but also, and more generally, at all those articulations that might be interpreted in terms of a historical explanation. It is as if neo-Kantianism sensed, within such an aspiration, an unacknowledged affinity with the method of critical-historical reconstruction employed by Marx.

---

81    Gadamer 2004, p. 6.

82    Habermas 1987b, p. 183.

83    See Weber 1975, p. 55, note 2. As emerges from a letter to his mother, dated January 1884, Weber read Dilthey during his military service in Strasbourg (Weber 1936, pp. 90–1).

84    Weber 1975, p. 55, note 2; p. 59, note 10; p. 73, note 52; p. 75, note 60.

85    Weber 1975, p. 90.

86    Dilthey 2002, pp. 168ff, 179ff.

87    Troeltsch 1922, pp. 517–18, 519. Within the context of neo-Kantianism's discursive world, this negative judgement could not be any harsher. Troeltsch speaks of a 'complete regression into a purely quantitative naturalist view' (Troeltsch 1922, p. 519).

## 17.4    The Displacement of History and Culture into the Sphere of Ideological Values

After southwest German neo-Kantianism had cleared the way by excluding, with the aid of its concept of 'nature', every attempt to discover what is general and rule-governed within history and culture, the stage could be taken by *value*. In his 1899 lecture on *'Kulturwissenschaft und Naturwissenschaft'* ['Cultural Science and Natural Science'], Rickert opposes to value-free *nature* a *culture* that is 'affected with meaning and value'.[88] If nature is the paragon of something that has developed by itself and is left to its own development, culture refers to what men have created in a value-affected and meaningful way, or to 'whatever is at least *fostered* intentionally for the sake of the *values* attaching to it'.[89] The discursive arrangement is structured in such a way that the most varied aspects of human practice fall, almost automatically, within the sphere of 'value'. In *The Limits of Concept Formation in Natural Science*,[90] culture will then refer to the 'domain of what is valuated and cultivated in a normatively general way', as well as to the 'value with regard to which things obtain the individual significance that everyone must recognise in them'. Weber also holds that empirical reality becomes culture 'because and to the extent that we relate it to ideas of value', and that it encompasses those components of reality 'which become meaningful to us by virtue of that relation'.[91]

The definitions play with the ambiguity of the word 'value' [*Wert*]: it may refer to the ability to distinguish various degrees of relevance in a practically 'evaluating' way, an ability without which non-human and human animals would be unable to survive. If this is what is termed 'value', then the term refers, for example, to the identification of use values that are indispensable for the satisfaction of needs. Another semantic level refers to what Marx addressed by means of his metaphors 'realm of necessity' and 'realm of freedom',[92] i.e. the distinction between, on the one hand, means/end relations required for the reproduction of life and, on the other, self-determined forms of life in which individuals posit and practice, as an end in itself, what seems worth living to them. Haug has called this aspect of the human positing of ends in themselves the 'cultural dimension', thereby distinguishing it from the 'higher' values of

---

88    Rickert 1962, p. 81.
89    Rickert 1962, p. 19.
90    Rickert 1902, p. 578.
91    Weber 1988d, p. 175; compare pp. 180–1.
92    Marx and Engels 1975–2005, vol. 37, p. 807.

the ideological.[93] The 'evaluating' approach to life that manifests itself in such cultural self-activity is something other than the orientation, called for by Rickert, to what is 'evaluated as normatively general'. Nor would a materialist theory of culture attempt to describe it by reference to particular 'value ideas'; rather, it would start from the life practices of the individuals who draw these distinctions.[94]

Marx already demonstrated that the ambiguity of the term 'value' lends itself well to semantic displacements with reference to the field of economics in his engagement with Wagner's *Lehrbuch der politischen Ökonomie* ['Handbook of Political Economy'].[95] Neo-Kantianism makes use of this ambiguity in order to abandon the cultural to the higher instances of the ideological. Rickert is concerned with a 'sphere of what is value-like' [*Sphäre des Wertartigen*] that is neither physically nor psychically real, but which is considered 'higher' because it has a 'meaning' that 'merely psychic being does not need to dispose of'.[96] That which is supposed to constitute, in Dilthey, the unity of life as such is consistently articulated as 'merely psychic'. Instead of providing history and culture with their foundation, it is just their 'material', becoming historically significant only insofar as it 'is linked to a world of non-psychic formations of meaning'.[97] In his critique of 'psychologistic' philosophies of history, Weber also states that, in contrast with mere emotional content, 'value' is 'something which appears to us to demand "validity"'.[98] Rickert goes in search of that 'which has ceased to be identical with the merely psychic', that which 'represents the historical realisation, in the form of cultural artefacts, of normatively general values as law, morality and ethical life, as art, religion and philosophy'.[99]

---

93    Haug 2011, pp. 44ff; see Haug 1980, pp. 10–11.

94    'Not only do we require no "values" to assess this dimension, but it is precisely in this positing of ends in themselves that we discover an acute criterion by which to assess "values"' (Haug 1980, p. 12).

95    The key example of 'underhand manoeuvring' in Wagner's 'theory of value' consisted in re-baptising the general use value of objects for the satisfaction of human needs as the general category of 'value', in order then to 'deduce' from this general 'concept of value' both use and exchange value and subjective values (Marx and Engels 1975–2005, vol. 24, pp. 536ff).

96    Rickert 1929, pp. 185, 543, 545.

97    Rickert 1929, pp. 183–4.

98    Weber 1975, p. 182.

99    Rickert 1929, p. 525.

Together, the instances cited constitute what Marx described as the 'superstructure of ideological strata',[100] i.e. of those 'higher' divisions of state intellectuals that Adam Smith, in his distinction between productive and unproductive labour, 'relegated *economically* to the same class as clowns and menial servants'—a 'peculiar profanation precisely of those functions which had hitherto been surrounded with a halo and had enjoyed superstitious veneration'.[101] Later, bourgeois society realised the necessity to '[reproduce] in its own form everything against which it had fought in feudal or absolutist form'.[102] Instead of choosing the digression of considering the 'structure of mental life', like Dilthey, Rickert directly invokes the superordinate sphere within which the mandarins operate. The 'normatively general values' he is concerned with are withdrawn from and at the same time elevated above the empirical psychic life they are supposed to affect; they are bound up with the ideological powers as society's real beyond.

Rickert organises the same sort of denial of everyday life competencies when he invokes the value of the 'individual' against what is 'general' and 'rule-governed'. He undergirds the concept of the 'historical individual' with the notion of an individual 'in the narrow sense', an individual that represents both that which is 'particular and unique' and that which is 'indivisible'.[103] The distinction between the essential and the inessential does not coincide, as in Dilthey, with the dividing line between the physical and the psychic; instead, it traverses both realms: what distinguishes the diamond from a piece of coal in the world of bodies and what distinguishes Goethe from an average individual in the world of personalities is the value expressed in them. Both their uniqueness and their indivisible unity rest on our 'relating them to a value'.[104] For history is not interested in the 'individuality of all men', but only in that individuality which expresses a general value by virtue of its model character.[105] Accordingly, the historical individual is defined as that reality which must

---

100  Marx 1969–71a, p. 287.

101  Marx 1969–71a, p. 175. 'All these illustrious and time-honoured occupations—sovereign, judge, officer, priest, etc.,—with all the old ideological professions to which they give rise, their men of letters, their teachers and priests, are *from an economic standpoint* put on the same level as the swarm of their own lackeys and jesters' (Marx 1969–71a, pp. 300–1). According to Marx, Smith's 'hatred of the unproductive government' reveals the standpoint of the 'still revolutionary bourgeoisie, which has not yet subjected to itself the whole of society' (Marx 1969–71a, p. 300).

102  Marx 1969–71a, p. 175.

103  Rickert 1902, p. 342.

104  Rickert 1902, p. 352.

105  Rickert 1902, p. 357.

'form a unique and unitary manifold for everyone by relating to a general value'.[106] Thus, in contrast with Marx, Rickert is concerned not with real individuals and the societal relations they enter into, but with mere embodiments of ideological values, which the philosopher of value has decided to consider the marks of genuine individuality.[107] Weber will transfer this elitist conception of man to politics when he opposes the overwhelming process of bureaucratisation by appealing to special 'individuals' such as the leading entrepreneur and politician (see above, Chapter 12.2). 'His thought is determined not by an individualism associated with the notion of equality, but by an interest in the representative individual, in the extraordinary character who bears great responsibility and sets himself off from "everyman"', Hennis aptly remarks, even if he fails to relate this to Weber's neo-Kantianism and merely mentions, in an arbitrary manner, the context of Nietzsche and Burckhardt.[108]

It is one of the antinomies of such an ideological construct that the concepts banished from historical and cultural science with the aid of the idiographic method later return there as the epitome of values. This is true, for example, of the concept of *generality*: against the 'generality' of the 'natural sciences', which finds expression in laws, Rickert sets a 'second generality', represented by values that are universally valid but not accessible to everyone: the historical individual is 'significant for *everyone* by virtue of that in which it is *different from everything else*'.[109] Thus, for example, what is significant about Goethe is precisely that 'by virtue of which he differs from every other specimen of the concept of man'.[110] In this way, cultural theory is given the ideological function of crystallising history in the form of 'model images' that subjects imitate without ever being able to equal them.[111] With the aid of this construct, Rickert posits an instance of 'generality' that can no longer be reclaimed antagonistically, as it is explicitly oriented towards domination: one can no longer appeal to it by reference to rights that ought to be generalised; one must simply subordinate

---

106   Rickert 1902, p. 368.

107   What Rickert addresses by the concept of the individual is negotiated by Windelband in terms of the distinction between 'individuals' and 'persons'. All people are individuals, but this does not yet make them 'persons': 'The great mass of people, which ultimately seems to exist only for the procreation of the species, has no more than a potential personality' (Windelband 1914, p. 337).

108   Hennis 1987, p. 212.

109   Rickert 1902, pp. 358–9; Rickert 1986, p. 90.

110   Rickert 1902, pp. 358.

111   On the ideological workings of representation as model/image, see Haug's studies on art in the Nazi state: Haug 1986, pp. 146ff.

oneself to it.[112] Rickert needs the ideologisation of the general in order to be able to justify the ethical individual's 'integration' into the 'individual whole'.[113] Because the concept of the 'historical individual' is not identical with a single personality, according to Rickert, the conclusion that imposes itself is 'that the curbing of individuality may become an ethical duty'.[114] Rickert argues that whoever has learned to think historically knows that the ethical renunciation of personal idiosyncrasies serves the 'individualisation of life'.[115]

Rickert explains what the expressions 'historical individual' and 'individual whole' mean concretely by reference to the *nation*, which he views as the most important of all human communities.[116] The 'worldview of natural science' is incapable of grasping their ethical significance, because it thinks effusively and in terms of humanity in its entirety.[117] Opposed to this 'general' and 'largely content-free' concept of man is the 'individual whole' of the nation. Treating it as a 'historical individual' entails the postulate of an ethical duty 'to be, first and foremost, the member of a nation'.[118] What Rickert propounds against 'naturalism' is directed at Kant himself by Lask; Kant's 'valuation' appears not as 'integration into a totality, but as subsumption under a general concept'—it is only in Fichte that one notes the 'tremendous progress in the individualisa-tion of valuation which consists in the insertion, between the individual and humanity, of the nation as an independent value formation'.[119]

Like *generality, development* also returns—via the detour of values. Of course the historian needs to think of processes as 'necessary unities' while 'internally dividing them into a number of stages' and 'presenting them as a 'vast series of different phases', Rickert emphasises.[120] 'Each stage is only to be seen as a necessary component part of the whole individual process of implementing a general cultural value', Burger summarises.[121] What is decisive, Weber adds, is that such laws of development and periodisations are not thought of as

---

112   To 'natural law', which he associates with the method of 'natural science' and with nation-alist thought, Rickert opposes the validity of historical law qua product of the historical development of culture: Rickert 1902, pp. 729ff.

113   Rickert 1902, p. 720.

114   Rickert 1902, p. 718.

115   Rickert 1902, p. 720.

116   Ibid.

117   Rickert 1902, pp. 720–1.

118   Rickert 1902, pp. 722–3.

119   Lask 1902, pp. 247–8, 264–5.

120   Rickert 1929, p. 437.

121   Burger 1976, p. 45.

'objective', but as theoretical constructs created by the scientist.[122] The neo-Kantian opposition of 'thought' and 'reality', 'culture' and 'nature' etc. allow him to combat the most diverse manifestations of 'developmental thought' while simultaneously working on the theory of occidental cultural development, which rests mainly on the differentiation of spheres of value. Tenbruck expresses surprise over the fact that Weber, who insisted throughout his life on the primacy of history's singularity with regard to 'objective' laws of development, 'suddenly aligns himself with the evolutionism of his day when it comes to matters of religion'.[123] This is however due not to some special status of religion, but to the adoption of a 'teleological and value-referencing' concept of development that seeks to overcome 'naturalist' evolutionism by transposing it to the level of values.[124]

What corresponds to the postulate of 'absolute values' on the side of the subject is not the concept of the 'internal' as such—Rickert describes it as 'vacuous'—,[125] but the concept of 'normal consciousness', coined by Windelband: a consciousness for which 'these values are simply *the* values' and which constitutes the standard of value by which to distinguish between higher and lower forms of ethical life in different peoples.[126] It becomes discernible thanks to the 'normative evidence' within which it presents itself, Windelband writes in his *Präludien* ['Preludes'].[127] Its recognition is the 'precondition of philosophy', just as philosophy is nothing but 'consideration of this normal consciousness'.[128]

## 17.5    The Distance between Kant and Rickert

The distance between such a philosophy of values and the Enlightenment philosophy of Kant has frequently been noted in the literature. Köhnke says of the southwest German philosophy of values that it rejects all inquiry into the development of values as unphilosophical.[129] The postulate of absolutely valid values that cannot be justified amounts to a 'leap into irrationality', and

---

122    See for example Weber 1988d, pp. 41ff, 144ff, 204ff, 358ff.
123    Tenbruck 1975, p. 682.
124    Schluchter 1991, p. 97.
125    Rickert 1929, p. 560.
126    Windelband 1914, pp. 253–4.
127    Windelband 1884, p. 48.
128    Windelband 1884, p. 44–5.
129    Köhnke 1986, p. 361.

this 'leap' takes the form of an 'authoritarian ideology'.[130] Wagner holds that resorting to the philosophy of values is incompatible with the critical tradition; he attempts to demonstrate that southwest German neo-Kantianism is no Kantianism at all, but rather based on Lotze's revival of the scholastic metaphysics of Anselm of Canterbury.[131] Wagner's main justification for this claim is that, differently than in Kant's transcendental philosophy, the state upon which a judgement is formulated has already been established in advance, instead of being constituted by means of the categorical synthesis of representations within the act of judgement. This means that the place of Kant's judging subject is taken by a dependent subject that cannot but accept given conditions.[132]

In fact, the relations of force have shifted markedly with regard to the definition of the bourgeois subject: the place of the Kantian subject, which was expected to constitute its reality in accordance with the categories of reason and 'rational' moral principles, has been taken by a subject of recognition that continually reaffirms its subordination to the ideological powers of the dominant order.[133] Philosophising no longer helps 'reason' assert itself against established authority; instead, the newly established philosophical authorities present the sciences subordinate to them with prescriptions as to what is 'rational' in the sense of the predominant values. Kant's philosophy, which the young Marx described, in 1842, as the 'German theory of the French revolution',[134] has here been transformed into the ideology of a German counterrevolution: an ethico-political project of the bourgeoisie that called all authority before the 'judgement-seat of reason', where, as Engels said, it was to 'justify its existence ... or give up existence',[135] turns into a philosophy of values associated with feudal-bourgeois mandarins, a philosophy that is directed *against* the 'rational' deduction and explication of values.

---

130  Köhnke 1986, pp. 419–20.

131  Wagner 1987, pp. 12–13, 72ff, 106–7. In Windelband's philosophy of values, one hears the voice not so much of Kant as of Lotze, Troeltsch already observed in his book on historicism: 'Windelband's theory is in fact a translation of Lotze's thought and metaphysics into the transcendental manner of thinking and language' (Troeltsch 1922, p. 552). It is in Lotze, Troeltsch argues, that the basic idea of an essential tension between the general and the particular, between general laws and individual realities originates, as does the 'transformation of Kant's ideas of reason into valid values' (ibid).

132  Wagner 1987, pp. 131, 134–5.

133  'In other words: judgements are to recognise reality in its thusness—no more' (Wagner 1987, p. 131).

134  Marx and Engels 1975–2005, vol. 1, p. 206.

135  Marx and Engels 1975–2005, vol. 24, p. 285.

Given the blatantly ideological character of this philosophy of values, the question arises what, if anything, distinguishes southwest German neo-Kantianism from a normative ideology. What is at stake here is the claim to being a *science* of values'; Rickert has considerable difficulty distinguishing the requisite 'theoretical' conception of value from the 'practical' positing of norms.[136] Thus what comes to the fore is the aspiration to a conception of science that is 'free of value judgements', an aspiration that is often, but wrongly, thought to have been invented by Weber.

---

136    See Rickert 1929, pp. 700ff.

# CHAPTER 18

# The 'Value Relation' as Bearer of 'Freedom from Value Judgements'

What was supposed to make a 'science of values' of the southwest German philosophy of values was the distinction between *value reference* [*Wertbeziehung*] and *value judgement* [*Werturteil*]. Windelband, who considers historiography and the examination of culture examples of 'value-affected cognition' [*werthaftes Erkennen*], contrasts such 'value-affectedness' with the 'weakliness of a moralisation and judgement of objects'; 'value-affectedness' is defined in terms of the scientific objects themselves 'only coming about by virtue of their relationship to a value'.[1] The value-relating method is to be 'distinguished with utmost clarity from the *evaluating* method', Rickert writes in *Kulturwissenschaft und Naturwissenschaft* ['Cultural Science and Natural Science'], because when history is at issue, values are relevant only to the extent 'that they are *in fact* valued by subjects'. The philosophy of values becomes a 'science' by virtue of refusing to value the values it deals with: 'it establishes only what *is*', relates the data of experience to values that are in fact valid and thus engages with values only by means of their effects.[2] In contrast with the willing and evaluating 'practical man', the historian and cultural scientist needs to enact a 'theoretical "referencing" of values' that involves considering history 'under the aspect of values'.[3] While 'value judgements' distinguish between good and evil, beautiful and ugly, valuable and worthless etc., the 'value-relation' divides reality into value-relevant (and thereby 'essential') and value-indifferent phenomena.[4] One might, for example, consider Luther's personality a boon or an evil, but no one can deny, according to Rickert, 'that he was relevant with regard to generally recognised values'.[5] To the extent that philosophy proceeds in a 'purely scientific' manner, it is concerned exclusively with the 'validity of values' and its theoretical comprehension.[6]

---

1  Windelband 1914, p. 240.
2  Rickert 1962, p. 87.
3  Rickert 1902, p. 356; compare p. 307.
4  Rickert 1929, p. 330.
5  Ibid.
6  Rickert 1929, p. 701.

## 18.1    A Commonality with Marx's Standpoint of Science

As its name indicates, the 'debate on value judgements' provoked by Weber turned almost exclusively on the possibility or impossibility of scientific freedom from value judgements, but not on the 'value relations' that are prior to such freedom and on whose basis it is supposed to function.[7] The more Weber's model imposes itself within the social sciences, the more it becomes part of anti-Marxism's standard repertoire for criticising Marxism's 'partisan' thought in the name of scientific 'freedom from value judgements'. The subordination of science to the communist party and its 'Marxist-Leninist' philosophy has repeatedly provided this critique with demonstrative confirmation.

And yet, considered by itself, the postulate of scientific 'freedom from value judgements' displays surprising affinities with Marx's understanding of an autonomous science that one must not accommodate to a 'viewpoint which is derived from *outside*, from *alien, external interests*'.[8] The young Marx of 1843 already opposed to the 'dogmatic criticism ... that struggles with its opposite' a 'true ... criticism' that can account for the contradictions of, say, the current constitution by '[grasping] their essence and necessity'.[9] And *Capital* is presented as the project of a 'free scientific inquiry' that exposes the internal logic of the phenomena examined without external additions and against the 'Furies of private interest'.[10]

---

7     In 1910, Weber made his participation at the Sociological Congress, the organisation of which he had himself suggested, conditional on the inclusion, in the congress statutes, of the principle 'that the association rejects, on principle and definitively, all propagandistic promotion of practical ideas' (Weber 1988b, p. 431). Compare his 1913 expert opinion on the value judgement controversy (reprinted in Baumgarten 1964, pp. 102ff), or the extended 1917 version (Weber 1988d, pp. 489ff). In a dissenting expert opinion written in 1914, Spranger attempts to demonstrate 'that it is a specific feature of the humanities to formulate "value judgements based on cognition"' (quoted in Keuth 1989, p. 39). Later controversies within the theory of science, including the controversy over positivism, have been described as rehashing the classic debate on value judgements (Keuth 1989, pp. 69ff, 93ff; compare Feix 1978, pp. 9ff).

8     Marx and Engels 1975–2005, vol. 31, p. 349. In this passage, Marx is criticising Malthus, whose '*sinning* against his science' he contrasts with Ricardo's scholarly forthrightness: 'But when a man seeks to *accommodate* science to a viewpoint which is derived not from science itself (however erroneous it may be) but from *outside*, from *alien, external interests*, then I call him "base"' (ibid.).

9     Marx and Engels 1975–2005, vol. 3, p. 91.

10    Marx and Engels 1975–2005, vol. 35, p. 10; compare vol. 37, p. 46; vol. 31, pp. 390–1.

It was this claim to scientific status that led Hilferding, for example, to describe the scientific system of Marxism as a 'logico-scientific, objective science that is free of value judgements' (in his 1909 book on *Finance Capital*).[11] However, this affinity with Weber is only apparent, because Hilferding identifies Marxism with the antiquated scientific ideal (rightly criticised by Weber) of a subject-independent 'objectivism', an ideal that elides the fact that scientific work is always undertaken from a particular standpoint. One might object to such an interpretation on the grounds that Marx described his main scientific work as a *Critique of Political Economy* and formulated its key concepts from the socialist perspective of 'social' or 'collective' production.[12] As critical science, Marxism contains the anticipation of a society without classes and domination, and it is oriented towards the self-determination of individuals.[13] Heuristically, such an anticipation allows one to distinguish, within the critique of the economy, the state and ideology under capitalism, between irrational forms and rational contents. The working class has 'no ideals to realize' but merely 'to set free the elements of the new society with which old collapsing bourgeois society itself is pregnant'.[14]

Thus, considered in and of themselves, Weber's and Marx's articulations of scientific 'freedom from value judgements' display relevant commonalities—especially with regard to their stance towards a 'partisanship' that comes from outside—, but these commonalities cease at the point where what the neo-Kantian paradigm describes as 'value judgements' is understood by Marx to inhere within the antagonistic structure of the scientific object itself. A more in-depth assessment would have to address, first and foremost, the way the postulate of freedom from value judgements relates to the type of critique known as 'determinate negation', whose 'no' comes not from outside but '[has] its standpoint within what is negated'.[15] But we do not need to engage with problems of the theory of science at greater length here. For in Weber, the postulate of freedom from value judgements only becomes significant by virtue

---

11    Hilferding 1923, p. XI.

12    On the relationship between the Marxian conception of science and the socialist perspective, see Haug's habilitation lecture, in which he criticises Hilferding for allowing the debate on value judgements to impose its concepts on him instead of questioning its character as science (Haug 1973, p. 145): 'The value judgement Hilferding refuses to recognise is rooted in the matter itself' (Haug 1973, p. 185).

13    See Projekt Ideologietheorie 1982, pp. 180ff.

14    Marx and Engels 1975–2005, vol. 22, p. 335.

15    Haug 1973, p. 179. On the concept of 'determinate negation', adopted from Hegel, see also Haug 1995b; on the distinction between utopian and scientific 'anticipation', see Rehmann 1994, pp. 366ff.

of the concept of the *value relation*, adopted from neo-Kantianism, and this concept implies incisive prescriptions both for the objects of science and for scientific method.

## 18.2    The Transposition of Ideological Values into the Theoretical 'Value Relation'

A first prescription limits the objects of investigation within history and culture to 'individuals' who act primarily in a value-oriented manner and are only admitted, as 'historical centres',[16] to the science of history and culture insofar as the values they relate to express a general aspiration of their culture. Oakes notes that this amounts to defining history in terms of mental life and as something distinct from social structures, relations and institutions.[17] The observation is somewhat imprecise, for as emerges from his polemic with Dilthey, Rickert is explicitly not concerned with mental, spiritual and psychic life as such, but with subordination to general, dominant and thereby 'valid' ideological values. On this understanding, 'freedom from value judgements' means that the implied ideological nature of history and culture is presented in a manner that is itself 'free of value judgements'.

The first thing this requires of scientists is that they be able to 'understand' and 'relive' the values of their historical subjects. Here, Rickert integrates Dilthey's hermeneutic categories, but not without first clarifying that they are only useful to the extent that they are strictly subordinated to ideological values: what needs to be 'understood' is not mental life as such, but the 'mental life of cultural individuals', which is constituted by values and thereby becomes 'meaningful'.[18] In this respect, the cognitive subject *is* a 'valuating' one in Rickert, but not in the sense of formulating 'value judgements' on its own authority; what is meant is subordination to an 'ought' that demands

---

16    To Rickert, 'historical centres' are animate and intellectual beings who position themselves with regard to dominant values; see Rickert 1929, pp. 506, 515.

17    See Oakes 1988a, p. 79: 'Rickert claims that the primary subject matter of history is mental life ... Only mental entities ... as opposed to the artefacts, relationships, institutions and structures ... valuate things or take a position on values'.

18    Rickert 1929, p. 611. Since Rickert's key point is that what is understood within history is 'always more than real, namely value-related and meaningful', the concept of an understanding [*Verstehen*] based on 'reliving' remains without a 'logically useful meaning' unless it is combined with 'our concept of a *value-relating individualising science of culture* whose essential material is provided by the meaningful mental life of cultural individuals' (Rickert 1929, p. 611; compare pp. 558ff, 574ff).

'recognition' as an absolutely valid value.[19] Weber appears to share this shift of emphasis; in his comments on the concept of 'understanding' [*Verstehen*] in the 'Methodological Foundations' of *Economy and Society*, he refers not to Dilthey, but to Rickert's *Limits of Concept Formation in the Natural Sciences* (as well as to Jaspers, Simmel and Tönnies).[20] To be sure, this contrasts with the fact that in 1913, in his expert opinion on freedom from value judgements, he proclaims a '"realistic" science of the ethical, whose explanations are based only on understanding'.[21] This is a more open definition of the object, one principally capable of integrating the 'realistic' question of how social antagonisms articulate themselves within the ethical. Weber organises slight shifts of meaning almost imperceptibly, without explicitly exiting the paradigm of the philosophy of values.[22] In any case, according to southwest German neo-Kantianism's concept of the value relation, the scientist needs to be, as Wegener says, highly 'responsive to cultural values' (meaning, for example, that a historian indifferent to religion cannot write a history of religion).[23] The scientist qua authoritative ideological subject is also subordinated; his psychic instances need to be prepared for and capable of being 'interpellated' by ideological values and powers; he should not examine their social foundations and reconstruct them in a historico-critical manner.

Over and above such receptiveness to ideological 'interpellation', the scientist also needs to perform the specific task of transposing the ideological values the subjects he examines have 'practically' subordinated themselves to onto the 'theoretical' level of a value relation, thereby constituting the object of his scientific inquiry as a unity of the validity of values.[24] The selection of

19    Rickert 1929, p. 690.
20    Weber 1978, p. 3; compare Weber 1988d, p. 427, note 1; p. 541. When Weber distances himself, in 'Roscher and Knies', from Simmel's theory of understanding, he justifies this in terms of its 'psychologism', but when he subscribes to the theory, he claims (against Simmel himself) that it is fully congruent with the standpoint of Rickert's theory of cognition (Weber 1988d, p. 92, note 1; pp. 92ff). For a more in-depth discussion, see Frisby 1988, pp. 585ff.
21    Quoted in Baumgarten 1964, pp. 115–16; compare Weber 1988d, p. 502.
22    Oakes concludes from such discrepancies that Weber did not fully grasp Rickert's theory of values (Oakes 1988b, p. 610). Instead of engaging in this sort of speculation, it would be more fruitful to attempt to analyse such semantic shifts as attempts at a historicisation and 'liquefaction' of neo-Kantianism (see Chapter 3.6).
23    Wegener 1962, p. 270.
24    One might term this transposition a 'primary ideological competence' of the scientist; the underlying receptiveness to interpellation would then represent a 'secondary ideological competence' (see Projekt Ideologietheorie 1982, p. 194).

what is essential and its separation from the inessential is based, in turn, on the general values of the culture. What was presented as the hallmark of the capacity for science turns out, under closer scrutiny, to be a transcendentalisation by means of which the 'value relation' is rendered inaccessible to subjective 'value judgements': the values constituting the 'value relation' are set off both from the real objects they are attached to and the valuations and aims of the subjects involved, forming an autonomous realm beyond the subject and the object.[25] The concept of the 'value relation' rests on a doctrine of two realms that distinguishes, within the philosophy of values, between the world of 'existence' and the world of 'validity' qua transcendental sphere. This transcendence of values, their subject-independent validity, is what Rickert calls their 'objectivity'.[26] Thanks to it, after 'generality' and 'development', a third previously eliminated aspect of reality is reintroduced by way of values. And it is on nothing other than this transcendence of values that the 'objectivity' of scientific concept formation depends, according to Rickert.[27]

### 18.3 Ideological 'Value-Affectedness' as a Condition of Admission to Science

To the extent that the called-for freedom from value judgements is supposed to function on such a foundation of values, not much is gained with regard to the development of a non-partisan science of society that takes into account the internal logics of development and contradictions of its object. Wegener says of the value relation that, as a figure of thought, it amounts to a 'logical circle', because on the one hand, cultural values are supposed to originate from the culture surrounding the scientist, and on the other hand they are supposed to constitute it.[28] This can be seen as the most visible symptom of an underlying ideological arrangement within which value-related phenomena are reflected in value-related phenomena, as in a hall of mirrors. A trajectory is traced from the value-related action of historical individuals to the 'understanding' and value-relation-constituting value-related action of the scientific subject and back. There is nothing to prevent the scientist from projecting his value-related standpoint back into history and 'recognising' it in its values (either as identical or as different). Ideological value-affectedness functions as a condition of

---

25    See Oakes 1988a, pp. 99–100.
26    Rickert 1929, p. 678.
27    Ibid.
28    Wegener 1962, p. 272.

admittance to science as such. The value judgement of the scientist, required for the identification of such value-affectedness, needs to be sublimated into a judgement of value attribution, and this in turn needs to integrate itself into the general values of the scientist's culture. In this respect, the value relation itself is a meta value judgement that is made to precede everything else and thereby rendered invisible; it produces a strategic arrangement that allows for certain value judgements while excluding others.[29]

The distinction between the value relation and value judgements makes it possible to retain the ideological as an a priori and constitutive factor of the scientific object, while simultaneously keeping at bay the concrete, 'value-judging' ideologies that compete with one another within the ensemble of ideological powers. In this way, the construal of a science that is both constitutive of values and free of value judgements allows one to balance contradictory demands: on the one hand, the science of history and culture needs to be guarded against the 'sociological' aspiration to identify social laws of movement, especially when such laws might reveal the transience of the dominant social order—this corresponds with the strategy of opposing to nature, which is 'free of value' and functions according to laws, a value-affected culture; on the other hand, it is a matter of constituting engagement with history as a science of experience that is free of specific worldviews, thereby buttressing it against 'valuating' claims—this is the point of the distinction between 'value relation' and 'value judgement'.

---

29    'This value judgement is introductory and not conclusive. It is not the finale, but the ouverture of a multi-part symphony of values' (Polack 1948, quoted in Wegener 1962, p. 82).

# CHAPTER 19

# Farewell to the Abstract Heaven of Ideas— Outlines of a Philosophical Paradigm Shift

## 19.1    The System of Values as Neo-Kantianism's Weakest Link

The critique of the neo-Kantian philosophy of values aims at a weak point of the construct that Weber has overcome and replaced by 'more modern' concepts: in order to be able to distinguish the 'value relation' qua valid meta value judgement from purely subjective value judgements, the 'southwest Germans' held that they needed to undergird it with a formal system of 'objective' values. Windelband divides the set of universally valid values into the subsets of the *true* (logic), the *good* (ethics) and the *beautiful* (aesthetics); these three spheres of value are traversed by the *sacred* (religion), of which he says that it disposes of no 'realm of values of its own' but consists rather in the 'metaphysical hue' that all values may obtain by virtue of their relationship to an otherworldly reality.[1] Rickert develops a formal hierarchy of spheres of value, basing it on the dichotomy of contemplation and activity; he thereby arrives at a sixfold system whose contemplative branch consists of (1) logic, (2) aesthetics and (3) mystical pantheism, while its active branch consists of (4) ethics, (5) erotics and (6) theistic religion.[2]

Due to its ahistoricity and purely formal character, this systematisation proved to be the weakest link in the southwest German philosophy of values. By and large, both contemporary and more recent critics have focused on and limited themselves to the refutation of this weakness, without objecting to the ideological tailoring of history and culture as such. The critique of neo-Kantianism continues to be organised in such a way that its modifications by

---

1  Windelband 1914, pp. 255, 388, 394. In subordinating philosophy to religion and thereby reversing Kant's dissociation of 'reason' from religious hegemony, Windelband sets himself off from the rival Marburg School, which interprets Kant's postulate of faith purely in the sense of accepting religion as true on the basis of reason (Windelband 1914, pp. 392–3). See the (somewhat uncritical) account in Ollig 1987, pp. 430–7.

2  Rickert 1913, p. 313; Rickert 1921, Appendix. In light of this, it is surprising that Habermas claims Rickert abandoned the aspiration of developing an a priori system of values upon completion of his 1899 treatise '*Kulturwissenschaft und Naturwissenschaft*' ['Cultural Science and Natural Science']. On Rickert's system of values, see for example the accounts in Troeltsch 1922, pp. 154–5, Schluchter 1979, pp. 30–1, and Oakes 1988a, pp. 135ff.

Weber remain largely unscathed. In order to understand this phenomenon, it is useful to preface consideration of Weber's modifications with a look at the underlying philosophical paradigm shift, which led to the neo-Kantian philosophy of values soon appearing outdated.

## 19.2    Croce's 'Ethico-Political History'

As announced in Nietzsche's reckoning with traditional philosophy, the 'old transcendentalisation' was no longer suited to the status of a dominant ideology, 'neither in its directly theological form nor in that of bashful theologies that postulate an abstract-ideal beyond. Philosophy needed to start from "this world"'.[3] A prime example for this tendency is Croce. Gramsci explains his popularity, inter alia, with reference to his dissolution of the philosophical 'system', which created the possibility for a 'greater affinity with life than that of any other speculative philosophy'.[4] Systematicity was no longer sought in an 'external, architectonic structure', but in a coherent solution to the problem of the historical process itself. This, Gramsci argues, is why Croce is so popular in the Anglophone world, which he claims has always displayed a preference for conceptions of the world 'that presented themselves not as grand and confusing systems, but as expressions of common sense augmented by critique and reflection, as the solution to moral, practical problems'.[5]

I will limit myself to discussing Croce's 1915 book *History: Its Theory and Practice*. Instead of superordinating a system of values to history, history is itself construed as a kind of beyond: the centrepiece of this approach is the concept of an 'ethico-political history' of moral and religious life, which is supposed to rise, as '*history*', above 'histories'.[6] Differently from the history of states, it also encompasses the development of moral institutions outside the state. The wars and peace settlements it discusses are declared or agreed by powers that 'are not pure power',[7] such that the emphasis is placed on the consensual aspect of ideological powers.[8] Being a history of spirit, and spirit being

---

3   Haug 1989, p. 184.

4   Gramsci 1975b, pp. 1215–17.

5   Gramsci 1975b, p. 1216; compare pp. 1225–6.

6   Croce 1930, p. 290; this passage is missing in the English translation (Croce 1921).

7   Croce 1930, p. 291; this passage is missing in the English translation (Croce 1921).

8   Gramsci, who describes Croce's 'ethico-political history' as an 'arbitrary and mechanical hypostatisation of the aspect of "hegemony"', relates its ethics to the 'activity of civil society'

a value—namely 'the only value that is possible to conceive'—, this history is also a 'history of values'.[9] It makes reference to those 'men of conscience who strive for moral perfection' and seeks to comprehend history as it affects us as 'moral persons'.[10] The neo-Kantian opposition of value relation and value judgement finds its corollary, here, in the distinction between the 'value of thought', which 'real' history is oriented toward, and the 'emotional value' of poetic or practicistic 'pseudo-histories'.[11] Differently from neo-Kantianism, the emphasis is placed not on the priority of the value relation with regard to value judgements, but on the 'transformation' of emotional values into intellectual values. For example, transforming a 'poetic' biography into a historical one requires us to 'repress our loves, our tears, our scorn' and ask 'what function the individual has fulfilled in social activity or civilisation'.[12]

Historical consciousness is conceptualised as a 'logical consciousness' that overcomes the valuating 'antitheses' of practical consciousness: 'For if there are no good and evil facts, but facts that are always good when understood in their intimate being and concreteness, there are not opposite sides, but that wider side that embraces both the adversaries and which happens just to be historical consideration'.[13] What neo-Kantianism achieves by means of a transcendentalisation of the value relation is here achieved in a neo-Hegelian manner, by working the value relation into a 'dialectical conception of progress'.[14] Gramsci has branded this attempt at preserving the thesis from the antithesis a 'degenerated and mutilated Hegelianism', tracing it back—as a manner of thinking associated with a 'passive revolution'—to a panic-stricken fear of Jacobinism.[15]

---

and its politics to 'initiative and coercion of the governmental and state type' (Gramsci 1975b, pp. 1222–5, 1234–5, 1302).

9    Croce 1921, p. 36.

10   Croce 1930, pp. 291, 289; this passage is missing in the English translation (Croce 1921).

11   Croce 1921, pp. 27ff.

12   Croce 1921, p. 37.

13   Croce 1921, p. 89. For this reason, history has no adversaries, according to Croce; rather, 'every adversary is at the same time its subject' (Croce 1921, p. 100).

14   Croce 1921, pp. 85–6.

15   Gramsci 1975b, p. 1220; compare pp. 1316–17.

## 19.3 The Turn from the Neo-Kantian Philosophy of Values to Neo-Hegelianism and Hermeneutics

Once German neo-Kantianism, in warding off historical materialist approaches and competing with the 'relativism' of historicism, had asserted ideological values in the form of an asocial and ahistorical apriorism, the pendulum swung the other way again, in this case as in others. One of the products of neo-Kantianism's decline was *neo-Hegelianism*: the *return to Hegel* initiated by Windelband, the founder of southwest German neo-Kantianism, around 1910 seemed necessary 'because the proposition "back to Kant" was failing as a bulwark against the materialism of the natural sciences and Marxism'.[16] A closely related phenomenon was the renewed appreciation of the hermeneutic currents associated with Dilthey, such that Berger is able to speak of a 'philosophical shift, from epistemology to hermeneutics'.[17] The claim to a superordinate function with regard to the single sciences resembles that of the neo-Kantian philosophy of values; according to Dilthey, hermeneutics is also to serve, qua link between philosophy and the historical sciences, 'to theoretically establish, against the constant incursions of romantic arbitrariness and sceptical subjectivity into the domain of history, that universal validity of interpretation upon which all certainty rests in historiography'.[18] Dilthey's student Spranger opposes to the 'abstract isolation and rigidity' of the neo-Kantian cognitive apparatus the task of 'conceiving of the forms of thought as being subject to historical development themselves'.[19] At first blush, this notion could remind one of the historicisation of forms of thought undertaken by Marx and Engels, but it is in fact part of a conservative countermovement whose method of understanding follows the principle 'that it is only within the historical that one can approach the suprahistorical'.[20]

'The Gordian knot of history has been cut through and from it an isolated, grey and thin thread has been extracted as means of guidance', Troeltsch remarks in a similarly critical vein, when he, in his 1922 book on historicism,

---

16    Laugstien 1990, p. 174.

17    Berger 1987, p. 299.

18    Dilthey 1900, p. 331.

19    Spranger 1905, p. 5.

20    Spranger 1905, p. 11. On Spranger's early work, see especially Löffelholz 1974. Spranger's ambiguous participation in the National Socialist state has been described as follows by Laugstien: 'It seems we are dealing (a) with a *conservative opponent of the Nazis* and (b) a *highly decorated representative of the fascist state* who was able (c) to continue representing, without any break, the West German republic after 1945. By and large, those who said (a) were reticent about also saying (b)' (Laugstien 1989, p. 32).

begins to distance himself from Rickert once more.[21] It was precisely because 'the great and central question' was, to him as well, that of how 'ultimate standards and unitary values' might be obtained from history itself that the construal of a fixed system of values struck him as useless;[22] he held that such an endeavour ran 'contrary to the flow and the infinity of becoming'.[23] According to Troeltsch, the construct becomes 'out of touch with life' [*lebensfremd*] in Rickert, and history turns into the 'picture book of ethics'.[24] Instead of developing out of history itself, the value system functions as a standard 'that hovers above history as something foreign, a product of pure reason' that can discover in the creations of history only 'material', and not its inner 'law'.[25] Following the neo-Kantian derealisation of history and culture, it is now once more a matter of orienting oneself to the 'internal motion of the object itself'; what is at stake is an interpenetration of object and method by virtue of which the object of historical life obtains its 'comprehensive, and entirely realistic right'.[26] Even 'development' is to be transferred back into the realm of the 'objective', although the 'peculiar object' of history within which the historian needs to 'take root' is interpreted, following Dilthey, in such a way that what is 'value-affected' can effortlessly be reintegrated into or extracted from it: as the 'creativity and internal life of the human soul'.[27] This is one of the points of disagreement with Weber, who in a discussion referred to Troeltsch's notion of development as 'Romantic humbug'.[28]

The hermeneutic critique focuses on a formalism that is accused of construing 'history' and the 'system of values' as abstract opposites, instead of organically combining them. With regard to this issue, Gadamer, for example, sides with Dilthey and opposes Rickert, formulating an argument (in *Truth and Method*) that is largely based on Heidegger's 'hermeneutics of facticity': what supports the structure of the historical world is not a set of facts derived from

---

21    Troeltsch 1922, p. 153.

22    Troeltsch 1922, p. 122.

23    Troeltsch 1922, pp. 151–2.

24    Troeltsch 1922, p. 156.

25    Troeltsch 1922, p. 154.

26    Troeltsch 1922, p. 233.

27    Troeltsch 1922, pp. 231, 234–5.

28    Troeltsch 1922, pp. 189–90, note 83. Troeltsch retaliated by criticising Weber for having contributed little to the historical representation of concrete developmental complexes: according to Troeltsch, Weber had 'brusquely rejected every intuitive representation that attempts to develop a sense of internal development and starts from developmental drives as a regression into dialectics, emanationist logic, Romanticism and historicism' (Troeltsch 1922, p. 567).

experience and subsequently related to values, but the 'inner historicity that belongs to experience itself'.[29]

Briefly put, the hermeneutical alternative to the neo-Kantian dichotomy of value judgement and value relation consists of a two-tiered reintegration into 'history': on the one hand, the various valuations of a historical event are conceptualised as the 'structure' of historical understanding, and on the other, the process of understanding, which is structured by contrary interpretations, is thought of as grounded within the object of history itself. According to Gadamer, history's genuine object is 'not an object at all, but the unity of the one and the other, a relationship that constitutes both the reality of history and the reality of the historical understanding'.[30] Here, contrary interpretations of, say, the French Revolution are not understood as *post hoc* value judgements; instead, 'perspectivalness' [*Perspektivität*], i.e. reference to the standpoints of the observers, is considered part and parcel of the historical object itself: 'It is a constitutive feature of its being that it presents itself in finite perspectives ... It is in the nature of the object itself to provide different possibilities of articulation and understanding'.[31] The focus on the ideological that Rickert ensures by means of the transcendentalisation of 'value relations' and their 'objective' values is achieved by Gadamer through a description of processes of understanding not as self-determined actions, but in the authoritarian language of the military, as 'being mustered into an event of traditioning' [*'Einrücken in ein Überlieferungsgeschehen'*] whose corollaries on the part of the subject are identified as the forms of subordination known as 'preservation, affirmation and cultivation' [*'Bejahung, Ergreifung und Pflege'*].[32] It is especially in the second part of *Truth and Method* that Gadamer accomplishes an 'aggressive rehabilitation of prejudicial thought while affirming the power of tradition ... and the unrestricted validity of authority and authorities'.[33]

---

29 Gadamer 2004, p. 217; compare pp. 342, 353.

30 Gadamer 2004, p. 299. According to Heidegger, the selection of history's potential objects has already occurred in the 'factical, existentiell choice of Dasein's historicality' (Heidegger 1962, p. 447). Dilthey already held that the object simultaneously contains a 'principle of selection' (Dilthey 2002, p. 186).

31 Berger 1987, p. 322; compare p. 318.

32 See Gadamer 2004, pp. 282, 291 (translation modified: the translation 'participating in an event of tradition' misses the authoritarian-military sense of *'Einrücken'*).

33 Orozco 2004, p. 13. In a discursive analysis of Gadamer's philosophical statements from the National Socialist period that is grounded in the theory of ideology, Orozco demonstrates that the political hermeneutics of this 'most successful philosopher of the German Federal Republic' (German conservative daily *Frankfurter Allgemeine Zeitung*) contributed to the internal stabilisation of German fascism.

To the extent that German fascism's 'purges' of philosophy affected neo-Kantianism, they were directed mainly against the Marburg School (Cassirer, Hönigswald, Cohen, Marck, Hoffmann, Liebert), which was rejected as the 'Jewish-liberal' current. But the journal *Logos*, which had been founded by Rickert in 1912 and had turned away from Kant and towards Hegel in 1921, under its editor Kroner, was handed over by the Reich Literature Chamber to two exponents of National Socialist right-wing Hegelianism (Glockner and Larenz); in 1935, it was refashioned into a journal for 'German' cultural philosophy.[34] As Laugstien demonstrates, the fascist state 'did not so much bring about the decline of neo-Kantianism as organise the funeral': 'The epistemological paradigm is relativized by more fundamental entities such as "history", "life" or "existence", and it serves as a popular target for abjurations of bookish academic philosophy'.[35]

The latter defended itself by claiming to be especially competent with regard to the articulation of everything value-related. In an essay published in 1933, Rickert sees himself as being on the defensive with regard to a 'Romantic' current that invokes Dilthey's 'entire man', Nietzsche's 'life' or Kierkegaard's 'existence' to deny philosophy's character as a science.[36] Against this view, which he relates directly to Heidegger's 1929 speech 'What is Metaphysics?', he wishes to retain the superordinated position of a 'philosophy qua science of the world in its entirety'.[37] The philosophy he defines as 'scientific' is one that is subordinated not to extra-theoretical interests, but only to philosophy's '*intrinsic values* ... which do not require the support of practical vital interests for their validity'.[38] Neo-Kantianism's distinction between value relations and value judgements is presented as drawing a line of demarcation between philosophy and the direct interventions of the Fascist state: it is precisely 'entire, i.e. willing and feeling ... man' to whom the totality of the world remains out of reach.[39] What Rickert defends is the specialised competence of the philosopher, who has '*detached* himself from all atheoretical vital and existential interests and attempts to think *purely* in a theoretical or scientific manner', thereby becoming capable of abstracting from his 'own existence'.[40]

---

34    See Laugstien 1990, pp. 157–8, 173–4.
35    See Laugstien 1990, p. 174.
36    Rickert 1933, p. 40.
37    Rickert 1933, p. 48.
38    Rickert 1933, p. 53.
39    Rickert 1933, p. 57.
40    Rickert 1933, p. 50.

Rickert's rejection of the 'philosophy of the movement' should not however be interpreted as a fundamental hostility to the National Socialist state. This can already be seen from the fact that he strives for a kind of division of labour between the 'two types of philosophy', extra-scientific worldviews and the scientific philosophy of philosophers.[41] What also emerges, however, is that the hermeneutic and vitalist attempts to overcome 'old-fashioned' neo-Kantianism are not as innocent as they first appear.

### 19.4    The Lacuna in the Critique of Southwest German Neo-Kantianism

This makes it all the more problematic that even recent critiques of neo-Kantianism seldom venture beyond the competing hermeneutic and vitalist countermodels. Habermas, whose theory of communication is in no small part developed (in *Knowledge and Human Interests*) on the basis of a careful study of Dilthey, albeit one that elides the political dimensions of Dilthey's hermeneutics,[42] has little more to oppose to Rickert's transcendental philosophy than the observation that the cultural meanings of empirically valid value systems have themselves emerged from 'value-oriented action'.[43] The ideological function of the concept of the value relation remains unchallenged. Schnädelbach concludes with the criticism that the neo-Kantian dichotomies of nature and culture, cognition and values etc. ought not to be introduced by means of transcendental logic, but rather 'accounted for by means of the hermeneutic efforts at self-understanding undertaken by real, historical individuals'.[44] Thus doubts are raised not about the alignment of culture with ideological values, but only about the justification offered for it. Oakes confronts Rickert with the opposite deduction, such that theoretical value relations are endorsed or rejected depending on subjective value judgements.[45] But such a reversal remains immanent to an ideological configuration; the

---

41    Rickert 1933, pp. 42ff.

42    See for example the extensive sections in Chapters II.7, II.8, III.9 and III.10. In accordance with his interest in the theory of communication, Habermas distinguishes, within Dilthey's work, between a 'monadological' view oriented towards solitary 'empathy' and a dialogical model based on everyday communicative action; Habermas relates the latter to Wittgenstein's 'language games' and then goes on to develop it by reference to Freud's 'hermeneutically'-oriented interpretation of dreams (Habermas 1987b, pp. 146, 167, 175–6, 214ff).

43    Habermas 1987b, p. 159, note 40.

44    Schnädelbach 1974, pp. 158–9.

45    Oakes 1988a, pp. 114ff, 126; Oakes 1988b, p. 612.

only difference is that this configuration is portrayed not from the perspective of the 'objective' validity of values, but from that of the ideological subject effect. Such a refutation has the additional disadvantage that the underlying assumption, namely that value relations develop organically from within free subjectivities, is far more unrealistic and illusory than the a priori existence of ideological instances as perceived, albeit in a reified form, by Rickert. Both versions elide the societal arrangements within which Rickert's 'objective' values are produced: relations of class, gender and state domination; the separation of manual and intellectual labour; the ensemble of ideological powers, their functionaries, practices and discourses.

According to Troeltsch, Weber adopted not just Rickert's general epistemological foundation but also his 'historico-logical theory of the constitution of the historical object', whereas he rightly rejected Rickert's authentic philosophy of history, namely the 'attribution of objectivity by reference to the valid system of objective values'.[46] But why should the notion of object constitution by means of value relations, which Weber adopted, not be part of Rickert's 'authentic' philosophy of history as well? The focus on a system of objective values, which has become part of the general paradigm of the scholarly literature on Weber, exposes to criticism only that which is in any case part of an outdated configuration of the ideological, a configuration that could no longer come to grips with the social antagonisms of the early twentieth century. Moreover, the neo-Kantian systems of value provided little orientation, if only because of their formalism, and Troeltsch himself accounts for the failure of Rickert's system of values to impress historians by reasoning soundly that they 'already dispose of their shared system of values without him'.[47] Thus while the critique of ideology bears down on that which has in any case already been rendered obsolete by 'history', the neo-Kantian construct of a science of history and culture that is both value-constituted and free of value judgements continues to prosper to this day, thanks to Weber and his followers.

What needs now to be examined is at what point Weber attempts—in accordance with the philosophical paradigm shift mentioned above—to restructure the southwest German neo-Kantianism he inherited, and at what point such a modernisation remains bound up with the fundamental ideological arrangement.

---

46    Troeltsch 1922, pp. 565–6.
47    Troeltsch 1922, p. 565.

# CHAPTER 20

# From the System of Values to the 'Clash of Values'—Weber's Reorganisation of the Neo-Kantian Philosophy of Values

In order to be able to examine Weber's restructuring of neo-Kantianism as an intervention into the ideological *dispositif* of bourgeois domination, I distinguish three aspects of his modifications: the shift from the 'system of values' to the value decision of the 'personality', the attempt to historicise the concept of the value relation and the adjustment of the neo-Kantian philosophy of values to the antagonisms of social interests.

## 20.1    The Ambivalence of the Value-Decisionist Concept of the Subject

What allows Weber to 'liquefy' the neo-Kantian conceptual apparatus is a shift of emphasis, from the validity of systems of values to the internal instances of a 'personality' constituted by 'ultimate' standards of value. As early as his essay on 'Roscher and Knies', he presents a concept of the personality that 'discovers "its" essence in the persistence of its internal relationship to certain ultimate "values" and "meanings" of life'.[1] It is these ultimate values—and not, say, needs or motivations—that 'become ends and thereby translate into teleologico-rational action' within a personality's activities.[2] In the essay on objectivity, he conceives of the 'innermost elements of the "personality"' as being comprised of the 'highest and most ultimate value judgements', those that 'determine our actions and give sense and meaning to our lives'.[3] Now it is the higher-order 'value judgements' that 'we experience as something "objectively" valuable', and a personality's 'dignity' results from the fact that it recognises values 'it relates its own life to'.[4] It is not particular values that matter, but the subject's ability to relate its life to 'values' in the first place, thereby providing that life with 'meaning'.

---

1    Weber 1975, p. 192.
2    Ibid.
3    Weber 1988d, p. 152.
4    Ibid.

By equating the reference to values with the meaningfulness of life, Weber can then go on to blend the concept of the 'personality' with that of the 'man of culture' [*Kulturmensch*], the latter also being defined in terms of such an ability to institute meaning: 'All cultural science has its transcendental premise not in our finding a particular or indeed any "culture" valuable, but in the fact that we are men of culture, equipped with the ability and the will to consciously take a stance on the world and provide it with meaning'.[5] While Rickert's considerations on cultural value are grounded in a transcendental realm of values, Weber relies on an 'ontology of the man of culture'.[6] His ability to 'relate' his life to values is expressed particularly clearly in the concept of the *decision*. Since what is meant are not common everyday decisions but 'value decisions',[7] Weber also sometimes speaks of 'ultimate' decisions.[8] They are what distinguish the 'personality' from the 'diffuse, vegetative "underground" of personal life'.[9] It is because of this unmediated opposition that Weber does not know what to make of Freudian psychoanalysis, in spite of his having carefully studied it.[10] Another contrast can be found in Gramsci, who defines the human being as a 'series of active relations': to develop a 'personality' means 'obtaining a consciousness of these relations', and to change one's own personality is to change these circumstances.[11]

In Weber's view, what distinguishes a 'consciously lived' life from one that 'floats along' in nature's thrall, is a 'chain of ultimate decisions ... by virtue of which the soul chooses ... its own destiny, as in Plato'.[12] According to Henrich, the reference to Plato is to the end of the *Politeia*, which Weber 'reinterpreted

---

5     Weber 1988d, p. 180.

6     Wegener 1962, pp. 117, 124.

7     Weber 1988d, p. 511.

8     See for example Weber 1988d, pp. 507, 604, 608; Weber 1984–2009, vol. I/17, pp. 101, 104.

9     Weber 1975, p. 192.

10    See Marianne Weber 1975, pp. 380ff.

11    Gramsci 1975b, pp. 1344–5. Thus, according to Gramsci, an individual philosopher's historical personality is also 'determined by the active relationship between him and his cultural environment, which he seeks to transform, an environment that responds to what the philosopher does and functions as "teacher" by forcing him to engage in ongoing self-criticism' (Gramsci 1975b, p. 1331). The critique that Gramsci then formulates can also be applied to Weber's value decision: 'These days, when the "thinker" contents himself with his own, "subjectively" free thought, he provokes ridicule, for the unity of science and life is an active unity, and it is there that freedom of thought first realises itself' (Gramsci 1975b, p. 1332).

12    Weber 1988d, pp. 507–8.

to suit his meaning'.[13] In fact, it was in this passage that Plato developed the notion of a metempsychosis by which the immortal soul chooses a new life following the death of the body.[14] The final sentence of *Science as a Vocation*, in which Weber relates fulfilment of one's human and professional duty, the 'demands of the day', to the choice of one's destiny, whereby 'everyone finds and obeys the daemon who holds the threads of *his* life',[15] also evokes the final section of Plato's *Politeia*: there, the goddess of destiny, Lachesis, provides everyone with his chosen demon as a guardian, and this guardian then fastens the soul to the spindle of necessity.[16]

Weber's orientation towards 'ultimate' value decisions creates a beyond that leaves all genuine problems of conscious 'life conduct', from the requisite analysis of one's situation to the integration of contradictory social demands, far behind.[17] The 'personality' of the man of culture is construed as an ideological subject, in the double meaning of 'subordination' [*assujetissement*] and 'free subjectivity' elaborated on by Althusser:[18] it subordinates itself to supreme values and simultaneously experiences this subordination as a free choice by which it determines its own destiny.[19] While such articulations can also be found in Windelband and Rickert, the shift of emphasis described indicates a more general paradigm shift that one can follow Laugstien in describing as a 'reconfiguration of the discursive order, from *consciousness* to *existence*'.[20] Schluchter speaks of an 'existentialist turn' in Weber's worldview, one reflecting the fact 'that between Kant and Weber, the works of Schopenhauer and Nietzsche had been produced'.[21] Since Schluchter is interested only in categorising Weber in terms of the history of ideas, he misses the ambiguity of this 'turn'.

For such a shift can mean various things, depending on its context. On the one hand, the farewell to the neo-Kantian value world of the true, the good and

---

13   Henrich 1952, p. 128, note 4.

14   Plato, *Politeia*, Book x, 617 d/e.

15   Weber 2008, p. 52.

16   See Plato, *Politeia*, Book x, 620 d/e.

17   On the concept of 'life conduct' as a category within the science of the subject (distinct from the concept of lifestyle), see Holzkamp 1995.

18   Althusser 1971, p. 182.

19   What Althusser describes as the 'subject effect' was already criticised by Nietzsche in *Beyond Good and Evil*, by reference to freedom of the will: a delusional longing to be 'that very *causa sui*, and, with a courage greater than Münchhausen's, pulling yourself by the hair from the swamp of nothingness up into existence' (Nietzsche 2002, p. 21).

20   Laugstien 1989, p. 45.

21   Schluchter 1991, p. 286.

the beautiful makes it possible to set the concepts of the value relation and of culture off from that of the norm in a way that Windelband and Rickert could not, despite their formalism. This can already be seen from the claim, mentioned above, to develop a 'realistic' science of the ethical that is not itself an 'ethics', as well as in those passages in which Weber appears to use the concept of the value relation only in the operative sense of a scholarly cognitive interest.[22] When dealing with ethical conservatism, Weber sometimes displays an irreverence that can go so far as to assume the character of a deconstruction of ideological norms, as when, for example, he notes that prostitution is as much a 'cultural phenomenon' as religion.[23] And compared to traditional moral philosophies, Weber's emphasis on specific value decisions accurately reflects the fact that every individual is repeatedly faced with the concrete necessity of choosing from various 'values' and their possible interpretations in such a way as to render them relevant to its actions. According to Tugendhat,[24] the Enlightenment's invocation of the volition and autonomy of the individual is 'the only conceivable non-transcendental instance' by reference to which given norms can be questioned and practical undertakings justified.

On the other hand, Weber's shift from the paradigm of consciousness to that of 'existence' also amounts to an existentialisation of ideological subjection that can also be found—with specific connections—in fascism's conceptual ideologues.[25] According to Henrich's summary of Weber's position, 'what is basically willed in all values, in spite of the clashes between them, is resolution itself'.[26] Henrich however fails to notice the ambivalence of such abstraction. Within Weber's value decision, the value-deciding individual is removed from its relations of work and reproduction, on the basis of whose rules of

---

22    Thus, for example, in his expert assessment on the debate on value judgements, he wishes to remind his readers 'that the expression "value relation" merely refers to the philosophical interpretation of that specific scholarly "interest" that is in charge of selecting and shaping the object of an empirical investigation' (Weber 1988d, p. 511; compare Baumgarten 1964, p. 122).

23    Weber 1988d, p. 181.

24    Tugendhat 1993, pp. 202–3.

25    For example, the *Projekt Ideologietheorie* discovered an existentialisation of ideological subordination in Mussolini's transformation from a left socialist to the founder of fascism, this being related to a dissociation of faith from the social body of concepts: 'Within the articulation struggle-mortal risk-faith, we discern the decided retention of the status of ideological subjection as such' (Projekt Ideologietheorie 1980, p. 48; compare p. 50).

26    Henrich 1952, p. 129.

reciprocity and cooperation one might develop a 'morality of mutual respect'.[27] In Weber, there is no 'structural interconnection between the for-me and the for-others' that is rooted in social practice, one from which a sustainable ethics might be derived,[28] and as in his model of politics, there is no prospect of an 'association in which the free development of each is the condition of the free development of all'.[29]

Where access to the ethico-political is denied 'from below', there is nothing to prevent its functionalisation 'from above'. Weber's heaven of values has been cleared of all determinate values while simultaneously being established as an unquestionable instance by means of the dualism of 'is' and 'ought'. The subject type outlined in Windelband's account of 'normal consciousness', a subject to whom values 'simply are values', assumes the traits of a decisionist subject type, characterised by an indeterminate and vacuous resolution to 'serve' a 'cause', whatever it may be. Hennis's claim that what characterises Weber's conception of man is primarily 'devotion' is not altogether unfounded.[30] If Windelband and Rickert's postulate of absolutely valid but unjustifiable values is 'irrational', as Köhnke demonstrates,[31] then the same is true of Weber's value decisionism.[32]

In his critique of Kant's categorical imperative, Gramsci refers to Socratic ethics, in which the moral will 'is based on the intellect, on wisdom, so that bad action is due to ignorance etc., and the search for critical insight provides the basis for a higher morality'.[33] Weber takes the opposite position: on his

---

27  Tugendhat 1984, p. 162. In 1993, Tugendhat adopts Rawls's concept of the 'cooperative being', using it to justify his concept of a 'morality of mutual respect' without recourse to 'higher truths' and without a 'free-floating decisionist volition"' (Tugendhat 1993, pp. 56, 82, 86, 96, 196, 224). For an evaluation and a critique of this account, see Haug 1996b, pp. 138ff, 143–4.

28  Haug 1996b, pp. 128, 141.

29  Marx and Engels 1975–2005, vol. 6, p. 506.

30  Hennis 1987, pp. 99–100, 236.

31  Köhnke 1986, pp. 419–20.

32  This value decisionism has been noted from various perspectives: according to Troeltsch, Weber juxtaposed to causal science a 'personal endorsement of values that takes a stand on certain issues' as something that is entirely extra-scientific and therefore all the more significant practically (Troeltsch 1922, pp. 570–1). He notes critically that Weber scorned 'all scientific justification of . . . personally endorsed values' (Troeltsch 1922, p. 569). Oakes criticises Weber's 'sociological theory of values' for retaining the decisionist solution to the problem of values (Oakes 1988a, pp. 151–2). In Schluchter's account, the problem is played down to a 'decisionist residuum' (Schluchter 1991, p. 310).

33  Gramsci 1975b, p. 1484.

account, whatever is done 'rationally' is ultimately grounded in 'irrational' value decisions.


## 20.2    The Limits of Weberian Historicisation

It is on this basis that one can account for the difficulties Weber encounters in his efforts to historicise the neo-Kantian concept of the value relation. Instead of criticising the apriorism of the neo-Kantian concept of value, he tries to circumvent it by introducing, differently from Rickert, the concept of 'value ideas'. He describes them as being not just 'subjective', but also 'historically mutable according to the character of the culture and of the thoughts governing people's minds'.[34] This amounts to an almost imperceptible shift in the meaning of the concept of the value relation:[35] because the cultural problems that people concern themselves with constantly constitute themselves anew, the contours of what becomes meaningful to us remain 'fluid'.[36] Here, Weber approaches a concept of history that is generally termed 'perspectivism' in the literature on the philosophy of history, where it is also related to Nietzsche's remarks on the necessarily perspectival character of historiography.[37] The 'objectivity' of socio-scientific cognition now no longer depends on a system of 'objective' values; it depends, 'in the last instance', on the relationship to 'value ideas' which can themselves, however, 'not be established as valid on the basis of the empirical material'.[38] This of course begs the question of what is gained by such a shift of emphasis. What is decisive to scientific 'cognitive value' is still the 'faith, proper to all of us in one form or another, in the supra-empirical validity of higher and ultimate value ideas, within which we anchor the meaningfulness of our existence'.[39] In claiming that this faith in supreme value ideas and their monopoly on the provision of meaning is compatible

---

34    Weber 1988d, p. 183.

35    According to Wegener, Weber has transformed the neo-Kantian value relation into a 'value content relation', within which one no longer relates to a 'value in itself' but to 'that which one judges valuable' (Wegener 1962, p. 120).

36    Weber 1988d, p. 184.

37    See for example Schnädelbach 1974, p. 82. A prime example is provided by the second part of Nietzsche's *Untimely Meditations*, where he accounts for the divergent conceptions of history associated with 'monumental', 'antiquarian' and 'critical history' in terms of the specific social interests of the historiographic subjects (Nietzsche 1997, pp. 67–72, 72–5, 87–100).

38    Weber 1988d, p. 213.

39    Ibid.

with the historical transformation of value standards,[40] Weber is not engaging in any substantive innovation; the claim is one of the most current affirmations of ideological concepts of value.[41] While Weber points out, in this context, that 'the *concrete* configuration of the value relation' is subject to historical change,[42] the same is obviously not true (or at least not to the same extent) of the 'supreme' value ideas that are valid 'supra-empirically', and which, by virtue of this contrast, come to resemble Rickert's 'objective' values. Thus the very distinction between the extra-historical and the historical that Weber meant to overcome is reproduced: supreme value ideas shed 'light' on the ever-changing 'finite part of the tremendous and chaotic stream of events'.[43] Since the promised internal relation cannot be demonstrated, the aspects of value continue to bear down on history from above. And when Weber attempts to describe, in the often quoted conclusion of his essay on objectivity, the historical paradigm shift by which science alters its position and its conceptual apparatus, he continues to make science 'contemplate the stream of events from the heights of thought'.[44]

In spite of its modification by Weber, the concept of the value relation retains the gaze from above against which Marx and Engels developed the aspiration, in the *German Ideology* (1845/46), to 'leap out of' philosophy and begin studying actuality 'like an ordinary man'.[45] Gramsci characterised Croce's philosophy as a 'retranslation of the realistic historicism of the philosophy of praxis into speculative language',[46] and something similar can be said for Weber, even though Weber's 'speculative language' is of course composed not of neo-Hegelian but rather of a combination of neo-Kantian and hermeneutic-vitalist articulations. His efforts at historicisation soon stalled, and he limited himself

---

40    Ibid.

41    After all, the systems of value posited by Windelband and Rickert are also formal systems that prudently leave the contentual determination of their realms of value to 'history'. Rickert describes his system of values as an 'open system', within which one needs to leave space for the 'incompleteness of historical life' (quoted in Troeltsch 1922, p. 152).

42    Ibid.

43    Weber 1988d, pp. 213–14.

44    'But at some point there is a change of hue: the meaning of the aspects thoughtlessly exploited becomes dubious, and the path begins to disappear in the dusk. The light of the major cultural problems falls further afield. Then science also prepares to alter its conceptual apparatus and contemplate the stream of events from the heights of thought' (Weber 1988d, p. 214).

45    Marx and Engels 1975–2005, vol. 5, p. 236.

46    Gramsci 1975b, p. 1233.

to rhetorical invocations of the infinite 'current' of events.[47] Their metaphysical pathos is a symptom of the impossibility of a genuine historicisation within the theoretical-discursive formation that Weber positions himself in: both the orientation of the historical and cultural sciences to ideological values and the underivable nature of those values as posited by neo-Kantianism are retained.

## 20.3    The Eternal Struggle over Values—Weber and Nietzsche

And yet Weber appears immune to this very criticism, thanks to his emphasis on an implacable and irresolvable struggle over values. Peukert was prompted by this to oppose to the notion of a continuity between Rickert and Weber the hypothesis that Weber began from Nietzsche and then adopted the instruments provided by Rickert.[48] Peukert bases his hypothesis mainly on Hennis, who proposed a reconstruction of Weber's scholarly project that starts from Weber's encounter with Nietzsche's work, which Hennis dates to 1894.[49] Turner claims that Nietzsche's 'perspectivism' is the epistemological foundation of Weber's concept of the social sciences, using this claim to argue that Weber is germane to present issues insofar as his work touches on questions raised by postmodernism.[50] By contrast, Schluchter, for example, confronts the Nietzschean faction within Weber scholarship with the argument that Weber distanced himself from Nietzsche in as 'principled' a manner as that in which he distanced himself from Marx, adding that Nietzschean 'undertones' are not to be found in the 'mature', but only in the young Weber (e.g. the one of the Freiburg inaugural address).[51] In spite of its avowed 'freedom from value judgements', the debate is strongly overdetermined by political reception interests:

---

47    'The stream of unfathomable events flows endlessly toward eternity' (Weber 1988d, p. 184). Weber says of the historical disciplines that they are blessed with perennial youth, because in them, 'the constantly progressing river of culture constantly provides new ways of looking at problems' (Weber 1988d, p. 206). And so on. Revealing insights into the discursive context of such articulations are provided by Troeltsch's book on historicism; see for example the sections on Simmel and Bergson (Troeltsch 1922, pp. 572ff, 632ff).

48    Peukert 1989, p. 17; compare pp. 25–6.

49    Hennis 1987, pp. 171ff, 189.

50    Turner 1996, pp. XIV, XXXII. 'In short, Nietzsche's so-called "perspectivism" became a part of Weber's basic epistemology of the social sciences' (Turner 1996, p. XIV). 'Weber's perspectivism, his concern for the legacy of Nietzsche ... and his anxiety with respect to the limitations of rationality and reason are all themes which have entered directly into the debate over postmodernism' (Turner 1996, p. XXXII).

51    Schluchter 1991, p. 79, note 129; pp. 177–8, note 18; compare p. 33, note 22; p. 47, note 49.

while some consider Nietzsche's influence a sufficient guarantee of Weber's farewell to ideology and his compatibility with postmodernism, others tend to exclude the 'domination-affirming critic of ideology' Nietzsche together with his revolutionary antipode Marx from the ideological consensus of pluralistic democracy.[52]

What calls for debate are the regulatory value standards themselves, Weber writes in his essay on objectivity, and such debate, he adds, needs to take place not just between class interests, but also between worldviews, although they are of course 'to a considerable extent' dependent on their link with 'class interests'.[53] Much as with Weber's acknowledgement of 'class struggle' in the debates on social policy (see above, Chapter 13.2), his acknowledgement of a struggle over values is directly opposed to the Katheder socialist project of an overarching 'ethical' political economy that provides every conceivable cultural ideal 'with the stamp of the "ethical"', thereby 'lumping together all kinds of values in an imprecise manner and self-deceptively eliding the conflicts between the various ideas'.[54] What Weber is able to point out against such a political economy is that its poorly thought out general terms, such as *agricultural interests*, *state interests* or *worker interests*, reveal themselves to be 'bundles of muddled and contrary value relations'.[55]

The strength of this argument immediately becomes apparent when one compares it, say, with the 'dialectical' elimination of contradictions attempted in Croce's 'garbled Hegelianism' (see above, Chapter 19.2). The supreme ideals that stir us most powerfully take effect 'for all time only by struggling with other ideals', ideals that are 'as sacred to others as ours are to us'.[56] Of course, the claim that this will be the case 'for all time' suggests that the underivability of values posited by neo-Kantianism is not left behind but only modified, the predicate of perpetuity being shifted from ideological values to the struggle over them. In his essay on the significance of 'freedom from value judgements', specifically in the more recent part of the essay's 1917 publication that he added to the original 1913 version, Weber sides with the 'exponents of the notion of a collision of values', defending them against the accusation of 'relativism'.[57]

---

52    Haug 1993, p. 18; for an exhaustive analysis of Nietzsche's combination of ideology-
      critique and radical aristocratism, see Losurdo 2004, chapter 10, 11 and 14; see also
      Rehmann 2007.

53    Weber 1988d, p. 153.

54    Weber 1988d, pp. 148, 156.

55    Weber 1988d, p. 210.

56    Weber 1988d, pp. 153–4.

57    Weber 1988d, p. 508.

A genuine philosophy of values must not fail to recognise that even the most orderly 'conceptual scheme of "values"' cannot do justice to the decisive fact, that of an 'insurmountable fight to the death' between different values, according to Weber.[58] It is true, he continues, that the spheres of value intersect and intertwine in people's articulation of opinions, and that common people in particular fail to notice this 'blending of morally hostile values', but paying attention to it is precisely what Weber identifies as the task of science.[59]

In 'Science as a Vocation', Weber elaborates on the 'unresolvable conflict' of value systems by reasoning that it is precisely the not-beautiful that can be sacred, just as the not-good can be beautiful and the true needs to be neither beautiful nor sacred. In formulating this argument, which is obviously directed against Windelband's system of the true, the good, the beautiful and the sacred, Weber refers directly to Nietzsche.[60] He is presumably making reference to the *Genealogy of Morals*,[61] where Nietzsche opposes the aristocratic 'value equation' of the good, the aristocratic, the strong and the beautiful to the transvaluation implemented by the priestly caste, and in particular by the Jewish 'priestly people': a transvaluation by which the 'lowly' and 'ugly' become the 'good' and the 'pious'.[62] 'The well-being of the majority and the well-being of the few are opposite viewpoints of value';[63] under the heading of 'Rome against Judea, Judea against Rome', they have struggled against one another for millennia: 'there has hitherto been no greater event than *this* struggle, *this* question, *this* deadly contradiction'.[64]

Thus this reference seems to support the hypothesis of Hennis and Peukert, namely that Weber took Nietzsche as his starting point. Wagner, who holds that Weber's methodological 'early writings' were influenced by Rickert, also holds that in 'Science as a Vocation', Weber steps out of neo-Kantianism's force field, and that he does so under the influence of Nietzsche.[65] Yet what exactly this Nietzschean starting point, with the aid of which Weber is supposed to have

---

58    Weber 1988d, p. 507.

59    Ibid.

60    Weber 2008, p. 44.

61    Thematic parallels aside, this is likely because Weber referred mainly to this book by Nietzsche in a different context, his religio-sociological discussion of 'resentment'. See the introduction to his *Economic Ethics of the World Religions*, published in English as 'The Social Psychology of the World Religions' (Weber 1946b, pp. 270ff; see Weber 1984–2009, vol. I/19, pp. 88ff; Weber 1988e, pp. 241ff) and *Economy and Society* (Weber 1978, pp. 494ff).

62    Nietzsche 1989, p. 34; Nietzsche 1999, vol. 5, p. 267.

63    Nietzsche 1989, p. 56; Nietzsche 1999, vol. 5, p. 289.

64    Nietzsche 1989, p. 52; Nietzsche 1999, vol. 5, pp. 285–6.

65    Wagner 1987, pp. 157–8, 159ff.

overcome Rickert's neo-Kantianism, consisted of is not something the Nietzschean faction within Weber scholarship sheds any light upon. Hennis believes he has identified the central category of Weber's scholarly query in Weber's talk about the development of a 'type of *human being*' [*Menschentum*],[66] and he holds that this category picks up on Nietzsche's key question.[67] Wagner is content to merely point out a shared 'tragic transcendence',[68] and Peukert speaks of Weber having adopted Nietzsche's 'radical relativism with regard to values',[69] in spite of Weber explicitly rejecting just such a relativism.[70] Moreover, it is questionable whether Nietzsche's approach is even properly characterised as 'relativism with regard to values', since what Nietzsche is explicitly concerned with (in, for example, the *Genealogy of Morals*) is a '*critique*' of moral values',[71] one he consistently develops from the elitist perspective of individuals that rule without any hindrance and mediation.[72] Turner brings about a similar downplaying of Nietzsche's undertaking when he claims that Nietzsche's philosophy is characterised primarily by its relationship to the values and practices of everyday life, which revolve, according to Turner, around 'reciprocity and emotion'.[73] If these authors were to take their own hypothesis seriously, they would have to demonstrate that Weber subjected the neo-Kantian philosophy of values to a critique of ideology as radical as the one Nietzsche formulated against the Kantianising philosophy of his own time.[74]

But Nietzsche's radical critique of ideology is precisely what Weber could *not* adopt, and this for the simple reason that Nietzsche's rejection of any 'compromise-formation' between the ruling and the subaltern classes would jeopardise his own Fordist project of a historical bloc between industrial capitalists and

---

66     See for example Weber 2001, p. 106.

67     Hennis 1987, p. 22.

68     Wagner 1987, pp. 155ff.

69     Peukert 1989, p. 18.

70     Weber 1988d, p. 508.

71     Nietzsche 1989, p. 20.

72     'The nature of law, religion and morality as compromises indicates to him that the underclasses are also represented in these instances and may appeal to them, whereas powerful individuals are constrained to accept checks on their power' (Haug 1993, p. 18).

73     Turner 1996, p. XIII. 'The core of Nietzsche's philosophy was an attachment to "the little things" of everyday life. Nietzsche thought that the values and practices of everyday life, which were centred on reciprocity and emotion, were being transformed' (Turner 1996, p. XIII).

74     On this, see the first part of *Beyond Good and Evil*, 'On the Prejudices of Philosophers' (Nietzsche 2002).

labour aristocracy (see above, Chapter 13). And unlike Nietzsche, the Weber of 'Science as a Vocation' is *not* concerned with articulating values as value oppositions between the ruling and the ruled; instead he wishes to show that by and large, the value spheres of the beautiful, the good, the true and the sacred do not correlate with one another, their relationship being, rather, one of competition.[75] In 'Science as a Vocation', Weber bases his argument on Windelband's model of values, whereas in his 'Intermediary Consideration', where he attempts to demonstrate the irreconcilable opposition between the 'religious ethic of fraternity' and the spheres of the economic, the political, the aesthetic and the scientific,[76] he relies mainly on Rickert's system of values.[77] In both variants, what is at issue are the spheres of underivable ideological values that the neo-Kantian philosophy of values distinguishes between. Weber confirms this himself by referring to them as 'gods' that rise from their graves in the shape of 'impersonal forces' and strive to control our lives.[78] On the one hand, he breaks with Windelband and Rickert—and this certainly with the aid of Nietzsche—insofar as he rejects the outdated notion of a unification of value spheres by means of a meta-ideology or 'science', but at the same time, he resituates the problem raised by Nietzsche within the internal relations of the ideological: the struggle over values, which Nietzsche identified primarily as one between the 'master morality' and the 'moralism of resentment' as practised by the subaltern, has now been transposed to a relation between the ideological instances and their distinct areas of applicability.

This new formulation of the problem (as the problem of how opposed 'spheres of value' are perceived and processed) entails an affinity not so much with Nietzsche as with Marx, to whose ideologico-critical perspective Weber could not be more opposed.

---

75    Weber 1984–2009, vol. I/17, pp. 99–100; Weber 1988d, pp. 603–4.

76    Weber 1946c, pp. 327ff; Weber 1984–2009, vol. I/19, pp. 485ff; Weber 1988e, pp. 541ff.

77    See Schluchter 1991, p. 297, note 255.

78    Weber 1984–2009, vol. I/17, p. 101; Weber 1988d, p. 605.

# CHAPTER 21

# Weber's Concept of Spheres of Value as a Modernisation of Ideological Societalisation

## 21.1    Ideology's 'Law of Complementarity'

In the *1844 Manuscripts*, Marx discovers a particular way in which the ideological operates so 'that each sphere applies to me a different and opposite yardstick—ethics one and political economy another'.[1] The distinction between the spheres of the state, right, morality and religion is one Marx discovered in Hegel's 1821/33 *Elements of the Philosophy of Right*, and which he evaluated carefully in his 1843 *Contribution to the Critique of Hegel's Philosophy of Right*. But what Hegel conceptualises from the point of view of the state (the 'crown of the edifice'), and what he views as 'subaltern moments' of morals embodied in the state, is analysed by Marx in regards to bourgeois society and the private property constituting it.[2] At this point in time, Marx still views the emergence of opposed spheres as being determined, in a general way, by the 'nature of estrangement', because each sphere 'focuses attention on a particular field of estranged essential activity, and each stands in an estranged relation to the other'.[3]

In his later writings, this aspect is conceptualised more precisely. In 'On The Jewish Question', Marx is especially interested in the polar structure formed by the spheres of the political state and bourgeois life, a structure that emerges with bourgeois society and splits individuals into abstract citizens on the one hand and bourgeois private persons on the other: wherever the political state develops, 'man—not only in thought, in consciousness, but in reality, in life— leads a twofold life, a heavenly and an earthly life: life in the political community, in which he considers himself a communal being, and life in civil society, in which he acts as a private individual'.[4]

---

1  Marx and Engels 1975–2005, vol. 3, p. 310.
2  Marx and Engels 1975–2005, vol. 3, pp. 107–9. 'Private property entails a system of divisions, and right and morality are ligaments determined by these divisions' (Haug 1993, p. 158).
3  Marx and Engels 1975–2005, vol. 3, p. 310.
4  Marx and Engels 1975–2005, vol. 3, p. 154.

The *German Ideology* (1845/46) reinterprets the antagonistic 'spheres' as ideological forms of thought and practice, inserted into the structure of domination and related to 'practical powers' that 'come to stand above people', such that they 'determine' and 'subordinate' them, appearing within the imagination as '"holy" powers'.[5]

This is precisely what Weber is referring to when he speaks metaphorically about 'gods' that rise from their graves and strive to control our lives.[6] When he speaks out against the traditional model of an overarching and universally valid meta-ideology, insisting on an irreconcilable cleavage between the spheres of value and the religious ethic of fraternity, the market-regulated economy, the politics of force and so on,[7] he is thematising the immediate manifestation of a complex of effects that one might follow Haug in describing as 'ideology's law of complementarity': as a rule, the dominant order does not reproduce itself by means of a one-to-one representation of ideological realms, as if an identical principle were reflected everywhere (as in Lukács's principle of 'reification'); instead, the private-egotistical workings of bourgeois society are compensated for in 'imaginary countersocieties', albeit in a way that leaves private property unaffected.[8] When for example Marx described religion as the 'sigh of the oppressed creature', the '*opium* of the people' or 'the imaginary flowers on the chain',[9] he is concerned with such a paradox of domination being stabilised by means of counterworlds.

What distinguishes both Weber and Marx from Nietzsche is the insight that successful compensation requires representation of the 'subaltern' in the ideological instances right, religion and morality. In Weber's case, this emerges particularly clearly in his religio-sociological engagement with Nietzsche's 'brilliant essay' on *resentment*,[10] *On the Genealogy of Morals*. Weber interprets Nietzsche's exposure of the Judaeo-Christian 'slave uprising within morality' in such a way as to allow for extraction of a positive element of 'ethical rationalisation' from the hopes of redemption articulated by the subaltern; this positive element can then be integrated into the 'Western' ideal-type of religious

---

5      Marx and Engels 1975–2005, vol. 5, p. 245.
6      Weber 1984–2009, vol. I/17, p. 101; Weber 1988d, p. 605.
7      Weber 1984–2009, vol. I/19, pp. 485ff; Weber 1988e, pp. 541ff.
8      See Haug 1993, pp. 19, 147, 199.
9      Marx and Engels 1975–2005, vol. 3, p. 175.
10     Weber 1946b, p. 270; Weber 1984–2009, vol. I/19, p. 88; Weber 1988e, p. 241.

development.[11] From the perspective of an effective reproduction of authority, Nietzsche's critique of values is inapt insofar as its frontal attack on the positions the subaltern occupy within the ideological imaginary would also eliminate the integrating effect of values.

The differences between Marx and Weber emerge more clearly against the background of this commonality. Marx is interested in the functional relationship the various 'spheres of value' enter into within the reproduction of relations of domination; Weber accepts them as cut and dried phenomena and contents himself with noting their contrariety. Weber interprets the complementary structure of the ideological as an eternal struggle of the gods; what Marx observes about it is the displacement of social competencies to superordinate instances and its effects of alienation. Weber defines the personality of the 'man of culture' in terms of constant subordination to supreme value ideas; Marx takes the opposite view, namely that the proletarians need to 'overthrow' the state (and the 'supreme value ideas' that cohere by virtue of it) in order 'to assert themselves as individuals'.[12] Weber naturalises the ideological forces by means of the ambivalent concept of 'spheres of value', whereas Marx historicises them with an eye to a classless society in which the human beings will be able to 're-absorb' them in themselves,[13] much as they will regulate the productive complex by means of their 'common mind' and bring their metabolism with nature under their 'common control'.[14]

The weakness of the Marxian alternative is also the apparent plausibility of the absence of alternatives that Weber presides over: it remained unclear how such an immediate reappropriation by 'socialised man' might be implemented in societies with a highly developed division of labour and in the absence of the market and the state.[15] The Marxian notion of a 'human emancipation',

---

11    See the relevant sections of the *Social Psychology of the World Religions* (Weber 1946b, pp. 275ff; Weber 1984–2009, vol. 1/19, pp. 94ff; Weber 1988e, pp. 246ff) and of *Economy and Society* (Weber 1978, pp. 494–9, 933–4). To be sure, what is at issue in the 'rational' element of redemption that Weber extracts from morality's appropriation from below is an imaginary liberation from suffering that places the faithful in a 'permanent state', thereby making them 'internally immune' to suffering (Weber 1946c, p. 327; Weber 1984–2009, vol. 1/19, p. 484). What remains is an anti-Judaic articulation by which Weber attributes the 'essentially negative power' of resentment and its 'glorification of suffering, of ugliness and of being despised', its 'specific ethic of meekness and non-resistance' primarily to the post-exile 'pariah people', the Jews (Weber 1952, pp. 3ff, 375–6; see Weber 1988f, pp. 3ff, 391–2).

12    Marx and Engels 1975–2005, vol. 5, p. 53.

13    Marx and Engels 1975–2005, vol. 3, p. 168.

14    Marx and Engels 1975–2005, vol. 37, pp. 256, 807.

15    Marx and Engels 1975–2005, vol. 37, p. 807.

which sees man recognising and organising his *forces propres* as immediately 'social forces',[16] developed as an immediate reversal of Rousseau's account of the bourgeoisie's 'political emancipation', in the course of which man needs to be deprived of his (private-egotistical) *forces propres* so that they can be replaced with alien (social) forces.[17] For considerable time, the image of the future was characterised (like its associated critical perspective) by a communism of immediacy that was based on an abstract negation of parliamentarism, thereby paving the way for an unchecked state monopolism.

Marx's silence on the problem of democratic forms of mediation and constitutional limits has rightly become the focus of Marxist self-criticism following the collapse of authoritarian and bureaucratic socialism. According to Nicos Poulantzas, what was missing in Marxist theory was a dialectic strategy of democratising the existing state apparatus by 'combining the transformation of representative democracy with the development of forms of direct, rank-and-file democracy or the movement of self-management'.[18] This lacuna within Marxism has also helped provide the Weberian concept of spheres of values with the aura of a 'pluralist' and thus democratic alternative. In what follows, I seek to demonstrate that this prevailing interpretation thoroughly misunderstands the significance of the Weberian concept of spheres of value.

## 21.2    Weber's Concept of Spheres of Value and the German 'Power Pragma' During the First World War

Weber's acknowledgement of a 'polytheism of values' reconciles those interpreters of Weber who disagree on the question of Nietzsche's influence: Peukert praises Weber for constituting science as a 'site of rational discourse by which to clarify vital issues in spite of divergent value horizons', attributing to

---

16    Marx and Engels 1975–2005, vol. 3, p. 168.

17    In Rousseau's *Social Contract*, which Marx had excerpted a short time before, in the *Kreuznach Notebooks* of July/August 1843 (Marx and Engels 1979–1989, 1992 ff, MEGA, vol. IV.2, pp. 91–101), the one who wishes to 'institutionalise' a people is faced with the following necessity: 'Il faut qu'il ôte à l'homme ses forces propres pour lui en donner qui lui soient ètrangères' ['He has to take from man his own powers, and give him in exchange alien powers which he cannot employ without the help of other men'] (quoted in Marx and Engels 1975–2005, vol. 3, p. 168).

18    Poulantzas 1978, p. 260. According to Poulantzas, the Marxist perspective of the 'withering away of the state' needs to be reconceptualised as a twofold process in which the 'extension and deepening of political freedoms and the institutions of representative democracy ... are combined with the unfurling of forms of direct democracy and the mushrooming of self-managements bodies' (Poulantzas 1978, p. 256).

him a scientific pluralism in the sense of 'rule-governed conflict resolution'—
'austere, but guided by fair rules'.[19] In an almost literal repetition of this assessment, Schluchter discovers in Weber's theory of science a theory of conflict
that aims for the enlightened, non-delusory and rule-governed resolution of
social conflict.[20] Weber's value decisionism is underhandedly transformed
into an 'ethic of dialogue', centred, according to Schluchter, on the imperative:
'You shall expose your ethical conviction to a discussion on values'.[21] Habermas
believes he can take from Weber, as hallmarks of Western modernity, a decen-
tred conception of the world and the 'differentiation of cultural value spheres
with their own inner logics', albeit with certain modifications related to the theory of communication.[22] The new regulatory device of value-dialogical conflict
resolution replaced the old philosophical beyond of the true, the good and the
beautiful. From various camps within the reception of Weber, an apparently
'democratic' discursive world is constructed within which the significance of
the Weberian concept of spheres of values to the ideological reproduction of
class societies and their relations of domination can no longer be thematised.

What is universally praised, within the scholarly literature on Weber, as a
pluralist and rational conception of values, has its immediate source in the
German military campaigns of the First World War. Weber first uses the expression 'polytheism of values' in February 1916, in 'Between Two Laws', a reader's
letter opposing Christian pacifism. Weber's argument amounts to the claim
that such a pacifism would be ruinous for Germany, because it contradicts the
'power pragma' of a great people, and with it one's responsibility to history. 'One
should leave the gospel aside when reasoning on this matter', Weber decrees,
unless one is willing to be 'serious' and follow Tolstoy in consistently opting
for a radical exodus from capitalist societies, whose products one should then
cease to consume.[23] This argument, which Weber reiterates in 1918/19, both in
'Politics as a Vocation' and in 'Science as a Vocation',[24] makes use of a pseudo-
radical phraseology in order to exclude Christian potentials for resistance
from the realms of political and economic domination: Weber claims that the
gospel is ultimately opposed to every 'regularity' of the social world, 'if this

---

19    Peukert 1989, pp. 21, 26.
20    Schluchter 1991, p. 306.
21    Schluchter 1991, p. 328.
22    Habermas 1984, p. 186; Habermas 1987a, p. 315.
23    Weber 1984–2009, vol. I/15, pp. 97–8; Weber 1988a, p. 144.
24    'All or nothing' is the decisive issue with regard to the absolute ethic of the gospel, accord-
      ing to Weber. He describes the gospel as an 'ethic of indignity—except for a saint' (Weber
      2008, p. 197). In 'Science as a Vocation', this claim is followed by a contrast between 'reli-
      gious dignity' and 'manly dignity' (Weber 2008, p. 45).

world is to be one of worldly "culture", and thus of the beauty, dignity, honour and grandness of the "creation".[25] This formulation alludes implicitly to
Nietzsche, who traced Christianity back to the 'instinctive hatred of reality'
in his *Antichrist*.[26] Weber integrates what Nietzsche asserts in the form of a
frontal attack on the positions the 'subaltern' occupy within the realm of the
religious into the concept of a system of 'controlled demarcation' between the
various social realms. To this end, he refers back to an argument formulated by
the 'sober empiricist' John Stuart Mill: starting from experience, one will never
arrive at God—especially not at a God of mercy, Weber adds—but at polytheism, i.e. at a struggle between various binding 'series of values':[27] whoever is in
the 'world' must '*choose* which of these Gods he will obey or when he ought to
and will obey the one and when the other'.[28]

   This short text is more revealing of Weber's concept of spheres of value than
the sublimated versions in which he no longer speaks of the 'power pragma'
of an undisturbed military policy but of the rational 'entelechies' of world
orders,[29] the self-limitation of science, its freedom from value judgements and
the like.[30] In 1843, Marx was still confronted with a so-called 'Christian state' in
Germany, which acknowledged 'the *Bible* as its *Charter*' and which one needed
to confront with 'the *words* of Holy Scripture' in order to force it into a 'mental

---

25   Weber 1984–2009, vol. I/17, p. 98; Weber 1988d, p. 145.

26   Nietzsche 1968, p. 152; Nietzsche 1999, vol. 6, p. 212. According to Nietzsche, Judaeo-
     Christian religion constitutes a rejection of 'all that represents the ascending movement
     of life, well-constitutedness, power, beauty, self-affirmation on earth' (Nietzsche 1968,
     p. 144; Nietzsche 1999, vol. 6, p. 192). In concrete terms, what is meant by the 'world'
     negated by Christianity is, for example, '[b]eing a soldier, being a judge, being a patriot,
     defending oneself; preserving one's honour; desiring to seek one's advantage; being *proud*'
     (Nietzsche 1968, p. 160; Nietzsche 1999, vol. 6, p. 211).

27   Weber is referring to an essay on 'Theism' that Mill published, along with two earlier essays,
     in 1874, as *Three Essays on Religion*; a German translation was published in 1875. The multi-
     plicity of natural phenomena tempts one to interpret these phenomena as the product of
     heterogeneous forces, Mill argues, so that belief in gods is 'immeasurably more natural' to
     the human mind than belief in a single creator and master of Nature (Mill 1998, p. 129).

28   Weber 1984–2009, vol. I/15, p. 98; Weber 1988a, p. 145.

29   Weber 1984–2009, vol. I/19, pp. 485, 487; Weber 1988e, pp. 541, 544.

30   In later writings, in which the expression 'polytheism of values' or 'value orders' recurs
     (e.g. Weber 1984–2009, vol. I/17, p. 99), the immediately politico-military meaning of his
     demand is relegated to the background. This is also true of the well-known opposition
     between the different spheres of value in the 'Intermediary Consideration', published a
     short time earlier (in December of 1915; see Weber 1984–2009, vol. I/19, pp. 485ff; Weber
     1946c, pp. 327ff).

derangement'.[31] In Weber's polytheism of values, the possibility of forcing the state into such contradictions has been eliminated. Ideological values are kept at the disposal of state, military and economic authority, but they cannot be invoked against it. In proceeding thus, Weber continues, by other means, the project begun by Rickert when he attempted to define the 'general' content of values: in Rickert's case, invocation of the 'general', in the sense of universal rights, was precluded insofar as the 'general' was said to be relevant to all only insofar as it is *different from everyone*' (see above, Chapter 17.4). Now, the possibility of asserting the 'general' against the particular interests of domination is precluded by a regionalisation and particularisation of the ideological itself, which is divided into distinct and incompatible 'spheres of value'. The concept of spheres of value is the ideological formula for the corporatist 'compartmentalisation' with the aid of which Weber wishes the antagonisms of class society to be regulated (see above, Chapter 13.5).

Such a shielding of state power from the possibility of appeals formulated from below can hardly be described as 'democratic'. This is true not only if one follows Marx in regarding the Paris Commune, the 'reabsorption of the State power by society',[32] as the paradigm of democracy; it is also true if one subscribes to the self-understanding of parliamentary democracy, which invokes the universal values of general human and participatory rights. If democracy, 'by its very nature, means the equal participation of all in the common mastering of a common task', as Abendroth has said,[33] then it runs contrary to the particularist concept of an exercise of authority that is secured by measures of a controlled demarcation, functioning smoothly and, in this sense, 'rationally'. If the state is understood as 'something abstracted from the collectivity of citizens', Gramsci writes, there results 'the absence of a real democracy, of a real national collective will, and hence, because of this passivity of individuals, the need for a more or less disguised despotism of the bureaucracy'.[34] Weber's

---

31   Marx and Engels 1975–2005, vol. 3, p. 158. 'Criticism is, therefore, fully justified in forcing the state that relies on the Bible into a mental derangement in which it no longer knows whether it is an *illusion* or a *reality*, and in which the infamy of its *secular* aims ... comes into insoluble conflict with the sincerity of its *religious* consciousness' (ibid).

32   Marx and Engels 1975–2005, vol. 22, p. 487. Freedom consists in 'converting the state from an organ superimposed upon society into one completely subordinated to it', Marx writes in the 1875 *Critique of the Gotha Programme* (Marx and Engels 1975–2005, vol. 24, p. 94). On Marx's concept of democracy, see also H. Wagner 1995 and Heuer 1995.

33   Abendroth 1975, p. 26.

34   Gramsci 2007, p. 63.

concept of spheres of values also promotes the very bureaucratisation of the state that Weber warns against in his anti-bureaucratic rhetoric.

One can describe Weber's particularist model of spheres of value as 'modern', provided one does not think of such 'modernisation' in normative terms, but rather in those outlined, say, in the 'pragmatic' definition of Peukert—as the 'linkage of an industrial capitalist economy and class structure with formal bureaucratic authority and social integration, scientific-technological mastery of the world and a rationally ordered, disciplined life conduct'.[35] However, a concept of modernity thus 'free of value judgements' could also be applied to a fascist type of catch-up Fordisation. Peukert himself points out the line of continuity linking the 'rationalisation movement' of the 1920s, which was 'drunk with modernisation', and within which Weber's concepts of modernisation first took hold in Germany, to a 'fascist politics that retained the element of coercion associated with rationalisation projects'.[36] And while the philosophers active in the fascist state rejected the French Revolution's articulations of natural right almost to a man, they were quite able to latch on to aspects of the particularisation of ideological socialisation promoted, *inter alia*, by Weber's 'polytheistic' model of spheres of value. This is evident, for example, in Nicolai Hartmann, who paved the way for the Nazis, in 1933, by dismantling the 'universal human perspective' of philosophy and 'degeneralising, particularising and historicising' the ideological.[37]

### 21.3 The Dichotomy of the Ethics of Conviction and the Ethics of Responsibility as an Ideological Pitfall

Another basic feature of Weber's conception of ethics can be extrapolated, as through a magnifying glass, from his anti-pacifist stance. Schluchter euphemistically describes it as a 'criticist ethics of responsibility based on a theory of conflict':[38] since class and state domination dress up as 'this world', 'the world' or 'reality', their critique necessarily appears otherworldly, unworldly and hostile to reality.

Such action from outside the 'entelechies of the world', entirely 'irrational' with regard to its effects, is described as the 'ethics of conviction' in Weber's 1913 'Expert Opinion on the Debate on Value Judgements', as well as in the

---

35    Peukert 1989, p. 78.
36    Peukert 1989, p. 81.
37    Haug 1989, p. 184.
38    Schluchter 1991, p. 333.

1915 'Intermediary Consideration'.[39] Conversely, the terms 'ethic of success' or 'ethic of responsibility' (the latter term will be used by Weber in 'Politics as a Vocation')[40] encompass the entire reality of ethical action that starts from the 'world' and takes account of the consequences of a value decision. Weber presents us with two distinct and complementary versions of this opposition: what he places in the foreground is the distinction, free from value judgements, between two equally justified maxims 'of a strictly "formal" character', which he claims supplement one another and only constitute the 'real man' and politician with a calling when they appear in conjunction.[41] Under the surface of this sublimated formalism, Weber lashes out with full force against sermon-on-the-mount pacifists, syndicalists and revolutionary socialists, attributing irresponsibility and incoherence to all of them.[42]

Weber's distinction became an openly political issue in the German Federal Republic in 1981, when Chancellor Helmut Schmidt justified the deployment of Pershing missiles in terms of Weber's 'ethic of responsibility'. The pastor and former senator of the interior for West Berlin Heinrich Albertz responded that he viewed Weber's distinction as 'false and dangerous', because it can be invoked, according to Albertz, to justify any political decision.[43] Roth discusses Weber's ethico-political frontlines against the background of the NATO Double-Track Decision, concluding that Weber's dichotomy of the ethics of responsibility and the ethics of conviction was no longer sustainable in light of the destructive potential of modern armaments systems.[44] By contrast, Schluchter views the political frontlines as 'superficial' and claims that the formalism of

---

39    See Baumgarten 1964, p. 124; Weber 1988d, p. 514; Weber 1984–2009, vol. I/19, pp. 497–8; Weber 1988e, p. 553.

40    Weber 1984–2009, vol. I/17, pp. 237ff; see Weber 2008, pp. 198–9 (translation modified).

41    Weber 1988d, p. 505; Weber 1984–2009, vol. I/17, p. 250, Weber 1988a, p. 559.

42    Weber 2008a, p. 196. 'The follower of the ethic of conviction only feels himself "responsible" for ensuring that the flame of pure conviction, the flame, for example, of protest against the injustice of the social order, is not extinguished' (Weber 1984–2009, vol. I/17, p. 238; see Weber 2008a, p. 199). While the pacifism of those with an ethic of conviction regularly turns into the violence of the millenarian prophet, according to Weber (Weber 1984–2009, vol. I/17, p. 240; see Weber 2008a, pp. 199–200), he sees the revolutionary soldier of faith as being forced to satisfy the 'resentment' of his followers (Weber 1984–2009, vol. I/17, p. 245; see Weber 2008a, p. 203). In nine out of ten cases, Weber adds, those with an ethic of conviction are mere 'windbags' (Weber 1984–2009, vol. I/17, p. 250; see Weber 2008a, p. 205).

43    Quoted in Roth 1987, pp. 219–20.

44    Roth 1987, pp. 201ff, 219ff.

the conflict-theoretical 'ethics of personality' needs to be considered independently, as it constitutes the 'core of the matter'.[45]

What Schluchter fails to notice is that the alternative presented to those called upon to make a 'decision on values' is a pitfall: because critique and the capacity for resistance have, as examples of an 'ethics of conviction', been excluded from the world orders, the 'ethics of responsibility' has no other option, within the compartmentalised 'entelechies' and in spite of all claims to the contrary,[46] than to legitimate existing 'practical constraints', or at best to juggle competing logics of domination. 'There are two possibilities', Weber writes to Michels on 4 August 1908: *either* 'my right is not of this world' *or* the affirmation of culture 'along with *accommodation* to the sociological conditions of all "technology"', be it economic, political, or what have you'.[47] If one chooses the second possibility, i.e. regulation based on the 'ethics of responsibility', then not only does all talk of revolution become a 'farce', but the notion that 'the "domination of man by man" might be eliminated by some form of democracy, and be it the most elaborate' becomes 'a *utopia*'.[48]

The conceptual game Weber plays with the concepts of the ethics of conviction and the ethics of responsibility circles a gap. What is absent is what the young Marx dissociates from the form of morality and retains qua ethical content, namely 'the *categoric imperative to overthrow all relations* in which man is a debased, enslaved, abandoned, despicable being'.[49] While it is true that Marx already abandons such language in *The German Ideology*, relegating morality to the 'ideological forms' that 'subordinate' men,[50] his critique of morality aims at the ideological form of morality and not against the capacities for an upright gait that inhere in it.[51] The ethico-political prospect of a self-determined association free of domination structures the late Marx's scientific analyses as much as it structured the idealistic humanism of his early writings. According to Wielenga, the 'materialist and militant humanism' of the mature Marx is characterised by a combination of materialist analysis and self-transforming

---

45    Schluchter 1991, p. 337.
46    One such claim to the contrary is that there can be no talk of the ethics of conviction being identical with irresponsibility, and the ethic of ultimate ends with the absence of conviction (Weber 2008a, p. 196). But the division into dichotomies has a logic of its own, which determines the significance of the individual elements.
47    Weber 1984–2009, vol. II/5, pp. 615–16.
48    Weber 1984–2009, vol. II/5, p. 616.
49    Marx and Engels 1975–2005, vol. 3, p. 182.
50    Marx and Engels 1975–2005, vol. 5, pp. 36, 245.
51    See Haug 1993, pp. 162–3, 171ff.

practice that has itself 'a highly ethical relevance, though Marx would not call it that'.[52]

In his engagement with Tugendhat, Haug proposes moving beyond moral-philosophical decisionism by means of Gramsci's concept of 'catharsis', which denotes the constitution of the ethico-political, the transition of a political class from the economic-corporatist phase to the phase of the struggle for hegemony. According to Haug, this involves an 'impetus towards generalisation that causes the individual to transgress its boundaries and pushes particularism past the corporatist limit'.[53] In Weber, the laborious ascension to the ideological superstructures that the term 'catharsis' refers to can be associated only with the bourgeoisie; Weber is unable to conceptualise the process in a general way. What is missing in Weber is the 'interlinking of my very own development with the free development of all', the 'wherefore' of a political ethic, 'the gain in political agency by the articulation of something that tends to create a bond between everyone'.[54]

---

52    Wielenga 1984, p. 327.
53    Haug 1996b, pp. 143–4; compare p. 126.
54    Haug 1996b, pp. 141, 143–4.

# CHAPTER 22

# Ideal-Typical Conceptualisation's Blind Spot

In the scholarly literature on Weber, the concept of the 'ideal type' is typically considered the crowning achievement of his theory of science. From the 1904 essay on objectivity, where Weber coins the concept, to *Economy and Society*'s 'sociological theory of categories', the 'ideal type' determines Weber's concept formation in the fields of cultural science and sociology, such that Mommsen can speak of the 'fundamental theoretical concept of Weber's main theoretical work'.[1] Accounts of the concept's genesis differ: Marianne Weber sees the concept as having already been used, 'in the same sense', in Jellinek's general theory of the state,[2] and Hennis makes the same claim with reference to Lange's *History of Materialism*;[3] Tenbruck holds that the theoretical conception of Simmel's *Philosophy of Money* was decisive,[4] while Kühne attributes this role to the 'thought objects' of Tönnies's 'pure sociology', adding that they have been purged of even the faintest trace of history.[5] Burger treats the concept as a 'rather original synthesis' of the problems discussed in the 'methodological debate' within German and Austrian economics, problems that neither Menger's abstract-theoretical nor Schmoller's Romantic-historicist method was able to solve.[6] On this view, Weber reinterpreted the concepts both of classical economy and of Menger's 'theory of marginal utility' as 'ideal types', thereby arriving at a methodological position that coincided neither with the position of Menger nor with that of Schmoller, but rather integrated many elements from both.[7]

If nothing else, the explanatory plausibility of the 'ideal type' can be seen from the fact that it allowed Weber to provide even the 'specifically Marxist "laws"' with a place within his theory of science: they may be heuristically fruitful as 'developmental constructs', when one 'uses them to compare reality

---

[1]  Mommsen 1974, p. 65.

[2]  Marianne Weber 1975, p. 314.

[3]  Hennis 1996, pp. 197–8.

[4]  Tenbruck 1959, pp. 622ff.

[5]  Kühne 1971, p. 311.

[6]  Burger 1976, pp. 9, 141ff.

[7]  Burger 1976, p. 150; compare Weber 1988d, pp. 189–90.

to them', but they become 'dangerous' when 'thought of as empirically valid or even as real ... "efficient forces", "tendencies" and so on'.[8]

## 22.1 The Ideal Type as a Deliberately One-Sided Conceptual Construct

According to Weber, the 'ideal type' is a mental image that combines certain historical relations and processes into a 'cosmos of *conceptual* relations that is free of internal contradictions'. By virtue of its conceptual 'purity', which one does not encounter in reality, it assumes the character of a '*utopia* ... obtained by conceptual enhancement of certain elements of reality'.[9] Its relationship to empirical evidence is limited to its function of 'pragmatically *illustrating* and rendering comprehensible' a number of 'ascertained' or 'suspected' relations and effects.[10] Instead of representing reality, it functions as a 'purely ideal *liminal concept* ... by which reality is *measured* in order to render more clear certain meaningful elements of its empirical content, and with which it is *compared*'.[11] The ideal type is explicitly not the 'average' of the phenomena it describes; it results, on the one hand, from the 'one-sided exaggeration of one or *several* aspects' and, on the other, from the 'combination' of those single phenomena 'that can be accommodated to the one-sidedly emphasised aspects' so as to form a unified mental construct.[12] For example, the ideal type of a 'capitalist culture' is comprised of the abstraction of a purely capitalist professional structure and the 'utopia' of a culture dominated only by the private capitalist interest in valorisation.[13] In the 'Methodological Foundations' of *Economy and Society*, Weber uses the term to construe a 'conceptually pure type of rational action' by reference to which the 'irrational' and 'affectually determined' complexes of meaning at work in people's behaviour can be represented as 'deviations'.[14] Such ideal-typical constructs, which one will perhaps

---

8   Weber 1988d, p. 205.
9   Weber 1988d, pp. 190–1.
10  Weber 1988d, p. 191.
11  Weber 1988d, p. 194.
12  Ibid.
13  Weber 1988d, pp. 191–2. In *History and Class Consciousness* (1923), Lukács will engage in such an ideal-typical construction with the aid of his concept of reification, without any reflection on how he thereby abstracts from non-commodified relations (see for example Lukács 1971, pp. 88–9, 154–5). This makes him the exponent of a philosophical model within Marxism that Althusser has described as that of 'expressive totality' (Althusser and Balibar 1997, p. 17; compare Projekt Ideologietheorie 1982, pp. 51ff).
14  Weber 1978, pp. 4–5; Weber 1988d, pp. 544–5.

encounter in reality as rarely as a physical reaction predicted 'on the assumption of an absolute vacuum', state 'what course a given type of human action would take if it were strictly rational, unaffected by errors and emotional factors and if, furthermore, it were completely and unequivocally directed to a single end'.[15]

But in what way is such a 'one-sided' emphasis on 'aspects', to which historical phenomena are expected to 'subordinate' themselves, any different from an arbitrary invention or an ideological construct? Verifying the formation of concepts by means of a developmental logic rooted in the object under investigation is out of the question for Weber, since he rejects every relation of representation, invoking the authority of Kant to justify this, and postulates the 'discursive nature of our cognition'.[16] In this context, he refers back implicitly to Dilthey's justification of the human sciences: in the social sciences in particular, which involve 'mental' processes that need to be 'empathetically "*understood*"', there is no such thing as an 'objective' scientific analysis that can be formulated independently of one-sided emphasis on certain aspects, Weber argues.[17] 'It is not the "*objective*" relations of "*things*" but the *ideal* relations of *problems* that underlie the areas of operation proper to the sciences'.[18] As soon as the 'quality' of a socio-economic process is at issue, the thrust of the scholar's cognitive interests becomes decisive.[19]

## 22.2    The *Rendezvous Manqué* with Marx

Within the opposition of 'ideal-typical' to objectivist concept formation, there is a recurrence of the *rendezvous manqués* that we analysed with reference to the dichotomies of nature and culture, law and value, etc. That Marx and Weber were more akin in their rejection of a standpoint-independent objectivism than Weber himself thought possible has already emerged from our discussion of the 'Theses on Feuerbach' (see above, Chapter 16.2). The question concerning research's guiding cognitive interests, which Weber con-

---

15    Weber 1978, pp. 9, 20; Weber 1988d, pp. 548, 560.
16    Weber 1988d, pp. 195, 208. For Kant, human cognition is 'discursive' when it operates through concepts, not through intuition (Kant 1900, p. 108). Lask also speaks of the 'discursive character of our cognition' (Lask 1902, p. 30); Weber presumably adopted the formulation from him.
17    Weber 1988d, pp. 170, 173.
18    Weber 1988d, p. 166.
19    Weber 1988d, p. 161.

fronts the naïve objectives of 'ethical political economy' with, is also at the centre of Marx's critique of science and his methodological reflections. After all, in *Capital*, Marx is himself engaging—in a methodologically conscious manner—in what one could characterise as 'ideal-typical' concept formation, as when he analyses the development of the form of value as under laboratory conditions, that is to say, in a form more pure than has ever existed in reality.[20] Throughout Marx's critique of political economy, the orientation to a classless society free of domination 'introduces a perspective into the subject matter even when it is not explicitly called by its name'.[21] The dualism of 'objective' and 'subjective', 'reality' and 'cognitive interest', of a 'mimetic' concept formation independent of the standpoint of the scientist and an 'ideal-typical' concept formation detached from the scientific object, is a product of Weber's engagement with the Marxism of the Second International and obscures the controversy between Weber and Marx rather than shedding light on it. But surely Marx would never have claimed that the laws of tendency obtained by him are significant only when they are *not* 'thought of as *real*... "effective forces", "tendencies" etc.'[22] While, for example, the ideal-typically obtained 'law of value' is not encountered in a pure form empirically, it does exist as a tendency operating in reality, one that 'violently' asserts itself in the accidental and fluctuating exchange relations associated with private commodity production based on the division of labour, much as the 'law of gravity... asserts itself when a house falls about our ears'.[23]

The difference lies mainly in the way in which the object under investigation and the guiding cognitive interest are defined. In his engagements with 'metaphysical' materialism, Marx arrives at the insight that the philosophical opposition of 'matter' and 'mind' needs to be abandoned, analysing the conditions of capitalist domination and estrangement starting from people's practical modes of production and reproduction. Weber turns against the epistemologies of a subject-independent objectivism by taking recourse to the *cultural meaning* of the life phenomena under examination: it is 'our' attribution of meaning that is crucial to the selection of material and to concept formation; 'we' are the ones who select from the infinite multiplicity of events the ones that relate to the *'ideas of cultural value* by which we approach reality'; an

---

20    Marx and Engels 1975–2005, vol. 35, pp. 57ff.

21    Haug 1973, pp. 152–3.

22    Weber 1988d, p. 205.

23    Marx and Engels 1975–2005, vol. 35, p. 86.

ideal type's selective principles depend on the perspective from which 'we' are able to 'consider [cultural phenomena] as meaningful to us'.[24]

Given Weber's opposition to 'ethical political economy', this can be read, to an extent, as a critical exposure of the standpoint-dependence of scientifically dressed-up value judgements. In any case, by deducing such value judgements from given cultural values, Weber destroys the illusion that they develop organically from the examined reality itself. Moreover, and as we have seen (see above, Chapter 20.1), he wants his conception of the 'conditionality of cultural cognition on value ideas' to be understood as being itself free of value judgements, i.e. independent of the ethical assessment of valuable phenomena.[25] But his critique remains half-hearted: instead of inquiring into the social standpoints associated with political economy's ethical value judgements, and into their functionality for domination, he includes them in his 'we' and contents himself with pointing out the cultural and social standpoint-dependence of cognition as such. The argument operates within an abstract dualism of subject-independent objectivity and value-guided cognition, instead of overcoming this dualism by developing a 'philosophy of praxis'.

'There is no light at the foot of the lighthouse'—in his *Principle of Hope*, Bloch formulates this dictum to illustrate that what is closest to the subject remains invisible to it.[26] It is precisely the decisive instance, the one that the selection and prioritisation of objects of inquiry depend on, that remains in the dark in Weber: who are the social actors referred to as 'we', the ones who attribute 'cultural meaning' to historical events or deny it to them? And what determines the 'value ideas' that the aspects responsible for one-sided emphasis are oriented to 'in the last instance'?[27] This discursive lacuna is the site at which the value problem of the ideological catches up with Weber's attempt to constitute sociology as a 'science of reality' opposed to the prevailing tendency to strive to assess the 'ethical' value of things. The argument is circular: whether the ideal type is purely an intellectual game or a case of scientifically fruitful concept formation can only be decided by reference to its 'success with regard to the cognition of concrete cultural phenomena', but the criteria of success turn out to be dependent on 'our' attribution of meaning.[28]

Finally, Weber sees the point of his dispute with ethical political economy as being 'merely' that of 'exposing the often *very subtle* line that separates sci-

24    Weber 1988d, pp. 178, 192.
25    Weber 1988d, p. 181.
26    Bloch 1986, p. 295.
27    Weber 1988d, p. 213.
28    Weber 1988d, pp. 193–4.

ence from faith'.[29] Even the 'Katheder socialists' could have endorsed such a cautious critique. The attempt to found a sociological 'science of reality' gets stalled halfway, because Weber, in a skewed attack on a naïve objectivism, eliminates the reference to reality altogether. His argument focuses, in a one-sided way, on the demarcation between scientific statements and 'value judgements', but it prevents insight into the ideological determinants of the conceptual arrangement itself. This is mainly due to the fact that Weber has adopted, in his value decisionism, the neo-Kantian postulate of principally underivable 'values'. In particular, what is absent in his work is a reflection on how the retrojection of current 'cultural meanings' onto one's historical material might be curbed methodologically.[30]

## 22.3    The Capitalist Orientation of Weber's Sociological Ideal Types

Weber's concept of the 'ideal type' can be both supplemented and critically corrected by inscribing the appropriate social subject into his lacuna. The 'we' that Weber leaves undefined in his discourse on the theory of science emerges elsewhere, as when he outlines the political consensus of the editors and regular contributors to the journal *Archiv für Sozialwissenschaft und Sozialpolitik*: these 'men', who are concerned with the well-being and social advancement of workers, approve of capitalist development 'for now', not because of its quality, but because they consider it 'practically unavoidable', and because a principled struggle against it appears to them as an 'impediment to the working class's ascension into the light of culture'.[31] 'Whatever capitalism may do to man, it must, according to Weber, first and before all evaluation, be understood as necessary reason', Marcuse comments,[32] thereby simultaneously exposing the ideological foundation, constituted by 'value relations', of the 'freedom from value judgements' Weber lays claim to. The organic intellectual of the bourgeoisie, who argues, in his political writings, in favour of a Fordist modernisation of

---

29    Weber 1988d, p. 212.

30    With regard to ethnology, which has long placed the problem of inadvertent retrojection at the centre of its methodological self-reflection, Meillassoux calls for reconstructing the social behaviour of the individuals observed by objectifying their situation, their conditions of life, their practical relationship to nature and their mutual relationships. According to Meillassoux, it is only by means of such a historical materialist method of inquiry that 'social personae can be placed in a coherent context again, thereby becoming capable of presenting themselves in their subjectivity' (Meillassoux 1994, p. 319).

31    Weber 1988d, p. 159.

32    Marcuse 1969, p. 202.

the economy, the state and culture, now presents himself as a social scientist who is forced, by his sober realism, to accept, 'without value judgements', not just Germany's 'power pragma' and increasing bureaucratisation, but also capitalism qua force of destiny.[33] What is expressed in talk of 'the working class's ascension into the light of culture' is the aimed-for historical bloc of bourgeoisie and labour aristocracy, which we identified as the key goal in our analysis of Weber's political interventions (see above, Chapter 13.4).

If one follows Weber's considerations on the significance of the various 'ideas of cultural value' to ideal-typical concept formation, one needs to also decipher his own concepts from the point of view of this strategic option. As Mommsen observes, Weber construes the network of his ideal types in such a way 'as to allow the genuine problems of value to permeate it as far as possible'.[34] In fact, in *Economy and Society*, he develops the ideal-typical 'construction of a purely rational course of action'[35] in such a way as to teleologically tailor it, on the political level, to the state, and particularly to its 'legal', impersonal and bureaucratic form of authority, whereas on the economic level, he tailors it to the 'market struggle' and the market- and income-oriented calculus of money and capital.[36]

The line of development oriented to a 'rational' capitalism is formulated on the level of '*formal* rationality', which Weber distinguishes from '*material* rationality', the latter being concerned with the provision of goods to certain groups of people, thus belonging to the realm of 'valuing postulates' [*wertende Postulate*].[37] Thus it is precisely the qualitative questions arising within economic life that are linked by him to the sphere of 'value judgements'. The type of rationality that is based on standpoints of use value thereby suffers a *de facto* exclusion from sociology: at best, considerations of 'material rationality' appear as impediments to economic rationalisation, as is the case again today with regard to the prevailing neoliberal strategies on the one hand and welfare regulations or ecological concepts of 'sustainable development' on the other. Weber is interested solely in 'formal' rationality, which he conceives of

---

33   According to Marcuse, Weber's concept of destiny 'generalizes the blindness of a society which reproduces itself behind the back of the individuals, of a society in which the law of domination appears as objective technological law'. A science that is not committed to the abolition of such a 'fate' is 'pledged', on Marcuse's view, 'not to reason, but to the reason of established domination' (Marcuse 1969, p. 215).

34   Mommsen 1974, p. 66.

35   Weber 1978, p. 6.

36   Weber 1978, pp. 54–5, 72–4, 90ff, 107ff, 215ff.

37   Weber 1972, p. 44; see Weber 1978, p. 85 (translation modified).

as 'purely technical'.[38] What proves 'regular in the sense of having proven itself, in formal rational terms', in the historian's own society becomes the 'universal yardstick by which to assess actions and the comprehensibility of motives', Lefèvre observes.[39]

That the rationality of capitalist domination determines this ideal type, which is supposedly 'free of value judgements', can already be seen from Weber's argument that strict capital accounting, supposedly the acme of economic rationality, is bound up with 'the social phenomena of "shop discipline" and approbation of the means of production, and that means: with the existence of a "system of domination"'.[40] Specifically in terms of this *relation of domination*, the private capitalist economy is more 'rational' than the planned economy, since the latter needs to make use primarily of 'ideal motives of what is in the broadest sense an altruistic type' when mobilising its workers: because since the non-owning have no choice, under capitalism, but 'to comply with the authority of others in order to obtain any return at all for the utilities they can offer on the market', the 'risk of going entirely without provisions' functions as a 'decisive element of the motivation of economic activity'.[41] What Marx criticised as the 'dull compulsion of economic relations'[42] has become, in Weber, the *telos* of formal rationality.

Marcuse remarks that Weber's analysis 'took into its "pure" definitions of formal rationality valuations peculiar to capitalism',[43] and Lefèvre considers Weber's methodological formalisation a 'theoretical reenactment of capital's own engagement with reality'.[44] Paradoxically, there also inheres within this formally abstract 'reenactment' the critical potential that Lukács and the Frankfurt School, for example, were able to latch on to.[45]

---

38    Weber 1978, p. 86.
39    Lefèvre 1971, p. 27.
40    Weber 1978, p. 198.
41    Weber 1978, p. 110.
42    Marx and Engels 1975–2005, vol. 35, p. 726.
43    Marcuse 1969, p. 223.
44    Lefèvre 1971, p. 56.
45    For example, Marcuse also identifies Weber's formal abstraction as the point at which his 'analysis becomes self-criticism', insofar as it shows 'the degree to which capitalist rationality itself abstracts from man, to whose needs it is "indifferent", and in this indifference becomes ever more productive and efficient, calculating and methodical, thus erecting a "shell of bondage", furnishing it (quite luxuriously), and universalizing it' (Marcuse 1969, p. 224). On the way Lukács and 'critical theory' engaged with Weber's concept of 'rationality', see also Habermas 1984, pp. 345ff.

It is symptomatic of the relations of power at work within Weber's reception that the insight into the capitalist functionality of Weberian 'rationality' was abandoned again by Habermas, notwithstanding his claim to continuing the tradition of 'critical theory': as early as 1968, in a piece written on the occasion of Marcuse's seventieth birthday, Habermas summarises Marcuse's critique of Weber's 'rationality' in such a way as to elide those passages in which Marcuse deciphers the specifically capitalist logic of that 'rationality'; Habermas focuses instead on the passages that formulate a critique of technology.[46] As a result, Marcuse's ideology-critical insight into the specific capitalist orientation of Weber's concept of rationalisation got lost in Habermas's interpretation. What also got lost was Marcuse's alternative design for technology and science and therefore the possibility to connect critical theory organically with the urgent issues of ecological sustainability: whereas Marcuse advocated a fundamental 'change in the direction of progress', that would arrive 'at essentially different concepts of nature',[47] Habermas argued that there is, with regard to the nature of technology and science as domains of 'purposive-rational action', no realistic alternative. Instead of challenging the capitalistic mode of production and its profit-driven overexploitation of natural resources, he shifted the critique to the domain of an alternative project of 'interaction' and 'communicative reason'.[48] Having adopted, in his *Theory of Communicative Action*, Schluchter's interpretation, according to which it is the *purposive-rational* orientation of social action that crowns Weber's typology,[49] Habermas goes on to criticise Weber for having theoretically neglected, within his conception of rationality, the significance of 'value rationality', as opposed to 'purposive rationality'; Habermas then lays a claim to elaborating on this neglected aspect himself, by means of his theory of communication.[50]

But the critique of Weber's 'purposive rational' reductionism misses the mark in two ways. On the one hand, it attacks Weber's concept of rationality just where it is materially powerful, namely where it allows one to articulate

---

46    Habermas 1987c, pp. 111ff.

47    Marcuse 1969, pp. 223–4; see Marcuse 1966, pp. 166–7, 236.

48    For a critique of Habermas's misleading interpretation of Marcuse, his return to Weber's fatalism and his abandoning of critical theory's radical critique, see Rehmann 2013, pp. 99–111.

49    Schluchter 1979, p. 192.

50    Habermas 1984, pp. 281ff, 284–5.

forms of 'social action' in terms of their given constellations of interests.[51] On the other hand, it limits itself to criticising Weber for attributing excessive importance to 'purposive rationality', thereby overlooking, of all things, its underlying, specifically bourgeois reductionism: instead of dissecting it analytically and separating it from the capitalist determination of its form, Habermas adopts it en bloc, in order to place a 'value rational' compensation at its side. Leaving the entire domain of 'purposive-rational actions' organised by capitalism unchallenged, Habermas deprives critical theory of its critical sting.

In the essay on objectivity, Weber develops the ideal type as a concept within the theory of science; in parallel with this, he develops the ideal type of the 'spirit of capitalism' with reference to the historical object of inquiry that is ascetic Protestantism. Not only does this ideal type determine the inquiries that structure the *Protestant Ethic*; it also radiates out from there to determine the conceptual configurations of Weber's comparative *Economic Ethics of the World Religions*, as well as those of his studies on Western rationalism as such. Starting from the first part of the *Protestant Ethic*, I will now investigate, in an exemplary fashion, the relations of hegemony within which the ideal-typical composition of a Protestant-capitalist originary spirit takes place and the selection procedures that govern this process.

---

51    According to Michael Löwy, 'le constat brutal de Weber sur la contradiction irréductible des valeurs et son analyse des résultats aliénants de la rationalité instrumentale sont un point de départ plus fécond pour l'analyse de la société moderne que les rêves de réconciliation linguistique des valeurs de Habermas- d'ailleurs largement inspirés de la doctrine des "valeurs consensuelles" du sociologue américain Talcott Parsons. Le monde moderne ressemble beaucoup plus à la "guerre des dieux" wébérienne qu'à une aimable "discussion publique" d'intérêts et valeurs opposés' (Löwy 2003, p. 188).

# PART 4

# The Ideal-Typical Construction of an Originary Protestant-Capitalist Spirit

∵

# CHAPTER 23

# The Ethico-Political Stakes of a 'Purely Historical Account'

If the function of the beginning of an essay is to present to the reader the investigation's political stakes, without any detours, then Weber's introduction to the *Protestant Ethic* succeeds very well. The first sentence already formulates a sociological thesis that relates the study of the Protestant spirit of the sixteenth and seventeenth centuries to contemporary issues: Weber asserts the 'overwhelmingly Protestant' character of capital ownership and entrepreneurship, of the educated strata of the workforce and of those employees of modern firms who have received advanced technical training or been trained as salesmen.[1] Thus, the problem posed in the *Protestant Ethic* is bound up, from the outset, with the project of German capitalism's economic, political and ideological modernisation: the very social subjects whose constitution as a bloc has become the core problem for a new bourgeois hegemony in the transition to Fordism now constitute the starting point of a 'purely historical account'.[2] If entrepreneurs, the 'labour aristocracy' and the scientific-technical intelligentsia are overwhelmingly Protestant, the investigation's political relevance is obvious. Weber is primarily addressing those who have an interest in the formation of such a bloc, and he thematises what ought therefore to also interest them, namely the emergence and the effects of the Protestant formation of capitalism's modern economic subjects. The readers Weber is attempting to convince of the relevance of his study are obviously those factions of the bourgeoisie that are open to modernisation, and those Protestant circles that strive for a position as 'organic intellectuals' within the projected modernisation process.

In light of this topical issue, formulated in the opening sentences of the *Protestant Ethic*, it is difficult to see how the internal link between Weber's account of the 'spirit of capitalism' in terms of Protestantism and his project of Fordisation could be overlooked within the scholarly literature. When

---

1  Weber 1950, p. 35. In what follows, and unless otherwise noted, citations are from the final, 1920 version of the *Protestant Ethic* (on which Weber 1950—the translation by Talcott Parsons—is based); I only quote from the first version where it differs significantly from the final version.

2  Weber 1950, p. 182.

Schluchter writes that what Weber is concerned with thematically in the *Protestant Ethic* is the 'individual peculiarity of modern culture',[3] he expresses, in an exemplary fashion, a type of reception that is still prevalent, and which avoids analytically deciphering the social context by means of unspecific and overly general terms such as 'modern' and 'culture'. There is of course no lack of interpretations that situate Weber's study in the context of 'modern capitalism', but they do this mainly in terms of the question (formulated by Weber himself) to what extent the thesis on Protestantism can adequately explain 'modern capitalism', instead of proceeding in the opposite direction and asking to what extent Fordism's need of a new productivist ethic determines Weber's formulation of the query and his conceptual strategy. As for critical theory's analysis of Weber, it focuses on demonstrating that his key concepts are subordinated to the capitalist standpoint of valorisation and therefore unable to adequately grasp the object under investigation.[4] This ideology-critique remains valid and relevant, but it is too general in the sense that it does not grasp Weber's specific project of an early Fordist modernisation project.

If Weber's introduction to the *Protestant Ethic* points us to the contemporary issue of bourgeois hegemony, his political interventions repeatedly amount to the call for a new 'ethic'. That overcoming bourgeois immaturity requires, first and foremost, adequate educational work, and that no economic aspect can replace such work, is something we already learned from the Freiburg inaugural address.[5] As early as 1894, Weber wished to contribute to an ethical constitution of the bourgeoisie as a self-confident and independent class by means of the emergence of a homogeneous stock market elite (see above, Chapter 10), and his critique of the institution of the entailed estate was directed at the bourgeoisie's 'feudal pretensions', which stalled the development of a specifically bourgeois ethic (see above, Chapter 11.2). Conceptualised as an ethic of the upper bourgeoisie, it simultaneously unfolds its effects across the classes: the search was for a 'German form', founded on 'inner distance and reservedness', which could also serve the lowermost strata of society as a 'model'.[6] As for the 'ethical' integration of the labour aristocracy, it was to be promoted by the appeal to 'manly' worker honour, which Weber built into the ideological socialisation of German imperialism by relating it to soldierly and social-Darwinist notions (see above, Chapter 13.3). As emerges from our analysis of the essay on the American sects, the thesis on Protestantism easily accommodates the need

3   Schluchter 1991, p. 65.
4   See especially Marcuse 1969, pp. 205ff, 214, 223, and Lefèvre 1971, pp. 56ff, 90, 107.
5   Weber 1994a, p. 27.
6   Weber 1984–2009, vol. I/15, pp. 388–9; Weber 1988a, pp. 284–5.

for a Fordist regulation of the way of life, undergirding it with a complementary counter-image, one conceived of from the inside out (see above, Chapter 3).

The illusion of an apolitical sociology of religion rests mainly on Weber's claim of scientific cognition's 'freedom from value judgements'. It is only once that Weber formulates a value judgement and profession of faith in the *Protestant Ethic*, namely in the context of his concluding vision, which sees outer goods obtaining, within the 'iron cage' of capitalism, an 'irresistible force' over people, engendering within them a 'mechanized petrification, embellished with a sort of convulsive self-importance'.[7] Thus, the one time the *Protestant Ethic* turns into a critique of capitalism, Weber thinks of himself as having left the realm of scientific inquiry. But as we have already seen in our discussion of the 'value relation' and the 'ideal type' (see above, Chapters 18 and 22), the problem of an ideological overdetermination of science is not situated where Weber says of himself that he is articulating a 'value judgement', but where he tacitly constructs the network of his ideal types in such a way 'as to allow the genuine problems of value to permeate it as far as possible'.[8] The instance of valuation the *Protestant Ethic* allows itself to be 'permeated' by is thus the attempt to confront the German bourgeoisie with a Puritan-capitalist habitus as 'norm of bourgeois existence', and what Weber presents as a 'purely historical' account, untainted by value judgements or professions of faith, turns out to be the 'attempt to contribute to the renaissance of this bourgeois-Puritan class consciousness'.[9] I pursue this remark below, without falling into the trap of trying to directly deduce Weber's sociology of religion from certain political statements. The link between Weber's political interventions and his scientific work, which is ostensibly 'free of value judgements', is not to be sought, primarily, on the level of the occasional congruence of contents, but rather in the conceptual arrangement of the material itself.

The inner connection between Weber's various research projects also emerges from the boost in his productivity between 1903 and 1904, by means of which Weber was able to free himself, at least initially, from his depressive nervous disorder. The 'streams' that Marianne Weber saw as '[flowing] along side by side' are at the same time interconnected.[10] The *Protestant Ethic* assumes an intermediate position between the political critique of the *entailed estate* and

---

7    Weber 1950, pp. 181–2. In the first version of the *Protestant Ethic*, Weber speaks of a ' "Chinese" petrification' (Weber 1905, p. 109), which he will go on to examine in his 1915 study on Confucianism (see Weber 1951).

8    Mommsen 1974, p. 66.

9    Mommsen 1974, pp. 100, 417.

10    Marianne Weber 1975, p. 326.

the methodological reflections on socio-scientific *objectivity*. If the interlocking bourgeois-feudal interests Weber examines by reference to the example of the entailed estate are characteristic of a German backwardness that is to be over-come with the aid of the *Protestant Ethic*, among other things, then the 'spirit of capitalism' reconstructed in that work can simultaneously be considered a first application of the concept of the 'ideal type', developed in the 'essay on objectivity', to a historical subject matter.[11] In the last chapter, the Fordist mod-ernisation of the economy, the state and culture was identified as the organis-ing centrepiece of ideal-typical concept formation (see above, Chapter 22.3); now, we need to verify whether, and if so in what way, this also applies to the concrete ideal type that is the 'spirit of capitalism'. Since this ideal type deter-mines not just the queries formulated in the *Protestant Ethic* and the essay on 'Protestant Sects', but also those formulated in the later *Economic Ethics of the World Religions*, exposure of its principles of construction simultaneously pro-vides us with a key to the theoretical structure of Weber's sociology of religion in its entirety.

In the sections that follow, I will attempt to decipher, in terms of the theory of hegemony, the way in which Weber traces the 'spirit of capitalism' back to ascetic Protestantism. This includes the following steps:

- In order to demonstrate that Weber's basic methodological operation con-sists in isolating the 'inner peculiarity', I compare his introductory remarks on Protestant and Catholic attitudes in Germany with other methods of denominational comparison, and especially with a study by Weber's stu-dent Martin Offenbacher, which Weber (wrongly) claims to rely on in the first chapter of the *Protestant Ethic*.
- The next step concerns the links to the discursive world of 'cultural Protestantism', which I will interpret not just as a phenomenon proper to the history of ideas, but also and primarily as a relevant ideological forma-tion of Germany's ruling power bloc. One immediately relevant context is the '*Kulturkampf*', which Weber intended to conduct on the level of 'conscience', rather than politically.
- A comparison with the leading theologian of cultural Protestantism, Albrecht Ritschl, shows that on the one hand, Weber sides with German cultural Protestantism in its twofold hostility to Catholicism and Jacobinism, while on the other hand, he restructures this hostility both in terms of domestic and in terms of foreign policy. A specific feature of this restructur-ing consists in an Anglo-American turn, significantly influenced by Georg

---

11    Marshall 1982, pp. 45, 51–2, 95, 119; compare Marianne Weber 1975, pp. 335–6.

Jellinek's account of human rights, which traces those rights back to independentism.

- Weber defines the concept of the 'spirit of capitalism' in terms of an underlying reversal of means and ends; in doing so, he has been influenced, primarily, by Simmel's *Philosophy of Money*, which was itself informed by elements of Marx's analysis of the form of value.

- Finally, the concept is related to the approaches to political economy developed by the 'younger historical school', of which Sombart and Weber are considered exponents. Since Weber developed the category in the course of a direct engagement with the first edition of Sombart's *Modern Capitalism*,[12] I will focus on a comparison of these two works. Such a comparison can also serve as an example by which to consider the debate on whether the 'spirit of capitalism' is to be traced back to the Reformation or the Renaissance, a debate that yields important insights for the theory of hegemony.

The starting point of my textual analysis is the first chapter of the *Protestant Ethic*, in which Weber discusses the relationship between denomination and social stratification. For before he can historically deduce the nexus of Protestantism and the 'spirit of capitalism', he needs to perform a basic methodological operation, one that allows him to sever the 'internal' disposition of subjects from their social contexts.

---

12    Sombart 1902.

# CHAPTER 24

# The Basic Operation: Isolation of the 'Mental and Spiritual Particularities'

Weber's finding that Protestantism is ahead of other religious denominations with regard to modernisation relies on a study of the economic situation of the various denominations in the Grand Duchy of Baden, written by his student Martin Offenbacher and published in 1901. It is from Offenbacher that Weber takes his 'facts and figures', as he himself writes.[1] Moreover, he uses the title of the study, *Religious Affiliation and Social Stratification* [*Konfession und soziale Schichtung*], as the title of his first chapter. One needs to compare the two texts to notice that virtually the entire chapter is directed against Offenbacher's interpretation of the statistical material and opposes a contrary interpretation to it. In the process, interesting deviations from Offenbacher's argument and account become apparent.

## 24.1     The Critique of Offenbacher's Comparison of Denominations

According to Offenbacher, Eastern Germany and the Rhineland already reveal how the differences in status between the various denominations are ultimately a product of 'historical development'.[2] While some attempts were made, in Baden, to account for the inferiority of Catholicism in 'anthropological terms', the available evidence was not sufficient for deciding the question of whether or not the social differences of the various religions 'lie in the peculiarities of the denominational communities themselves'.[3] This careful assessment is related to the fact that Offenbacher imposes a specific constraint on his socio-logical inquiry: initially, he writes, one needs to take into account the external aspects influencing the situation of the denominations, examining 'the land and the people as the natural and ... cultural foundations upon which the current status of the two denominations rests'. It is only when the entirety of these aspects fails to explain the differentials discovered that one should turn to explanations based on the internal qualities of the denominational

---

1   Weber 1950, p. 35, note 4.

2   Offenbacher 1901, p. 1.

3   Ibid.

communities: 'We will find that there is no need to do this to any significant extent'.[4] By contrast, Weber's sociological introduction is intended to demonstrate that the inner peculiarity of the denominations is decisive to their social status.

Offenbacher justifies his explanation by pointing out that the Protestants were early to settle in the more economically developed territories of Baden (particularly north of the river Alb) and were thus favoured, independently of the will of those involved, by 'nature' and the 'course of *historical events*'.[5] He argues that while it was surely no coincidence that the regions where a monetary economy developed early on were also the first to adhere to the Reformation in the sixteenth century, what was 'decisive' to the distribution of denominations was, 'generally speaking, not the social and intellectual status of the mass of the population, but the denomination of the territorial sovereign, which was not normally related to economic aspects, but due partly to political and partly to purely personal reasons', as a result of the principle '*cuius regio eius religio*'.[6]

Weber picks up on one aspect of this explanation when he reports the view, explicitly attributed to Offenbacher,[7] that Protestantism's modernisation advantage can in part be traced back to distant 'historical reasons', 'in which religious affiliation is not a cause of the economic conditions, but to a certain extent appears to be a result', reasons the Protestant continues to profit from economically.[8] To be sure, Offenbacher explicitly does not speak, in his discussion of the denominational policy of the territorial sovereigns, of economic causes, but of the 'political' or 'personal' decisions of the sovereigns. It appears that Weber shifts Offenbacher's consideration into the realm of the economic so as to be able to set off more strongly his own explanation, based on internal religious reasons: he argues that one needs to inquire into the causes of the unusually pronounced predisposition towards the Reformation displayed by the economically most developed areas, adding that the divergent degrees of education and participation in modern technical and commercial activities evident within the two denominations can 'undoubtedly' be traced back to 'mental and spiritual peculiarities acquired from . . . the type of education

---

4  Offenbacher 1901, p. 2.
5  Offenbacher 1901, pp. 2, 12, 14–15.
6  Offenbacher 1901, p. 15.
7  Weber 1950, p. 35, note 4.
8  Weber 1950, p. 35.

favoured by the religious atmosphere of the home community and the parental home'.[9]

The remark on education makes reference to the following results of Offenbacher's study: (1) the share of Catholics who have undergone higher education is far lower than might be expected given their share of the total population, and that of Protestants far higher;[10] (2) while Catholics are still relatively well represented at secondary schools (because of the high number of prospective students of theology),[11] they are poorly represented at grammar and middle schools, especially in the promising subjects of chemistry, construction and engineering;[12] (3) to the extent that skilled workers employed in large industry are recruited interlocally, the number of Protestants among them is higher than that of Catholics.[13]

These denominational statistics have been criticised, particularly by Samuelsson, who focuses on the figures provided for Baden's technical secondary schools:[14] Samuelsson points out that Weber overlooked a crucial miscalculation on the part of Offenbacher, who stated the share of Protestants at technical secondary schools as 69 percent instead of 59 percent;[15] moreover, Samuelsson argues, both Offenbacher and Weber neglect the *absolute* number of students, which was so low, in the case of the Protestants at technical secondary schools (1,500 students as opposed to 4,500 at academic secondary

---

9    Weber 1950, p. 39. What Weber places beyond doubt in this passage is discussed far more carefully in his 1908/09 study *Die Psychophysik der industriellen Arbeit* ['The Psychophysics of Industrial Labour']: there, he writes that the extent to which Catholicism coincides with divergent degrees of suitability to work is a problematic issue, as the factor Catholicism can no longer be isolated (Weber 1984–2009, vol. I/11, p. 280, note 35a; Weber 1988b, p. 162, note 1).

10   Offenbacher's finding is based on an analysis of academic and technical secondary schools, higher vocational schools, technical schools and higher secondary schools during the period 1885–95. The Catholic share of students was 19 percent lower than one would have expected on the basis of their share of the overall population; that of the Protestants was 11 percent higher and that of the Jews 8.5 percent higher (Offenbacher 1901, pp. 16–17).

11   The share of Catholic students was 46 percent, that of Protestants 43 percent, the Catholic share of the overall population being 61.3 percent. Of the Catholics graduating from secondary school in the period 1891–94, 42 percent went on to study theology, so that the number of Catholics pursuing 'worldly' vocational training can be assumed to have been even lower (Offenbacher 1901, p. 17).

12   Offenbacher 1901, pp. 16–17, 20.

13   Offenbacher 1901, pp. 42, 48, 50.

14   Samuelsson 1961, pp. 140ff.

15   See Weber 1950, p. 38, note 8.

schools), that one cannot draw any conclusions from it; Samuelsson also faults Offenbacher and Weber for failing to compare the shares of Catholics and Protestants at technical secondary schools with their shares of the population in the corresponding *school districts*, pointing out that on such a comparison, there was virtually no disparity to be found.[16] Thus the denominational statistics boiled down to the trivial finding 'that in certain towns with a particularly large Protestant majority in a country otherwise predominantly Catholic there were more Protestants than Catholics at the secondary schools'.[17]

These objections, the substance of which is also confirmed by Turksma,[18] are significant mainly because Weber relies especially on Offenbacher's results on technical and higher secondary schools in formulating his revision of Offenbacher's assessment. While Offenbacher accounts for the differences in the degree of education in terms of the more favourable pecuniary circumstances of the Protestants, arguing that these circumstances facilitated access to professions requiring a costly education,[19] Weber emphasises that the denominational disparities in the '*type* of higher education' cannot be explained in terms of financial standing, but only in terms of inner disposition.[20]

This already allows one to observe that Weber's argument tries to derive its plausibility mainly from the weaknesses of a (real or alleged) economism. Against it, Weber articulates a conviction that is widely accepted as common sense, namely that not everything can be accounted for in terms of what is (in whatever sense) 'material'. Secondary literature usually overlooks that Weber frames the problem in a way that only allows for an either-or response: if it proves insufficient to trace the Catholic 'educational deficit' back to financial standing, then this is reason enough, for Weber, to consider an explanation in terms of 'internal' reasons to have been proven correct—the abstract opposition of economic and ideal causes does not allow one to take additional or mediating socio-historical and ideological determinants into account.

That such an isolation of the denominational factor is by no means unavoidable can be seen, *inter alia*, from Ludwig Cron's study of the correlation

---

16    In the school districts with secondary schools (those of Karlsruhe, Mannheim, Ettenheim, Mosbach, Billingen and Weinheim), the Protestant share of the total population was also higher than the Catholic share (about 55 percent). 'Thus, school by school and district by district it appears that the proportions of school children classified by religious faith are almost exactly the same as the corresponding proportion of the total populations of the appropriate district' (Samuelsson 1961, p. 141).

17    Samuelsson 1961, p. 142.

18    Turksma 1962, pp. 460, 465, 467–8.

19    Offenbacher 1901, pp. 20–1.

20    Weber 1950, p. 38 (emphasis added).

between denomination and university attendance; roughly contemporary with Offenbacher's investigation, Cron's study formulates a different interpretation of similar statistical results: the Catholic deficit in the natural sciences, mathematics and political economy was especially marked when the students came from an artisan or peasant background; it became less marked in the case of middle-tier civil servants, and in the case of the sons of Catholic industrialists, it turned into an advance vis-à-vis the sons of Protestant industrialists.[21] It is no coincidence that Weber does not make the slightest reference to this study. On Cron's view, the case of the industrialists demonstrates especially clearly 'to what extent the economic situation needs to be emphasised over religious motivation when considering access to higher education', for it was there that the denomination's influence on the choice of subject yielded to other considerations 'that brought about a virtual reversal of circumstances'.[22] 'Within intellectually and economically privileged circles, the Catholic type of student increasingly disappears and comes to resemble the Protestant type'.[23] Baumeister concludes that one can see from recent micro-level investigations how closely the characteristics of particular religious denominations overlapped and interacted with social characteristics, e.g. urban and rural relations.[24] For example, if one were to compare urban and rural Catholics, one would note the same differences that Offenbacher noted between Protestants and Catholics—thus Samuelsson with regard to the two denominations' relative shares in aggregate capital investment.[25] Using the same evidence and the same method, one could just as well have shown that geographic, climatic or racial factors are responsible for economic disparities: 'it is all a question of "ideal types"'.[26]

Regardless of what importance one wishes to attribute to the religious factor from case to case, it is clear that the typically 'Catholic' professional and

---

21   Cron 1900, pp. 84ff.

22   Cron 1900, p. 93.

23   Cron 1900, p. 112.

24   Baumeister 1987, p. 71. According to Baumeister, Cron was 'the first to successfully compare and assess the relative importance of socio-economic circumstances and religious attitudes in an empirically stringent manner and with an eye to a concrete area of social behaviour' (Baumeister 1987, p. 67). This was possible, according to Baumeister, because of a method 'that did not analyse the denominational factor as a constant term, as is usually done, but rather as a variable that strongly shapes behaviour in traditional, pre-industrial areas of society' (ibid).

25   Samuelsson 1961, p. 144.

26   Samuelsson 1961, pp. 146–7.

educational conducts emphasised by Weber need to be analysed as multiply overdetermined superpositional phenomena.

## 24.2    On the Social Profile of the Catholic Bloc

Weber's treatment of Offenbacher makes clear how little his argument is determined by the denominational statistics themselves, and how strongly it is determined by his own investigational intentions. The modified set-up of Cron's investigation would already suffice to take one back from Weber's direct link between educational standing and denominational professional ethic to the complex interrelationship between denominational identity, geographic distribution, social stratification, inner dispositions and so on.[27] This would also alter the thrust of the inquiry into causes: one question that would then be brought into view would be the one concerning the social conditions and ideological structures that allowed Catholicism to remain rooted in the peasant and artisan sectors. Gramsci, for example, notes the Catholic Church's extraordinary ability 'to remain in contact with "simple minds" ' while preventing the detachment of the intellectually higher-ranking strata from the lower strata and mediating between religion and the common sense of the people.[28] To be sure, the church does not accomplish these tasks with an eye to elevating 'simple minds' to the level of intellectuals; instead, it means to 'leave them to their primitive philosophy of common sense'.[29] Accordingly, the price to be paid for the 'abstractly rational and correct relationship' between intellectuals and common people is that of having to employ disciplinary means to maintain their unity 'on the low level of the masses',[30] whereas the *philosophy of praxis* is concerned with 'constructing a moral and intellectual bloc' that will render the intellectual progress of the masses 'politically possible'.[31] Here, Gramsci's diagnosis displays a point of contact with the critique formulated by the German 'reform Catholics'; around the turn of the century, they offered as one reason for the Catholic 'educational deficit' that the educated Catholic strata were practising an anti-intellectualism similar to that of the pious rural

---

27    'We thought it ... inappropriate to claim without further ado that the denominational position has a decisive effect on the type of studies undertaken. Many factors interpose themselves between the two' (Cron 1900, p. 111).

28    Gramsci 1975b, pp. 1382–3, 1396–7.

29    Gramsci 1975b, p. 1384.

30    Gramsci 1975b, p. 1385.

31    Ibid.

population: they displayed plenty of reverence for the clergy but thought little of science, considering it a threat to Christian dogma.[32]

Thus a hegemony-theoretical investigation might account for the deficits 'in the form of higher education' that Weber emphasises as the profile of (and price to be paid for) the formation of a bloc whose centre of gravity lay in rural and small-town areas as well as in peasant and petty bourgeois strata, and which involved intellectuals being prevented, by authoritarian and disciplinary means, from exiting the unity of the bloc.[33] Such a Gramscian perspective would also show how one-sided it is to portray the social dispositions of the Catholic bloc purely from the standpoint of a 'modern' and 'educated' Protestantism, i.e. as backward and retrograde: Catholicism's culture of clubs and associations, far stronger and more intense than that of Protestantism,[34] can, as Nipperdey has shown,[35] also be interpreted as a relevant modernisation factor. As early as the ideological crisis that followed the First World War, Catholicism's capacity to form an inter-class bloc would prove a significant advantage over the Protestant church.[36] In the Weimar Republic, Catholic mobilisation gave rise to a distinct anti-socialist bloc that rivalled the fascist achievement of hegemony until the Reich Concordat with the Vatican blasted it apart in 1933. And in spite of the collaboration between the National Socialist state and the Catholic church, it remains true for the period after 1933 that the struggle over the church, to the extent that it was conducted as a 'war of

---

32    This was the view of Georg von Hertling, among others. Hertling was the 'chief ideologue' of Germany's educated Catholic laity, chairman of the *Görres Society* and later prime minister of Bavaria; in 1896, he was the first to speak of a Catholic 'educational deficit' (see Baumeister 1987, pp. 50ff). Nipperdey says with reference to Hertling that such self-criticism expressed the growing unease inspired in Catholic academics by the anti-intellectualism of the clerics, the popular associations and Catholic popular culture in general (Nipperdey 1993, p. 75).

33    See Gramsci 1975b, pp. 1383, 1385. Such disciplinary measures were also brought to bear upon Germany's 'Reform Catholics', whose 'modernism' was condemned as heresy and declared anathema by Pope Pius X in his 1907 encyclical *Pascendi dominici gregis* (see Baumeister 1987, p. 93).

34    In 1929, only 7.25 percent of the Protestant youth was organised in Protestant youth organisations, whereas 32 percent of the Catholic youth was organised in Catholic youth organisations (see Schellenberger 1975, p. 6).

35    Nipperdey 1988, pp. 27, 31, 61.

36    For example, 50,000 people left the Catholic church in 1920, whereas 315,000 left the Protestant churches—more than six times as many (see Rehmann 1986, p. 17; see also the entries on '*Kirchenaustritt*' [secession from a church] in Höfer and Rahner 1957–65, and in Galling and von Campenhausen 1957–65.

position' over ideological competencies of socialisation, was conducted mainly against the 'deep multi-tiered structure' of the Catholic Church.[37]

### 24.3   Weber's Departure from Offenbacher's Model of Interaction

While Offenbacher and Weber share a deficit-based approach, Offenbacher's study at least has the advantage of presenting the interaction of economic, political, church-historical and religious determinants. For example, he accounts for the relationship between wealth differentials and denomination in terms of the fact that 'the general shock to tradition that occurred in the sixteenth century, due to the imposition of the monetary economy, was one of the worldly forces promoting the Reformation, but was also itself dramatically boosted by the break with the traditional church authorities'.[38] Thus what is proposed is an explanation that one might describe, on the basis of the late Engels, as a *model of interaction* [*Wechselwirkung*].[39] This model also involves the 'mental and spiritual peculiarities' acquired through 'education' that Weber emphasises, but only as one factor among others: (1) the Catholic cult is more costly than the Protestant one, and while the Catholics spent considerable sums on monasteries, the Protestants were able to profitably invest their wealth in business enterprises; (2) the situation in Baden was influenced by French expatriates who came mainly from the property-owning strata and often settled in Protestant areas; (3) the free towns, and particularly those most developed in economic terms, were strongholds of Protestantism;[40] (4) the Catholic position within modern economic life suffered from an '*acquired mental* peculiarity, which in turn was produced by the overwhelming influence of a powerful cultural force'.[41]

---

37    See Rehmann 1986, pp. 44ff, 62ff.

38    Offenbacher 1901, p. 23.

39    'If some younger writers attribute more importance to the economic aspect than is its due, Marx and I are to some extent to blame', Engels writes self-critically in a letter to Joseph Bloch dated 21/22 September 1890: 'We had to stress this leading principle in the face of opponents who denied it, and we did not always have the time, space or opportunity to do justice to the other factors that interacted upon each other' (Marx and Engels 1975–2005, vol. 49, p. 36). 'It is in the interaction [*Wechselwirkung*] of all these factors and amidst an unending multitude of fortuities ... that the economic trend ultimately asserts itself as something inevitable' (Marx and Engels 1975–2005, vol. 49, p. 35). See Engels's letter to Conrad Schmidt, 27 October 1890 (Marx and Engels 1975–2005, vol. 49, p. 60).

40    Offenbacher 1901, pp. 22–3.

41    Offenbacher 1901, p. 24.

Reading Weber's introduction to the *Protestant Ethic* with this explanatory model in mind, one discovers a skilful arrangement of arguments that has lastingly fooled the authors of much of the scholarly literature on Weber: at first blush, it seems as if Weber were arguing against a monocausal economic model of determination to which he needs to oppose the significance and autonomy of ideal motives. In reality, however, he is setting himself off against a model that posits the *interaction* of economic, political and religious factors; he isolates one of its aspects and posits its predominance with regard to the others.[42] In doing so, he is concerned not only with emphasising the confessional factor as opposed to the economic factor; he also seeks to privilege the 'intrinsic character' over the 'external' circumstances of the denominations: 'Thus the principal explanation of this difference must be sought in the permanent intrinsic character of their religious beliefs, and not [only] in their temporary external historico-political situations'.[43] I have placed the word 'only' in brackets because it is missing in the first edition.[44] The fact that Weber adds it in the second edition is symptomatic of how the emphasis on the persistent internal habitus of the denomination can be revoked if necessary. The logic of the sentence is now oddly skewed: the first part of the sentence ('the principal explanation…') declares that a denomination's external, 'historico-political situation' is secondary, while the second part of the sentence ('not only…') limits itself to denying the exclusive relevance of an 'external' explanation.

The distinction is anything but pedantic. The *co-determination* of 'internal' dispositions, which display a certain autonomy with regard to external constellations, could be integrated into a historical materialist sociology, to the extent that the latter is not economistic, but rather open to the analysis of hegemonic processes. This is the sense in which E.P. Thompson, for example, lays claim to complementing Marx's economic analysis by focusing on the question of how the experiences of people who find themselves living under specific relations of production are practically lived and culturally and ideologically processed.[45] But this is something other than the aspiration to *replace*

---

42    This is overlooked not just in the prevailing reception of Weber, whose exponents attempt
       to demonstrate the superiority of Weber with regard to Marx, but also by most of Weber's
       critics, who eschew contextual analysis of Weber's argument. By contrast, Turksma can
       note the following, thanks to his textual comparison between Weber and Offenbacher:
       'Right from the start, Weber thus makes the *"geistige Eigenart"* the centre, and he further
       does with Offenbacher's argument as he pleases. The historico-political contingency disappears
       in a casual remark. The geographical element is missing' (Turksma 1962, p. 465).

43    Weber 1950, p. 40.

44    Weber 1904, p. 6.

45    See Groh in Thompson 1980, p. 23.

a historical reconstruction with the attempt to deduce everything from an internal disposition, especially if that internal disposition is supposed to have led a life of its own for centuries, independently of 'external' constellations. The latter approach would amount to an idealist countermodel that stands in the way of an integral social history, i.e. a social history that relates structures and ideological and cultural dispositions to one another. The very place at which Gramsci sought to overcome economism by developing the concept of hegemony[46] would here be occupied by the speculative construct of a static internal 'essence' of the denominations.

## 24.4    Weber's Vacillation between a 'Strong' and a 'Weak' Thesis on Protestantism

The ambivalence apparent in the above comparison between the first and the second edition concerns one of the fundamental issues associated with the *Protestant Ethic* and the controversies provoked by it. The sentence structure is symptomatic of a double bottom in Weber's argument, one that Parkin has characterised as constant vacillation between a 'strong' and a 'weak' thesis on Protestantism:[47] the weak thesis posits an analogy between the 'Protestant ethic' and the 'spirit of capitalism', as well as the interaction of both with the development of the capitalist system, whereas the strong thesis proclaims a causal relationship.[48] Critics who focus on Weber's 'strong' thesis, attempting to identify in his work a 'spiritualist' deduction of capitalism,[49] are easily refuted by quotations that see Weber denying that he wishes to deduce the capitalist economic system from the Reformation and claiming that he is concerned with the investigation of 'elective affinities' [*Wahlverwandtschaften*] between certain forms of religious faith and professional ethics, a 'tremendous confusion of interdependent influences'.[50]

---

46   Gramsci writes that economism within the theory of historiography needs to be combated 'by developing the concept of hegemony' (Gramsci 1975c, pp. 1595–6). For a comprehensive discussion, see Haug 1985, pp. 142–55; see also Haug 1988, pp. 34ff.

47   'Weber tends to shift back and forth between two rather different lines of argument— what might be called a strong thesis and a weak thesis' (Parkin 1982, p. 43).

48   Compare Morris 1987, pp. 63ff.

49   In a letter to Rickert dated 2 April 1905, Weber himself characterises the *Protestant Ethic* as 'a sort of "spiritualistic" construction of the modern economy' (quoted in Marianne Weber 1975, p. 356).

50   Weber 1950, p. 91; compare p. 174; see Weber 1987, p. 285; Weber 1988d, pp. 169, 189.

But then he opposes Sombart, whom he describes as discussing the entrepreneurial ethic as an effect of capitalism, by emphasising that he (Weber) needs to consider the opposite thesis.[51] With reference to Sombart again, albeit without mentioning him explicitly, Weber claims that the question concerning the driving forces of modern capitalism does not so much arise on the level of the supplies of money that can be valorised capitalistically as on that of the spirit of capitalism: 'Where it appears and is able to work itself out, it produces its own capital and monetary supplies as the means to its ends, but the reverse is not true'.[52]

Finally, when Weber attempts to explain, in his posthumously published *Economic History*, 'what ultimately created capitalism', his concluding answer places all the emphasis on the concept of the 'rational', and this concept, in turn, derives its modern specificity primarily from the Reformation and ascetic Protestantism.[53] Rachfahl remarks that in spite of his claims to the contrary, Weber treats the Protestant ethic as a factor so powerful as to leave its mark on everything 'and absorb everything completely'.[54] Parkin also concludes that Weber was concerned primarily with proving the 'strong thesis'.[55]

The determinational relationship between Protestantism, the spirit of capitalism and capitalism exercised not just Rachfahl, Fischer, Troeltsch and Weber in their early debates, between 1907 and Weber's 1910 'Anti-Critical Postscript', but also subsequent generations. As a rule, the exponents of the various textual interpretations found in the secondary literature argue over 'misunderstandings' prompted by the thesis on Protestantism,[56] instead of reflecting on Weber's methodological decision to isolate the 'inner peculiarity', which helps to explain his vacillation between a 'strong' and a 'weak' thesis.

This cannot, however, be explained by reference to the subject of Weber's study, the religious constellations of the sixteenth and seventeenth centuries; it can only be explained by reference to certain early twentieth century

---

51    Weber 1950, p. 43, note 19.

52    Weber 1950, pp. 68–9. In the first edition of the *Protestant Ethic*, the spirit of capitalism's creation of money is emphasised even more clearly: '*da* schaffte *er sich die Geldvorräte als Mittel seines Wirkens*'—['it *produced* its own capital and monetary supplies as the means to its ends'] (Weber 1904, p. 29).

53    Weber 1923, pp. 302, 312ff.

54    Rachfahl in Weber 1987, p. 266; compare p. 269.

55    'Despite all his customary qualifications and caveats, he is undoubtedly concerned to show that early Protestant beliefs made an unparalleled impact upon the conduct of economic life' (Parkin 1982, p. 44).

56    The fruitlessness of this topos can be seen, in an exemplary fashion, from Fischoff's survey of the controversy; see Fischoff 1978, pp. 351, 361–2, 365.

discursive formations, within which efforts to 'ethically' mobilise economic subjects met with the ideological formation of 'cultural Protestantism'.

## 24.5    The Ethical Mobilisation of Economic Subjects

Weber's ambiguity becomes explicable as soon as one considers the addressees of his political project: if he wishes to unleash within the bourgeoisie the forces of self-moralisation that he holds are required by Fordist rationalisation, then he needs to emphasise the 'inner peculiarity' of the subjects with all his strength and at the risk of engaging in speculation. This one-sidedness, methodologically backed by the concept of the 'ideal type', has to be such that it can be qualified or partially revoked whenever empirical demonstration proves difficult.

When Weber speaks out against economist explanatory models, one needs to be aware that various frontlines are involved. As a rule, he is communicating not only with Marxism, which he received mainly through the lens of the Second International's determinism as shaped by Kautsky,[57] but also—like Germany's 'historical school' in its entirety—with the spontaneously economistic forms of thought proper to his own class. Marshall overemphasises this in formulating the thesis that in the *Protestant Ethic*, Weber is not debating with the ghost of Marx, but with that of Adam Smith.[58] There is much to suggest that Weber was debating with both ghosts at once, and that this overlap was precisely what contributed to the success of the *Protestant Ethic*. The main starting point for Weber's engagement with the bourgeoisie is, as Gramsci would have said, a relatively underdeveloped, merely 'corporatist'-economic stage of bourgeois class consciousness, which has yet to work its way up to an 'ethico-political form'.[59]

These strategic stakes can be recognised clearly when Weber presents his addressees with the problem of 'traditionalism'. In doing so, he is concerned with demonstrating that the 'traditionalist' attitude to work cannot be overcome purely by economic incentives: raising piece-rate wages may under certain circumstances lead to the worker contenting himself with the wages he has hitherto received and reducing his daily output accordingly. Likewise, reducing wages will not necessarily lead to a rise in performance; it can just

---

57    On Weber's and Troeltsch's reception of Kautsky, see Bosse 1970, pp. 92, 98–9, 145–6.

58    'Weber is debating, not with the ghost of Marx, but—via German historical economics—with that of Adam Smith' (Marshall 1982, p. 33).

59    Gramsci 1996, pp. 179ff; Gramsci 1975b, pp. 1244–5.

as well lead to a decline in performance: either because a 'physiologically insufficient' wage weakens labour power and leads to 'survival of the unfit',[60] or more generally in the case of work that rests on responsibly conducted, qualified work with sensitive machines.[61] By contrast, Weber discerns in Pietist workers both the capacity for mental concentration and a sense of duty with regard to work, economy and self-control.[62] Weber's perspective is consistently that of the capital owner who attempts to increase the intensity of the labour performed by his wage workers, the duration of the work day (and the productivity of labour) being given. And much as in the 1895 Freiburg inaugural address, where Weber addresses the issue of political modernisation, Weber concludes that the requisite professional attitude can be directly engendered neither by higher nor by lower wages; it can only be the product 'of a long and arduous process of education'.[63]

Once the significance of economic attitudes to capitalist modernisation has been recognised, there remains a second preconception, widespread in the bourgeoisie, that needs to be eliminated: Weber consistently speaks out against a 'popular' and 'modern' interpretive scheme that associates Catholicism with outdated, ascetic 'unworldliness' and Protestantism with 'joyful worldliness' in the Enlightenment sense.[64] He finds an example of such a misinterpretation in Offenbacher's comparison between the Catholic who wants to sleep well and the Protestant who likes to eat well.[65] Strictly speaking, this example is inappropriate. For the 'Catholic' need to sleep well has nothing to do, in and of itself, with 'unworldliness' and 'asceticism'; with regard to culture, it would rather have to be considered—like the Protestant's hearty meal—an example of 'joyful worldliness'. The fact that Weber nevertheless associates it with

---

60  This negative 'selection' develops along an East-West axis: 'The present-day average Silesian mows, when he exerts himself to the full, little more than two-thirds as much land as the better paid and nourished Pomeranian or Mecklenburger, and the Pole, the further East he comes from, accomplishes progressively less than the German' (Weber 1950, p. 61).

61  Weber 1950, pp. 59, 61.

62  Weber 1950, pp. 62–3. In his 1908/09 study *'Zur Psychophysik der industriellen Arbeit'* ['On the Psychophysics of Industrial Labour'], Weber quantifies the performance differential between Pietist workers and average workers as 38 or 39 percent (Weber 1984–2009, vol. I/11, pp. 278–9; Weber 1988b, pp. 160–1).

63  Weber 1950, p. 62.

64  Weber 1950, pp. 40–2.

65  Weber 1950, p. 41. 'In the vernacular, one jokes: you can either eat well or sleep well. In the present case, the Protestant likes to eat well, whereas the Catholic wants to sleep well' (Offenbacher 1901, p. 68).

ascetic unworldliness is itself symptomatic of how he surrenders the cultural to the ideological aspect of a moral mobilisation of work performance.

Weber does not make this explicit, but his argument is directed primarily against the leading 'cultural Protestant' theologian Albrecht Ritschl, in whose *History of Pietism* Lutheran Protestantism is defined as 'attention to the world', whereas Catholicism is defined as ascetic 'unworldliness' (see below, Chapter 25.4). Here, Weber's critique concerns the characterisation of Protestantism. For if Protestantism were to be defined as 'attention to the world', it would merely function as a kind of early form of purely rationalist, irreligious worldviews, and not specifically in the manner of 'purely religious motives'.[66] Weber's counterargument is that a worldly utilitarianism 'would never have been capable of motivating such tremendous sacrifices for non-rational ideal ends'.[67] In fact, the economic superiority of Great Britain went hand in hand with a 'record of piety',[68] and 'otherworldliness' and asceticism were not contrary to participation in capitalist entrepreneurship, but historically bound up with it.[69] Finally, the bourgeoisie did not flock to 'liberty', but to a Puritan tyranny that regimented its behaviour: in order to defend this Puritan tyranny, the bourgeoisie developed a 'heroism' that 'bourgeois classes as such have seldom before and never since displayed'.[70]

Thus, the opening passages of the *Protestant Ethic* already link the contemporary problem of a competitive economic attitude with the religio-sociological object of inquiry that is the 'heroic' genesis of such an attitude. The bourgeois economic ethos that Weber considers vital is to be provided with a Protestant foundation. The 'ethico-political' stage of bourgeois class consciousness that Weber aims at is given an 'ethico-religious' anchorage.

In performing this operation, Weber relies on the discursive material of German cultural Protestantism, which he simultaneously provides with a specifically Anglo-American twist.

---

66    Weber 1950, p. 90.
67    Weber 1950, pp. 125–6.
68    Weber 1950, p. 145.
69    Weber 1950, pp. 41–2.
70    Weber 1950, p. 37.

# CHAPTER 25

# From German 'Cultural Protestantism' to Anglo-American 'Civil Religion'

## 25.1    Cultural Protestantism as a Religious Ideology of Bourgeois Modernisation

'*Cultural Protestantism*' has asserted itself as the term for the ideological link between bourgeois class interests and Protestant 'values', both within the literature on the history of theology and in that of the social sciences. Its first documented use dates to about 1904; the term originally functioned as an orthodox exonym for a modernist current within theology, whose exponents preferred to refer to themselves as 'new Protestants' or 'liberal theologians'. The term did not become a positive endonym until the 1920s.[1]

The term was popularised mainly by Karl Barth, who used it to refer not to a certain current within theology, but to the type of theology that prevailed throughout the nineteenth century, a theology that Barth broke with during the First World War and in opposition to which he developed his 'dialectical theology'. The decisive reason for this break was the fact that in August 1914, 'more or less all' of Barth's theological teachers publicly endorsed the military policy of Wilhelm II. 'Grown mad over their ethos, I became aware that I would no longer be able to adhere to their ethic and dogmatism, their Bible exegesis or their account of history either, that the theology of the 19th century would henceforth be a theology without a future to me', Barth reports retrospectively in a 1957 lecture.[2] He uses 'cultural Protestantism' as an ideology-critical term, which refers to those who surrender the sacred word of God to the dominant 'culture'. Like the reformers of the sixteenth century, Barth enacts the break with the dominant theology in the form of an 'orthodoxy' that condemns the synthesis of 'Christianity' and 'culture' as an instance of sinful human hubris and from the standpoint of a diastatic separation between 'gospel' and 'culture', 'faith' and 'religion'.

The theological critique of ideology was so incisive that theologians and historians of theology are still working hard today to eliminate its effects. The pattern followed by these efforts can be illustrated with reference to

---

1    See Graf 1984, pp. 265, 226; see also Graf 1990, pp. 232ff.
2    Barth 1960, pp. 574–5.

F.W. Graf, who discusses cultural Protestantism with an eye to discovering in it traditions suitable to the articulation of a *theologically justified* acceptance of the German Federal Republic's parliamentary democracy, which is of course itself a cultural Protestant approach.[3] To this end, he proceeds, without further ado, to attribute Barth's 'dialectical theology' to the general critique of culture articulated by antiliberal intellectuals, which allows him to associate it with the conservative revolution and, by way of it, with the 'German Christians' (i.e. the most radical fascist faction in the Protestant Church).[4] He is aided in this not only by the ambiguity of the concept of liberalism, but also by that of the German adjective 'bürgerlich', which allows him to attribute to dialectical theology an 'aggressive critique of bürgerliche Kultur' while simultaneously suggesting that the National Socialist movement, which stepped forward to reorganise the bourgeois camp, was characterised by a 'basic anti-bourgeois stance'.[5] Under the pretence of engaging in a long overdue historical differentiation of Barth's critique, Graf engages in a church-historical revisionism that stands the historical antagonisms of the struggle over the church on their head. In reality, the 'German Christians' were quite capable, to the extent that they came to represent the interests of the state, of situating themselves within the tradition of cultural Protestantism, of which one of their leading theologians, Emanuel Hirsch, claimed that it amounted to 'tracing back' everything worldly to its religious foundation.[6] By contrast, Barth's theology became, under German fascism, the backbone of the Confessing Church's efforts at self-defence.[7] In Hübinger's most recent study of the relationship between cultural Protestantism and politics, the displacement of the theological critique of ideology is completed: the extensive index of names does not include that of Karl Barth, which appears only in the bibliography.[8]

---

3  Namely, by means of the reception of 'those undogmatic patterns in the theological interpretation of politics that were developed, in their classical form, by cultural Protestant academic politicians such as Rade, Baumgarten, Troeltsch and Mulert' (Graf 1990, p. 239).

4  See Graf and Tanner 1990, pp. 191, 198–9, 200; Graf 1984, p. 253.

5  Graf 1990, p. 238; Graf and Tanner 1990, pp. 198–9. On the widespread abuse of this ambiguity of the term 'Bürgertum', see Projekt Ideologietheorie 1980, pp. 54ff, and Rehmann 1999.

6  Hirsch 1954, p. 156. See also Hirsch's 'reader', published in 1938, on the modern *'Reconfiguration of Christian Thought'*, a sourcebook for students of theology in the National Socialist state that included cultural Protestant religio-philosophical texts by the likes of Kant, Fichte, Schelling, Schleiermacher and Baur, but none by Rousseau or the liberals Rade and Troeltsch, who were considered 'left wing'.

7  See Rehmann 1986, pp. 110–24.

8  Hübner 1994, pp. 322, 338.

'Cultural Protestantism' is defined in quite divergent ways. Used in a broad sense, the term refers to the 'general reshaping of traditional Christian items of faith into specifically bourgeois norms and cultural ideas'.[9] According to Barth, the theology of the eighteenth century is already characterised by a tendency toward 'bourgeoisification' [*Verbürgerlichung*] and 'moralisation' that imposes itself in combination with Christianity's 'statification' and 'philosophisation': in a 'process that is increasingly accepted as natural', the property- and estates-based interests of the bourgeoisie 'become the defining forces at work within religio-ecclesiastical issues, which are themselves increasingly defined by the bourgeoisie'.[10] Used more narrowly, the term refers only to the period from the foundation of the German Reich in 1871 to the First World War and to the theological school of Ritschl, whose leading exponents were Harnack, Hermann and Rade, as well as to the 'religio-historical school' that emerged from it and was associated with Ernst Troeltsch, the author from whom Max Weber adopted the greater part of his implicit 'theology'.[11] According to Hübinger, the 'cultural Protestantism' that was characterised by an anti-clerical thrust rallied the bourgeois counter-elites against the traditional aristocracy, counter-elites that were oriented to a civil-religious bolstering of the Reichs's political culture and assumed an affinity between free Christianity and the norms of bourgeois life conduct.[12]

Summarising the various definitions, one can say that 'cultural Protestantism' denotes a 'becoming bourgeois' of Protestant theology which comprises rivalling currents and can be described, in terms of the history of ideas, both as an effect of the Enlightenment on theology and as a 'passive revolution' of theology against the Enlightenment. Barth describes this twofold character when he credits the 'emotional theology' [*Gefühlstheologie*] of Schleiermacher (1768–1834), not without a certain irony, with having 'completed and overcome the Enlightenment, overcome and completed it', and to have done so 'beyond Rousseau's outbursts, beyond Lessing's struggles, beyond Kant's critique'.[13]

Hübinger notes that Weber also 'retained an affinity for the cultural Protestant milieu throughout his active life' and 'assumed a typically cultural

---

9      Graf 1984, pp. 215–16.

10     Barth 1960, pp. 73–4.

11     On the 'narrow' meaning of the term '*cultural Protestantism*', see, *inter alia*, Amelung 1976, p. 1340, and Schneemelcher 1980, p. 779. Schick limits cultural Protestantism to the period between 1890 and 1914 (Schick 1970, pp. 2–3). On the influence Troeltsch's theology exerted on the *Protestant Ethic*, see Graf 1987, p. 136; see also Graf 1988, pp. 325ff.

12     Hübinger 1994, pp. 22–3.

13     Barth 1960, p. 368.

Protestant perspective of inquiry' in his sociology of modernity.[14] In what follows, I will seek to develop an understanding of 'cultural Protestantism' that goes beyond the common classifications in terms of the history of ideas and conceptualises it as an influential ideological formation in Wilhelmine Germany. What appears, in Barth's critique, as a surrender of the gospel to the dominant culture can be reconstructed from the societal constellations of the time and in terms of the theory of hegemony. Thus I will not be inquiring, at this point, into the cultural Protestant theologies that Weber integrates into the part of the *Protestant Ethic* that is concerned with the history of religion, but rather into cultural Protestantism's contemporary ethico-political frontlines, along which Weber positions himself by means of his concept of a Protestant-capitalist spirit.

### 25.2    *'Kulturkampf'* and the *'Debate on Inferiority'*

As Nipperdey observes,[15] the sociological studies produced around the turn of the century tended to account for the 'deficits' of the Catholics in the manner of Offenbacher and Cron, that is, in terms of geographical or socio-economic factors: to account for them in terms of a different 'spirit' was an endeavour initially undertaken less by serious scholars than by speculating journalists. This observation already signals how inappropriate it would be to consider Weber's emphasis on the 'inner peculiarity' no more than a result of methodological discussions among scholars. Its origins lie, rather, in the self-conception of a Protestant leadership and its intellectuals, which is to say it needs itself to be reconstructed as an effect of hegemony.

It is obvious that the *Protestant Ethic* inscribes itself into the context of a Protestant stance proper to the period of the *Kulturkampf.* As early as the 1880s, Weber 'shared, without qualifications, the liberal *Kulturkampf* stance of the time', Mommsen observes, adding that 'throughout his life', Weber 'never abandoned the *Kulturkampf* mentality he had passionately adhered to as a young man'.[16] Weber was significantly influenced by national-liberals such as his uncle Hermann Baumgarten, who was convinced of the world-historical mission of an 'ethico-political Protestantism'.[17] When the *Kulturkampf* was officially ended by a 'peace law' issued in April of 1887, Baumgarten published

14    Hübinger 1994, pp. 3, 113.
15    Nipperdey 1993, p. 76.
16    Mommsen 1974, pp. 13, 132.
17    Roth 1993b, p. 89.

the anti-Catholic pamphlet *Römische Triumphe* ['Roman Triumphs'], in which he accounted for the Catholic 'triumph' in terms of such factors as the capacity of clerical agitators to stir up common people against the privileged and more educated Protestants.[18]

On 25 April 1887, the 23-year-old Weber wrote Baumgarten a letter that expresses both Weber's partisanship within the *Kulturkampf* and his critique of its political form: the ' "peace" quietly declared' with the Catholic church reveals, according to Weber, that the Protestant motives were purely political, and not conscientious. But this, he adds, amounts to the admission of a 'grave injustice', namely that of having abused, for external reasons and thus unconscionably, the conscience of the Catholic people.[19] What follows from this self-criticism is not, as one might assume, an abandonment of the confessional struggle, but rather its resumption on a different basis. What is hardest to bear about this defeat, Weber writes, is that the moral injustice prevents us 'from ever taking up the struggle again in the manner in which it needs to be taken up if it is to lead to victory'.[20] Thus the project of conducting the struggle against Catholicism not in an immediately political fashion, but on the level of *conscience*, is announced early on.[21]

The first version of the *Protestant Ethic* also contains a direct reference to the *Kulturkampf*, which was deleted from the second, 1920 version: the Centre Party delegate Adolf Gröber, who had presented parliament with a pro-Catholic 'Proposition on Tolerance', invoking religious tolerance in Catholic Maryland, prompts Weber to remark that while the Catholic church might be able to accept a tolerance based on political expediency, it would never be able to accept tolerance qua religious principle. He adds that the psychological foundation of liberty in the Puritan countries is the hostility to authority displayed by the Quakers and other Protestant sects.[22] Weber returns to this theme in *Economy and Society*: he quotes the Centre Party delegate Mallinckrodt, who had admitted before the Reichstag that Catholic freedom of conscience consists in being allowed to obey the Pope, and develops the view that no ecclesiastical

---

18    See ibid., p. 90.

19    Weber 1936, p. 234.

20    Ibid.

21    Much like Baumgarten, Weber wanted the struggle to be 'conducted on the basis of inner motives', Mommsen comments (Mommsen 1974, p. 13; compare p. 6). That Weber rejected the state-political *Kulturkampf* can be seen, for example, from his criticism of the 'misguided methods' used by Bismarck (Weber 1984–2009, vol. I/15, p. 447), or from his notes for a political speech to be held at a DDP rally in January of 1919, where one reads, under the heading 'church': 'no *Kulturkampf*' (Weber 1984–2009, vol. I/16, p. 171).

22    Weber 1905, p. 43, note 78.

institution of salvation, including the Calvinist one, can guarantee freedom of conscience; only the sects are able to do so.[23] What both passages have in common is the argumentative strategy of responding to a 'German' *Kulturkampf* theme with a specifically Anglo-American achievement.

The displacement of the *Kulturkampf* from state politics to *ethics* is also no original Weberian accomplishment. Towards the end of the nineteenth century, the politico-administrative *Kulturkampf* was continued in the *debate on inferiority*. It turned mainly on the degree of modernity proper to the two denominations and saw the 'liberal' current within Protestant theology claiming the 'practico-cultural superiority of the Protestant spirit over Roman Catholic piety, which was alleged to be purely world-renouncing'.[24] As Baumeister shows,[25] the notion of Catholic *inferiority* developed as a Protestant response to the Centre Party's 'parity campaign': the Catholic call for 'parity', which dominated public debate since the 1880s, concerned access to the key positions within the state administrations of Prussia and the Reich, as well as within the judiciary and the system of higher education. One important disputed terrain was the 'scientific objectivity' of statistical investigations. In 1893, the Centre Party published lists detailing the composition of the civil service's higher echelons, first for Westphalia and then for all of Prussia; the first major result was the publication, in 1897, of a Catholic memorandum on 'Parity in Prussia', whose second, extended edition was distributed to Prussian civil servants and politicians in 1899. What was at stake throughout this campaign was the demonstration that Catholics were subject to political 'discrimination', or that there existed a 'system of exclusion' that began with entry-level employment and asserted itself by means of a close-knit network of selection mechanisms, as well as by means of student associations, the reserve officer corps, selection procedures that precluded open competition, affiliation with a certain milieu, etc.

By contrast, the counter-concept of 'Catholic inferiority' represses the structural causes of discrimination and replaces them with the assumption of an 'internal' inferiority. It is easy to see that this concept represents the consolidation of a 'Protestant' view of Catholic Germany. However, the denominational frontline is rendered more complex by the fact that this view was also adopted by 'reform Catholics' such as Emile de Laveleye, Herman Schell, Karl Muth, G. von Hertling, Albert Ehrhard and others,[26] albeit in combination with the discrimination thesis, which these authors retained, and the proposal

---

23    Weber 1978, p. 1209.
24    Graf 1984, p. 263.
25    Baumeister 1987, pp. 15ff, 24, 26–7, 40.
26    See Laveleye 1875, Schell 1897, Muth 1898, von Hertlin 1899 and Ehrhard 1902.

to overcome Catholicism's current deficits by means of its 'modern' forces.[27] This constellation was an unfavourable one for the Catholic camp, since every Catholic self-criticism, no matter how nuanced, was received by the denominational opponent as confirmation of his own inferiority thesis. Naturally, Weber does not pass up the opportunity to support his claims about Protestant superiority with references to Catholic publications, mentioning Schell, von Hertling and Laveleye in particular.[28]

The same Weber who exposed Wilhelmine Germany's selection mechanisms in his critique of the entailed estate, the reserve officer corps and the student associations (see above, Chapter 11) completely elides these determinants in his account of Catholicism's 'deficit'. The opening passages of the *Protestant Ethic*, where Weber isolates the 'intrinsic character', already take sides in the denominational competition over positions within the state apparatus and civil society. For the two rivals are positioned in such a way that the Catholic side is forced to place the emphasis of its arguments on the structural causes of its subaltern status in an almost historically materialist rhetoric, whereas the Protestant side tends to legitimate its social superiority by reference to the features of its internal essence. Weber latches onto this self-conception, that of a dominant power bloc that is in a position to interpret its 'Protestant' hegemony as being 'inwardly' justified. To be sure, this was preceded by a defeat on the political level, namely the official termination of the '*Kulturkampf*'; said defeat prompted, by way of compensation, a further increase in the emphasis placed on inward superiority.

Thus the isolation of the intrinsic character involves not just support for the 'Protestant' and opposition to the 'Catholic' side, but also support for an upper social stratum (which articulated itself in Protestant terms) and opposition to the 'people' (which articulated itself in Catholic-clerical terms). Moreover, Weber's operation reproduced within itself the bourgeoisie's integration into the ruling power bloc, which rested, to a significant extent, on the fact that the denominational dispute distracted the liberals from their project of political democratisation. The very unleashing of the '*Kulturkampf*' by Bismarck was motivated, at least in part, by the fear of an eventual rapprochement between the liberals and the Centre Party. The underlying strategy for the homogenisation of the ruling power bloc has frequently been described as an instance of 'secondary' or 'negative integration', whereby one opponent was declared an 'enemy of the Reich' and placed under police surveillance, while tactical

27    See Baumeister 1987, pp. 75ff, 85ff; Nipperdey 1988, pp. 33ff.
28    Weber 1950, p. 35, note 3; Weber 1950, p. 44, note 23.

alliances were formed with the other.[29] With regard to foreign policy, such 'enemies of the Reich' included both the 'ultramontane' papacy and France, considered not just a national, but also an 'ethical, religio-denominational enemy'.[30] On the one hand, this two-front battle allowed the liberals to act out their democratic impulses by combating the 'reactionary' Catholic church;[31] on the other, it ensured that they kept their distance from the 'irreligious' Jacobinism of the French Revolution, which in turn was to be explained, on this view, in terms of the weakness of French Catholicism. The manner in which the opposition between bourgeois democracy and *ancien régime* was transposed to the terrain of denominational oppositions emerges from an observation made by Nipperdey: while the French philosophers of the counterrevolution had identified Protestantism as the source of secularisation, the Enlightenment and revolution, the German liberals turned the argument around and presented Protestantism as the modern device for overcoming revolution by means of reforms.[32]

Weber provided the problematic of Catholic inferiority with a 'fixed place ... in the "subconscious" of the social and historical sciences', according to Baumeister, who describes this process as a sublimated and scientifically 'purged' confessionalism.[33] Baumeister argues that the period around 1900 saw the most varied social and political problems being 'perceived as "denominational" in a manner that seems downright outlandish by today's standards. This was true of the rise of the labour movement as much as of the increasing number of suicides or shifts in the international balance of power'.[34] Baumeister interprets this as the 'crisis symptom of a changing, insecure society' that processed its upheavals by means of the old denominational categories.[35] In order to understand the historical significance of this denominational processing, it is worth taking a brief look at the history of the relationship between Catholicism and Protestantism.

---

29    See Sauer 1970, pp. 430ff; Wehler 1973, pp. 96ff.

30    Köhle-Hezinger 1976, p. 283.

31    In his memoirs, Bebel notes that the liberals itched to 'distract from their willingness to sacrifice bourgeois liberties by grandiloquently blowing the horn of *Kulturkampf*' (Bebel 1911, p. 218).

32    'The liberals turned the argument around: Protestantism is indeed connected with progress and modernity, but Protestantism is not revolution; it is constant reform. The Catholic countries are the ones with these kinds of revolution, provoked by despotism, corruption, and laziness' (Nipperdey 1993, p. 77).

33    Baumeister 1987, pp. 11, 101.

34    Baumeister 1987, pp. 74–5.

35    Ibid.

In a 'discursive archaeology' of sorts, Paul Münch reconstructs the 'Weber thesis before Weber' from the sixteenth to the nineteenth century; reversing Merton's characterisation of Weber as a 'sociological giant' carrying the later 'dwarves' on his shoulders, Münch concludes that Weber was, at best, 'a giant standing on the shoulders of dwarves'.[36] The metaphor aims at Weber's dependence on ideologues who transformed the Reformation's economic results (secularisation of church property, elimination of the 'unproductive' church orders, a reduction in the number of holidays) into a myth of Protestant superiority, from the period of European denominational consolidation onward.[37] Long-term studies show that as social constellations changed, so did the perception of denominational differences. For example, there was less emphasis on these differences during the enlightened absolutism of the eighteenth century, as can be seen from the fact that all theologians of the period defined 'the Christian's role in the world' in similar terms, regardless of their denomination.[38] Accordingly, the tendency to explain denominational differences in economic and political terms prevailed. For example, in his study of the interdenominational debates on the economic backwardness of the Catholic countries that were conducted during the 1870s and 1880s, Strohm concludes that the way the problem was considered then was more realistic than Weber's invocation of a Protestant 'spirit'. For instance, account was taken of the sociological phenomenon that the Protestant dynasties of inheritance were better equipped for long-term economic planning than the clerical electoral dynasties of the Catholic countries.[39]

---

36   Münch 1993, p. 71; compare pp. 52–3.

37   According to Münch, the sixteenth century did not see the two denominations displaying significant differences in terms of their (equally traditionalist) economic ethics or their treatment of able-bodied mendicants (Münch 1993, pp. 54, 60). In the late sixteenth century, however, William Perkins's *Treatise of the Vocations or Callings of Men* (1597) introduced the stereotype of the lazy Catholic, who bleeds the land of money and sends the money to Rome (Münch 1993, p. 55). 'From then on, confessional enemies no longer appeared only as adversaries in the creed but also experienced a basic social stigmatization as a pack of unproductive outcasts' (Münch 1993, p. 56).

38   'The decent, orderly, industrious, and content Citizen, who quietly and steadily went about his other business, represented the ideal of the good Christian for all the confessions' (Münch 1993, p. 57).

39   Strohm 1966/72, pp. 242, 247, 253. Strohm sees in these debates, conducted mainly in the *Journal von und für Deutschland* ('Journal From And For Germany'), the first 'beginnings of religio-sociological cognition of reality' (Strohm 1966/72, p. 237). It is revealing of the nature of interconfessionalism that the publicist Sartori was able to look to both the

In the first third of the nineteenth century, the relationship between the denominations was still characterised by tolerance, but animosity increased in the 1830s, and especially following German unification under Prussia: the Protestants celebrated Luther as a German patriot, and 'Catholic' became a synonym for un-German, ultramontane, uncivilised and lazy.[40] In parallel with the deterioration of the relationship between the denominations, there also occurred a paradigm shift, from the mostly political explanatory models of the late eighteenth century to the 'spirit'-based explanations typical of the *Kulturkampf*.[41]

The isolation of the 'inner peculiarity' and its denominationalist definition, which Weber so effectively anchored in sociology's 'subconscious', as Baumeister says, thus need to be considered products of an intricately composed myth. This myth is based on an explanatory model that proceeds from a speculative inside outward, and in which the denominations' multiply determined positional differences within the economy, the state and civil society are reduced to a static 'essence'. As for the myth's concrete social dynamic in the late nineteenth century, it derives from Protestantism's effective alliance with other ideological fields, particularly those of nationalism and the prevailing values of diligence and dutifulness. This alliance was driven, in turn, by the frontlines in the *Kulturkampf*, which saw the ruling power bloc combating not just Catholicism, but also the 'legacy' of the French Revolution and the threat of Marxist Social Democracy.

## 25.3 Protestant 'Culture' as an Integrational Cipher in the Crisis of Orientation

That 'there is something Protestant about the machine' was a well-known saying by the theologian and abbot of Loccum, Gerhard Uhlhorn,[42] one Friedrich Naumann was particularly fond of citing. The Protestant articulation of

---

state 'rationalism' of Protestant Prussia under Frederick II and Austria's reform Catholic 'Josephinism' (Strohm 1966/72, pp. 246–7).

40    Münch 1993, p. 58. Compare Köhle-Hezinger's nuanced stadial model of the Catholic-Protestant relationship, in which the spectacular 'Cologne event' of 1837 (the imprisonment of Cologne's archbishop on the orders of the Prussian state) and the period following the foundation of the Reich are considered moments of maximum tension (Köhle-Hezinger 1976, pp. 92–8).

41    Münch 1993, p. 71.

42    Uhlhorn 1887, pp. 8–9.

economic and technological progress is not unique to Weber but part of the basic repertoire of the 'debates on culture' conducted around the turn of the century; these debates can be considered the immediate context of Weber's thesis. Weber's intervention meets with a social constellation in which political solutions to the crisis of hegemony were stalled. As Bruch's, Hübinger's and Graf's studies on *Kultur und Kulturwissenschaften um 1900* demonstrate, the intellectual debates on models of social organisation were primarily conducted in the 'pre-political space' of culture.[43] Like Weber, the various disciplines inquired into the 'cultural significance' of their subjects,[44] and the term 'cultural history' assumed the 'sound of an integrating code within the increasingly differentiated system of the single sciences'.[45] This code performed the task that the history of states could no longer perform: it brought about an 'integrational effect that was able to link all spheres of life, from Israelite prophecy to Marx's theory of surplus value and Lamprecht's "sensitivity of the soul"'.[46] The transcendence of state history that Croce claimed to have achieved by means of his 'ethico-political history' (see above, Chapter 19.2) was here to be brought about by means of the concept of cultural history.

Bruch, Hübinger and Graf, who uncritically adopt the concept of 'culture' current in the turn of the century's 'debates on culture', speak of the bourgeoisie's 'acute need for "cultural societalisation" [*kulturelle Vergesellschaftung*], i.e. for binding patterns of interpretation, values and rules of conduct that could be resorted to whenever decisions needed to be taken'. On this account, the leading cultural sciences laid a claim to providing society with 'consensually accepted cultural norms and values, thereby laying the foundation for the community's political integration'.[47] The very definition of 'cultural societalisation' in terms of values and norms that are both 'binding' and 'consensually accepted' indicates that what is here presenting itself in the general cloak of 'the cultural' is nothing other than the ideological: as with the concept of culture in the neo-Kantian philosophy of values (see above, Chapter 17.4), what is at stake here are not self-determined ways of life that social groups autonomously posit as ends in themselves and by which they articulate their claim to a fulfilled life, but rather suitable modalities of a societalisation-from-above.[48]

---

43    Bruch, Hübinger and Graf 1989, p. 15.

44    Bruch, Hübinger and Graf 1989, p. 16.

45    Hübinger 1989, p. 26.

46    Bruch, Hübinger and Graf 1989, p. 17.

47    Bruch, Hübinger and Graf 1989, pp. 14–15. Compare Hübinger 1994, pp. 21ff.

48    On the concept of 'the cultural' or the 'cultural moment' and its distinction from the ideological, see Haug 2011, pp. 41ff, 46ff; see Rehmann 2013, pp. 250ff.

Moreover, and this is a peculiarity of the German history of ideology, the bourgeois concept of 'culture' was directed primarily against French 'civilisation'. The social content of this opposition changed fundamentally: as Elias has shown,[49] the concept of culture was associated, in the eighteenth century, with an inward and powerful sense of spirituality by which the weak bourgeois intelligentsia lived its opposition to a courtly society whose model was France. 'Civilisation' became the twofold counter-image of foreignness and class domination, whereas in 'culture', the bourgeois elements were kept away from every sort of political activity. After the French Revolution, what had begun as a social antithesis became a national one. Jehle remarks that during the eighteenth century, France was present within Germany in the form of the aristocratic elite, whereas the French Revolution fundamentally altered the situation: 'It was the French Revolution that turned German aristocrats into haters of the French, even as it inspired in French aristocrats a love for the country that promised them shelter from the revolution'.[50]

A century later, the protagonists of the 'debates on culture' were still searching for 'German' models of integration that could buttress the upcoming capitalist modernisation process without the violent ruptures of the French Revolution while preventing the 'deterioration of values' caused by the Enlightenment, materialism and socialism. It was understood that unlike 'material' civilisation, 'culture' is shaped by ethical practice and guided by moral imperatives. The centrepiece of the religio-ethical understanding of culture was the concept of the *personality*, whose religious origins were universally accepted in the various Protestant camps. Accordingly, the most diverse works examined the internal relationship of religion, education and the constitution of the personality.[51] Interdisciplinary cooperation was frequent, as when historians and theologians searched for common 'swathes of historical continuity'.[52] One of Protestant theology's more important contributions consisted in 'presenting the Reformation as the normative origin of modernity and thereby outlining the ideal image of a true modernity shaped by a purely Christian genesis'.[53] The historians of the so-called 'Ranke renaissance' played an important role in this project; they were concerned to 'genetically combine' the legacy of Luther, the

---

49  Elias 1939, pp. 21, 38.

50  Jehle 1996, p. 42. 'Since the French Revolution, it has always been the opposition between the two countries that has driven and determined the resolution of their respective internal contradictions' (Jehle 1996, p. 44).

51  Graf 1989, pp. 123–4.

52  Bruch 1989, p. 79.

53  Graf 1989, p. 118.

classicism of the late eighteenth century and the anti-Napoleonic wars of liberation of 1813.[54] Nipperdey observes that the more secular society became,
the more frequently religious categories were used to formulate explanations
of reality that non-churchgoers with a Protestant background could identify
with just as well as liberal Protestants: 'a mixture of universalistic speculations,
self-righteousness, and prejudices'.[55]

Graf explains the contradiction between religious interpretations and ongoing secularisation by arguing that as theologians lost their status as a 'functional
elite', they compensated for this by self-confidently asserting themselves as a
'value elite':[56] on the one hand, the theological faculties within the system of
university education suffered a continuous loss of importance between 1890
and 1914 (for example, students of theology represented an ever smaller percentage of the student body as a whole); on the other hand, Protestant theology
began to view itself as 'having been called upon to become the ethico-political
leadership of the new nation state'.[57] Graf accounts for this sense of mission
firstly in terms of theology's major contribution to the 'international significance of German scholarship' (for example, Germany's liberal academic theology and historico-critical Bible studies exerted a strong influence on Great
Britain and the USA) and secondly in terms of the high repute theologians
enjoyed among the representatives of other 'cultural sciences', which invoked
the cohesive power of religion and attributed to theology 'an especially important role in the formulation of new cultural values by which to master the crisis
of integration and meaning'.[58]

Theology met with such appreciation throughout the 'educated circles', to
which it was linked by a multiform network of 'minor theological publications'
promoting the popularisation of the new insights into the religious and cultural history of Christianity.[59] The theologian Otto Baumgarten (a cousin of
Max Weber) claimed that to the extent that it is organised in the form of a
church, religion becomes subject to processes of auto-dissolution, even as it
becomes more potent than ever as a 'general ferment of culture', increasing the

---

54    Bruch 1989, p. 76.

55    Nipperdey 1993, p. 78.

56    Graf 1989, p. 106.

57    Graf 1989, pp. 105–6.

58    Graf 1989, p. 107. According to Nipperdey, the late nineteenth century sees the historico-
      critical subdisciplines of theology becoming an 'intellectual superpower that also exerted
      a lasting influence on the laity's attitude to religion (Nipperdey 1988, p. 73).

59    Graf 1989, pp. 108–9.

'intensity of the inner Christian culture'.[60] What presents itself, here, as general culture is of course primarily the cultural ideology of the educated bourgeoisie, Protestantism's stimulation of inter-class cohesion being relatively weak (compared to Catholicism). Graf concludes that it is only when this context is borne in mind that one can even understand 'why the theme of religion played such an important role within the process of sociology's constitution as an independent cultural science, especially in the cases of Georg Simmel and Max Weber'.[61]

This cultural Protestant sounding board of the period around 1900 also represents one of the reasons for the influence exerted by the *Protestant Ethic*. Within the German constellation of a bourgeois-Junker class compromise, the bourgeoisie's achievement of hegemony depended upon its ability to provide its ethico-political claim to leadership with a religious foundation. Even if Weber described himself, in a letter to Tönnies dated 19 February 1909, as 'absolutely "tone-deaf"' with regard to religion',[62] he had a keen sense of this religious precondition of hegemony.

### 25.4    Ritschl and Weber: A New Arrangement of Ethical Resources

Having so far concentrated on Weber's placement with regard to the ethico-political frontlines of German cultural Protestantism, I will now attempt to demonstrate how he tries to reconfigure those frontlines. An obvious standard of comparison is provided by the conception of Protestantism developed by the leading cultural Protestant theologian Albrecht Ritschl (1822–89), whose significance to those parts of the *Protestant Ethic* that deal with the history of religion is similar to that of Schmoller with regard to Weber's interventions into political economy and social policy, or Rickert's with regard to his 'theory of science': Ritschl provides Weber's argument with both its starting point and its counterfoil. Ritschl's significance to the *Protestant Ethic* can already be seen from the numerous footnotes in which Weber engages with Ritschl's main theological work, *Rechtfertigung und Versöhnung* ['Justification and Reconciliation'], three volumes, 1870–4, as well as with his *Geschichte des Pietismus* ['History of Pietism'], three volumes, 1880–6.[63] Ritschl was to

---

60    Quoted in Graf 1989, p. 111.

61    Graf 1989, p. 112.

62    Weber 1984–2009, vol. II/6, p. 65.

63    Graf notes that Ritschl is the theologian most frequently criticised by Weber in the *Protestant Ethic* (Graf 1993, p. 42).

the consolidation of cultural Protestantism as an influential ideology of the ruling power bloc what Schleiermacher was to the constitution of a cultural Protestant religiosity of the educated classes. To Karl Barth, Ritschl is 'the prototype of the national-liberal German burgher in the age of Bismarck', standing upon the foundation of his 'life ideal' with unprecedented decidedness.[64] In their history of theology, Stephan and Schmidt emphasise the self-confidence of his thought, which they claim was inwardly bound up with the 'sense of security proper to a bourgeoisie that is proud of its culture' and which, they add, hung over his theology like a shadow.[65] Ritschl's theology represents, first and foremost, a triumph over the 'precarious intellectual situation' of the 1840s, a situation that had been brought about by the attack of the left Hegelians but gradually yielded, in the course of the 1850s and 1860s, to a more stable state in which 'the revolutionary spirits were cast away again'.[66] Gabriel observes that Ritschl attempted to mediate between orthodox-confessional and liberal theology, and that this corresponded to the rapprochement between feudal and bourgeois-liberal forces after 1848: 'Thus Ritschl becomes the leading theologian of the Bismarck era'.[67] According to Graf, Ritschl sought to overcome German society's crisis of integration by an inwardly renewed Lutheranism: 'He proclaimed a patriotic Lutheran bourgeoisie ... to be the most important force of cultural advancement'.[68] This is related to the church-historical project of 'linking the Reformation and modernity while eliding Pietisim'.[69] The glorification of the vocation of a 'worldly'-oriented bourgeoisie secured him considerable influence within the popular theology of the educated elites.[70]

I will use as an example the comparison between the denominations undertaken by Ritschl in the first part of his three-volume *History of Pietism*. There, Ritschl develops the basic criteria of assessment that allow him to describe Pietism as a symptom of Protestantism's decline. 'Lutheranism' provided the yardstick that Ritschl deduces neither from Luther's scriptural principle (*sola*

---

64    Barth 1960, p. 567.
65    Stephan and Schmidt 1973, p. 274.
66    Timm 1967, p. 70. During the revolution of 1848/49, Ritschl joined a constitutionalist citizen's association in Bonn; this association had been founded in opposition to a more radical democratic association and hoped for a constitutional state on the Prussian model. When the democrats began taking 'violent measures', Ritschl hastily departed for Cologne in order to enlist the aid of the Prussian military stationed there, an action motivated by his 'dutiful interest in the public order'; see Timm 1967, p. 81.
67    Gabriel 1975, p. 50.
68    Graf 1993, p. 46.
69    Wichelhaus 1965, p. 45.
70    Schick 1970, p. 20.

scriptura), nor from his theology of justification (sola fide), but purely from his conception of the state and of vocation. Luther's conception of the state implies that the state is instituted by God and buttresses the religious community; his conception of vocation is geared to the 'ideal of Christian life' or the notion that the 'yardstick of qualitative perfection' is to be found not in unworldly monasticism but in the 'faithful fulfilment of one's vocation'.[71] It is precisely the priority of worldly vocations that Ritschl considers decisive, because they are the 'practical expression' of the fact that 'Christianity is conceived of not as fleeing the world, but as fulfilling and pervading it'.[72]

Whatever departs from this image of Luther and Lutheranism is articulated as a relapse into Catholicism, which Ritschl defines in terms of the concept of 'unworldliness'. Its first characteristic feature is the Franciscan orientation towards the early Christian ideal of poverty, which saw the prescription to go through the world without a bag, money or a staff, given by Jesus to his disciples, being applied 'literally' to the members of the congregation.[73] Thus the cultural Protestant concept of the 'world' functions, here, as a social one and constitutes the opposite pole with regard to a Christian option for the poor.[74] The concept of 'asceticism' is used as a synonym of 'unworldliness';[75] other elements include mysticism and contemplation.[76] The Catholic-Protestant denominational opposition serves Ritschl as a projection surface that allows him to eliminate from his own denomination whatever runs contrary to his project of modernisation.

The Baptist movements of the sixteenth century number among the first victims of this elimination process; Ritschl traces them back to the 'Catholic-ascetic Christianity of the Middle Ages', and more specifically to the Franciscan third orders.[77] What Ritschl considers 'Catholic' is primarily the Baptist call to renounce all property and the ascetic critique of luxury and festive culture.[78] By contrast, what Ritschl considers 'Catholic' in Calvin is not the evocation

---

71    Ritschl 1880, pp. 38–9, 44.

72    Ritschl 1880, p. 41.

73    Ritschl 1880, pp. 13–14.

74    It would be worth investigating to what extent Weber continues to convey this social meaning of the cultural Protestant concept of the 'world' in his basic religio-sociological concepts, such as 'adjustment to the world', 'rejection of the world', 'overcoming of the world', 'intramundane', etc.

75    Ritschl 1880, p. 15.

76    Ritschl 1880, pp. 47, 50–1, 56, 60–1.

77    Ritschl 1880, pp. 29ff.

78    Ritschl 1880, pp. 24, 26.

of an early Christian ideal of poverty,[79] but rather the assertion that the Bible calls for a church discipline independent of the state; given the existence of Christian authorities, Ritschl considers this assertion outdated, anti-state and unchristian. The very 'manner' in which Calvin deduces church discipline from the New Testament qua 'inspired book of law' evokes the Franciscan position and comes close to monastic unworldliness, according to Ritschl.[80] A second factor consists in the antipathy Calvin expressed towards convivial recreation and public games.[81] Overall, Ritschl argues, Calvinism seeks to 'imitate the early church, both in terms of its constitution and of its unworldly ethic...as far as its existence within the state allows'.[82] Thus Calvinism represents a tempered, but equally dangerous early Christianity that has lodged itself within the state.

Since Ritschl thinks of himself as the theologian of the 'Prussian Union of Churches' (founded in 1817 by Frederick William III of Prussia and consisting of the Lutheran Church and the Reformed Church of Prussia), he cannot fully reject the reformed current, but needs rather to divide it: he places the 'German' camp, consisting of Lutheranism and Zwinglianism, on one side, and 'extra-German' Calvinism on the other.[83] The line of division is dictated by nationalist hostilities, and especially by Franco-German hostility. For the decisive feature of Calvinist church discipline consists, according to Ritschl, in its French national character, construed as a combination of the tendency towards 'unfree lawfulness' (the 'inclination to allow oneself to be disciplined in every regard') and the 'drive towards equality'.[84] By contrast, the sense of individual and ethical 'liberty' is typically 'German'.[85] Against bourgeois discourses that link liberty, equality and fraternity, 'equality' is construed, in the name of 'liberty', as 'coercion', or, in the discourse of theology, as 'lawfulness'. In the field of theological concept formation, Ritschl articulates the hostility of a 'Caesaristically' constituted Junker-bourgeois bloc towards the French Revolution and its supporters.

---

79   Ritschl does credit Calvin with having considered the 'communist tendency' of the Jerusalem congregation (see Apostles 5, 32–37) an exception, and with having denied its prescriptive character (Ritschl 1880, p. 110). Like the Lutheran one, the Calvinist 'organisation of life' is 'linked to vocational practice and integration in the state' (Ritschl 1880, p. 73).

80   Ritschl 1880, pp. 72–6.

81   Ritschl 1880, p. 77.

82   Ritschl 1880, p. 96.

83   Ritschl 1880, p. 63.

84   Ritschl 1880, pp. 73, 75.

85   Ritschl 1880, p. 74.

But Ritschl's religio-historical set-up generates ever new opponents: since Calvinism spread to England and then to North America, the anti-French stance becomes opposition to the religious traditions of the Anglo-Saxon world. Ritschl already detects an anti-state and thus 'Catholic' stance in the Scottish Calvinist John Knox (1505–72), who deduced the state form from the will of the people, thereby attributing the people with a right to resistance.[86] The Dutch and French diasporas in London, which had no state to protect them and were thereby bound to consider Christ the direct head of the church, tended in a similar direction. Ritschl sees the spread of Calvinism to England leading primarily to the 'independentism' of the English Revolution, whose 'ascetic saintliness' he interprets as a 'regression' to the 'trajectory of Baptism' and thus to the 'Franciscan Reformation'.[87]

This is essentially the theological and historical arrangement that Weber finds before him and takes as his starting point.[88] In order to understand the need for its restructuring, one has to realise that Ritschl's projection of the German Empire's hostilities onto the field of theological history threatened to lead into a dead end in several respects. (1) With regard to foreign policy, these hostilities reflected German Bonapartism's fruitless opposition to all of its Western rivals (France, England and America); during the First World War, this opposition combined with the conflict with Russia and led to the military defeat of the 'Triple Alliance' (Germany, Austria-Hungary and Italy). (2) As far as domestic policy is concerned, these hostilities revealed a dangerous paralysis of the ruling power bloc with regard to the modernisation required by the system. For behind medieval 'Catholicism' and 'Baptism' lies Bismarckian Caesarism's two-front battle against the Catholic Centre Party and the Social Democrats.[89] To this was added the hostility of the 'national liberal' Ritschl towards 'political liberalism', which is represented, within Ritschl's church-historical projection, both by Calvinism and by Pietism.[90] When, in 1887, the Progressive Party and the Centre Party joined forces with the Social Democrat

---

86    Ritschl 1880, p. 77.

87    Ritschl 1880, pp. 78–9.

88    There is no need to further pursue Ritschl's church-historical construct here. The exclusion of Calvinism is significant to the overall structure of his history of Pietism insofar as he does not trace Pietism to Lutheranism, but to the Calvinist church of the Netherlands (see Ritschl 1880, pp. 101, 369, 596).

89    Graf confirms this: 'This double political stance against Catholicism and the Social Democrats also marked his construction of history ... It was meant to assert the superiority of National-Liberal Protestantism over Catholicism and Social Democracy' (Graf 1993, p. 43).

90    Ritschl 1880, p. 267.

Party to oppose Bismarck's military policy, Ritschl attempted to demonstrate, in an official speech at the Georg-August-University in Göttingen, that all three parties rested upon 'the principles, proper to natural law, of the community of goods and of the origin of the state in an agreement of men', and that these principles, in turn, originate in medieval Catholicism:[91] 'The Roman Catholic, the socialist and the specifically liberal conception of the state have as their common basis the false opposition between fantastic natural law and historical law'.[92]

The more clearly Weber recognises these dead ends, the more urgent becomes the task of overcoming the blockades by a new arrangement of ethical resources. Weber is by no means the only one opposed to the Ritschl School. For on the one hand, he resorts to a church historiography that predates Ritschl, and whose exponents include Baur, Goebel, Hundeshagen, Schneckenburger and Müller; these historians were more inclined to present Calvinism and/or Baptism as the more authentic and simultaneously the more modern form of Protestantism. And on the other hand, he can make use of the comprehensive theological and religio-historical works of Ernst Troeltsch, who was himself a student of Ritschl and broke conclusively with the Ritschl School in 1902, i.e. just two years before the *Protestant Ethic* was written.[93]

The very way in which Weber defines his object of inquiry in the *Protestant Ethic* is revealing of the way he reorganises Ritschl's account of Protestantism. By specifying, in the title of the second section, that the Protestant ethic is the 'Practical Ethics of the Ascetic Branches of Protestantism', he distinguishes his object of inquiry from Lutheranism. While the Lutheran concept of vocation is considered an essential foundation of the new professional ethos, it is no longer anything more than its prerequisite: the 'Protestant ethic' is conceived of both as a specific modification of Lutheranism and as its counter-concept.

Weber distinguishes four currents as the historical bearers of this Protestant ethic: (1) Calvinism 'in the form which it assumed in the main area of its influence in Western Europe, especially in the seventeenth century'; (2) Pietism, which Weber (like Ritschl) sees as originating mainly in English and Dutch

---

91    Ritschl 1887, p. 55.

92    Ritschl 1887, p. 61.

93    Troeltsch enacted this break in his work *Die Absolutheit des Christentums und die Religionsgeschichte* ['The Absoluteness of Christianity and the History of Religion'], in the preface to which he opposed to the 'dogmatic method' of the Ritschl school (and especially of Wobbermin, Traub and Reischle) his own 'historical method': 'In spite of numerous affinities, this is a case of one self-contained view opposing another' (Troeltsch 1902, p. IX).

Calvinism and then spreading to Lutheranism in the seventeenth century; (3) Methodism, which only took shape within the English state church in the mid-eighteenth century; (4) the Baptist, Mennonite and Quaker sects, which developed from the Baptist movement.[94] In the course of Weber's study, it turns out that the four components can essentially be reduced to just two: since Weber considers both continental Pietism and Anglo-Saxon Methodism 'secondary movements' and 'milder forms of the consistent ascetic ethics of Puritanism', Calvinism and the sects that developed from Baptism remain as the two most important and autonomous bearers of Protestant asceticism.[95]

Outwardly, the changes to Ritschl's arrangement are minor. Weber adopts both Ritschl's portrayal of Calvinism and the Baptist movements as exponents of an 'ascetic' life ideal and his conception of Pietism as an offshoot of English and especially Dutch Calvinism. To be sure, Ritschl did not discuss England's Calvinist-Puritan Pietism and the Methodism that developed from it, a fact that provides Troeltsch with an opportunity to mock his theological mentor for his poor knowledge of English.[96] It is not in the particular attributions that the opposition lies, but in the basic assessment of Protestant *asceticism*: what Ritschl discussed as a relapse into Catholic 'unworldliness' is presented by Weber as the origin of a 'spirit of capitalism', and what Ritschl celebrated as a religion oriented towards both the authoritarian state *and* modernity is now considered an impediment to progress.

Weber's reorganisation of the church-historical setup is simultaneously a reorganisation of the foreign and domestic policy frontlines projected into it: (1) In Ritschl's church-historical projection, the Baptists represent Social Democracy and Calvinism represents a bourgeoisie that is susceptible to democracy; in Weber, this constellation undergoes a social and political trans-valuation: by making 'ascetic Protestantism' the product of these two elements, Weber provides the aimed-for alliance between the bourgeoisie and the labour aristocracy with a religious foundation. (2) In Ritschl's construct, a 'German', Lutheran-dominated union stands opposed both to Catholic France and to the Protestantism of England, whereas Weber, by his upgrading of Puritanism and sects, seeks to latch on to the religious traditions of the Anglo-American world. It is there in particular that he finds the ethical resources required for the renewal of Germany's ruling power bloc. 'The fact that our nation has never

---

94    Weber 1950, pp. 95, 144.

95    Weber 1950, p. 144, note 168.

96    '[T]he accidental fact that he [Ritschl] did not know English gave to his views and to those of his followers a very considerable and a very unfortunate twist' (Troeltsch 1960, p. 941, note 424).

gone through the school of severe asceticism, in *no* form whatsoever, is ... the source of everything I find detestable in it (and in myself)', he writes to Adolf von Harnack on 5 February 1906.[97] However, the basic cultural Protestant hostilities towards Catholicism, the French Enlightenment and the French Revolution remain unaltered.

### 25.5    Jellinek and Weber: Linking up with Anglo-American Mythistory

According to Roth, the *Protestant Ethic* marks both the endpoint of a long tradition of liberal orientation towards England and the beginning of a growing interest in America, which was seen as a possible opponent or ally within the imperialist rivalry with England.[98] With regard to Weber's specifically Americanist and simultaneously anti-French stance, Georg Jellinek's treatise on the *Declaration of Human Rights* is especially significant. In the first edition of the *Protestant Ethic*, Weber points out that he owes to this book 'the stimulus to engage again with Puritanism'.[99] In a memorial address held in honour of the deceased Jellinek in 1911, Weber notes that Jellinek's 'demonstration of religious influences in the genesis of the "human rights"' provided him with the most essential stimuli for the 'investigation of the importance of religious elements in areas where one would not expect to find them'.[100] In particular, Weber adopts Jellinek's view that religious freedom of conscience is the 'oldest' and 'most basic Right of Man because it comprises all ethically conditioned action'.[101]

'The principles of 1789 are really the principles of 1776', thus the central thesis of Jellinek's study:[102] the declaration of human rights issued by the French national assembly in August of 1789 is traced back not to Rousseau's *Contrat social*, in which liberty allegedly consists only in participation in the state, but rather to the Bill of Rights, the constitution of Virginia issued in 1776; the intellectual origins of the Bill of Rights, in turn, are situated in the late sixteenth century reformed church of England.[103] It was in early *independentism*, accord-

---

97    Weber 1984–2009, vol. II/5, p. 33.

98    Roth 1993b, pp. 91, 93.

99    Weber 1905, p. 43, note 78; the passage is missing in the 1920 edition.

100   Quoted in Marianne Weber 1975, p. 476.

101   Weber 1978, p. 1209.

102   Jellinek 1919, p. 71. I quote from the third edition of the book.

103   Jellinek 1919, pp. 6ff, 12ff, 41ff.

ing to Jellinek, that there first developed a 'sovereign individualism within the domain of religion', and this independentism was then transferred to the domain of politics in the form of guaranteed freedom of religion: the state qua contract of sovereign elements, agreed upon for the protection of conscience.[104] In America, unrestricted freedom of conscience was first practised in 1636, in the state of Providence founded by the independent Roger Williams; in 1647, it was first written into law (in Rhode Island).[105] Since on this account freedom of religion is of key importance, with other calls for human rights organised around it,[106] Jellinek considers it a proven fact that the legal codification of the individual's inalienable rights has 'religious', not 'political' origins: 'What has until now been considered the work of the revolution is in fact a product of the Reformation and its struggles'.[107]

*Either* French *or* American, *either* political *or* religious—such oppositions prevent the insight that rising bourgeois classes can develop organic intellectuals who articulate ethico-political projects in various ideological forms, both within 'politics' and within 'religion', and that to the extent that they do so within religion, they can do so in various denominations. The purpose of the inappropriate either/or logic is to sever human rights from the French Enlightenment's philosophy of natural law, so that said human rights can then be given both a religious, Protestant and a modern Americanist significance. Roth places Jellinek's and Weber's interpretation within the context of Germany's hostility to France and reads it both as an expression of this hostility and as a reaction to it, by which human rights (having been rendered 'un-French') were to be rendered palatable to Protestant conservatives.[108]

This is another indication that the modernisation of the ruling power bloc continued to be conceived of as a 'passive revolution' against the effects exerted by the French Revolution, which Jellinek's American-Protestant deduction of human rights is also consistently directed against: in contrast with French-dominated Europe, America never aimed to *replace* positive religion with the notion of human enlightenment, and while the American states with their

---

104   Jellinek 1919, p. 43.

105   Jellinek 1919, pp. 47, 50.

106   Jellinek 1919, p. 65.

107   Jellinek 1919, p. 57.

108   Given German hostility to France and the French Enlightenment, it is no coincidence, according to Roth, 'that Jellinek and Weber, partly in conformity with and partly in reaction to these trends, shifted the origins of human rights back to the religious seventeenth century and the Anglo-American realm' (Roth 1993a, p. 22).

bills of rights developed into 'well-ordered communities' where 'one never heard laments about the state-dissolving consequences of their principles', the French upended the foundations of their political system by 'overhastily adopting foreign institutions'.[109]

Jellinek makes the French Revolution's human rights stem from Puritanism; in the same way, and as if by a division of labour between the two scholars, Weber pursues the project of accounting for the 'spirit of capitalism' in terms of Protestantism. The two interpretations have been combined and have become the standard account of Western modernity, particularly under the influence of the American Weberians associated with Parsons. Zaret considers this a residue of the old 'Whig history', one that has been refuted by more recent research or at least strongly relativised by the investigation of other factors.[110] Zaret himself opposes to the continuity thesis an explanatory approach that views the proclamation of tolerance and freedom of conscience as a reaction of the educated classes to the English Revolution and as a triumph over it: the liberal separation of religion and politics was the response of the Enlightenment thinkers around Locke and the 'moderate' church leaders of the Restoration period to the problem of 'contested authority'.[111] One might speak, in Gramsci's terminology, of a crisis of hegemony, caused by a radical sectarian Protestantism's temporary predominance within the state and the military on the one hand, and by the internecine struggles of the rival sects on the other: 'It was no longer possible to assume that religion would stabilize the social order: in politics, religion could facilitate the mobilization of popular grievances'.[112] The starting point for a mobilisation from below was the Protestant *conscience*: 'For when poorer Protestants consulted their consciences, they did not always find the abiding respect for property that God seemed to implant in more affluent consciences'.[113]

Here, the 'antagonistic reclamation' of Protestant values leads to a situation in which the religious is displaced from its predominant position within ideological socialisation.[114] Clerical and extra-clerical 'Enlightenment thinkers' develop liberal-democratic ideologies that separate religion from politics and replace Puritan theology with 'natural religion'.[115] The social bearers of the new

---

109   Jellinek 1919, pp. 33, 55; compare pp. 70–1.

110   Zaret 1989, p. 168.

111   Zaret 1989, pp. 165, 170, 176.

112   Zaret 1989, p. 172.

113   Ibid.

114   On the concept of 'antagonistic reclamation', see Haug 1993, pp. 84ff; Rehmann 2013, p. 260.

115   Zaret 1989, p. 170.

ideology are 'cohesive groups' within English society's intellectual establishment who have generally climbed from the middle strata of the bourgeoisie to the gentry and aristocracy, breaking with their Puritan upbringing in the process: 'Most grew up in Puritan families but all rejected Calvinist theology and the sectarian ideal of a holy Commonwealth'.[116] This is precisely the case of Benjamin Franklin, by reference to whom Weber attempts to illustrate the ideal type of the 'spirit of capitalism' (see below, Chapter 26.1).

Zaret's critique, which limits itself to discussing the relationship between Puritanism and liberal ideology, may here serve as an example of a type of explanation that relates shifts within the domain of the ideological to the oppositions within society and its hegemonic constellations. Considered from this vantage point, evolutionism within the history of ideas reveals its weakness: it deduces ideas from ideas without determining their position within the various ideological formations or analysing the way they function within ideological socialisation. This is true of Weber in much the same way as it is true of Jellinek, Weber's anti-evolutionist rhetoric notwithstanding. Borkenau speaks, in 1934, of an 'isolating and causal view' having prevented Weber from taking into account the 'process of social transformation' that separates early from late Calvinism.[117] Tawney, who adopts key elements of Weber's thesis, also criticises the elision of Puritanism's internal antagonisms: 'The issue between divergent doctrines was fought out within the Puritan movement itself. Some won; others lost'.[118]

The material by reference to which Weber attempts to demonstrate the link between Puritanism and the 'spirit of capitalism' (Baxter in particular) is from the late seventeenth century, 'immediately before the change to utilitarianism',[119] i.e. from the period after 1660, when English Puritanism was confronted with the failure of Cromwell's 'kingdom of God' and the victory of the Restoration. Lehmann explains the fact that most Puritans concentrated on religious edification and the fulfilment of their professional duties in terms of their defeat and elimination from politics.[120] Lehmann criticises Weber for generalising the post-revolutionary motivational structure of disappointed pastors, whose halted political commitment ('quietism') became economic activism.[121]

---

116   Zaret 1989, p. 165.

117   Borkenau 1971, pp. 154, 158.

118   Tawney 1938, pp. 313, note 32.

119   Weber 1950, p. 156, note 3.

120   Lehmann 1988, p. 540.

121   Lehmann 1988, pp. 541–42. Lehmann sees this economic activism, which Weber describes as a psychological effect of the Calvinist doctrine of predestination, as a transformation of eschatological expectations into worldly ascetic orientations. According to Lehmann,

Gramsci has criticised this as the view of history proper to a 'passive revolution', his example being Croce, whose *History of Europe* begins not with the French Revolution but with the Restoration of 1815. Since this view of history fails to take notice of the aspect of struggle, through which the opposed forces are formed and a new ethico-political system emerges, it represents only the 'passive' aspect of the revolution.[122]

Not only does Weber's thesis rely on a post-revolutionary, depoliticised Puritanism, but he also overlooks the instances in which a petty bourgeois and artisan Protestant social ethos stood in the way of a specifically capitalist spirit. Kilian, for example, is able to show plausibly that in New England, capitalist 'possessive individualism' had to assert itself against the embittered resistance of a traditionalist Puritan clergy before the clerics adapted their theology to the altered power relations, a process that involved major crises.[123] The spirit of capitalism is engendered mainly by a 'counterculture' of newly wealthy merchants whose material base was the 'triangular slave trade between Massachusetts, Africa and the Caribbean'.[124] But the adaptation of a modern European natural law that will help constitute 'possessive individualism', particularly in its Lockean variant, will be achieved primarily by some factions of New England's clergy, which thereby attempt to get the better of their opponents within the church.[125] As soon as one resituates the relationship between Puritanism and capitalism within the context of complex ideological struggles, it becomes possible to reinterpret Weber's evolutionist conception of a continuous internal development of spirit as an essentialised and reified version of a contradictory interaction: as the 'product of a process of mediation' that involved 'certain elements of Puritanism ... being reworked and provided with a new social purpose'.[126]

According to Zaret, the deduction of liberal ideology from Protestantism is more mythic than real, and the main reason the continuity thesis persists is that it corresponds with an Anglo-American civil religion that is preserved by means of countless rituals within the American educational system, as well

---

this transformation was rendered necessary by the long crisis of the seventeenth century and took place within various religious reform movements. The reconfiguration of eschatological expectations 'resulted, in Puritanism as much as in Jansenism and Pietism, in something like a high voltage network of professional ethic energy' (Lehmann 1980, p. 147).

122    Gramsci 1975b, p. 1227.
123    Kilian 1979, pp. 40ff.
124    Kilian 1979, pp. 42, 101–2.
125    Kilian 1979, pp. 59, 74ff.
126    Kilian 1979, p. 48.

as by political rhetoric.[127] This conformity with the Anglo-American foundational myth is also the main reason for the exceptionally vigorous reception of Weber's *Protestant Ethic* in the USA: seeking to confront the German present with the mirror of the Anglo-Saxon past, Weber adopted America's bourgeois-liberal account of its origins, in which Puritanism was considered a precursor of liberalism and the political struggles for liberty were traced back to religious struggles.[128] In doing so, he was in agreement with a broad public that considered the relationship between Puritanism, political liberty and America's status as a world power beyond doubt. Talcott Parsons, who was introduced to the *Protestant Ethic* as an exchange student in Heidelberg in the 1920s, was so fascinated by this relationship that he decided to translate the book into English. This development, which one can describe, following Roth, as the reimporting of an Anglo-American export, made the *Protestant Ethic* a powerful instance of American 'mythistory'.[129]

Thus, if Weber gives the German nationalist positions of Ritschl and others that he latches on to a new twist, he does so primarily by inserting himself into an Anglo-American 'mythistory'. It goes without saying that this is a questionable operation in historiography and religious studies. Its efficacy consists mainly in the ideological endeavour of linking the myths of German cultural Protestantism with those of civil religion.

According to Troeltsch, Weber's 'own important discovery' is not so much to be seen in his concept of 'ascetic Protestantism', already rudimentarily developed by Ritschl and Schneckenburger, but rather in his 'setting of this conception within the whole framework of universal, economic history and history of civilization'.[130] Weber achieves this cultural and economic contextualisation mainly by means of a 'spirit of capitalism' whose ideal-typical concept

---

127    Zaret 1989, p. 176.

128    Roth 1993a, pp. 2–3; Roth 1993b, p. 84.

129    Roth 1993a, pp. 3–4. 'As it was, the original Whig interpretation, adapted by Weber for polemical reasons, was reimported by Parsons and others into the Anglo-American realm and helped reinforce the American orthodox understanding of an inherent connection between Protestantism and liberal democracy... The exportation and reimportation of Protestant self-interpretation, if not self-congratulation, appears to me an important element in accounting for the American receptivity to the Weber Thesis' (Roth 1993a, p. 3). To be sure, Roth's assumption that Weber adopted the liberal view of history 'for polemical reasons' underestimates the significance of this orientation for the whole theoretical setup of Weber's sociology of religion and authority: what was ultimately at stake therein was the assertion of a new American mode of production by means of adequate ethical superstructures.

130    Troeltsch 1960, p. 987, note 510.

formation anticipates the mythic aspects of the thesis on Protestantism and capitalism.

In light of this, I shall now consider the *Protestant Ethic*'s second introductory passage, in which Weber, inspired by Simmel's *Philosophy of Money*, uses the example of Benjamin Franklin to introduce the category of the 'spirit of capitalism'.

# CHAPTER 26

# Weber and Simmel: The Psychological 'Deepening' of Marxian Value Form Analysis

## 26.1    Benjamin Franklin's Ethos—Utilitarian or Puritan?

The concept of the *spirit of capitalism* cannot be defined in advance, Weber writes, but needs first to be illustrated in a provisional manner and then 'gradually put together' from its historically real components.[1] Benjamin Franklin serves as the example by which to provisionally illustrate the concept. Weber quotes extensively from two texts by Franklin, namely *Necessary Hints to Those That Would be Rich* (1736) and *Advice to a Young Tradesman* (1748), where Franklin admonishes young businessmen not to waste any time—'remember that time is money'—, since to do so is not only to lose the corresponding sum of money, but also its potential offspring to the thousandth generation, money being 'the *prolific, generating nature*'.[2]

Franklin is here articulating a logic of gain that Aristotle already characterised as 'chrematistics' in his *Politics*, and to which he opposed his concept of a (use-value-oriented) 'economics'.[3] According to Weber, Franklin is articulating a specifically capitalist ethos, which he sums up in Kürnberger's words: 'They make tallow out of cattle and money out of men'.[4] On Weber's

---

1    Weber 1950, p. 47.

2    Quoted in Weber 1950, pp. 48–9. 'Remember that money is of the *prolific, generating nature*. Money can beget money, and its offspring can beget more, and so on ... He that kills a breeding sow destroys all her offspring to the thousandth generation. He that murders a crown destroys all that it might have produced, even scores of pounds' (Franklin 1904a, p. 235; compare Franklin 1904b, pp. 26–7).

3    Aristotle criticises the salesmanship [*kapelike*] practised predominantly by metics as contrary to nature, because it aims at maximum gain. He directs the same criticism at interest and usury, which cause money to generate more money (see *Politics*, Book I, 1257b 28–35; 1258a, 1–10, 40–b8). Chrematistics is contrary to nature because it 'makes money, this mere means of exchange, an end in itself and engages in exchange for its sake' (Haacke 1994, p. 53; compare pp. 54–5). See also the discussion in the first volume of Marx's *Capital* (Marx and Engels 1975–2005, vol. 35, p. 163, note 1). What distinguishes Franklin from Aristotle, however, is the insight that value is determined by labour (see Marx and Engels 1975–2005, vol. 35, p. 61, note 1).

4    Quoted in Weber 1950, p. 51.

view, what distinguishes Franklin's mindset from Fugger's pursuit of gain is a specific 'ethical' quality, namely the 'idea of a duty of the individual toward the increase of his capital', as he writes in the final version of the *Protestant Ethic*.[5] In the first version, Weber spoke, less specifically, of 'increasing his assets'.[6] Here, Weber deemed it necessary to set not just the special 'ethical' colouration, but also the specifically capitalist character of this ethos off from other efforts to increase one's wealth. Thus the difference between the modern 'spirit of capitalism' and other variants of the spirit of gain lies in a specific ethical bond that ties the capital owner to the autonomised capitalist valorisation interest, whose violation appears not just as a 'foolishness', but also as 'forgetfulness of duty'.[7]

It is no coincidence that Weber uses the example of Franklin to illustrate this spirit. The great intellectual of the founding of the US state, co-author both of the 1776 Declaration of Independence and of the 1787 Constitution, whose public embrace of Voltaire in Paris symbolised the alliance between the French and the American Enlightenments, plays a role in the *Protestant Ethic* that is similar to that of bourgeois human rights in Jellinek: the 'father of all Yankees', as Carlyle called him,[8] has to be separated from the context of the Enlightenment and associated with a Protestant religious tradition. With regard to his economic views, Franklin is linked both to the Physiocrats and to Adam Smith, who read *The Wealth of Nations* to him 'chapter by chapter' prior to its publication in 1776, as Brentano reports.[9] Marx describes Franklin as one of the first economists since William Petty to have understood the determination of value by labour.[10]

To be sure, Franklin is not unproblematic as a starting point for Weber's demonstration that Puritanism and capitalism are related. For the person in whom Weber sees the spirit of capitalism manifested in 'almost classical purity' is one he is forced to admit was *not* a Puritan but a 'colourless deist', whose ethos has been 'coloured with utilitarianism' [*utilitarisch gewendet*]—after all, in order to be safe from the claims of creditors, the young businessman counselled by Franklin needs first and foremost to *appear* an honest man.[11] How can ascetic Protestantism culminate in a stance that is dominated by other ideological

5       Weber 1950, p. 51.
6       Weber 1904, p. 14.
7       These are additions to the 1920 edition of the *Protestant Ethic* (Weber 1950, p. 51).
8       Quoted in Kilian 1979, p. 48.
9       Brentano 1916, p. 157.
10      Marx and Engels 1975–2005, vol. 35, p. 60, note 1.
11      Weber 1950, pp. 48, 53; compare Franklin 1904a, p. 236.

patterns? This is the question raised by Samuelsson, who thereby considers Weber's deduction from religious origins as good as falsified.[12]

In fact, an explanation of Franklin's ethos could just as well start from the 'empirical schools of philosophy, then coming to the fore in England'; this is the approach chosen by Sombart, for example.[13] While Weber claims Franklin traced his insight into the utility of virtue back to divine revelation,[14] Franklin himself states in his *Autobiography* that he already began to have doubts about such revelations at the age of 15, adding that he became a deist and then became convinced that the moral values prescribed by religion need to be considered from the point of view of their contribution to our 'felicity of life'.[15] He stated that revelation as such has no meaning to him, since the actions commanded or forbidden by religion 'might be forbidden *because* they were bad for us, or commanded *because* they were beneficial to us, in their own natures'—'it was, therefore, every one's interest to be virtuous who wished to be happy even in this world'.[16] Franklin makes an exception for attendance of church services, arguing that they are characterised by a fixation on sectarian doctrine and a neglect of moral and civic education: 'not a single moral principle was inculcated or enforc'd, their aim seeming to be rather to make us Presbytarians than good citizens'.[17] In order to further his moral advancement, he elaborates his own 'articles of faith' and founds a masonic lodge (the *Junto*) with fixed rituals, where debates on issues of morality, politics and natural philosophy are held every Friday.[18] To the extent that his catalogues of virtues invoke 'religious principles'—a supreme being, its providence, the immortality of the soul, obedience to authorities—, they are intended to capture a general essence common to all religions.[19] Thus Franklin articulates an aspiration common to all Enlightenment philosophy of religion, from Rousseau and Lessing to Kant, namely that of extracting from the revealed religions their inner core of 'civil', 'natural' or 'rational' religion, a religion no longer based on sacred events or

---

12    Samuelsson 1961, p. 55.

13    Sombart 1958, p. 223.

14    Weber 1950, p. 49.

15    Franklin 1904c, pp. 149–50.

16    Franklin 1904c, pp. 150, 201.

17    Franklin 1904c, p. 187.

18    Franklin 1904c, p. 153. On Franklin's articles of faith, see Franklin 1904d, pp. 319ff; on the club rules of the *Junto*, which aimed at mutual moral advancement, see Franklin 1904e, pp. 331ff.

19    Franklin 1904c, pp. 185–6, 200.

texts, but on people's moral consciousness.[20] Bellah, among others, pointed out the accordances with Rousseau's *Social Contract*.[21] Franklin's implicit theology is that of a secularised and bourgeoisified civil religion.

Weber brackets these transformations of religiosity by inserting a level of inquiry that is, so to speak, situated below concrete religious ideologies, namely the religiously determined level of 'those psychological sanctions which, originating in religious belief and the practice of religion, gave a direction to practical conduct and held the individual to it'.[22] Thus Franklin's 'utilitarian colouring' appears as a sort of surface phenomenon proper to the history of ideas, underneath which lies the deep structure of a 'professional duty' that Weber sees as having been anticipated in Luther's theology and then fully developed in Calvinism and the Baptist sects. Instead of dissecting Franklin's 'spirit' into its various determinants, Weber resorts to the organic metaphor of theological 'roots' that may have died and been replaced by utilitarian thisworldliness, but which have nevertheless left 'important traces' within the secularised ethic.[23]

Here as elsewhere, the notion of a primarily religious determination is made to appear plausible by means of an ambivalence in the argument: on the one hand, Weber points out that a purely utilitarian interpretation would be too 'simple', since it rules out the possibility of 'type[s] of feeling' shared with the religious notions of Puritanism—an argument that is immediately plausible with regard to the 'weak' thesis on Protestantism.[24] To be sure, if one accepted this argument, one would still have to engage with Bosse's objection that Weber is unable to demonstrate 'that the causally active "religious elements"—the Protestant ethos—really are *religious* elements' and not, say, a state of mind rendered possible by an economic, political and social constellation that has merely assumed a religious form.[25] What is ultimately at stake here is the thesis, both neo-Kantian and cultural Protestant, of an 'autonomy' of religious consciousness, which Weber adopted mainly from Troeltsch.[26]

---

20    In Franklin, how people's moral consciousness is anchored in religion becomes irrelevant: 'And this persuasion, with the kind hand of Providence, or some guardian angel, or accidental favorable circumstances and situations, or all together, preserved me ... from my want of religion' (Franklin 1904c, p. 151).

21    Bellah 2002, p. 516; compare Rousseau 1959, pp. 340–1.

22    Weber 1950, p. 97.

23    See for example Weber 1950, pp. 97, 170.

24    Weber 1950, p. 53.

25    Bosse 1970, p. 63.

26    Compare the way Weber and Troeltsch agree on the 'purely religious motives' of the reformers (Weber 1950, p. 90; Troeltsch 1960, pp. 564–6). Troeltsch developed this idea in

Over and above this, however, Weber constructs a set-up that attributes the level of life conduct, relevant to human action, to religion, leaving the Enlightenment with the status of a derivative end product without any determining power of its own. Comparison between the first and the second version of the *Protestant Ethic* reveals that here too, Weber vacillates between a 'strong' and a 'weak' thesis: in 1905, he writes that psychological sanctions stemmed from 'religious ideas that were predominantly purely religious', but in 1920, he qualifies this by writing that they were '*to a large extent* derived from the peculiarities of the religious ideas behind them'.[27] As with Weber's isolation of the 'inner peculiarity' (see above, Chapter 24), the course is set by means of a conceptual set-up that characterises some of the phenomena under investigation as essential and interior, and others as inessential and exterior. The shift to a deeper, 'psychological' level also has the advantage of being beyond the reach not just of social history, but also of the history of ideas; it is thus immune to objections from these two fields. A contextual analysis of the religio-historical part of the *Protestant Ethic* shows that Weber jumps back and forth between theological dogma and speculative psychology, practising a theo-psychological method of deduction that is characteristic of cultural Protestant theology from Schleiermacher and Ritschl to Schneckenburger and Troeltsch.[28]

What is ambivalent, however, is not just Weber's explanation for the specifically *ethical* colouration of Franklin's 'spirit of capitalism', but also his definition of its specifically *capitalist* character.

## 26.2    From the Capitalist Standpoint of Valorisation to the 'Human' Interest in Acquisition

Let us compare the first definition of the 'spirit of capitalism' with another one: 'In fact, the *summum bonum* of this ethic, the earning of more and more

---

his concept, derived from Kant, of a 'religious a priori' that is anchored in the essence of reason and by virtue of which 'everything real and in particular all values were related to an absolute substance qua point of departure and yardstick' (Troeltsch 1913, p. 494; compare Troeltsch 1895, pp. 400–1, 406; Troeltsch 1904, pp. 29–30, 117ff, 123ff; Troeltsch 1905, pp. 26–7, 44ff).

27    Weber 1905, p. 3; Weber 1950, pp. 97–8 (emphasis added).

28    Weber bases his argument mainly on the dogmatic-historical literature that organises religion along certain psychological ideal types, as Graf observes: 'German-speaking Protestant theologians of the nineteenth century mostly followed a psychological classification that allowed not only for the independence of religion, but also for the instructive power of religious ideas' (Graf 1993, p. 31).

money, combined with the strict avoidance of all spontaneous enjoyment of life, is above all completely devoid of any eudemonistic, not to say hedonistic, admixture. It is thought of so purely as an end in itself, that from the point of view of the happiness of, or utility to, the single individual, it appears entirely transcendental and absolutely irrational. Man is dominated by the making of money, by acquisition as the ultimate purpose of his life. Economic acquisition is no longer subordinated to man as the means for the satisfaction of his material needs'.[29]

At first blush, Weber seems to have modelled the capitalist ethic directly on the analyses in the first section of *Capital*, where Marx discusses how money goes from being a mere medium of exchange (C–M–C) to being an 'end in itself'.[30] On Marx's account, the 'change of form' first occurs when money is hoarded; the hoarder attempts to hold gold as money, '[acting] in earnest up to the Gospel of abstention' and, in this labour of Sisyphus, 'makes a sacrifice of the lusts of the flesh to his gold fetish'.[31] The 'change of form' is continued by the more 'astute' capitalist, who, instead of withdrawing money from circulation, makes it circulate over and over, and whose immediate aim is never use value, but the 'restless never-ending process of profit-making': 'This boundless greed after riches, this passionate chase after exchange-value, is common to the capitalist and the miser; but while the miser is merely a capitalist gone mad, the capitalist is a rational miser'.[32]

To be sure, one could ask again to what extent Franklin even displays the *anti-hedonist ethos* of monetary gain outlined by Weber (and required by him so he can posit asceticism as the link between Puritanism and the spirit of capitalism). In fact, the 42 year old does just what Fugger refuses to do the same year, citing his fondness for monetary gain as the reason: he shuts down his business so as to henceforth dispose of the 'leisure' his philosophical studies and enjoyments require.[33] Baumgarten sees Franklin not as an ascetic but as an Epicurean whose praise of monetary gain is subordinated to the idea of

---

29    Weber 1950, p. 53.

30    Marx and Engels 1975–2005, vol. 35, pp. 140, 163–4.

31    Marx and Engels 1975–2005, vol. 35, p. 144.

32    Marx and Engels 1975–2005, vol. 35, pp. 163–4.

33    'When I disengaged myself... from private business, I flatter'd myself that, by the suffi-
      cient tho' moderate fortune I had acquir'd, I had secured leisure during the rest of my life
      for philosophical studies and amusements' (Franklin 1904c, p. 242). By contrast, Fugger
      rejected the advice of a business associate who had suggested he retire, stating that 'he
      thought otherwise, he wanted to make money as long as he could' (see Sombart 1902,
      p. 396; Weber 1950, pp. 51–2).

happiness.[34] After all, the same period sees Franklin penning a bacchanalian song in which he mocks the accumulation of wealth for its own sake, intemperate love and the thirst for power as matters for 'dull asses' who gnaw on the shells while missing the kernels.[35] In a 1779 letter, he laments the personality of the 'miser', who gives up 'any kind of a comfortable living ... and the joys of benevolent friendship for the sake of accumulating wealth': 'Poor man ... you pay too much for your whistle'.[36]

What is more important than the characterisation of Franklin is a significant shift that occurs within the definition of the 'spirit of capitalism' itself: the valorisation interest of the capital owner, explicitly emphasised by Weber at the outset, has underhandedly become an autonomous 'gain'. This is related to the fact that Weber now cloaks his initial definition of a spirit of capitalism that seeks to make money from people under the overly general language of 'man'. Lefèvre comments that here, 'man' is quite obviously understood to be a 'man who is acting as a capitalist'.[37]

The main factor in this shift is the influence of Simmel's 1900 book *The Philosophy of Money*, which Weber had read a short time earlier and whose contents he works into the subchapter on the 'spirit of capitalism'. It was in Simmel's book that Weber discovered a 'preformulation' of the methods he would go on to apply in the *Protestant Ethic*, Schnabel observes.[38] According to Frisby, Weber's remarks on the spirit of capitalism need to be read as a response to Simmel, and in particular to his detailed discussion of the predominance of means over ends.[39] While this link is widely recognised in the scholarly literature on Weber, it usually goes unnoticed that Simmel, in turn, conceived of his teleology of means and ends as a response to 'historical materialism', so that Weber is also responding to Marx, albeit indirectly.[40]

When Simmel articulates the transformation of money from a mere means to a coveted end in itself as a 'symbol' of practical life in general,[41] he translates

---

34    Baumgarten 1936, pp. 94–5, 100.

35    'Then toss off your glasses and scorn the dull asses / who, missing the kernel, still gnaw the shell: / What's love, rule, or riches? Wise Salomon teaches: They're vanity, vanity, still' (quoted in Baumgarten 1936, p. 96).

36    Quoted in Baumgarten 1936, pp. 103–4; compare Brentano 1916, p. 151.

37    Lefèvre 1971, p. 41.

38    Schnabel 1976, p. 288.

39    Frisby 1988, pp. 584, 591; compare Marshall 1982, pp. 33–4.

40    See for example Simmel's Preface to *The Philosophy of Money* (Simmel 1990, p. 56) and the 1901 self-advertisement documented in the appendix to the German edition (Simmel 1989, p. 719).

41    Simmel 1990, p. 232.

the Marxian analysis of the form of value back into a suprahistorical philosophy. Marx mainly discusses the positing of money as an end in itself in the context of the shift from an exchange of commodities that is mediated by money
(C–M–C) to an increase in value that is mediated by commodities (M–C–M'),
by which value acquires the 'occult quality of being able to add value to itself'.[42]
What Marx, picking up on the Aristotelian distinction between 'economics'
and 'chrematistics', analyses as a change in the form and function of money
'evolves from our innermost being in which the soul determines our relation
to life' in Simmel.[43] What is presented, in Marx, as a function-historical caesura within the genesis of capital appears, in Simmel, as an anthropological
constant that merely finds its 'fulfilment' in money.[44] Simmel replaces the
Marxian analysis of the form of value with the general psychological law of a
'metempsychosis' of the end in itself:[45] the end is achieved all the more readily
'the more our strength is focused and concentrating on producing... means',
so that 'one cannot promote the final purpose better than to treat the means as
if it were the end in itself'.[46] According to Simmel, the 'antedating of the final
purpose' nowhere occurs as radically as in the middle term that is money—the
more perfectly it functions as a means, the more it assumes the psychological
significance of an end in itself: its value as a means increases 'right up to the
point at which it is valid as an absolute value and the consciousness of purpose
in it comes to an end'.[47]

The re-translation of Marx's analysis of the forms of value and money is
part of Simmel's basic methodological intention, namely 'to construct a new
storey beneath historical materialism', such that 'economic forms themselves
are recognized as the result of more profound valuations and currents of psychological or even metaphysical pre-conditions'.[48] In tracing economic forms
back to 'interiority's great provinces of interest', he seeks to provide exemplary
evidence for the view 'that at any point on the most indifferent and least ideal
surface of life, a plumbline can be sunk into its most profound depths'.[49] This
objective is not unique to Simmel; he largely brings up to date the 'psycho-
genetic' approach of Dilthey (see above, Chapter 17.3), which also proved influ-

---

42    Marx and Engels 1975–2005, vol. 35, pp. 164–5.
43    Simmel 1990, p. 232.
44    Ibid.
45    Simmel 1990, p. 231.
46    Simmel 1990, pp. 230–1.
47    Simmel 1990, p. 232.
48    Simmel 1990, p. 56.
49    Simmel 1989, p. 719.

ential in the 'historical school' of political economy.[50] The price to be paid for such attempts to 'deepen' Marx's analysis is a speculative degree of generality that rescinds Marx's analytic efforts to distinguish between differences of form and function. By transposing the Marxian analyses of the forms of value and money to the overly general level of a psychological contemplation of essences, he eliminates the critique of capitalist alienation and domination inherent in them.

Thus in appropriating the results of Simmel's philosophy of money, Weber is already basing himself on a variant of 'passive revolution' within the development of social theories that has adopted single elements of the Marxian analysis in a subdued form. Here too, Weber will not leave unchanged what he has adopted: while Simmel reacted to Marx by formulating an ahistorical psychology, Weber attempts to newly historicise the results of that psychology (as Sombart will also do, albeit in a different manner).

### 26.3    The Formal Resemblance of Money and God

What Weber also takes from Simmel is the link between the positing of money as an end in itself and religion. The analogy is not new, but rather pre-shaped by a long Judaeo-Christian tradition of the critique of mammon. The excerpts from James Mill's 1823 book *Eléments d'économie politique* that the young Marx compiled in 1844 contain the idea that money, by mediating people's social interaction, becomes a 'real God' while its 'cult becomes an end in itself'.[51] And within the circuit M–C–M', in which the commodity value expressed in money becomes 'an independent substance, endowed with a motion of its own', the commodity value 'differentiates itself as original value from itself as surplus-value... as the father differentiates himself from himself qua the son'.[52] To be sure, there is an important difference between these formulations and the traditional metaphors of religious articulations of money: Marx discerns a reversal of bourgeois economy that displays a religious form not just in money, but also at the more fundamental level of the commodity. The commodity only

---

50    For example, in 1893 Schmoller picks up on Diltheyan ideas and claims the theory of political economy requires a descriptive and analytic psychology. It is a matter, he argues, of articulating a hierarchy of psycho-ethical causes 'that explain all social developments and that are as decisive for the realm of political economy as for those of the law, politics, the church and society' (quoted in Krause and Rudolph 1980, pp. 92–3).

51    Marx and Engels 1975–2005, vol. 3, p. 212.

52    Marx and Engels 1975–2005, vol. 35, p. 165.

appears to be a simple and natural thing at first blush; in reality—and because of its dual nature as use value and value—, it is 'a very queer thing, abounding in metaphysical subtleties and theological niceties'.[53] The commodity 'stands with its feet on the ground' as use value, but as social value, i.e. the quantity of socially necessary labour time contained in it, it is 'transcendent' [*übersinnlich*].[54] Marx uses the term 'fetish' to designate the deep religious aspect of bourgeois commodity production—the 'artefact' that exercises power over its makers:[55] under the conditions of a private production characterised by the division of labour, the producers only interact with each other socially when they exchange their products, which is to say they produce without knowing whether or not what they produce is actually required. By ceding their social nature to commodities, they create a situation in which they must suffer the social context violently asserting itself behind their backs as an alien, reified force, much as the 'law of gravity... asserts itself when a house falls about our ears'.[56]

Simmel removes money from the context of a private commodity production characterised by the division of labour and sums up the traditional religious analogies by formulating a psychological hypothesis: as the unifying point of countless series of ends, money is significantly related, 'in its psychological form', to the notion of God, whose deeper essence is 'that all diversities and contradictions in the world achieve a unity in him'.[57] Such divine unity of opposites can be interpreted as a specific function of the ideological, that of condensing antagonistic forces in a 'compromise', thereby holding the social totality together.[58] It is precisely when the religious loses this function that money becomes 'the centre in which the most opposed, the most estranged and the most distant things find their common denominator and come into

---

53    Marx and Engels 1975–2005, vol. 35, p. 81.

54    Ibid.

55    The word 'fetish', which derives from the Portuguese '*feitiço*' and thereby from the Latin '*facticium*' and '*facere*' ['to make'], means 'artefact, although "powerful work" is also implied, so that the Portuguese word *feitiço* has the meaning of "spell"' (Haug 1976, p. 167). In the parlance of the Portuguese missionaries, the term referred to 'object deities'; Marx polemically reverses the Christian view of 'heathen' deities: 'What is this African fetishism compared to the European fetishim, in which the entire organisation of social production ... is left to the internal dynamic of artefacts ...!' (Haug 1976, pp. 167–8).

56    Marx and Engels 1975–2005, vol. 35, p. 86.

57    Simmel 1990, p. 236.

58    On the categories of 'condensation' and 'compromise' as transferred from Freud's interpretation of dreams to a theory of the ideological, see Projekt Ideologietheorie 1982, pp. 189ff, 201; cf. Rehmann 2013, pp. 254ff.

contact with one another'.[59] Godlike, it stands above the series of existence 'as an integrating force that supports and permeates every single element'.[60] It was in terms of this formal psychological resemblance that Simmel accounted for the religious worldview's common 'hostility' towards money: 'for too many people money signifies the end of the telological sequences and lends to them such a measure of unified combination of interests, of abstract heights, of sovereignty over the details of life, that it reduces the need to search for such satisfactions in religion'.[61] Much as Sombart would later do,[62] Simmel establishes the link to religion mainly by means of the 'monotheistic schooling' of the Jews: having, in the course of millennia, grown habituated to looking up to a unitary supreme being and to consider it 'the goal and intersection of all particular interests', they necessarily submitted, in economics, to value, which 'presents itself as the encompassing unity and the common focal point of all sequences of purpose'.[63]

Weber will not adopt this link, since he denies the significance of the Jews to the 'rational' organisation of commercial and industrial labour, and thereby to the 'new and distinctive forms of modern capitalism'.[64] But similarly to Simmel, he articulates the positing of economic gain qua end in itself as something religious from the outset, something 'entirely transcendental'.[65] What stands in the way of this new transcendence is the 'traditionalism' that has developed in the various social classes: 'A man does not "by nature" wish to earn more and more money, but simply to live as he is accustomed to live and to earn as much as is necessary for that purpose'.[66] Here, Weber latches on to the hostility of the German 'historical school' towards the explanation and justification of the pursuit of economic gain in terms of 'natural law'.[67] To think about how 'the customary wage may be earned with a maximum of comfort and a minimum of exertion' is *natural*, but what is required is a stance that breaks with this calculus, such that labour 'must ... be performed as if it were an absolute end in itself, a calling'.[68] Before Weber ventures onto the terrain of the religious, he has already paved the way for this step by a conceptual set-up

---

59  Simmel 1990, p. 236.
60  Simmel 1990, p. 485.
61  Simmel 1990, p. 237.
62  Sombart 1911, pp. 226ff; Sombart 1998, pp. 232–5.
63  Simmel 1990, p. 237.
64  See for example Weber 1978, pp. 612ff.
65  Weber 1950, p. 53.
66  Weber 1950, p. 60.
67  See Marshall 1982, p. 25; Hennis 1988, p. 50.
68  Weber 1950, pp. 61–2.

inherent in the way he develops his query: he divides the domain of labour into a principally idle 'nature' and an economic outlook that 'detaches itself' from nature and 'transcends' it.

The opposition is structured in such a way that the active side calls immediately for a religious interpretation. One side is associated with the egotistical private individual's 'purposive rationality', which tends towards idleness, while on the other side there remains only the overarching morality of the calling and of economic gain. Within this opposition, it becomes inconceivable that labour might itself be a site of self-activity and self-realisation. But this was precisely the perspective from which Marx posited that labour (once it has been freed from its enslaving subordination to the division of labour) is 'life's prime want'.[69] Weber's concept of labour does not include the standpoint of use value, and skill-related and cooperative joy oriented towards social utility is thereby also absent from it: the domain of labour is exhaustively partitioned into traditionalism and the interest in valorisation.

### 26.4     From the Ethos of Acquisition to the Work Ethos

Considering Weber's initial introduction of the concept from this vantage point, one can see clearly that he has modified his definition of the 'spirit of capitalism' not once but *twice*: he starts from the capitalist's ethically charged interest in valorisation and arrives, via the concept of *economic gain*, at the concept of the *work* ethos.

Let us consider more clearly how Weber enacts this shift in meaning. He points out that if one were to ask Franklin why one should make money out of people, he would reply, as in his *Autobiography*, with the Solomonic proverb his father impressed upon him: 'Seest thou a man diligent in *his business*? He shall stand before kings'.[70] But the link to the transformation of people into money is one Weber has himself construed: in Franklin, the Solomonic proverb is not quoted as a reply to the question concerning capitalist exploitation

---

69    Marx and Engels 1975–2005, vol. 24, p. 87. According to Frigga Haug, 'from his early to his later period, Marx consistently retains the prospect of freeing labour from its tortuously "inverted" character and making it a collective self-activity that is associated with pleasure. This is the golden thread in Marxian thought' (F. Haug 1994, p. 418). In *critical psychology*, the needs that aim at an extension of the social control of reality are described as ' "productive" needs' (Holzkamp-Osterkamp 1976, pp. 23ff) or as the 'productive … aspect of human relations of need' (Holzkamp 1983, p. 242).

70    Proverbs 22:29, quoted in Weber 1950, p. 53. The emphasis is Weber's, not Franklin's.

as posed by Weber, but as elucidating the importance of diligence and thrift for professional advancement in general.[71] Moreover, the aspect of the achievement of cultural hegemony is also involved, for Franklin has just presented himself as the founder of a public subscription library in Philadelphia that has become a model for all of America and elevated the educational level of 'common tradesmen and farmers' to such an extent that it has become equal to that of the 'gentlemen' of other countries.[72]

Weber elides the obvious link between the proud 'standing before kings' of the Solomonic proverb and Franklin's project of creating a broad literary culture. In his assessment of Franklin, Weber emphasises vocational and professional proficiency as the be-all and end-all of Franklin's morality,[73] and this virtue now appears as the response to Weber's construed opening question concerning the motives behind capitalist exploitation. We thus see Weber laboriously working to make the 'ethos' of the capitalist appropriation of surplus value converge with a work ethos that one might also—taken by itself—interpret as 'craftman's pride'. Brentano suggested the latter interpretation, although he also fails to mention, for apologetic reasons, Franklin's 'chrematistic' way of thinking.[74] It would be equally plausible to interpret Franklin's work ethos as an intellectual passion of learning; this is in fact suggested by the context (the foundation of the public subscription library). What 'standing diligently in one's business' has to do with making money out of people is never analysed.

Nor does the next step in Weber's argument move matters forward: Weber argues that a characteristic and, in a sense, even constitutive feature of the 'social ethic of capitalistic culture' consists in one's peculiar 'duty in a calling', namely the 'obligation which the individual is supposed to feel ... towards the content of his professional activity, no matter in what it consists, in particular no matter whether it appears on the surface as a pure valorisation of his labour power, or only of his immovable property [*Sachgüterbesitz*] (as capital)'.[75]

But why should individuals feel dutifully bound to what their professional activity 'consists' in, when this content appears wholly indifferent? Weber is combining two fundamentally different statements: a work ethos oriented towards use value would indeed be bound up with the specific content of one's

---

71     Franklin 1904c, pp. 185–6.

72     'These libraries have improved the general conversation of the Americans, made the common tradesmen and farmers as intelligent as most gentlemen from other countries' (Franklin 1904c, p. 172; see also pp. 171 and 182ff).

73     Weber 1950, p. 53.

74     Brentano 1916, p. 148.

75     Weber 1950, p. 54; translation modified.

profession, which would thereby not be arbitrary; a work ethos that is under the sway of the standpoint of valorisation and dominated by an abstract interest in economic gain would disregard labour's concrete content, limiting the sense of duty to the mere expenditure of labour power, engaged in for the purpose of obtaining a corresponding sum of money.

Empirically, the two attitudes can overlap just as well as they can conflict— but in either case, one would have to distinguish between them when searching for a 'spirit of capitalism'. The English language has the advantage of providing words for the different aspects of human productive activity, Marx points out: 'work' refers to qualitatively defined use-value-oriented activity, whereas 'labour' refers to quantitatively measured value-creating activity.[76]

I have spontaneously assumed that Weber's professional ethos needs to be understood as a work ethos. But it is when Weber speaks of 'immovable property' [*Sachgüterbesitz*], at the latest, that one understands that he is primarily thinking of an 'ethos' of capital valorisation; the valorisation of capital is in fact the context in which he introduces the notion of a 'spirit of capitalism'. But then what is meant by a 'pure valorisation of *his* labour power'? Suddenly, everything becomes ambiguous: if Weber is using the possessive pronoun to refer to the wage worker as the personal bearer of his own labour power, then why does he refer to the worker, who alienates his labour power, as labour power's 'valoriser'? Or is the 'individual' that valorises 'his labour power' the same as the one that valorises its immovable property? If that is the case, a new ambiguity immediately results: does Weber wish to claim that the diligent entrepreneur 'valorises' his own labour power, or does he mean that the entrepreneur, qua capitalist, profits from the labour power he purchases on the labour market? Does the possessive pronoun then refer to the labour power of 'his' workers (the workers subordinate to him)? The 'sentiment' to which the matter presents itself thus would not be as 'unbiased' as Weber assumes; Weber would in fact be describing precisely the biased standpoint of the one whose calling it is to combine, under his command, his constant and his variable capital.

## 26.5    Capitalist or Entrepreneurial Spirit?

Thus the criticism Marx directs at *classical political economy* also applies to Weber: both confuse two quite different forms of private property, namely property based on one's own labour and property based on the exploitation

---

76    Marx and Engels 1975–2005, vol. 35, p. 56, note 1.

of other people's labour: 'It [political economy] forgets that the latter not only is the direct antithesis of the former, but absolutely grows on its tomb only'.[77]

Marx discusses this opposition by reference to the colonisation of North America, where the wage workers who had emigrated from England became self-employed farmers as soon as they had earned a little money in the factories. The resulting labour shortage causes the degree of exploitation of wage workers to remain 'indecently low',[78] and the workers also lack a sense of dependence.[79] Compared to the immiserated proletarians of the motherland, they appear educated, affluent and 'enterprising'.[80] This development is suppressed in two ways: on the one hand, the state increases the price of land, thereby barring the way to self-employment; on the other hand, higher immigration quotas create a reserve army of labour that undermines the position of labour vis-à-vis the capitalists.[81] Capitalist private property, Marx concludes, has as its fundamental condition the 'annihilation of self-earned private property'.[82]

Like the different kinds of private property, the 'capitalist' and the 'entrepreneurial' spirit stand opposed to one another in this account. This raises the question of whether what Weber encountered in the middle-class sects of America was really the 'spirit of capitalism' or rather one of its antipodes, namely the initiative of emigrants who had managed to escape the early capitalist misery of their home countries. To be sure, the opposition between the two is not written in stone. Like others used by Marx, the distinction is not immediately empirical, but analytic. The most diverse combinations are possible, and under the conditions of capitalist hegemony, even anticapitalist impulses can be recast as dynamic new manifestations of the 'spirit of capitalism'. Within a consolidated capitalist functional context, 'entrepreneurs' will only be successful to the extent that they adapt to the objective mental and emotional forms of capital's movements. And the capitalist, whatever his actual 'spirit', tends towards the construction of a self-conception that foregrounds his successful 'entrepreneurship' and relegates his function for capital to the background.

The Marx of *Capital* is only interested in the capitalist insofar as the capitalist 'represents' capital.[83] Gramsci, however, submits the capitalist entrepreneur

77    Marx and Engels 1975–2005, vol. 35, p. 752.

78    Marx and Engels 1975–2005, vol. 35, p. 756.

79    Marx and Engels 1975–2005, vol. 35, pp. 756–7.

80    Wakefield, quoted in Marx and Engels 1975–2005, vol. 35, p. 757.

81    Marx and Engels 1975–2005, vol. 35, pp. 759–61.

82    Marx and Engels 1975–2005, vol. 35, p. 761.

83    Marx and Engels 1975–2005, vol. 35, pp. 163, 241, 312, 595.

to an analytic distinction between his function for capital and his entrepreneurial function, describing the latter as an intellectual activity that requires technical skill as well as the capacity for leadership [*capacità dirigente*], both of which he needs to demonstrate within production and outside it, i.e. within the organisation of society.[84] Accordingly, Gramsci criticises the tacit equation of capitalism with industrialism (in an article by Burzio, on the crisis of the West) and suggests replacing the concept of the 'capitalist spirit' with that of an 'industrial spirit' [*spirito industriale*].[85] In his efforts to extract economic activism from its capitalist form, he speaks—with reference both to Calvinism and to the late medieval '*comuni*'—of a new 'active attitude of enterprise and initiative' [*di intraprendenza e iniziativa*], of a 'spirit of economic enterprise' [*spirito di intrapresa economica*] or of the spirit of initiative [*spirito di iniziativa*].[86]

Considered with these distinctions in mind, Weber's concept of the 'spirit of capitalism' can be seen to comprise the most contrary meanings. What was initially defined as a valorisation interest that takes on a life of its own goes on to take the entirety of ascetic attitudes to work under its wing and speaks in their name. Marcuse observes that Weber's analysis 'took into its "pure" definitions of formal rationality valuations peculiar to capitalism';[87] in the present case, this is concretely achieved by virtue of capital's appropriation and subordination of labour in society, which is then unconsciously reproduced within social science. By eschewing an analytic distinction between the standpoints of use value and exchange value—differentiating between the two is something he could have learned from Simmel—,[88] Weber allows the ideological function to dominate science. The concept of the 'spirit of capitalism' achieves in one way what the capitalist self-conception as an 'entrepreneur' achieves in another: entrepreneurship and capitalism, the spirit of initiative and the capitalist determination of its form are amalgamated into a homogeneous unity—the formation of a conceptual 'bloc' that correlates with the aimed-for historical bloc consisting of the bourgeoisie and the labour aristocracy.

84    Gramsci 1975c, p. 1513.
85    Gramsci 1975a, p. 83; see Gramsci 1992, p. 181.
86    See Gramsci 2007, pp. 194, 115; Gramsci 1975b, pp. 1267, 1275, 1389.
87    Marcuse 1969, p. 223.
88    In the *Philosophy of Money*, there is at least one instance of Simmel drawing a clear distinction between the standpoint of use value and that of exchange value: he writes that the care given to the specific quality of things (to never throw away a piece of string, to look for every lost pin) is not to be confused with 'avarice', which is focused on monetary value, thereby rendering specific qualities indifferent (Simmel 1990, p. 246).

On the one hand, Weber adopts from Simmel the psychologistic neutralisation of the Marxian analysis of the form of value; on the other hand, he criticises the related ahistorical equation of the monetary economy with capitalism, which he claims fails to grasp the specific quality of 'Western capitalism'.[89] One characteristic feature of Weber's concept of the 'spirit of capitalism' is that it combines conceptual haziness with a close focus on a specific historical formation: on the one hand, the concept is overly general and blurs distinctions such as those between the ethos of valorisation and the work ethos or between the standpoint of use value and that of exchange value; on the other hand, the principle of the 'ideal type' entails a consistent narrowing down of the concept, so that it refers only to certain culturally 'significant' and therefore 'one-sidedly' emphasised aspects.

The immediate context of Weber's historical placing of the 'spirit of capitalism' is provided by the works of the 'younger historical school', of which he is himself considered a member, and in particular by the works of the early Sombart. This context needs to be reconstructed in order to see how Weber abstractly isolates certain aspects of the 'spirit of capitalism' in order to then merge them into an ideal type.

---

89     Weber 1988e, p. 5, note 1. In *Roscher and Knies*, Weber announced a 'systematic critique' of
        Simmel (Weber 1975, p. 158, note 55), but he never produced such a critique. The critique
        formulated by Othmar Spann, to which Weber refers in the passage cited, is criticised by
        Weber for remaining indebted to a 'psychologistic concept of society' (quoted in Frisby
        1988, p. 587). In a fragment on Simmel that was presumably written around 1908 but not
        published at the time ('*Georg Simmel als Soziologe und Theoretiker der Geldwirtschaft*'
        ['Georg Simmel as Sociologist and Theorist of the Monetary Economy']), Weber hints at
        the criticism that the analogical method by which Simmel accesses 'meaning' is question-
        able (see Frisby 1988, pp. 586–7).

# CHAPTER 27

# Werner Sombart's 'Overcoming' of Marxism

## 27.1    The Historical School as 'Digestive Science' (Rosa Luxemburg)

The 'older historical school' of political economy, whose members included Wilhelm Roscher (1817–94), Bruno Hildebrandt (1812–78) and Karl Knies (1821–98), emerged in the 1840s. It was a specifically 'German' reaction both to the French Revolution and to the 'Western' cosmopolitanism of classical political economy from Smith to Ricardo.[1] It was ostensibly concerned with opposing the 'surgical extraction' of the economy from the 'living body' of popular life and the life of the state, and in particular the 'narrow egotistic psychology' according to which social actors are guided, in their economic behaviour, only by economic considerations, as opposed to ethical motives.[2] If Machiavelli banished ethics from politics, Adam Smith performed the same operation for political economy, criticises Knies, who emphasises the significance of the 'ethico-political moment' for political economy and speaks of the discipline being 'elevated' to the status of a 'moral and political science'.[3]

At first glance, this seems to represent an integral approach to studying social practices. But behind this pathos of wholeness, there lies the definition of political economy as a 'state economy' concerned with 'judging men and ruling them'.[4] The *historical school* developed from cameralism, which became the discipline of state science due to the Prussian path of capitalist development.[5] Marx describes cameralism as 'a medley of smatterings, through whose purgatory the hopeful candidate for the German bureaucracy has to pass'.[6] And the *historical school of law*, a second precursor of the historical school of political economy, is discussed by him as a symptom of the 'German state of affairs', which involved Germany adopting not the revolutions of other countries, but their restorations, so that Germany is situated 'below the level of history': it is

---

1   According to Braunreuther, historicism in political economy 'was related to reactionary-Romantic aspirations directed against the French Revolution' (Braunreuther 1978, p. 116). On the contrast between the historical school and classical political economy, see Winkel 1977, pp. 92ff, 117–18; Krause and Rudolph 1980, pp. 2, 43; Marshall 1982, p. 29; Hennis 1988, pp. 50–1.

2   Knies 1883, pp. 436–7.

3   Knies 1883, pp. 438, 440.

4   Roscher, quoted in Knies 1883, p. 437.

5   Braunreuther 1978, pp. 111–12.

6   Marx and Engels 1975–2005, vol. 35, p. 14; compare Engels in vol. 16, p. 465.

a 'school of thought that legitimizes the infamy of today with the infamy of yesterday, a school that stigmatizes every cry of the serf against the knout as mere rebelliousness once the knout has aged a little and acquired a hereditary significance and a history'.[7] In the *Theories of Surplus Value*, Marx says of Roscher's political economy that it 'proceeds "historically" and, with wise moderation, collects the "best" from all sources, and in doing this contradictions do not matter; on the contrary, what matters is comprehensiveness ... All systems are thus made insipid, their edge is taken off and they are peacefully gathered together in a miscellany'.[8] Marx calls this the vulgar economic 'graveyard' of political economy as a science: the more political economy is 'perfected', the more its empiricist 'vulgar element' breaks away from it and confronts it as its opposite.[9]

Schmoller is considered the founder of the 'younger historical school'; the theorists identified with it include (besides Sombart and Weber) Lujo Brentano, Karl Bücher, Eberhard Gothein and Georg Friedrich Knapp. The personal continuities with the Katheder socialists are not to be overlooked. In both cases, confronting Marx increasingly became the main concern, with different positions developing in a process of differentiation that was primarily determined by the various theorists' approach to Marx's analysis. Rosa Luxemburg characterised the younger historical school as a 'digestive science' whose secret cause was Marx: 'Under the oracular ramblings of the "historical school", one could hear the mischievous giggling of Marx's pitiless sarcasm'.[10] Luxemburg added that during the last quarter century (i.e. since the emergence of the younger historical school), 'overcoming Marx' had become a 'favourite pastime of German professors and a tried and tested way of applying for a private lectureship in Germany'.[11]

Much as on the practical terrain of social policy, a multi-tiered 'passive revolution' is enacted on the theoretical terrain of German political economy as well, with the aim of overcoming both classical political economy and the

---

7    Marx and Engels 1975–2005, vol. 3, p. 177. In his discussion of Roscher, Weber also notes that the historical school of political economy is dependent on the historical school of law, placing the emphasis on the former's telling reformulations of the latter's positions (Weber 1988d, pp. 9–10).

8    Marx and Engels 1975–2005, vol. 32, p. 501.

9    Ibid.

10   Luxemburg 1970–5e, p. 491.

11   Luxemburg 1970–5e, pp. 489, 491. For Rosa Luxemburg's critique of the historical school, see also Luxemburg 1970–5f, pp. 730ff, 772,782, 784; Luxemburg 1970–5g, p. 388; Luxemburg 1970–5d, pp. 163–4; Luxemburg 1970–5h, pp. 188, 223, 249, 260–1, 265; Luxemburg 1970–5h, pp. 525ff, 562, 646ff.

Marxian critique of political economy. With regard to specific issues, this 'passive revolution' is heterogeneous and characterised by disagreements that are sometimes quite forceful, but with regard to its basic thrust, it is remarkably coherent. Sombart and Weber, who pursue their project of overcoming Marx on the terrain of economic history, by discussing the question of how capitalism developed, also belong in this context. In Weber's case, however, the political stakes of this operation have already been sublimated to such an extent that they can only be discerned rudimentarily. The political aim is most manifest in Marx's student Sombart, whose concept of the 'spirit of capitalism' stems directly from his theoretical grapple with Marx.

### 27.2    The 'Further Development' of Marxism as a Glorification of Capitalism

While Weber claims his studies on the 'spirit of capitalism' developed from 'much older work' of his own,[12] it is widely recognised, in the scholarship on Weber, that this concept owes much to Weber's engagement with Sombart: the first, 1904/05 edition of the *Protestant Ethic* can be read as a direct response to Sombart's much discussed first edition of *Modern Capitalism* (1902), and in particular to the chapter on the 'Genesis of the Spirit of Capitalism'.[13] Weber also influenced Sombart's subsequent research, in particular *The Jews and Modern Capitalism* (1911), *The Quintessence of Capitalism* (1913) and the second, 1916/17 edition of *Modern Capitalism*, which Sombart called a 'completely new work'.[14] The supplemented notes to the final, 1920 version of Weber's *Protestant Ethic* contain a discussion of Sombart's divergent definition, in *The Quintessence of Capitalism*, of the 'spirit of capitalism', although Weber otherwise refers solely to the first edition of *Modern Capitalism*. In the preface to his *Gesammelte Aufsätze zur Religionssoziologie* 1920 ['Collected Essays on the Sociology of Religion'], however, Weber refers to the 'newest edition' of Sombart's 'fine main work on capitalism',[15] and in his posthumously published lectures on economic history, held during the 1919/20 winter semester, he also

---

12    Weber 1904, pp. 19–20; Weber 1950, p. 57, note 14.

13    See for example Käsler 1978, pp. 85, 87–8; Marshall 1982, pp. 37ff, 41ff, 52ff; Brocke 1987, p. 7; Appel 1992, p. 121; Lehmann 1993, p. 198; Lehmann 1996, p. 97.

14    'I have made use of no more than a tenth of the original text, and even this fraction of the old text has usually been integrated into completely new lines of thought' (Sombart 1916, p. IX).

15    Weber 1988e, p. 5, note 1; see Weber 1950, p. 185, note 2.

refers to the second edition of *Modern Capitalism*, although the bibliographical references were added by the editors.[16]

Werner Sombart (1863–1941) obtained his doctorate with a dissertation on the Roman *campagna* that was supervised by Schmoller. Prior to his 'aristocratic turn' around 1907/08,[17] Sombart was considered the member of the younger historical school most strongly influenced by Marx. He was the one to introduce the category of 'capitalism' into academic political economy, a category that Marx himself almost never used (unlike Engels).[18] The fact that Marx explicitly limited his critique of political economy to 'the capitalist mode of production, and the conditions of production and exchange corresponding to that mode',[19] indicates that unlike his successors, he cultivated a healthy scepticism towards any totalising category credited with being able to encapsulate the 'essence' of an entire society. Commenting on Sombart's 1894 article '*Zur Kritik des ökonomischen Systems von Karl Marx*' ['Towards a Critique of Karl Marx's Economic System'], Engels remarked: 'It is the first time that a German university professor succeeds on the whole in seeing in Marx's writings what Marx really says'.[20] Sombart's statement that 'the criticism of the Marxian system cannot consist of a refutation... but merely in a further development' struck Engels as particularly notable.[21] What is relevant to the thematic focus of Sombart's work is Engels's indirect call, formulated in a letter to Sombart dated 11 March 1895, to supplement *Capital* with a 'genuinely historical exposition'.[22]

In 1900, Kautsky states retrospectively that until 1896, he saw Sombart as 'one of our movement's next men', until Sombart's *Socialism and the Social Movement* (1896) demonstrated that his was an apolitical and thus entirely toothless Marxism.[23] The same year, Rosa Luxemburg got the 'fickle' Sombart into her sights, remarking that he was skipping ahead of the new imperialist world politics 'at an easy pace and with dainty gestures'.[24] Luxemburg concentrated on the strategy—also pursued by Weber—of a 'realistic' and 'historical'

16    See Weber 1923, pp. IV, 258, 265, 277, 301, 305.
17    Brocke dates this turn to the 'years before 1908' (Brocke 1987, p. 40), whereas Appel dates it to the period after the turn of the century, although he also dates its public perception to 1907/08 (Appel 1992, p. 15).
18    See Braudel 1979b, pp. 206–7.
19    Marx and Engels 1975–2005, vol. 35, p. 7.
20    Marx and Engels 1975–2005, vol. 37, p. 881.
21    Ibid.
22    Marx and Engels 1975–2005, vol. 50, p. 461.
23    Estate of Karl Kautsky, quoted in Brocke 1987, p. 27.
24    Luxemburg 1970–5f, p. 785.

method that presents the trade unions 'with unlimited prospects of economic advancement, only to conclude by denouncing *Social Democracy as the genuine obstacle to such advancement*'.[25] In 1906, during the debate on the mass strike, she sees this strategy bearing fruits within the trade unions, Sombart's theory having paved the way, on her view, for their abandonment of the political struggle. Luxemburg argues that Sombart developed his theory for the purpose of driving a wedge between the trade unions and Social Democracy, luring the trade unions 'onto the terrain of the bourgeoisie'.[26]

In 1902 Naumann praises what Kautsky and Luxemburg criticised in Sombart; Naumann speaks of a 'shedding of the purely dogmatic element that inheres in the Marxian concept of "capitalism"'.[27] When he speaks of 'dogmatism', Naumann has in mind not only the pillars of 'Kautskyanism' (e.g. the theories of immiseration, polarisation and collapse), which had been the object of debate since Bernstein's 1896 critique, but also the critique of capitalism itself: according to Naumann, an 'apocalyptic wind' blows through Marx's theory, whereas Sombart discusses capitalism 'without inner disapproval'.[28] Schmoller also noted this, when he says of Sombart, in 1902, that he engages in a 'glorification of capitalism'.[29]

Sombart himself consistently declares himself the executor of Marx's work; he retains this self-conception throughout every stage of his political development from socialism to 'National Socialism'. What separates him from Schmoller's 'historical school', he writes in the 1902 preface to the first edition of *Modern Capitalism*, is *Karl Marx*. To Sombart, Marx's name is synonymous with 'constructiveness in the arrangement of one's material ... the radical postulate of unitary explanations from final causes, the assembling of all social phenomena into a social system, in short: with what is specifically theoretical'.[30]

To be sure, this notion of what is 'specifically theoretical' does *not* correspond to the object of Marx's inquiry: when Sombart interprets *Capital* as aspiring to account for an entire social system in a 'unitary' manner and in terms of 'final causes', he overlooks not only the way in which Marx limits himself to discussion of the 'capitalist mode of production', but also Marx's leitmotif, the

---

25    Luxemburg 1970–5f, p. 782; compare p. 784.

26    Luxemburg 1970–5d, p. 164.

27    Quoted in Brocke 1987, p. 109.

28    Quoted in Brocke 1987, pp. 119–20.

29    Quoted in Brocke 1987, p. 138. In the same review of the first edition of *Modern Capitalism*, Schmoller accuses Sombart of adhering 'too strongly' to Marx's materialist philosophy of history (quoted in Brocke 1987, p. 146).

30    Sombart 1902, p. XXIX.

critique of alienation and domination. The totalising interpretation Sombart shares with the main currents of Marxism is also the starting point for his revision: the 'final causes' he wishes to trace social development back to are not economic relations but the 'motivation of living men', i.e. 'psychological motives' or 'teleological series' governing human action.[31] Sombart's break with Marxism is itself composed of contradictory elements: on the one hand, he is referring back, without knowing it, to an element of Marx's orientation towards praxis, an orientation that begins not from an economy without subjects but from the 'active life-process' of human beings;[32] on the other hand, he articulates this active side as the object of a 'historical psychology', which he considers one branch of a future 'peoples' psychology' [Völkerpsychologie].[33] Here as elsewhere, the economism of the Marxism of the period paved the way for an ethical 'overcoming' of Marx. When Sombart claims to speak in the name of the vital human qualities, this is of course a distraction: in order to curb the infinite variety of such psychological 'motives', Sombart limits himself to the 'dominant motivational series of the leading economic subjects'.[34] Weber's sociology of religion will follow him in opting for this consequential restriction by limiting its investigation to the leading 'culture bearers' [Kulturträger].[35]

Gramsci proposes studying the research trends evident in the social and economic history of different countries with an eye to their interaction with historical materialism, mentioning Sombart as an exponent of German political economy.[36] Guided by this proposal, I will concentrate, in what follows, on Sombart's early, 1902 history of the emergence of capitalism, a work that pursues two main questions: that of how certain economic subjects accumulate sufficient amounts of money for the formation of capital and that of how these same economic subjects develop a specific 'spirit of capitalism', by virtue of which there occurs a 'transubstantiation' of the buccaneer, the casual tradesman or the artisans into the *economical man* of classical political economy.[37]

---

31    Sombart 1902, pp. XVIII–XIX.

32    Marx and Engels 1975–2005, vol. 5, p. 36.

33    Sombart 1902, p. XXI.

34    'Only the motivational series of the leading economic subjects are relevant: in a capitalist economy, for example, these would not be those of wage labourers, but only those of entrepreneurs, not those of consumers, but those of producers and traders' (Sombart 1902, p. XXII).

35    Weber 1950, p. 30; Weber 1988e, p. 15; compare Weber 1946b, p. 268; Weber 1984–2009, vol. I/19, p. 86; Weber 1988e, p. 239.

36    Gramsci 2007, p. 359.

37    Sombart 1902, pp. 207–8, 218.

## 27.3    The Origin of Bourgeois Monetary Assets

One of the foundations of Sombart's analysis of the accumulation of money is his hypothesis that the high rates of profit and accumulation required for a large-scale accrual of wealth can be achieved neither by artisanal production nor by artisanal trade.[38] It is not here that the late pre-capitalist era's centres of monetary accumulation are to be sought, but rather (1) in the Catholic church, whose system of taxation led to the amassing of large sums of money in the midst of what was essentially a barter economy (the *Camera apostolica* as '*mater pecuniarum*'), (2) in the knightly orders, such as those of the Templars and the Knights of St. John, (3, 4) in the monarchies of France and England and (5) in the economy of the large landowners, whose income was increasingly monetarised.[39] The wealth of the cities (enumerated as point 6) was much less important, on Sombart's account, than the stock of money in these five centres: during the Middle Ages, probably only Venice, Milan and Naples had incomes similar to those of the Pope and the kings.[40]

Starting from this survey, Sombart's theory of the origin of bourgeois monetary assets develops in various directions. On the one hand, he concludes that urban bourgeois assets resulted largely from a 'transfer of wealth'.[41] One of the developments he has in mind is the 'becoming bourgeois of the formerly feudal financial administration' by which the fiscal rights (taxation of income, the charging of customs duty and so on) were leased or pawned to the *nuova gente*;[42] Sombart also mentions the 'usurious exploitation of landed property'.[43]

But for Sombart, this merely means that the search for the origins of bourgeois wealth has been shifted to another terrain. For the business of usury did not allow for the accrual of genuine wealth except among those who were already affluent: ' "He that has plenty of good shall have more": this proverb is even truer for the beginnings of wealth formation than for the later period'.[44] The question concerning 'primary wealth' needs to be posed differently depending on whether one is referring to Jews or Christians, according to Sombart: while

---

38    Sombart 1902, pp. 225–7.

39    Sombart 1902, pp. 237ff.

40    Sombart 1902, p. 245.

41    Sombart 1902, pp. 235, 245, 260.

42    Sombart 1902, p. 249. Sombart identifies this as one of the reasons for Germany's delayed development: 'When the time came for derivative wealth formation, the capitalists in England and France were able to tap the reserves of royal incomes, whereas their German colleagues had to sate themselves at the minor rivulets of episcopal and manorial finances' (Sombart 1902, p. 248).

43    Sombart 1902, pp. 257ff.

44    Sombart 1902, p. 269.

he claims the Jews retained the gold and jewellery they had acquired during the late Roman empire,[45] he considers the non-Jewish 'monetary aristocracy' the descendant of an urbanised hereditary aristocracy. On this view, the wealthy merchants of the 'patriciate' have nothing in common with the artisanal merchants, but descend from the 'families that originally resided in the cities, as owners of real estate', families that pocket an urban ground rent from the 'less privileged citizens' who settle on their urbanised land:[46] the bourgeoisie's 'original wealth' is an accumulated and monetarised ground rent that increases with the rising productivity of labour and is progressively invested in credit and usury transactions.[47] Its magnitude and degree of monetarisation determine the 'proportion' to which a city is able to participate in other forms of money accumulation.[48] Thus, according to Sombart, the superior wealth of the Italian and Flemish cities is to be explained in terms of their having 'forced the landed nobility, successfully and early on, to participate in urban life, i.e. to monetarise its rents, thereby providing their trade and their entire economic activities with a solid foundation in the form of significant assets'.[49]

Sombart's 'ground rent theory', often seen as rehashing the eighteenth century physiocratic theory of primary production, provoked fierce debates.[50] We will not pursue this for now, but focus instead on Sombart's view that his account amounts to a refutation of Marx's dictum that capital comes into the world 'dripping... with blood and dirt':[51] 'Capital did not come into the world as bloodily as Marx assumed. What occurred was a quiet and gradual tapping

---

45 Sombart 1902, p. 270.

46 Sombart 1902, pp. 284–5, 287–8.

47 Sombart 1902, pp. 291, 293, 298.

48 Sombart 1902, p. 294.

49 Sombart 1902, p. 296.

50 The association of Sombart with the Physiocrats can be traced back, in part, to Sieveking 1928 (on this, see Appel 1992, pp. 68, 210ff). Strieder, a student of Sombart, attempted to use the example of sixteenth century Augsburg to prove the validity of the ground rent theory but arrived at the opposite result, namely that significant wealth was achieved only through trade (see Kulischer 1929, pp. 398–9; Appel 1992, p. 43). Kulischer endorses Sombart's 'ground rent theory', albeit in a qualified form, as providing a valid account of one factor among others (Kulischer 1929, pp. 396ff); Dobb takes much the same view (Dobb 1970, pp. 95–6). Braudel uses the case of the 1661 corruption trial against the *surintendant* Fouquet to show that the French tax farmers had an aristocratic background and that ground rent was the source of the monetary assets that allowed them to provide the king with credit for a period of several generations (Braudel 1979b, pp. 480–1). Further examples can be found in Appel 1992, pp. 70–1, 268–9.

51 'If money, according to Augier, "comes into the world with a congenital blood-stain on one cheek," capital comes dripping from head to foot, from every pore, with blood and dirt' (Marx and Engels 1975–2005, vol. 35, p. 746).

of small particles of labour that went unnoticed by the working population but was destined to provide, in the course of time, the funds required by the capitalist economy'.[52] In making this claim, Sombart overlooks that Marx was examining a different phenomenon: not the origin of the bourgeoisie's monetary assets, which he presupposes as a given result 'handed down' from the Middle Ages in the forms of merchant's capital and usurer's capital,[53] but the genesis of *industrial* capital as buttressed by state despotism and constitutive of a new societal class relation, brought about by the separation of the (mainly agricultural) producers from their means of production and the draconian disciplining of the expropriated vagabonds, by which they were turned into wage labourers.[54] Another source identified by him was slave labour qua necessary condition and foundation ('pedestal') of free wage labour.[55]

While Sombart downplays the violence within the metropole that was associated, on Marx's analysis, with the genesis of capital,[56] he confirms that the process was one of utmost violence with regard to the relationship between the metropoles and the periphery. Sombart's chapter on the 'colonial economy' reads like a historical elaboration on the dispersed Marxian comments in *Capital* (to be found especially in Chapter XIX of the first volume), although of course Sombart never reveals his source. The violent assertion of unequal exchange relations and the profits achieved by means of slave labour are presented as necessary preconditions for the emergence of capitalism in Western Europe.[57] In particular, the colonial economy allows for accumulation on the basis of production-based profit before the conditions for capitalist

---

52    Sombart 1902, p. 292.
53    Marx and Engels 1975–2005, vol. 35, p. 738; compare Marx and Engels 1975–2005, vol. 37, p. 325.
54    Marx and Engels 1975–2005, vol. 35, pp. 707ff, 723ff.
55    Marx and Engels 1975–2005, vol. 35, pp. 739, 747.
56    For example, on Marx's analysis, violent expropriation and legislation against vagabondage were prerequisites of the constitution of the doubly 'free' wage labourer, but Sombart merely claims that there needed to be enough persons 'who, either because they did not want to or because they could not become independent producers or rentiers or ministers, voluntarily sought to earn their livelihood by means of wage labour performed for a capitalist entrepreneur' (Sombart 1902, p. 215). Sombart also vilifies the immiserated paupers as 'riff raff' (Sombart 1902, p. 216). Compare the way he describes, in the second edition of *Modern Capitalism*, the 'natural laziness, sloth, indolence' of early capitalism's paupers (Sombart 1916, pp. 798ff, 802).
57    Sombart 1902, pp. 326, 331.

production are in place:[58] 'We have grown rich because entire races and tribes have died and entire regions have been depopulated for our sake'.[59]

In order to allow for the genesis of modern capitalism, the ruthless exploitation of the colonies had to coincide with an increase in the supply of precious metals from Asia, Africa and especially America.[60] In the absence of this 'coincidence', and given that precious metals were otherwise scarce during the fifteenth century, Western European capitalism would 'hardly' have developed, 'or in any case only at an infinitely slow pace'.[61] This 'contingent' combination of circumstances prompts Sombart to polemicise against the 'absurdity of an abstract theory of capitalism', a polemic that appears to be directed against Marx.[62] And yet it was Marx who pointed out that the capitalist mode of production can only 'assume greater dimensions and achieve greater perfection' in countries where a sufficient sum of money is circulating, making 'the increased supply of precious metals since the sixteenth century ... an essential element in the history of the development of capitalist production'.[63]

Perhaps this idea, presumably taken from Marx, was what tempted Weber to claim, in his lectures on economic history, that Sombart had suggested the supply of precious metals was 'the only cause of capitalism's genesis'.[64] The passage is doubly imprecise: in fact, Sombart identified a number of reasons for the increase in monetary assets, and his argument presents the supply of precious metals as a decisive cause of the accelerated circulation of money, but not of the transformation of monetary assets into industrial capital.

### 27.4    Two Components of the 'Spirit of Capitalism'

Sombart's 'historical psychology' comes into play when he sets out to account for this last development; he attempts to explain the emergence of a new social formation by means of a 'psycho-genesis of capitalism'.[65] Sombart

---

58    Sombart 1902, p. 358.

59    Sombart 1902, p. 348.

60    Sombart 1902, pp. 359, 365ff, 370–1.

61    Sombart 1902, p. 359.

62    Ibid.

63    Marx and Engels 1975–2005, vol. 36, p. 342. Marx adds that this 'is not to be taken to mean that first a sufficient hoard is formed and then capitalist production begins'; rather, capitalist production 'develops simultaneously with the development of the conditions necessary for it' (ibid.).

64    Weber 1923, p. 301.

65    Sombart 1902, p. 391.

argues that the accumulated money obtains its 'character as capital' from certain 'purposes of capitalist enterprise', namely from the 'capitalist spirit' of the money's owners.[66]

From this one can see, first, that Sombart responds to a problem left undiscussed and unsolved by Marx, and second, how he shifts his argument to a different level. What Marx has to say about the historical question concerning the relationship of merchant's capital and usurer's capital to the genesis of the capitalist mode of production is at best vague and at worst tautological. He writes that the expansion of trade during the sixteenth and seventeenth centuries contributed 'overwhelmingly' to the rise of the capitalist mode of production, but adds that 'this was accomplished conversely on the basis of the already existing capitalist mode of production': one moment, the world market appears as the 'basis for this mode of production', the next, it is industry that revolutionises trade.[67] What proved important to subsequent scholarly debates on the emergence of capitalism was the distinction between the putting-out system, in which the merchant gains control of production and appropriates surplus labour on the basis of the old mode of production, and the 'really revolutionising path', which sees the rising artisanal producer becoming simultaneously a merchant and a capitalist.[68]

Thus, if Sombart had wished to implement Engels's suggestion of supplementing *Capital* with a 'genuinely historical exposition' of capitalism's genesis,[69] he would have had to break down capital's 'arrival' in production according to its diverse variants (state manufactures, the putting-out system, the transformation of master artisans into capitalists, among others). On this basis, he could then have examined the emergence of different mentalities in terms of a 'historical psychology'. Instead of such historical elaboration, Sombart engages in a methodological break, including within his own approach: when examining the accumulation of money, Sombart sought to describe its economic origins and the associated transfers of wealth, but when it comes to accounting for the transition to industrial capital, he recasts the problem as that of

---

66    Sombart 1902, p. 378.

67    Marx and Engels 1975–2005, vol. 37, p. 331.

68    Marx and Engels 1975–2005, vol. 37, p. 332. Compare the competing interpretations in the debate between Dobb and Sweezy: Dobb emphasised the predominance of the 'really revolutionising path' in England since the early seventeenth century, i.e. the transformation of artisans into capitalists (Dobb 1970, pp. 131ff, 141–2), whereas Sweezy held that such upward social mobility remained a marginal phenomenon (Sweezy 1976, pp. 46ff). See also Dobb's response to Sweezy, documented in Sweezy 1976, pp. 56–67.

69    Marx and Engels 1975–2005, vol. 50, p. 461.

accounting for a 'spirit of capitalism'.[70] Whatever this term may describe, however adequately, in the theories of Weber, Sombart and others, it is introduced as a stopgap that simultaneously functions as an 'emergency exit from the Marxian edifice', in Braudel's apposite phrase.[71] To be sure, in the face of a determinist Marxism understood, in accordance with the tradition of the Second and Third Internationals, as a 'science of laws' and 'theory of development', such an 'emergency exit' is also a way of articulating the active aspect of social initiative, albeit in such a way as to transpose it to the mental realm, which is to say one-sidedly.

Appel speaks of an 'anti-materialist ideologisation of the figure of the entrepreneur' that developed after the turn of the century; invoking Ringer's studies on the decline of the 'German mandarins', he interprets this ideologisation as a kneejerk reaction of intellectuals to the postwar period's putative tendencies towards massification.[72] The first thing that distinguishes Sombart's account from Weber's is its methodological decision to account for the concept of a 'spirit of capitalism' by amalgamating two distinct elements: it is only when the 'acquisitive drive' and 'economic rationalism' combine to form an 'organic unity' that one can speak of a new capitalist spirit, according to Sombart.[73]

Let us consider the first element first. By 'acquisitive drive', Sombart intends the 'elevation of the absolute means—money—to the status of highest end' as described by Simmel.[74] What Simmel presents as a universal law of human psychology is deduced historically by Sombart: on his account, the 'valuation of monetary property' intensifies in parallel with the increase in the accumulation of money; this, Sombart claims, already occurs in fourteenth century Italy,

---

70   To be sure, in 1913, Sombart will return to the genesis of industrial capital in his studies *Luxury and Capitalism* (Sombart 1913a) and *Krieg und Kapitalismus* ['War and Capitalism', Sombart 1913b]. See also the synoptic exposition in the second edition of *Modern Capitalism* (Sombart 1917, pp. 861–2, 865ff, 875ff, 884ff).

71   Braudel 1979b, p. 355. 'Sombart, comme à l'ordinaire, préfère poser le problème sur le plan des mentalités, de l'évolution de l'esprit rationnel, plutôt que sur celui de la société ou même de l'économie où il avait peur de suivre les cheminements de Marx' (Braudel 1979a, p. 452).

72   Appel 1992, pp. 55, 217ff, 227. Ringer states that his studies on the German mandarinate of the period between 1890 and 1933 were influenced by Max Weber's study of Confucianism (Ringer 1983, p. 15). On the 'ideal type' of the mandarinate in general, see Ringer 1983, pp. 12ff; on 'massification', see pp. 47ff; on Sombart as 'mandarin', see pp. 143ff, 171ff, 175–6, 346–7.

73   Sombart 1902, p. 391.

74   Sombart 1902, p. 383.

with the rest of Europe following suit in the fifteenth and sixteenth centuries.[75] But the craving for gold that manifested itself in the spread of robbery, in gold-digging and in alchemy only turned into the spirit of capitalism when it took hold of normal economic activity. It is then that there develops the altogether new idea 'that money can be earned by means of economic activity'.[76] Sombart identifies this mental leap with three social positions: (1) people from the lower estates who disposed of no extra-economic means by which to acquire money, 'pedantic usurers' and other 'sober natures lacking in brio'; (2) interaction with foreigners and interlocal trade; (3) colonial rule, the 'nursery of the capitalist spirit'.[77]

Sombart's discussion of economic activity as a means by which to acquire money already introduces the second element: now, economic life itself is trans-formed; it is dissolved into a series of calculi and then recomposed.[78] Sombart identifies Leonardo Fibonacci and Luca Pacioli as the progenitors of the result-ing 'economic rationalism'; Fibonacci laid the 'basis for exact calculation' in his 1202 work on mercantile bookkeeping, *Liter Abaci*,[79] and Pacioli's scholarly exposition of double-entry bookkeeping turned this method into 'a business resource accessible to everyone'.[80] In the second edition of *Modern Capitalism*, Sombart remarks that one could be in doubt as to whether capitalism created double-entry bookkeeping as a device for its purposes 'or whether it was double-entry bookkeeping from whose spirit capitalism was born'.[81] As Braudel notes, Sombart's eagerness to discover the origin of Western rationalism leads him to overlook the fact that Fibonacci learned how to use his reckoning tables in northern Africa: 'Fibonacci ... would better be cited as testifying to the sci-entific rationalisation of the Arabs'.[82] Moreover, double-entry bookkeeping spread slowly and did not contribute significantly to the success of the period's entrepreneurs,[83] whereas other effective tools such as bills of exchange, banks,

---

75    Sombart 1902, pp. 381, 383–4.

76    Sombart 1902, p. 388.

77    Sombart 1902, pp. 388ff.

78    Sombart 1902, p. 391.

79    Sombart writes that one could even consider the year 1202 the 'birthyear of modern capi-talism', as this was the year Venice began its military campaign against Constantinople, thereby initiating Europe's world-historical conquest of the orient (Sombart 1902, p. 392).

80    Sombart 1902, p. 393.

81    Sombart 1917, p. 118.

82    Braudel 1979b, p. 510.

83    Matthäus Schwartz, the accountant of the Fuggers, wrote in 1517 that merchants tended to note their business transactions on scraps of paper that they then pinned to the wall (Braudel 1979b, p. 510).

stock markets, discounting and so on were in use outside of Europe and its 'sacrosanct rationality'.[84]

There is an internal contradiction in Sombart's account that is symptomatic of his ambivalent reception. To Sombart, modern bookkeeping is the 'most consummate expression of specifically capitalist rationalism', since it renders capital independent of the entrepreneur's personality, confronting him with 'its own laws of motion', which operate independently of personal whims.[85] It is here at the latest that Sombart ought to have felt constrained by the internal logic of his subject matter to question the scope of his psychological explanatory model: the pursuit of gain that bookkeeping rationalises and renders independent of the entrepreneur's personality, and which Sombart describes, in the second edition of *Modern Capitalism*, as the 'essential core of capitalist enterprise',[86] is quite obviously not primarily a psychic phenomenon; it represents an objective *dispositif* that constrains the capitalist to function as 'capital personified' on pain of death.[87] In this respect, Schmoller is right to observe that in his efforts to formulate a historico-psychological account of capitalism, Sombart failed to 'penetrate' all of the notions he adopted from Marx.[88] This obviously entails that Sombart's 'overcoming' of Marx is still too bound up with what it seeks to overcome. This is also what Croce has in mind when he describes Sombart's 'intellectual history of the modern economic personality' (Croce is referring specifically to Sombart's 1913 *Quintessence of Capitalism*) as a flawed study that leaves a 'distressing impression' because it lacks a clear line of development:[89] 'The emphasis ought always to have been placed on the intellectual and moral development'.[90]

## 27.5    The 'Incorporation of the Proletariat into the National Community'

The general thrust of the bourgeois-conservative critique of the first edition of *Modern Capitalism* is that Sombart makes too many concessions to Marxism. Sombart's refutation of Marxism is in fact still too caught up in its struggle with the Marxian original to be considered successful. A number of university

---

84      Braudel 1979b, p. 512.

85      Sombart 1902, p. 394.

86      Sombart 1917, p. 102.

87      Marx and Engels 1975–2005, vol. 35, pp. 163, 312, 587.

88      Quoted in Brocke 1987, p. 145.

89      Croce 1930, p. 409.

90      Croce 1930, p. 411.

appointments (in Freiburg, Heidelberg and Karlsruhe) were revoked due to the interventions of Grand Duke Frederick, who held that Sombart was unsuited to the struggle against Social Democracy.[91]

Sombart responded to this pressure by pursuing the strategy of emphasising 'spirit' more strongly: in the second edition of *Modern Capitalism*, he formulates the basic notion 'that it is spirit which creates for itself a form adequate to it, thereby giving rise to a particular form of economic organisation'. He adds that while this notion can already be found in the first edition, he has now made it the 'guiding idea' of his exposition.[92] The capitalist spirit, now composed of the 'spirit of enterprise' and of the 'bourgeois spirit' [*Bürgergeist*],[93] now creates the modern army, structures the state, shapes technology and discovers the sites of precious metals.[94] Sombart thereby gives his account an idealist signature that is registered by his academic audience: most contemporary reviewers gratefully note his conspicuous abandonment of historical materialism and celebrate it as an overdue 'emancipation'. For example, a 1916 expert assessment commissioned by the Prussian minister of culture emphasises that under the influence of Weber's studies on Protestantism, Sombart has broken with the Marxist conception of history and arrived at a grand constructive synthesis: 'Intellectual forces come to stand ever more decidedly beside the economic process . . . The historian of culture who began as a Marxist has come to sing the praises of the state, without whose strong protection culture cannot thrive'.[95]

The later secondary literature tends to differ from the contemporary comments mainly in that it obfuscates the political issues at stake to the point of rendering them altogether unrecognisable. This is the case, for instance, when the difference between the first and the second edition of *Modern Capitalism* is identified as that between a 'monocausal' and a more comprehensive, 'polycausal' account of capitalism's genesis.[96] By contrast, Appel recognises

---

91    Brocke 1987, pp. 29–30, note 34.

92    Sombart 1916, p. 25.

93    In *The Quintessence of Capitalism*, Sombart employs this terminology to expand on his theory of two components of the capitalist spirit. He characterises the 'spirit of enterprise' as a synthesis of avarice, adventurousness and inventiveness (Sombart 1998, pp. 25, 91ff). The 'bourgeois spirit' is described as emerging in Florence in the late fourteenth century; Sombart uses this term to refer to the 'art of calculation' already discussed, as well as to rationalised economic behaviour [*masserizia*], mercantile reliability and bourgeois 'respectability' [*onestà*] (Sombart 1998, pp. 132ff, 168ff).

94    Sombart 1916, pp. 329, 331.

95    Becker, quoted in Brocke 1987, p. 427.

96    Lindenlaub 1967, pp. 317, 336; Brocke 1987, pp. 39, 41–2.

that 'the first edition is already quite multiform'.[97] He also formulates the more accurate claim with regard to the reasons for Sombart's revisions, arguing that Sombart was struggling for academic recognition and sought to 'accommodate' the expectations of his colleagues by placing greater emphasis on mental phenomena: 'In doing so, he was able to at least partly shake off the accusations of materialism'.[98]

Sombart's second strategy is that of juxtaposing to the economic determination of the 'materialist conception of history' a 'biologico-ethnological' one, as evident in his efforts to explain the capitalist spirit of usury in terms of Judaism's 'double morality'.[99] Sombart could have adopted this notion (and others) from Weber: in his *Ancient Judaism*, Weber characterised the Jewish mentality, that of a (putatively voluntary) pariah people, in terms of an underlying dualism of in-group and out-group morality.[100] But even after Sombart had gone on to view the Marxist-influenced labour movement as his main foe—a position he assumed, at the latest, in his 1924 book *Proletarischer Sozialismus* ['Proletarian Socialism'], which went on to become the standard reference for social conservatives opposed to Marxism and liberal capitalism—,[101] he states (in the 1927 preface to the third volume of *Modern Capitalism*) that his work aspires to be nothing other than 'a continuation and, in a sense, a perfecting of Marx's work': 'Everything that is good in my work is owed to the spirit of Marx'.[102] In January of 1933, he states in a radio lecture [*Mein Leben und Werk*, 'My Life and Work'] that he had attempted to extract from Marx's theory those elements 'that allow for the incorporation of the proletariat into the national community'.[103] Accordingly, he presents both his theoretical project of reconciling the 'historical school' with Marxism and his practico-political project of bringing together Social Democrats and bourgeois reformers in the Society for Social Reform as integral components of a class reconciliation conceived of in terms of a fascist 'community of the people' [*Volksgemeinschaft*]: it was a matter, he argues, of 'closing the gap that had opened up between the two halves of the people: the proletarian and the bourgeois half'.[104]

---

97    Appel 1992, p. 35.

98    Appel 1987, p. 82.

99    Sombart 1998, pp. 232–5, 265–6; Sombart 1916, pp. 909, 913–14; for an extended formulation of this view, see Sombart 1951.

100   Weber 1952, pp. 343ff.

101   Brocke 1987, p. 51.

102   Sombart 1927, p. XIX.

103   Quoted in Brocke 1987, p. 430.

104   Quoted in Brocke 1987, p. 431.

In Sombart's endorsements of Germany's fascist government, one discerns a sense of resignation, that of a man who has not been given the chance he hoped for. In a letter to Johann Plenge, the author of *The Ideas of 1914*, dated 24 September 1933, he expresses disappointment over the fact that the common 'paternity of National Socialism' is not being recognised by the Nazis: 'One wishes to have no intellectual fathers. All ideas begin with Year One of the "national revolution". I calmly resign myself to this destiny'.[105] Brocke overrates this statement by reading it as indicative of a 'broken' relationship to National Socialism.[106] The same year saw Sombart using his authority as chairman of the Association for Social Policy to exclude troublesome members; in 1935/36, the period of *Gleichschaltung*, he dissolved the Association, stating that 'the situation is no longer shaped by discussion, but by decision ... I for one say: thank God that this has happened'.[107]

That Sombart's political economy failed to assert itself within German fascism's economic policy was due not to any lack of endorsements of the fascist state but to his economic approach, which differed from that of the National Socialist modernisation project: in 1932, when Sombart proposed implementing a capitalist version of the 'planned economy', to be combined with the project of a 're-ruralisation' of the German economy,[108] his proposal was mainly discussed in the national conservative circles associated with the journal *Die Tat*, whose editors, Zehrer and Zimmermann, were students of Sombart. The Strasser brothers mainly mediated the proposal's reception within the National Socialist leadership—Otto Strasser had also been a student of Sombart.[109] Influenced by Keynes, Sombart (and the Gereke plan he co-authored) did not propose relieving entrepreneurs of their burdens, but rather increasing public

---

105   Quoted in Brocke 1987, p. 56, note 90.

106   Brocke 1987, p. 56.

107   Quoted in Boese 1939, pp. 283–4. On the occasion of Sombart's seventy-fifth birthday (in 1938), Ermsleben, his city of birth, declared him a 'fellow combatant of Adolf Hitler in the intellectual world'. Sombart held a speech of thanks in which he assured his audience that he had always felt a National Socialist and would always remain true to the idea of National Socialism (quoted in Brocke 1987, p. 55).

108   Sombart proposed that in pursuing 'proximate' autarchy, the state should take measures to increase the percentage of the population residing in rural areas from 30 percent to at least 42.5 percent, the level recorded in an 1882 census (see Brocke 1987, p. 417). The 'planned economy' proposed by Sombart was to display the following features: (1) 'totality'; (2) 'uniformity' (i.e. 'planning must be central'); (3) a 'manifoldness' that was to include the capitalist firm, characterised by the 'far-reaching personal responsibility of its director' (quoted in Brocke 1987, pp. 403ff).

109   Appel 1992, pp. 237–8, 241.

and private purchasing power by means of improvements to infrastructure, particularly in the areas of transportation, communication and agriculture; with regard to agriculture, Sombart had in mind both small farms and cooperatives. While the measures implemented by the new economic minister Hjalmar Schacht drew inspiration from the Keynesian project of an active business-cycle policy, they focused not on re-ruralisation, but on an enforced armaments policy.[110] In the late 1930s, if not earlier, economic policy was dominated by the ordoliberal theories of Walter Eucken and Alfred Müller-Armack, the later 'fathers of the social market economy' of the German Federal Republic, theories that distanced themselves both from the 'subjectivism' of the historical school and from Sombart's 'anti-capitalism'.[111]

---

110    Appel 1992, pp. 239, 241.
111    Appel 1992, pp. 249ff.

# CHAPTER 28

# Weber's Dislodgement of the 'Spirit of Capitalism' from Capitalism

## 28.1    A Tautological Conceptual Arrangement

When Weber speaks of the 'spirit of capitalism', he is explicitly referring to the spirit of 'modern', i.e. 'Western European and American' capitalism.[1] The reference to 'Western Europe', of course, cannot be intended geographically, for the Catholic countries are absent from Weber's 'Western Europe' even when they number among Europe's westernmost countries (France, Spain and Portugal). Behind Weber's ideal-typical emphasis on Protestant features, one clearly discerns the contours of an Anglo-American hegemony with which Weber confronts backward Germany.

Even during the earliest controversies prompted by the *Protestant Ethic*, Weber was accused of arbitrarily excluding other factors relevant to the 'spirit of capitalism', and the accusation has since been repeated in countless variants. For example, Brentano invokes the capitalist career of his own Italo-Catholic family and argues that Weber's main error consists in his neglect of the 'pagan emancipation from traditionalism', which he associates first with the spread of Roman law during the Middle Ages and then with the 'empiricist philosophy' of the Physiocrats and Adam Smith.[2] Sombart accounts for the spirit of capitalism in America in terms of migration, which, he claims, represents a process of selection of the fittest in and of itself.[3] Fischer then invokes Sombart to emphasise the role played by 'capitalist forms of enterprise' during the period prior to the Reformation, interpreting Luther's emphasis on professional work as an 'adjustment of the world of religious notions to the given economic situation'.[4] Rachfahl draws attention to the research of Pirenne,[5] which demonstrated the emergence of a Dutch early capitalism in the rural textile industry of Flanders prior to the arrival of Calvinism, and emphasises

---

1    Weber added this specification to the second edition of the *Protestant Ethic*: Weber 1950, p. 47; compare Weber 1904, p. 15.
2    Brentano 1916, pp. 133ff, 153ff, 157.
3    Sombart 1916, pp. 882ff; Sombart 1998, pp. 302–3.
4    Fischer 1978a, pp. 17–18; Fischer 1978b, p. 40.
5    Pirenne 1905.

Calvinism's later takeover by a 'rationalist libertinism'.[6] 'To quote Marc Bloch, capitalism has as many birth certificates as there are historians studying the subject', Samuelsson concludes,[7] having arrived at the result that even leading American entrepreneurs made use, in their self-presentations, of the most varied ideological resources, from Puritanism and utilitarianism to social Darwinism: 'From a variety of philosophies they picked out whatever contributed to the defence of their own conduct, riches and power'.[8]

Weber is able to pre-empt some of these objections by emphasising his 'weak thesis' and pointing out the provisional character of his deliberate ideal-typical simplification, as when he concludes by mentioning the significance of 'humanist rationalism', 'empiricism', technological development and the 'totality of social conditions, especially economic'.[9] The more weighty criticism is, however, the methodological one that he has already defined the 'spirit of capitalism' in terms of ascetic Protestantism to such an extent that the correlation he sets out to prove has already been decided on in advance, by means of a tautological posing of the question. For example, Marshall observes that '[t]he Protestant ethic and the spirit of modern capitalism are defined in terms of each other'.[10] Weber has in fact devised both ideal types in such a way as to make them fit closely together: Protestantism's features fit the profile of the capitalist ethos perfectly.[11] For example, when Weber decides to discuss Calvinism not by reference to Calvin but only 'in the form to which it had evolved by the end of the sixteenth and in the seventeenth centuries in the great areas where it had a decisive influence and which were at the same time the home of capitalistic culture',[12] he limits himself, from the outset, to a hegemonic constellation within which Protestantism and capitalism have already linked together effectively.

---

6  Rachfahl 1978, pp. 98–9, 135.

7  Samuelsson 1961, p. 149.

8  Samuelsson 1961, p. 78; compare pp. 70–1.

9  Weber 1905, p. 109; Weber 1950, p. 183.

10  Marshall 1982, p. 68.

11  Brentano already speaks of a *petitio principii*, whereby the spirit of capitalism is conceived of in such a way 'as to necessarily provide that which one wishes to prove' (Brentano 1916, p. 131). According to Samuelsson, the structure of Weber's argument is circular: first he introduces the concept of the 'spirit of capitalism' as a specific feature of Protestantism, and then he shows that Protestants display this feature (Samuelsson 1961, p. 66). Referring to Weber's concept of rationality, Lefèvre speaks of the 'tautologically coercive character' of the method of historical reconstruction (Lefèvre 1971, p. 50).

12  Weber 1950, p. 220, note 7.

Much of the scholarly literature on the *Protestant Ethic* does no more than move to and fro within this circular arrangement, sometimes apologetically and sometimes critically. In what follows, I will attempt to reconstruct the ideological determinants of this conceptual set-up. This becomes possible as soon as one observes, from the vantage point of Sombart's work, the stages of abstraction that underlie the ideal-typical 'composition' of the spirit of capitalism.

## 28.2     The Exclusion of Sombart's 'Adventure Capitalism'

In a lengthy insertion into the second edition of the *Protestant Ethic* that appears to be directed at Sombart, Weber characterises the spirit of capitalism by speaking of economic behaviour being predominantly oriented towards a 'rational utilisation of capital' and a 'rational capitalistic organization of labour'.[13] If one brackets, for the time being, the question of what is meant by 'rational', the defining features that remain are the emergence of capitalist forms of enterprise and the capitalist shaping of work. As in Sombart, the 'spirit of capitalism' appears to represent the historical site at which capitalism, or a mentality anticipating it, no longer represents a 'parasitic' epiphenomenon of the feudal world, but rather takes a hold of and begins to organise production itself.[14]

But Weber does not in fact venture onto the terrain of the capitalist organisation of enterprise and work; he places all the emphasis on the concept of the 'rational'. The sober, planning orientation of the 'spirit of capitalism' is contrasted by him with the hand-to-mouth existence of the peasant, the 'privileged traditionalism of the guild craftsman' and (in a 1920 addition) to 'adventurers' capitalism, oriented to the exploitation of political opportunities and irrational speculation'.[15] With regard to their rejection of peasant and artisan 'traditionalism', Weber and Sombart agree. But the second opposite term, that of a political and irrationally speculative 'adventure capitalism', excludes everything that Sombart describes as the 'spirit of enterprise': avarice, speculation, pillage, state manufactures, overseas trade, the slave and the

---

13    See Weber 1950, p. 58; compare Weber 1904, p. 20.

14    Hobsbawm demonstrates the weakness of a 'parasitic' capitalism that develops on the soil of feudalism by reference to the decline of Italy and the Netherlands during the seventeenth century (Hobsbawm 1965, pp. 18–19, 41–42).

15    Weber 1950, p. 76; compare Weber 1904, p. 34.

colonial economy.[16] To be sure, it is not easy to see how a trading company that speculates on the enormous price differentials afforded by the spice trade, calculates its operating profit and makes use of insurance can be described as 'irrational'. Weber organises his exclusion of everything that does not correspond to his notion of capitalist spirit by means of a series of associations. He takes from Sombart's romanticising account of the pillage-oriented and mercantile-capitalist spirit of enterprise the combination of the 'inner attitude of the adventurer' with a 'ruthlessness in acquisition' unfettered by ethical constraints.[17] However, he projects these traits onto the pre-capitalist and non-European countries in which, he claims, the pursuit of gain appeared 'more intense' and 'more unscrupulous' than, say, in England.[18] This leads him to the astonishing claim that modern capitalism has as little use for the 'business man who seems absolutely unscrupulous in his dealings with others' as for the undisciplined worker.[19] Thus the traditionalist camp includes the peasant, the craftsman, the freebooter and the oriental trader.[20] On the opposite pole of the conceptual set-up, the rational and Protestant spirit no longer refers, as in the concept's original definition, to the unfettered pursuit of economic gain as an end in itself, but rather to the ethical 'restraint, or at least a rational tempering of this irrational impulse' (of acquisitiveness).[21] Thus the concept of the 'spirit of capitalism', which oscillates between capitalist valorisation and the work ethic, undergoes yet another semantic change.

### 28.3   Purging the Capitalist Spirit of the Materiality of Capitalist Domination

The exonerating function of such a dichotomy is plain to see. In spite of its idealist or *völkisch* 'overcoming' of Marx, Sombart's account of bourgeois

---

16   See Sombart 1998, pp. 63ff; Sombart 1917, pp. 25ff.

17   Weber 1950, p. 58. On Sombart's account, the raids were led by 'men ... who were full of romance and yet possessed a keen eye for realities ... [T]hey were the forerunners of the capitalist undertakers of to-day' (Sombart 1998, p. 70). In the second edition of *Modern Capitalism*, the 'spirit of enterprise' refers to the 'Romantic aspect of the spirit of early capitalism' (Sombart 1917, vol. 2.1, pp. 24ff).

18   Weber 1950, pp. 56–7.

19   Weber 1950, p. 57.

20   'An unconvincing mixture of fictitious illustrations, composite instances drawn from diverse times and places, and anecdotal empirical examples', Marshall comments (Marshall 1982, p. 45).

21   Weber 1950, p. 17; Weber 1988e, p. 4; compare Weber 1978, pp. 629–30.

monetary wealth and of the entrepreneurial spirit still displayed too many aspects of the material reality of capitalist domination: state and church apparatuses that accumulate money, businessmen who collect taxes and customs duty and, last but not least, a colonial economy, genocide and slave labour. Sombart's opposition to the bourgeois myth of origin, according to which capitalism was born from the skilled crafts, and his focus on the lines of continuity linking capitalism to the elites of the old society would prove useful to later studies of capitalism. This can be seen from the example of the numerous, sometimes approving and sometimes critical references to Sombart found in Braudel's work, which draws a sharp distinction between 'capitalism' and the crafts-based, middle-class market economy with its underlying subsistence-oriented material civilisation.[22] Not unlike Sweezy in the 1950s debate between Sweezy and Dobb, Braudel asserts the 'exteriority' of capitalism with regard to the market economy, sometimes in opposition to Marx.[23] He mainly has in mind the large mercantile capitalists who occupied a strategic position within the intersection between the major currents of commodity exchange and the centres of political decision-making, and who were able—thanks to their privileged access to information and state support—to continuously circumvent the rules of the market economy.[24] The large trading companies were usually headed by self-contained family dynasties that disposed of a sufficient number of bases of operation within the state apparatuses.[25] In accordance with a 'treacherous law of small numbers', a consistently small group of privileged persons ruled from century to century.[26] Wallerstein, who also supports Sweezy's 'circulationist' theory of capitalism's origins,[27] even holds that historical capitalism was a reaction, on the part of the feudal classes, to the dissolution of the system of landed property; he argues that capitalism allowed the feudal classes to reverse the trend towards an egalitarian system of small

---

22    Braudel 1979a, pp. 7–8; 1979c, pp. 545–6.

23    Braudel 1979b, p. 514. From 1950 onward, Paul Sweezy developed his account of capitalism's emergence from the 'extra-systemic' cause of long-distance trade, thereby opposing the view of Maurice Dobb, whose 1946 book *Studies in the Development of Capitalism* places the emphasis on the contradictions immanent to the feudal system, and in particular on the contradiction between the growing need for income on the part of the feudal classes and the feudal system of production's inability to satisfy this need (see Dobb 1970, pp. 33ff; Sweezy 1976, pp. 33ff; Frank 1977, pp. 94ff).

24    Braudel 1979b, p. 353.

25    Braudel 1979b, pp. 393–94.

26    Braudel 1979b, pp. 415–16.

27    Wallerstein 1974, p. 393.

producers and safeguard the continuity of the ruling families:[28] '[T]he correct basic image is that capitalism was brought into existence by a landed aristocracy which transformed itself into a bourgeoisie because the old system was disintegrating'.[29]

One might respond by asking whether such an explanatory approach does not render claims about capitalism's genesis 'from above' overly absolute. For example, in Wallerstein, the unbroken continuity of domination entails that a bourgeois revolution never occurred.[30] Dobb already confronted Sweezy with the question of what the seventeenth century English civil war's genuine point of contention is supposed to have been.[31] But what is of decisive importance with regard to Weber's 'spirit of capitalism' is that it abstracts both from the feudal-bourgeois continuities emphasised by Wallerstein and from the key role played by the absolutist state. Marx's observation on capitalism's genesis from 'blood and dirt', which Sombart rejected with regard to the metropole but confirmed for the periphery, has disappeared altogether in Weber's ideal-typical concept formation.[32]

## 28.4    The Detachment of the Spirit from the Economic Form

It is easy to see why Weber does not articulate his opposition to Marxism on the terrain of the Marxian critique of alienation and domination but chooses a frontline more favourable to him, namely that of a 'naïve historical materialism' that can only conceive of the spirit of capitalism as a 'reflection' of material conditions in the ideal superstructure.[33] He justifiably opposes a mechanistic Marxism of derivation by pointing out the possibility that the spirit of capitalism may have *predated* capitalist development.[34] It is no coincidence that later scholars have largely followed him in this choice, which makes it easy to score points against Marxism. Schluchter, for example, holds that Weber's refusal to reduce the 'ideal superstructure' to a 'material base', or political domination

28    Wallerstein 1983, pp. 42–3.

29    Wallerstein 1983, pp. 104–5.

30    Ibid.

31    Dobb in Sweezy 1976, p. 65.

32    In praising the superiority of Weber's 'theoretical reflection', which he claims Sombart 'never equalled', Lehmann overlooks that this 'superiority' over Sombart's eclecticism comes at the cost of substantial elisions (Lehmann 1996, pp. 107–8; compare Lehmann 1993, p. 207).

33    Weber 1950, p. 55.

34    Weber 1950, p. 55; see Weber 1987, pp. 47–8, 171–2.

to the economy, constitutes an 'important point' on which Weber differs from Marx.[35]

What is discussed as a basic difference between Weber and Marx is in fact first and foremost a difference between two distinct objects of study. In his critique of political economy, Marx did not trace the activity of bourgeois economic subjects back to their 'psychology', but rather analysed the economy's functional relations as 'objective forms of thought' that all actors (the buyer and the seller, the capitalist and the wage worker, etc.) need to adopt if they are to act successfully, regardless of their particular psychic disposition. Thus the accusation commonly levelled at Marx by the 'historical school', namely that he operates on the basis of a 'narrow' psychology, is inappropriate: Marx never laid any claim to providing a capitalist 'psychology'; he limited himself to studying capitalism's predefined 'forms of individuality', which are anchored in economic and ideological practices.[36] Marx never systematically examined the way individuals adopt such forms of individuality, nor would he have been able to do so within the framework of a critique of political economy. For the concrete mode assumed by the practical adoption of a form of individuality depends on concrete individualities, their social positions, their way of life and their hegemonic context. Contrary to a widespread conception of Marxism that is evident among both Marxists and non-Marxists, Marx never held that innovations must always occur within the economic 'base' before they can ascend to the ideological 'superstructure'. Such an economistic interpretation is already given the lie by the fact that Marx and Engels did not thematise the ideological primarily as a phenomenon of consciousness, but as a material and relatively autonomous instance: as a number of 'practical forces' (the state, law, religion, the school etc.) that appear as ' "holy" powers' within the imagination.[37] In the *Grundrisse*, Marx observes that Roman law, by developing the categories of the

35   Schluchter 1991, p. 107.

36   Sève 1972, pp. 152–3. According to Sève, the Marx of *Capital* was only able to develop his critique of political economy as a science by resisting the temptation to engage in the sort of psychology still evident in the 1844 *Paris Manuscripts* and limiting himself to a theory of individuality's general historical forms (Sève 1972, pp. 149–50).

37   Marx and Engels 1975–2005, vol. 5, p. 245; compare p. 36. Accordingly, the autonomisation of consciousness is theorised on the basis of the 'division of labour' (Marx and Engels 1975–2005, vol. 5, p. 245). In the 'Preface' to *A Contribution to the Critique of Political Economy*, the 'ideological forms' are thematised not just as forms of consciousness, but as forms in which class oppositions are practically fought out (Marx and Engels 1975–2005, vol. 29, p. 263). The first 'ideological power over man' is the state, the late Engels writes (Marx and Engels 1975–2005, vol. 26, pp. 392–3), and the state is by no means a phenomenon of consciousness, but rather a 'power, having arisen out of society, but placing itself

'juridical person, precisely of the individual engaged in exchange', was able to 'anticipate' the law of the future bourgeois society.[38] The possibility of such an anticipation is related to what he describes as the 'uneven development' of material production and superstructural instances, e.g. artistic development.[39] The theoretical framework goes beyond what Engels has in mind when he speaks of the relative autonomy and 'retroactive action' of the superstructure upon the economic base. What is now acknowledged is that an element of the superstructure might precede the economic base instead of simply acting back upon it.[40]

Thus a historical materialist and a Weberian analysis do not have to disagree on the principal question of whether or not capitalist forms of practice and thought may be anticipated by religion, ethics and other ideologies. For example, Borkenau, who invokes 'dialectical materialism' in his study of the transition from the feudal to the bourgeois worldview [*Der Übergang vom feudalen zum bürgerlichen Weltbild*],[41] is able to combine Weber's hypothesis—namely that in the case of the social strata influenced by Calvinism, the 'capitalist way of thinking' precedes the capitalist way of life—with a socio-historical analysis, arriving at a partial confirmation of Weber's claims: according to Borkenau, early Calvinism was initially the faith of a heterogeneous conglomerate of the most varied non-capitalist strata (mainly the petty gentry and artisans), who responded to money capital's encroachment on social relations by adjusting to this development.[42] This analysis is based on a conception of religion that emphasises the *anticipation* of future developments, much like Marx: 'New religions render difficult processes of adjustment possible, which is to say they channel the available forces in the direction of a way of life that does not yet exist'.[43]

---

above it, and alienating itself more and more from it' (Marx and Engels 1975–2005, vol. 26, p. 269). See Rehmann 2013, pp. 58ff.

38    Marx 1973, p. 246; Marx and Engels 1975–2005, vol. 28, p. 177.

39    Marx 1973, p. 109.

40    See Engels to Schmidt, 27 October 1890, Marx and Engels 1975–2005, vol. 49, pp. 59–60. On the status of *anticipation* within Marxism, especially in Marx, Luxemburg, Bloch, Benjamin, Gramsci and Brecht, see Rehmann 1994, pp. 364ff.

41    Borkenau 1971, p. 159.

42    Borkenau 1971, p. 157.

43    Borkenau 1971, p. 159. The anticipation of future social relations is implicit in Marx's well-known definitions of religion as the '*expression* of real suffering and a *protest* against real suffering', or as the 'sigh of the oppressed creature' (Marx and Engels 1975–2005, vol. 3, p. 175). Compare Marx's discussion of religion in terms of the world having 'long dreamed of possessing something of which it has only to be conscious in order to possess it in

Once again, one of Weber's strong points consists in his giving expression, up to a point, to the orientation towards real life practice that was lost in the Marxism of his day, that of the Second International, whereas his main weakness consists in the way he chooses to fill in the lacuna. His argument begins with the 'weak' thesis according to which capitalist economic 'form' and the corresponding 'spirit' generally stand 'in some sort of adequate relationship to each other, but not in one of necessary interdependence'.[44] This means that a capitalist business can be organised in a traditionalist manner, just as a craft business such as Benjamin Franklin's printing office can be organised in accordance with the 'spirit of capitalism'.[45] Accordingly, Weber construes his account of the radical transformation of the textile industry's putting-out system in such a way as to posit a static technological base; the transformation manifests itself purely in a mental shift: there occurs no transition to the closed workshop or to machinofacture; what happens is that 'some young man' from one of the families involved in the putting-out system moves to the countryside, takes sales into his own hands, intensifies surveillance of the weavers and reinvests his profits instead of treating them as rent.[46] That Weber considers this type of entrepreneur politically significant to his own time can already be seen from the way he contrasts the entrepreneur's propensity for investment and 'cool self-control and frugality' with the entailed estate and its conspicuous displays of affluence.[47]

It is no coincidence that Weber's account, intended to be 'free of value judgements', here lapses into the pathos of a heroic story: the 'unusually strong character' and the special 'ethical qualities' by which the entrepreneur wins the trust of his customers and workers are presented as the keys to his success.[48] In his account of the 'spirit of enterprise', Sombart rhapsodises on the 'vigorous, adventurous, victory-accustomed, brutal, greedy conquerors of the very grandest sort';[49] Weber opposes to this figure the 'men who had grown up in the hard school of life, calculating and daring at the same time, above all temperate and reliable, shrewd and completely devoted to their business, with strictly bour-

---

reality' (Marx and Engels 1975–2005, vol. 3, p. 145). Within Marxism, the significance of religion qua utopian dream-story is mainly elaborated by Ernst Bloch (see for example Bloch 1986, pp. 1183ff).

44    Weber 1950, p. 64.
45    Ibid.
46    Weber 1950, p. 67.
47    Weber 1950, p. 63.
48    Weber 1950, p. 69.
49    Sombart 1920, p. 94.

geois opinions and principles'.[50] The controversy on the heroic origins of the capitalist class also involves two competing, but also complementary myths of masculinity.

According to Marianne Weber, Weber's account of the revolutionary transformation of the textile industry's putting-out system was based on the history of Weber's own Westphalian family. The model for the traditionalist type of entrepreneur, she says, was Weber's paternal grandfather, the Bielefeld-based linen dealer Karl August Weber (1796–1872), who lived on, in the memory of his grandson, as an amiable patrician gentleman: 'making money was neither an end in itself nor a sign of success, but was primarily a means to a comfortable life that was appropriate to one's class. Accordingly the pace of life was slow'.[51] As for the account of the capitalist spirit, it was informed, on Marianne Weber's account, by her husband's uncle Karl David Weber (1824–1907), who relocated the sale of domestically-produced linen to the countryside following the decline of the Bielefeld-based business. Marianne Weber reports that Karl David Weber resorted to 'ungentlemanly', modern capitalist business methods in order to recreate his business from the ashes: in order to sidestep the wholesalers, he travelled the country himself and 'set the poverty-stricken small farmers of the Senne, who managed to coax only potatoes and buckwheat out of the sand, at looms and provided them with yarn'.[52]

What renders this account interesting is not so much the link to Weber's family history in and of itself as the fact that Marianne Weber departs from Max Weber by describing the innovations introduced within the family business as a response to critical economic conditions. For Marianne Weber says of the Bielefeld trading house that prior to its renewed success, it 'declined because of technical innovations', which the elderly grandfather Karl August Weber was no longer able to adapt to.[53] As Roth shows, the decline of Bielefeld's linen industry was related to the crisis of the European textile industry following the Napoleonic wars. Under pressure from the cheaper British produce, the linen salesmen were faced with only two options: mechanising production or expanding the putting-out system. Because the mechanisation of production was too costly, they opted, in a 'traditionalist' manner, for quality over quantity, and were crushed by the competition of the cheaper British products, like the Weber family's business in 1861.[54] It was only the son, Karl David Weber, who

---

50    Weber 1950, p. 69.
51    Marianne Weber 1975, p. 25.
52    Marianne Weber 1975, p. 172.
53    Marianne Weber 1975, p. 24.
54    Roth 1993b, pp. 99–100.

opted for the putting-out system as a solution, recruiting about a thousand paupers as cheap labour.[55]

Taking Weber at his word when he invokes his own family history,[56] one notes that it contradicts his conceptualisation in several ways. To begin with, it was the pressures of an economic crisis that were decisive, not the development of a new spirit.[57] Moreover, adjustment to the new circumstances was brought about not by social climbers from the middle classes, to whom Weber normally attributes the 'spirit of capitalism', but by the son of one of the leading families. Thus the suggestion that the business was created anew and from below, by 'some young man', is misleading. More importantly, Weber's heroic spirit of capitalism does not, in this case, denote a rise from the status of producer to that of the industrial capitalist who engages in 'rational' economic activity (what Marx described as the 'really revolutionising path'), but rather the reactionary strategy of a 'catch-up', 'semi-peripheral' capitalism that seeks to compensate for its inferiority by intensifying exploitation: 'Without revolutionising the mode of production, it only worsens the condition of the direct producers ... and appropriates their surplus-labour on the basis of the old mode of production'.[58] Finally, Weber's uncle does not even seem to have been characterised by an ascetic, Protestant stance: according to Marianne Weber's memoirs, he inclined most towards Islam.[59]

Weber not only considers the disjunction of economic form and spirit possible, as signalled by his 'weak' thesis; such a disjunction is in fact constitutive of his conceptualisation.[60] The social bearers of the 'spirit of capitalism' are consistently *not* the large entrepreneurs of the mercantile patriciate, the monopolists of overseas trade, the major banks of issue, putting-out systems etc., but the 'rising strata of the lower industrial middle classes', the 'rising middle and small bourgeoisie'.[61] Instead of distinguishing between different components of the 'spirit of capitalism', Weber chooses one that appears compatible with ascetic Protestantism and presents it as the whole. 'When I say "horses", I only mean grey horses', Rachfahl comments mockingly. 'When I write about "horses", this should be read as: "horses in my sense of the word", i.e. grey horses'.[62]

---

55    Roth 1993b, p. 100.

56    In 1911, Weber declared himself proud of his bourgeois ancestry and his link to Westphalian linen [*Die Handelshochschulen*] (quoted in Roth 1993b, p. 102).

57    'Economic pressures ... were paramount' (Roth 1993b, pp. 100–1).

58    Marx and Engels 1975–2005, vol. 37, pp. 332–3.

59    See Roth 1993b, p. 101.

60    Weber signals the transition from the 'weak' to the 'strong' thesis by remarking that the disjunction of form and spirit was 'regularly' the case (Weber 1950, p. 49).

61    Weber 1950, p. 65, note 23.

62    Rachfahl in Weber 1987, p. 260; compare p. 256.

Most importantly, he consistently situates his ideal type in the very places where actually-existing capitalism's centres of power are *not* located. Weber's capitalist spirit was absent, for example, in fourteenth- and fifteenth-century Florence, which constituted the money and capital market of all major political powers, whereas it thrived 'in the backwoods small bourgeois circumstances of Pennsylvania in the eighteenth century, where business threatened for simple lack of money to fall back into barter'.[63] Prior to all capitalist development, it flourished in Massachusetts, a state founded, for 'religious' reasons, by the petty bourgeois, artisans, yeomen and preachers, whereas the neighbouring southern states of the union, founded by large capitalists for business reasons, had capitalist enterprises, but hardly any capitalist spirit.[64] The ideal-typical onesidedness by which Weber focuses on ascetic Protestantism is premised on the methodological decision to sever all organic ties between economic forms and the 'ethos' of those acting within them. The first controversies with Fischer and Rachfahl already see Weber's hermetic construct giving rise to the to-ing and fro-ing of irritated 'misunderstandings' that has continued to characterise the debate to this day: due to the unmediated leap from economic form to spirit, the attempts at refuting Weber undertaken by his critics grasp at nothing, being formulated in terms of political economy and economic history. For the concept of an 'ideal type', or of something that explicitly does not stand in any determinate relation to reality, can by definition *not* be criticised in the name of reality. Thus, in his 'Anti-Critical Postscript', Weber can backtrack to the claim that he speaks of the spirit of capitalism because the attitudes thus referred to seem to 'us' to 'somehow be specifically "adequate" to capitalism ... without necessarily being associated with it in the majority of cases or even in the average case'.[65] If neither the majority nor the ideal average of capitalism's forms of organisation can tell us anything about it, then its efficacy can be neither verified nor falsified on this level—'Weber's method is unwarrantable'.[66]

Until now, my comparison between Sombart and Weber has served to characterise Weber's spirit of capitalism *negatively* or in terms of that which it elides; in what follows, I use the example of Weber's and Sombart's controversy over Leon Battista Alberti to pursue the question of what hegemonic constellation Weber's ideal-typical concept formation aims at *positively*.

---

63    Weber 1950, p. 75.
64    Weber 1950, pp. 75ff.
65    Weber 1987, p. 284; see Weber 2001, p. 94.
66    Samuelsson 1961, p. 150.

# CHAPTER 29

# Weber's Perspective: Capitalist Spirit as a Popular Mass Movement

## 29.1    Renaissance Man or Reformation Man?

In the first edition of *Modern Capitalism*, the classic representative of Sombart's 'capitalist spirit' is Jakob Fugger, who tells a salesman weary of his work and preparing for retirement that he (Fugger) has something else in mind and 'wanted to make money as long as he could'.[1] Weber responds to this quotation, but interprets it as no more than an ethically indifferent 'expression of commercial daring' and contrasts it with Benjamin Franklin's 'ethically coloured maxim for the conduct of life'.[2] In his critique of the *Protestant Ethic*, Rachfahl responds by asking: 'How does Weber know that Fugger did not feel an inner duty toward his profession, that he was not also taken with the notion that man has a duty to perform the task life has placed before him faithfully and conscientiously?'[3]

One could continue by asking how Weber knows that the pious, Puritan businessman, to whom he attributes an 'amazingly good, we may even say a pharisaically good, conscience in the acquisition of money',[4] is not plagued by his conscience in much the same way as the Catholic businessman who bequeaths the greater part of his wealth to the church in the hope of obtaining salvation? The religious proviso against excessive acquisition of money [*Deo placere vix potest*], considered typically Catholic by Weber,[5] was brought to bear quite forcefully on the Puritan salesman Robert Keayne, who was reprimanded by his congregation for his 'profiteering'; plagued by his conscience, he bequeathed his money to the city of Boston so that it might build a parish hall. Kilian, who analyses Keayne's testament, considers it a typical document of the early phase of American Puritanism, when the clergy was still strong

---

1  Quoted in Sombart 1902, p. 396.

2  Weber 1950, pp. 51–2. To Weber, there is nothing specifically modern about Fugger. Weber sees Fugger as representing a type of capitalist that has existed since the age of the pharaohs: 'for as long as we have had a history' (Weber 1987, p. 161; see Weber 2001, p. 69).

3  Rachfahl 1978, p. 108.

4  Weber 1950, p. 176.

5  Weber 1950, pp. 64ff.

enough to 'check the advance of possessive individualism':[6] the testament reflects a proximate power balance between clergymen and salesmen, theological precepts and worldly success, and it is 'torn to and fro between economic rationalism and the strict social doctrine of New England Puritanism'.[7]

These objections provide an indication that definitions of the spirit of capitalism that abstract from forms of social praxis and their associated relations of hegemony are built on the sand of 'empathetic' speculation. This is also evident in the subsequent development of Weber's and Sombart's controversy over the writings of the Italian architect and writer Leon Battista Alberti (1404–1472).

Initially, the dual construct Sombart presented in the 1902 edition of *Modern Capitalism*—an acquisitive drive that takes on a life of its own combined with rational bookkeeping—provided Weber with the model with which to contrast his specifically 'modern', Protestant and ethical concept of the spirit of capitalism. In *Der Bourgeois* (English edition: *The Quintessence of Capitalism*), Sombart responded mainly by means of an ethical expansion of the second component of his construct. In 1902, he had spoken of an economic rationalism shaped by double-entry bookkeeping; now (in 1913), he speaks of the 'bourgeois spirit' [*Bürgergeist*] encompassing a broad spectrum of 'bourgeois virtues' over and above 'the art of calculation'.[8] In doing so, he integrates a previously neglected theme that Weber had articulated into his own model, albeit in such a way as to strip that theme of its Protestant and ethical character. One cannot trace the bourgeois virtues back to the Puritan and Quaker ethic, Sombart argues, for in Alberti's *I Libri della Famiglia*, one already finds everything that Defoe and Benjamin Franklin later spoke of in English:[9] the rationalisation and economisation of economic conduct, mercantile reliability and observance of contracts, bourgeois 'respectability' [*onestà*] and the mathematical ability to dissolve the world into figures and transform these figures into a system of earnings and expenses.[10] Nothing has changed in the world of bourgeois virtue during the four centuries since the *Quattrocento*, Sombart concludes.[11] As in the first, 1902 version of Sombart's argument, the two components of the spirit

---

6    Kilian 1979, p. 38.
7    Kilian 1979, p. 36; compare Bailyn 1965, p. 41; Henretta 1993, pp. 329ff.
8    Sombart 1998, pp. 103ff; Sombart 1920, pp. 135ff.
9    Sombart 1920, pp. 136, 149, 334.
10   Sombart 1998, pp. 103ff, 125ff.
11   Sombart 1920, p. 157.

of capitalism, both that of the 'vigorous' adventurer and that of the virtuous citizen, coincide with the figure of the Renaissance man.[12]

Weber, who usually addresses Sombart with the utmost deference,[13] responds to this appropriation of his framing of the problem, which was originally oriented towards Protestantism, with irritated annoyance: *The Quintessence of Capitalism* is 'by far the weakest of [Sombart's] larger works', he writes,[14] a 'book with a thesis [*Thesenbuch*] in the worst sense'.[15] In formulating his principles of thrift, Alberti has in mind only the management of one's budget, not acquisition, Weber argues; Alberti's reflections on money concern only the investment of one's wealth, not the valorisation of capital, he adds, and nowhere in his work does one find anything corresponding to Franklin's maxim 'time is money'.[16] Moreover, Alberti's work is not an 'ethic', Weber argues, but merely a compilation of 'worldly wisdom' that criticises carelessness in monetary matters as unreasonable, not as an 'ethical defect'.[17]

In order to be able to follow the controversy, I make reference, below, to Alberti's four-book *On the Family*, the first three of which were written around 1434, and the fourth around 1441. I will be quoting both from the 1960 Italian edition [*Opere Volgari*] and from the 1969 English translation.

## 29.2    The Interminability of the Controversy on the Spiritual Origin of Capitalism

Weber's last argument, which denies the ethical character of Alberti's *On the Family*, is only sustainable if one refuses, from the outset, to consider anything an *ethic* that is not a Protestant ethic in the Weberian sense. For example, Alberti not only considers idleness [*ozio*] useless and harmful; he also considers it a 'nest and lair of vice'.[18] For the idler knows neither honour nor shame [*non sente onore e vergogna*]. Thus idleness spawns depravity [*lascivia*], and depravity gives rise to contempt of the law, which leads to the demise of

---

12    Sombart 1920, p. 95. 'In Sombart, the spirit of capitalism bears the hue of the Renaissance, in Weber that of the reformation' (Hintze 1929, quoted in Brocke 1987, p. 335).

13    As when Weber emphasises how much his study owes to Sombart's 'important works, with their pointed formulations, and this even, perhaps especially, where they take a different road' (Weber 1950, p. 198, note 14).

14    Weber 1950, p. 191, note 19.

15    Weber 1950, p. 201, note 29.

16    Weber 1950, p. 194, note 9.

17    Weber 1950, pp. 196–7, note 12.

18    Alberti 1969, pp. 132; Alberti 1960, pp. 165–6.

nations.[19] Conversely, the ethical qualities of diligence and industry [*diligenza e industria*] function as wellsprings of wealth, much as their absence, in the form of carelessness, indolence and sluggishness [*negligenza, ignavia e tardità*], leads to poverty.[20]

In his effort to deny the *ethical* character of *On the Family*, Weber argues that in that work, religious conceptions are 'not *yet*' linked to the recommendation of thrift, whereas such a link is 'no *longer*' evident in Franklin.[21] It is precisely between this 'not yet' and this 'no longer' that the stakes of the *Protestant Ethic* are situated. Weber's argument that the religious element in Alberti is 'colourless'[22] might be related to the fact that the honesty of the family [*onestà*] is at the centre of Alberti's system of values, with religious considerations—and considerations of economic gain—grouped around it.[23] But the claim that Alberti *never* treats religious motives as reference points in his recommended life conduct is not accurate,[24] since Alberti does require such motives to provide a creation-theological justification of his ethic: man has been created to please God, and since even plants and animals are active, man pleases God by being 'up and going',[25] especially by engaging in major undertakings.[26] Man comes into the world 'to make good use of the world [*per usare le cose*], and he is born to be happy'.[27] While one could perhaps question whether Alberti's ethic is religiously based in the sense suggested by Sombart's image of the pious Catholic,[28] it is certainly buttressed by religious considerations, which is also the predominant strategy in Franklin. By articulating his lesson on economic and life conduct as divinely ordained and sacred,[29] Alberti

---

19    Alberti 1969, p. 132; Alberti 1960, p. 166.

20    Alberti 1969, p. 146; Alberti 1960, p. 185.

21    Weber 1950, p. 196, note 12.

22    Ibid.

23    *Honour* has a godlike status itself: it is the most pious [*religiosissima*] mother of all peace and happiness; one should seek its counsel in all affairs, always seek to satisfy its standards and conform only to it (Alberti 1969, pp. 140–50; Alberti 1960, pp. 192–3).

24    Weber 1950, p. 56, note 12.

25    Alberti 1969, pp. 133–4; Alberti 1960, pp. 167ff.

26    Alberti, 1969, p. 136; Alberti 1960, p. 171.

27    Ibid.

28    Sombart 1920, pp. 292–3.

29    Gianozzo, who has missed his morning prayer because of the intense conversations being held in his family, is assured by Lionardo that his lesson on economic and life conduct is no less pleasing in the sight of God than if he had gone to mass; after all, he has taught 'many good and most sacred things' (Alberti 1969, p. 230) [*'tante buone e santissime cose'*] (Alberti 1960, p. 316).

is doing precisely what Weber denies he does, namely 'exploiting' religion for his ethical valorisation of the accumulation of wealth [*accumulare ricchezze*].

Alberti is referring concretely to activities such as buying and selling, lending and claiming money: activities that are 'solely directed to making a profit' [*suggetti solo al guadagno*].[30] These pecuniary activities [*essercizii pecuniarii*] are wrongly thought of as menial and disreputable, Alberti argues, for wealth helps one obtain friendship and praise, can help one achieve both fame and renown and is of great use to the nation, as it fills the coffers of the state.[31] If one accepts the analysis of Hans Baron,[32] according to which the Franciscan ideal of voluntary poverty prevailed in the Florence of the Trecento roughly until the 1378 Ciompi revolt, then Alberti is an example of how a fundamental shift in values asserted itself during the *Quattrocento*.[33] The Alberti family itself was a prime example of the combination of virtue and wealth; the family gave rise, in the most varied countries, to the most important merchants [*conosciuti grandissimi mercatanti*], becoming one of Florence's most wealthy dynasties and one of the few that was able to retain its wealth over time.[34]

But if what is presented in Alberti's work is an ethic, the question remains in what sense the spirit it expresses is a specifically *capitalist* spirit. In the third book, *Oeconomicus*, Alberti devotes himself mainly to praising thrift as a 'holy thing' [*santa cosa la masserizia*];[35] Sombart interprets this as expressing a new bourgeois virtue, one directed against all forms of the seigniorial lifestyle,[36] whereas Weber interprets it as an element of traditional budget management also found in the ancient writers that Alberti draws inspiration from (such as Xenophon, Cato and Varro).[37] Sombart's interpretation is supported by the fact that Alberti develops his concept of thrift to counter wastefulness [*prodigalità*], and behind this latter concept, one easily discerns the various estates of feudal society, not just princes and aristocrats, but also priests and the Pope.[38] Alberti also opposes avarice [*avarizia*], which is unable

---

30    Alberti 1969, p. 142; Alberti 1960, p. 180.

31    Alberti 1969, p. 142; Alberti 1960, p. 181.

32    Baron 1992, pp. 46, 67ff, 84ff.

33    The threats posed by the poverty ideal of the Fraticelli led to the 'influence *paupertas* exerted in bourgeois circles... ending abruptly' towards the late 1370s (Baron 1992, p. 84).

34    Alberti 1969, pp. 143ff; Alberti 1960, pp. 182ff.

35    Alberti 1969, p. 160; Alberti 1969, p. 209.

36    Sombart 1920, pp. 138–9.

37    Weber 1950, p. 197, note 12.

38    See Alberti 1969, pp. 160–1 (Alberti 1960, pp. 208–9); on princes, see Alberti 1969, pp. 236–7 (Alberti 1960, pp. 326–7); on priests and the Pope, see Alberti 1969, pp. 261ff (Alberti 1960, pp. 364ff).

to put to use what it owns when necessary.[39] The whole art of thrift does not so much consist in conserving things as in using them when needed [*in usarle a'bisogni*].[40] Thus Alberti distances himself from the social type of the miser, who, instead of 'throwing his money again and again into circulation', in the manner required by the Alberti family's wool wholesaling, decides to 'save his money from circulation'.[41] The counterpart to the miser is the merchant, for whom it is advantageous to have 'ink-stained fingers', so that no one gets it into their head that he might not be fully aware of his accounts.[42] What emerges from this is a 'rational' capitalist standpoint, which, as Weber himself explains, aims at large business transactions in order to economise on work.[43] While Franklin's equation of time with money is not found in Alberti in quite those terms, Alberti also speaks of time as a 'precious thing' [*cosa preziosa*], of which one must not waste a single hour.[44] Samuelsson is right to criticise Weber for his tendency to inflate differences in the language used by Alberti and Weber into principal intellectual oppositions.[45]

On the other hand, one could argue in favour of Weber's interpretation by pointing out that Alberti's recommendations of thrift largely refer to the economics of the household [*casa*] and the country estate [*possessione* or *villa*], whereas little is said about the Alberti family's main line of business, the wholesaling and processing of wool. From the impassioned descriptions of the country estate—far from the 'mad goings-on' of the cities, providing the family with affordable meals and the most reliable and respectable income—, one can see how strongly Alberti is influenced by ancient literature's accounts of rural life, and in particular by Xenophon's *Oikonomikos*. Weber concludes from this that Alberti should be relegated to the category of the ancient *oikonomia*, without considering the possibility that Alberti might be using traditional ideological trappings to articulate a new social perspective. Weber's wish for clear categorisation prompts him—and Sombart, even though Sombart is arguing the opposite case—to overlook the fact that Alberti's text contains different and contradictory logics.

---

39    Alberti 1969, p. 161; Alberti 1960, p. 211.

40    Alberti 1969, p. 163; Alberti 1960, p. 214.

41    Marx 1976, pp. 254–5.

42    Alberti 1969, p. 197; Alberti 1960, p. 265.

43    Weber 1950, p. 197, note 12; compare Alberti 1969, p. 196; Alberti 1960, p. 203.

44    Alberti 1969, p. 172; Alberti 1960, p. 227.

45    'Minor variations of phraseology ... are inflated to major importance even though two different languages and a time-gap of 300 years are involved' (Samuelson 1961, p. 63).

Thus the overall enterprise that is to provide the family with a respectable income consists of three departments [*membri*]: the household, the estate and the business properly speaking [*la bottega*].[46] When one considers the relative importance attributed to each of them, there emerges a picture very different from that of an apparent nostalgia for the *casa* and the *villa*. The division of labour stipulated by Alberti allots to the father of the family the privileges of income and acquisition outside the household [*guadagnare e acquisitare di fuori*], as well as the associated responsibility of socialising with 'respectable' persons, while the father's wife is responsible for managing the household and directing and supervising the servants.[47] While the bulk of the third book is devoted to the question of how to instruct the wife so that she will perform these tasks well, it remains clear that they are 'minor matters', whereas the conduct of business is a 'manly' and respectable undertaking.[48] The question of which form of property is to be preferred, landed property or monetary assets, is addressed by Alberti in the form of a controversy between the older Gianozzo, who wishes money to be nothing but a means of circulation, and the younger Adovardo, who praises it as the 'root of all things' and the 'sinews of any kind of work', pointing out the advantages of usury.[49] It is the older Gianozzo, whom Alberti occasionally presents as an exponent of Aristotelian economics, who formulates a compromise that is acceptable to both parties and would prove compatible with capital's valorisation strategies until modernity: 'I am not in favor ... of having only lands or only money. Better have some of this and some of that, some stowed far away and located at a variety of places'.[50] Such an allocation of capital investments is not at all atypical of the 'practical' spirit of actually-existing capitalism, notwithstanding the fact that Weber wishes to exclude it from his ideal type of the 'spirit of capitalism'.[51]

---

46    Alberti 1969, p. 202; Alberti 1960, p. 273.

47    Alberti 1969, p. 235; Alberti 1960, p. 280.

48    The business is described as a *'faccenda virile e lodatissima'*, a virile and most praiseworthy undertaking, whereas Alberti uses the diminutive form of the word *'faccenda'* [undertaking] when referring to the management of the household; he speaks of *'faccenduzze di casa'* (Alberti 1969, p. 208; Alberti 1960, p. 282).

49    Alberti 1969, pp. 232–3; Alberti 1960, pp. 324ff.

50    Alberti 1969, p. 235; Alberti 1960, p. 324.

51    The controversy over the relative merits of landed property and monetary assets recurred, in an almost identical form, in late seventeenth-century England; see Pocock 1975, pp. 450–1. Wallerstein even holds that the historical transition from rent to profit as posited by the 'classical economists' is a myth, the actual historical development having been just the opposite: 'Every capitalist attempts to transform profit into rent. The main goal of every "bourgeois" is to become an "aristocrat"' (Wallerstein 1995, p. 323; compare p. 313).

'Si le capitalisme peut se reconnaitre à l'esprit et se peser au poids des mots, alors Max Weber a tort', writes Braudel, who is inclined to agree with Sombart's interpretation of Alberti.[52] While Marx dated the 'age of capitalism' from the sixteenth century, he perceived the sporadic beginnings of capitalist production (i.e. not just of mercantile capitalism) in the fourteenth and fifteenth centuries, the earliest of them in Italy.[53] It was there that '[m]anufactures first flourished', Marx and Engels write in *The German Ideology*,[54] and in *Anti-Dühring*, Engels refers to Italy as 'the first nation of capitalists in history', the nation that coined the word 'capital'.[55] The expression '*il capitale*', derived from the Medieval Latin '*caput*' ['head, main sum'], was in fact first used in thirteenth-century Italy.[56] Sombart considers the Florentine cloth industry the first genuinely capitalist industry. [57]

Alberti reports that his family ordered enough wool from distant Flanders to keep the woolworkers of Florence and a large part of Tuscany busy;[58] the basis for this was an advanced system of wool production that involved an extensive rural putting-out system during the thirteenth and fourteenth centuries but saw the final stages of production (milling and dyeing) performed in the city and under the merchant's surveillance, such that the dawn of manufacture coincided with the decline of the putting-out system.[59] From about the mid-fourteenth century, the upper Italian towns no longer limit themselves to dyeing the raw wool and cloth shipped from the north in order to then sell them to the east; instead, they begin to produce wool and cloth themselves, and in doing so combine a rural putting-out system with urban manufacture: 'L'Arte della Lana va dominer Florence'.[60] Initially, it was not Venice but Florence, already the centre of European banking around 1300, where production reached the stage of manufacture.[61] The leading merchants simultaneously or subsequently engaged in trade, banking, stock market speculation, putting out and manufacture.

---

52    Braudel 1979b, p. 517.

53    Marx 1976, p. 876.

54    Marx and Engels 1975–2005, vol. 5, p. 67.

55    Marx and Engels 1975–2005, vol. 25, p. 195; compare vol. 27, p. 365.

56    'Il est détecté sans conteste en 1211 et, dès 1283, dans le sens de capital d'une société marchande. Au XIVe siècle, il est presque partout, chez Giovanni Villani, chez Boccace, chez Donato Velluti' (Braudel 1979b, p. 201).

57    Sombart 1920, p. 129.

58    Alberti 1969, p. 146; Alberti 1960, p. 188.

59    Braudel 1979b, pp. 289–90.

60    Braudel 1979c, p. 63.

61    Braudel 1979c, pp. 95, 105.

L'éventail marchand, industriel, bancaire, c'est-à-dire la coexistence de plusieurs formes de capitalismes, se déploie déjà à Florence au XIIIe siècle.[62]

However, Marx's work also features passages that seem to contradict this interpretation. In the *Grundrisse*, Marx argues that supremacy with regard to monetary wealth is not sufficient for bringing about a 'dissolution into capital'; otherwise, the decline of the older property relations in ancient Rome and Byzantium would have led to free labour and capital, and not to the domination of the city by the country.[63] In Florence, the transition from money to capital is largely stalled as well, due to the power of the guilds: '*Manufactures may develop sporadically, locally, in a framework which still belongs to a quite different period, as e.g. in the Italian cities alongside the guilds*'.[64] For this reason, other scholars, more careful than Sombart and Braudel, speak of a 'semi-capitalist stage', pointing out that in spite of the considerable size of the sites of production, artisanal forms of property and production as determined by the guild [*Arte della Lana*] continued to prevail: all of production was ultimately controlled by large merchants who provided the producers with their raw materials and organised sales, but the late fifteenth century still saw manufacturing split up between about 270 workshops.[65] This structure— mercantile supervision of a persistently decentralised productive structure— may help explain why Alberti describes his economic activity as consisting mainly of personal surveillance; he uses the image of a spider, the strands of whose web start from himself and radiate outward.[66] 'The wealth of Florence did not become the basis for an accumulation of capital, which would have reshaped relations of production in such a way as to increasingly separate the producers from their conditions of production. Only this would have entailed

---

62    Braudel 1979c, p. 539.

63    Marx and Engels 1975–2005, vol. 28, p. 430.

64    Ibid.

65    Lopez 1980, pp. 466–7; Burke 1984, pp. 262–3; compare Anderson 1974, pp. 157–8. According to Perry Anderson, the 'premature development' of mercantile capital in the towns of northern Italy stalled the development of a strong nation state. 'Paradoxically it was the economic advance of Northern Italy that condemned it to a long cycle of political backwardness hereafterwards' (Anderson 1974, p. 169; see also p. 143). This also rendered impossible the imposition of capitalist relations of production by means of absolutist authority.

66    Alberti 1969, p. 206; Alberti 1960, p. 279.

the transformation of money into capital', writes Deppe.[67] On this basis, one could argue that Weber's 'spirit of capitalism' refers only to the early bourgeois mentality that announces the capitalist transformation of production itself. But of course, Weber would reject such a linking of 'form' and 'spirit'. Moreover, such a 'mental' opposition between mercantile and industrial capital presupposes the separation of commodity production from commodity circulation, something that does not exist empirically in developed capitalism.

The debate's focus on *the* spirit of capitalism entailed the replacement of one onesided account by another. Neither of the two disputants is interested in analysing the text's contradictory standpoints and the ideological compromises formed between them. Weber purges Alberti's *On the Family* of all chrematistics, whereas Sombart fails to comment on the work's orientation to pre-capitalist ideological patterns. In translating the key concept of *onestà* as 'bourgeois honesty' from the outset,[68] Sombart renders invisible the facts that the significance of this central value is contested and that Alberti is working to rehabilitate and present as respectable the pursuit of economic gain, which those of 'large and liberal spirit' [*l'animo magno e liberale*] still considered disreputable.[69] To this is added, in Sombart, an inconsistency in the argument that pulls the ground from under his basic intention: in discussing Alberti's relationship to the 'spirit of antiquity', Sombart suddenly discovers that the pursuit of economic gain and economic rationalism, previously celebrated by him as innovative distinguishing features of Alberti's 'capitalist spirit', were already 'fully developed' in Cato and others.[70] He thereby unwittingly confirms Weber's categorisation. Weber immediately detects this weakness in Sombart's argument and makes the most of it.[71] Finally, Sombart uses the 'illegitimate child' Alberti as an example in order to illustrate his 'law of mixed blood', according to which, when seigniorial and bourgeois blood mix, it is the latter that prevails.[72]

In the ideologically overdetermined competition over whose is the valid myth of origin—Braudel speaks of a 'retrospective sociology, one that has

---

67    Deppe 1987, p. 151.
68    Sombart 1920, p. 163.
69    Alberti 1969, p. 141; Alberti 1960, p. 180.
70    Sombart 1920, p. 290.
71    Weber 1950, p. 56, note 12.
72    Sombart 1920, pp. 278–9. 'What streams of merchant blood must have blended with the noble blood of this family to render such a transformation possible!' (Sombart 1920, p. 279).

gone astray'—,[73] Sombart is no less wrong than Weber to refuse to recognise any difference between Renaissance man and 'Reformation man', or between the Protestant ethic and Thomism.[74] Florentine cloth production was already declining when Alberti wrote *On the Family* (between 1434 and 1441), and the economy no longer achieved the dynamism it had displayed until the early fourteenth century—a consequence, in part, of international trade's centre of power being relocated from the southeast to the northwest.[75] What Weber explains in denominational terms, talking it up as the key feature of the *modern* spirit of capitalism, is entirely missed by Sombart: the hegemony of a northern European (and later north American) capitalism and the impetus this capitalism received 'from below', from a new entrepreneurship that was forming within production.[76] And of course a 'spirit of capitalism' that assimilates itself defensively to pre-bourgeois relations of hegemony is not of the same hue as one that sets out to conquer society's ideological superstructures, or one that has already obtained hegemony and needs to defend itself against a socialist labour movement.

If Braudel is right to disagree with Weber's analysis of the spirit of capitalism, it could still be the case that Weber has simply couched a valid argument in the wrong framework. For this reason, we need to ask whether there is another theme hidden behind the search for origins that Weber undertakes within the history of ideas, a theme that calls for a different theoretical approach.

### 29.3    The Hidden Theme: The Bourgeoisie's Popular-National Achievement of Hegemony

The above-mentioned deep layer of 'psychological sanctions' that 'gave a direction to practical conduct and held the individual to it' give an indication of what Weber is interested in.[77] Weber distinguishes between a 'doctrine' and the 'motives to practical action' that are determined by the desire for salvation.[78] In contrast with mere 'doctrine', the 'ethos' Weber is concerned with disposes

---

73    Braudel 1979b, p. 507.

74    To the extent that any system of religion is involved in the emergence of the bourgeois virtues, 'it is the Catholic one. The Protestant ethic was unable to do anything but adopt what Thomism had created' (Sombart 1920, p. 334).

75    See Deppe 1987, pp. 127–8, 142–3.

76    Kofler 1966, pp. 291ff, 297, 308; compare Dobb 1970, pp. 141–2, 166.

77    Weber 1950, p. 97.

78    Weber 1950, p. 73, note 29.

of effective 'psychological sanctions' that intervene, in an orienting manner, on the level of action, and it is this, Weber emphasises against Sombart, that is the point of the entire essay.[79] In fact, the distinction provides the consistently maintained framework not only of the *Protestant Ethic*, but of Weber's sociology of religion in its entirety: 'it is not the ethical *doctrine* of a religion, but that form of ethical conduct upon which premiums are placed that matters... [S]uch conduct constitutes "one's" specific "ethos" in the sociological sense of the word'.[80]

There is an interesting overlap between Weber's 'sociological' concept of the ethos and the problem that most interests the Gramsci of the tenth *Prison Notebook* in Croce's broad concept of religion, and because of which he adopts that concept, in a slightly modified form, as part of his terminology. If one leaves the mythical element aside, one finds, in each and every religion, a core 'that consists in a consciousness of reality and in a corresponding ethic' [*concezione della realtà e in un etica conforme*], Croce wrote in his *History of Europe*.[81] Gramsci elaborates on one aspect of this observation: namely that a worldview transcends the confines of the 'closely circumscribed intellectual strata' and spreads among the masses, becoming a 'faith', a 'moral will', a corresponding form of life and behaviour.[82] Gramsci relates the terms *faith, norm* and *morality* to the development of social agency: what is at stake is the transformation of a theoretical activity qua 'creation of a new way of thinking' into an incentive to act, action being understood as the 'creation of new history'. This requires the ethico-political ability 'to replace all preceding conceptions and opinions throughout the life of the state'.[83] One historical example of such a 'dissemination of a world-view' is Paul the Apostle, whom Gramsci analogises, in this context, with Lenin's historical function.[84]

In his definition of the 'spirit of capitalism', Weber is also concerned, among other things, with the point at which said spirit emerged as a 'mass

---

79    Weber 1950, p. 56, note 12.

80    Weber 1946a, p. 321. In a letter to Count Keyserling dated 12 November 1912, Weber identifies as one of the achievements of the *Protestant Ethic* its distinction between the 'content' of a revealed religion and the characteristics by which the faithful can gauge their certainty of salvation: it is starting from these characteristics, Weber argues, that one can examine the 'apparatus' of a given religion (quoted in Baumgarten 1964, p. 448).

81    Croce 1935, p. 19; Croce 1953, pp. 17–18.

82    See Gramsci 1975b, pp. 1217, 1251, 1271, 1292; on the use Gramsci makes of Croce's broad concept of religion, see also Rehmann 1991, pp. 181–2.

83    Gramsci 1975b, p. 1217.

84    Gramsci 2007, pp. 183–4.

phenomenon' and became a 'way of life common to whole groups of men'.[85] In order to set it off effectively against Sombart's 'bourgeois virtues', Weber links the distinction between 'doctrine' and 'ethos' to a definition of the social positions of the intellectuals involved. The extent of the difference becomes clear, he writes, when one compares the writings of the 'Renaissance *littérateur*' Alberti, written for the humanist patriciate and never much noticed outside scholarly circles, with the writings of Franklin, written for the masses of the bourgeois middle class:[86] 'But how can anyone believe that such a literary theory could develop into a revolutionary force at all comparable to the way in which a religious belief was able to set the sanctions of salvation and damnation on the fulfilment of a particular... manner of life?'[87] The young Marx expected a 'radical' theory (one that treats the human being as the 'root') to seize the masses, thereby becoming a 'material force';[88] Weber identifies ascetic Protestantism as such a life-changing force, at least with regard to the bourgeoisie.

It is as if Gramsci continued writing at the point where Weber indicates without pursuing the point, the social differences between intellectuals. His starting point is Croce's assessment, in his *History of the Baroque Age in Italy*, that the Renaissance remained 'aristocratic', failed to spread to the people and never became 'habit (*costume*) or "prejudice"', i.e. a collective conviction and faith'. The Reformation, however, 'was very much characterised by this ability to penetrate the popular masses [*penetrazione popolare*], although it paid for this with a stalling of its internal development'.[89] Gramsci adds that Lutheranism and Calvinism initially created a 'popular culture' and a 'broad national-popular movement' [*un vasto movimento popolare-nazionale*], providing resistance to the armies of the Counterreformation with a solid foundation; it was only later that they brought forth a new group of intellectuals and a corresponding high culture.[90]

The perspective from which Gramsci discusses this dialectic of popular and high culture is of course not that of the emergence of the spirit of capitalism, but that of an 'intellectual and moral reform'. This expression is used by him to refer to formations as diverse as Marxism, the French Revolution and the Protestant reformations, which were anchored in popular movements and

---

85    Weber 1950, pp. 55, 57.

86    Weber 1950, p. 56, note 12.

87    Ibid.

88    Marx and Engels 1975–2005, vol. 3, p. 182.

89    Croce 1929, pp. 11–12; see also Gramsci 1996, pp. 140–4: Gramsci 1975c, p. 1858.

90    Gramsci 1996, p. 142; Gramsci 1975c, p. 1859.

aimed at a cultural emancipation of the subaltern classes and the construction of a 'collective national-popular will'.[91] The immediate context is the problem, much exploited by Croce, that 'official' Marxism had adapted itself to a 'philosophical vulgar materialism'.[92] Faced with this vulgarisation, Gramsci set his hope on Marxism's 'absolute historicism', i.e. on its self-reflexive capacity to apply its 'demystifying critique to itself':[93] Much as the 'intellectual crudeness of Reformation man' at least represented the prelude to classical German philosophy, Marxism, which became a determinist 'religion' by virtue of its linking up with common sense,[94] can discover within itself the elements it requires to transcend this primitive stage. When Croce identifies the 'inferior current' that has emerged within Marxism with the philosophy of praxis as such, he assumes the Renaissance man's stance on the Protestant Reformation, notwithstanding the fact that he has himself criticised that stance as elitist and aristocratic.[95] Gramsci treats the Reformation and the Renaissance as comprehensive 'models of cultural development', without which one cannot comprehend the 'molecular process by which a new culture asserts itself'.[96] His perspective is that of an 'integral culture' that boasts all the mass features of the Protestant Reformation and the French Enlightenment, in addition to the classicism of Greek culture and the Renaissance.[97]

While the Renaissance was able to combine, via the period's numerous immigrants, with the formation of nation states across Europe, it had a

---

91  Gramsci 1975c, p. 1560. Gramsci first uses the expression 'intellectual and moral reform' in the third notebook (Gramsci 1996, p. 39); he adopts it (indirectly, via Sorel) from Ernest Renan's eponymous 1871 book, *La réforme intellectuelle et morale* (Gramsci 1975c, pp. 1683, 1860). Renan's perspective was however utterly reactionary: immediately after France's defeat in the Franco-Prussian War of 1871, he used the expression as a generic term to refer to a strategy of crisis resolution that involved the restoration of the ruling dynasty and the aristocracy as a '*race à part*' within France, and the enforcement, in foreign policy, of a colonialism articulated in racist terms (see Renan 1967, pp. 115, 122, 132, 141ff). Charles Maurras considered the book one of his 'bibles' (see the preface by Revel in Renan 1967, p. 9).

92  Gramsci 1996, pp. 140–4.

93  See Thomas 2009, pp. 249, 253.

94  When one lacks the initiative in the struggle, Gramsci argues, mechanical determinism becomes 'a formidable force of moral resistance, of cohesion, of patient perseverance ... It is an "act of faith" in the rationality of history transmuted into an impassioned teleology that is a substitute for the "predestination," "providence," etc. of religion' (Gramsci 2007, p. 353; compare Gramsci 1975b, p. 1389).

95  Gramsci 2007, p. 154; Gramsci 1975b, p. 1293.

96  Gramsci 2007, p. 192.

97  Gramsci 1975b, p. 1233.

'reactionary' function within Italy, namely that of paving the way for the Counterreformation.[98] Gramsci characterises it as the 'economic-corporative phase of Italian history'.[99] What he considers decisive is a specific weakness in the hegemony of the urban bourgeoisie: the urban bourgeoisie was unable to '[break] loose from narrow-minded corporatism', constitute itself as an independent and autonomous class, produce a cultural and intellectual organisation to counter the church and then create the superstructures of an 'integral state civilization'.[100] Because the economically active bourgeoisie failed to produce intellectuals with close ties to the people, with the aid of whom it could have worked its way from the economic base to society's various functional levels, the Renaissance assumed the character of a 'recuperation' [*riscossa*] and 'bulwark' against 'a certain heterodox and romantic restlessness' that first burgeoned in the period of the communes and later gained the upper hand during the Reformation period.[101] Even if the first elements of the Renaissance were of popular origin, as Gramsci follows Ezi Levi in assuming,[102] the crafting of the Tuscan dialect into an 'illustrious vulgar tongue' remained limited to professional literati and was reabsorbed by the courts: a cultural compromise, not a revolution.[103] To Gramsci, the rapid transition from the Renaissance to the Counterreformation was ultimately due to the absence of a 'popular-national bloc' within the field of religion; conversely, the Reformation was successful because it disposed of such a bloc.[104]

Thus the criterion of a bourgeois *mass movement*, addressed by Weber in what is little more than an aside, is re-articulated, in Gramsci, as an issue within the theory of hegemony. From this perspective, the question that arises is not that of whether or not Alberti was inspired, like Franklin, by the 'spirit of capitalism'; the question is whether this 'spirit' renders possible a bourgeois transformation of society as a whole. Gramsci denies this. To him, Alberti represents the type of bourgeois he refers to as *borghese*;[105] this type of bourgeois directs his attention at what is 'private' [*particolare*]: 'the bourgeois as an individual who develops within civil society and who has no concep-

---

98    Gramsci 2007, p. 342; Gramsci 1975c, pp. 1908–10, 1912–14, 2350.
99    Gramsci 2007, p. 96.
100   Gramsci 1996, p. 367.
101   Toffanin, approvingly cited in Gramsci 1996, p. 401.
102   Gramsci 2007, pp. 96–7.
103   Gramsci 2007, p. 7.
104   Gramsci 1975b, 1129–30.
105   Gramsci 1996, p. 349; compare Gramsci 1975b, p. 696.

tion of political society outside his "particular" sphere'.[106] Alberti would have rejected the proposition of getting involved in politics by arguing that what is important for a man is 'to live for himself, not for the community [*vivere a se, non al comune*], to care for one's friends, certainly, as long as this does not lead one to neglect one's own affairs'.[107] According to Gramsci, Alberti's political abstinence amounts to an effective endorsement of the Catholic Church, 'which is the de facto federal centre, due to its intellectual and political hegemony'. Thus Alberti embodies an Italian bourgeois current of thought that is linked to the 'Guelphs' (followers of the Pope),[108] whereas a different, Ghibelline (pro-imperial) current, led by Machiavelli, looked to the founding of a strong nation state and opposed the predominance of the Catholic church for this reason.[109]

When one reconsiders the debate between Weber and Sombart from the perspective of Gramsci's hegemony-theoretical framing of the problem, one notices a *strength* of Weber's argument that he is not able to make full use of given the way the debate is conducted, as an inquiry into the origins of capitalism formulated in terms of the history of ideas. Unlike Sombart, Weber has a precise intuitive grasp of the difference between a private-bourgeois tradesman's spirit and an expansive ideology that is bound up with the rise of the bourgeoisie and aims at a reconfiguration of the way society is organised, as well as of people's entire life conduct and subjectivity. Not only is Sombart not interested in this difference, which is of key importance from the point of view of the theory of hegemony, but the way he conceptualises the two components of his 'capitalist spirit' renders them virtually useless as ethical sources of a hegemony encompassing all of society: Sombart's 'spirit of enterprise' is too strongly informed by the images of the avaricious and violent adventurer, and the virtues of his 'bourgeois spirit' are tailored to the existence of the private *borghese*, to whom Sombart attributes petty-mindedness and miserliness. These descriptions also disarticulate the project of renewing bourgeois hegemony during the transition to Fordism—a project with regard to which

---

106    Gramsci 1996, p. 338: compare Gramsci 1975a, pp. 614–15; Gramsci 1975c, pp. 1912–14.

107    Alberti 1969, p. 177; Alberti 1960, p. 233.

108    The party of the Guelphs was founded in response to the *Trecento*'s social tensions, giving direct expression to the political influence of the 'major dynasties', without the mediation of the guilds (Deppe 1987, p. 163). Alberti's critique of papal avarice is part of a larger, successful attempt to win the Pope as a 'friend', in spite of his bad character; after all, one had financially supported his assumption of office (Alberti 1969, p. 261; Alberti 1960, p. 364). Alberti himself held an office within the Roman curia for thirty years, from 1432 onward (see the introduction to the German edition of Alberti: Alberti 1962, p. VII).

109    Gramsci 1996, pp. 337–8; Gramsci 1975c, pp. 1912–14.

Sombart, to whom Schmoller attributes an 'aestheticising Epicureanism',[110] corresponds to the intellectual type of the *Renaissance man*.

Weber, by contrast, appears as an ethico-political *reformer* who wishes to modernise German capitalism according to a Puritan-Americanist model. His opposition to the bourgeoisie's corporatist consciousness, evident on the first pages of the *Protestant Ethic* (see above, Chapter 24.5), finds its logical sequel in the debate with Sombart. The bourgeois qua *borghese* is neither willing nor able to spark off an ethico-political movement, and this is as true of him in the Renaissance period as it is in Weber's day. What emerges is a hegemonic project that links the ethical requirements of the pending Fordist modernisation of the economy, the state and civil society to a radical transformation that is supposed to assume, differently from the aristocratic Renaissance, the character of a popular movement.

But what is the significance, in terms of the theory of hegemony, of the fact that Weber subsumes, under the rubric of a 'spirit of capitalism', the popular-national qualities Gramsci discusses from the point of view of the subaltern classes achieving hegemony? I can only provide a rough, concluding sketch of how Weber tailors the religious movements whose 'economic ethic' he claims to analyse to fit under the bonnet of his capitalist modernisation project.

---

110    Quoted in Brocke 1987, p. 146.

# CHAPTER 30

# Outlook: The Social Components of Weber's Orientalist Sociology of Religion

As we have seen in the preceding chapters, the currents of 'ascetic Protestantism' are selected and treated in such a way as to fit effortlessly into the readymade ideal type 'spirit of capitalism'. The latter is defined as Protestant from the outset, and the way the Protestant currents are presented makes it seem as if they led necessarily to capitalism. Thus they also correspond to the ideal type's implicit rules of composition, which we were able to identify most clearly when contrasting Weber with Sombart. What is established in advance is that the spirit sought for has been purged of capitalism's reality of domination and that it initially emerges *from within* (from the depths of religious consciousness), before it becomes an iron cage. Moreover, Weber sets the spirit of capitalism off sharply against the business logics of mercantile capital, defining it as a feature of an industrialism that arises from within the middle class. Another ideal-typical component links the spirit of capitalism to an expansive bourgeois mass movement, thereby drawing a line of division between it and the mere business sense of the private citizen. Easy reception of the concept is assured by virtue of the fact that the capitalist spirit can oscillate arbitrarily between the capitalist ethos of valorisation, the pursuit of monetary gain and a work ethic, as long as Weber has identified its psychological motive as ascetic-Protestant.

What is especially consequential with regard to the arrangement of Weber's religio-historical material is the link he posits between capitalist spirit and mass movement: because Weber conceptualises the capitalist spirit in such a way that it includes—differently from Alberti's 'literati'—the hegemonic efficacy of popular-national movements, he needs to ensure in turn that these movements coincide with the capitalist spirit. To be sure, this is a precarious undertaking, since the religious movements invoked by Weber partly owed their popular anchorage to the oppositional articulations by which they condemned early capitalism's 'mammonism' and its 'societies monopolia' (Luther). Within the framework of the ideal-typical conceptual set-up, there are only two ways of solving this problem: either the anticapitalist articulations are taken note of and excluded from the spirit of capitalism as instances of 'traditionalism', or they are repressed and neutralised, so that the religious current they are associated with can be interpreted in terms of the 'spirit of capitalism'.

In the *Protestant Ethic*, the first method is exemplarily evident in Weber's ambivalent depiction of Luther. On the one hand, Weber adopts the prevailing cultural Protestant interpretations (particularly those of Ritschl and Eger), which consider the concept of vocation as found in Luther's Bible translation the basis of the modern notion of an intramundane vocation;[1] on the other hand, Weber concludes that because of its 'traditionalist' economic ethic, Luther's worldview is in no way internally related to the spirit of capitalism.[2] Weber justifies this claim by arguing that Luther bases his critique of usury and interest on a 'conception of the nature of capitalistic acquisition', i.e. on one that is (from the capitalist standpoint) 'definitely backward', and in particular on the notion of the unproductive nature of money.[3] Weber makes reference to Luther's 1540 'admonishment' *To the Clergy, to Preach Against Usury*, which invokes the Aristotelian argument that money does not increase by itself and cannot bear fruit like a tree or a field.[4]

Such articulations gave Marx cause to exploit the analytic and polemical wealth of Luther's critique of money and put it to use in his own critique of the capitalist mode of production. Marx sees the strength of Luther's critique of usury as consisting, among other things, in the fact that it is directed not against money lending alone (like Proudhon's critique), but more principally against the transformation of money from a mere means of circulation (C–M–C) into the end-in-itself of commodity circulation (M–C–M'); in other words, it is directed not just against usurious, but also against mercantile capital.[5] Marx uncovers a critique of capitalism whose arguments are formulated from the perspective of small-scale, use-value-oriented commodity production; in Weber, this very critique and its social content are rendered invisible by means of the concept of 'traditionalism', which is applied both to Luther's indebtedness to the Bible's condemnation of the 'godless' pursuit of economic gain and

---

1   Weber 1950, pp. 79ff, 84–5. The passages cited in support of this interpretation are 1 Corinthians 7, 20 and Jesus Sirach 11, 20–1. However, a closer textual comparison shows that Weber projects his semantics of vocation back from the eighteenth and nineteenth centuries to the sixteenth century.

2   Weber 1950, p. 80.

3   Weber 1950, pp. 72–3.

4   Luther 1914, p. 360; compare Aristotle, *Politics*, 1257 and 1258.

5   See for example the careful appraisals of the 'dean of German political economists' in the *Grundrisse*, the *Contribution to the Critique of Political Economy, Theories of Surplus Value* and *Capital*: Marx and Engels 1975–2005, vol. 29, pp. 448, 378, 364; Marx 1969–71b, pp. 527ff; Marx and Engels 1975–2005, vol. 35, p. 199; vol. 37, pp. 230, 391–2.

to his orientation towards state authority following the break with Müntzer.[6] As in his interventions into the politics of his day, Weber identifies both conservative submission to authority and use-value-oriented anticapitalism with 'traditionalism'. While Weber requires the Reformation's popularity for his project of capitalist modernisation, he is not interested in discovering its social causes or its revolutionary dynamic.[7]

Weber already applies his second method to the theological starting point of his account, the doctrine of 'double predestination' (i.e. predestination both of the elect and of the damned). This doctrine was not, however, invented by Calvin; it was first theologically elaborated by Augustine and mainly represented, within the Catholic tradition, by Jansenism. The dogma's century-old pre-Protestant history is enough to render problematic the determining role Weber attributes to it with regard to the emergence of the spirit of capitalism. His reductive focus on the bourgeoisie can here be seen from the fact that out of the many different applications of the Calvinist doctrine of predetermination, he only mentions its application to the salvation of the *individual* believer. And yet he must have known, e.g. from the book by Max Scheibe he cites,[8] that in the first edition of his 1536 *Institutio*, Calvin applied the notion of predestination primarily to the collective subject that was the new church qua community of the saved: because the salvation of the elect is rooted in God's eternal providence, the members of this community can never lose their state of grace, Calvin writes, which is to say that whatever setbacks they may suffer, they will never fall prey to damnation. The correlative notion of eternal damnation is logically assumed, but it remains 'in the background', at least initially, and is only 'touched upon in passing'.[9] The argument is part and parcel of intense interpellations that call on believers to consider themselves elect, and it serves the function of deterministically buttressing the confidence and perseverance of the communities of religious refugees. In contrast with that of later Calvinism, early Calvinism's notion of predestination referred not so much to the successful individual as to the new ecclesiastical community, at the heart of which stood the city of Geneva as the 'new Jerusalem', besieged and eventually liberated.[10] What Weber overlooks is that Calvin's concept of predestination has a semantic thread woven into it that linked the experience

---

6    Weber 1950, pp. 82ff.

7    See for example Blickle's studies of the 'communalist' dynamic of the 'communal Reformation' (Blickle 1987 and Blickle 1992).

8    Weber 1950, p. 103, note 13.

9    Scheibe 1897, pp. 9, 14.

10   See Bürgin 1960, pp. 144, 145–6.

of the Calvinists' Europe-wide persecution to the persecuted's chiliastic fanta-
sies of reversal as articulated in the Revelation of St. John. With reference to the
secularised Marxist variant of such determinism, Gramsci spoke of the form of
religion proper to the subaltern, and in spite of all his criticisms, he insisted
that given unfavourable relations of power, this form of religion can become
'a formidable force of moral resistance, of cohesion, of patient perseverance'.[11]
By gearing everything to the 'spirit of capitalism', Weber fails to do justice to
this popular dynamic, reductively eliminating the social polyvalence of his
religious material.

   When dealing with the religious, Weber consistently abstracts from the
aspect Marx described as the 'sigh of the oppressed creature' and *'protest
against real suffering'*.[12] This is especially clear in the case of the Baptists,
whose gospel of poverty had prompted Ritschl to identify them as precur-
sors of Social Democracy and exclude them from Protestantism (see above,
Chapter 25.4). When Weber rehabilitates them as the 'second independent
source of Protestant asceticism',[13] he does so at the cost of eliding their origins
in the popular Reformation. The image of the Baptism he presents is that of a
placid quietism; he eliminates everything about the Baptist movement that
was eschatological and looked to the establishment of the 'kingdom of God'
in a social revolutionary sense. According to Weber, the basis of the Baptist
ethic consists of the attitude of 'silent waiting'; by his silence, the believer
brings about the 'deep repose of the soul in which alone the word of God can
be heard'.[14] Weber explicitly disregards the 'half-communistic communities of
the early period',[15] even though the 'silent waiting' of the Baptists, their retreat
from a 'godless' world, cannot be understood without consideration of the preceding failure of their 'kingdom-of-God' utopias (both in the military defeats of
the Peasant War in 1525 and in the 1535 suppression of the Münster commune).[16]
Here as elsewhere, Weber employs the method that Gramsci criticised Croce's
*History of Europe* for: he retains only the 'passive' aspect of the revolution and
disregards the aspect of struggle, through which a new ethico-political system

11    Gramsci 2007, p. 353; Gramsci 1975b, p. 1389.
12    Marx and Engels 1975–2005, vol. 3, p. 175.
13    Weber 1950, p. 144.
14    Weber 1950, pp. 148–9.
15    Weber 1959, p. 149.
16    On this, see for example the analyses of Goertz (Goertz 1987 and Goertz 1988).

emerges.[17] He is interested only in what remains when the 'intensity of the search for the Kingdom of God' yields gradually to 'sober economic virtue'.[18]

If in Weber's account Calvinism's primary effect is that of unleashing the acquisitive energy of private commerce, then a Baptism become bourgeois shapes the virtues of economic honesty ('honesty is the best policy').[19] As Weber argues (and as will later be argued more elaborately by Troeltsch), this is the stable combination that constitutes 'ascetic Protestantism' as a type, thereby giving rise to the modern lifestyle and personality type of 'Americanism'.[20] Within this religio-historical set-up, one can clearly discern the two components of the productivist alliance between the industrial bourgeoisie and the worker aristocracy that Weber and other German 'modernisers' are working to promote: Fordism's historical bloc is the hidden *telos* of the *Protestant Ethic*. Whatever stands in the way of this bloc's formation is eliminated from the religio-historical material. As in politics, Weber distances himself from both a 'lofty' and a 'lowly' rival: from social-conservative, statist or detached ideologies that correspond to the 'Renaissance' model and lack the cohesive force to achieve the requisite popular support, and from resistant, popular-democratic or revolutionary tendencies that might threaten the integration of the subaltern into the envisioned historical bloc.

What does this mean for the theoretical set-up of Weber's comparative 'Economic Ethic of World Religions'? It is obvious that the combination of ascetic Protestantism and capitalist spirit, which turned out to be a religious articulation of an anticipated historical bloc of Fordism, is not only the main subject of the *Protestant Ethic*, but also the *telos* of Weber's subsequent studies on the world religions. The capitalistic class bias incorporated in the ideal-type of 'occidental rationalisation' is projected upon a global stage and reveals itself as a Eurocentrism that looks at the non-European cultures with the declared objective of demonstrating the social and (primarily) religious causes of their *deficit*, namely their inability to engender a Western type of capitalist spirit. To portray non-European cultures as 'others' caught in a constitutive 'state of minority', fundamentally lacking the ethical qualities of the European model, is of course a fundamental characteristic of what Edward Said has analysed

---

17    Gramsci 1975b, p. 1227.

18    Weber 1950, p. 176.

19    Weber 1950, pp. 150–1.

20    Both Weber (Weber 1950, p. 53) and Troeltsch (Troeltsch 1960, pp. 577–8) mention the personality type of 'Americanism'. One of Troeltsch's merits, vis-à-vis Weber's account in the *Protestant Ethic*, is that he distinguishes between early and later manifestations both of Calvinism and of Baptism.

as 'Orientalism'. According to Said, 'Weber's studies of Protestantism, Judaism and Buddhism blew him (perhaps unwittingly) into the very territory originally charted and claimed by the Orientalists'.[21] Sara Farris has used Said's approach and shown that Weber's ideal-typical construction of the economic ethic of world religions is intimately intertwined with an Orientalist view that denied that the non-European cultures could develop a 'personality'.[22] Andrew Zimmerman analysed Weber's comparative studies on world religions as a culturalist sublimation of his earlier, predominantly anti-Polish racism: 'Weber used religion as other thinkers used race, to characterise and explain the politics, economics, and psychology of fixed populations... Culture functions just as effectively to reduce history to an elaboration of stereotyped identities'.[23] As in other Orientalist approaches, the construct of the 'other' is used to define the European 'self'. Weber's comparison of world religions is a Eurocentric monologue that explains the global supremacy of the 'West' in terms of the inner ethical virtues of its leading *culture bearers*. Weber is thus doing what he himself has analysed as a 'theodicy of good fortune' by which the fortunate need to know that they have a right to their good fortune and thus deserve it.[24]

Yet Weber is projecting not just a capitalist and Eurocentric perspective onto the screen of religious world history, but also a specific Fordist class alliance between bourgeoisie and labour aristocracy. This allows us to situate his conceptual arrangement more precisely. In fact, the ideal-typical construct of a Western rationalisation of the religious that extends from the 'giants' of the Old Testament prophets to ascetic Protestantism displays similar requirements as the historical bloc of Fordism: the class foundation needs to be 'urban' and 'bourgeois' (or proto-bourgeois), and the intellectual agents need to be organically linked to the people without becoming revolutionary. If both the 'literati' of Confucianism, who in their doctrine of 'adjustment to the world' represent the bureaucratic civil servants of Weber's time, and the 'world-rejecting' prophets of Hinduism and Buddhism stalled the development of a 'spirit of capitalism', one important reasons for this was—on Weber's view—their failure to establish an effective hegemony over the lower strata of the populace, which therefore remained stuck in 'magic'. Conversely, Weber also holds that

---

21    Said 2003, p. 259.

22    Farris 2010b, and 2013. See Weber 1951, p. 235; Weber 1958, p. 342.

23    Zimmerman 2006, p. 68; see Zimmerman 2010, pp. 216–17. See also Hund 2010 and Hund 2014.

24    Weber 1942, p. 271; see Enrique Dussel's analysis of Eurocentric accounts of 'modernity' that transform a phenomenon proper to the system centre-periphery into a manifestation of inner ethical qualities (1998, pp. 4ff).

all chiliasm up until the Baptist revolution is based on an irrational *loss* of faith, by which 'the belief is dropped that an everlasting tension exists between the world and the irrational metaphysical realm of salvation'.[25] By writing eschatological hopes off as irrational desires for revenge, rather than considering them an expression of irrational circumstances, Weber 'brands chiliasm—or innerworldly hope in its most concentrated form—as irrational and surgically removes it from the history of rationalism', Kippenberg notes critically.[26]

It is here, in this surgical removal of the 'sigh of the oppressed creature', that the relevant opposition between Weber's and Marx's treatments of religious matters is to be found. It is an opposition between different research perspectives, and ultimately between the underlying social projects. But the dichotomy of religious ethic and economic basis that both determinist Marxists and Weber epigones feel at home in to this day is part of an outdated paradigm. Gramsci proposed a more fruitful approach: that of transferring decontextualised complexes of ideas back into the functional relations of ideological instances. Considered from this perspective, Weber's main contribution is that of having demonstrated the relative autonomy and efficacy of the religious, not least in regards to the anticipation of future constellations. A reinterpretation of Weber's sociology of religion in terms of the theory of hegemony must preserve this strength while simultaneously overcoming the often speculative character of Weber's theo-psychological deduction. The most important task for such a reinterpretation would however be that of freeing research from the narrow, bourgeois-capitalist and 'cultural Protestant' focus that Weber has given it.

---

25    Weber 1946c, p. 340; MWG I/19, p. 499.
26    Kippenberg 1991, p. 79, note 45.

# Bibliography

Abendroth, Wolfgang 1975, 'Demokratie als Institution und Aufgabe', in *Arbeiterklasse, Staat und Verfassung*, Frankfurt on the Main: Europäische Verlagsanstalt.

Adorno, Theodor W. and Max Horkheimer 1997 [1947], *Dialectic of Enlightenment*, London: Verso.

Alberti, Leon Battista 1960 [1433–41], *I libri della famiglia*, in *Opere volgari*, volume 1, Bari: Laterza.

———— 1962 [1433–41], *Über das Hauswesen: Übersetzt von Walther Kraus*, Zürich: Artemis.

———— 1969 [1433–41], *The Family in Renaissance Florence: A translation by Renée Neu Watkins of* I Libri Della Famiglia *by Leon Battista Alberti, with an Introduction by the translator*, Columbia: University of South Carolina Press.

Aldenhoff, Rita 1988, 'Max Weber und der Evangelisch-soziale Kongress', in *Max Weber und seine Zeitgenossen*, edited by Wolfgang J. Mommsen and Wolfgang Schwentker, Göttingen: Vandenhoeck & Ruprecht.

Althusser, Louis 1971, 'Ideology and Ideological State Apparatuses', in *Lenin and Philosophy, and Other Essays*, London: New Left Books.

Althusser, Louis and Étienne Balibar 1997 [1965], *Reading Capital*, London: Verso.

Amelung, Eberhard 1976, 'Kulturprotestantismus', in *Historisches Wörterbuch der Philosophie*, edited by J. Ritter and K. Gründer, Basel: Schwabe.

Anderson, Perry 1976, *The Antinomies of Antonio Gramsci*, London: New Left Books.

———— 1979, *Lineages of the Absolute State*, London: Verso.

Anter, Andreas 1995, *Max Webers Theorie des modernen Staates, Herkunft, Struktur und Bedeutung*, Berlin: Duncker & Humblot.

Apel, Karl 1939, *Die soziale Frage im Lichte der Verhandlungen des Evangelisch-sozialen Kongresses*, Dissertation, Marburg University.

Appel, Michael 1987, 'Der "Moderne Kapitalismus" im Urteil zeitgenössischer Besprechungen', in *Sombarts 'Moderner Kapitalismus': Materialien zur Kritik und Rezeption*, edited by Bernhard vom Brocke, Munich: Deutscher Taschenbuch Verlag.

———— 1992, *Werner Sombart: Historiker und Theoretiker des modernen Kapitalismus*, Marburg: Metropolis.

Assoun, Paul-Laurent 1984, 'Cognition', in *Dictionnaire critique du marxisme*, edited by Georges Labica and Gérard Bensussan, Paris: Presses universitaires de France.

———— 1985, 'Loi', in *Dictionnaire critique du marxisme*, edited by Georges Labica and Gérard Bensussan, Paris: Presses universitaires de France.

Aston, Trevor (ed.) 1965, *Crisis in Europe 1560–1660: Essays from 'Past and Present'*, London: Routledge & Kegan Paul.

Baden, Max 1927, *Erinnerungen und Dokumente*, Berlin: Ritter.

Bader, Michael, Johannes Berger, Heiner Ganssman and Jost v. d. Knesebeck 1987 [1976], *Einführung in die Gesellschaftstheorie: Gesellschaft, Wirtschaft und Staat bei Marx und Weber*, Frankfurt on the Main: Campus.

Bailey, Edward 1985, *Civil Religion in Britain*, Bristol: Network for the Study of Implicit Religion.

Bailyn, Bernard 1965, *The New England Merchants in the Seventeenth Century*, Cambridge: Harvard University Press.

Baratella, Nils and Jan Rehmann 2005, 'Kritik in postkritischen Zeiten—Zu Boltanski/Chiapello: *Der neue Geist des Kapitalismus*', *Das Argument*, 261: 376–88.

Baratta, Giorgio 1900, '"Die Hegemonie geht aus der Fabrik hervor": Gramsci zu Amerikanismus und Sozialismus', in *Utopie und Zivilgesellschaft: Rekonstruktionen, Thesen und Informationen zu Antonio Gramsci*, edited by Uwe Hirschfeld und Hartmut Rügemer, Berlin: Elefanten Press.

Barbalet, Jack 2008, *Weber, Passion and Profits: 'The Protestant Ethic and the Spirit of Capitalism' in Context*, Cambridge: Cambridge University Press.

Barkin, Kenneth D. 1970, *The Controversy over German Industrialization, 1890–1902*, Chicago: University of Chicago Press.

Baron, Hans 1992 [1988], *Bürgersinn und Humanismus im Florenz der Renaissance*, Berlin: Wagenbach.

Barth, Karl 1960 [1946], *Die protestantische Theologie im 19. Jahrhundert: Ihre Vorgeschichte und ihre Geschichte*, 2 volumes, Zürich: Evangelischer Verlag.

Bauer, Otto 1980 [1937], 'Max Adler. Ein Beitrag zur Geschichte des "Austromarxismus"', in Werkausgabe, volume 9, Vienna: Europa-Verlag.

Baumeister, Martin 1987, *Parität und katholische Inferiorität: Untersuchungen zur Stellung des Katholizismus im Deutschen Kaiserreich*, Paderborn: Schöningh.

Baumgarten, Eduard 1936, *Die geistigen Grundlagen des amerikanischen Gemeinwesens 1: Benjamin Franklin: Der Lehrmeister der amerikanischen Revolution*, Frankfurt on the Main: Klostermann.

———— 1964, *Max Weber: Werk und Person, Dokumente ausgewählt und kommentiert von Eduard Baumgarten*, Tübingen: Mohr.

Bebel, August 1911, *Aus meinem Leben: Zweiter Teil*, Stuttgart: Dietz.

Beetham, David 1988, 'Gaetano Mosca, Vilfredo Pareto und Max Weber: ein historischer Vergleich', in *Max Weber und seine Zeitgenossen*, edited by Wolfgang J. Mommsen and Wolfgang Schwentker, Göttingen: Vandenhoeck & Ruprecht.

Bellah, Robert N. 1978, 'Religion and the Legitimation of the American Republic', *Society*, 15, 4: 16–23.

———— 2002 [1967], 'Civil Religion in America', in *A Reader in the Anthropology of Religion*, edited by Michael Lambek, Oxford: Blackwell.

Bendix, Reinhard 1960, *Max Weber: An Intellectual Portrait*, Garden City, NY: Doubleday & Company, Inc.

Benseler, Gustav Eduard 1990, *Benselers griechisch-deutsches Schulwörterbuch, bearbeitet von Adolf Kaegi*, Leipzig: Teubner.

Bensussan, Gérard 1986, 'Crises du marxisme', in *Dictionnaire critique du marxisme*, edited by Georges Labica and Gérard Bensussan, Paris: Presses universitaires de France.

Berger, Johannes 1987 [1967/68], 'Historische Logik und Hermeneutik', in *Materialien zur Neukantianismus-Diskussion*, edited by Hans-Ludwig Ollig, Darmstadt: Wissenschaftliche Buchgesellschaft.

Berger, Stephen D. 1973 [1971], 'Die Sekten und der Durchbruch in die moderne Welt: Zur zentralen Bedeutung der Sekten in Webers Protestantismus-These', in *Seminar: Religion und gesellschaftliche Entwicklung, Studien zur Protestantismus-These Max Webers*, edited by Constans Seyfarth and Walter M. Sprondel, Frankfurt on the Main: Suhrkamp.

Bergmann, Theodor 1994, 'Agrarfrage', in *Historisch-Kritisches Wörterbuch des Marxismus*, edited by Wolfgang Fritz Haug, Frigga Haug and Peter Jehle, Hamburg: Argument.

Bernays, Marie 1912, 'Berufswahl und Berufsschicksal des modernen Industriearbeiters', *Archiv für Sozialwissenschaft und Sozialpolitik*, 35: 123–76.

Bharadwaj, Krishna and Sudipta Kaviraj (eds) 1989, *Perspectives on Capitalism: Marx, Keynes, Schumpeter and Weber*, New Delhi: Sage.

Blickle, Peter 1987, *Gemeindereformation: Die Menschen des 16. Jahrhunderts auf dem Weg zum Heil*, Studienausgabe, Munich: Oldenbourg.

——— 1992 [1982], *Die Reformation im Reich: Zweite, überarbeitete und erweiterte Auflage*, Stuttgart: Ulmer.

Bloch, Ernst 1974 [1954], 'Zweierlei Kant-Gedenkjahre', in *Immanuel Kant zu ehren*, edited by Joachim Kopper and Rudolf Malter, Frankfurt on the Main: Suhrkamp.

——— 1986 [1954], *The Principle of Hope*, Oxford: Blackwell.

Boltanski, Luc, and Ève Chiapello 2005, *The New Spirit of Capitalism*, London: Verso.

Böckler, Stefan and Johannes Weiß (eds) 1987, *Marx oder Weber? Zur Aktualisierung einer Kontroverse*, Opladen: Westdeutscher Verlag.

Boese, Franz 1939, *Geschichte des Vereins für Sozialpolitik 1782–1932, Im Auftrage des Liquidationsausschusses verfasst vom Schriftführer*, Berlin: Duncker & Humblot.

Borkenau, Franz 1971 [1934], *Der Übergang vom feudalen zum bürgerlichen Weltbild, Studien zur Geschichte der Manufakturperiode*, Darmstadt: Wissenschaftliche Buchgesellschaft.

Bosse, Hans 1970, *Marx, Weber, Troeltsch: Religionssoziologie und marxistische Ideologiekritik*, Munich: Kaiser.

Bourdieu, Pierre 2000, *Das religiöse Feld: Texte zur Ökonomie des Heilsgeschehens*, Konstanz: UVK.

Bracher, Karl Dietrich 1978, *Die Auflösung der Weimarer Republik: Eine Studie zum Problem des Machtverfalls in der Demokratie*, Königstein: Athenäum.

Braudel, Fernand 1979a, *Civilisation matérielle, économie et capitalisme, XVe–XVIIIe siècle, 1: Les structures du quotidien: Le possible et l'impossible*, Paris: Colin.

―――― 1979b, *Civilisation matérielle, économie et capitalisme, XVe–XVIIIe siècle, 2: Les jeux de l'échange*, Paris: Colin.

―――― 1979c, *Civilisation matérielle, économie et capitalisme, XVe–XVIIIe siècle, 3: Le temps du monde*, Paris: Colin.

Braunreuther, Kurt 1978, *Studien zur Geschichte der politischen Ökonomie und der Soziologie, Teil II*, Berlin: Akademie-Verlag.

Braverman, Harry 1974, *Labor and Monopoly Capital: The Degradation of Work in the Twentieth Century*, New York: Monthly Review.

Brecht, Bertolt 1968, *Gesammelte Werke 20: Schriften zur Politik und Gesellschaft*, Frankfurt on the Main: Suhrkamp.

―――― 1976 [1929–31], *Saint Joan of the Stockyards*, translated by Frank Jones, London: Methuen.

Brentano, Lujo 1871, *Die Arbeitergilden der Gegenwart 1: Zur Geschichte der englischen Gewerkvereine*, Leipzig: Duncker & Humblot.

―――― 1872, *Die Arbeitergilden der Gegenwart 2: Zur Kritik der englischen Gewerkvereine*, Leipzig: Duncker & Humblot.

―――― 1916, *Die Anfänge des modernen Kapitalismus: Festrede gehalten in der öffentlichen Sitzung der K. Akademie der Wissenschaften am 15. März 1913*, Munich: Verlag der K. B. Akademie der Wissenschaften.

Breuer, Stefan 1993, *Anatomie der konservativen Revolution*, Darmstadt: Wissenschaftliche Buchgesellschaft.

Breuilly, John 1988, 'Eduard Bernstein und Max Weber', in *Max Weber und seine Zeitgenossen*, edited by Wolfgang J. Mommsen and Wolfgang Schwentker, Göttingen: Vandenhoeck & Ruprecht.

Brocke, Bernhard von (ed.) 1987, *Sombarts 'Moderner Kapitalismus': Materialien zur Kritik und Rezeption*, Munich: Deutscher Taschenbuch Verlag.

Bröckling, Ulrich, Susanne Krasmann and Thomas Lemke (eds) 2000, *Gouvernementalität der Gegenwart: Studien zur Ökonomisierung des Sozialen*, Frankfurt on the Main: Suhrkamp.

Bruch, Rüdiger vom 1989, 'Kulturstaat—Sinndeutung von oben', in *Kultur und Kulturwissenschaften um 1900: Krise der Moderne und Glaube an die Wissenschaft*, edited by Rüdiger vom Bruch, Friedrich Wilhelm Graf and Gangolf Hübinger, Stuttgart: Steiner.

Brüggen, Willi 1999, 'Der verstummte Seufzer der bedrängten Kreatur, Moderne-Begriff: Jan Rehmanns Analyse von Max Webers Wertprinzipien', *Freitag* 28, July 9.

Buci-Glucksmann, Christine 1977, 'Über die politischen Probleme des Übergangs: Arbeiterklasse, Staat und passive Revolution', *Sopo (Sozialistische Politik)*, 41, 9.

———— 1980, *Gramsci and the State*, London: Lawrence and Wishart.

Buci-Glucksmann, Christine and Göran Therborn 1981, *Le défi social-démocrate*, Paris: Maspéro.

———— 1982, *Der sozialdemokratische Staat: Die 'Keynesianisierung' der Gesellschaft*, Hamburg: VSA.

Burger, Thomas 1976, *Max Weber's Theory of Concept Formation: History, Laws and Ideal Types*, Durham: Duke University Press.

Bürgin, Alfred 1960, *Kapitalismus und Calvinismus: Versuch einer wirtschaftsgeschichtlichen und religionssoziologischen Untersuchung der Verhältnisse in Genf im 16. und beginnenden 17. Jahrhundert*, Winterthur: Keller.

Burke, Peter 1984, *Die Renaissance in Italien*, Berlin: Wagenbach.

Cachon, Jean-Luc 1986, 'Nature', in *Dictionnaire critique du marxisme*, edited by Georges Labica and Gérard Bensussan, Paris: Presses universitaires de France.

Caire, Guy 1983, 'Aristocratie ouvrìere', in *Dictionnaire critique du marxisme*, edited by Georges Labica and Gérard Bensussan, Paris: Presses universitaires de France.

Conrad, Else 1906, *Der Verein für Socialpolitik und seine Wirksamkeit auf dem Gebiet der gewerblichen Arbeiterfrage*, Jena: Fischer.

Croce, Benedetto 1911, *La filosofia di Giambattista Vico*, Bari: Laterza.

———— 1921 [1915], *Theory and History of Historiography*, translated by Douglas Ainslie, London: Harrap.

———— 1926, *Cultura e vita morale: Intermezzi polemici*, Bari: Laterza.

———— 1929, *Storia dell'età barocca in Italia*, Bari: Laterza.

———— 1930, 'Theorie und Geschichte der Historiographie und Betrachtungen zur Philosophie der Politik, Nach der dritten Auflage', in *Gesammelte politische Schriften in deutscher Übertragung*, bearbeitet und übersetzt von H. Feist und R. Peters, volume I/4, Tübingen: Mohr.

———— 1935, *Geschichte Europas im neunzehnten Jahrhundert*, Zürich: Europa-Verlag.

———— 1951 [1896], *Materialismo storico ed economica marxistica*, Bari: Laterza.

———— 1953, *Storia d'europa nel secolo decimonono*, Bari: Laterza.

Cron, Ludwig 1900, *Glaubens-Bekenntnis und höheres Studium, Aus den Akten der Universitäten Heidelberg und Freiburg und der Technischen Hochschule Karlsruhe 1869–1893*, Heidelberg: Wolff.

Deichgräber, Karl 1971, *Charis und Chariten, Grazie und Grazien*, Munich: Heimeran.

Deppe, Frank 1987, *Niccolò Machiavelli: Zur Kritik der reinen Politik*, Cologne: Pahl-Rugenstein.

Deppe, Frank, Georg Fülberth and Jürgen Harrer (eds) 1978 [1977], *Geschichte der deutschen Gewerkschaftsbewegung*, Cologne: Pahl-Rugenstein.

D'Eramo, Marco 2002 [1995], *The Pig and the Skyscraper: Chicago, A History of Our Future*, London: Verso.

Dilthey, Wilhelm 1923, *Briefwechsel zwischen Wilhelm Dilthey und dem Grafen Paul Yorck v. Wartenburg 1877–1897*, Halle: Niemeyer.

——— 1924 [1895/96], 'Beiträge zum Studium der Individualität', in *Gesammelte Schriften*, volume v, Leipzig: Teubner.

——— 1924 [1894], 'Ideen über eine beschreibende und zergliedernde Psychologie', in *Gesammelte Schriften*, volume v, Leipzig: Teubner.

——— 1924b [1900], 'Die Entstehung der Hermeneutik', in *Gesammelte Schriften*, volume v, Leipzig: Teubner.

——— 1958 [1890], 'System der Ethik', in *Gesammelte Schriften*, volume x, Leipzig: Teubner.

——— 1989 [1883], *Introduction to the Human Sciences*, edited and with an Introduction by Rudolf A. Makkreel and Frithjof Rodi, Princeton: Princeton University Press.

——— 2002 [1910], *The Formation of the Historical World in the Human Sciences*, edited with an introduction by Rudolf A. Makkreel and Frithjof Rodi, Princeton: Princeton University Press.

Dobb, Maurice 1970, *Studies in the Development of Capitalism*, London: Routledge.

Dörrie, Heinrich 1981, Art. 'Gnade', in *Reallexikon für Antike und Christentum*, vol. 11, Stuttgart.

Downton, J.V. 1973, *Rebel Leadership: Commitment and Charisma in the Revolutionary Process*, New York: Free Press.

Du Bois, W.E.B. 1906, 'Die Negerfrage in den Vereinigten Staaten', *Archiv für Sozialwissenschaft und Sozialpolitik*, 22: 31–79.

Dussel, Enrique 1998, 'Beyond Eurocentrism: The World System and the Limits of Modernity', in *The Cultures of Civilization*, edited by Fredric Jameson and Masao Miyoshi, Durham and London: Duke University Press.

Ebbinghaus, Angelika 1984, *Arbeiter und Arbeitswissenschaft: Zur Entstehung der 'Wissenschaftlichen Betriebsführung'*, Opladen: Westdeutscher Verlag.

Ebertz, M.N. 1987, *Das Charisma des Gekreuzigten: Zur Soziologie der Jesusbewegung*, Tübingen: Mohr.

Ehrhard, Albert 1902, *Der Katholizismus und das zwanzigste Jahrhundert im Lichte der kirchlichen Entwicklung der Neuzeit*, Stuttgart: Roth.

Elias, Norbert 1939, *Über den Prozess der Zivilisation, Soziogenetische und psychogenetische Untersuchungen 1: Wandlungen des Verhaltens in den westlichen Oberschichten des Abendlandes*, Basle: Haus zum Falken.

Eliasberg, Wladimir 1966 [1926], 'Die Psychotechnik und die Motivationsstufen der Arbeit', in *Industriesoziologie I. Vorläufer und Frühzeit 1835–1934,* edited by Friedrich Fürstenberg, Neuwied: Luchterhand.

Farris, Sara 2010a: 'New and Old Spirits of Capitalism', *International Review of Social History,* 55, 2: 331–40.

———— 2010b, 'An "Ideal Type" Called Orientalism: Selective Affinities between Edward Said and Max Weber', *Interventions: International Journal of Postcolonial Studies,* 12, 2: 265–84.

———— 2013, *Max Weber's Theory of Personality: Individuation, Politics and Orientalism in the Sociology of Religion,* Leiden, Boston: Brill.

Feix, Nereu 1978, *Werturteil, Politik und Wirtschaft: Werturteilsstreit und Wissenschaftstransfer bei Max Weber,* Göttingen: Vandenhoeck & Ruprecht.

Feldman, Gerald D. 1974, 'Der deutsche Organisierte Kapitalismus während der Kriegs- und Inflationsjahre 1914–1923', in *Organisierter Kapitalismus: Voraussetzungen und Anfänge,* edited by Heinrich August Winkler, Göttingen: Vandenhoeck & Ruprecht.

Ferri, Franco (ed.) 1977, *Politica e storia in Gramsci: Atti del convegno internazionale di studi gramsciani, Firenze, 9–11 dicembre 1977,* volume 1: *Relazioni a stampa,* Rome: Editori riuniti.

Fischer, H. Karl 1978a [1907], 'Kritische Beiträge zu Professor Max Webers Abhandlung "Die Protestantische Ethik und der Geist des Kapitalismus", Replik auf Herrn Professor Max Webers Gegenkritik', in *Die protestantische Ethik II: Kritiken und Antikritiken,* edited by Johannes Winkelmann, Gütersloh: Mohn.

———— 1978b [1908], 'Protestantische Ethik und "Geist des Kapitalismus", Replik auf Herrn Professor Max Webers Gegenkritik', in *Die protestantische Ethik II. Kritiken und Antikritiken,* edited by Johannes Winkelmann, Gütersloh: Mohn.

Fischoff, Ephraim 1978 [1944], 'Die protestantische Ethik und der Geist des Kapitalismus: Die Geschichte einer Kontroverse', in *Die protestantische Ethik II: Kritiken und Antikritiken,* edited by Johannes Winkelmann, Gütersloh: Mohn.

Ford, Henry 1922, *My Life and Work,* Garden City: Doubleday.

Foster, John, Brett Belamy and Richard Clark York 2010, *The Ecological Rift: Capitalism's War on the Earth,* New York: Monthly Review Press.

Fraenkel, Ernst (ed.) 1959, *Amerika im Spiegel des deutschen politischen Denkens: Äußerungen deutscher Staatsmänner und Staatsdenker über Staat und Gesellschaft in den Vereinigten Staaten von Amerika,* Cologne: Westdeutscher Verlag.

Frank, Andre Gunder 1977, 'On So-Called Primitive Accumulation', *Dialectical Anthropology,* 2: 87–106.

Franklin, Benjamin 1904a [1748], 'Advice to a young Tradesman', in *The Works of Benjamin Franklin in Twelve Volumes,* compiled and edited by John Bigelow, volume 2, New York: Putnam.

——— 1904b [1736], 'Necessary hints to those who would be rich', in *The Works of Benjamin Franklin in Twelve Volumes*, compiled and edited by John Bigelow, volume 2, New York: Putnam.

——— 1904c [1791/93], 'Autobiography', in *The Works of Benjamin Franklin in Twelve Volumes*, compiled and edited by John Bigelow, volume 1, New York: Putnam.

——— 1904d [1728], 'Articles of Belief and Acts of Religion', in *The Works of Benjamin Franklin in Twelve Volumes*, compiled and edited by John Bigelow, volume 1, New York: Putnam.

——— 1904e [1728]: 'Rules for a Club Established for Mutual Improvement', in *The Works of Benjamin Franklin in Twelve Volumes*, compiled and edited by John Bigelow, volume 1, New York: Putnam.

Freud, Sigmund 1949 [1921], *Group Psychology and the Analysis of the Ego*, New York: Liveright.

Friemert, Chup 1980, 'Die Organisation des Ideologischen als betriebliche Praxis', in *Faschismus und Ideologie*, edited by Projekt Ideologietheorie, Berlin: Argument.

Frisby, David 1988, 'Die Ambiguität der Moderne: Max Weber und Georg Simmel', in *Max Weber und seine Zeitgenossen*, edited by Wolfgang J. Mommsen and Wolfgang Schwentker, Göttingen: Vandenhoeck & Ruprecht.

Fürstenberg, Friedrich (ed.) 1966, *Industriesoziologie I: Vorläufer und Frühzeit 1835–1934*, Neuwied: Luchterhand.

Gabriel, Hans-Jürgen 1975, *Christlichkeit der Gesellschaft? Eine kritische Darstellung der Kulturphilosophie von Ernst Troeltsch*, Berlin: Union.

Gadamer, Hans-Georg 2004 [1960], *Truth and Method*, London: Continuum.

Galling, Kurt and Hans von Campenhausen (eds) 1957–65, *Die Religion in Geschichte und Gegenwart*, Tübinen: Mohr.

Giancotti, Emilia 1995, 'Determinismus I', in *Historisch-Kritisches Wörterbuch des Marxismus*, edited by Wolfgang Fritz Haug, Frigga Haug and Peter Jehle, Hamburg: Argument.

Gneuss, Christian and Jürgen Kocka (eds) 1988, *Max Weber: Ein Symposium*, Munich: Deutscher Taschenbuch Verlag.

Goertz, Hans-Jürgen 1987, *Pfaffenhass und groß Geschrei: Die reformatorischen Bewegungen in Deutschland 1517–1529*, Munich: Beck.

——— 1988, *Die Täufer: Geschichte und Deutung*, Munich: Beck.

Goetze, Dieter 1987, *Castro—Nkrumah—Sukarno: Eine vergleichende soziologische Untersuchung zur Strukturanalyse charismatischer politischer Führung*, Berlin: Reimer.

Gorges, Irmela 1980, *Sozialforschung in Deutschland 1872–1914, Gesellschaftliche Einflüsse auf Themen und Methodenwahl des Vereins für Socialpolitik*, Königstein: Hain.

Göhre, Paul 1896, *Die evangelisch-soziale Bewegung, Ihre Geschichte und ihre Ziele*, Leipzig: Grunow.

—— 1913 [1891], *Drei Monate Fabrikarbeiter und Handwerksbursche*, Leipzig. Grunow.

Gosh, Peter 2008, *A Historian Reads Max Weber. Essays on the Protestant Ethic*, Wiesbaden: Harrassowitz Verlag.

Graf, Friedrich Wilhelm 1984, 'Kulturprotestantismus: Zur Begriffsgeschichte einer theologiepolitischen Chiffre', *Archiv für Begriffsgeschichte*, 28: 214–68.

—— 1987, 'Max Weber und die protestantische Theologie seiner Zeit', *Zeitschrift für Religions- und Geistesgeschichte*, year 39.

—— 1988, 'Fachmenschenfreundschaft: Bemerkungen zu "Max Weber und Ernst Troeltsch" ', in *Max Weber und seine Zeitgenossen*, edited by Wolfgang J. Mommsen and Wolfgang Schwentker, Göttingen: Vandenhoeck & Ruprecht.

—— 1989, 'Rettung der Persönlichkeit: Protestantische Theologie als Kulturwissenschaft des Christentums', in *Kultur und Kulturwissenschaften um 1900: Krise der Moderne und Glaube an die Wissenschaft*, edited by Rüdiger vom Bruch, Friedrich Wilhelm Graf and Gangolf Hübinger, Stuttgart: Steiner.

—— 1990, 'Kulturprotestantismus', in *Theologische Realenzyklopädie*, edited by Gerhard Krause and Gerhard Müller, Berlin: De Gruyter.

—— 1993, 'The German Theological Sources and Protestant Church Politics', in *Weber's Protestant Ethic: Origins, Evidence, Contexts*, edited by Hartmut Lehmann and Guenther Roth, New York: Cambridge University Press.

Graf, Friedrich Wilhelm and Klaus Tanner 1990, 'Kultur II. Theologiegeschichtlich', in *Theologische Realenzyklopädie*, edited by Gerhard Krause and Gerhard Müller, Berlin: De Gruyter.

Graf, Ruedi 2001, 'Review of Jan Rehmann, *Max Weber: Modernisierung als passive Revolution*', *Widerspruch*, 40: 194–8.

Gramsci, Antonio 1965, *Lettere dal carcere*, Turin: Einaudi.

—— 1966, *La questione meridionale*, Rome: Editori riuniti.

—— 1971, *Costruzione del partito comunista*, Turin: Einaudi.

—— 1975a [1929–32], *Quaderni del carcere, Volume primo: Quaderni 1–5 (1929–1932)*, Turin: Einaudi.

—— 1975b [1930–3], *Quaderni del carcere, Volume secondo: Quaderni 6–11 (1930–1933)*, Turin: Einaudi.

—— 1975c [1932–5], *Quaderni del carcere, Volume terzo: Quaderni 12–29 (1932–1935)*, Turin: Einaudi.

—— 1992 [1929–35], *Prison Notebooks*, edited with introduction by Joseph A. Buttigieg, translated by Joseph A. Buttigieg and Antonio Callari, volume 1, New York: Columbia University Press.

———— 1995 [1930–3], *Gefängnishefte 6: Philosophie der Praxis, Hefte 10–11*, Herausgegeben von Wolfgang Fritz Haug, Hamburg: Argument.

———— 1996 [1929–35], *Prison Notebooks*, edited with introduction by Joseph A. Buttigieg, translated by Joseph A. Buttigieg and Antonio Callari, volume 2, New York: Columbia University Press.

———— 2007 [1929–35], *Prison Notebooks*, edited with introduction by Joseph A. Buttigieg, translated by Joseph A. Buttigieg and Antonio Callari, volume 3, New York: Columbia University Press.

Greiff, Bodo von 1976, *Gesellschaftsform und Denkform. Zum Zusammenhang von wissenschaftlicher Erfahrung und gesellschaftlicher Entwicklung*, Frankfurt on the Main: Campus.

Haacke, Stephanie 1994, *Zuteilen und Vergelten: Figuren der Gerechtigkeit bei Aristoteles*, Vienna: Turia & Kant.

Habermas, Jürgen 1984 [1981], *The Theory of Communicative Action 1: Reason and the Rationalization of Society*, translated by Thomas McCarthy, Boston: Beacon Press.

———— 1987a [1981], *The Theory of Communicative Action 2: Lifeworld and System, A Critique of Functionalist Reason*, Boston: Beacon Press.

———— 1987b [1968], *Knowledge and Human Interests*, translated by Jeremy J. Shapiro, Cambridge: Polity Press.

———— 1987c [1968], 'Technology and Science as Ideology', in *Toward a Rational Society*, translated by Jeremy J. Shapiro, Cambridge: Polity Press.

Hahn, Barbara 2006, 'Review of Radkau, *Max Weber: Die Leidenschaft des Denkens*', *Sehepunkte: Rezensionsjournal für Geschichtswissenschaften*, 6, 2, available at www .sehepunkte.de/2006/02/9048.html.

Haug, Frigga 1988, 'Rosa Luxemburg und die Politik der Frauen', in *Küche und Staat: Die Politik der Frauen*, edited by Frigga Haug and Kornelia Hauser, Berlin: Argument.

———— 1994, 'Arbeit', in *Historisch-Kritisches Wörterbuch des Marxismus*, edited by Wolfgang Fritz Haug, Frigga Haug and Peter Jehle, Hamburg: Argument.

———— 2003, ' "Schaffen wir einen neuen Menschentyp": Von Henry Ford zu Peter Hartz', *Das Argument*, 252: 606–17.

———— 2007, *Rosa Luxemburg und die Kunst der Politik*, Hamburg: Argument.

Haug, Frigga and Kornelia Hauser (eds) 1988, *Küche und Staat: Die Politik der Frauen*, edited by Frigga Haug and Kornelia Hauser, Berlin: Argument.

Haug, Wolfgang Fritz 1973 [1972], 'Die Bedeutung von Standpunkt und sozialistischer Perspektive für die Kritik der politischen Ökonomie', in *Bestimmte Negation, 'Das umwerfende Einverständnis des braven Soldaten Schwejk' und andere Aufsätze*, Frankfurt on the Main: Suhrkamp.

———— 1976 [1974], *Vorlesungen zur Einführung ins* Kapital, Cologne: Pahl-Rugenstein.

———— 1980, 'Standpunkt und Perspektive materialistischer Kulturtheorie', in *Materialistische Kulturtheorie und Alltagskultur*, edited by Wolfgang Fritz Haug and Kaspar Maase, Berlin: Argument.

———— 1984, 'Die Camera obscura des Bewusstseins: Kritik der Subjekt/Objekt-Artikulation im Marxismus', in *Die Camera obscura der Ideologie*, edited by Projekt Ideologietheorie, Berlin: Argument.

———— 1986, *Die Faschisierung des bürgerlichen Subjekts: Die Ideologie der gesunden Normalität und die Ausrottungspolitiken im deutschen Faschismus, Materialanalysen*, Berlin: Argument.

———— 1987, 'Nach dem Fordismus: Post-Fordismus? Überlegungen im Anschluss an Jürgen Häusler und Joachim Hirsch', Das Argument, 165: 672–6.

———— 1989, 'Nicolai Hartmanns Neuordnung von Wert und Sinn', in *Deutsche Philosophen 1933*, edited by Wolfgang Fritz Haug, Hamburg: Argument.

———— 1993, *Elemente einer Theorie des Ideologischen*, Hamburg: Argument.

———— 1994, 'Abbild', in *Historisch-Kritisches Wörterbuch des Marxismus*, edited by Wolfgang Fritz Haug, Frigga Haug and Peter Jehle, Hamburg: Argument.

———— 1995a, 'Denkform', in *Historisch-Kritisches Wörterbuch des Marxismus*, edited by Wolfgang Fritz Haug, Frigga Haug and Peter Jehle, Hamburg: Argument.

———— 1995b, 'bestimmte Negation', in *Historisch-Kritisches Wörterbuch des Marxismus*, edited by Wolfgang Fritz Haug, Frigga Haug and Peter Jehle, Hamburg: Argument.

———— 1996a, 'Was kommt nach dem fordistischen Marxismus?', *Das Argument*, 214: 183–99.

———— 1996b, *Philosophieren mit Brecht und Gramsci*, Berlin: Argument.

———— 1997, 'ehern', in *Historisch-Kritisches Wörterbuch des Marxismus*, edited by Wolfgang Fritz Haug, Frigga Haug and Peter Jehle, Hamburg: Argument.

———— 1999, 'Eine neue Entschlüsselung Max Webers', *Sozialismus*, 26, 4: 55–6.

———— 2011, *Die kulturelle Unterscheidung: Elemente einer Philosophie des Kulturellen*, Hamburg: Argument.

Häusler, Jürgen and Joachim Hirsch 1987, 'Regulation und Parteien im Übergang zum "Post-Fordismus"', *Das Argument*, 165: 651–71.

Hegel, Georg Wilhelm Friedrich 1892 [1819–28], *Lectures on the History of Philosophy*, volume 1, London: Kegan Paul.

———— 1896 [1819–28], *Lectures on the History of Philosophy*, volume 3, London: Kegan Paul.

Heidegger, Martin 1962 [1927], *Being and Time*, New York: Harper.

Hennis, Wilhelm 1987, *Max Webers Fragestellung: Studien zur Biographie des Werks*, Tübingen: Mohr.

———— 1988, 'Eine "Wissenschaft vom Menschen": Max Weber und die deutsche Nationalökonomie der Historischen Schule', in *Max Weber und seine Zeitgenossen*, edited by Wolfgang J. Mommsen and Wolfgang Schwentker, Göttingen: Vandenhoeck & Ruprecht.

——— 1996, *Max Webers Wissenschaft vom Menschen: Neue Studien zur Biographie des Werks*, Tübingen: Mohr.

Henretta, James A. 1993, 'The Protestant Ethic and the Reality of Capitalism in Colonial America', in *Weber's Protestant Ethic: Origins, Evidence, Contexts*, edited by Hartmut Lehmann and Guenther Roth, New York: Cambridge University Press.

Henrich, Dieter 1952, *Die Einheit der Wissenschaftslehre Max Webers*, Tübingen: Mohr.

Herkommer, Sebastian 1998, 'Eine ideologietheoretische Max Weber-Lektüre', *Z. Zeitschrift Marxistische Erneuerung*, 36.

Hertling, Georg von 1899, *Das Princip des Katholizismus und die Wissenschaft: Grundsätzliche Erörterungen aus Anlass einer Tagesfrage*, Freiburg: Herder.

Heuer, Uwe-Jens 1995, 'Demokratie/Diktatur des Proletariats', in *Historisch-Kritisches Wörterbuch des Marxismus*, edited by Wolfgang Fritz Haug, Frigga Haug and Peter Jehle, Hamburg: Argument.

Hilferding, Rudolf 1915, 'Arbeitsgemeinschaft der Klassen?', *Der Kampf*, 8.

——— 1923 [1910], *Das Finanzkapital: Marx-Studien—Blätter zur Theorie und Politik des wissenschaftlichen Sozialismus*, Vienna: Volksbuchhandlung.

Hinrichs, Peter 1981, *Um die Seele des Arbeiters: Arbeitspsychologie, Industrie- und Betriebssoziologie in Deutschland 1871–1945*, Cologne: Pahl-Rugenstein.

Hintze, Otto 1929, 'Der moderne Kapitalismus als historisches Individuum: Ein kritischer Bericht über Sombarts Werk', *Historische Zeitschrift*, 139: 457–509.

Hirsch, Emanuel 1938, *Die Umformung des christlichen Denkens in der Neuzeit: Ein Lesebuch*, Tübingen: Mohr.

——— 1954 [1949], *Geschichte der neueren evangelischen Theologie im Zusammenhang mit den allgemeinen Bewegungen des europäischen Denkens*, volume 5, Gütersloh: Bertelsmann.

Hirsch, Joachim 1985, 'Auf dem Wege zum Postfordismus? Die aktuelle Neuformierung des Kapitalismus und ihre politischen Folgen', *Das Argument*, 151: 325–42.

——— 1990, *Kapitalismus ohne Alternative? Materialistische Gesellschaftstheorie und Möglichkeiten einer sozialistischen Politik heute*, Hamburg: VSA.

Hirsch, Joachim and Roland Roth 1986, *Das neue Gesicht des Kapitalismus: Vom Fordismus zum Post-Fordismus*, Hamburg: VSA.

Hirschfeld, Uwe and Werner Rügemer (eds) 1990, *Utopie und Zivilgesellschaft: Rekonstruktionen, Thesen und Informationen zu Antonio Gramsci*, Berlin: Elefanten Press.

Hobsbawm, Eric J. 1965 [1954], 'The crisis of the seventeenth century', in *Crisis in Europe 1560–1660: Essays from 'Past and Present'*, edited by Trevor Aston, London: Routledge & Kegan Paul.

Höfer, Josef and Karl Rahner (eds) 1957–65, *Lexikon für Theologie und Kirche*, Freiburg: Herder.

Holzkamp, Klaus 1983, *Grundlegung der Psychologie*, Frankfurt on the Main: Campus.

———— 1995, 'Alltägliche Lebensführung als subjektwissenschaftliches Grundkonzept', *Das Argument*, 212: 817–46.

Holzkamp-Osterkamp, Ute 1976, *Grundlagen der psychologischen Motivationsforschung 2: Die Besonderheit menschlicher Bedürfnisse—Problematik und Erkenntnisgehalt der Psychoanalyse*, Frankfurt on the Main: Campus.

Hübinger, Gangolf 1989, 'Kapitalismus und Kulturgeschichte', in *Kultur und Kulturwissenschaften um 1900: Krise der Moderne und Glaube an die Wissenschaft*, edited by Rüdiger vom Bruch, Friedrich Wilhelm Graf and Gangolf Hübinger, Stuttgart: Steiner.

———— 1994, *Kulturprotestantismus und Politik: Zum Verhältnis von Liberalismus und Protestantismus im wilhelminischen Deutschland*, Tübingen: Mohr.

Hund, Wulf D. 2010, 'Negative Societalisation: Racism and the Constitution of Race', in *Wages of Whiteness & Racist Symbolic Capital* edited by Wulf D. Hund, Jeremy Krikler, and David Roediger, Berlin: Lit.

———— 2014, 'Rassismus im soziologischen Denken: Von Adam Smith bis Max Weber', in *Racism Analysis Yearbook* (forthcoming).

Jacobs, Kurt 1995, 'Destruktivkräfte', in *Historisch-Kritisches Wörterbuch des Marxismus*, edited by Wolfgang Fritz Haug, Frigga Haug and Peter Jehle, Hamburg: Argument.

Jäger, Michael 1994, 'Ableitung', in *Historisch-Kritisches Wörterbuch des Marxismus*, edited by Wolfgang Fritz Haug, Frigga Haug and Peter Jehle, Hamburg: Argument.

Jaspers, Karl 1989a [1921], 'Max Weber: A Commemorative Address', in *Karl Jaspers on Max Weber*, edited with introduction and notes by John Dreijmanis, translated by Robert J. Whelan, New York: Paragon House.

———— 1989b [1932], 'Max Weber: Politician, Scientist, Philosopher', in *Karl Jaspers on Max Weber*, edited with introduction and notes by John Dreijmanis, translated by Robert J. Whelan, New York: Paragon House.

Jehle, Peter 1994, 'Alltagsverstand', in *Historisch-Kritisches Wörterbuch des Marxismus*, edited by Wolfgang Fritz Haug, Frigga Haug and Peter Jehle, Hamburg: Argument.

———— 1996, *Werner Krauss und die Romanistik im NS-Staat*, Hamburg: Argument.

Jellinek, Geog 1919 [1895], *Die Erklärung der Menschen- und Bürgerrechte: Ein Beitrag zur modernen Verfassungsgeschichte*, Dritte Auflage unter Verwertung des handschriftlichen Nachlasses, durchgesehen und ergänzt von Walter Jellinek, Munich: Duncker & Humblot.

Jessop, Bob 1988, 'Postfordismus: Zur Rezeption der Regulationstheorie bei Hirsch', *Das Argument*, 169: 380–90.

Kant, Immanuel 1900 [1787], *Critique of Pure Reason*, New York: Collier.

Käsler, Dirk 1972, *Max Weber: Sein Werk und seine Wirkung*, Munich: Nymphenburger Verlagshandlung.

———— (ed.) 1976, *Klassiker des soziologischen Denkens 1: Von Comte bis Durkheim*, Munich: Beck.

———— (ed.) 1978, *Klassiker des soziologischen Denkens 2: Von Weber bis Mannheim*, Munich: Beck.

———— 1996, 'Freiheit für Max Weber: Wilhelm Hennis will ihn den Händen seiner Interpreten entreißen', *Frankfurter Allgemeine Zeitung*.

———— 2006, 'Natur, Nerven und Pollutionen', *Der Spiegel*.

Kellenbenz, Hermann (ed.) 1980, *Handbuch der europäischen Wirtschafts- und Sozialgeschichte 2: Europäische Wirtschafts- und Sozialgeschichte im Mittelalter*, Stuttgart: Klett-Cotta.

Keuth, Herbert 1989, *Wissenschaft und Werturteil: Zu Werturteilsdiskussion und Positivismusstreit*, Tübingen: Mohr.

Kilian, Martin 1979, *Die Genesis des Amerikanismus: Zum Verhältnis von amerikanischer Ideologie und amerikanischer Praxis 1630–1789*, Frankfurt on the Main: Campus.

Kippenberg, Hans G. 1991, *Die vorderasiatischen Erlösungsreligionen in ihrem Zusammenhang mit der antiken Stadtherrschaft: Heidelberger Max-Weber-Vorlesungen 1988*, Frankfurt on the Main: Suhrkamp.

Kleger, Heinz and Alois Müller (eds) 1986, 'Mehrheitskonsens als Zivilreligion? Zur politischen Religionsphilosophie innerhalb liberal-konservativer Staatstheorie', in *Religion des Bürgers: Zivilreligion in Amerika und Europa*, edited by Heinz Kleger and Alois Müller, Munich: Kaiser.

Knies, Karl 1883 [1853], *Die politische Oekonomie vom geschichtlichen Standpuncte*, Braunschweig: C.A. Schwetschke und Sohn.

Kocka, Jürgen 1974, 'Organisierter Kapitalismus oder Staatsmonopolistischer Kapitalismus? Begriffliche Vorbemerkungen', in *Organisierter Kapitalismus: Voraussetzungen und Anfänge*, edited by Heinrich August Winkler, Göttingen: Vandenhoeck & Ruprecht.

Kofler, Leo 1966, *Zur Geschichte der bürgerlichen Gesellschaft*, Neuwied: Luchterhand.

Köhle-Hezinger, Christel 1976, *Evangelisch-katholisch: Untersuchungen zu konfessionellem Vorurteil und Konflikt im 19. und 20. Jahrhundert, Vornehmlich am Beispiel Württembergs*, Tübingen: Tübinger Vereinigung für Volkskunde.

Köhnke, Klaus Christian 1986, *Entstehung und Aufstieg des Neukantianismus: Die deutsche Universitätsphilosophie zwischen Idealismus und Positivismus*, Frankfurt on the Main: Suhrkamp.

Kouri, E.I. 1984, *Der deutsche Protestantismus und die soziale Frage 1870–1919: Zur Sozialpolitik im Bildungsbürgertum*, Berlin: de Gruyter.

Krätke, Michael 1995a, 'Bürokratie', in *Historisch-Kritisches Wörterbuch des Marxismus*, edited by Wolfgang Fritz Haug, Frigga Haug and Peter Jehle, Hamburg: Argument.

———— 1995b, 'Beamte', in *Historisch-Kritisches Wörterbuch des Marxismus*, edited by Wolfgang Fritz Haug, Frigga Haug and Peter Jehle, Hamburg: Argument.

———— 1995c, 'Börse', in *Historisch-Kritisches Wörterbuch des Marxismus*, edited by Wolfgang Fritz Haug, Frigga Haug and Peter Jehle, Hamburg: Argument.

Krause, Werner and Günther Rudolph 1980, *Grundlinien des ökonomischen Denkens in Deutschland 1848 bis 1945*, Berlin: Akademie-Verlag.

Krebs, Hans-Peter 1990, 'Führt die Philosophie ein geschichtliches Eigenleben? Gramscis Umgang mit Giambattista Vico und der Geschichte der Philosophie', *Das Argument*, 182: 531–41.

Kross, Editha 1995, 'Chartismus', in *Historisch-Kritisches Wörterbuch des Marxismus*, edited by Wolfgang Fritz Haug, Frigga Haug and Peter Jehle, Hamburg: Argument.

Krüger, Dieter 1983, *Nationalökonomen im wilhelminischen Deutschland*, Göttingen: Vandenhoeck & Ruprecht.

——— 1988, 'Max Weber und die "Jüngeren" im Verein für Sozialpolitik', in *Max Weber und seine Zeitgenossen*, edited by Wolfgang J. Mommsen and Wolfgang Schwentker, Göttingen: Vandenhoeck & Ruprecht.

Kühne, Eckehard 1971, *Historisches Bewusstsein in der deutschen Soziologie: Untersuchungen zur Geschichte der Soziologie von der Zeit der Reichsgründung bis zum Ersten Weltkrieg auf wissenssoziologischer Grundlage*, Marburg: Bläschke und Ducke.

Küttler, Wolfgang 1999, 'Review of Rehmann: *Max Weber: Modernisierung als passive Revolution*', *Das Argument*, 229: 119–22.

Kulischer, Josef 1929, *Allgemeine Wirtschaftsgeschichte des Mittelalters und der Neuzeit 2: Die Neuzeit*, Munich: Oldenbourg.

Lange, Frederick Albert 2000 [1866], *The History of Materialism, and Criticism of its Present Importance*, 3 volumes, London: Routledge.

Lask, Emil 1902, *Fichtes Idealismus und die Geschichte*, Tübingen: Mohr.

Laugstien, Thomas 1989, 'Die protestantische Ethik und der "Geist von Potsdam": Sprangers Rekonstruktion des Führerstaats aus dem Prinzip persönlicher Verantwortung', in *Deutsche Philosophen 1933*, edited by Wolfgang Fritz Haug, Hamburg: Argument.

——— 1990, *Philosophieverhältnisse im deutschen Faschismus*, Hamburg: Argument.

——— 1995, 'Artikel Determinismus II', in *Historisch-Kritisches Wörterbuch des Marxismus*, edited by Wolfgang Fritz Haug, Frigga Haug and Peter Jehle, Hamburg: Argument.

——— 1997, 'Erkenntnistheorie', in *Historisch-Kritisches Wörterbuch des Marxismus*, edited by Wolfgang Fritz Haug, Frigga Haug and Peter Jehle, Hamburg: Argument.

Laveleye, Émile de 1875, *De l'avenir des peuples catholiques: Étude d'économie sociale*, Paris: Baillière.

Leborgne, Daniele and Alain Lipietz 1996, 'Postfordistische Politikmuster im globalen Vergleich', *Das Argument*, 217: 697–712.

Lefèvre, Wolfgang 1971, *Zum historischen Charakter und zur historischen Funktion der Methode bürgerlicher Soziologie: Untersuchung am Werk Max Webers*, Frankfurt on the Main: Suhrkamp.

Lehmann, Hartmut 1980, *Das Zeitalter des Absolutismus: Gottesgnadentum und Kriegsnot*, Stuttgart: Kohlhammer.

—— 1988, 'Asketischer Protestantismus und ökonomischer Rationalismus: Die Weber-These nach zwei Generationen', in *Max Webers Sicht des okzidentalen Christentums: Interpretation und Kritik*, edited by Wolfgang Schluchter, Frankfurt on the Main: Suhrkamp.

—— 1993, 'The Rise of Capitalism: Weber versus Sombart', in *Weber's Protestant Ethic: Origins, Evidence, Contexts*, edited by Hartmut Lehmann and Guenther Roth, Cambridge: Cambridge University Press.

—— 1996, *Max Webers 'Protestantische Ethik': Beiträge aus Sicht eines Historikers*, Göttingen: Vandenhoeck & Ruprecht.

Lehmann, Hartmut and Guenther Roth (eds) 1993, *Weber's Protestant Ethic: Origins, Evidence, Contexts*, Cambridge: Cambridge University Press.

Lehmbruch, Gerhard and Philippe C. Schmitter (eds) 1982, *Patterns of Corporatist Policy-Making*, London: Sage.

Lenin, Vladimir Ilyich 1960–78a [1918], 'Next Immediate Tasks of the Soviet Government', in *Collected Works*, volume 27, Moscow: Progress Publishers.

—— 1960–78b [1917], 'The Impending Catastrophe and How to Combat It', in *Collected Works*, volume 25, Moscow: Progress Publishers.

—— 1960–78c [1916], 'Imperialism, the Highest Stage of Capitalism', in *Collected Works*, volume 22, Moscow: Progress Publishers.

—— 1960–78d [1907/08], 'The Agrarian Programme of Social Democracy in the First Russian Revolution', in *Collected Works*, volume 13, Moscow: Progress Publishers.

—— 1960–78e [1899], 'The Development of Capitalism in Russia', in *Collected Works*, volume 3, Moscow: Progress Publishers.

—— 1960–78f [1905] 'Social Democracy's Attitude Towards the Peasant Movement', in Collected Works, volume 9, Moscow: Progress Publishers.

—— 1960–78g [1917], 'The Tasks of the Revolution', in *Collected Works*, volume 26, Moscow: Progress Publishers.

—— 1960–78h [1909], 'Materialism and Empirio-criticism', in *Collected Works*, volume 14, Moscow: Progress Publishers.

Levy, Carl 1988, 'Max Weber und Antonio Gramsci', in *Max Weber und seine Zeitgenossen*, edited by Wolfgang J. Mommsen and Wolfgang Schwentker, Göttingen: Vandenhoeck & Ruprecht.

Lindenlaub, Dieter 1967, *Richtungskämpfe im Verein für Sozialpolitik: Wissenschaft und Sozialpolitik im Kaiserreich vornehmlich vom Beginn des 'Neuen Kurses' bis zum Ausbruch des Ersten Weltkrieges (1890–1914)*, Wiesbaden: Steiner.

Lipp, Wolfgang 1985, *Stigma und Charisma: Über soziales Grenzverhalten*, Berlin: Reimer.

Löffelholz, Michael 1974, *Philosophie, Politik und Pädagogik im Frühwerk Eduard Sprangers 1900–1918*, Hamburg: Buske.

Löwy, Michael 2013, *La cage d'acier: Max Weber et le marxisme wébérien*, Paris: Stock.

Lopez, Roberto S. 1980, 'Italien: Die Stadtwirtschaft vom 11. bis zum 14. Jahrhundert', in *Handbuch der europäischen Wirtschafts- und Sozialgeschichte 2: Europäische Wirtschafts- und Sozialgeschichte im Mittelalter*, edited by Hermann Kellenbenz, Stuttgart: Klett-Cotta.

Losurdo, Domenico 1996, *Il revisionismo storico: Problemi e miti*, Bari: Laterza.

――― 2004, *Nietzsche, il ribelle aristocratico: Biografia intellettuale e bilancio critico*, Torino: Bollati Boringhieri.

Lübbe, Hermann 1960, 'Neukantianismus', in *Religion in Geschichte und Gegenwart*, volume 4, edited by Kurt Galling and Hans von Campenhausen, Tübingen: Mohr Siebeck.

――― 1987 [1963], 'Neukantianischer Sozialismus', in *Materialien zur Neukantianismus-Diskussion*, edited by Hans-Ludwig Ollig, Darmstadt: Wissenschaftliche Buchgesellschaft.

Lukács, György 1971 [1923], *History and Class Consciousness: Studies in Marxist Dialectics*, Cambridge: MIT Press.

――― 1980 [1954], *The Destruction of Reason*, London: Merlin.

Luther, Martin 1914 [1540], 'An die Pfarrherren, wider den Wucher zu predigen', in *Kritische Gesamtausgabe*, volume 51, Weimar: Böhlau.

Luxemburg, Rosa 1970–5a [1899], 'Hohle Nüsse', in *Gesammelte Werke*, volume 1/1, Berlin: Dietz.

――― 1970–5b [1914], 'Zwischen Hammer und Amboss', in *Gesammelte Werke*, volume 3, Berlin: Dietz.

――― 1970–5c [1916], 'Die Krise der Sozialdemokratie', in *Gesammelte Werke*, volume 4, Berlin: Dietz.

――― 1970–5d [1906], 'Massenstreik, Partei und Gewerkschaften', in *Gesammelte Werke*, volume 2, Berlin: Dietz.

――― 1970–5e [1900], 'Die "Deutsche Wissenschaft" hinter den Arbeitern', in *Gesammelte Werke*, volume 1/1, Berlin: Dietz.

――― 1970–5f [1899/1900], 'Zurück auf Adam Smith!', in *Gesammelte Werke*, volume 1/1, Berlin: Dietz.

――― 1970–5g [1903], 'Im Rate der Gelehrten', in *Gesammelte Werke*, volume 1/2, Berlin: Dietz.

――― 1970–5h [1909/16], 'Einführung in die Nationalökonomie', in *Gesammelte Werke*, volume 5, Berlin: Dietz.

Machiavelli, Niccolò 1970 [ca. 1517], *The Discourses*, edited with an introduction by Bernard Crick, translated by Leslie J. Walker, with Revisions by Brian Richardson, London: Penguin.

————— 2005 [1532], *The Prince*, translated by Peter Bondanella, with an Introduction by Maurizio Virolo, Oxford: Oxford University Press.

Mackenbach, Werner 1995, 'Bonapartismus', in *Historisch-Kritisches Wörterbuch des Marxismus*, edited by Wolfgang Fritz Haug, Frigga Haug and Peter Jehle, Hamburg: Argument.

Maier, Charles S. 1974, 'Strukturen kapitalistischer Stabilität in den zwanziger Jahren: Errungenschaften und Defekte', in *Organisierter Kapitalismus: Voraussetzungen und Anfänge*, edited by Heinrich August Winkler, Göttingen: Vandenhoeck & Ruprecht.

Mangoni, Luisa 1977, 'Il problema del fascismo nei "Quaderni del carcere"', in *Politica e storia in Gramsci, Atti del convegno internazionale di studi gramsciani, Firenze, 9–11 dicembre 1977*, edited by Franco Ferri, Rome: Editori riuniti.

Marcuse, Herbert 1966, *One-Dimensional Man: Studies in the Ideology of Advanced Industrial Society*, Boston: Beacon Press.

————— 1969, 'Industrialization and Capitalism in the Work of Max Weber', in *Negations: Essays in Critical Theory*, translated by Jeremy J. Shapiro, Boston: Beacon Press.

Markner, Reinhard 1995, 'Bürgerliche Gesellschaft', in *Historisch-Kritisches Wörterbuch des Marxismus*, edited by Wolfgang Fritz Haug, Frigga Haug and Peter Jehle, Hamburg: Argument.

Marshall, Gordon 1982, *In Search of the Spirit of Capitalism: An Essay on Max Weber's Protestant Ethic Thesis*, New York: Columbia University Press.

Marx, Karl 1969–71a, *Theories of Surplus-Value, Part I*, translated by Emile Burns, edited by Salomea Wolfovna Ryazanskaya, Moscow: Progress Publishers.

————— 1969–71b, *Theories of Surplus-Value, Part III*, Moscow: Progress Publishers.

————— 1973 [1939], *Grundrisse: Foundations of the Critique of Political Economy (Rough Draft)*, translated by Martin Nicolaus, London: Penguin Books.

————— 1976, *Capital: A Critique of Political Economy, Vol I*, translated by Ben Fowkes, London: Penguin Books.

————— 1981, *Capital: A Critique of Political Economy, Vol III*, translated by David Fernbach, London: Penguin Books.

Marx, Karl and Friedrich Engels 1957, *Marx-Engels Werke* (MEW), 42 volumes, Berlin: Dietz Verlag.

————— 1975–2005 [1835–95], *Collected Works* (MECW), 50 volumes, London: Lawrence & Wishart.

————— 1979–1989, 1992 and following: *Marx-Engels Gesamtausgabe* (MEGA), Berlin/ DDR-Amsterdam.

Massing, Otwin 1976, 'Auguste Comte', in *Klassiker des soziologischen Denkens 1: Von Comte bis Durkheim*, edited by Dirk Käsler, Munich: Beck.

Mayer, Jakob Peter 1956 [1943], *Max Weber in German Politics: A Study in Political Sociology*, London: Faber and Faber.

McNeill, William H. 1986, *Mythistory and other Essays*, Chicago: University of Chicago Press.

Meeks, W.A. 1983, *The First Urban Christians: The Social World of the Apostle Paul*, New Haven: Yale University Press.

Meillassoux, Claude 1994, 'Anthropologie', in *Historisch-Kritisches Wörterbuch des Marxismus*, edited by Wolfgang Fritz Haug, Frigga Haug and Peter Jehle, Hamburg: Argument.

Merleau-Ponty, Maurice 1955, *Les Aventures de la Dialectique*, Paris: Gallimard.

Merquior, J.G. 1988, 'Georges Sorel und Max Weber', in *Max Weber und seine Zeitgenossen*, edited by Wolfgang J. Mommsen and Wolfgang Schwentker, Göttingen: Vandenhoeck & Ruprecht.

Meyer, Ahlrich 1969, 'Mechanische und organische Metaphorik politischer Philosophie', *Archiv für Begriffsgeschichte*, 13: 128–99.

Michels, Robert 1916 [1911], *Political Parties: A Sociological Study of the Oligarchical Tendencies of Modern Democracies*, London: Jarrold and Sons.

——— 1927, 'Grundsätzliches zum Problem der Demokratie', *Zeitschrift für Politik*, 17.

Migliorini, Bruno 1983, *Storia della lingua italiana*, Florence: Sansoni.

Mill, John Stuart 1998 [1875], *Three Essays on Religion: Nature, The Utility of Religion, Theism*, Amherst: Prometheus.

Mitzman, Arthur 1970, *The Iron Cage: An Historical Interpretation of Max Weber*, New York: Knopf.

——— 1988, 'Persönlichkeitskonflikt und weltanschauliche Alternativen bei Werner Sombart und Max Weber', in *Max Weber und seine Zeitgenossen*, edited by Wolfgang J. Mommsen and Wolfgang Schwentker, Göttingen: Vandenhoeck & Ruprecht.

Mommsen, Wolfgang J. 1959, *Max Weber und die deutsche Politik 1890–1920*, Tübingen: Mohr.

——— 1971, 'Die Vereinigten Staaten von Amerika im politischen Denken Max Webers', *Historische Zeitschrift*, 213: 358–81.

——— 1974 [1959], *Max Weber und die deutsche Politik 1890–1920, Zweite überarbeitete und erweiterte Auflage*, Tübingen: Mohr.

——— 1988a, 'Einleitung', in *Max Weber und seine Zeitgenossen*, edited by Wolfgang J. Mommsen and Wolfgang Schwentker, Göttingen: Vandenhoeck & Ruprecht.

——— 1988b, 'Robert Michels und Max Weber: Gesinnungsethischer Fundamentalismus versus verantwortungsethischen Pragmatismus', in *Max Weber und seine Zeitgenossen*, edited by Wolfgang J. Mommsen and Wolfgang Schwentker, Göttingen: Vandenhoeck & Ruprecht.

Mommsen, Wolfgang J. and Wolfgang Schwentker (eds) 1988, *Max Weber und seine Zeitgenossen*, Göttingen: Vandenhoeck & Ruprecht.

Morris, Brian 1987, *Anthropological Studies of Religion: An Introductory Text*, Cambridge: Cambridge University Press.

Mottek, Hans, Walter Becker and Alfred Schröter 1974, *Wirtschaftsgeschichte Deutschlands: Ein Grundriss, 3: Von der Zeit der Reichsgründung 1871 bis zur Niederlage des faschistischen deutschen Imperialismus 1945*, Berlin: Deutscher Verlag der Wissenschaften.

Mühlmann, W.E. 1961, *Chiliasmus und Nativismus: Studien zur Psychologie, Soziologie und historischen Kasuistik der Umsturzbewegungen*, Berlin: Reimer.

Münch, Paul 1993, 'The Thesis Before Weber: An Archaeology', in *Weber's Protestant Ethic. Origins, Evidence, Contexts*, edited by Hartmut Lehmann and Guenther Roth, Cambridge: Cambridge University Press.

Müssiggang, Albert 1968, *Die soziale Frage in der historischen Schule der deutschen Nationalökonomie*, Tübingen: Mohr.

Muth, Karl 1898, *Veremundus: Steht die katholische Belletristik auf der Höhe der Zeit, Eine literarische Gewissensfrage von Veremundus*, Mainz: F. Kirchheim.

Naumann, Friedrich 1911 [1906], *Neudeutsche Wirtschaftspolitik*, Berlin: Fortschritt.

Nemitz, Rolf 1979, ' "Mut zur Erziehung" als konservativer Spontaneismus', *Das Argument*, 113.

Nietzsche, Friedrich 1968 [1888], *Twilight of the Idols; The Anti-Christ*, London: Penguin.

―――― 1989 [1886/88], *On the Genealogy of Morals; Ecce Homo*, New York: Vintage.

―――― 1997 [1874], *Untimely Meditations*, edited by Daniel Breazeale, translated by R.J. Hollingdale, Cambridge: Cambridge University Press.

―――― 1999, *Kritische Studienausgabe*, edited by Giorgio Colli and Mazzino Montinari, Munich: de Gruyter.

―――― 2002 [1886], *Beyond Good and Evil: Prelude to a Philosophy of the Future*, Cambridge: Cambridge University Press.

Nipperdey, Thomas 1988, *Religion im Umbruch: Deutschland 1870–1918*, Munich: Beck.

―――― 1993, 'Max Weber, Protestantism, and the Context of the Debate around 1900', in *Weber's Protestant Ethic: Origins, Evidence, Contexts*, edited by Hartmut Lehmann and Günther Roth, Cambridge: Cambridge University Press.

Nolte, Ernst 1963, 'Max Weber vor dem Faschismus', *Der Staat: Zeitschrift für Staatslehre, öffentliches Recht und Verfassungsgeschichte*, 2: 1–24.

Nusser, Karl Heinz 1986, *Kausale Prozesse und sinnerfassende Vernunft: Max Webers philosophische Fundierung der Soziologie und Kulturwissenschaften*, Freiburg: Alber.

Oakes, Guy 1988a, *Weber and Rickert: Concept Formation in the Cultural Sciences*, Cambridge: MIT Press.

―――― 1988b, 'Max Weber und die Südwestdeutsche Schule: Der Begriff des historischen Individuums und seine Entstehung', in *Max Weber und seine Zeitgenossen*, edited by Wolfgang J. Mommsen and Wolfgang Schwentker, Göttingen: Vandenhoeck & Ruprecht.

Offenbacher, Martin 1901, *Konfession und soziale Schichtung: Eine Studie über die wirtschaftliche Lage der Katholiken und Protestanten in Baden*, Tübingen: Laupp.

Ollig, Hans-Ludwig 1987 [1985], 'Die Religionsphilosophie der Südwestdeutschen Schule', in *Materialien zur Neukantianismus-Diskussion*, edited by Hans-Ludwig Ollig, Darmstadt: Wissenschaftliche Buchgesellschaft.

Orozco, Teresa 2004 [1995], *Platonische Gewalt: Gadamers politische Hermeneutik der NS-Zeit*, Hamburg: Argument.

Ostrogorsky, Maurice 1903a/b, *La démocratie et l'organisation des partis politiques*, 2 volumes, Paris: Calmann-Lévy.

Paggi, Leonardo 1970, *Gramsci e il moderno principe I. Nella crisi del socialismo italiano*, Rome: Editori riuniti.

Parkin, Frank 1982, *Max Weber*, London: Tavistock.

Pêcheux, Michel 1983, 'Ideologie—Festung oder paradoxer Raum?', *Das Argument*, 25: 379–87.

Peukert, Detlev 1989, *Max Webers Diagnose der Moderne*, Göttingen: Vandenhoeck & Ruprecht.

Philip, André 1926, *Le problème ouvrier aux États Unis*, Paris: Alcan.

Plessen, Marie-Louise 1975, *Die Wirksamkeit des Vereins für Socialpolitik 1872–1890: Studien zum Katheder- und Staatssozialismus*, Berlin: Duncker & Humblot.

Pocock, J.G.A. 1975, *The Machiavellian Moment: Florentine Political Thought and the Atlantic Republican Tradition*, Princeton: Princeton University Press.

Poulantzas, Nicos 1978, *State, Power, Socialism*, translated by Patrick Camiller, London: Verso.

Projekt Ideologietheorie 1980, *Faschismus und Ideologie*, 2 volumes, Berlin: Argument.

———— 1982 [1979], *Theorien über Ideologie*, Berlin: Argument.

———— 1984, *Die Camera obscura der Ideologie*, Berlin: Argument.

Rachfahl, Felix 1978 [1909], 'Kalvinismus und Kapitalismus', in *Die protestantische Ethik II. Kritiken und Antikritiken*, edited by Johannes Winkelmann, Gütersloh: Mohn.

Radkau, Joachim 1998, *Das Zeitalter der Nervosität: Deutschland zwischen Bismarck und Hitler*, Munich: Hanser.

———— 2005, *Max Weber: Die Leidenschaft des Denkens*, Munich: Hanser.

———— 2011, *Max Weber: A Biography*, translated by Patrick Camiller, Cambridge: Polity.

Rehmann, Jan 1986, *Die Kirchen im NS-Staat: Untersuchung zur Interaktion ideologischer Mächte*, Berlin: Argument.

———— 1991, 'Gramsci und die Religionsfrage: Ein Beitrag zum christlich-marxistischen Dialog', *Widerspruch: Beiträge zur sozialistischen Politik*, 21: 179–83.

———— 1994, 'Antizipation', in *Historisch-Kritisches Wörterbuch des Marxismus*, edited by Wolfgang Fritz Haug, Frigga Haug and Peter Jehle, Hamburg: Argument.

———— 1995, 'Charisma', in *Historisch-Kritisches Wörterbuch des Marxismus*, edited by Wolfgang Fritz Haug, Frigga Haug and Peter Jehle, volume 2, Hamburg: Argument.

———— 1999, " 'Abolition' of Civil Society? Remarks on a Widespread Misunderstanding in the Interpretation of 'Civil Society' ", *Socialism and Democracy*, 13, 2: 1–18.

——— 2007, Review article on Domenico Losurdo's "Nietzsche: il ribelle aristocratico: Biografia intellettuale e bilancio critico", *Historical Materialism*, 15, 2: 173–93.

——— 2008, 'Kalvinismus/Puritanismus', in *Historisch-Kritisches Wörterbuch des Marxismus*, edited by W.F. Haug and P. Jehle, volume 7/1, Hamburg: Argument.

——— 2013, *Theories of Ideology: The Powers of Alienation and Subjection*, Leiden: Brill.

Reich, Wilhelm 1971 [1933/42], *Die Massenpsychologie des Faschismus*, Cologne Kiepenheuer & Witsch.

Renan, Ernest 1967 [1871], *La réforme intellectuel et morale*, Paris: Union générale d'éditions.

Rickert, Heinrich 1902, *Die Grenzen der naturwissenschaftlichen Begriffsbildung: Eine logische Einleitung in die historischen Wissenschaften*, Tübingen: Mohr.

——— 1913, 'Vom System der Werte', *Logos*, 4: 295–327.

——— 1921, *System der Philosophie, Erster Teil: Allgemeine Grundlegung der Philosophie*, Tübingen: Mohr.

——— 1929 [1902], *Die Grenzen der naturwissenschaftlichen Begriffsbildung. Eine logische Einleitung in die historischen Wissenschaften*, Fifth Edition, Tübingen: Mohr.

——— 1933, 'Wissenschaftliche Philosophie und Weltanschauung', *Logos*, 22: 37–57.

——— 1962 [1926], *Science and History: A Critique of Positivist Epistemology*, translated by George Reisman, edited by Arthur Goddard, Princeton: D. Van Nostrand.

——— 1986 [1902], *The Limits of Concept Formation in Natural Science: A Logical Introduction to the Historical Sciences (abridged edition)*, edited and translated by Guy Oakes, Cambridge: Cambridge University Press.

Riesebrodt, Martin 1985, 'Vom Patriarchalismus zum Kapitalismus: Max Webers Analyse der Transformation der ostelbischen Agrarverhältnisse im Kontext zeitgenössischer Theorien', *Kölner Zeitschrift für Soziologie und Sozialpsychologie*, 37: 546–67.

Rifkin, Jeremy 1992, *Beyond Beef: The Rise and Fall of the Cattle Culture*, New York: Dutton Books.

Ringer, Fritz K. 1983 [1969], *Die Gelehrten: Der Niedergang der deutschen Mandarine 1890–1933*, Stuttgart: Klett-Cotta.

Ritschl, Albrecht 1880, *Geschichte des Pietismus 1: Der Pietismus in der reformierten Kirche*, Bonn: Adolph Marcus.

——— 1887, 'Festrede zur Feier des 150-jährigen Bestehens der Georg-August-Universität in Göttingen am 8. August 1887', in *Drei akademische Reden*, Bonn: Adolph Marcus.

Ritter, Joachim and Karlfried Gründer 1971–2007, *Historisches Wörterbuch der Philosophie*, Basle: Schwabe.

Röhrich, Wilfried 1972, *Robert Michels: Vom sozialistisch-syndikalistischen zum faschistischen Credo*, Berlin: Duncker & Humblot.

Rollmann, Hans 1993, '"Meet me in St. Louis": Troeltsch and Weber in America', in *Weber's Protestant Ethic: Origins, Evidence, Contexts*, edited by Hartmut Lehmann and Guenther Roth, Cambridge: Cambridge University Press.

Rosenthal, Claudius 1999, 'Der Arbeiter und sein Anteil an den Gütern, Politik im Irdischen: Jan Rehmann hat mit Gramsci Max Weber gelesen', *Süddeutsche Zeitung*.

Roth, Guenther 1987, *Politische Herrschaft und persönliche Freiheit: Heidelberger Max-Weber-Vorlesungen 1983*, Frankfurt on the Main: Suhrkamp.

———— 1989, 'Marianne Weber und ihr Kreis', in Marianne Weber, *Max Weber. Ein Lebensbild*, Munich: Piper.

———— 1993a, 'Introduction', in *Weber's Protestant Ethic: Origins, Evidence, Contexts*, edited by Hartmut Lehmann and Guenther Roth, Cambridge: Cambridge University Press.

———— 1993b, 'Weber the Would-Be Englishman: Anglophilia and Family History', in *Weber's Protestant Ethic. Origins, Evidence, Contexts*, edited by Hartmut Lehmann and Guenther Roth, Cambridge: Cambridge University Press.

———— 2001, *Max Webers deutsch-englische Familiengeschichte 1800–1950: Mit Briefen und Dokumenten*, Tübingen: Mohr Siebeck.

Rousseau, Jean-Jacques 1959 [1762], 'Du Contrat social ou Essai sur la forme de la République (Première Version)', in *Oeuvres complètes*, édition publiée sous la direction de Bernhard Gagnebin et Marcel Raymond, volume 3, Paris: Gallimard.

Rustow, Dankwart A. (ed.) 1970, *Studies in Leadership*, New York: Braziller.

Samuelsson, Kurt 1961 [1957], *Religion and Economic Action*, Stockholm: Svenska Bokförlaget.

Said, Edward W. 2003 [1978], *Orientalism*, 25th anniversary edition, New York: Vintage Books.

Sauer, Wolfgang 1970 [1966], 'Das Problem des deutschen Nationalstaats', in *Moderne deutsche Sozialgeschichte*, edited by Hans-Ulrich, Cologne: Kiepenheuer & Witsch.

Scaff, Lawrence A. 2011, *Max Weber in America*, Princeton: Princeton University Press.

Schäfers, Bernhard 1967, 'Ein Rundschreiben Max Webers zur Sozialpolitik', *Soziale Welt*, 18: 261–71.

Scheibe, Max 1897, *Calvins Prädestinationslehre: Ein Beitrag zur Würdigung der Eigenart seiner Theologie und Religiosität*, Halle: Ehrhardt Karras.

Schell, Hermann 1897, *Der Katholicismus als Princip des Fortschritts*, Würzburg: Göbel.

Schellenberger, Barbara 1975, *Katholische Jugend und Drittes Reich: Eine Geschichte des katholischen Jungmännerverbandes 1933–1939 unter besonderer Berücksichtigung der Rheinprovinz*, Mainz: Grünewald.

Schick, Manfred 1970, *Kulturprotestantismus und soziale Frage: Versuche zur Begründung der Sozialethik vornehmlich in der Zeit von der Gründung des Evangelisch-Sozialen Kongresses bis zum Ausbruch des 1. Weltkrieges (1890–1914)*, Tübingen: Mohr.

Schiffer, Irvine 1973, *Charisma: A Psychoanalytic Look at Mass Society*, Toronto: University of Toronto Press.

Schluchter, Wolfgang 1979, *Die Entwicklung des okzidentalen Rationalismus: Eine Analyse von Max Webers Gesellschaftsgeschichte*, Tübingen: Mohr.

———— 1980, *Rationalismus der Weltbeherrschung: Studien zu Max Weber*, Frankfurt on the Main: Suhrkamp.

———— (ed.) 1988, *Max Weber Sicht des okzidentalen Rationalismus: Interpretation und Kritik*, Frankfurt on the Main: Suhrkamp.

———— 1991, *Religion und Lebensführung 1: Studien zu Max Webers Kultur- und Werttheorie*, Frankfurt on the Main: Suhrkamp.

———— 1996, *Neubeginn durch Anpassung? Studien zum ostdeutschen Übergang*, Frankfurt on the Main: Suhrkamp.

Schmitt, Carl 2008 [1928], *Constitutional Theory*, Durham: Duke University Press.

Schmitter, Philippe C. 1979 [1974], 'Still the Century of Corporatism?', in *Trends Toward Corporatist Intermediation*, edited by Philippe C. Schmitter and Gerhard Lehmbruch, London: Sage.

———— 1982, 'Reflections on Where the Theory of Neo-Corporatism has gone and Where the Praxis of Neo-Corporatism may be going', in *Patterns of Corporatist Policy-Making*, edited by Gerhard Lehmbruch and Philippe C. Schmitter, London: Sage.

Schmitter, Philippe C. and Gerhard Lehmbruch (eds) 1979, *Trends Toward Corporatist Intermediation*, London: Sage.

Schmoller, Gustav 1903, 'Werner Sombart, Der moderne Kapitalismus', *Jahrbuch für Gesetzgebung, Verwaltung und Volkswirtschaft im Deutschen Reich*, 27.

———— 1920, *Zwanzig Jahre deutscher Politik (1897–1917): Aufsätze und Vorträge*, Munich: Duncker & Humblot.

Schnabel, Peter-Ernst 1976, 'Georg Simmel', in *Klassiker des soziologischen Denkens 1: Von Comte bis Durkheim*, edited by Dirk Käsler, Munich: Beck.

Schnädelbach, Herbert 1974, *Geschichtsphilosophie nach Hegel: Die Probleme des Historismus*, Freiburg: Alber.

Schneemelcher, Wilhelm 1980, 'Kulturprotestantismus', in *Evangelisches Soziallexikon*, edited by Friedrich Karrenberg, Stuttgart: Kreuz-Verlag.

Schön, Manfred 1988, 'Gustav Schmoller und Max Weber', in *Max Weber und seine Zeitgenossen*, edited by Wolfgang J. Mommsen and Wolfgang Schwentker, Göttingen: Vandenhoeck & Ruprecht.

Schreiber, Ulrich 1984 [1982], *Die politische Theorie Antonio Gramscis*, Berlin: Argument.

Schreiter, Jörg 1988, *Hermeneutik—Wahrheit und Verstehen: Darstellung und Texte*, Berlin: Akademie-Verlag.

Schulin, Ernst 1988, 'Max Weber und Walter Rathenau', in *Max Weber und seine Zeitgenossen*, edited by Wolfgang J. Mommsen and Wolfgang Schwentker, Göttingen: Vandenhoeck & Ruprecht.

Schulze-Gaevernitz, Gerhart von 1890, *Zum socialen Frieden*, 2 volumes, Leipzig: Duncker & Humblot.

Schumpeter, Joseph A. 1934, *The Theory of Economic Development: An Inquiry into Profits, Capital, Credit, Interest, and the Business Cycle*, translated by Redvers Opie, Cambridge: Harvard University Press.

Schwentker, Wolfgang 1988, 'Leidenschaft als Lebensform: Erotik und Moral bei Max Weber und im Kreis um Otto Gross', in *Max Weber und seine Zeitgenossen*, edited by Wolfgang J. Mommsen and Wolfgang Schwentker, Göttingen: Vandenhoeck & Ruprecht.

Sen, Asok 1989, 'Weber, Gramsci and Capitalism', in *Perspectives on Capitalism: Marx, Keynes, Schumpeter and Weber*, edited by Krishna Bharadwaj and Sudipta Kaviraj, New Delhi: Sage.

Senghaas, Dieter (ed.) 1979, *Kapitalistische Weltökonomie: Kontroversen über ihren Ursprung und ihre Entwicklungsdynamik*, Frankfurt on the Main: Suhrkamp.

Sève, Lucien 1972, *Marxismus und Theorie der Persönlichkeit*, Frankfurt on the Main: Marxistische Blätter.

Seyfarth, Constans and Walter M. Sprondel (eds) 1973, *Seminar: Religion und gesellschaftliche Entwicklung: Studien zur Protestantismus-These Max Webers*, Frankfurt on the Main: Suhrkamp.

Simmel, Georg 1989 [1900], *Philosophie des Geldes*, herausgegeben von David P. Frisby und Klaus Christian Köhnke, in *Gesamtausgabe*, volume 6, Frankfurt on the Main: Suhrkamp.

——— 1990 [1900], *The Philosophy of Money*, edited by David Frisby, translated by Tom Bottomore and David Frisby, London: Routledge.

Sinclair, Upton 1971 [1906], *The Jungle*, Cambridge: Bentley.

Sohm, Rudolf 1923 [1892], *Kirchenrecht 1: Die geschichtlichen Grundlagen*, Berlin: Duncker & Humblot.

Sohn-Rethel, Alfred 1971, *Warenform und Denkform: Aufsätze*, Frankfurt on the Main: Europäische Verlagsanstalt.

——— 1978 [1970], *Intellectual and Manual Labour: A Critique of Epistemology*, London: Macmillan.

Sombart, Werner 1888, *Die römische Campagna: Eine sozialökonomische Studie*, Leipzig: Duncker & Humblot.

——— 1893, 'Review of Max Weber, *Die römische Agrarfrage*', Zeitschrift für Social- und Wirtschaftsgeschichte 1: 349–56.

——— 1902, *Der moderne Kapitalismus 1: Die Genesis des Kapitalismus*, Leipzig: Duncker & Humblot.

——— 1911, *Die Juden und das Wirtschaftsleben*, Leipzig: Duncker & Humblot.

——— 1913a, *Luxus und Kapitalismus: Studien zur Entwicklungsgeschichte des modernen Kapitalismus 1*, Leipzig: Duncker & Humblot.

418BIBLIOGRAPHY

—— 1913b, *Krieg und Kapitalismus: Studien zur Entwicklungsgeschichte des modernen Kapitalismus 2*, Leipzig: Duncker & Humblot.

—— 1916, *Der moderne Kapitalismus: Historisch-systematische Darstellung des gesamteuropäischen Wirtschaftslebens von seinen Anfängen bis zur Gegenwart 1: Die vorkapitalistische Wirtschaft, Die historischen Grundlagen des modernen Kapitalismus, Zweite, neugearbeitete Auflage*, Leipzig: Duncker & Humblot.

—— 1917, *Der moderne Kapitalismus: Historisch-systematische Darstellung des gesamteuropäischen Wirtschaftslebens von seinen Anfängen bis zur Gegenwart 2: Das europäische Wirtschaftsleben im Zeitalter des Frühkapitalismus, vornehmlich im 16., 17. und 18. Jahrhundert, Zweite, neugearbeitete Auflage*, Leipzig: Duncker & Humblot.

—— 1920 [1913], *Der Bourgeois: Zur Geistesgeschichte des modernen Wirtschaftsmenschen*, Leipzig: Duncker & Humblot.

—— 1927, *Der moderne Kapitalismus: Historisch-systematische Darstellung des gesamteuropäischen Wirtschaftslebens von seinen Anfängen bis zur Gegenwart 3: Das Wirtschaftsleben im Zeitalter des Hochkapitalismus*, Leipzig: Duncker & Humblot.

—— 1951 [1911], *The Jews and Modern Capitalism*, Glencoe: Free Press.

—— 1998 [1920], *The Quintessence of Capitalism: A Study of the History and Psychology of the Modern Business Man*, London: Routledge.

Sorel, Georges 1908, *Réflexions sur la violence*, Paris: Librairie de "pages libres".

—— 1916 [1908], *Reflections on Violence*, London: Ruskin House.

Spranger, Eduard 1905, *Die Grundlagen der Geschichtswissenschaft: Eine erkenntnistheoretisch-psychologische Untersuchung*, Berlin: Reuther & Reichard.

—— 1923: 'Rickerts System', *Logos*, 12: 183–98.

Stephan, Horst and Martin Schmidt 1973 [1938], *Geschichte der evangelischen Theologie in Deutschland seit dem Idealismus*, Berlin: de Gruyter.

Strohm, Theodor 1966/72, 'Konfession und industriegesellschaftliche Entwicklung— Über die Anfänge religionssoziologischer Wirklichkeitskenntnis', *Theologia Viatorum*, 11.

Sweezy, Paul 1976, *The Transition from Feudalism to Capitalism*, introduced by Rodney Hilton, London: New Left Books.

Tawney, R.H. 1938 [1922], *Religion and the Rise of Capitalism: A Historical Study*, Harmondsworth: Penguin.

Taylor, Frederick Winslow 1919, *The Principles of Scientific Management*, New York: Harper & Brothers.

Tenbruck, Friedrich H. 1959, 'Die Genesis der Methodologie Max Webers', *Kölner Zeitschrift für Soziologie und Sozialpsychologie*, 11: 573–630.

—— 1975, 'Das Werk Max Webers', *Kölner Zeitschrift für Soziologie und Sozialpsychologie*, 27.

Theiner, Peter 1983, *Sozialer Liberalismus und deutsche Weltpolitik: Friedrich Naumann im Wilhelminischen Deutschland*, Baden-Baden: Nomos.

———— 1988, 'Friedrich Naumann und Max Weber: Stationen einer politischen Partnerschaft', in *Max Weber und seine Zeitgenossen*, edited by Wolfgang J. Mommsen and Wolfgang Schwentker, Göttingen: Vandenhoeck & Ruprecht.

Thomas, Peter 2006, 'Being Max Weber', *New Left Review*, 41: 147–58.

———— 2009, *The Gramscian Moment: Philosophy, Hegemony and Marxism*, Leiden: Brill.

Thompson, Edward P. 1980, *Plebeische Kultur und moralische Ökonomie: Aufsätze zur englischen Sozialgeschichte des 18. und 19. Jahrhunderts,* ausgewählt und eingeleitet von Dieter Groh, Frankfurt on the Main: Ullstein.

Timm, Hermann 1967, *Theologie und Praxis in der Theologie Albrecht Ritschls und Wilhelm Hermanns: Ein Beitrag zur Entwicklungsgeschichte des Kulturprotestantismus*, Gütersloh: Mohn.

Tocqueville, Alexis de 1904 [1835], *Democracy in America*, New York: Appleton.

Tönnies, Ferdinand 2001 [1920], *Community and Civil Society*, edited by Jose Harris, translated by Jose Harris and Margaret Hollis, Cambridge: Cambridge University Press.

Tribe, Keith 1983, 'Prussian Agriculture—German Politics: Max Weber 1892–7', *Economy and Society*, 12, 2: 181–226.

Troeltsch, Ernst 1895, 'Die Selbständigkeit der Religion', *Zeitschrift für Theologie und Kirche*, 5: 361–436; 6: 71–110, 167–218.

———— 1902, *Die Absolutheit des Christentums und die Religionsgeschichte*, Tübingen: Mohr.

———— 1904, *Das Historische in Kants Religionsphilosophie: Zugleich ein Beitrag zu den Untersuchungen über Kants Philosophie der Geschichte*, Berlin: Reuther & Richard.

———— 1905, *Psychologie und Erkenntnistheorie in der Religionswissenschaft: Eine Untersuchung über die Bedeutung der Kantischen Religionslehre für die heutige Religionswissenschaft, Vortrag, gehalten auf dem International Congress of Arts and Sciences in St. Louis*, Tübingen: Mohr.

———— 1913 [1909], 'Wesen der Religion und der Religionsgemeinschaft', in *Gesammelte Schriften 2: Zur religiösen Lage, Religionsphilosophie und Ethik*, Tübingen: Mohr.

———— 1922, 'Der Historismus und seine Probleme, Erstes Buch: Das logische Problem der Geschichtsphilosophie', in *Gesammelte Schriften 3*, Tübingen: Mohr.

———— 1960 [1912], *The Social Teachings of the Christian Churches*, translated by Olive Wyon, with an Introduction by H. Richard Niebuhr, New York: Harper.

Tucker, Robert C. 1968: 'The Theory of Charismatic Leadership', *Daedalus: Journal of the American Academy of Arts and Sciences*, 97, 2.

Tugendhat, Ernst 1984, *Probleme der Ethik*, Stuttgart: Reclam.

———— 1993, *Vorlesungen über Ethik*, Frankfurt on the Main: Suhrkamp.

Turksma, L. 1962, 'Protestant Ethic and Rational Capitalism: A Contribution to a never ending Discussion', *Social Compass*, 9: 445–73.

Turner, Bryan S. 1996 [1981], *For Weber: Essays on the Sociology of Fate*, London: Sage.

Uhlhorn, Gerhard 1887, *Katholicismus und Protestantismus gegenüber der socialen Frage*, Göttingen: Vandenhoeck & Ruprecht.

Verein für Socialpolitik 1890, 'Verhandlungen des Vereins für Socialpolitik 1890', in *Schriften des Vereins für Socialpolitik 47*, Leipzig: Duncker & Humblot.

——— 1905, 'Verhandlungen des Vereins für Socialpolitik 1905', in *Schriften des Vereins für Socialpolitik 116*, Leipzig: Duncker & Humblot.

Vico, Giambattista 2001 [1744], *New Science: Principles of the New Science Concerning the Common Nature of Nations, Third Edition, Thoroughly Corrected, Expanded and Revised by the Author*, translated by David Marsh with an introduction by Anthony Grafton, London: Penguin.

Wagner, Gerhard 1987, *Geltung und normativer Zwang: Eine Untersuchung zu den neu-kantianischen Grundlagen der Wissenschaftslehre Max Webers*, Freiburg: Alber.

Wagner, Gerhard and Heinz Zipprian 1987 [1985], 'Max Weber und die neukantian-ische Epistemologie', in *Materialien zur Neukantianismus-Diskussion*, edited by Hans-Ludwig Ollig, Darmstadt: Wissenschaftliche Buchgesellschaft.

Wagner, Hartmut 1995, 'Demokratie', in *Historisch-Kritisches Wörterbuch des Marxismus*, edited by Wolfgang Fritz Haug, Frigga Haug and Peter Jehle, Hamburg: Argument.

Wallerstein, Immanuel 1974, 'The Rise and Future Demise of the World Capitalist System: Concepts for Comparative Analysis', *Comparative Studies in Society and History*, 16, 4: 307–415.

——— 1983, *Historical Capitalism*, London: Verso.

——— 1995, 'Bourgeoisie 11', in *Historisch-Kritisches Wörterbuch des Marxismus*, edited by Wolfgang Fritz Haug, Frigga Haug and Peter Jehle, Hamburg: Argument.

Ward, W.R. 1988, 'Max Weber und die Schule Albrecht Ritschls', in *Max Weber und seine Zeitgenossen*, edited by Wolfgang J. Mommsen and Wolfgang Schwentker, Göttingen: Vandenhoeck & Ruprecht.

Wassenberg, Arthur F.P. 1982, 'Neo-Corporatism and the Quest for Control: The Cuckoo Game', in *Patterns of Corporatist Policy-Making*, edited by Gerhard Lehmbruch and Philippe C. Schmitter, London: Sage.

Weber, Alfred 1955, *Einführung in die Soziologie*, Munich: Piper.

Weber, Marianne 1975 [1926], *Max Weber: A Biography*, New York: Wiley.

Weber, Max 1894, 'Die Ergebnisse der deutschen Börsenenquête', *Zeitschrift für das gesamte Handelsrecht*, 43, 28.

——— 1904, 'Die protestantische Ethik und der "Geist" des Kapitalismus, Teil 1', *Archiv für Sozialwissenschaft und Sozialpolitik*, 20: 1–54.

——— 1905, 'Die protestantische Ethik und der "Geist" des Kapitalismus, Teil 11', *Archiv für Sozialwissenschaft und Sozialpolitik*, 21: 1–110.

——— 1906a, '"Kirchen" und "Sekten" in Nordamerika: Eine kirchen- und sozialpolitische Skizze', *Die christliche Welt*, 20, 24: 558–62.

——— 1906b, '"Kirchen" und "Sekten" in Nordamerika: Eine kirchen- und sozialpolitische Skizze', *Die christliche Welt*, 20, 25: 577–83.

——— 1923, *Wirtschaftsgeschichte: Abriss der universalen Sozial- und Wirtschaftsgeschichte, aus den nachgelassenen Vorlesungen*, herausgegeben von Siegmund Hellmann und Melchior Palyi, Munich: Duncker & Humblot.

——— 1936, *Jugendbriefe*, herausgegeben von Marianne Weber, Tübingen: Mohr.

——— 1946a [1904/05], 'The Protestant Sects and the Spirit of Capitalism', in *From Max Weber: Essays in Sociology*, New York: Oxford University Press.

——— 1946b [1915], 'The Social Psychology of the World Religions', in *From Max Weber: Essays in Sociology*, New York: Oxford University Press.

——— 1946c [1915], 'Religious Rejections of the World and Their Directions', in *From Max Weber: Essays in Sociology*, New York: Oxford University Press.

——— 1950 [1920], *The Protestant Ethic and the Spirit of Capitalism*, translated by Talcott Parsons, with a Foreword by R.H. Tawney, New York: Scribner.

——— 1951 [1916], *The Religion of China: Confucianism and Taoism*, translated by Hans H. Gerth, Glencoe, Illinois: The Free Press.

——— 1952 [1917–1919], *Ancient Judaism*, translated by Hans H. Gerth and Don Martindale, Glencoe, Illinois: The Free Press.

——— 1958 [1916–17], *The Religion of India: The Sociology of Hinduism and Buddhism*, translated by Hans H. Gerth and Don Martindale, New York: The Free Press.

——— 1972 [1921/22], *Wirtschaft und Gesellschaft: Grundriss der verstehenden Soziologie*, Tübingen: Mohr.

——— 1975 [1903], *Roscher and Knies: The Logical Problems of Historical Economics*, New York: Free Press.

——— 1978 [1921/22], *Economy and Society: An Outline of Interpretive Sociology*, edited by Guenther Roth and Claus Wittich, Berkeley: University of California Press.

——— 1984–2009 [1891], 'Die römische Agrargeschichte in ihrer Bedeutung für das Staats- und Privatrecht', in *Max Weber Gesamtausgabe, herausgegeben von Horst Baier, M. Rainer Lepsius, Wolfgang J. Mommsen, Wolfgang Schluchter and Johannes Winckelmann*, volume I/2, Tübingen: Mohr.

——— 1984–2009 [1892], 'Die Lage der ostelbischen Landarbeiter im ostelbischen Deutschland', in *Max Weber Gesamtausgabe, herausgegeben von Horst Baier, M. Rainer Lepsius, Wolfgang J. Mommsen, Wolfgang Schluchter and Johannes Winckelmann*, volume I/3, Tübingen: Mohr.

——— 1984–2009 [1892–99], 'Landarbeiterfrage, Nationalstaat und Volkswirtschaftspolitik. Schriften und Reden 1892–1899', in *Max Weber Gesamtausgabe, herausgegeben von Horst Baier, M. Rainer Lepsius, Wolfgang J. Mommsen, Wolfgang Schluchter and Johannes Winckelmann*, volume I/4, Tübingen: Mohr.

———— 1984–2009 [1905–12], 'Zur Russischen Revolution von 1905: Schriften und Reden', in *Max Weber Gesamtausgabe, herausgegeben von Horst Baier, M. Rainer Lepsius, Wolfgang J. Mommsen, Wolfgang Schluchter and Johannes Winckelmann*, volume I/10, Tübingen: Mohr.

———— 1984–2009 [1906–1908], 'Briefe 1906–1908', in *Max Weber Gesamtausgabe, herausgegeben von Horst Baier, M. Rainer Lepsius, Wolfgang J. Mommsen, Wolfgang Schluchter and Johannes Winckelmann*, volume II/5, Tübingen: Mohr.

———— 1984–2009 [1908–12], 'Zur Psychophysik der industriellen Arbeit: Schriften und Reden 1908–1912', in *Max Weber Gesamtausgabe, herausgegeben von Horst Baier, M. Rainer Lepsius, Wolfgang J. Mommsen, Wolfgang Schluchter and Johannes Winckelmann*, volume I/11, Tübingen: Mohr.

———— 1984–2009 [1909–1910], 'Briefe 1909–1910', in *Max Weber Gesamtausgabe, herausgegeben von Horst Baier, M. Rainer Lepsius, Wolfgang J. Mommsen, Wolfgang Schluchter and Johannes Winckelmann*, volume II/6, Tübingen: Mohr.

———— 1984–2009 [1914–18], 'Zur Politik im Weltkrieg: Schriften und Reden 1914–1918', in *Max Weber Gesamtausgabe, herausgegeben von Horst Baier, M. Rainer Lepsius, Wolfgang J. Mommsen, Wolfgang Schluchter and Johannes Winckelmann*, volume I/15, Tübingen: Mohr.

———— 1984–2009 [1918–20], 'Zur Neuordnung Deutschlands: Schriften und Reden 1918–1920', in *Max Weber Gesamtausgabe, herausgegeben von Horst Baier, M. Rainer Lepsius, Wolfgang J. Mommsen, Wolfgang Schluchter and Johannes Winckelmann*, volume I/16, Tübingen: Mohr.

———— 1984–2009 [1915–20], 'Die Wirtschaftsethik der Weltreligionen: Konfuzianismus und Taoismus, Schriften 1915–1920', in *Max Weber Gesamtausgabe, herausgegeben von Horst Baier, M. Rainer Lepsius, Wolfgang J. Mommsen, Wolfgang Schluchter and Johannes Winckelmann*, volume I/19, Tübingen: Mohr.

———— 1984–2009 [1916–20], 'Die Wirtschaftsethik der Weltreligionen: Hinduismus und Buddhismus', in *Max Weber Gesamtausgabe, herausgegeben von Horst Baier, M. Rainer Lepsius, Wolfgang J. Mommsen, Wolfgang Schluchter and Johannes Winckelmann*, volume I/20 Tübingen: Mohr.

———— 1987, *Die protestantische Ethik II: Kritiken und Antikritiken*, edited by Johannes Winkelmann, Hamburg: Siebenstern.

———— 1988a [1921], *Gesammelte politische Schriften*, herausgegeben von Johannes Winckelmann, Tübingen: Mohr.

———— 1988b [1924], *Gesammelte Aufsätze zur Soziologie und Sozialpolitik*, herausgegeben von Marianne Weber, Tübingen: Mohr.

———— 1988c [1924], *Gesammelte Aufsätze zur Sozial- und Wirtschaftsgeschichte*, herausgegeben von Marianne Weber, Tübingen: Mohr.

———— 1988d [1922], *Gesammelte Aufsätze zur Wissenschaftslehre*, herausgegeben von Johannes Winckelmann, Tübingen: Mohr.

———— 1988e [1920], *Gesammelte Aufsätze zur Religionssoziologie I*, Tübingen: Mohr.

———— 1988f [1921], *Gesammelte Aufsätze zur Religionssoziologie III*, herausgegeben von Marianne Weber, Tübingen: Mohr.

———— 1994a [1895], 'The Nation State and Economic Policy', in *Political Writings*, Cambridge: Cambridge University Press.

———— 1994b [1917], 'Suffrage and Democracy in Germany', in *Political Writings*, Cambridge: Cambridge University Press.

———— 1994c [1918], 'Parliament and Government in Germany under a New Political Order', in *Political Writings*, Cambridge: Cambridge University Press.

———— 2001, *The Protestant Ethic Debate, Max Weber's Replies to his Critics, 1907–1910*, edited by David J. Chalcraft and Austin Harrington, translated by Austin Harrington and Mary Shields, Liverpool: Liverpool University Press.

———— 2008a [1919], 'Politics as a Vocation', in *Max Weber's Complete Writings on Academic and Political Vocations*, edited by John Dreijmanis, New York: Algora.

———— 2008b [1917/19], 'Science as a Vocation', in *Max Weber's Complete Writings on Academic and Political Vocations*, edited by John Dreijmanis, New York: Algora.

Weber, Thomas 1994, 'Anatomie II', in *Historisch-Kritisches Wörterbuch des Marxismus*, edited by Wolfgang Fritz Haug, Frigga Haug and Peter Jehle, Hamburg: Argument.

———— 1995, 'Bedeutung', in *Historisch-Kritisches Wörterbuch des Marxismus*, edited by Wolfgang Fritz Haug, Frigga Haug and Peter Jehle, Hamburg: Argument.

Weeks, Kathi 2011, *The Problem with Work: Feminism, Marxism, Antiworks Politics, and Postwork Imaginaries*, Durham and London: Duke University Press.

Wegener, Walther 1962, *Die Quellen der Wissenschaftsauffassung Max Webers und die Problematik der Werturteilsfreiheit der Nationalökonomie: Ein wissenschaftssoziologischer Beitrag*, Berlin: Duncker & Humblot.

Wehler, Hans-Ulrich 1970 [1966], *Moderne deutsche Sozialgeschichte*, Cologne: Kiepenheuer & Witsch.

———— 1973, *Das deutsche Kaiserreich 1871–1918*, Göttingen: Vandenhoeck & Ruprecht.

———— 1974, 'Der Aufstieg des Organisierten Kapitalismus und Interventionsstaates in Deutschland', in *Organisierter Kapitalismus: Voraussetzungen und Anfänge*, edited by Heinrich August Winkler, Göttingen: Vandenhoeck & Ruprecht.

———— 1995, *Deutsche Gesellschaftsgeschichte 3: Von der 'Deutschen Doppelrevolution' bis zum Beginn des Ersten Weltkrieges 1849–1914*, Munich: Beck.

Weinzen, Hans 1994, 'Arbeiteraristokratie', in *Historisch-Kritisches Wörterbuch des Marxismus*, edited by Wolfgang Fritz Haug, Frigga Haug and Peter Jehle, Hamburg: Argument.

Weiß, Johannes 1981, *Das Werk Max Webers in der marxistischen Rezeption und Kritik*, Opladen: Westdeutscher Verlag.

Wichelhaus, Manfred 1965, *Kirchengeschichtsschreibung und Soziologie im neunzehnten Jahrhundert und bei Ernst Troeltsch*, Heidelberg: Winter.

Wielenga, Bastian 1984, *Introduction to Marxism*, Bangalore: Centre for Social Action.

—— 1995, 'Dorfgemeinschaft', in *Historisch-Kritisches Wörterbuch des Marxismus*, edited by Wolfgang Fritz Haug, Frigga Haug and Peter Jehle, Hamburg: Argument.

Wilson, Bryan R. 1973: *Magic and the Millenium: A Sociological Study of Religious Movements of Protest Among Tribal and Third-World Peoples*, London: Harper & Row.

Windelband, Wilhelm 1884, *Präludien: Aufsätze und Reden zur Einleitung in die Philosophie*, Freiburg: Mohr.

—— 1914, *Einleitung in die Philosophie*, Tübingen: Mohr.

—— 1915 [1894], 'Geschichte und Naturwissenschaft', in *Präludien: Aufsätze und Reden zur Philosophie und ihrer Geschichte 2*, Tübingen: Mohr.

Winkel, Harald 1977, *Die deutsche Nationalökonomie im 19. Jahrhundert*, Darmstadt: Wissenschaftliche Buchgesellschaft.

Winkler, Heinrich August (ed.) 1974, *Organisierter Kapitalismus: Voraussetzungen und Anfänge*, Göttingen: Vandenhoeck & Ruprecht.

Worsley, Peter 1968, *The Trumpet Shall Sound: A Study of 'Cargo Cults' in Melanesia*, New York: Schocken.

Wulff, Erich 1969, 'Grundfragen transkultureller Psychiatrie', *Das Argument*, 50: 227–60.

Zaret, David 1989, 'Religion and the Rise of Liberal-democratic Ideology in 17th Century England', *American Sociological Review*, 54, 2: 163–79.

Zimmerman, Andrew 2006, 'Decolonizing Weber', in *Postcolonial Studies*, 9, 1: 53–79.

—— 2010, *Alabama in Africa: Booker T. Washington, the German Empire, and the Globalization of the New South*, Princeton and Oxford: Princeton University Press.

# Name Index

# Subject Index